Fodor's 2000

Arizo

D1188526

Fodor's Travel Publications, Inc. • New York, Toronto, London, Sydney, Auckland

CONTENTS

3

MAPS

Circled letters in text correspond to letters on the photographs. For more information on the sights pictured, turn to the indicated page number Ⓐ〉 on each photograph.

DESTINATION ARIZONA

The splendor of Arizona's natural landmarks is reason enough to visit. But there is more to the state than beautiful vistas. Traces of a rich, layered history mark the awesome terrain and inspire artists, artisans, and the discerning shoppers who buy their work. Arizona's cuisines are captivating; its brilliant skies enthrall lovers of the outdoors. Take time to absorb the calming lessons of the heat and the majestic landscape—on the still waters of a magnificent lake at sunset or beside a fountain on an awning-shaded patio over lunch—and a bit of Arizona will stay with you forever.

THE GRAND CANYON AND NORTHWEST ARIZONA

Ⓐ 47

The Grand Canyon, one of nature's longest-running works in progress, both exalts and humbles the human spirit. It all started some 65 million years ago when massive upheavals created a tableland known as the Colorado Plateau. Later, the Colorado River, which arrived a mere 10 million years ago, started scouring down the plateau and in the process laid bare aeons of geological history encoded in stone that itself dates back as much as 1.3 billion years—a quarter of the age of the earth. These days, a fine time of sightseeing can be had just by setting up a lawn chair and staying put: As the sun moves across the sky, the play of light and shadow on the vividly colored buttes, monuments, and canyon walls changes the hues of the landscape before your very eyes. But except for painters and photographers, few visitors stay rooted—in the Grand

Ⓑ 71

© 38

D 53

Canyon National Park, which preserves this fabulous landscape, there are simply too many other options. You can view the spectacle not only from the ©**South Rim,** the most popular vantage point, but also from the air. Or, astride a mule, you might ride along 19th-century miners' trails descending deep into the canyon's Ⓔ**Inner Gorge** for an overnight at Phantom Ranch, at the bottom. Or you could travel aboard an inflatable rubber raft along the Ⓑ**Colorado River,** whose placid reaches alternate with rapids to create one of the world's most outrageous thrill rides. Soothing body and soul at day's end is the log-and-stone Ⓐ**El Tovar Hotel,** nearing the century mark itself. The handsome Ⓓ**Cameron Trading Post,** a study in south-

western style, also makes a fine base for canyon forays. You can buy some of the region's finest Navajo, Hopi, Zuni, and Pueblo jewelry, rugs, and craftwork here and admire some of the very finest pieces at the superb gallery. It's a perfect way to get back in touch with the grandeur of human endeavor.

Ⓔ 71

THE GRAND CANYON AND NORTHWEST ARIZONA

F ⟩ 58

The ⓖ**North Rim** of the Grand Canyon is the rim less traveled, and its devotees don't mind a bit. They like the elbow
room and willingly travel the extra miles to see views that out-
dazzle even the stunners farther south. The appropriately named
ⓕ**Point Sublime** stands out, but Toroweap Overlook also rewards your journey, and Bright Angel Point, Point Imperial,
and Cape Royal are as spec-
tacular—and more accessible.
As if the canyon itself weren't

G ⟩ 53

H ⟩ 55

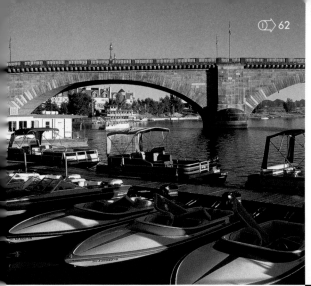

① ➤ 62

enough, northwestern Arizona also lures anglers with oversize trout near Ⓗ**Lees Ferry** and, in Lake Havasu City, with a bit of Britannia in the form of Ⓘ**London Bridge**—the real thing, shipped over from Eng-

Ⓙ ➤ 60

land in pieces to span a neck of man-made Lake Havasu. Anglophiles get a kick out of the town's faux-British touches; Anglophiles into water sports like the place even better. Meanwhile, Americana reigns around Ⓙ**Kingman,** a local transportation hub where you can cruise along legendary Route 66, that pre-interstate icon of American restlessness and the call of the open road. Not far from Kingman is the Ⓚ**Oatman Hotel,** centerpiece of a ghost town with a main street straight out of a Western movie, where the Old West really does come to life.

Ⓚ ➤ 62

THE NORTHEAST

Most residents of northeast Arizona are Navajo and Hopi, and, although modems and pickup trucks are part of daily life now, traditions endure that predate the conquistadors. Portions of high desert country are holy to those who live here—almost all of this land is majestic. Throughout the area, wind and frost have created magical effects in stone, such as the swirled rock formations (actually petrified dunes) in sunset-hued

Ⓒ▷87

Ⓐ**Antelope Canyon**. At places like the Ⓑ**Monument Valley Navajo Tribal Park,** Susie Black and other traditional rug makers create their own magic. The Ⓒ**White House Ruin** in breathtaking Canyon de Chelly and ruins at Betatakin and Keet Seel at Navajo National Monument are eloquent reminders of how ancient peoples wrested shelter from this fierce land, building pueblos dwarfed by the surrounding rocks. At Ⓓ**Lake Powell,** Glen Canyon Dam inverted the equation: Here, man dominated nature, and the lake so created is a spectacular meeting of earth and water.

Ⓓ▷98

NORTH-CENTRAL ARIZONA

Ⓐ▷112

Ⓑ▷132

For more than a thousand years, people have found this slice of Arizona irresistible. The predecessors of the Native Americans who created the jewelry so beautifully showcased in the Ⓑ**Museum of Northern Arizona** built prodigiously all across this area of the Colorado Plateau between the 8th and 15th centuries. North and south of Flagstaff, the home of this museum and the area's major population center, the Sinagua people put up impressive houses in total harmony with the natural world around them. You can see their sturdy cliff dwellings rising high on the sides of the red-rock bluffs at the

Ⓒ▷141

Ⓐ**Montezuma Castle National Monument,** among North America's best-preserved prehistoric ruins, and at the fascinating Ⓔ**Walnut Canyon National Monument,** whose dry climate and sheltered site have left many of the hundreds of Sinagua homes in close-to-perfect condition. Still other remains, lower to the ground, befitting the area's wide horizons, grace the nearby Ⓓ**Wupatki National Monument.** Archaeological evidence shows that the Sinagua traded widely in the area but that settlement here and at other local sites was repeatedly hampered by eruptions of the cone that forms the centerpiece of what is now Ⓒ**Sunset Crater Volcano National Monument.** Today, 900 years after the last eruption, the haunting bleakness of the land bespeaks the power of the earth's inner fires, just as the blooming prickly pear cactus bespeaks the desert's power to bring forth surprising beauty.

Ⓔ 140

13

NORTH-CENTRAL ARIZONA

The laid-back towns of north-central Arizona are as bewitching as the landscape. One exceptional place to enjoy both is Prescott, whose cool mountain heights and curiously New Englandlike architecture lure Phoenix residents fleeing southern heat. Another is funky Ⓕ**Jerome,** a former copper-mining boom town that was all but abandoned in 1953. It was discovered by hippies in the 1960s and now charms visitors with its bawdy history, its boutiques, and, thanks to its location on high ground, its spectacular views. From Jerome you can see the Ⓖ**San Francisco Peaks,** north of Flagstaff, beloved of cross-country and downhill skiers and snowboarders in winter and hikers in fall, when the aspen groves blaze with gold. Some visitors come to celebrated Ⓘ**Sedona** to mountain-bike along nearby trails bordered by pines and to absorb the breathtaking loveliness of spots like Ⓙ**Boynton Canyon.** New Age thinkers make their way here from both coasts in the

Ⓕ⟩114

Ⓖ⟩242

belief that the area is rich with "power points" or "vortices" that concentrate the planet's energy and create a perfect environment for the nourishment and alignment of the soul. Locals rue the karma that brought developers to town in the 1980s, for the builders' visions were blind to the town's vintage quirks. On the positive side, Sedona's growth has made it easy to find lovely lodgings and beguiling restaurants, galleries, and shops like those in the elegant Ⓗ**Tlaquepaque** complex. Drinking in the wonder of the land that surrounds the town, even skeptics may put their disbelief on hold.

PHOENIX
AND CENTRAL
ARIZONA

One of America's fastest-growing metropolitan areas, Phoenix started booming in the mid-19th century, when it rose atop the ancient Hohokam civilization's ruins, now partially excavated at Pueblo Grande Museum and Cultural Park. Easterners flooded Phoenix in the 1920s in search of clean air; celebrities, including every president except Herbert Hoover, stayed at posh resorts such as the fabled Ⓐ**Arizona Biltmore.** The wonderful and equally famous ⒷⒹ**Heard Museum** illuminates other facets of local culture. Its architecture reflects Arizona's Spanish Colonial heritage; the collections (and events like the Hoop Dancing Competition) showcase the traditions of Native American artists from ancient times to the present. Also worth noting are the Arizona Science Center, the Phoenix Art Museum, and vibrant international dining. Nature surrounds you: you can hike within minutes of downtown—in 17,000-acre South Mountain Park or to ©**Squaw Peak,** a local landmark with a splendid view.

Ⓑ⟩ 155

©⟩ 150

Ⓓ⟩ 155

PHOENIX AND CENTRAL ARIZONA

Rising where the Sonoran Desert butts up against the Superstition Mountains, Phoenix anchors a metropolitan area that also includes Scottsdale, Tempe, and some 20 other communities surrounded by a landscape of stunning beauty. Frank Lloyd Wright was so taken with the area when he consulted on Phoenix's Biltmore resort in 1927 that he built a sprawling winter home,

Taliesin West, on 600 rugged acres outside Scottsdale, now open to visitors on guided tours (which include the lovely adjacent gardens). Suburban Papago Salado's vivid, compact Ⓔ**Desert Botanical Garden,** which displays thousands of species of native cactus and other desert plants, is another place to get in touch with the landscape. You can also saddle up a gentle mount for a guided ride in the Ⓕ**Sonoran Desert,** take a mountain-biking adventure into the foothills, or hop aboard a hot-air balloon to survey it all from on high. Because Central Arizona is prime resort country,

Ⓔ▷158

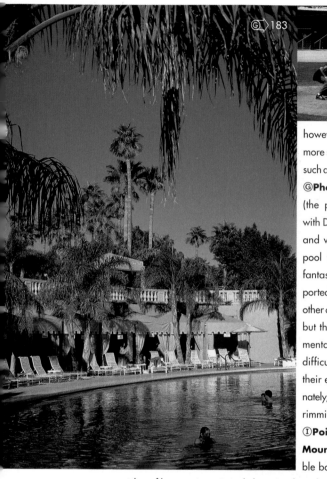

G⟩ 183

H⟩ 202

however, most pleasures are more sedate. At pricey resorts such as Scottsdale's renowned **GPhoenician,** luxury reigns (the place comes complete with Dutch Master paintings), and when you hop into the pool for a dip, it's easy to fantasize you've been transported to Babylon. Golf is another opportunity for exertion, but the challenges are often mental: the scenery makes it difficult for golfers to keep their eyes on the ball. Fortunately, panoramas such as that rimming the course at the **IPointe Hilton on South Mountain** make even a double bogey sting a bit less. If your idea of heaven is to sit and cheer (and maybe lift pencil to scorecard or nacho to mouth), come to Mesa's **HHoHoKam Park** and hope you catch Chicago Cubs slugger Sammy Sosa ruining yet another pitcher's day. Elsewhere, you can watch any number of other big-league stars tuning up during spring training—you'll never get closer to them. In summer, an Arizona Diamondbacks game is worth the trip if only to experience the stadium: It's one of the wonders of the baseball world, complete with a swimming pool beyond the outfield.

I⟩ 191

A 234

Far from the world of tennis whites, eastern Arizona casts its own riveting spell, by turns verdant or stark and haunting. The White Mountains, northeast of Phoenix, contain the world's largest stand of ponderosa pines, as well as alpine meadows decked with wildflowers and some of the cleanest air you'll ever breathe. If you love the outdoor life, you may well fall in love with this place. Side by side to the northeast lie a few of the region's more interesting landmarks: Homolovi Ruins State Park is home to five ancestral

EASTERN ARIZONA

B 243

Hopi pueblos. The ⑧**Painted Desert** assumes hues from blood red to pink, then back again, as the sun rises, climbs, and sets. And ⑩**Petrified Forest National Park** protects a forest of trees that stood when dinosaurs walked the earth, turned to stone over aeons as if touched by the hand of a vengeful god—the pieces of petrified log look deceptively like driftwood cast upon an oceanless beach. Ancient petroglyphs mark the rocks here, as they do in Ⓐ**Lyman Lake State Park.** Delving deep into such ancient mysteries, amateur diggers at the White Mountain Archaeological Center at Ⓒ**Raven Site Ruins** learn from professionals. If you stop to pitch in, be prepared to get hooked: Few things are more thrilling and moving than retrieving a piece of the human saga.

C 235

TUCSON

With its 700,000 residents augmented by legions of "snowbirds" who come for the winter, Tucson isn't that much smaller than Phoenix. Yet while Phoenix revels in its status as a modern American metropolis, Tucson retains the feel of a small southwestern town. Claiming that Phoenix has paved over the desert in its sprawl, Tucsonians say the serenity of their mostly arid land imparts an easygoing personality to their city. A walk in verdant ⑩**Sabino Canyon,** a favorite of hikers that's within the

Ⓒ 263

Ⓓ 261

city limits, does nothing to dispel that notion. Neither does a stroll among the towering cacti of Ⓐ**Saguaro National Park.** The desert may seem empty of life as you walk through it, but the superb zoo and botanical garden known as the Ⓒ**Arizona-Sonora Desert Museum** demonstrates otherwise by showing you rattlesnakes, prairie dogs, the American kestrel, and other wildlife. To get a look at the kind of wild life that was lived in Tucson a century ago—if Hollywood's version of the truth is to be trusted—stop at the Ⓑ**Old Tucson Studios,** where that quick-draw past is theatrically re-created.

TUCSON

Colonial Spain and Mexico left a strong imprint on Tucson's art, architecture, cuisine, and culture. Locals boast that the best Mexican food anywhere north of the border is served right here, and you may find it hard to disagree after a few meals at the restaurants along 4th Avenue, among other culi-

nary landmarks. In downtown's El Presidio Historic District, traditional Mexican adobes and wide-porched Territorial homes underscore the city's Hispanic heritage. In the Ⓔ**Barrio Historico** neighborhood to the south, a contemporary mural adds a grace note to 19th-century buildings that make you feel as if you've been transported back to the days when Arizona belonged to Mexico. To turn back the clock still farther, head for the lovely Ⓖ**Mission San Xavier del Bac,** founded more than three centuries ago when imperial Spain ruled the region; the church still serves the community for which it was built. Close as you feel

Ⓕ▷282

G⟩263

to Mother Spain at spots like this, the Wild West never feels far away either. At the vintage 1919 ⓕ**Hotel Congress** you'll find live rock music in a setting that's art deco with a Western twist, and at hostelries such as Tanque Verde Ranch and the ①**White Stallion Ranch,** slow horseback rides through the desert are the order of the day and rodeos go on every week. Head farther west to one of the local spas, perhaps world-famous Canyon Ranch or the beautiful ⓗ**Miraval,** whose holistic wellness programs are rooted in Asian philosophies—the realignment of your body and soul begins as soon as you set foot on the grounds, which are themselves an invitation to reflection, contemplation, and serenity. But then, that's what Tucson is about. It is that rarest of urban destinations: a town that offers all the worldly pleasures yet manages, through its beauty and mellow ways, to make you feel as though you've left the world behind.

①⟩276

ⓗ⟩274

Deep in southern Arizona, there is a town called Why. Though the name is simply a phonetic rendition of the town's original name—Y—the label anticipates doubts that travelers might have about the area ("Why bother?"). Mountain-and-desert scenery as splendid as any in Arizona is one reason, starting with the remarkable fauna and rock formations at Ⓔ**Chiricahua National Monument.** Enduring pockets of the Old West in the form of ghost towns are another. Ⓐ**Pearce** died in the 1930s, when gold deposits ran dry, and remains as photogenic as they come. Douglas is also a time capsule, home to the palatial Ⓒ**Gadsden Hotel,** where local ranchers meet for drinks and Tiffany skylights recall the

SOUTHERN ARIZONA

Ⓐ 313

Ⓑ 307

HERE LIES
Lester Moore
Four Slugs
From A 44
No Les
No More

© 312

town's glorious heyday. Once-notorious Tombstone, not in the least ghostly, hums with commerce and reenactments of gunfights, most notably the confrontation in which the Earps and Doc Holliday shot it

Ⓓ 319

out with the Stantons at the OK Corral. Participants with slow reflexes often ended up in Ⓑ **Boot Hill Graveyard,** sometimes with a peculiar epitaph. In southern Arizona, the old frontier is not the only frontier: At Ⓓ **Kitt Peak National Observatory,** astronomers gaze into the universe, joined by more than a few travelers who have made the stunning drive through the Tohono O'odham Reservation to behold the world's final frontier. Witnessing the miracle of the starriest sky imaginable, you might find a whole new meaning for that query, *why?*

Ⓔ 312

GREAT ITINERARIES

Lake
Mead

Highlights of Arizona
14 days

Ghostly Native American ruins, chamber music in Sedona, color-soaked canyons, shopping in Tucson: Arizona is full of history, culture, and good times. Start or end this survey with a few days in Phoenix.

PRESCOTT, JEROME, AND SEDONA
2 days. From Phoenix, head northwest to take a look around Prescott, "Everyone's Hometown," and its old-fashioned town square, Victorian homes, and pine-covered foothills. The near-ghost town of Jerome clings to the mountainside nearby. Surrounded by windswept sandstone, Ⓐ Sedona is breathtaking, as well.
☞ *The Verde Valley, Jerome, Prescott, and Sedona in Chapter 3*

GRAND CANYON
2 days. The Grand Canyon is truly one of the wonders of the world. Whether you raft the Colorado, ride a mule, tackle a hike, or gaze from the terrace of a rim-side hotel, time here is always an adventure.
☞ *The South Rim and Environs, The North Rim and Environs, in Chapter 1*

Ⓐ 121

NAVAJO NATIONAL MONUMENT AND MONUMENT VALLEY
1 day. Tram tours led by Navajo guides roll past the sandstone mesas and spires of Monument Valley, where private cars can't go. At Navajo National Monument,

linger among the cliff dwellings and ponder the lives of those who came before.
☞ *Navajo Nation North in Chapter 2*

CANYON DE CHELLY
2 days. Journey into magical Canyon de Chelly on foot, on horseback, or in a guided four-wheel-drive vehicle to view Native American ruins and the magnificent sandstone landscape.
☞ *Navajo Nation East in Chapter 2*

HOPI MESAS
2 days. Rising above the desert floor, the Hopi Mesas are home to some of the oldest inhabited villages in the United States.
☞ *The Hopi Mesas in Chapter 2*

PAINTED DESERT AND PETRIFIED FOREST
1 day. If rocks could talk, those in Petrified Forest National Park and the Painted Desert would tell how aeons of wind and rain polished the remains of a primeval swamp into gem-colored hills filled with fossils.
☞ *Petrified Forest National Park and the Painted Desert in Chapter 5*

CORONADO TRAIL TO TUCSON
1 day. On the scenic Coronado Trail you will find treasure in abundance: aspen and fir forests, lakes stocked with trout, and wildlife.
☞ *The White Mountains in Chapter 5*

TUCSON
2 days. While in Tucson, check out the beautiful San Xavier del Bac mission and the El Presidio Historical District surrounding the Museum of Art.
☞ *Exploring Tucson in Chapter 6*

SAGUARO NATIONAL PARK
1 day. Both the east and the west sections of Saguaro National Park put you face to face with the eponymous

cactus. Experience desert plants and animals at the Arizona-Sonora Desert Museum. At Old Tucson Studios, movies are still being filmed.
☞ *Exploring Tucson in Chapter 6*

The Old West
12 days

Desperadoes, Indian warriors, galloping ponies, lawmen riding into the sunset: In Arizona, the Wild West is never far away. You can relive the romance at the state's historic locales, starting or ending with a stay in Tuscon.

GHOST TOWNS
4 days. Start in Benson, where you can hop a train to the ghost towns of Charleston and Fairbank. Guns still blaze and villains fall in Tombstone—but only during staged fights. Be sure to check out the OK Corral. Later, explore quaint Bisbee, now an artists' haven of restored Victorian homes and upscale bistros. After a morning in tumbledown Gleeson and Pearce, move on to Fort Bowie National Historic Site, where U.S. soldiers once skirmished with Cochise's Apaches. Down-town Willcox looks like the cow town it is and has two Western-history museums.
☞ *Southeast Arizona in Chapter 7*

SOUTH OF TUCSON
1 day. To appreciate the Spanish influence on small towns along the meandering Santa Cruz River, tour the mission at Tumacacori National Historic Park. Up the road is Tubac, site of Arizona's first European settlement and the Tubac Presidio State Historic Park and Museum.
☞ *Side Trips near Tucson in Chapter 6*

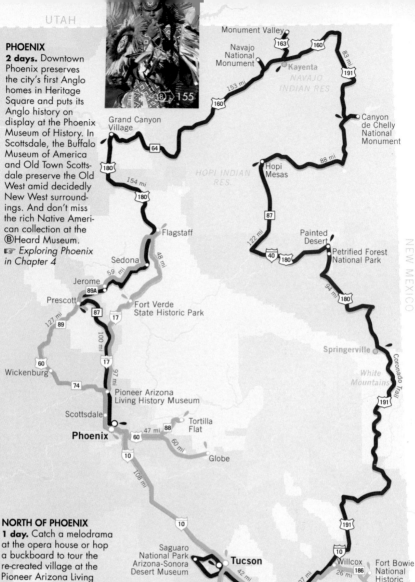

PHOENIX

2 days. Downtown Phoenix preserves the city's first Anglo homes in Heritage Square and puts its Anglo history on display at the Phoenix Museum of History. In Scottsdale, the Buffalo Museum of America and Old Town Scottsdale preserve the Old West amid decidedly New West surroundings. And don't miss the rich Native American collection at the Ⓑ Heard Museum.
☞ *Exploring Phoenix in Chapter 4*

NORTH OF PHOENIX

1 day. Catch a melodrama at the opera house or hop a buckboard to tour the re-created village at the Pioneer Arizona Living History Museum. In Wickenburg, home to many fine guest ranches, you'll find a tranquil site where justice was meted out: the Jail Tree.
☞ *Side Trips near Phoenix in Chapter 4*

THE VERDE VALLEY

2 days. Gold once lured folks to Prescott, giving rise to the former red-light district known as Whiskey Row; stop at Sharlott Hall Museum for a glimpse of the town's past. Old mine tunnels honeycomb the land around Jerome, where museums memorialize the local mining bonanza.
☞ *The Verde Valley, Jerome, Prescott, and Sedona in Chapter 3*

FLAGSTAFF

1 day. The natural beauty of this area leaves no doubt as to why Anglos settled here. To see how they lived, stop in downtown's restored Historic Railroad District and at Riordan State Historic Park.
☞ *Flagstaff in Chapter 3*

CENTRAL ARIZONA

1 day. Learn about life on an Old West military outpost at Fort Verde State Historic Park, then sample frontier fare in Tortilla Flat. Protected by two mountain ranges, once-flourishing Globe retains the charm of its mining days.
☞ *The Verde Valley, Jerome, Prescott, and Sedona in Chapter 3 and Side Trips Around the Apache Trail in Chapter 4*

FODOR'S
CHOICE

Even with so many special places in Arizona, Fodor's writers and editors have their favorites. Here are a few that stand out.

NATURAL WONDERS

Canyon de Chelly National Monument, Navajo Nation. These ancient cliff dwellings are in profound harmony with their natural surroundings. ☞ p. 86

Ⓗ **Desert Botanical Garden, Phoenix.** An early morning walk through the desert gives perhaps the best and most pleasant view of the flora and fauna. ☞ p. 158

Grand Canyon, North Rim. The only way to get to know the canyon is to hike or ride a mule down through the geological eras to the bottom of the chasm. ☞ p. 57

Ⓓ **Red Rocks, Sedona.** Picnic or hike among Sedona's natural monuments and feel the wonder of the place. ☞ p. 123

Ⓔ **Saguaro National Park, Tucson.** You'll see the world's largest stand of saguaro cacti here, as well as fascinating petroglyphs made by the Hohokam people. ☞ p. 264

Taliesin West, Scottsdale. Architect Frank Lloyd Wright's winter residence ingeniously integrates indoor and outdoor space. ☞ p. 160

SCENIC DRIVES

Coronado Trail. The steep 123-mi stretch of highway from Springerville to Clifton is dramatic as it winds from verdant meadows down into the Sonoran Desert. ☞ p. 238

Ⓘ **Flagstaff to Sedona via Oak Creek Canyon.** Another stunning canyon, this one is quiet and tree-lined on its low end, towering and majestic as it looks toward Sedona. ☞ p. 123

Jerome to Prescott. The winding road through Prescott National Forest is one of Arizona's most breathtaking mountain drives. ☞ p. 117

Point Sublime, Grand Canyon. The panorama along the dirt road leading out to the point is one of the most awesome views you'll ever witness from the comfort of your car. ☞ p. 58

Texas Canyon. Is it possible to tire of canyons? Not when they are like this one—hung with massive boulders in astonishing formations apparently defying gravity. ☞ p. 315

Ⓖ **Tucson to Kitt Peak.** About 20 mi southwest of Tucson you enter the Tohono O'odham reservation, eventually ascending to a world-renowned observatory. ☞ p. 319

U.S. 163 to Utah. The drive between Kayenta and the Goosenecks of Utah's San Juan River takes in magical scenery. The winding, water-carved canyon of the San Juan River is a fascinating counterpart to the Grand Canyon. ☞ p. 96

FLAVORS

Ⓑ **Janos at La Paloma, Tucson.** The innovative Southwestern cuisine of chef-owner Janos Wilder keeps the crowds coming year-round. $$$$ ☞ p. 272

Restaurant Hapa, Phoenix. Thai, Chinese, and other astonishingly flavorful Asian-hybrid entrées and desserts add up to one big-time dining experience. $$$ ☞ p. 170

The Kramers at the Manzanita Restaurant Lounge, Cornville. The sophistication of the Continental fare here is unexpected, considering the location. $$ ☞ p. 113

Such Is Life, Phoenix. In Moises Treves's corner of Phoenix you can taste cactus, chicken Maya, garlic shrimp—delicious regional Mexican food. $$–$$$ ☞ p. 177

Prescott Brewing Company, Prescott. Four drafts are brewed on the premises and served with good pub fare. $ ☞ p. 119

COMFORTS

Ⓙ **The Boulders, Phoenix.** The Valley's most serene and secluded luxury resort hides among hill-size granite boulders in the foothills town of Carefree. $$$$ ☞ p. 187

Ⓒ **The Phoenician, Phoenix.** French-provincial furnishings, fine European paintings, and spacious rooms make this the most elegant hotel in town. Its desert garden shelters hundreds of succulents, and the Terrace Dining Room offers the most lavish Sunday brunch in the city. $$$$ ☞ p. 183

Ⓕ **Arizona Inn, Tucson.** With almost all that you would want from a landmark inn—period furnishings, fireplaces, quiet and friendly service, even a midtown location—you won't be disappointed. $$$–$$$$ ☞ p. 278

Ⓐ **Briar Patch Inn, Sedona.** It may not be in the heart of Sedona, but its lovely location in Oak Creek Canyon sets it apart. $$–$$$$ ☞ p. 126

Wahweap Lodge at Lake Powell. A central source for Lake Powell recreation, Wahweap has cruises, river excursions, boat rentals, waterskiing, and a restaurant—it's a nearly all-in-one resort. $$ ☞ p. 102

Grand Canyon Lodge, North Rim. On the North Rim you can avoid the crowds as you enjoy the mighty abyss. The historic, rustic Grand Canyon Lodge has spectacular canyon views. $–$$ ☞ p. 58

Casa Tierra Bed & Breakfast, Tucson. In an adobe building, this fine B&B outside town is great for a desert getaway. $$ ☞ p. 276

Cameron Trading Post, Cameron. With its trading-post charm, this may well be the best base for seeing both the north and south rims of the Grand Canyon, as well as nearby Navajo-Hopi country. $ ☞ p. 53

1 THE GRAND CANYON AND NORTHWEST ARIZONA

To appreciate the Grand Canyon, you must see it for yourself. Even the finest photographs fail to deliver a fraction of the impact of a personal glimpse into this vast, beautiful scar on the surface of our planet—277 mi long, 18 mi across at its widest spot, and more than a mile below the rim at its deepest point. The Grand Canyon is the quintessence of the high drama of the American western landscape. Nearby, Lake Mead, the Hoover Dam, and the gambling halls of Laughlin, Nevada, have their appeals, too.

By William E.
Hafford and
Edie Jarolim

Updated by
Kim
Westerman

MILLIONS OF WORDS have been devoted to describing the Grand Canyon, but writers generally have conceded that the earth's greatest gorge is beyond the scope of language. Southwestern author Frank Waters has come closer than most to capturing its power. "It is the sum total," he writes, "of all the aspects of nature combined in one integrated whole. It is at once the smile and frown upon the face of nature. In its heart is the savage, uncontrollable fury of all the inanimate Universe, and at the same time the immeasurable serenity that succeeds it. It is Creation." Less eloquently, but no less spiritedly, an 1892 visitor remarked, "By Joe! This canyon takes the whole shooting-match!"

More than 65 million years ago, a long series of violent geological upheavals created a domed tableland, today called the Colorado Plateau. Then the Colorado River, racing south through present-day Utah, began chewing at the uplifted region. The river is responsible for much of the still ongoing erosion, but many side gullies and canyons were formed by melting snow and fierce rainstorms that sent water rushing into the gorge through smaller tributaries. Softer rock formations were washed away by the Colorado and carried to the distant sea; the harder formations remained as great cliffs and buttes. Above the river line are otherworldly stone monuments with colors that range from muted pastels to deep purples, vibrant yellows, fiery reds, and soft blues. You'll see the palette shift with the hours: The colorful scene created by the mid-morning sunlight is repainted by the setting sun, each masterpiece slightly different from that which preceded it.

This is also a land of ancient peoples. In some of the deepest, most inaccessible reaches of the Grand Canyon, evidence of early human habitation exists. Stone ruins high in the cliffs reveal the secrets of cultures 8,000 to 10,000 years old. In higher country, above both the North and South rims, are the remains of prehistoric Pueblo settlements that were active until about AD 1350. A period of harsh and sustained drought, climatic change, soil erosion, and overuse of local resources is thought to have caused the people to seek more favorable lands. Modern-day Hopi and New Mexican Pueblo peoples view themselves as descendants of the earlier inhabitants, whose former dwellings, they believe, hold ancestral spirits.

In 1540 a band of Spanish soldiers under the command of Captain García López de Cárdenas became the first white men to look into the canyon. The members of the expedition, dispatched by Francisco Coronado to find the fabled golden cities of Cibola, found the Grand Canyon instead. Spanish Franciscan missionary and explorer Francisco Tomás Garcés visited a Havasupai Indian village in the canyon in 1776, and Lieutenant Joseph Ives went on an official mission for the U.S. government to explore the area in 1857–58. Ives did not like the region much, writing in his report to Congress that "it seems intended by nature that the Colorado River, along the greater portion of its lonely and majestic way, shall be forever unvisited and undisturbed." That was indeed the case until 1869, when John Wesley Powell, a one-armed Civil War hero, adventurer, and scholar, put rough-hewn boats into the Colorado and let the swirling white water of the mighty river take him along its length. After Powell came countless other explorers, fortune hunters, and visitors to prove Ives wrong.

At the end of the 19th century almost all development at or near the canyon was related to mining. The earliest trails down into the canyon were built by miners searching for precious minerals. Shortly after the turn of the century, the Santa Fe Railroad completed a line to the canyon's South Rim, which, combined with Theodore Roosevelt's 1903 visit, drew public interest to the site; in 1919 it was declared a national park. Today close to 5 million visitors come each year from around the world to peer into the gorge.

Your first view of the Grand Canyon will last a lifetime. After a half dozen lookouts, however, your sense of wonder will begin to diminish—it's difficult to establish a personal relationship with so much grandeur. Traveling along the rim, you will soon tire of putting your nose up against all this beauty, safely, almost antiseptically. So take the plunge: Even a short hike down any of the trails will open up a totally new perspective on the scale of this massive abyss.

Pleasures and Pastimes

Dining

Throughout Grand Canyon country and northwestern Arizona, restaurants cater to tourists who seek standard American fare, prepared quickly and offered at reasonable prices. An exception to this general rule is the fine-dining restaurant and service at El Tovar, the oldest hotel in the canyon. Restaurants are open daily unless otherwise noted, and dress throughout this recreational area is casual (though you may want to don your hole-free jeans for the El Tovar dining room).

Hiking

Hiking opportunities range from leisurely walks on well-defined paths through gently rolling country to arduous multiday treks to the bottom of the canyon—and across to the other rim if you'd like. Some popular trails are outlined in this chapter; park rangers or visitor-center personnel can provide you with information about other routes.

Lodging

The Fred Harvey Company opened the El Tovar Hotel on the South Rim in 1905, heralding the development of Grand Canyon Village. Now there are more than 900 motel and hotel rooms in the Village, but even that number of accommodations is insufficient in summer. The North Rim is less crowded but has limited lodging facilities. Make reservations as soon as your itinerary has been decided, even as early as a year in advance. The South Rim's National Park Service Visitor Center in Grand Canyon Village posts the availability of hotel rooms inside the park and in the nearby town of Tusayan. If you can't find accommodations in the immediate area of the South Rim, you'll probably find something in the nearby communities of Williams or Flagstaff (☞ Flagstaff *in* Chapter 3). Prices at many of the hotels and motels in Grand Canyon country are lower in spring, fall, and winter.

Mountain Biking

Mountain-bike enthusiasts revel in the network of dirt access roads that lace the North Rim, among them a 17-mi muscle tester that leads to Point Sublime, overlooking the inner canyon's Granite Gorge and its fierce rapids. A network of trails fans out north of Point Sublime, leading to other vistas to the west; mountain bikers who follow those trails are likely to have the place to themselves during most of the year.

Rafting

Many who have made the white-water trip down the Colorado River through the Grand Canyon say it is the adventure of a lifetime. Trips embark from Lees Ferry, below Glen Canyon Dam near Page, Arizona. Those that run the length of the canyon can last from three days to three weeks. Shorter treks, also starting at Lees Ferry, let passengers off at Phantom Ranch at the bottom of the Grand Canyon (about 100 mi). These pass through a great amount of white water, including Lava Falls rapids (on longer trips), considered the wildest navigable rapids in North America. For those who would like a more tranquil turn on the Colorado, there are also one-day, quiet-water raft excursions that begin below Glen Canyon Dam near Page.

Exploring the Grand Canyon and Northwest Arizona

The Grand Canyon stretches across northwest Arizona. Its popular South Rim includes Grand Canyon Village, Village Rim, East Rim Drive, and West Rim Drive. The drive to the less-visited North Rim, in the Arizona Strip—a 12,000-square-mi tract of land isolated from the rest of the state by the Colorado River—takes in views of the Painted Desert to the east. Havasu Canyon, south of the middle part of the national park, provides another respite from the crowds. To the northwest is Lake Mead, the largest man-made body of water in the United States, formed by the construction of giant Hoover Dam.

Numbers in the text correspond to numbers in the margin and on the South Rim and East Rim Drive, South Rim and West Rim Drive, North Rim, and Northwest Arizona and Lake Mead maps.

Great Itineraries

If you're in a hurry, a visit of three days will make you feel like you've "done" the Grand Canyon; a lengthier stay of 10 days or so is enough to make you feel like an old hand—particularly if you're able to experience some white-water rafting on the Colorado River. A few extra days will allow for a trip to the Lake Mead area. Reservations for area destinations are frequently made up to a year in advance; even diversions such as rafting trips and mule rides into the canyon can require reservations made more than six months ahead.

IF YOU HAVE 2 OR 3 DAYS

Spend the first night in ⛰ **Williams** ㉓. The next morning, board the historic **Grand Canyon Railway,** which takes you to the South Rim of the canyon. Spend the afternoon visiting **Grand Canyon Village** and then perhaps take in the informative IMAX film in nearby **Tusayan** (taxis or a shuttle bus will take you there). Spend the night at ⛰ **Grand Canyon Village** and the next morning take a tour of the **Village Rim** ⑨–⑭ or build up an appetite with a short hike before lunch, then take the 3:15 train back to Williams.

If you don't want to be at the Grand Canyon itself, try hiking in the less-frequented ⛰ **Havasu Canyon.** Hike 8 mi down into the canyon to the small village of Supai and the Havasupai Lodge. You'll want to spend at least two days in this hiker's heaven. On the morning of the third day, give yourself plenty of time and water to climb back out of the canyon, or consider riding up by mule.

IF YOU HAVE 4 OR 5 DAYS

You will have time to ponder the marvels of the Grand Canyon, both from above as well as from below. After a night at the ⛰ **Grand Canyon Village,** take the mule-pack expedition down the **Bright Angel Trailhead** ⑬, stopping along the way for a picnic lunch on a plateau with breathtaking views. Arrive at ⛰ **Phantom Ranch** for dinner and a night's sleep, then return by mule pack to the **South Rim** and another night or two in the Grand Canyon area.

IF YOU HAVE 7 TO 10 DAYS

You will have time for a memorable expedition that includes hiking the canyon as well as experiencing the thrill of white-water rafting along the Colorado River. If time allows, drive through the Arizona Strip to

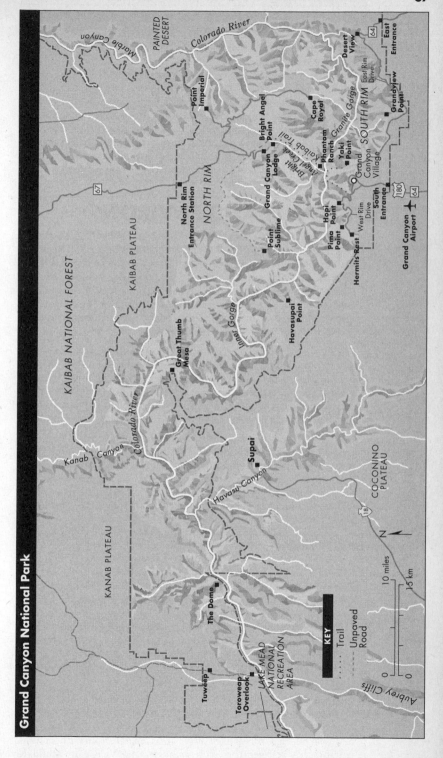

Grand Canyon National Park

the North Rim. Alternatively, head to the northwest to visit **Lake Mead** ㊲ and view **Hoover Dam** ㊳.

When to Tour the Grand Canyon and Northwest Arizona

If you can arrange it, try to visit the Grand Canyon in the fall or spring. You might encounter cold weather during those periods, but chances are good that most days will be clear and pleasantly cool or even warm. In autumn and spring, when the crowds have thinned, reservations are much easier to come by, and in some cases prices drop. Also consider a winter visit to the South Rim. Snow on the ground only enhances the site's sublime beauty. The North Rim, however, is inaccessible from mid-October to mid-May, when heavy snows close the area's highways and facilities.

THE SOUTH RIM AND ENVIRONS

The approach to the South Rim of the Grand Canyon is across the relatively level surface of the 7,000-ft Coconino Plateau, so you won't see the great gorge until you're past Tusayan, practically at its edge. Truth be told, the South Rim is a bit of a circus in summer. Most of Grand Canyon Village was laid out before the park service existed; the area is not well equipped to accommodate the crowds that converge on the area every summer—there are only 1,400 parking spaces for the nearly 6,000 cars that enter each day.

The Park Service is currently constructing a visitor transportation system to eliminate private vehicle traffic along the South Rim. When it is completed in 2002, it will transport visitors via light rail from the town of Tusayan to a new visitor center (☞ *below*). Alternate-fuel buses will run between points of interest from Desert View to Hermit's Rest, and extensive greenways will be open to pedestrians and bicyclists.

Until then, if you can visit during the winter months, you'll be able to navigate the South Rim with little difficulty. Lodging reservations inside the park (except for Phantom Ranch) this time of year are usually available with only two or three weeks' notice, and the best-maintained hiking trails (Bright Angel and South Kaibab) are less trafficked, if potentially icy. *See* the Beating the Crowds at the Canyon Close-up box, *below,* for how to make your high-season visit more manageable.

Tusayan and Environs

81 mi northwest of Flagstaff on U.S. 180.

The town of Tusayan, 2 mi south of Grand Canyon National Park's south entrance, has dining, lodging, and other facilities. Its main attraction is an **IMAX theater** that screens an exciting 34-minute film, *Grand Canyon—The Hidden Secrets,* shown on a 70-ft-high screen. The script is informative, and some of the shots—especially those of boats running the rapids—are positively dizzying. ⊠ *AZ 64/U.S. 180,* ☎ *520/638-2203.* ⊡ *$8.* ☉ *Mar.–Oct., daily 8:30–8:30; Nov.–Feb., daily 10:30–6:30; shows every hr on the ½ hr.*

Lodging

$$$ ⊞ **Grand Canyon Suites.** This all-suites hotel has guest quarters decorated in a variety of western themes, such as Route 66, Zane Grey, and Wild Bill Hickok. All have sitting areas separate from the bedrooms. Microwaves, refrigerators, coffeemakers, and VCR's are standard amenities. Unlike many lodgings in the area, the hotel has no pool or whirlpool. ⊠ *Box 3251, Grand Canyon 86023,* ☎ *520/683-3100 or 888/538-5353,* ℻ *520/638-2747. 32 rooms. AE, MC, V.*

BEATING THE CROWDS AT THE CANYON

I T'S HARD TO COMMUNE with one of nature's great spectacles when you've just spent two hours looking for a parking spot and are now being asked to step out of the range of someone's video camera. During the Canyon's busiest tourist season, not even a descent into the canyon itself guarantees a getaway. If you do intend to visit between May and November—"high" season gets longer every year—you'll need to make your plans at least six months in advance. Once you arrive, you'll find it may be in your best interests to simply avoid the South Rim this time of year. Even when the park's new visitor transportation system (F The South Rim and Environs) is completed, all but eliminating automobile traffic, there will still be lots of people around. Here are three alternative ways of experiencing the Canyon while everyone else is in line at the south entrance:

Take the road less travelled. Approach is everything if your goal is to avoid the masses. Most tourists come to the south entrance of the Grand Canyon via highways 64 and 180 from Flagstaff. It's a pleasant enough route, but if you take Highway 89 instead, you'll have the option of stopping off at Sunset Crater and Wupatki national monuments on your way (☞ Chapter 3). You'll be treated to a view of the Painted Desert to the east (☞ Chapter 5), and you'll also pass through a corner of the Navajo reservation (☞ Chapter 2). Along the road are native artisans selling jewelry, pottery, and rugs.

You can stop to stretch your legs in Cameron (about 50 mi north), and have a brain-awakening bowl of spicy green chili at the Cameron Trading Post before continuing on. Get on Highway 64 west for the 35-mi drive to Desert View, where the road turns into East Rim Drive, also known as Desert View Drive, about

5 mi beyond the less crowded east entrance of the park. If you continue west on the East Rim Drive, you'll reach the visitor's center at South Rim in 20 mi.

Skip the South Rim altogether. At Cameron, instead of turning west towards the east entrance of the park, keep heading north on Highway 89. The North Rim of the Grand Canyon is 10 mi from the South Rim as the crow flies, but by car the journey from Flagstaff to the North Rim will log more than 200 mi on your odometer and consume five hours of your vacation. Is it worth the effort? Unequivocally.

Highway 89 to the North Rim closes to visitors after the first big winter snow, usually in December, and doesn't reopen until spring. But if you're visiting between May and November, plan to stay overnight at the Grand Canyon Lodge and try to arrive at Cape Royal (23 mi southeast of the hotel, and a meandering three-hour drive from Cameron) for the most spectacular sunset anywhere, regardless of the weather. On the Kaibab Plateau, at an elevation of 7,876 ft, Cape Royal is densely forested, the most mountainous area in the park. The air is crystalline even in high summer.

Let the conductor do the driving. If you're pressed for time, or simply don't want the hassle of taking a car into the park, make the sleepy town of Williams your base for exploring. A turn-of-the-century steam locomotive or vintage diesel train (depending on the season) departs every morning from the Williams Depot at 9:30 sharp for a 2¼-hr jaunt to Grand Canyon Village on the South Rim. The train departs the village at 3:15 PM (☞ Williams, *below*) so you can do the round-trip in one day, but it's nice to spend a night in the park (☞ Grand Canyon Village, *below*) and return the following afternoon.

$$–$$$ ⌷ **Quality Inn.** The airy atrium here, which has a spa and lounge, distinguishes this chain motel. You can access first-floor rooms from the atrium or from the parking lot. All the rooms, in soothing shades of light blue, peach, or tan, have coffeemakers and two sinks. A buffet breakfast at the full-service restaurant will fortify you for a day at the canyon. ⊠ *AZ 64/U.S. 180, Box 520, Grand Canyon 86023,* ☏ *520/ 638–2673 or 800/221–2222,* FAX *520/638–9537. 176 rooms. Restaurant, lounge, minibars, pool. AE, D, DC, MC, V.*

$$ ⌷ **Best Western Grand Canyon Squire Inn.** About 2 mi south of the park entrance, this motel lacks some of the historic charm of the older lodges at the canyon rim, but it has more amenities—including a bowling alley, a cowboy museum in the stylish lobby, and an upscale gift shop. Spacious rooms have southwestern-style furnishings. Ask for one with a view of the woods; others face the highway. ⊠ *AZ 64/U.S. 180, Box 130, Grand Canyon 86023,* ☏ *520/638–2681 or 800/622–6966,* FAX *520/638–2782. 250 rooms, 4 rooms accessible to people with disabilities. Coffee shop, dining room, lounge, pool, beauty salon, sauna, 2 tennis courts, bowling, exercise room, billiards, video games, travel services. AE, D, DC, MC, V.*

$$ ⌷ **The Grand Hotel.** Opened in 1998, this stone-and-timber structure in the heart of the Tusayan strip has clean, generic motel rooms with one king or two queen beds; an extra few bucks buys you a small balcony. The large barbeque-and-steaks restaurant features live country-and-western singers and Native American dance performances each evening, and a local medicine man offers a variety of Native American workshops to guests. Kinks in service and a sometimes indifferent staff can intrude on an otherwise pleasant stay. ⊠ *Box 3319, Grand Canyon 86023,* ☏ *520/638–3333,* FAX *520/638–3131. 120 rooms. Restaurant, bar, no-smoking rooms, indoor pool, hot tub, exercise room, meeting room. AE, DC, MC, V.*

$–$$ ⌷ **Red Feather Lodge.** Some of the rooms are worn around the edges, but this motel is still a good value, largely because of the pool, whirlpool, and game room for kids. A restaurant on the premises serves American and Native American food. ⊠ *Box 1460, Grand Canyon 86023,* ☏ *520/638–2414 or 800/538–2345,* FAX *520/638–9216. 230 rooms. Dining room, pool, hot tub. AE, DC, MC, V.*

⌂ **Grand Canyon Camper Village.** The village has 250 RV hookups, some partial, some full ($23 for two people, plus $2 for each additional person over the age of 12), and 100 tent sites ($15 for two people). ⊠ *Off AZ 64/U.S. 180, Box 490, Grand Canyon 86023,* ☏ *520/638– 2887.* ☉ *Year-round.*

⌂ **Ten X Campground.** This spot has 70 sites, water, and pit toilets for $10 per day but no hookups or showers. No reservations are accepted. ⊠ *Kaibab National Forest, 9 mi south of Grand Canyon National Park east of AZ 64/U.S. 180. Tusayan Ranger District:* ⊠ *Box 3088, Grand Canyon 86023,* ☏ *520/638–2443.* ☉ *May 1–Sept. 30.*

Outdoor Activities and Sports

HORSEBACK RIDING
You can rent gentle horses at the **Apache Stables** at Moqui Lodge (⊠ U.S. 180, ☏ 520/638–2891) for $22 an hour or $36 for two hours. A four-hour East Rim ride goes for $57.50, a campfire horse and hay-wagon ride for $27 ($7.50 if you ride in the wagon rather than on your own horse). The stables open in March, and rides are offered, weather permitting, through the end of November.

Approaching the South Rim

❶ Mather Point, about 4 mi north of the south entrance, gives you the first glimpse of the canyon from one of the most impressive and accessible vista points on the rim; from it, you can see nearly one quarter of Grand Canyon. This overlook, named for the National Park Service's first director, Stephen Mather, yields extraordinary views of the Inner Gorge and the numerous buttes that rise out of the eroded chasm: Wotan's Throne, Brahma Temple, Zoroaster Temple, and many others. The Grand Canyon Lodge, on the North Rim, is almost directly north from Mather Point and only 10 mi away—yet you have to drive nearly 210 mi to get from one spot to the other.

★ **❷** The National Park Service **Visitor Center,** in Grand Canyon Village just west of Yavapai Point, has park rangers on hand to answer questions and aid in planning Grand Canyon excursions; short movies and slide shows on the canyon are presented regularly; and there's a bookstore. A daily schedule for ranger-led hikes and evening lectures is also posted. Buses and taxis leave from here for the IMAX theater in Tusayan (☞ *above*).

An exhibit area profiles the area's natural and human history. The first inhabitants were probably nomadic Paleo-Indians, arriving more than 10,000 years ago. Artifacts that were found in caves deep in the canyon were left by a later Archaic culture. They are perfectly preserved figurines of animals, made from willow twigs more than 4,000 years ago— thus predating Homeric Greece by 1,000 years. About 2,200 years ago, ancestral Pueblo culture began to develop around the canyon. The museum also traces the arrival of explorers Captain García López de Cárdenas, John Wesley Powell, and others. Late in 2000 a new visitor center, the **Canyon View Information Plaza,** will open east of Yavapai Point. It will provide orientation and activities and will eventually serve as the hub of the park's new visitor transportation system (☞ *above*). ⊠ *East side of Grand Canyon Village, about 1 mi east of El Tovar Hotel,* ☎ *520/638–7888.* ⊡ *Free.* ☉ *Memorial Day–Labor Day, daily 8–6; rest of yr, daily 8–5.*

Outdoor Activities and Sports

If you'd like a little exercise and great views of the canyon, it's an easy hike from the back of the visitor center to the El Tovar Hotel (☞ Grand Canyon Village, *below*). Walk through a pretty wooded area for about ½ mi, where the path then runs along the rim for another ½ mi or so.

East Rim Drive

The breathtaking East Rim Drive proceeds east for about 25 mi along the South Rim from Grand Canyon Village to Desert View. Before beginning the drive, consider stopping to see the exhibits and attend the free lectures offered by park naturalists at Yavapai Observation Station, ¾ mi east of the visitor center. There are four marked picnic areas along the route and rest rooms at Tusayan Museum and Desert View.

❸ Yaki Point, east of Grand Canyon Village on AZ 64, provides an exceptional view of Wotan's Throne, a majestic flat-top butte named by François Matthes, a U.S. Geological Survey scientist who developed the first topographical map of the Grand Canyon. Due north is Buddha Temple, capped by limestone. Newton Butte, with its flat top of red sandstone, lies to the east. At Yaki Point the popular **Kaibab Trail** starts the descent to the Inner Gorge, crosses the Colorado over a steel suspension bridge, and wends its way to rustic Phantom Ranch (☞ Dining and Lodging, *below*), the only lodging facility at the bottom of the Grand Canyon. If you plan to go more than a mile, carry water with

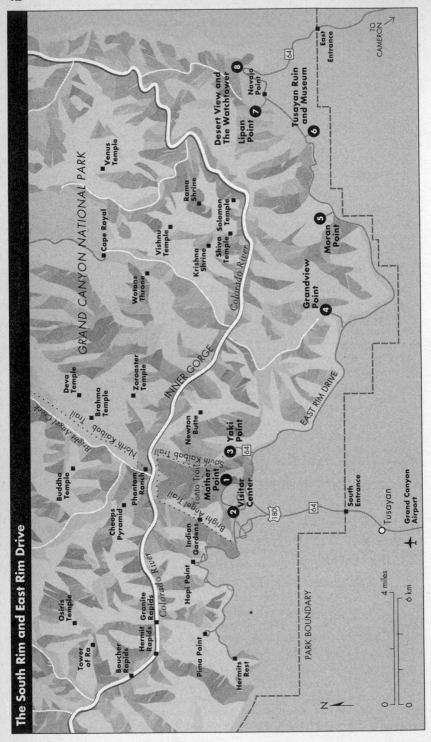

The South Rim and East Rim Drive

GRAND CANYON NATIONAL PARK

Venus Temple

Cape Royal

Rama Shrine

Vishnu Temple

Solomon Temple

Shiva Temple

Krishna Shrine

Wotans Throne

Desert View and The Watchtower

Lipan Point

Navajo Point

Tusayan Ruin and Museum

East Entrance

TO CAMERON

64

8

7

6

Colorado River

INNER GORGE

Moran Point

5

Grandview Point

4

EAST RIM DRIVE

Deva Temple

Brahma Temple

Zoroaster Temple

Newton Butte

Yaki Point

3

Mather Point

1

Visitor Center

2

64

North Kaibob Trail

Bright Angel Creek

South Kaibab Trail

Buddha Temple

Phantom Ranch

Tonto Trail

Cheops Pyramid

Indian Gardens

Bright Angel Trail

Hopi Point

180

64

South Entrance

Tusayan

Grand Canyon Airport

Colorado River

Granite Rapids

Hermit Rapids

Osiris Temple

Tower of Ra

Boucher Rapids

Pima Point

Hermits Rest

N

PARK BOUNDARY

0   4 miles

0   6 km

you (☞ Hiking *in* Outdoor Activities and Sports, *below*). If you encounter a mule train, the animals have the right-of-way. Move to the inside of the trail and wait as they pass.

④ About 7 mi east of Yaki Point, **Grandview Point,** at an altitude of 7,496 ft, has large stands of ponderosa pine, piñon pine, oak, and juniper. The view from here is one of the finest in the canyon. To the northeast is a group of dominant buttes, including Krishna Shrine, Vishnu Temple, Rama Shrine, and Shiva Temple. A short stretch of the Colorado River is also visible. Directly below the point and accessible by the Grandview Trail is Horseshoe Mesa, where you can see ruins of the Last Chance Copper Mine. Grandview Point was also the site of the Grandview Hotel, constructed in the late 1890s but closed in 1908; logs salvaged from the hotel were used for the Kiva Room of the Desert View and the Watchtower (☞ *below*).

⑤ **Moran Point,** about 5 mi east of Grandview Point, was named for American landscape artist Thomas Moran, who painted Grand Canyon scenes from many points on the rim but was especially fond of the play of light and shadows from this location. He first visited the canyon with John Wesley Powell in 1873, and his vivid canvases helped persuade Congress to create a national park at the Grand Canyon. "Thomas Moran's name, more than any other, with the possible exception of Major Powell's, is to be associated with the Grand Canyon," wrote the noted canyon photographer Ellsworth Kolb, and it is fitting that Moran Point is a favorite spot for photographers and painters.

Three miles east of Moran Point on the south side of the highway is
⑥ the entrance to the **Tusayan Ruin and Museum,** which contains evidence of early habitation in the Grand Canyon and information about ancestral Pueblo people. *Tusayan* comes from a Hopi phrase meaning "country of isolated buttes," which certainly describes the scenery. The partially intact rock dwellings here were occupied for roughly 20 years around AD 1200 by 30 or so Indian hunters, farmers, and gatherers; they moved elsewhere, like so many others, pressured by drought and depletion of natural resources. A museum and a bookstore display artifacts, models of the dwellings, and exhibits on modern tribes of the region. Free 30-minute guided tours—as many as five during the summer, fewer in winter—are given daily. ⊠ *East Rim Dr., 3 mi east of Moran Point,* ☎ *520/638–2305.* ▭ *Free.* ⊙ *Daily 9–5.*

⑦ **Lipan Point,** a mile northeast of Tusayan Ruin, is the canyon's widest point. From here you can get an astonishing visual profile of the gorge's geologic history, with a view of every eroded layer of the canyon. You can also see Unkar Delta, where a wide creek joins the Colorado to form powerful rapids and a broad beach. Anasazi farmers worked the Unkar Delta for hundreds of years, growing corn, beans, and melons.

Just over 1 mi east of Lipan Point lies 7,461-ft **Navajo Point,** the probable site of the first Spanish descent into the Canyon, in 1540. Just west of Navajo Point—the highest elevation on the South Rim—is the head of the unmaintained Tanner Trail, a rugged route once favored by gold prospectors, rustlers (it's also called Horsethief Trail), and bootleggers.

⑧ **Desert View and The Watchtower** make for a climactic final stop. From the top of the 70-ft stone-and-mortar watchtower, built in 1932 by the Fred Harvey Company and the Santa Fe Railroad in the style of Native American structures, even the muted hues of the distant Painted Desert to the east and the 3,000-ft-high Vermilion Cliffs rising from a high plateau near the Utah border are visible. In the chasm below, angling to the north toward Marble Canyon, an imposing stretch of the

Colorado River reveals itself. The Watchtower houses a glass-enclosed observatory with powerful telescopes. ⊠ *The Watchtower,* ☎ *520/638–2736; 520/638–2360 trading post.* ⊡ *Free; 25¢ to climb Watchtower.* ☉ *Daily 8–7 or 8–8 in summer, daily 9–5 in winter.*

Dining and Lodging

$ ✕⊡ **Phantom Ranch.** Built in 1932 on the site of a hunting camp, this group of wood-and-stone buildings is set among a grove of cottonwood trees at the bottom of the canyon. For hikers (who need a backcountry permit to come down here), dormitory accommodations—20 beds for men and 20 for women—are available, as are two cabins (one sleeps four, the other 10). Seven additional cabins are reserved exclusively for mule riders; lodging, meals, and mule rides are offered as a package (☞ Guided Tours *in* The Grand Canyon and Northwest Arizona A to Z, *below*). The restaurant at Phantom Ranch, probably the most remote eating establishment in the United States, has a limited menu. All meals are served family style, with breakfast, dinner, and box lunches available. Food and lodging reservations should be made from nine to 11 months ahead. ⊠ *Amfac Parks and Resorts, 14001 E. Iliff, Suite 600, Aurora, CO 80014,* ☎ *303/297–2757,* FAX *303/297–3175. 4 dormitories with shared bath and 2 cabins for hikers, 7 cabins with shower outside for mule riders. Dining room. AE, D, DC, MC, V.*

⚠ **Bright Angel.** This free campground (32 sites available) is en route to Phantom Ranch, close to the bottom of the canyon. There are toilet facilities and running water but no showers. A backcountry permit is required to stay here. ⊠ *Backcountry Office, Box 129, Grand Canyon 86023,* ☎ *520/638–7875.* ☉ *Year-round.*

⚠ **Desert View Campground.** Fifty RV and tent sites, flush toilets, and water but no hookups are available here for $10 per night, with no reservations. ⊠ *23 mi east of Grand Canyon Village off AZ 64; Box 129, Grand Canyon 86023,* ☎ *520/638–7875.* ☉ *May–Sept.*

⚠ **Indian Garden.** About halfway down the canyon is this free campground with 15 sites, located en route to Phantom Ranch. Running water and toilet facilities are available, but there are no showers. A backcountry permit, which serves as a reservation, is required. ⊠ *Box 129, Grand Canyon 86023,* ☎ *520/638–7875.* ☉ *Year-round.*

Outdoor Activities and Sports

HIKING

South Kaibab Trail, starting near Yaki Point on East Rim Drive near Grand Canyon Village, connects at the bottom of the canyon (after the Kaibab Bridge across the Colorado) with the **North Kaibab Trail.** Plan on two to three days if you want to hike the gorge from rim to rim (if you do this, we recommend that you descend from the North Rim, as it is more than 1,000 ft higher than the South Rim). South Kaibab Trail is steep, descending 4,800 ft in just 7 mi, with no water or campgrounds (there are portable toilets at Cedar Ridge, 2¼ mi from the trailhead) and very little shade. The trail corkscrews down through some spectacular geology, closely following the 300-million-year-old Supai and Redwall formations; look for (but don't remove) fossils in the limestone when you take your frequent water breaks. If you're going back up to the South Rim, ascend **Bright Angel Trail.** Accommodations for hikers along the way include the campgrounds at Indian Garden and Bright Angel, or Phantom Ranch (☞ Dining and Lodging, *above*).

Shopping

Desert View Trading Post (⊠ East Rim Dr., near the Watchtower at Desert View, ☎ 520/638–2360) sells a mix of traditional southwestern souvenirs and authentic Native American pottery.

Grand Canyon Village

Grand Canyon Village and the Village Rim can be explored on foot (about 1 mi round-trip); a paved pathway over level ground runs along the rim. Cars can be left at the nearby El Tovar parking lot.

⑨ Hopi House, a multistory structure of rock and mortar, was modeled after buildings found in the Hopi village of Oraibi, Arizona, the oldest continuously inhabited community in the United States (☞ The Hopi Mesas *in* Chapter 2). Part of an attempt by the Fred Harvey Company to encourage Southwest Indian crafts at the turn of the century, Hopi House was established as one of the first curio stores in the Grand Canyon.

★ ⑩ A few yards to the west of Hopi House is the historic **El Tovar Hotel** (☞ Dining and Lodging, *below*). Built in 1905 to resemble the great hunting lodges of Europe, this log structure underwent a renovation in 1998 yet retains the ambience of its early days. If the weather is cool, stop in front of the stone fireplace to warm your hands. The rustic lobby, with its numerous stuffed and mounted animal heads, is a great place for people-watching, and the back porch provides a front-row seat for viewing the canyon.

★ ⑪ A trail at the rim leads west toward **Lookout Studio.** Built in 1914 to compete with the Kolbs' photographic studio (☞ *below*), the building was designed by architect Mary Jane Colter to resemble a Hopi pueblo. The combination lookout point, museum, and gift shop has a collection of fossils and geologic samples from around the world. An upstairs loft provides another excellent overlook into the mighty gorge below.

⑫ A half dozen yards west of Lookout Studio are a few steps that descend to the **Kolb Studio,** built in 1904 by the Kolb brothers as a photographic workshop. If you look out the window, you can see Indian Gardens, where, in the days before a pipeline was installed, Emery Kolb descended 3,300 ft each day to get the water he needed to develop his prints. Perhaps the exercise was beneficial: He operated the studio until he died in 1976 at age 95. The gallery here is worth checking out— painting, photography, and crafts exhibits are presented from mid-April through November. There's also a bookstore.

★ ⑬ **Bright Angel Trailhead,** a few feet from Kolb Studio, is the starting point for perhaps the best known of all the trails that descend to the bottom of the canyon. Originally a bighorn sheep path that was later used by the Havasupai Indians, it was widened in 1890–91 for prospectors and has since become a well-maintained avenue for mule and foot traffic. If you intend to go very far—the trail descends 5,510 ft to the Colorado River—you should have the proper equipment and notify the park-service representatives at the visitor center before you go.

Directly east of Bright Angel Trailhead are railroad tracks over which the Santa Fe trains once passed. Here you'll see the barn that houses some of the tour mules; it's worth a brief stop, especially for children.

⑭ Farther east, **Bright Angel Lodge** was built in 1935 of Oregon pine logs and native stone; rustic cabins are set off from the main building. The rocks used to make the "geologic" fireplace are arranged in the order in which they are layered in the Grand Canyon, and the history room displays memorabilia from the South Rim's early years. The lodge's soda fountain has the distinction of selling the most Breyer's ice cream in the United States.

The South Rim and West Rim Drive

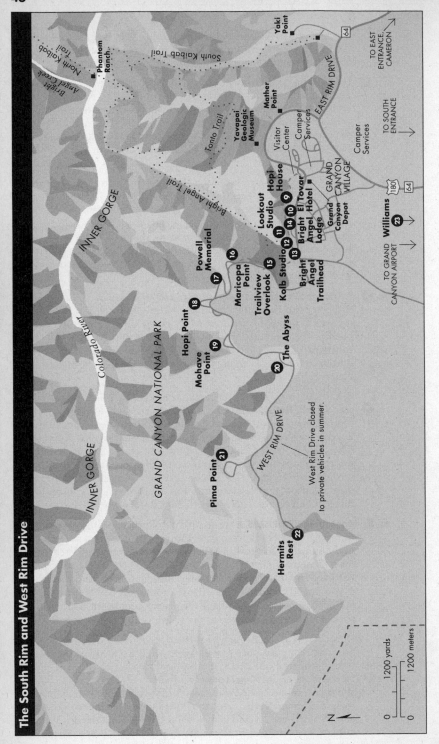

Dining and Lodging

$$–$$$$ ✕🎬 **El Tovar Hotel.** Built in 1905 of native stone and pine logs and re-
★ modeled in 1998, the Fred Harvey Company's El Tovar is reminiscent
of a grand European hunting lodge. It maintains its excellent reputa-
tion for service, though at a time when indoor plumbing is no longer
a luxury, rooms don't seem as posh as they once might have. Some are
small, but all are nicely appointed, and a number have canyon views.
The hotel's restaurant has a long-standing local reputation for good
food served in a classic 19th-century room of hand-hewn logs and
beamed ceilings. The Southwest-inspired menu changes seasonally but
includes a daily vegetarian special along with fish, poultry, and meat
dishes. The local game is always a good choice. ✉ *Amfac Parks and
Resorts, 14001 E. Iliff, Suite 600, Aurora, CO 80014,* ☎ *303/297–
2757,* 𝖥𝖠𝖷 *303/297–3175. 70 rooms, 10 suites. Bar, dining room, room
service. AE, D, DC, MC, V.*

$–$$$ ✕🎬 **Bright Angel Lodge.** Mary Jane Colter designed this 1935 log-and-
stone structure that sits within a few yards of the canyon rim and blends
superbly with the natural environment. Most rooms in the main lodge
share baths; cabins, some with fireplaces and/or canyon views, are scattered among the pines: Visitors can expect historic charm and bargain
prices, not luxury accommodations. The Bright Angel coffee shop is
open for breakfast, lunch, and dinner; the more upscale but still casual Arizona Steak House serves dinner only. ✉ *Amfac Parks and Resorts, 14001 E. Iliff, Suite 600, Aurora, CO 80014,* ☎ *303/297–2757,*
𝖥𝖠𝖷 *303/297–3175. 11 rooms with bath, 13 rooms with ½ bath, 6
rooms with shared bath, 42 cabins with bath. Restaurant, bar, coffee
shop, beauty salon. AE, D, DC, MC, V.*

$–$$$$ 🎬 **Grand Canyon National Park Lodges.** The Fred Harvey Company
has seven lodges on the South Rim. El Tovar (☞ *above*) and Bright
Angel (☞ *below*)are outstanding, but Maswik Lodge, Yavapai Lodge,
Moqui Lodge, Kachina Lodge, and Thunderbird Lodge are all com-
fortable, if not luxurious. The setting, rather than the amenities, is the
draw here, so it's a good idea to bring a flashlight as the wooded grounds
are dimly lighted. In addition to lodge rooms, Maswik has inexpen-
sive rustic cabins. Moqui, which is only open from March through
November, is on U.S. 180, just outside the national park; the others
are in Grand Canyon Village. ✉ *Amfac Parks and Resorts, 14001 E.
Iliff, Suite 600, Aurora, CO 80014,* ☎ *303/297–2757,* 𝖥𝖠𝖷 *303/297–
3175. 855 rooms with bath. Restaurant, 2 cafeterias (at Yavapai Lodge
and Maswik Lodge). AE, D, DC, MC, V.*

▵ **Mather Campground.** There are 97 RV and 190 tent sites (no
hookups), flush toilets, water, showers, and a laundromat at Mather;
the cost is $10 per site. No reservations are accepted from December
to March. *Grand Canyon Village; reservations through* ✉ *Destinet,
Box 85705, San Diego, CA 92138,* ☎ *800/365–2267; 858/452–0150
outside the U.S.* ⊙ *Year-round.*

▵ **Trailer Village.** This campground in Grand Canyon Village has 78
RV sites with full hookups for $18 per site. ✉ *Amfac Parks and Re-
sorts, 14001 E. Iliff, Suite 600, Aurora, CO 80014,* ☎ *303/297–2757,*
𝖥𝖠𝖷 *303/297–3175.* ⊙ *Year-round.*

Nightlife and the Arts

Nightlife in these parts consists of watching a full moon above the soar-
ing buttes of the Grand Canyon, roasting marshmallows over a crack-
ling fire, crawling into your bedroll beside some lonely canyon trail,
or attending a free evening program on area history. The following Grand
Canyon properties have cocktail lounges: **El Tovar Hotel** (piano bar),
Bright Angel Lodge (live entertainment), **Maswik Lodge** (sports bar),
and **Moqui Lodge** (live entertainment).

In September the **Grand Canyon Chamber Music Festival** (⊠ Box 1332, Grand Canyon 86023, ☎ 520/638–9215) is held in the Shrine of the Ages auditorium at the South Rim visitor center. Call or write for schedule information and advance tickets. A **lecture series** on scientific topics, cosponsored by the National Park Service and the Grand Canyon Association, coincides with the chamber-music festival; ask for details at the area lodges or the visitor center.

Outdoor Activities and Sports

HIKING

The well-maintained Bright Angel Trailhead (☞ *above*) is one of the most popular and scenic hiking paths from the South Rim to the bottom of the canyon (9 mi). Rest houses are equipped with water at the 1½- and 3-mi points from May through September and at Indian Gardens year-round. Water is also available at Bright Angel Campground, 9¼ mi below the trailhead. Plateau Point, about 1½ mi below Indian Gardens, is as far as you should go on a day hike. Bright Angel Trail is the easiest of all the footpaths into the canyon, but because the climb out from the bottom is an ascent of 5,510 ft, the trip should be attempted only by those in good physical condition and should be avoided in midsummer due to extreme heat. The top of the trail, a tight set of switchbacks called Jacob's Ladder, can be icy in winter. Note that you will be sharing the trail with mule trains, which have the right-of-way.

Shopping

Nearly every lodging facility and retail store at the South Rim stocks Native American artifacts and Grand Canyon souvenirs. After a while, all the merchandise begins to look alike, but most of the items sold here are authentic. The **El Tovar Hotel Gift Shop** (⊠ Grand Canyon Village, ☎ 520/638–2631) carries Native American jewelry, rather expensive casual wear, and souvenir gifts. **Hopi House** (⊠ East of El Tovar Hotel, ☎ 520/638–2631), which opened in 1905, still has one of the widest selections of Native American artifacts—some of museum quality and not for sale—in the vicinity of the Grand Canyon. **Verkamp's** (⊠ across from El Tovar Hotel, ☎ 520/638–2242) is in a 1906 building where a huge buffalo head surveys those browsing the fine artwork and crafts.

West Rim Drive

Originally called Hermit Rim Road, West Rim Drive was constructed by the Santa Fe Company in 1912 as a scenic tour route. Ten overlooks spread out over an 8-mi leg, and each of them is worth a visit. You need to return on the same road, so consider stopping at half of the overlooks on the way out and the others on the way back; access to the lookout points is easy from both sides of the road. West Rim Drive has many hairpin turns, so be sure to observe the posted speed limits. In summer West Rim Drive is closed to auto traffic because of congestion. From Memorial Day weekend to October 1, a free shuttle bus (☞ Getting Around *in* The Grand Canyon and Northwest Arizona A to Z, *below*) makes most of the stops described below.

⑮ Trailview Overlook provides a dramatic view of the Bright Angel and Plateau Point trails as they zigzag down the canyon. In the deep gorge to the north flows Bright Angel Creek, one of the few permanent tributary streams of the Colorado River in the region. Toward the south is an unobstructed view of the distant San Francisco Peaks, Arizona's highest mountains (the tallest is 12,633 ft), as well as of Bill Williams Mountain (on the horizon) and Red Butte (about 15 mi south of the canyon rim).

16 Less than a mile from Trailview Overlook, **Maricopa Point** merits a stop not only for the arresting scenery, which includes the Colorado River below, but also for its towering opening and defunct mine. On your left as you face the canyon are the Orphan Mine and (below) a mine shaft and cable lines leading up to the rim. The copper ore in the mine, which started operations in 1893, was of excellent quality, but the cost of removing it finally brought the venture to a halt in 1966. The Battleship, the red butte directly ahead of you in the canyon, was named during the Spanish-American War, when battleships were in the news.

★ **17** About ½ mi beyond Maricopa Point, the large granite **Powell Memorial** stands as a tribute to the first man to ride the wild rapids of the Colorado River through the canyon in 1869. John Wesley Powell measured, charted, and named many of the canyons and creeks of the river. It was here that the dedication ceremony for Grand Canyon National Park took place on April 3, 1920.

18 From **Hopi Point** (elevation 7,071 ft) you can see a large section of the Colorado River; although it appears as a thin line, the river is nearly 350 ft wide below this overlook. Across the canyon to the north is Shiva Temple, which remained an isolated section of the Kaibab Plateau until 1937. In that year, Harold Anthony of the American Museum of Natural History led an expedition to the rock formation in the belief that it supported life that had been cut off from the rest of the canyon. Imagine the expedition members' surprise when they found an empty Kodak film box on top of the temple. Directly below Hopi Point lies Dana Butte, named for a prominent 19th-century geologist. In 1919, an entrepreneur proposed connecting Hopi Point, Dana Butte, and the Tower of Set across the river with an aerial tramway, a technically feasible plan that fortunately has not been realized.

19 Four-fifths of a mile to the west of Hopi Point, **Mohave Point** also has striking views of the Colorado River and of 5,401-ft Cheops Pyramid, the grayish rock formation behind Dana Butte. Granite and Salt Creek rapids can also be seen from this spot.

20 **The Abyss** (elevation 6,720 ft) is one of the most awesome stops on West Rim Drive, revealing a sheer drop of 3,000 ft to the Tonto Platform. From the Abyss you'll also see several isolated sandstone columns, the largest of which is called the Monument.

21 **Pima Point** provides a bird's-eye view of the Tonto Platform and the Tonto Trail, which wends its way through the canyon for more than 70 mi. Also to the west, two dark, cone-shape mountains—Mt. Trumbull and Mt. Logan—are visible on clear days. They rise in stark contrast to the surrounding flat-top mesas and buttes.

★ **22** **Hermits Rest,** the westernmost viewpoint, and the Hermit Trail that descends from it (☞ *below*) were named for the "hermit" Louis Boucher, a 19th-century French-Canadian prospector who had a number of mining claims and a roughly built home down in the canyon. Canyon views from here include Hermit Rapids and the towering cliffs of the Supai and Redwall formations. The stone building at Hermits Rest sells curios and refreshments and has the only rest rooms on West Rim Drive.

Outdoor Activities and Sports
HIKING
The steep, 9-mi Hermit Trail beginning at Hermits Rest (8 mi west of Grand Canyon Village) is suitable only for experienced long-distance hikers. The trail is in generally good condition, but there is a tricky passage that was damaged by rock slides in 1993. For much of the year,

no water is available along the way; ask a park ranger about the availability of water at Santa Maria Springs and Hermit Creek. The route leads down to the Colorado River and has inspiring views of Hermit Gorge and the Redwall and Supai formations. Six miles from the trailhead you'll come across the scattered ruins of Hermit Camp, which the Santa Fe Railroad ran as a tourist camp from 1911 until 1930.

Williams

 55 mi south of Grand Canyon Village, 30 mi west of Flagstaff on I–40 and AZ 64. Use I–40 exits 161, 163, or 165.

Once a tough turn-of-the-century town of saloons, bordellos, and opium dens, Williams gained some respectability with the construction of one of the first Harvey Houses, the original Fray Marcos, completed in 1908. It is said to be the first poured-concrete building in Arizona. The bordello is now a bed-and-breakfast, the saloon and opium den are a Mexican restaurant, and the Fray Marcos is a luxury hotel.

Often considered just a jumping-off point for the Grand Canyon (it's only an hour away from the South Rim by car and a little more than two hours by train), Williams retains its own funky frontier charm despite a proliferation of motels and fast-food restaurants on its main street (named, like the town itself, after mountain man "Crazy Bill" Williams). The wooded area (elevation 6,700 ft) is temperate in summer, and in winter a small ski center operates (☞ Outdoor Activities and Sports, *below*). Many of the neon signs on Bill Williams Avenue hark back to the days when it was known as Route 66. Indeed, Williams was not bypassed by I–40 until 1984. Antiques shops with reasonable prices and retailers selling Native American crafts and jewelry line this main drag of historic buildings and period lampposts.

The **Williams Visitor Center,** which also houses the Chamber of Commerce and Forest Service office, is a 1901 passenger-train depot whose brick walls still show graffiti scrawled by early railroad workers and hoboes. ✉ *200 W. Railroad Ave., at Grand Canyon Blvd.,* ☎ *520/635–1418 or 520/635–4061.* ☉ *Daily 8–5.*

In 1989 the **Grand Canyon Railway** re-inaugurated service along a route established in 1901. The 65-mi trek from Williams Depot to the South Rim (2½ hours each way) takes the vintage train through prairie, ranch, and national park land to the log-cabin train station in Grand Canyon Village. The ride includes refreshments, commentary, and corny but fun onboard entertainment by Wild West characters. Passengers ride in restored 1923 cars and enjoy complimentary soft drinks in Coach Class. Club Class, with its fully stocked mahogany bar and complimentary morning pastries and coffee, costs an additional $20. A First Class ($50 upgrade), Deluxe Observation Class, or Luxury Parlor Car (both $70 upgrade) ticket gets you continental breakfast and complimentary afternoon champagne and snacks. The company also operates Farwest Airlines and offers air-and-rail packages between Phoenix and the South Rim.

Even if you don't take the train, it's worth visiting the **Williams Depot,** built in 1908 to replace the terminal where the visitor center now resides. Attractions here include a passenger car and the locomotive of a turn-of-the-century steam train, a gift shop where you can find kitschy souvenirs like a tie that plays "I've Been Working on the Railroad," and Max and Thelma's, a full-service restaurant. The small **Railroad Museum** is next to the depot in the original dining room of the old Harvey House. The museum holds an interesting collection of old railroad and Harvey-girl photographs and is a good place to learn about the history of the Grand Canyon Railway, which once carried American presidents, Franklin D. Roosevelt among them, on their whistle-stop campaigns through the West. ⊠ *Williams Depot: N. Grand Canyon Blvd., at Fray Marcos Blvd.,* ☎ *800/843–8724 for railway reservations and information.* ▣ *Round-trip fare $50 plus 8.8% tax and $6 national park entrance fee.* ⊙ *Departs daily from Williams at 9:30 AM, from the South Rim at 3:15 PM.*

Ⓒ Children enjoy the **Grand Canyon Deer Farm,** where visitors can pet pygmy goats, llamas, and deer, including the tiny fawns born every June and July. ⊠ *100 Deer Farm Rd., 8 mi east of Williams off I–40's Exit 171,* ☎ *520/635–4073.* ▣ *$5.* ⊙ *Mar.–May, daily 9–dusk; June–Aug., daily 8–dusk; Sept.–Oct., daily 9–dusk; Nov.–Feb., daily 10–5 in good weather.*

Dining and Lodging

$–$$ ✕ **Pancho McGillicuddy's.** Originally the Cabinet Saloon, this restaurant is on the National Register of Historic Places. Gone are the spittoons and pipes—the smoke-free dining area now has a Mexican decor, which sets the scene for such specialties as armadillo eggs, the local name for deep-fried jalapeños stuffed with cheese. ⊠ *141 Railroad Ave.,* ☎ *520/635–4150. MC, V.*

$–$$ ✕ **Rod's Steak House.** You can't miss this steak house with the plastic Angus cow out front. Obviously the emphasis here is on meat—sizzling mesquite-broiled steaks, prime rib, and the like. Steaks are often overcooked, so order yours a bit rarer than you actually want it. A children's menu is available. ⊠ *301 E. Rte. 66,* ☎ *520/635–2671 or 800/562–5545. D, MC, V.*

$ ✕ **Cruisers Café 66.** Route 66 icons fill this renovated gas station, formerly Tiffany's Lube Lounge. The menu and the spirit of the place remain lively—and the spiffed-up decor retains old gasoline logos and a couple of gas pumps. Standard American dishes are your best bet; stay away from the pasta. ⊠ *233 W. Rte. 66,* ☎ *520/635–2445. AE, DC, MC, V.*

$ ✕ **Grand Canyon Coffee Café.** You'll find the best espresso drinks in town here, along with wonderful sandwiches on homemade focaccia. Try an egg-cream soda with Ghirardelli chocolate if you're feeling nostalgic. You'll enjoy the Harley-Davidson artifacts that fill the space—some of them are for sale. ⊠ *125 W. Rte. 66,* ☎ *520/635–1255. No credit cards. Closed Sun.*

$$–$$$ ▥ **Sheridan House Inn.** This bed-and-breakfast, opened in 1998, provides a more civilized alternative to crowded Grand Canyon National Park lodgings. The inn, nestled among pine trees just a few blocks from Route 66, has large, quiet rooms decorated with taste. Hearty breakfasts (like eggs Benedict and buttermilk pancakes) will ready you for the hour-long drive to the Canyon. Steve and Evelyn Gardner are gracious hosts who'll be happy to help you plan your itinerary. Steve, a former restaurant chef, serves hors d'oeuvres every afternoon. ⊠ *460 E. Sheridan Ave., 86046,* ☎ *520/635–9441 or 888/635–9345. 7 rooms, 3 suites. Exercise room. Full breakfast. AE, D, MC, V.*

$$ ▥ **Fray Marcos Hotel.** This hotel across from the train station was designed to resemble the depot's original Fray Marcos lodge. Neoclassical Greek columns flank the grand entrance, which leads into a lobby with a 35-ft-high ceiling, maple balustrades, an enormous flagstone fireplace, and gigantic oil paintings of the Grand Canyon by local artist Kenneth McKenna. Bronzes by Frederic Remington, from the private collection of hotel owners Max and Thelma Biegert, also adorn the lobby. The southwestern-style rooms have large bathrooms. Adjacent to the lobby is Spenser's, a pub with an ornate hand-carved bar from England. A 100-room expansion is due to open in spring of 2000; the hotel also operates a full-service hookup RV park next door. ⊠ *235 N. Grand*

Canyon Blvd., 86046, ☎ *520/635–4010 or 800/843–8724. 89 rooms. Bar. AE, DC, MC, V.*

$–$$ ▦ **Red Garter.** A restored bordello dating from 1897 now houses a small bed-and-breakfast furnished to retain an old-fashioned feel. Ask for the "Best Gal's" room, with its own sitting room overlooking the train tracks. Despite the inn's location, all four rooms (two are interior, with skylights but no windows) are very quiet, as the only train traffic is the Grand Canyon Railway, with one daily arrival and departure. Even if you don't stay here, the fresh goodies at the on-site bakery are worth a stop. ⊠ *137 W. Railroad Ave., 86046,* ☎ *520/635–1484 or 800/328–1484. 4 rooms. Continental breakfast. AE, D, MC, V. Closed Jan.–mid-Feb.*

$ ▦ **Mountainside Inn Gateway to the Grand Canyon.** At the east entrance to town, this motel has comfortable rooms, a good American restaurant, and live country-and-western bands in summer. ⊠ *642 E. Rte. 66, 86046,* ☎ *520/635–4431 or 800/462–9381,* ℻ *520/635–2292. 95 rooms, 1 suite. Restaurant, pool, hot tub. AE, D, DC, MC, V.*

$ ▦ **Quality Inn Mountain Ranch & Resort.** Six mi east of town, the warm lights and friendly staff of this motel beckon. Rooms are basic and predictable, and included with the room rate is a full breakfast in the coffee shop, which has views of the San Francisco Peaks. In season, evening hayrides complete with singing cowboys, staged gun fights, and a cookout are offered on the grounds. ⊠ *6701 E. Mountain Ranch Rd., 86046,* ☎ *520/635–2693,* ℻ *520/635–4188. 73 rooms. Restaurant, bar, coffee shop, no-smoking rooms, pool, hot tub, 2 tennis courts, horseback riding. AE, D, MC, V.*

△ **Flintstones Bedrock City.** You'll find 28 tent sites and 32 partial RV hookups in a cartoon-kitsch setting here. Basic rates are $13 per site for two people; add $2 for electricity hookup, $2 for water hookup, and $1.50 for each additional person. Facilities include a gift shop full of Flintstones memorabilia, a diner, and pay showers. ⊠ *Grand Canyon Hwy. (30 mi south of Grand Canyon National Park at U.S. 180/AZ 64 junction), HC 34, Box A, 86046,* ☎ *520/635–2600.* ☾ *Apr.–Oct. (may open earlier or close later, depending on weather).*

Outdoor Activities and Sports

FISHING

Fishing for trout, crappie, catfish, and smallmouth bass is popular at a number of lakes surrounding Williams. For information on obtaining a fishing license, contact the **Arizona Game and Fish Department** (☞ Fishing *in* The Grand Canyon and Northwest Arizona A to Z, *below*).

SKIING

The **Williams Ski Area** (⊠ Box 953, 86046, ☎ 520/635–9330) is usually open mid-December through March; take South 4th Street for 2 mi, and then turn right at the sign and go another 1½ mi. There are four groomed runs (including one for beginners) and other downhill trails as well as areas suitable for cross-country enthusiasts.

Havasu Canyon

141 mi from Williams (to head of the Hualapai Trail), west on I–40 (to Seligman) and AZ 66, north on Indian Hwy. 18. Note: Last gas is at the junction of AZ 16 and Hwy. 18.

Havasu Canyon, south of the middle part of the national park and away from the crowds, possesses a Shangri-la–like beauty. It is the home of about 500 Havasupai, a tribe that has populated this isolated country for centuries. Their name means "people of the blue water," and you'll know why when you see the canyon's waterfalls, as high as 200 ft, cascading over red cliffs into travertine pools surrounded by thick foliage and sheltering trees. Eight-mile-long **Hualapai Trail** twists into the canyon along the edges of sheer rock walls. Be sure to call ahead if you plan to hike the trail—or ride a horse or mule down for about $70. You'll definitely want to spend the night if you're hiking or riding (☞ Dining and Lodging, *below*). The hurried can take a helicopter: **Papillon Helicopters** (☎ 800/528–2418) operates an excursion from Tusayan to Supai for $440 per person, which includes the horseback and guide fee. Note: All visitors are charged a $12 fee to enter the Havasupai tribal lands. *Havasupai Tourist Enterprise,* ⊠ *Supai 86435,* ☎ *520/448–2141 for general information; 520/448–2111 for lodging reservations.*

Dining and Lodging

$ ╳☶ **Havasupai Lodge.** The lodge and restaurant are at the bottom of Havasu Canyon and are operated by the Havasupai tribe. The restaurant serves three meals a day, generally sandwiches and fast-food-type fare, and a daily special; dinner prices are about $8–$10. ⊠ *Supai 86435,* ☎ *520/448–2111. 24 rooms. Restaurant. No credit cards; call for payment guidelines and restrictions.*

CAMPING

For information about camping in Havasu Canyon, call the **Havasupai Tourist Enterprise** (☎ 520/448–2121).

THE NORTH RIM AND ENVIRONS

The North Rim, within the 12,000-square-mi Arizona Strip, draws only about 10% of the Grand Canyon's visitors but is, many believe, even more gorgeous than the South Rim. There's plenty to see on the long drive to the rim, which is about 210 mi whether you start out from the South Rim of the canyon or from Flagstaff. This trip is not an option during the winter, when heavy snows block highway access and facilities are closed.

Cameron Trading Post

㉔ *53 mi north of Flagstaff on U.S. 89; 57 mi east of Grand Canyon Village on AZ 64.*

Most of the jewelry, rugs, baskets, and pottery sold at the historic **Cameron Trading Post** (☎ 520/679–2231 or 800/338–7385) are made by Navajo and Hopi artisans, but some are created by New Mexico's Zuni and Pueblo Indians. Come armed with knowledge of Native American artisanship if you're looking at high-ticket items, some of which are sold at a separate gallery. Also on the post are a restaurant, a cafeteria, a grocery store, a butcher shop, and a post office. An outlet of the **Navajo Arts and Crafts Enterprises** (⊠ AZ 64/U.S. 89, ☎ 520/679–2244) stocks authentic Navajo products.

Dining and Lodging

$ ╳☶ **Cameron Trading Post.** Southwestern-style rooms at this modern
★ two-story complex have carved-oak furniture, tile baths, and balconies overlooking the Colorado River. The original native-stone landscaping—including fossilized dinosaur tracks—of the 1930s inn previously on this site was retained, as was the small, well-kept garden with lilacs, roses, and crab-apple trees. Call ahead for reservations; the motel is usually booked in high season. A cafeteria—hot and cold sandwiches and other buffet-style fare—has an antique back bar and light fixtures. Service here is faster than at the older dining room, which has original tinwork ceilings, a kiva fireplace, and oak sideboards. The homemade green chili, served with Indian fry bread, is phenomenal. The trading post is on the Navajo reservation, so no alcohol is served here.

The North Rim

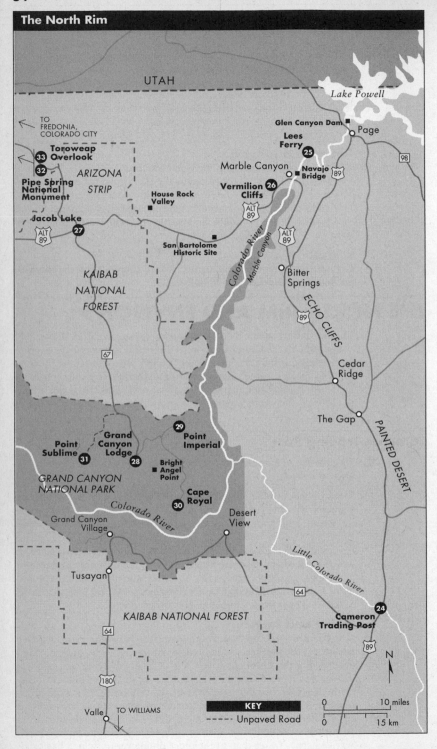

UTAH

Lake Powell

TO FREDONIA, COLORADO CITY

Glen Canyon Dam

Page

Lees Ferry

(25)

Marble Canyon

Navajo Bridge

(33) Toroweap Overlook

(32)

ARIZONA STRIP

Pipe Spring National Monument

House Rock Valley

Vermilion Cliffs (26)

ALT 89

ALT 89

Jacob Lake

ALT 89 (27)

San Bartolome Historic Site

Colorado River

Marble Canyon

ALT 89

Bitter Springs

KAIBAB NATIONAL FOREST

89

ECHO CLIFFS

67

Cedar Ridge

The Gap

(29) Point Imperial

PAINTED DESERT

Point Sublime

Grand Canyon Lodge

(31)   (28)

Bright Angel Point

Cape Royal

(30)

GRAND CANYON NATIONAL PARK

Colorado River

Grand Canyon Village

Desert View

Little Colorado River

Tusayan

64

KAIBAB NATIONAL FOREST

Cameron Trading Post (24)

89

N

64

180

Valle   TO WILLIAMS

KEY

- - - Unpaved Road

0   10 miles

0   15 km

✉ *Box 339, Cameron 86020,* ☎ *520/679–2231 or 800/338–7385 ext. 414,* FAX *520/679–2350. 62 rooms, 4 suites. Restaurant, cafeteria, grocery. AE, DC, MC, V.*

⚠ **Cameron RV Park.** This park, open year-round, is adjacent to the Cameron Trading Post. There are 60 spaces with hookups; the fee for each is $15 per day. There are no public rest rooms or showers. ✉ *U.S. 89,* ☎ *520/679–2231 or 800/338–7385,* FAX *520/679–2350.* ☉ *Year-round.*

En Route　The route north from Cameron Trading Post on U.S. 89 affords a wide and unobstructed view of the **Painted Desert** off to the right. The desert, which covers thousands of square miles and extends far to the south and east, is a vision of harsh beauty, with windswept plains and mesas, isolated buttes, and barren valleys in soft pastel patterns. The sparse vegetation is mostly desert scrub, which provides sustenance for only the hardiest wildlife. Most of the undulating hills belong to the Chinle formation, deposited more than 200 million years ago and containing countless fossil records of ancient plants and animals.

About 30 mi north of Cameron Trading Post, the Painted Desert country gives way to sandstone cliffs that run for many miles off to the right. Brilliantly hued, and ranging in color from light pink to deep orange, the **Echo Cliffs** rise to more than 1,000 ft in many places. They are also essentially devoid of vegetation, but in a few places high up you'll spot thick patches of tall cottonwood and poplar trees, nurtured by springs and water seepage from the rock escarpments.

At Bitter Springs, 60 mi north of Cameron, U.S. 89A branches off from U.S. 89, running north and providing views of **Marble Canyon,** the geographical beginning of the Grand Canyon but outside the national park. Like the rest of the Grand Canyon, Marble Canyon has been carved by the force of the Colorado River. Traversing a gorge nearly 500 ft deep is **Navajo Bridge,** a narrow steel span built in 1929 and listed on the National Register of Historic Places. Formerly used for car traffic, it now functions only as a pedestrian overpass; a newer, wider bridge, built 120 ft downriver, was dedicated in 1995.

Lees Ferry Area

76 mi north of Cameron Trading Post, U.S. 89 to U.S. 8.

★ ㉕　A turnoff at Marble Canyon Lodge, about 1 mi past Navajo Bridge in the small town of Marble Canyon, leads to historic **Lees Ferry,** 3 mi away. On a sharp bend in the Colorado River at a break in the Echo Cliffs, Lees Ferry is considered mile zero of the river, the point from which all distances on the river system are measured. This spot, one of the last areas in the mainland United States to be completely charted, was first visited by non–Native Americans in 1776, when Spanish priests Fray Francisco Atanasio Domínguez and Fray Silvestre Velez de Escalante tried but failed to cross the Colorado. Explorer John Wesley Powell also visited in 1870 on an expedition with Mormon leaders. After the ferry was established, it became part of the Honeymoon Trail, a gateway to Utah for young couples who wanted their civil marriages in Arizona sanctified at the Latter-Day Saints temple in St. George. It also became a crossing and a supply point for miners and other pioneers who shaped the American West.

Lees Ferry retains a number of vestiges of the mining era, but it's now primarily known as the spot where most of the Grand Canyon river rafts put into the water. In addition, huge trout lurk in the river near here, so there are several places to pick up angling gear and/or a guide (☞ Fishing *in* Outdoor Activities and Sports, *below*).

★ ㉖   West from the town of Marble Canyon, rising to the right of the highway, are the sheer, spectacular **Vermilion Cliffs,** in many places more than 3,000 ft high. Keep an eye out for condors; these giant endangered birds were reintroduced into the area in the winter of 1996–97. Early reports suggest that the birds, once in captivity, are surviving well in the wilderness.

Dining and Lodging

$ ✕🏨 **Lees Ferry Lodge.** Geared toward the Lees Ferry trout-fishing trade, this lodge will outfit you, guide you, and freeze your catch (if it's legal size). At the end of the day you can sit out on one of the garden patios of this rustic 1929 building, constructed of native stone and rough-hewn beams. Rooms are charming, if a bit quirky in their plumbing. The hotel's Vermilion Cliffs Bar and Grill is a popular gathering spot for river raft guides and it serves good American fare—especially the steaks and seafood—in an authentic western setting. ⊠ *4 mi west of Navajo Bridge on U.S. 89A, HC 67, Box 1, Marble Canyon 86036,* ☎ *520/355–2231. 9 rooms with shower, 1 5-person trailer with shower. Restaurant. MC, V.*

$ ✕🏨 **Marble Canyon Lodge.** This Arizona Strip lodge opened in 1929
★ on the same day the Navajo Bridge was dedicated. Three types of accommodations are available: rooms with lace curtains, brass beds, and hardwood floors in the original building; standard motel rooms in the newer building across the street; and two-bedroom apartments, each bedroom containing a queen and a single bed, in a small, newer complex built in 1992. Guests can sit on the porch swing of the native-rock lodge building and look out on the Vermilion Cliffs and the desert, or they can play the piano that was brought over from Lees Ferry in the 1920s. Zane Grey and Gary Cooper are among the well-known former guests. The restaurant serves steaks, seafood, pasta, and sandwiches. ⊠ *¼ mi west of Navajo Bridge on U.S. 89A, Marble Canyon 86036,* ☎ *520/355–2225 or 800/726–1789,* 𝖥𝖠𝖷 *520/355–2227. 52 units. Restaurant, coin laundry, private airstrip. D, MC, V.*

$ 🏨 **Cliff Dwellers Lodge.** Built in 1949 in the Marble Canyon area of the Arizona Strip, this dining and lodging complex sits at the foot of the Vermilion Cliffs. Rooms in the modern motel building are attractive and clean. ⊠ *U.S. 89A, 9 mi west of Navajo Bridge, HC 67–30, Marble Canyon 86036,* ☎ *520/355–2228 or 800/433–2543,* 𝖥𝖠𝖷 *520/355–2229. 22 rooms. Restaurant, bar, grocery. D, MC, V.*

Outdoor Activities and Sports

FISHING

The Colorado River in the Lees Ferry area is known for good-size German brown and rainbow trout. Marble Canyon Lodge (☞ Dining and Lodging, *above*) sells Arizona fishing licenses.

Lees Ferry Anglers (⊠ HC 67, Box 2, Marble Canyon 86036, ☎ 520/355–2261; 800/962–9755 outside AZ) operates guided fishing trips, starting from $225 per day; it practices year-round catch and release.

En Route   As you continue the journey to the North Rim, the immense blue-green bulk of the Kaibab Plateau stretches out before you. About 18 mi past Navajo Bridge, a sign directs you to the **San Bartolome Historic Site,** an overlook with plaques that tell the story of the Domínguez-Escalante expedition of 1776. At **House Rock Valley,** a large road sign announces the House Rock Buffalo Ranch, operated by the Arizona Division of Wildlife. A 23-mi dirt road leads to the home of one of the largest herds of American bison in the Southwest. You may drive out to the ranch, but be aware that you may not see any buffalo—the expanse of their range is so great that they frequently cannot be spotted from a car.

As it nears its junction with AZ 67, U.S. 89A starts climbing to the top of the **Kaibab Plateau,** heavily forested, rife with animals and birds, and more than 9,000 ft at its highest point. The rapid change from barren desert to lush forest is dramatic.

Jacob Lake

㉗ *25 mi west of town of Marble Canyon on U.S. 89A, at AZ 67.*

Jacob Lake junction is a good place to stop for groceries and gas. The forest service's **Kaibab Plateau Visitor's Center** (☏ 520/643–7298) here is open from May through mid-October.

Dining and Lodging

$ ✕🖬 **Jacob Lake Inn.** Basic cabins and standard units are available at this modest 5-acre complex in Kaibab National Forest. All rooms overlook the highways. The bustling lodge center, a popular stop for those heading to the North Rim, has a grocery, a coffee shop, a restaurant, and a large gift shop. ⊠ *AZ 67/U.S. 89A, 86022,* ☏ *520/643–7232. 11 motel units, 3 family units, 22 cabins. Restaurant, café, grocery. AE, D, DC, MC, V.*

🔺 **Demotte Campground.** This forest-service campground 29 mi south of Jacob Lake is open from late May or early June through October. It has 22 single-unit (RV or tent) sites, but no hookups, for $10 per day. There are interpretive campfire programs in summer. No reservations are accepted. ⊠ *Off AZ 67. Business address:* ⊠ *Southwest Natural and Cultural Heritage Association, Box 620, Fredonia 86022,* ☏ *520/643–7633 in season; 520/643–7395 off-season.* ⊙ *June–Oct.*

🔺 **Jacob Lake Campground.** Fifty-six family and group RV and tent sites (no hookups) are available for $10 per vehicle per day here. On summer evenings, rangers present interpretive programs. No reservations are accepted (except for groups of 10 or more). It's open year-round, but there are no facilities or running water in winter; fees are only charged from mid-April through October. ⊠ *U.S. 89A/AZ 67. Business address:* ⊠ *Southwest Natural and Cultural Heritage Association, Box 620, Fredonia 86022,* ☏ *520/643–7633 in season; 520/ 643–7395 off-season.* ⊙ *Year-round.*

🔺 **Kaibab Lodge Camper Village.** This campground has 50 tent sites ($10 for two people) and 80 RV and trailer sites ($20 for a pull-through with full hookups, $10 without hookups). Fire pits and more than 70 picnic tables are available in this wooded spot, located near a gas station, store, and restaurant. Reservations are accepted. Camper Village is open mid-May to November, weather permitting. ⊠ *AZ 67, ¼ mi south of U.S. 89A. Reservations:* ⊠ *Box 3331, Flagstaff 86003,* ☏ *520/643–7804 in season; 520/526–0924; 800/525–0924 (outside AZ) in winter;* ℻ *520/527–9398.* ⊙ *Mid-May–Nov.*

En Route AZ 67 runs south from U.S. 89A to the North Rim; the route passes through one of the thickest stands of ponderosa pine in the United States. Visitors frequently see mule deer and Kaibab squirrels, which live only on the plateau; you can recognize them by their all-white tails and the long tufts of white hair on their ears. Keep an eye out for mountain lions, elk, and black bears, too.

The North Rim

44 mi south of Jacob Lake on AZ 67.

★ **㉘** The historic **Grand Canyon Lodge** is literally at the end of the road (AZ 67). Built in 1928 by the Union Pacific Railroad, the massive stone structure is listed on the National Register of Historic Places. Its huge lounge area has hardwood floors, high-beam ceilings, and a marvelous view of the canyon through plate-glass windows. Don't forget to pay your respects to Brighty, the faithful burro of children's-book fame, honored by a bronze sculpture near the lounge's west entrance. On warm days visitors sit in the sun and drink in the surrounding beauty at an equally spacious outdoor viewing deck, where park-service employees deliver free lectures on geology and history. Lunch, dinner, or a snack in the lodge's rock-and-log dining room is an integral part of the North Rim experience; the food is good and reasonably priced. If you don't want a full meal, just buy a drink at Pizza Place, sit out on the viewing deck, and watch the sun set over the canyon.

★ The trail to **Bright Angel Point,** one of the most awe-inspiring overlooks on either rim, starts on the grounds of the Grand Canyon Lodge and proceeds along the crest of a point of rocks that juts into the canyon for several hundred yards. The walk is only 1 mi round-trip, but it's an exciting trek because there are sheer drops just a few feet away on each side of the trail. In a few spots where the route is extremely narrow, metal railings along the path ensure visitors' safety. The temptation to clamber out to precarious perches to have your picture taken is great, but be very careful: Every year several people die from falls at the Grand Canyon.

The **Transept Trail** begins near the corner of the lodge's east patio. This 3-mi (round-trip) trail stays near the rim for part of the distance before it plunges into the forest, ending at the North Rim Campground and General Store, 1½ mi from the lodge.

㉙ Eleven miles northeast of Grand Canyon Lodge is one of the North Rim's most popular lookouts, **Point Imperial,** the highest vista point (elevation 8,803 ft) at either rim, offering magnificent views of both the canyon and the distant country for many miles around: the Vermilion Cliffs to the north, the 10,000-ft Navajo Mountain to the northeast in Utah, the Painted Desert to the east, and the Little Colorado River canyon to the southeast.

★ ㉚ **Cape Royal,** another popular lookout, is about 23 mi southeast of Grand Canyon Lodge. A short walk on a paved road from the parking lot leads to this southernmost viewpoint on the North Rim. In addition to a large slice of the Grand Canyon, Angel's Window, a giant, erosion-formed hole, can be seen through the projecting ridge of Cape Royal. At Angel's Window Overlook, ⅓ mi north of here, **Cliff Springs Trail** starts its 1-mi route (round-trip) through a forested ravine. The trail, narrow and precarious in spots, passes ancient dwellings, winds beneath a limestone overhang, and terminates at Cliff Springs, where the forest opens on another impressive view of the canyon walls.

㉛ An excellent option for those who want to get off the beaten path, the trip to **Point Sublime** is intended only for visitors driving vehicles with high-road clearance (pickups and four-wheel-drive vehicles). It is also necessary to be properly equipped for wilderness road travel: Check with a park ranger or at the information desk at Grand Canyon Lodge before taking this journey. The road winds for 17 mi through gorgeous high country to Point Sublime, an overlook that lives up to its name. You may camp here only with a permit from the Backcountry Office at the park ranger station (☞ Hiking *in* The Grand Canyon and Northwest Arizona A to Z, *below*).

Dining and Lodging

$–$$ ✕🛏 **Grand Canyon Lodge.** This historic property, constructed mainly in the 1920s and '30s, is the premier lodging facility in the North Rim area. The main building has limestone walls and timbered ceilings. Additional lodging options include small, rustic cabins; larger cabins (some with a canyon view and some with two bedrooms); and traditional motel rooms in newer units. You might find marinated pork kebabs, grilled swordfish, or linguine with cilantro on the dining room's dinner menu. ⊠ *Amfac Parks and Resorts, 14001 E. Iliff, Suite 600, Aurora, CO 80014,* ☎ *303/297–2757,* FAX *303/297–3175. 44 rooms, 157 cabins. Bar, dining room, cafeteria. AE, D, MC, V.*

$ 🏠 **Kaibab Lodge.** In a wooded setting 5 mi from the North Rim entrance, this 1920s property contains rustic cabins with simple furnishings. When they're not out gazing into the abyss, guests can sit around a stone fireplace (it can be chilly up here in spring and early fall). This is a popular base for cross-country skiers in winter. The lodge is open mid-May to early November for the summer season. ⊠ *AZ 67, HC 64, Box 30, Fredonia 86022,* ☎ *520/638–2389. 24 cabins with shower. Restaurant. D, MC, V.*

🔺 **North Rim Campground.** The only designated campground inside Grand Canyon National Park, 3 mi north of the rim, has 83 RV and tent sites (no hookups) for $10 per day. *Reservations through* ⊠ *Destinet, Box 85705, San Diego, CA 92138,* ☎ *800/365–2267; 858/452–0150 outside the U.S.* ☉ *Mid-May–Oct.*

Outdoor Activities and Sports

MULE RIDES

Canyon Trail Rides (☎ 435/679–8665 off-season; 520/638–2292 after May 15 at Grand Canyon Lodge) conducts short mule rides suitable for children on the easier trails along the North Rim. A one-hour ride, available to those six and older, runs about $12. Half-day trips on the rim or into the canyon (minimum age eight) cost $35; full-day trips (minimum age 12), which include lunch and water, go for $85. These excursions are very popular, so try to make reservations in advance. Rides are available daily from May 15 to October 15.

Elsewhere in the Arizona Strip

The Arizona Strip, sometimes called the American Tibet because it's so isolated, holds only two small towns: Fredonia, known for farming and lumbering, and Colorado City, home to a polygamous Mormon sect that has lived here for more than a century. The combined population of these two towns is less than 7,000; fewer than 700 permanent residents—including 150 members of the Kaibab-Paiute tribe—live in the rest of the strip. Services in this part of the state are extremely limited; top off your tank when you find a gas station, and keep an ample supply of drinking water in your car.

③ **Pipe Spring National Monument,** 90 mi from the North Rim and 14 mi from Fredonia, is one of the few reliable sources of water in the Arizona Strip. The park contains a restored rock fort and ranch, with exhibits of southwestern frontier life; in summer there are living-history demonstrations that focus on such things as ranching operations or weaving. The fort was intended to fend off Indian attacks (which never came because a peace treaty was signed before it was finished). It ended up functioning mainly as headquarters for a dairy operation and in 1871 became the first telegraph station in the Arizona territory. About ½ mi north of the monument is a campground, a picnic area, and a casino run by the Kaibab-Paiute tribe. The slots draw busloads of people to this remote spot. ⊠ *HC 65, Box 5, Fredonia 86022,* ☎ *520/643–7105.* 🎟 *$2.* ☉ *Historic structures daily 8–4:30; visitor center/museum daily 8–5.*

Six miles back toward Fredonia from Pipe Spring on AZ 389, a dirt
road leads 50 mi south through starkly beautiful uninhabited country
to **Toroweap Overlook,** a lonely and awesome viewpoint over one of
the narrowest stretches of the canyon (less than 1 mi across). The overlook also contains the deepest sheer cliff (more than 3,000 ft straight
down). From this vantage point, you can see upstream to sedimentary
ledges, cliffs, and talus slopes. Looking downstream, you can see miles
of the lava flow that forms steep deltas, some of which look like black
waterfalls frozen on the cliff. Be sure you have plenty of gas, drinking
water, good tires, and a reliable car; a high-clearance vehicle (one that
sits high up off the ground, like a pickup truck) is best for this trip.
Don't try to go in wet weather, when the dirt road is likely to be
washed out. There's a ranger station near the rim as well as a primitive campground. If you plan to return the same day, you should make
motel reservations in advance at an Arizona Strip motel.

NORTHWEST ARIZONA

If the Grand Canyon is the most dramatic natural attraction in northwest Arizona, it's by no means all there is to see. Towns like Kingman
hark back to the glory days of the old Route 66, while the ghost towns
of Chloride and Oatman bear testament to the mining madness that
once reigned in the region. Water-sports fans, or those who just want
to laze on a houseboat, will enjoy Lake Havasu, over which London
Bridge surrealistically presides.

Kingman

112 mi west of Williams via I–40 or Rte. 66.

Route 66 cuts through the town of Kingman (population 13,000), which
is surrounded on three sides by rugged hills. The neon-lined roadway
here is named for native son Andy Devine, the gravelly voiced actor
who played sidekick in innumerable westerns. Because I–40, U.S. 93,
AZ 68, and Route 66 all converge in Kingman, which is also served
by Amtrak, Greyhound, and America West airlines (offering three
flights a day from Phoenix), it is a hub for local attractions like Hoover
Dam, Laughlin, and Lake Havasu.

The **Kingman Area Chamber of Commerce** (✉ 333 W. Andy Devine
Ave., ☎ 520/753–6106) carries T-shirts, postcards, and the usual
brochures to acquaint you with local attractions. The **Mohave County
Museum of History and Arts** (✉ 400 W. Beale St., ☎ 520/753–3195)
includes an Andy Devine Room with memorabilia from Devine's Hollywood years, an exhibit of carved Kingman turquoise, and a diorama
depicting the expedition of Lt. Edward Beale, who led his ill-fated camel-
cavalry unit to the area in search of a wagon road along the 35th parallel. Follow the White Cliffs Trail from downtown, and you'll see the
deep ruts cut into the desert floor by the wagons that eventually came
to Kingman after Beale's time.

The **Bonelli House** (✉ 430 E. Spring St., ☎ 520/753–1413), an excellent example of the Anglo-Territorial architecture popular in the early
1900s, is one of 62 buildings in the business district listed on the National Register of Historic Places. A 15-mi drive from town up Hualapai Mountain Road will take you to **Hualapai Mountain Park** (☎ 520/
753–0739), where more than 2,200 wooded acres at elevations ranging from 6,000 to 8,400 ft hold 6 mi of hiking trails as well as picnic
areas, rustic cabins, and RV and tenting areas.

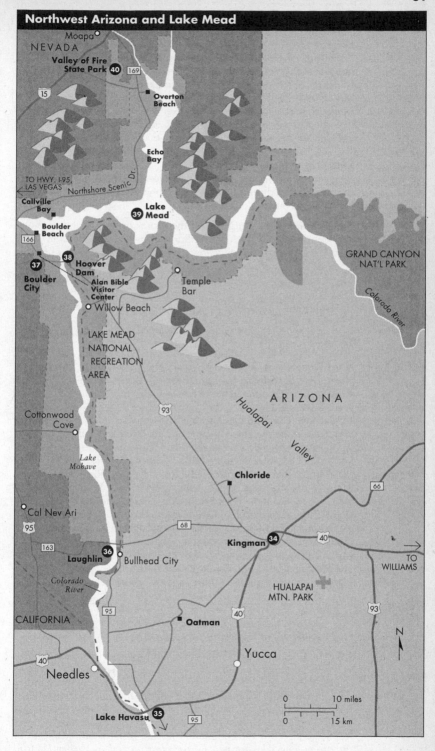

Northwest Arizona and Lake Mead

NEVADA

Moapa

Valley of Fire
State Park (40) 169

15

Overton
Beach

Echo
Bay

TO HWY. I-95,
LAS VEGAS
Northshore Scenic Dr.

Callville
Bay

Boulder
Beach

166

Lake
Mead (39)

GRAND CANYON
NAT'L PARK

Colorado River

37

38 Hoover
Dam

Boulder
City

Alan Bible
Visitor
Center

Temple
Bar

Willow Beach

LAKE MEAD

NATIONAL

RECREATION

AREA

A R I Z O N A

Cottonwood
Cove

93

Hualapai

Valley

Lake
Mohave

Chloride

66

Cal Nev Ari

95

68

Kingman 34

40

TO
WILLIAMS

163

Laughlin 36 Bullhead City

Colorado
River

HUALAPAI
MTN. PARK

93

CALIFORNIA

95

Oatman

40

40

Needles

Yucca

N

Lake Havasu 35

95

0   10 miles

0   15 km

OFF THE
BEATEN PATH

If you take U.S. 93 north from Kingman, in about 12 mi you'll come to a marked turnoff for the ghost town of **Chloride,** which takes its name from a type of silver ore mined in the area. Many buildings were lost to fires that ravaged the town in its heyday, but some historic treasures still stand, including the old bank vault, now a museum; the 1890 Jim Fritz house; and the Tennessee Saloon, now a general store and dance hall. Don't miss the huge murals painted on the rocks at the outskirts of town by western artist Roy Purcell, who worked the mines here in his youth. One copper mine, owned by the Duval Corporation, is still in operation at Chloride; you might see their huge ore trucks barrel down the road.

Lodging

Kingman has about three dozen motels, most of them along Andy Devine Avenue. Most of the major chains are represented, including Days Inn, Motel 6, and Super 8.

$ ☷ **Brunswick Hotel.** Antiques fill the rooms of this downtown hotel remodeled in 1997. With the addition of in-room phones and TV's, as well as new carpeting, it's now a cut above the chains that line this strip. ⊠ *315 E. Andy Devine Ave., 86401,* ☎ *520/718–1800. 12 rooms with shared bath, 8 suites. Restaurant. Full breakfast. AE, D, MC, V.*

$ ☷ **Quality Inn.** This chain member has comfortable rooms and a spiffy coffee shop stocked with Route 66 memorabilia. ⊠ *1400 E. Andy Devine Ave., 86401,* ☎ *520/753–4747 or 800/221–2222. 98 rooms. Coffee shop. AE, D, DC, MC, V.*

En Route   A worthwhile stop on your way from Kingman to Lake Havasu, the ghost town of **Oatman** is reached via old Route 66 (now 68). It's a straight shot across the Mohave Desert valley for a while, but then the road narrows and winds precipitously for about 15 mi through the Black Mountains. (This road is public, but beyond a narrow shoulder the land is privately owned and heavily patrolled, thanks to still-active gold mines throughout these low but rugged hills.) Oatman's main street is right out of the Old West; scenes from a number of films, including *How the West Was Won,* were shot here. It still has a remote, old-time feel: Many of the natives carry sidearms, and they're not acting. You can wander into one of the three saloons or visit the Oatman Hotel, where Clark Gable and Carole Lombard honeymooned in 1939 after they were secretly married in Kingman, but the burros that often come in from nearby hills and meander down the street are the town's real draw. A couple of stores sell hay to folks who want to feed these "wild" beasts, which at last count numbered about a dozen and which leave plenty of evidence of their visits in the form of "burro apples"—so watch your step.

Lake Havasu

35 *60 mi southwest of Kingman.*

Lake Havasu is renowned for its London Bridge—not the London Bridge of the nursery rhyme, but London Bridge all the same. A brilliant stroke of entrepreneurship turned what might have been just another desert town on the Colorado into a crowd-drawing curiosity: When the City of London put the sinking bridge, erected in 1831, up for sale in 1967, developer Robert McCulloch decided it would make the perfect centerpiece for the community he had planned on the shores of the 46-mi-long lake formed by the construction of Parker Dam in 1938. He bought the historic bridge for nearly $2.5 million, had it dismantled stone by stone, shipped to the United States, and reassembled (all 10,000 tons of it) to span a narrow arm of Lake Havasu.

An Olde English theme is played to the hilt here: A Tudor-style village replete with pub, red London telephone booths, Beefeaters, and other Britobilia abuts the base of the bridge. But Havasu City is on a lake, and in Arizona after all, so the sunshine, water sports, and fishing can amuse visitors after they've seen the surprising span. The weather is wonderful in spring, fall, and winter, but summers see temperatures that exceed 100°F for weeks at a time. Among the recreational opportunities on and around Lake Havasu are houseboat, ski-boat, Jet Ski, and sailboat rentals; marinas, RV parks, and campgrounds; and golf, tennis, and guided fishing expeditions.

Those interested in exploring the desert—including old mines and a wildlife refuge—might consider booking a four-wheel-drive tour with **Outback Adventures** (⊠ 1350 McCulloch Blvd., ☎ 520/680–6151).

Dining and Lodging

Many tourists make this stop a day trip on their way to Laughlin or Vegas, but there are plenty of accommodations if you'd like to rest a pace in this kitschy town. The area has several RV parks and campgrounds, more than 25 lodgings—from inexpensive roadside motels to posh resorts—and more than 45 restaurants. Of the chain hotels in town, the Best Western and the Holiday Inn are your best bets.

$–$$ ✕ **Shugrue's.** Perhaps the best restaurant for miles, Shugrue's is an offshoot of a popular Sedona spot. Pastas, salads, and sandwiches are all fairly reliable, and there are views of the bridge from almost every table. ⊠ *1425 McCulloch Blvd.,* ☎ *520/453–1400. AE, MC, V.*

$ ✕ **Chico's Tacos.** This is a decent Mexican fast-food choice. The salsa bar offers several fresh salsas of various degrees of spiciness. ⊠ *1641 McCulloch Blvd.,* ☎ *520/680–7010. No credit cards.*

$$$$ 🏨 **Havasu Springs Resort.** An increasingly popular Lake Havasu vacation option is to rent a houseboat by the week. These portable lodgings are good choices for large groups, as they sleep up to 12 people. ⊠ *2581 Hwy. 95, Parker 85344,* ☎ *520/667–3361,* ℻ *520/667–1098. Kitchens on board. No credit cards.*

$–$$$$ 🏨 **London Bridge Resort.** If you want to be close to the bridge, this kitschy hotel is a dependable choice. The decor is a strange mix of Tudor and southwestern; other than that, rooms are standard chain accommodations. There's a mediocre Mexican restaurant on the premises. ⊠ *1477 Queen's Bay, 86403,* ☎ *520/855–0888 or 800/624–7939,* ℻ *520/855–9209. 170 rooms. Restaurant, 3 pools, golf course, beach. AE, D, MC, V.*

$–$$$ 🏨 **Island Inn.** Though there's nothing remarkable about this hotel, it's one of the newer options in the area. The large rooms are immaculate, if nothing to write home about. ⊠ *1300 W. McCulloch Blvd., 86403,* ☎ *520/680–0606 or 800/243–9955,* ℻ *520/680–4218. 117 rooms. Pool, hot tub. AE, D, MC, V.*

SOUTHEAST NEVADA

Just across the Nevada border lies a wealth of attractions that can greatly expand a visit to the Grand Canyon and northwest Arizona. Seeming worlds away from the canyon, a bridge across the Colorado river leads to a hubbub of human activity in the casinos of Laughlin. Hoover Dam, a towering monument to the control of nature, provides an entirely different sort of contrast. And Lake Mead slakes even the most powerful desert thirst.

Laughlin, Nevada

36 *32 mi west of Kingman on U.S. 93 to AZ 68 into Nevada.*

Wayne Newton may play Vegas, but Laughlin is Waylon Jennings territory. Though it's often considered just a smaller version of Las Vegas, Laughlin has a character of its own, with gambling halls lining Casino Drive along the Colorado River. Don Laughlin bought an eight-room motel and opened the first casino here in 1966, and basically built the town from scratch. The town didn't really take off until the early 1980s, when the success of Laughlin's Riverside Hotel-Casino, which drew gamblers and river rats from northwestern Arizona, southeastern California, and even southern Nevada, attracted other casino operators who took advantage of the affordable riverfront property.

Today Laughlin is the state's third major resort area. It generally attracts older, retired travelers who spend at least part of the winter in Arizona—the sandstone bluffs above Laughlin are lined with their RVs, bearing license plates from all over the United States and Canada—and a younger resort-loving crowd that prefers the low-minimum tables, the cheap food and lodging, and the slots galore to the intensity of Las Vegas. The dealers are generally friendlier, the bettors more relaxed, and, especially when compared with the shuttered rooms in Las Vegas, Laughlin casinos have an airy feeling, lent by large picture windows that overlook the Colorado. Laughlin's outdoor activities include water sports, golf, tennis, and strolls along the tree-lined River Walk.

Except for the **Regency Casino** (⊠ 1950 S. Casino Dr., ☎ 702/298–2439), all of Laughlin's major casinos have hotel rooms.

Lodging

$–$$$$ 🏨 **Flamingo Hilton.** You'll think you're in Vegas when you pull up at the Flamingo, a hotel right in the middle of the action. The casino at the largest resort in Laughlin has 1,500 slot and video machines and a sports book. The Flamingo's 3,000-seat outdoor amphitheatre, on the banks of the Colorado River, hosts big-name entertainers. The large guest rooms are surprisingly (and pleasingly) subdued, if a bit pricey by Laughlin standards. The ubiquitous buffet-style restaurant is inexpensive, and the hotel offers packages that include dining options. ⊠ *1900 S. Casino Dr., 89029,* ☎ *702/298–5111 or 800/352–6464,* FAX *702/298–5116. 1,912 rooms. 4 restaurants, pool, 3 tennis courts, casino, showroom, airport shuttle, car rental. AE, D, DC, MC, V.*

$–$$$ 🏨 **Harrah's.** An enormous, gaudy, but comfortable hotel with its own sandy beach has large rooms with Colonial Mexican–style decor. Big-name entertainers perform in the Fiesta Showroom and at the Rio Vista Outdoor Amphitheater. The William Fisk Steakhouse serves fine Continental fare, and the buffet is one of the largest in town. ⊠ *2900 S. Casino Dr., 89028,* ☎ *702/298–4600 or 800/447–8700. 1,157 rooms. 5 restaurants, lounge, 2 pools, hot tub, health club, shops, showroom, chapel. AE, D, DC, MC, V.*

$–$$ 🏨 **Avi Hotel and Casino.** This property has a long beachfront along the Colorado River. It's a couple of miles from the main gambling drag, so it's a bit quieter than other hotels in the area. Rooms are spacious and comfortable, and the restaurant, which serves typical buffet fare, is open 24 hours a day. ⊠ *10000 Aha Macav Pkwy., 89029,* ☎ *702/535–5555 or 800/284–2946. 301 rooms. Restaurant, casino. AE, D, MC, V.*

$ 🏨 **Colorado Belle.** This Circus Circus–owned place is a Nevada anomaly: a riverboat casino that's actually on a river! The nautical-theme rooms have views of the Colorado River, and there's a brewpub on the premises. ⊠ *2100 S. Casino Dr., 89028,* ☎ *702/298–4000 or 800/477–*

4837, FAX 702/298–3697. *1,230 rooms. 6 restaurants, pool, hot tub, laundry service and dry cleaning. AE, D, DC, MC, V.*

$ ⊞ **Golden Nugget Laughlin.** This is a mini version of the Las Vegas Golden Nugget. It has a tropical atrium familiar to anyone who's seen the Nugget's big-sister casino, the Las Vegas Mirage. ⊠ *2300 S. Casino Dr., 89028,* ☎ *702/298–7111 or 800/237–1739,* FAX *702/298–7279. 304 rooms. 4 restaurants, lounge, pool, hot tub. AE, D, DC, MC, V.*

$ ⊞ **Lake Mohave Resort.** On the Arizona side of the river across from Laughlin, this older motel has large rooms, most with lake views, that are suitable for families. A nautical-themed restaurant overlooks the marina, where there's a bait and tackle shop. ⊠ *Katherine Landing, Bullhead City, AZ 86430,* ☎ *520/754–3245 or 800/752–9669. 51 rooms. Restaurant, boating. D, MC, V.*

$ ⊞ **Pioneer Hotel and Gambling Hall.** You can spot this small (by casino standards) hotel, owned by the Santa Fe Hotel and Casino in Las Vegas, by looking for the neon mascot, River Ric, on the sign; he's Vegas Vic's brother. Granny's Gourmet Room serves Continental and American cuisine. ⊠ *2200 S. Casino Dr., 89028,* ☎ *702/298–2442 or 800/ 634–3469,* FAX *702/298–5256. 416 rooms. 2 restaurants, lounge, pool, hot tub. AE, D, DC, MC, V.*

$ ⊞ **Ramada Express.** For visitors seeking a refuge from children, this is the place. The Gamblers Tower in this railroad-theme hotel and casino is reserved for adults, and there is an adults-only pool and kid-free restaurants. The 53,000-square-ft casino has state-of-the-art slots and a sports book. A miniature train takes you on a free ride around 27 landscaped acres. ⊠ *2121 S. Casino Dr., 89028,* ☎ *702/298–4200 or 800/ 272–6232. 1,501 rooms. 5 restaurants, lounge, pool, hot tub, airport shuttle. AE, D, DC, MC, V.*

$ ⊞ **River Palms Resort Casino.** A large balcony overlooks the table games in the 65,000-square-ft casino here. For those seeking a quiet retreat, the hotel's south wing is adjacent to the outdoor pool and hot tub, away from the sizzling slots. ⊠ *2700 S. Casino Dr., 89028,* ☎ *702/298–2242 or 800/835–7903,* FAX *702/298–2179. 1,000 rooms. 4 restaurants, pool, hot tub, health club, showroom, airport shuttle. AE, D, DC, MC, V.*

$ ⊞ **Riverside Resort.** This is the original Laughlin joint, still owned by Don Laughlin himself. The Gourmet Room restaurant serves Continental and American cuisine. Check out the **Loser's Lounge,** with its graphic homage to famous losers, such as the *Hindenburg,* the *Titanic,* and the like. There's also a 900-space RV park. ⊠ *1650 S. Casino Dr., 89029,* ☎ *702/298–2535 or 800/227–3849,* FAX *702/298–2614. 1,405 rooms. 6 restaurants, lounge, 2 pools, hot tub, nightclub, showroom. AE, D, DC, MC, V.*

Boulder City, Nevada

③⑦ *76 mi northwest of Kingman via U.S. 93.*

About 8 mi west of Hoover Dam, Boulder City is a small town with a movie theater, numerous gift shops and eateries, and several hotels and motels. Developed in the early 1930s to house the 4,000 Hoover Dam workers and to deter them from spending their hard-earned dollars on wine, women, and Las Vegas, Boulder City is the only community in Nevada where gambling is illegal. There are, however, several roadside casinos just outside the town limits. After the dam was completed, the town shrunk by more than half, kept alive by the management and maintenance crews of the dam and Lake Mead. But Boulder City slowly recovered and is now a vibrant little Southwest town.

Be sure to stop at the **Boulder City/Hoover Dam Museum** (⊠ 444 Hotel Plaza, ☎ 702/294–1988), which preserves and displays artifacts relating to the workers and construction of Boulder City and Hoover Dam. Across the street is the historic **Boulder Dam Hotel** (⊠ 1305 Arizona St., ☎ 702/293–3510), built in 1932 (and restored in 1960). Check out the lobby, which looks the same today as it did when it first opened. In the hotel is the **Boulder City Chamber of Commerce** (⊠ 1305 Arizona St., ☎ 702/293–2034), a good place to gather information on the history of Hoover Dam and historic sights around town. You can spend an enjoyable couple of hours strolling the main streets downtown, popping into Indian and Mexican gift shops, antiques and jewelry stores, and galleries.

Hoover Dam

★ ③⑧ *67 mi northwest of Kingman via U.S. 93.*

The visual impact of Hoover Dam's incredible mass and height makes it a popular stop on a visit to the Lake Mead area. Congress authorized the funding of the $175 million dam in 1928 to control floods and generate electricity. Completed in 1935, the dam is 727 ft high (the equivalent of a 70-story building) and 660 ft thick at the base (more than the length of two football fields). Its construction required 4.4 million cubic yards of concrete, enough to build a two-lane highway from San Francisco to New York.

Originally referred to as Boulder Dam, the structure was officially named Hoover Dam in recognition of President Herbert Hoover's role in the project. More than 700,000 people a year (34 million since the tours began in 1937) take the Bureau of Reclamation's 45-minute guided tour, which leads visitors deep inside the structure for a look at its inner workings. Tours leave every few minutes from the exhibit building at the top of the dam; the guides are well informed and entertaining. A visitor center on the Nevada side contains a theater with three revolving sections, an exhibition gallery, an observation tower, and a five-story parking garage. ⊠ *U.S. 93 east of Boulder City,* ☎ *702/293–8321.* ⊠ *$8.* ☉ *Tours daily 8:30–5:30 in summer, 9–4 in winter.*

Lake Mead

③⑨ *67 mi northwest of Kingman on U.S. 93.*

Lake Mead (Colorado River water backed up behind the Hoover Dam) is the largest man-made reservoir in the country: It covers 229 square mi, and its irregular shoreline extends for 550 mi. You can get information on the lake's history, ecology, and recreational opportunities, as well as driving maps and accommodations information, at the **Alan Bible Visitors Center** (☎ 702/293–8990), the National Park Service's visitors center for the Lake Mead area. It's just northeast of Boulder City, at the intersection of U.S. 93 (also called Nevada Highway here) and Lakeshore Scenic Drive (NV 166), and is open daily 8:30 to 4:30.

Lakeshore Scenic Drive (NV 166) wends its way along the beautiful shore of Lake Mead. A drive of about an hour will take you along the north side of the lake, where you'll find several recreation areas and marinas. People who come to Lake Mead to swim find **Boulder Beach** the Nevada site closest to Arizona, only a mile or so from the visitors center. **Echo Bay,** roughly 40 mi northeast of Boulder Beach, is the best place to swim in the lake because it's got better sand and is less crowded than the other beaches. All over the lake, anglers fish for largemouth bass, catfish, trout, and black crappie, but striped bass provide the most sport. Houseboating is a favorite pastime; you can rent houseboats, along with speedboats, ski boats, and Jet Skis at the various marinas. Divers have a fantastic choice of underwater sights to explore, including the entire town of St. Thomas, a farming community that was inundated by the lake in 1937. Other activities abound, such as waterskiing, sailboarding, and snorkeling.

Lodging

$$$–$$$$ ⊞ **Seven Crown Resorts.** This is a good resource for houseboat rentals, an increasingly popular vacation option, especially for large groups. The boats come equipped with full kitchens and air-conditioning, and they can sleep up to 14 people. The beauty of renting a houseboat is that you can cruise down the lake and park where you please for as long as you like. ⊠ *Box 16247, Irvine, CA 92623,* ☎ *800/752–9669. D, MC, V.*

$ ⊞ **Temple Bar Resort.** This upgraded motel right on the Arizona shore of the lake is a good choice if you want a quiet room; the hotel's remote location ensures peace. The restaurant, which serves typical American fare, has outdoor seating overlooking the water. ⊠ *Temple Bar, AZ 86643,* ☎ *520/767–3211 or 800/752–9669. 22 rooms. Restaurant. D, MC, V.*

⚠ **Temple Bar Campground.** Space is available on a first-come, first-served basis at this 153-site facility on the Arizona shore of the lake, but there are usually plenty of unoccupied sites on all but the busiest holiday weekends. All sites have a picnic table and fire ring. The nightly fee is $10. ⊠ *Box 16247, Irvine, CA 92623,* ☎ *520/767–3401 or 800/752–9669.* ☉ *Open year-round.*

Outdoor Activities and Sports

BOATING

Rental options include houseboats, patio boats, fishing boats, and ski boats—pick up a list of marinas at the Alan Bible Visitors Center (☞ *above*). Houseboat rentals are available at: **Callville Bay Resort and Marina** (☎ 800/255–5561) or at **Echo Bay Resort** (☎ 702/394–4000 or 800/752–9669). You'll find boat rentals, a beach, camping facilities, a gift shop, and a restaurant at **Lake Mead Marina** (⊠ Boulder Beach, ☎ 702/293–3484).

CRUISES

A 1½-hour cruise of the Hoover Dam area on a 250-passenger sternwheeler is available through **Lake Mead Cruises** (⊠ Lake Mead Marina, near Boulder Beach, ☎ 702/293–6180). A 15-mi motorized raft trip on the Colorado from the base of Hoover Dam down Black Canyon to Willow Beach is offered by **Gray Line Tours** (☎ 702/384–1234 or 800/634–6579).

Valley of Fire

④⓪   *60 mi northeast of Boulder City on Hwy. 169; less than 2 mi west of upper arm of Lake Mead.*

When your drive up Lakeshore Scenic Drive reaches the upper arm of the lake, about a mile past Overton Beach, look for the sign announcing the Valley of Fire State Park. Turn left here to reach the Visitors Center.

The 56,000-acre Valley of Fire State Park was dedicated in 1935 as Nevada's first state park. Valley of Fire takes its name from its distinctive coloration, which ranges from lavender to tangerine to bright red, giving the vistas along the park road an otherworldly appearance. Here the incredible rock formations have been weathered into unusual shapes that suggest elephants, beehives, ducks, cobras, even pianos. Mysterious petroglyphs (carvings etched into the rock) and pictographs (pictures drawn or painted on the rock's surface), are believed to be the work of the Basketmaker and Anasazi Pueblo people, who lived along the nearby Muddy River between 300 BC and 1150 BC. The most spectacular petroglyphs are found just off the park road, beyond the visitors center on a flat cliff face reached by a 100-step staircase.

The **Valley of Fire Visitors Center** has a large variety of displays on the park's history, ecology, archaeology, and recreation, as well as slide shows and films, an art gallery, and information about the 50 campsites within the park. The park is open year-round; the best times to visit, especially during the heat of the summer, are sunrise and sunset, when the light is especially spectacular. ⊠ *Hwy. 169 (Box 515), Overton 89040,* ☎ *702/397–2088.* ⊙ *Daily 8:30–4:30.*

OFF THE
BEATEN PATH

LOST CITY MUSEUM – The Overton area, along with its little bedroom community, Logandale, just north of it along the highway, is one of the finest treasure chests of Anasazi history and artifacts in the American Southwest. Lost City was a major outpost of the ancient Anasazi culture, which reigned during the early part of this millennium, then disappeared around 1150. In and around the museum is an immense collection of artifacts, including basketry, weapons, extensive black-and-white photographs of the excavation of Lost City in 1924, and a restored Basketmaker pit house. To visit the Lost City Museum from Valley of Fire, turn around on the park road and head back to the "T" intersection at the entrance to the Valley of Fire. Turn left and drive roughly 8 mi into Overton. Turn left at the sign for the museum and cross the railroad tracks into the parking lot. ⊠ *721 S. Hwy. 169,* ☎ *702/397–2193.* ☞ *$2.* ⊙ *Daily 8:30–4:30.*

THE GRAND CANYON AND NORTHWEST ARIZONA A TO Z

Arriving and Departing

By Bus
Greyhound Lines (☎ 800/231–2222) provides bus service to Flagstaff, Williams, and Laughlin. **Nava-Hopi Tours** (☎ 520/774–5003 or 800/892–8687) operates buses from and to the South Rim of the Grand Canyon from early April to late October.

By Car
If you are driving to Arizona from the east, or coming up from the southern part of the state, the best access to the Grand Canyon is from Flagstaff. You can take U.S. 180 northwest (81 mi) to Grand Canyon Village on the South Rim. Or, for a scenic route with stopping points along the canyon rim, drive north on U.S. 89 from Flagstaff, turn left at the junction of AZ 64 (52 mi north of Flagstaff), and proceed north and west for an additional 57 mi.

To visit the North Rim of the canyon, proceed north from Flagstaff on U.S. 89 to Bitter Springs. Then take U.S. 89A to the junction of AZ 67, which leads to the North Rim, a distance of approximately 210 mi from Flagstaff.

If you are crossing Arizona on I–40 from the west, your most direct route to the South Rim is on AZ 64 (U.S. 180), which runs north from Williams for 58 mi to Grand Canyon Village.

For more about routes to the Grand Canyon, *see* the Beating the Crowds at the Canyon Close-up box, *above*.

By Plane

AIRLINES

The many carriers that fly to the Grand Canyon from Las Vegas include **Air Nevada** (☎ 800/634–6377), **Air Vegas** (☎ 800/255–7474), **Las Vegas Airlines** (☎ 800/634–6851), and **Eagle Scenic Airlines** (☎ 800/634–6801). **Scenic Airlines** (☎ 800/445–8738 from Phoenix) operates two daily flights from Phoenix to Grand Canyon Airport.

America West Express (☎ 800/235–9292) serves **Laughlin/Bullhead City International Airport** (☎ 520/754–2134) and flies to Bullhead City and Lake Havasu. Laughlin is also served by **Reno Air** (☎ 800/736–6247). **Flamingo Hilton Laughlin Reservations** (☎ 888/528–4454) provides visitor packages from dozens of U.S. cities.

AIRPORTS

McCarran International Airport (☎ 702/261–5743) in Las Vegas is the primary air hub for flights to **Grand Canyon National Park Airport** (☎ 520/638–2446). You can also make connections into the Grand Canyon from **Sky Harbor International Airport** (☎ 602/273–3300) in Phoenix.

FROM THE AIRPORT

The **Tusayan/Canyon Airport Shuttle** (☎ 520/638–0821) operates between Grand Canyon Airport and the nearby towns of Tusayan and Grand Canyon Village; it makes hourly runs daily between 8:15 AM and 5:15 PM, with additional trips in the summer months.

Fred Harvey Transportation Company (☎ 520/638–2822 or 520/638–2631) offers 24-hour taxi service at Grand Canyon Airport, Grand Canyon Village, and the nearby village of Tusayan; taxis also make trips to other destinations in and around Grand Canyon National Park.

By Train

Amtrak (☎ 800/872–7245) provides daily service to Arizona from both the east and west, with its most convenient stop (for Grand Canyon access) at Flagstaff. The *Southwest Chief* stops at the Needles, California, Amtrak station, whence an Amtrak Thruway bus shuttles passengers to Laughlin. From Flagstaff, bus connections can be made for the final leg of the trip to the South Rim through **Nava-Hopi Tours** (☞ By Bus, *above*).

Getting Around

By Car

Most of Arizona's scenic highlights are many miles apart, and a car is the most practical mode of transportation for touring the state. However, you won't really need one if you're planning to visit only the Grand Canyon's most popular area, the South Rim. Many people choose to fly to the Grand Canyon and then hike, catch a shuttle or taxi, or sign on for bus tours or mule rides in Grand Canyon Village. Caution: When driving off major highways in low-lying areas, watch for rain clouds. Flash floods from sudden summer rains can be deadly.

In the summer, roads leading to the South Rim near Grand Canyon Village and the parking areas along the rim are badly congested. If you visit from October through April, you should experience only light to moderate traffic. The more remote North Rim has no services available from late October through mid-May. Reaching elevations of more than 8,000 ft, the road is open for day use only until the first heavy snowfall of the year (generally in November or December), at which point roads close until spring. The South Rim stays open to auto traffic all year, though access to the West Rim is restricted in summer because of overcrowded roads.

By Shuttle Bus

In the South Rim area, free summer shuttle buses operate between Grand Canyon Village and the West Rim about every 15 minutes from 6:30 AM to 6:45 PM, late May through September. In addition, during these months free shuttles go to Yaki Point on a more limited basis. **Mayflower** runs a year-round shuttle taking hikers from the South Rim's Backcountry Office (across from the visitor center, ☎ 520/638–7888), Maswik Lodge, and Bright Angel Lodge to South Kaibab Trailhead at Yaki Point; there are two departures every morning. Check for times upon arrival. From May.15 through the end of October, **Trans Canyon Van Service** (☎ 520/638–2820), a South Rim to North Rim shuttle, leaves from Bright Angel Lodge at 1:30 PM and arrives at the North Rim at about 6 PM; the return from Grand Canyon Lodge is at 7 AM, with arrival at the South Rim at about noon. The fare is $60 each way ($100 round-trip), and a 50% deposit is required two weeks in advance.

Contacts and Resources

Banks

There is a 24-hour teller machine at the **Bank One** (☎ 520/638–2437) South Rim office, across from the visitor center in Grand Canyon Village. No banking facilities are located within Grand Canyon National Park at the North Rim.

Bicycling

Bicycles are not permitted on any of the Grand Canyon's designated trails, but there are miles of scenic paved thoroughfares in the national park. The park roads have narrow shoulders and are heavily trafficked; use extreme caution. There are no rentals or tours available at either North or South Rim.

Car Rentals

Major companies serving Phoenix and Flagstaff include **Avis** (☎ 800/331–1212), **Budget** (☎ 800/527–0700), and **Hertz** (☎ 800/654–3131).

Emergencies

Ambulance (☎ 911). **Fire** (☎ 911). **Police** (☎ 911).

SOUTH RIM

Grand Canyon Health Center (✉ Grand Canyon Village, ☎ 520/638–2551 or 520/638–2469) offers physician services and receives patients weekdays 8–5:30, Saturday 9–noon. After-hours care and 24-hour emergency services are also available. Dental care (☎ 520/638–2395) is by appointment only.

NORTH RIM

The **North Rim Clinic** (✉ Grand Canyon Lodge, Cabin 1, ☎ 520/638–2611 ext. 222) is staffed by a nurse practitioner. The clinic is open for walk-ins and appointments Friday through Monday 9–noon and 3–6, and Tuesday 9–noon.

PHARMACIES

At the South Rim, the well-stocked **Grand Canyon Clinic Pharmacy** (☎ 520/638–2460) in Grand Canyon Village is open weekdays 8:30–5 year-round and also Saturday morning in the summer; it's generally closed for an hour at lunchtime during the week. There is no pharmacy at the North Rim.

Entrance Fees

Fees levied by the National Park Service vary depending on your method of entering Grand Canyon National Park. If you arrive by automobile, the fee is $20, regardless of the number of passengers. Individuals arriving by bicycle or on foot pay $10. The entrance gates are open 24 hours but are generally supervised from about 7 AM until 6:30 or 7 PM. If you arrive when there's no one at the gate, you may enter legally without paying.

Fishing

Contact the **Arizona Game and Fish Department** (✉ 2222 W. Greenway Rd., Phoenix 85023, ☎ 602/942–3000) for a fishing license.

Food and Camping Supplies

SOUTH RIM

Babbitt's General Store has three locations in the South Rim area: at Grand Canyon Village (☎ 520/638–2262), in the nearby village of Tusayan (☎ 520/638–2854), and at Desert View (☎ 520/638–2393) near the park's east entrance. The main store, in Grand Canyon Village, is a department store that has a deli and sells a full line of camping, hiking, and backpacking supplies in addition to groceries.

NORTH RIM

The **North Rim General Store** (☎ 520/638–2611), inside the park across from the North Rim Campground, carries groceries, some clothing, and travelers' supplies.

Guided Tours

BY BOAT

Wilderness River Adventures (☎ 800/992–8022) offers a seven-day excursion that includes hiking and white-water rafting along the Colorado River.

BY BUS

From late May to late September, a free **shuttle bus service** is offered by the National Park Service (☞ Getting Around by Shuttle Bus, *above*) in the South Rim area. This does not provide a guided tour, but you can get a good feel for the region by taking advantage of trips through Grand Canyon Village, to Yavapai Museum, and to Hermits Rest on the West Rim. The **Fred Harvey Transportation Company** (☎ 520/638–2822 or 520/638–2631) in Grand Canyon Village operates daily motorcoach sightseeing trips along the South Rim and to destinations as far away as Monument Valley on the Navajo reservation. Prices range from $12 for short trips to $80 for all-day tours. Children's half-price fares apply to those under 16 for in-park tours, under 12 on the longer out-of-park tours. For schedules, call the **South Rim Reservations** number (☎ 520/638–2401) or inquire at any Grand Canyon Lodge transportation desk (☞ Visitor Information, *below*).

BY MULE

Mule trips down the precipitous trails to the Inner Gorge of the Grand Canyon are nearly as well known as the canyon itself. But it's hard to get reservations unless you make them months in advance, especially in summer; write to the **Reservations Department** (✉ Amfac Parks and Resorts, 14001 E. Iliff, Suite 600, Aurora, CO 80014, ☎ 303/297–2757, FAX 303/297–3175). These trips have been conducted since the early 1900s, and no one has ever been killed by a mule falling off a cliff. Nevertheless, the treks are not for the faint of heart or people in questionable health. Riders must be at least 4 ft 7 inches tall, weigh less than 200 pounds, and understand English. Pregnant women are not allowed to ride, and children under 15 must be accompanied by an adult. The all-day ride to Plateau Point costs $102 (lunch included).

An overnight with a stay at Phantom Ranch at the bottom of the canyon (☞ East Rim Drive, *above*) is $250.25 ($447.50 for two) for one night, $347.50 ($589 for two) for two nights; meals are included in these prices.

BY PLANE

Flights over the Grand Canyon by airplane or helicopter are offered by a number of companies operating either from Grand Canyon Airport or from heliports in Tusayan.

Air Grand Canyon (☎ 520/638–2618 or 800/247–4726) and **Grand Canyon Airlines** (☎ 520/638–2407 or 800/528–2413) fly small planes; **AirStar Airtours** (☎ 520/638–2622 or 800/962–3869), **Papillon Helicopters** (☎ 520/638–2419 or 800/528–2418), and **Kenai Helicopters** (☎ 520/638–2412 or 800/541–4537) operate whirlybirds. Prices and length of flights vary greatly with tours, but they start at about $55 per person for short airplane flights and $90 per person for short helicopter runs. Inquiries and reservations can also be made at any Grand Canyon Lodge transportation desk (☞ Visitor Information, *below*).

BY TRAIN

See Grand Canyon Railway *in* Williams, *above*.

ON FOOT

The **Grand Canyon Field Institute** (✉ Box 399, Grand Canyon 86023, ☎ 520/638–2485) leads educational guided hikes around the canyon from April through October. Tour topics include everything from archaeology and backcountry medicine to photography and landscape painting.

For a very personalized tour of the Grand Canyon and surrounding sacred sites, contact **Marvelous Marv** (✉ Box 544, Williams 86046, ☎ 520/635–4948), the Indiana Jones of Williams, whose knowledge of the area is as extensive as his repertoire of local legends.

Hiking

Overnight hikes in the Grand Canyon require a permit that can be obtained only by written or faxed request to the **Backcountry Office** (✉ Box 129, Grand Canyon 86023, ☎ 520/638–7875, FAX 520/638–2125). Permits are extremely limited—only 1,600 are issued each year—and the office strongly recommends that reservations be made a full year in advance due to the ever-growing number of visitors to the park. The cost is $20 per permit plus $4 per night for each member of your party. If you arrive without a permit, go to the Backcountry Office at either rim: South Rim near the entrance to Mather Campground, North Rim at the ranger station. There is a slim chance that a cancellation will leave a space available.

SAFETY TIPS

Carry water on hikes to the Inner Canyon—at least 1–1½ gallons per day. To avoid dehydration, drink frequently, about every 10 minutes, especially during summer months. Likewise, take food—preferably salty energy snacks such as trail mix and pretzels, along with bananas, fig bars, and other fructose-rich foods. Do not drink alcohol or caffeine, which accelerate dehydration; for the same reason, avoid processed sugar. Wear hiking boots that have been broken in and proven on previous hikes. Carry a first-aid kit. In case of a medical emergency, stay with the distressed person and ask the next hiker to go for help. Do not attempt to make the round-trip to the Colorado River in one day. The trek down is deceptively easy; the route back up is much longer than most other mountain day-hikes and very fatiguing. The Grand Canyon is unforgiving, and it claims several lives each year. Most of those deaths are avoidable.

Rafting

Although more than 25 companies currently offer excursions, reservations for raft trips (excluding smooth-water, one-day cruises) often need to be made more than six months in advance. For a complete list of river-raft companies, call 520/638–7888 from a touch-tone telephone and press 1-3-71, or write to request a *Trip Planner* (☞ Visitor Information, *below*). National Park Service white-water concessionaires include **Canyoneers, Inc.** (☎ 520/526–0924; 800/525–0924 outside AZ); **Diamond River Adventures, Inc.** (☎ 520/645–8866 or 800/343–3121); and **Outdoors Unlimited** (☎ 520/526–4546 or 800/637–7238). Smooth-water, one-day-trip companies include **Fred Harvey Transportation Company** (☎ 520/638–2822 or 502/638–2631) and **Wilderness River Adventures** (☎ 520/645–32796 or 800/992–8022). Prices for river-raft trips vary greatly, depending on type and length. Half-day trips on smooth water run as low as $40 per person; trips that negotiate the entire length of the canyon and take as long as 12 days can cost close to $2,000.

Road Service

SOUTH RIM

At Grand Canyon Village, the **Fred Harvey Public Garage** (☎ 520/638–2631) is a fully equipped AAA garage that provides auto and RV repair from 8 to 5 daily (closed 12–1 for lunch) as well as 24-hour emergency service. About ¾ mi down the road, across from the visitor center, **Fred Harvey Chevron** (☎ 520/638–2631) does minor repairs, oil and tire changes, and carries propane and diesel fuel.

NORTH RIM

The **Chevron** service station (☎ 520/638–2611), which repairs autos, is located inside the park on the access road leading to the North Rim Campground. No diesel fuel is available at the North Rim.

Safety Tips

Be careful when you or your children are near the edge of the canyon or walking any of the trails that descend into it. Guardrails exist only on portions of the rims. Before engaging in any strenuous exercise, be aware that the canyon rims are more than 7,000 ft in altitude. Being at this height can cause some people—even those in good shape—to become dizzy, faint, or nauseated. Before hiking into the canyon, assess the distance of the proposed hike against your physical condition. Although the descent may not be especially difficult, coming back up can be very strenuous. Take sufficient water and food on hikes into the canyon (☞ Hiking, *above*). During summer months, temperatures in the Inner Gorge can climb above 105°F.

Skiing

Though you can't schuss down into the Grand Canyon, you can cross-country ski in the woods near the rim when there's enough snow.

Babbitts General Store in the South Rim's Grand Canyon Village (☎ 520/638–2234 or 520/638–2262) rents equipment and can guide you to the best trails.

For downhill skiing, you may wish to visit the **Arizona Snowbowl** (☞ Flagstaff *in* Chapter 3), northwest of Flagstaff. It's larger than the Williams Ski Area (☞ Outdoor Activities and Sports *in* Williams, *above*), though still small by Rocky Mountain standards; it tends to be very crowded in season.

Telephones

You're likely to have a hard time getting through to the Grand Canyon: Trunk lines into the area are limited and often overloaded with people calling this most popular of Arizona's attractions. You'll get a fast busy signal if this is the case. In addition, when you do get through to the National Park Service or South Rim Reservations numbers—which handle many of the services listed in this chapter—you'll have to punch a lot of numbers on a computer-voice system before you reach the service you want. Be patient; it's possible to get through to a human being eventually. Writing ahead for the information-packed *Trip Planner* (☞ Visitor Information, *below*) is likely to save you a phone call. Remember, too, that the park does not accept reservations for backcountry permits by phone; they must be made in writing or by fax.

Traveling with Children

The Grand Canyon is family vacation country, and most activities can be enjoyed by all ages. Many of the daily activities at both the North and South rims, detailed in the free Grand Canyon newspaper, *The Guide,* will appeal especially to children. In addition, the Junior Ranger program, geared toward kids ages 4 through 12, introduces kids to the concept of caring for the national parks via an activities checklist found in *Young Adventurer,* a publication available at the South Rim Visitor Center and the Tusayan and Yavapai museums.

Visitor Information

Every arriving visitor at the South or North Rim is given a detailed map of the area. Centers at both rims also publish a free newspaper, *The Guide,* which contains a detailed area map; it is available at the visitor center and many of the lodging facilities and stores. The park also distributes "Accessibility Guide," a free newsletter that details the facilities accessible to travelers with disabilities.

In summer, transportation-services desks are maintained at **Bright Angel Lodge, Maswik Lodge,** and **Yavapai Lodge** in Grand Canyon Village; in winter, the one at Yavapai is closed. The desks provide information and handle bookings, sightseeing tours, taxi and bus services, mule and horseback rides, and accommodations at Phantom Ranch (at the bottom of the Grand Canyon). The concierge at **El Tovar** can also arrange most tours, with the exception of mule rides and lodging at Phantom Ranch.

Grand Canyon Lodge (✉ Amfac Parks and Resorts, 14001 E. Iliff, Suite 600, Aurora, CO 80014, ☎ 303/297–2757, FAX 303/297–3175) has lodging and general information about the North Rim year-round. For information on local services during the season in which the North Rim is open, generally mid-May through late October, depending on the weather, you can phone the lodge directly (☎ 520/638–2611).

Grand Canyon National Park (✉ Box 129, Grand Canyon 86023, ☎ 520/638–7888) is the contact for general information. Write ahead for a complimentary *Trip Planner,* updated regularly by the National Park Service.

Grand Canyon National Park Lodges (✉ Amfac Parks and Resorts, 14001 E. Iliff, Suite 600, Aurora, CO 80014, ☎ 303/297–2757, FAX 303/297–3175) can provide information on lodging, tours, and all other recreation inside the park at the South Rim.

North and South Rim Camping (✉ National Park Reservation Service, Box 85705, San Diego, CA 92138, ☎ 800/365–2267; 858/452–0150 outside the U.S.) provides information on camping in the park. When you call this computer-operated system, have the exact dates you'd like to camp on hand.

Williams and Forest Service Visitor Center (✉ 200 W. Railroad Ave., at Grand Canyon Blvd., Williams 86046, ☎ 520/635–4061), run jointly by the National Forest Service, the city of Williams, and the Williams Chamber of Commerce, has information on Williams, Kaibab Forest, and the entire Grand Canyon area.

Some other resources include: **Boulder City Chamber of Commerce** (✉ 1497 Nevada Hwy., Boulder City, NV 89005, ☎ 702/293–2034). **Kingman Area Chamber of Commerce** (✉ 333 W. Andy Devine Ave., Kingman 86401, ☎ 520/753–6106). **Lake Havasu Visitor and Convention Bureau** (✉ 314 London Bridge Rd., Lake Havasu City 86403, ☎ 520/453–3444 or 800/242–8278). **Laughlin Chamber of Commerce** (✉ 1725 Casino Dr., Box 77777, Laughlin, NV 89028, ☎ 702/298–2214 or 800/227–5245). **Laughlin Visitors Bureau** (✉ 1555 Casino Dr., ☎ 702/298–3022).

Weather
Weather information and road conditions for both rims, updated at 7 AM daily, can be obtained by calling 520/638–7888.

In general, the South Rim has summer temperatures that range from lows in the 50s to highs in the upper 80s. There are frequent afternoon thunderstorms. The area cools off quickly when the sun goes down, so bring a sweater or light jacket for the evening. Winter temperatures average lows around 20°F and highs near 50°F, with the mercury occasionally dropping below zero. In spring and fall, temperatures generally stay above 32°F and often climb into the 70s. The North Rim gets heavy winter snow and is thus open to the public only from mid-May through October. Temperatures during this open season range from lows in the 30s to highs in the 70s. As in the South Rim, afternoon rain is common; in May and October, it occasionally snows as well. As you proceed down either rim toward the canyon's Inner Gorge, temperatures rise. In summer along the Colorado River—at an elevation of about 2,400 ft—temperatures range from lows in the 70s to highs above 100°F. Winter sees lows in the 30s, highs around 50°F. It rarely snows at the bottom of the Grand Canyon, even in winter; snow on the rims usually turns to rain as it falls into the Inner Gorge.

2 THE NORTHEAST

To the Navajo and Hopi people who inhabit northeastern Arizona, the land is their spiritual guide, their history book, and the birthplace of their people. From the canyons of red sandstone, across the windswept desert, to the mountains of towering ponderosa pine, this is a region alive with sacred symbols, legends, and memories. Visitors are enchanted by the ancient ruins at the Navajo National Monument, Canyon de Chelly, Homolovi Ruins, the sculpted rock formations of Monument Valley, and the jade-green waters and rugged red cliffs of Lake Powell.

By William E.
Hafford

Updated by
Edward A.
Tomchin

NORTHEAST ARIZONA is a vast and magnificent land of lofty buttes, towering cliffs, and turquoise skies so clear horizons appear endless. Most of the land in the area belongs to the Navajo and Hopi peoples, who cling to ancient traditions based on spiritual values, kinship, and an affinity for nature. In many respects life on the Hopi Mesas has changed little over the last two centuries, and visiting this land can feel like traveling to a foreign country. Native American arts and crafts can be found in shops and trading posts, and in towns like Tuba City and Window Rock it's not uncommon to hear the gliding vowels and soft consonants of the Navajo language, a tongue as different from Hopi as English is from Chinese.

The Navajo reservation, formally known as the Navajo Nation, encompasses more than 25,000 square mi. In its approximate center sits the 4,000-square-mi Hopi reservation, a series of stone and adobe villages built on high mesas overlooking cultivated land. On Arizona's northern and eastern borders, where the Navajo Nation continues into Utah, Colorado, and New Mexico, the Navajo National Monument and Canyon de Chelly contain haunting cliff dwellings of ancient people who lived in the area 1,500 years ago. Glen Canyon Dam, which abuts the far northwestern corner of the reservation on U.S. 89, holds back more than 120 mi of emerald waters known as Lake Powell.

Most of northeast Arizona is desert country, but it is far from boring: Eerie and spectacular rock formations as colorful as desert sunsets highlight immense mesas, canyons, and cliffs; verdant stands of ponderosa pine cover the Chuska Mountains to the north and east of Canyon de Chelly. Navajo Mountain to the north and west in Utah soars over 10,000 ft, and the San Francisco Peaks climb to similar heights to the south and west by Flagstaff. According to the Navajo creation myth, these are two of the four mountainous boundaries of the sacred land where the Navajo first emerged from the earth's interior.

Pleasures and Pastimes

Camping
Camping is allowed only in posted authorized areas. Most campgrounds are primitive, in many cases nothing more than open, level areas where sleeping bags can be laid out or RVs parked; outside the Lake Powell area, a few sites, such as those in Monument Valley and Canyon de Chelly, have modern camping facilities.

Dining
Few communities in northeast Arizona have public eating establishments, but restaurants can be found in the following locations: Cameron, Tuba City, Page, Kayenta, Goulding's Trading Post–Monument Valley, Hopi Second Mesa, Keams Canyon, Chinle, Ganado, St. Michael's, Tsaile, Window Rock, and Fort Defiance. Fine dining is scarce, but you'll find very good Native American, Mexican, and southwestern cuisine, as well as standard American fare. Basic Navajo and Hopi fare consists mainly of fry bread, Indian-style tacos, and mutton stew. In the smaller reservation communities, only fast food may be available. Dining reservations are advisable in summer.

Fishing
Lake Powell holds varieties of bass, trout, bluegill, and pike, among others, and the Colorado River below Glen Canyon Dam is known for its large trout. Keep in mind that Lake Powell stretches into Utah; an appropriate permit is required for each locale. The eastern region of

the Navajo reservation has scattered lakes, most of them remote and small, but two of the more popular and accessible lakes are near Canyon de Chelly: Wheatfields Lake, on Indian Highway 12 about 11 mi south of the community of Tsaile, and Many Farms Lake, near the community of Many Farms, on U.S. 191. Permits are always required for fishing on the reservation (☞ Fishing *in* The Northeast A to Z, *below* for information about permits).

Hiking

Some of the best hikes in this region are in Canyon de Chelly, up the streambed between the soaring orange-and-white sandstone cliffs, with the remains of the ancient Anasazi communities frequently in view. Mummy Cave is especially worth a look, its three-story watchtower nearly perfectly preserved. The more weathered Antelope House and White House stand against the sweeping canyon cliffs as impressive reminders of a bygone era. The Navajo National Monument offers impressive hikes to two ruins: Betatakin, a settlement dating back to AD 1250, and Keet Seel, which dates back as far as AD 950. Both are in alcoves at the base of gigantic overhanging cliffs.

Hopi Ceremonies

The Hopi are well known for colorful ceremonial dances, many of which are supplications for rain, fertile crops, and harmony with nature. Most of these ceremonies take place in village plazas and kivas (underground ceremonial chambers) and last two days or longer; outsiders are permitted to watch only selected segments of very few ceremonies and are never allowed into kivas. The best known is the snake dance, in which participants carry poisonous snakes, but it has not been open to the public in recent years. Seasonal katsina dances performed at agricultural ceremonies have also been restricted, so it's best to inquire upon arrival. Each clan has its own sacred rituals, starting times, and dates, which are determined by tribal elders. Visitors should be respectful and adhere to the proper etiquette while observing dances.

Lodging

One of most important things to know when traveling in northeastern Arizona is which of the scattered communities have motels. Most motels throughout the northeast are clean, comfortable, and well maintained. Bed-and-breakfasts have begun to proliferate in Page, although zoning restrictions currently prevent them from being anything other than informal homestays. The town of Page is considering licensing larger B&B's with more facilities to give visitors more choices. At the time of this writing, the changes were still under consideration. Contact the Page/Lake Powell Chamber of Commerce (☞ Visitor Information *in* The Northeast A to Z, *below*) for a list of area B&Bs. During summer months, it is especially wise to make reservations.

Unless otherwise indicated, all rooms have air-conditioning, private baths, telephones, and TVs.

Native American Reservations

Visitors to the Navajo Nation and Hopi reservation have the opportunity to gain an understanding of the lives, past and present, of some of our land's true founding mothers and fathers. Both the Hopi and Navajo peoples are friendly to tourists, although the Hopi are far more protective of their privacy, customs, and laws. Observe the following when visiting either reservation:

- Do not wander across or through residential areas or disturb property. Always ask permission before taking photographs of the locals; you may have to pay to take the picture, and even if no money is requested, consider offering a dollar or two to the person whose photograph you have taken. The Navajo are very open about photographs; the Hopi do not allow photographs at all.

- Do not litter.

- No open fires are allowed; fires are permitted only in grills and fireplaces. Bring your own wood or charcoal. Do not attempt to cut or gather firewood on the reservations.

- Observe quiet hours from 11 PM until 6 AM at all camping areas.

- Do not disturb or remove animals, plants, rocks, or artifacts. They are protected by Tribal Antiquity and federal laws, which are strictly enforced.

- The possession and consumption of alcoholic beverages or illicit drugs is illegal. Do not bring them onto reservation lands.

- No off-trail hiking or rock climbing is allowed unless accompanied by a native guide.

- A tribal permit is required for fishing in lakes or streams. Violations of fish and game laws are punishable by heavy fines, imprisonment, or both.

- Off-road travel by four-wheel-drive vehicles, dune buggies, Jeeps, and motorcycles is not allowed unless accompanied by a native tour guide.

- Do not wear bathing suits or similar scanty clothing in public; it is offensive to the locals.

- Pets should be kept on a leash or in a confined area.

- Should you see a ceremony in progress while traveling, do not stop and watch uninvited or you will be asked to leave.

- On the Hopi reservation, taking photographs or making videos, tape recordings, or sketches of villages or ceremonies is strictly prohibited. Binoculars should never be used to observe people or villages. If you break these rules you run the risk of having your camera (not just the film), binoculars, recording devices, and sketch pads confiscated; you'll also be escorted off the reservation. These are the normal penalties, and there is no appeal. Each Hopi village has particular rules about visitors; check with the individual village Community Development Offices or call the Hopi Tribe Office of Public Relations (☞ Visitor Information *in* The Northeast A to Z, *below*) in advance for information. At all sacred events, neat attire and a respectful demeanor are requested; women should not expose their thighs or midriffs. Camping is permitted for a maximum of two nights, but only in designated areas.

- Be aware that relations between the Navajo and Hopi peoples are sometimes tense, owing to long-standing property disputes that have engaged the federal courts for years. It's simplest not to ask about it.

Shopping

Most visitors to the area are tempted by the beautiful pottery, turquoise and sterling-silver jewelry, handwoven baskets, Navajo wool rugs, and other examples of Native American crafts. Many trading posts also carry the work of some New Mexico tribes, including exquisite inlaid Zuni jewelry and the world-acclaimed pottery of the Pueblo people. Navajo and Hopi crafts, especially jewelry and pottery, are very similar in style; few lay people can differentiate between work by the two tribes.

Roadside stands often resemble hastily thrown together shacks, but they offer some outstanding values. Most products sold on the Hopi and Navajo reservations are authentic, but the possibility of imitations does exist. Trading posts are very reliable as are most roadside stands, but be wary of solo vendors hanging around parking lots. If you're planning on shopping on the Hopi Reservation or elsewhere outside the Navajo trading posts, it's a good idea to carry cash or traveler's checks. Phone lines in the region are sometimes unreliable, which can make credit-card use impossible. For more information, *see* Shopping *in* The Northwest A to Z, *below.*

Exploring the Northeast

The Navajo Nation, which encircles the Hopi reservation, occupies most of northeastern Arizona. The Canyon de Chelly is in the eastern part of the reservation. The Navajo National Monument and Monument Valley are in north central "Navajoland" (a term used by the Navajo in promotional material). In the northwestern corner of the Arizona portion of the reservation are Lake Powell and Glen Canyon Dam. Note: Northeastern Arizona is a sparsely inhabited area with few roads and services. Few establishments have numbered street addresses; even the post office operates on the basis of landmarks.

Numbers in the text correspond to numbers in the margin and on the Northeast Arizona map.

Great Itineraries

IF YOU HAVE 2–3 DAYS

If you're based in ⊞ **Holbrook** or ⊞ **Winslow,** you'll have an easy drive to some of the most interesting sights in northeastern Arizona. On your first day, visit **Canyon de Chelly** ③. On the second, set out for the **Hopi Mesas** ⑥–⑧, stopping along the way at the **Homolovi Ruins State Park** and the **Hubbell Trading Post National Historic Site** ④.

IF YOU HAVE 5 DAYS

On your first day drive to ⊞ **Cameron Trading Post,** explore the area, and spend the night at the motel there. The next morning, make your way north on U.S. 89 to **Tuba City** ⑨, the last stop for gas before heading east at Moenkopi on State Highway 264 for the **Hopi Mesas** ⑥–⑧. Have lunch at the **Hopi Cultural Center** then go south on State Highway 87 to visit the **Homolovi Ruins State Park.** Returning to Tuba City, head north on U.S. 160 toward ⊞ **Kayenta** ⑩, where you can spend your second night. Get up early the next day to visit the **Navajo National Monument** ⑭ and hike to Betatakin or Keet Seel pueblo (if you have made reservations in advance). Spend your third night at the lodge at ⊞ **Goulding's Trading Post** ⑬ in Monument Valley. The next day, visit **Monument Valley Navajo Tribal Park** ⑪, and then take U.S. 160 north to where it connects with U.S. 191 near the town of Mexican Water. Head south for Chinle, a good base for touring ⊞ **Canyon de Chelly** ③.

When to Tour the Northeast

Summer is a busy time in the Lake Powell area, and reservations for accommodations are essential. Travelers seeking a quieter vacation should plan to visit between early November and late March, when the crowds—and the prices—ebb. The first weekend of September after Labor Day is a good time to be at Window Rock, when the Navajo Nation Annual Tribal Fair takes place. It's the world's largest Native American fair, and includes a rodeo, traditional Navajo music and dances, food booths, and an intertribal powwow. August and September brings the Hopi Harvest Festival, a celebration featuring Harvest and Butterfly social dances. To keep up to date on the news and weather when traveling the Navajo and Hopi Nations, tune your radio to the following stations: 660 AM (KTNN), Window Rock; or 770 AM, 97.9 FM, and 107.3 FM (KOB).

ARIZONA'S NATIVE AMERICAN HIGHLIGHTS

"**B**EAUTY ALL AROUND ME . . . with it I wander." The words to this Navajo song capture the spirit of a visit to the ancient and modern homelands of Arizona's Native Americans. Take a trip into a world where the landscape shaped a civilization.

Phoenix and Environs (1 day). Begin your journey into Arizona's Native American heartland with a stop at the Deer Valley Rock Art Center near Phoenix, where you can wander among mysterious rock images painted by prehistoric artists. Other secrets reside at nearby Casa Grande Ruins National Monument, the remains of an unusual four-story structure. Overhanging cliffs protect the adobe walls at Tonto National Monument, and the handprints of early builders are still visible. (☞ Side Trips Near Phoenix, Side Trips Around the Apache Trail *in* Chapter 4.)

Eastern Arizona (1 day). A pleasant drive through cool mountains brings you to the ruins at Casa Malpais Archaeological Park, where you can almost hear the chants of long-gone dancers. Nearby, work alongside archaeologists at Raven Site Ruins and the White Mountain Archaeological Center. (☞ The White Mountains in Chapter 5.)

Canyon de Chelly (2 days). At the heart of Indian Arizona lie the towering crimson buttes, twisted spires, meandering creeks, and cliff dwellings of spectacular Canyon de Chelly. On the way here, don't miss the Anasazi-built Kinlichee Ruins and the Hubbell Trading Post National Historic Site, where you can admire and purchase the work of Navajo artisans. (☞ Navajo Nation East *below.*)

Hopi Indian Reservation (1 day). The Hopis' multi-unit, pueblo-style homes on First Mesa, Second Mesa, and Third Mesa look much as they did centuries ago, and the way of life has not changed much. Stop at the Hopi Cultural Center to learn about "the peaceful people" and sample Hopi cuisine. (☞ The Hopi Mesas *below.*)

Navajo Nation (1 day). As you stand under the sweeping sandstone cliffs at Navajo National Monument you can almost smell aboriginal cooking fires. Betatakin is the most accessible ruin, while the larger Keet Seel has plenty of nooks and crannies to investigate. (☞ Navajo Nation North *below.*)

Flagstaff and Environs (2 days). Wupatki National Monument, in the shadow of the Flagstaff's pine-covered San Francisco Peaks, is a high-country example of pueblo and granary ruins. Native flora make for a fragrant hike to the cliff dwellings of Walnut Canyon National Monument. South of Flagstaff, shaded walkways offer easy access to the well-preserved cliff dwelling at Montezuma Castle National Monument. Then stop at the visitors' center at Tuzigoot National Monument for a look at artifacts up to 1,000 years old. (☞ Chapter 3.)

Northeast Arizona

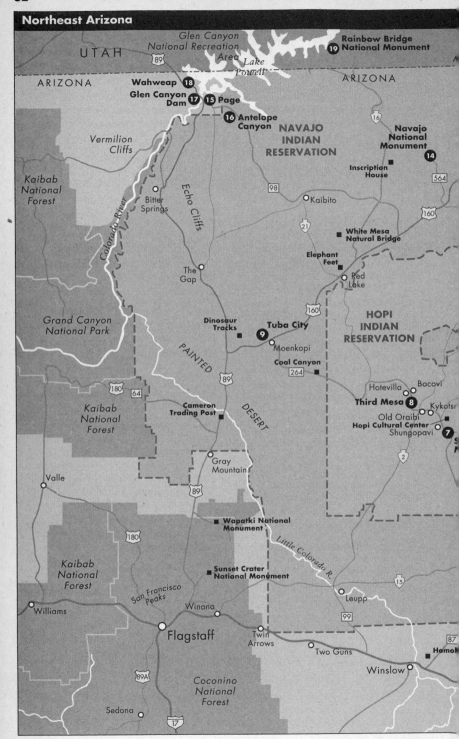

UTAH

Glen Canyon
National Recreation
Area Lake
Powell

19 Rainbow Bridge
National Monument

ARIZONA

89

ARIZONA

Wahweap **18**

Glen Canyon
Dam **17** **15** Page

16

16 Antelope
Canyon

NAVAJO
INDIAN
RESERVATION

Navajo
National
Monument

14

Inscription
House

564

Vermilion
Cliffs

Kaibab
National
Forest

Bitter
Springs

Colorado River

Echo Cliffs

98

Kaibito

160

21

White Mesa
Natural Bridge

Elephant
Feet

Red
Lake

The
Gap

160

HOPI
INDIAN
RESERVATION

Grand Canyon
National Park

PAINTED

Dinosaur
Tracks

Tuba City

9

Moenkopi

Coal Canyon

264

Hotevilla Bacovi

Third Mesa **8** Kykotsr

Old Oraibi

Hopi Cultural Center
Shungopavi **7**

180

64

Kaibab
National
Forest

89

DESERT

Cameron
Trading Post

2

Gray
Mountain

Valle

89

180

Wapatki National
Monument

Little Colorado R.

15

Kaibab
National
Forest

San Francisco
Peaks

Sunset Crater
National Monument

Leupp

99

Williams

Winona

Flagstaff

Twin
Arrows

Two Guns

87

Hamo

89A

Coconino
National
Forest

Winslow

Sedona

17

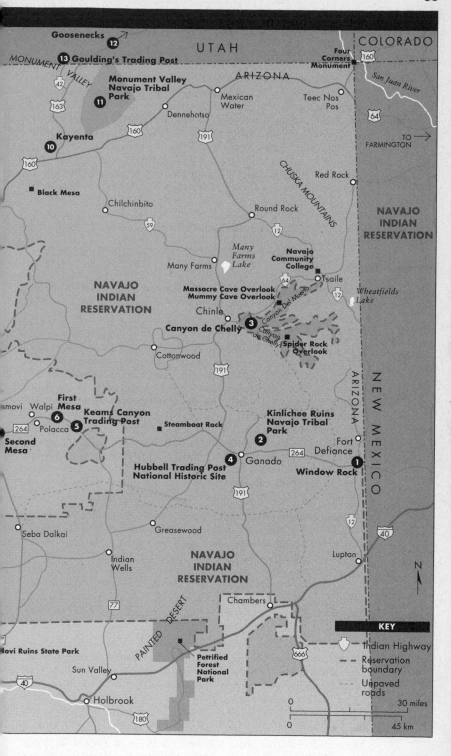

Goosenecks 12

13 Goulding's Trading Post

MONUMENT VALLEY

UTAH

COLORADO

Four Corners Monument 160

San Juan River

Monument Valley Navajo Tribal Park

42

11

Mexican Water

ARIZONA

Teec Nos Pos

64

TO FARMINGTON

163

Dennehotso

191

Kayenta

160

10

160

Black Mesa

Chilchinbito

59

Round Rock

Red Rock

CHUSKA MOUNTAINS

12

NAVAJO INDIAN RESERVATION

Many Farms Lake

Navajo Community College

NAVAJO INDIAN RESERVATION

Many Farms

Canyon Del Muerto

64

Tsaile

Wheatfields Lake

Massacre Cave Overlook
Mummy Cave Overlook

Chinle

12

Canyon de Chelly 3

Canyon de Chelly

Spider Rock Overlook

Cottonwood

191

First Mesa

smovi

Walpi

6

Keams Canyon Trading Post

Polacca 5

264

Second Mesa

Steamboat Rock

Kinlichee Ruins Navajo Tribal Park

2

ARIZONA

NEW MEXICO

Fort Defiance

1

264

Window Rock

Hubbell Trading Post National Historic Site

4

Ganado

191

Seba Dalkai

Greasewood

12

Lupton

40

Indian Wells

N

NAVAJO INDIAN RESERVATION

77

Chambers

PAINTED DESERT

KEY

Indian Highway

Reservation boundary

Unpaved roads

ovi Ruins State Park

666

Petrified Forest National Park

Sun Valley

40

0   30 miles

Holbrook

180

0   45 km

NAVAJO NATION EAST

Land has always been central to the history of the Navajo people: It's imbedded in their very name. The Tewa Indians were the first to call them *Navahu*—which means "large area of cultivated land." But according to the Navajo creation myth, they were given the name *ni'hookaa diyan diné*—"holy earth people"—by their creators. Today, among tribal members, they call themselves the diné. The eastern portion of the Arizona Navajo Nation (in Navajo, *diné bikéyah*) is a dry but often surprisingly green land, especially in the vicinity of the aptly named Beautiful Valley, south of Canyon de Chelly along U.S. 191. A landscape of rolling hills, wide arroyos, and small canyons, the area is dotted with traditional Navajo hogans (eight-sided domed houses made of mud, logs, or even contemporary building materials), sheepfolds, cattletanks, and wood racks. The region's easternmost portion is marked by tall mountains and towering sandstone cliffs cut by primitive roads that are generally accessible only by horse or four-wheel-drive vehicles.

Window Rock

❶ *192 mi from Flagstaff, east on I–40 and north on Indian Hwy. 12; 26 mi from Gallup, New Mexico, north on U.S. 666 and west on NM and AZ 264.*

Named for the immense arch-shape "window" in a massive sandstone ridge above the city, Window Rock is the capital of the Navajo Nation. With a population of fewer than 5,000, this community serves as the business and social center for Navajo families throughout the reservation. Window Rock is a good place to stop for food, supplies, and gas. It is also the home of the **Navajo Nation Council Chambers,** a handsome structure that resembles a large hogan. Visitors can observe sessions of the council, where 88 delegates representing 100 reservation communities meet on the third Monday of January, April, July, and October. **Window Rock Navajo Tribal Park**, near the Council Chambers, is where several Navajo religious ceremonies—most closed to outsiders—are held. ⊠ *Turn east off Indian Hwy. 12, about ½ mi north of AZ 264.*

The **Navajo Nation Museum,** on the grounds of the former Tse Bonito Park off AZ 264, is devoted to the art, culture, and history of the Navajo people, and has an excellent selection of books on the Navajo Nation. The Museum hosts exhibitions of native artists each season; call for a listing of shows. Next to the Navajo Nation Museum, the **Navajo Arts and Crafts Enterprises** (☞ Shopping, *below*) displays local artwork, including pottery, jewelry, and blankets. ⊠ *AZ 264, next to Navajo Nation Inn at junction of Indian Hwy. 12. Museum:* ☎ *520/871–6673.* ▣ *Free.* ☉ *Weekdays 1–5.*

If you're curious about wildlife in northeastern Arizona and its ties to Navajo culture and religion, stop at the **Navajo Nation Zoological Park.** Set amid sandstone monoliths on the border of Arizona and New Mexico, this unique zoo displays indigenous birds and animals that figure in Navajo legends—golden eagles, elk, and coyotes, among others. ⊠ *North off AZ 264 northeast of the Navajo Nation Museum* (☞ *above*), ☎ *520/871–6573.* ▣ *Free.* ☉ *Daily 8–5.*

Many all-Indian rodeos are held near the center of downtown at the **Navajo Tribal Fairgrounds.** The community hosts the annual July 4 Powwow, with a major rodeo, ceremonial dances, and a parade. The Navajo Nation Tribal Fair, much like a traditional state fair, is held in

RESERVATION REALITIES

BOTH THE NAVAJO AND HOPI base their culture on the land around them, but they are two distinct peoples, as different from each other as the French are from the Germans. The similarities and contrasts between them are reflected in the harsh realities of life on the reservation.

The Navajo refer to themselves as the diné (pronounced din-eh)—"the people"—and live on 17 million acres in Arizona, New Mexico, Utah, and Colorado. Although it is not officially part of the reservation, many Navajo consider southwestern Colorado part of their sacred land. The Hopi trace their roots back to the original settlers of the area, whom they call the Anasazi, or "ancient ones." Hopi culture is far more formal and structured than that of the Navajo, and their religion has remained much stronger and purer. But for both tribes, unemployment is very high on the reservation, and poverty is a constant presence.

Most Navajo and Hopi disapprove of the practice, but some panhandlers nevertheless cluster at shopping centers and view sites hoping to glean a few tourist dollars. They may ask for money to buy food or gasoline, but they usually spend their profits on illegal liquor. Visitors should respond to panhandlers with a polite but firm "no"; the phrases "she bay-so at-den" or "dough-da" (roughly translated, "no money") generally work. If you wish to help, make a donation to one of the legitimate organizations that raise funds at reservation grocery stores.

The sight of stray dogs, both starving and dead, is another unpleasant fact of life on the reservation. Among the Navajo in particular, dogs have never been held in high esteem, and in Navajo mythology dogs represent chaos and mischief. On both reservations, federal funding for animal control has been cut, and people struggling to make ends meet have few resources to devote to animal care. Visitors are encouraged not to feed the dogs, as this just exacerbates the problem.

Hopi mythology holds that a white-skinned people will save the tribe from its difficult life. Long ago, however, in the face of brutal treatment by the Anglos, most Hopi became convinced that their salvation would originate elsewhere. (Some Hopi now look to the Dalai Lama of Tibetan Buddhism for redemption.) As a result they occasionally take a brusque attitude toward non-Hopi visitors. Though not easy to witness, the disappointment of the Hopi and the despair of the Navajo are easy to understand after a visit to the reservation.

To learn more about the Navajo, visit http://www.navajocentral.org; to learn more about the Hopi, visit http://www.infomagic.com/äabyte/hopi.

– Ed Tomchin

early September. It offers standard county fair rides, midway booths, contests, shows, and the ubiquitous rodeo riding and bull-roping displays. Contact the Navajo Nation Fair Office (℡ 520/871–6282) for more information about both events.

Dining and Lodging

$ ✕ℍ **Navajoland Day's Inn.** This new lodging option in Window Rock offers standard-size rooms appointed with the chain's usual pastel-tone furniture. A Denny's Restaurant is on the property. ✉ *North side of Hwy. 264 west of Indian Hwy. 12, mailing address: Box 905, 86511,* ℡ *520/ 871–5690 or 800/329–7466,* 𝔽𝔸𝕏 *520/871–5699. 65 rooms, 8 suites. Indoor pool, hot tub, sauna, health club, meeting rooms. AE, DC, MC, V.*

Shopping

An outlet of the **Navajo Arts and Crafts Enterprises** (✉ Off AZ 264 and Indian Hwy. 12, next to Navajo Nation Inn, ℡ 520/871–4090 or 520/871–4095) stocks authentic tribal artworks. You'll occasionally find local artisans at work here.

Kinlichee Ruins Navajo Tribal Park

❷ *22 mi west of Window Rock off AZ 264.*

A marked road leads to this 640-acre park with dwellings built by the mysterious Anasazi, whom the Hopi call "the ancient ones." A self-guided trail—the park is always open—takes you past the ruins and exhibits, but visitors are not allowed into the kiva pit. There are picnic areas and a primitive campground where a camping fee of $1 per person may be collected.

Canyon de Chelly

★ **❸** *40 mi from Kinlichee Ruins Navajo Tribal Park, west on AZ 264 and north on U.S. 191.*

The nearly 84,000-acre Canyon de Chelly (pronounced d'*shay*) is one of the most spectacular national monuments in the Southwest. Its main gorges—the 26-mi-long Canyon de Chelly and the adjoining 35-mi Canyon del Muerto—have sheer, heavily eroded sandstone walls that rise to 1,000 ft. Ancient pictographs decorate some of the cliffs, and within the canyon complex there are more than 7,000 archaeological sites, some dating back almost 4,500 years. Gigantic stone formations rise hundreds of feet above streams, hogans, tilled fields, peach orchards, and grazing lands.

The first inhabitants of the canyons, the Anasazi, arrived more than 2,000 years ago. In AD 750, these Basket Makers disappeared and were replaced by Pueblo tribes who constructed stone cliff dwellings. The departure of the Pueblo people around AD 1300 is widely believed to have resulted from changing climatic conditions, soil erosion, dwindling local resources, disease, and internal conflict. Present-day Hopis see these people as their ancestors who, quite simply, left to find a better place to live. Beginning around AD 780, Hopi farmers settled here, followed by the Navajo around 1300. (The Navajo migrated from far northern Canada; no one is sure when they arrived in the Southwest. Despite evidence to the contrary, most Navajos hold that their people have always lived here.) Centuries-old traditions have been passed down to the Navajo families who now live, farm, and raise sheep in the area.

Both Canyon de Chelly and Canyon del Muerto have a paved rim drive (each takes about two hours) with views of the great canyon. Prehistoric ruins can be found near the base of cliffs and perched on high, sheltering ledges. The dwellings and cultivated fields of the present-day Navajo lie in the flatlands between the cliffs. The Navajo who inhabit the canyon today farm much the way their ancestors did.

The **South Rim Drive** (36 mi round-trip) of Canyon de Chelly starts at the visitor center and ends at **Spider Rock Overlook,** where cliffs plunge 1,000 ft to the canyon floor. Here you'll have a view of two pinnacles, Speaking Rock and Spider Rock; the latter rises about 800 ft from the canyon floor and is considered a sacred place. Navajo children are taught that Speaking Rock reports the names of bad boys and girls to Spider Woman, who carries them to her lair atop Spider Rock. Other highlights on the South Rim Drive are **Junction Overlook,** where Canyon del Muerto joins Canyon de Chelly; **White House Overlook,** from which a trail leads to the **White House Ruin,** with dwelling remains of nearly 60 rooms and several kivas; and **Sliding House Overlook,** where you can see ruins on a narrow, sloped ledge across the canyon.

The **visitor center** has exhibits on the history of the cliff dwellers and provides information on scheduled hikes, tours, and other programs within the national monument. ⊠ *AZ 7, 3 mi east of U.S. 191,* ☎ *520/ 674–5500.* ▣ *Free.* ☉ *Memorial Day–Labor Day, daily 8–6; Labor Day–Memorial Day, daily 8–5.*

The **North Rim Drive** (34 mi round-trip) of Canyon del Muerto also begins at the visitor center and continues northeast on Indian Highway 64 toward the town of Tsaile. Major stops include **Antelope House Overlook,** the site of a large ruin named for the animals painted on an adjacent cliff; the **Mummy Cave Overlook,** where two mummies were found inside a remarkably unspoiled pueblo dwelling, the monument's largest; and **Massacre Cave Overlook,** the last stop, which marks the spot where an estimated 115 Navajo were killed by the Spanish in 1805. (The rock walls of the cave are still pockmarked from the Spaniards' ricocheting bullets.) In Tsaile, Navajo medicine men worked in conjunction with architects to design the town's six-story **Navajo Community College** (⊠ Navajo Community College and Hatathli Museum on Indian Hwy. 12 just south of the junction with Indian Hwy. 64, ☎ 520/724–3311); admission is by donation and it's open weekdays 8:30–noon and 1–4. Because all important Navajo activities traditionally take place in a circle (a hogan is essentially circular), the campus was laid out in the round, with all of the buildings inside its perimeter. The college's **Hatathli Museum** is devoted to Native American culture. To the north of Tsaile are the impressive **Chuska Mountains,** covered with sprawling stands of ponderosa pine. There are no established hiking trails in the mountains, but up-to-date hiking information and backcountry-use permits (rarely granted if a Navajo guide does not accompany the trip) can be obtained at the **Navajo Nation Parks and Recreation Department** (☞ Hiking *in* The Northeast A to Z, *below*).

Dining and Lodging

Chinle is the closest town to Canyon de Chelly. There are three good lodgings with restaurants here, as well as a large supermarket and a campground. In late August each year, Chinle is host to the Central Navajo Fair, a public celebration complete with a rodeo, carnival, and traditional dances.

$–$$ ✕▣ **Holiday Inn Canyon de Chelly.** Formerly Garcia's Trading Post, this facility near Canyon de Chelly is less generic than you might expect: The territorial fort–style exterior gives an authentic rustic feel to the inn. Rooms, on the other hand, are predictably pastel and contemporary. The lobby restaurant, low-key by most standards, is the most upscale eatery in the area, serving well-prepared specialties like delicious mutton stew served with fry bread and honey. The hotel restaurant offers a box picnic ($6.95) for its guests and has a gift shop stocked with local Native American arts and crafts. ⊠ *Box 1889, Indian Rte. 7, Chinle 86503,* ☎ *520/674–5000,* FAX *520/674–8264. 108 rooms. Restaurant, pool. AE, D, DC, MC, V.*

$–$$ ✕⊡ **Thunderbird Lodge.** In an ideal location near the mouth of Canyon de Chelly, this pleasant establishment has stone and adobe units that match the architecture of the site's original 1896 trading post. Some rooms have roughly hewn beam ceilings, rustic wooden furniture, and Navajo decor. The staff is friendly and knowledgeable, and the manicured lawns and cottonwood trees create a resortlike atmosphere. Inexpensive soups, salads, sandwiches, and entrées, including charbroiled steaks, are prepared by an all-Navajo staff in the cafeteria. The lodge also offers truck tours of Canyon de Chelly (☞ Guided Tours *in* The Northeast A to Z, *below*). ⊠ *Box 548, ½ mi south of Canyon de Chelly visitor center, Chinle 86503,* ☎ *520/674–5841 or 800/679–2473. 72 rooms. Cafeteria. AE, D, DC, MC, V.*

$–$$ ⊡ **Best Western Canyon de Chelly Inn.** This two-story motel about 3 mi from Canyon de Chelly has cheerful rooms with modern oak furnishings and Native American–print bedspreads and drapes. All rooms have cable TV and coffeemakers. The on-site restaurant opens for breakfast at 6:30; traditional Navajo dinners are served until 9 PM. ⊠ *Box 295, Rte. 7 (¼ mi east of U.S. 191), Chinle 86503,* ☎ *520/674–5875, 520/674–5288, or 800/327–0354. 102 rooms. Restaurant, indoor pool. AE, D, DC, MC, V.*

$ ⊡ **Coyote Pass Hospitality.** You're not likely to encounter a more unusual lodging than this roving B&B run by the Coyote Pass clan of the Navajo Nation. It's not for everyone: You sleep on bedding on the dirt floor of a hogan (its location depends on the season, but most are near Canyon de Chelly), use an outhouse, and eat a Navajo-style breakfast—blue-corn pancakes and herbal tea, for instance—prepared on a wood-burning stove. If you don't mind roughing it a bit, this is a rare opportunity to immerse yourself in beautiful surroundings and Native American culture: The clan gives presentations on Navajo life every night. Guided hikes, nature programs, tours, and other meals are optional extras. Prices generally run about $85 for the first person and $15 for each additional person up to a maximum of eight people. The folks at Coyote Pass will also create a customized tour of the canyon suited to your purposes (hiking, camping, photography, etc.). ⊠ *Contact Will Tsosie, Box 91–B, Tsaile 86556,* ☎ *520/724–3383. Full breakfast. No credit cards.*

⚠ **Cottonwood Campground.** The 52 RV sites (maximum length 35 ft; no hookups) and 95 tent sites here are available free, on a first-come, first-served basis. Cottonwood trees shade the sites and picnic tables. Flush toilets and water are available from April to September. ⊠ *Canyon de Chelly National Monument, near visitor center, Chinle 86503,* ☎ *520/674–5500.* ☉ *Year-round.*

Outdoor Activities and Sports

HIKING

Only one hike within Canyon de Chelly National Monument—the **White House Ruin Trail** on the South Rim Drive—can be done without an authorized guide. The easy trail starts near White House Overlook and runs along sheer walls that drop about 550 ft. The hike leads to the White House Ruin (☞ *above*) and is 2½ mi round-trip.

Guided hikes to the interior of the canyons cost about $10 per hour with a three-hour minimum for groups of up to four people. (Don't venture into the canyon without a guide, or you'll face a stiff fine.) For overnights, you'll pay $20 more for the guide and about $30 for permission to stay on private land. From Memorial Day through Labor Day, free three-hour ranger-led hikes depart from the visitor center (☞ *above*) at 9 AM. Also during the summer, two- and four-hour hikes ($5 and $10) leave from the visitor center in the morning and afternoon. Some are strenuous and steep; visitors with health problems or a fear of heights should proceed with caution. Call ahead if you are interested in a hike: They're canceled occasionally due to local customs or events.

HORSEBACK RIDING

Justin's Horse Rental (⊠ Box 881, Chinle 86503, ☎ 520/674–5678), near the South Rim Drive entrance of Canyon de Chelly, conducts trips into the canyon for $10 per hour for each horse plus $10 per hour for a guide (two-hour minimum). A two-day, one-night guided excursion runs $190 per person and includes dinner and breakfast on the trail. The owner, Justin Tso, will gladly arrange longer or shorter rides through either canyon.

Hubbell Trading Post National Historic Site

④ *32 mi south of Canyon de Chelly, off AZ 264.*

John Lorenzo Hubbell, a merchant and friend of the Navajo, established this trading post in 1878. Hubbell taught, translated letters, settled family quarrels, and explained government policy to them, and during an 1886 smallpox epidemic, he turned his home into a hospital and ministered to the sick and dying. Hubbell died in 1930 and is buried near the trading post.

At the **visitor center,** National Park Service exhibits illustrate the post's history, and Navajo artisans frequently demonstrate jewelry and rug making. You may also take a self-guided tour of the grounds and visit the Hubbell Trading Post, which contains a fine display of Native American artistry (☞ Shopping, *below*). The visitor center also has a fairly comprehensive bookstore specializing in Navajo history, art, and culture; occasionally you may even find local weavers demonstrating their craft on the premises. ⊠ *AZ 264, 1 mi west of Ganado,* ☎ *520/755–3475.* ☑ *Free.* ☉ *Daily 8–5.*

Shopping

Hubbell Trading Post (⊠ Off AZ 264, 1 mi west of Ganado, ☎ 520/755–3254) is famous for its "Ganado red" Navajo rugs; the quality is outstanding but prices can be accordingly high—they range anywhere from $50 to around $20,000. It is hard to resist these beautiful designs and colors, and it's a pleasure just to browse around this rustic spot where Navajo artists frequently show their work. Documents of authenticity are provided for all works.

En Route About 20 mi west of the trading post, on AZ 264, you'll reach **Steamboat Rock,** an immense, jutting peninsula of stone that resembles an early steamboat, complete with a geologically formed waterline. At Steamboat Rock you are only 5 mi from the eastern boundary of the Hopi reservation.

THE HOPI MESAS

The Hopi Mesas and the small villages that line their tops have a feel of unfathomable antiquity. Generations of Hopitu, "the peaceful people," much like their Anasazi ancestors, have lived in these settlements of stone and adobe houses, which blend in with the earth so well that they appear to be natural formations. Television aerials, satellite dishes, and automobiles notwithstanding, these Hopi villages still impart the air of another time.

First Mesa, Second Mesa, and Third Mesa—the tall escarpments that form the center of the Hopi universe—have been so heavily touristed in recent years that access is now limited and visits require advance permission. Call the **Hopi Tribe Office of Public Relations** (☞ Visitor Information *in* The Northeast A to Z, *below*), which also provides phone numbers for village leaders and community development offices, for additional information and permission to visit certain areas.

To see the Hopi Mesas at a leisurely pace, stay at least one night either at the Hopi Cultural Center on Second Mesa in the heart of the reservation or, if you're planning to head north into Navajo country, in Tuba City (☞ *below*).

Keams Canyon Trading Post

❺ *48 mi west of Hubbell Trading Post on AZ 264.*

The trading post established by Thomas Keam in 1875 to do business with local tribes is now the area's main tourist attraction, offering a primitive campground, restaurant, service station, and gift shop and shopping center. An administrative center for the Bureau of Indian Affairs, Keams Canyon also has a number of government buildings.

The first 3 mi of the 8-mi wooded canyon running toward the northeast can be seen by car. At **Inscription Rock,** about 2 mi down the road, frontiersman Kit Carson engraved his name in stone. There are several picnic spots in the canyon.

Dining

$ ✕ **Keams Canyon Restaurant.** This typical roadside diner with Formica tabletops offers both American and Native American dishes, including Navajo tacos, made with Indian fry bread (not unlike a soft pizza crust) heaped with ground beef, chili, beans, lettuce, and grated cheese. It's open weekdays from 8 to 6 and weekends from 8 to 3. (Note: The adjacent motel is closed until further notice.) ⊠ *Keams Canyon Shopping Center, near AZ 264,* ☎ *520/738–2296. D, MC, V.*

Shopping

Keams Canyon Arts and Crafts (⊠ Keams Canyon, ☎ 520/738–2295), upstairs at the entrance to the Keams Canyon Restaurant, sells Hopi wares such as handcrafted jewelry, pottery, statuary, and artwork.

First Mesa

❻ *15 mi west of Keams Canyon, on AZ 264.*

On First Mesa you will initially approach Polacca; the older and more impressive villages of Hano, Sichomovi, and Walpi are at the top of the mesa. From Polacca, a paved road (off AZ 264) angles up to a parking lot near the village of Sichomovi. For permission to visit Hano, Sichomovi, and Walpi, or for information on the guided walking tours of these villages, call the **First Mesa Visitor's Center at Ponsi Hall.** ☎ *520/737–2262.* 🎫 *$5 (includes tour).* ☉ *Guided tours can be arranged 9–4 daily, except when ceremonies are being held.*

All the older Hopi villages have structures built of rock and adobe mortar in a simple architectural style. **Hano** actually belongs to the Tewa, a New Mexico Pueblo tribe that fled from the Spanish in 1696 and secured permission from the Hopi to build a new home on First Mesa. **Sichomovi** is built so close to Hano that only the residents can tell where one ends and the other begins. Constructed in the mid-1600s, this village is believed to have been built to ease overcrowding at Walpi, the highest point on the mesa.

★ **Walpi,** built on solid rock and surrounded by steep cliffs, frequently hosts ceremonial dances and can only be visited accompanied by a Hopi guide. Inhabited for more than 500 years, Walpi's cliff-edge houses—the mesa measures only 15 ft across at its narrowest point—seem to grow out of the nearby terrain. Today, only about 30 residents occupy this settlement, which has neither electricity nor running water. Walpi's surroundings make it less than an ideal destination for acrophobes.

Second Mesa

❼ *12 mi southwest of First Mesa, on AZ 264.*

Ideally located "at the Center of the Universe" is the **Hopi Cultural Center,** a good place to stop for the night (☞ Dining and Lodging, *below*), learn about the people and their reservation, and eat authentic Hopi cuisine. The museum is dedicated to the preservation of Hopi traditions and to presenting those traditions to non-Hopi visitors. There is a gift shop adjacent to the museum that sells works by local Hopi artisans at reasonable prices, and a modest picnic area on the west side of the building is a pleasant spot for lunch with a view of the Hopi Mesas. ✉ *On the north side of AZ 264, west of the junction at AZ 87,* ☎ *520/734–2401 (restaurant and motel), 520/734–6650 (museum).* ✎ *Museum $3.* ☉ *Mid-May–Oct., weekdays 8–5, weekends 9–4; rest of yr, weekdays 8–5.*

Shungopavi, the largest and oldest village on Second Mesa, may be reached by a paved road angling south off AZ 264, between the junction of AZ 87 and the Hopi Cultural Center. The famous Hopi snake dances (closed to the public) are held here in August during even-numbered years.

The small villages of Sipaulovi and Mishongnovi are off a paved road that runs north from AZ 264, about ⅓ mi east of the Hopi Cultural Center. **Mishongnovi,** the easternmost settlement, was built in the late 1600s. If you'd like to visit **Sipaulovi,** the most recently established village, call the Sipaulovi Village Community Center (☎ 520/737–2570) for permission and a guide.

OFF THE
BEATEN PATH
   HOMOLOVI RUINS STATE PARK – A short hour's side trip south on AZ 87 near I–40 is well worth the additional time. Homolovi, which means "place of the little hills," is a village established by Hopi ancestors around AD 1200 in the fertile lands near the Little Colorado River. The folks at Homolovi embrace visitors—maybe because of the old Hopi belief that each visitor brings much-needed rain. Strangely enough, the belief has been substantiated by precipitation records in recent years. The park has a museum of ancient Hopi artifacts (open whenever staff is on site; no phone), and is also the site of an ongoing archaeological excavation, a collaboration between Northern Arizona University students and teachers and native Hopi. The park offers 52 full-service camping/RV units ($15 per night or $75 per week), hiking trails, and picnic facilities. The campground is open year-round except Christmas, and costs are nominal ($10 per night or $50 per week). Pets are allowed on a leash, and the quiet hours in the campground (restricting use of generators, stereos, etc.) are 10 PM to 6 AM. The park's **Visitor Center** has displays and is staffed by a couple of archaeologists who love to talk about their work; it also offers books, maps, and a few craft items. Guided tours are available during the months of July and August. ☎ *520/289–4106, www.pr.state.az.us/parkhtml/homolovi.html.* ✎ *$4 per car for up to 4 people, $1 each additional person.* ☉ *Daily 8–5.*

Dining and Lodging

$ X▣ **Hopi Cultural Center Restaurant and Motel.** This Hopi-run establishment is the only place to eat or sleep in the immediate area, but because of its remote location it almost always has vacant rooms. The restaurant serves traditional Hopi dishes, including Indian tacos, Hopi blue-corn pancakes, fry bread (delicious with honey or salsa), and *nok qui vi* (a tasty stew made with tender bits of lamb, hominy, and mild green chilies). The motel offers clean, quiet rooms at reasonable rates. ▨ *AZ 264, 86403,* ☎ *520/734–2401. 33 rooms. DC, MC, V.*

Shopping

The **Hopi Arts and Crafts/Silvercrafts Cooperative Guild** (▨ West of the Hopi Cultural Center, ☎ 520/734–2463) hosts craftspeople selling their wares; you might even see silversmiths at work here. Shops at the **Hopi Cultural Center** (▨ AZ 264, ☎ 520/734–2401) carry the works of local artists and artisans. **Tsakurshovi** (▨ 1½ mi east of the Hopi Cultural Center, ☎ 520/734–2478) is a small, eclectic shop where Hopi come to buy katsina dolls and other ceremonial objects, such as bundles of sweetgrass and sage, deer hooves with which to make rattles, and ceremonial belts adorned with seashells. The proprietor's wife is one of the most renowned Hopi Basket Makers in the nation.

Third Mesa

❽ *8 mi northwest of Second Mesa, on AZ 264.*

At the eastern base of Third Mesa is the village of **Kykotsmovi**, known for its greenery and peach orchards. Hopi from Old Oraibi descended from the mesa to build this village in a canyon where it's perennially springtime. It's also the home of the Hopi Tribal Headquarters Chairman's Office and the Office of Public Relations (☞ Visitor Information *in* The Northeast A to Z, *below*), good sources of information regarding ceremonies and dances. Along AZ 264 are crafts shops and art galleries, as well as occasional roadside vendors. The Third Mesa villages are known for their baskets, katsina dolls, weaving, and jewelry.

Old Oraibi, a few miles west and on top of Third Mesa, is believed to be the oldest continuously inhabited community in the United States, dating from around AD 1150. It was also the site of a rare, bloodless conflict between two groups of the Hopi people; in 1906, a dispute, settled uniquely by a "push of war," a pushing contest, sent the losers off to establish the town of Hotevilla. Oraibi is a dusty spot, and as an act of courtesy, tourists are asked to park their cars outside and approach the village on foot.

Hotevilla and **Bacavi** are about 4 mi west of Oraibi, and their inhabitants are descended from the former residents of that village. The men of Hotevilla continue to plant crops and beautiful gardens along the mesa slopes.

En Route   Beyond Hotevilla, AZ 264 descends from Third Mesa, exits the Hopi reservation, and crosses into Navajo territory, past **Coal Canyon,** where Indians have long mined coal from the dark seam just below the rim. The colorful mudstone, dark lines of coal, and bleached white rock have an eerie appearance, especially by the light of the moon. Twenty miles west of Coal Canyon, at the junction of AZ 264 and U.S. 160, is the town of Moenkopi, the last Hopi outpost. Established as a farming community, it was settled by the descendants of former Oraibi residents.

Tuba City

❾ *50 mi northwest of Third Mesa on AZ 264.*

Tuba City, with about 12,000 permanent residents, is the administrative center for the western portion of the Navajo Nation. In addition to a motel, hostel, and a few restaurants, this small town has a hospital, a bank, a trading post and a movie theater. In late October, Tuba City hosts the Western Navajo Fair, a celebration combining traditional Navajo song dance with a parade, pageant, and countless arts and crafts exhibits. The octagonal **Tuba City Trading Post** (✉ Main St., Tuba City, ☎ 520/283–5441), founded in the early 1880s, sells groceries and authentic Navajo, Hopi, and Zuni rugs, pottery, baskets, and jewelry.

About 5½ mi west of Tuba City, between mileposts 316 and 317 on U.S. 160, is a small sign for the **Dinosaur Tracks.** More than 200 million years ago, dilophosaurus—a carnivorous bipedal reptile more than 10 ft tall—left tracks in soft mud that subsequently turned to sandstone. There's no charge for a look. Four miles west on U.S. 160 is the junction with U.S. 89. This is one of the most colorful regions of the **Painted Desert** (☞ Chapter 5), with amphitheaters of maroon, orange, and red rocks facing west; it's especially glorious at sunset.

Dining and Lodging

$ ✕ **Hogan Restaurant.** The main fare at this spot next to the Quality Inn Tuba City is southwestern and Mexican, but the menu also lists American and Navajo dishes. The chicken enchiladas and beef tamales are as good as any you'll find south of the border. The large dining room looks like a western coffee shop but incorporates Native American touches like pottery chandeliers. Breakfast is served here, too. ✉ *AZ 264/Main St., adjacent to Tuba City Motel and Trading Post,* ☎ *520/283–5260. AE, D, DC, MC, V.*

$ ✕ **Kate's Cafe.** A favorite of locals, this all-American café serves breakfast—try the vegetarian omelet—lunch, and dinner. Choose from hearty burgers, Kate's Club Sandwich, grilled chicken, or salads at lunchtime; dinner selections include three daily pasta specials and charbroiled New York strip steak. There may be a wait, but for local color and fine food at reasonable prices, this is the place. ✉ *AZ 264/Main St.,* ☎ *520/283–6773. No credit cards. No dinner Sun.*

$ ✕ **Tuba City Truck Stop Cafe.** Home cooking is what you'll get at this small, conveniently located fast-service restaurant. The popular Navajo vegetarian taco, available lunch and dinner, is a mix of beans, lettuce, sliced tomato, shredded cheese, and green chili served open face on succulent fry bread. Meatier options include mutton stew served with fry bread and hominy. It's open at 6 AM for breakfast and closes at 10 PM every day. ✉ *At the junction of AZ 264/Main St. and U.S. 160,* ☎ *520/283–4975. MC, V.*

$ ▥ **Grey Hills Inn.** Hotel students at Grey Hills High School run this unusual lodging, a former dormitory with large, clean accommodations. The beds are comfortable, and eclectic decor and kitschy paintings add character to the otherwise plain rooms. Bathrooms and showers are down the hall, and it's hard to find the inn's entrance in the large high school complex at night, but the rates are reasonable. A share of the inn's profits help support the students' class. ✉ *Off U.S. 160, ½ mi north of junction with AZ 264, mailing address: Box 160, 86045,* ☎ *520/283–6271 ext. 141; 520/283–4450 weekends and after school hrs. 32 rooms. MC, V.*

$ ▥ **Quality Inn Tuba City.** This property has a trading post and shops for essentials, gifts, and souvenirs. The standard rooms are spacious and well maintained, fine for an overnight stop before or after a visit to the Hopi Mesas. The on-site Hogan Restaurant (☞ *above*) serves basic fare. ⊠ *At the junction of AZ 264/Main St. and U.S. 160, mailing address: Box 247, 86045,* ☎ *520/283–4545 or 800/644–8383,* ℻ *520/283–4144. 80 rooms. Restaurant. AE, D, DC, MC, V.*

🏕 **Quality Inn Tuba City Campground.** This park adjacent to the Quality Inn (check in at the front desk) has 25 full hookup sites with cable TV, six tent sites, showers, laundry facilities, flush toilets, and RV dump stations. Sites run $12.75–$21; reservations are accepted through the hotel's 800 number. ⊠ *At the junction of AZ 264/Main St. and U.S. 160, mailing address: Box 247, 86045,* ☎ *520/283–4545 or 800/ 644–8383,* ℻ *520/283–4144.*

Shopping

The **swap meet** (⊠ Main St., behind the community center and next to the baseball field), held every Friday from 8 AM on, has good deals on jewelry, rugs, pottery, and other arts and crafts; there are also food concessions and booths selling herbs. The **Toh Nanees Dizi Shopping Center,** a half mile northeast of Tuba City on U.S. 160, has a pizza parlor, supermarket, and the Silver Screen Twin Theaters (☎ 520/283– 5255).

OFF THE BEATEN PATH   **CAMERON TRADING POST AND MOTEL** – Established in 1916, the Cameron Trading Post is one of the few remaining authentic trading posts in the Southwest. A convenient stop if you're driving from the Hopi Mesas to the Grand Canyon (☞ Chapter 1), it has reasonably priced dining, lodging, camping, and shopping. Fine authentic Navajo products are sold at an outlet of the Navajo Arts and Crafts Enterprises (⊠ U.S. 89, at junction with AZ 64, ☎ 520/679–2244). ⊠ *25 mi from Tuba City, west on U.S. 160 and south on U.S. 89.,* ☎ *520/679–2231.*

En Route   Twenty-two miles northeast of Tuba City on U.S. 160 is the tiny community of Red Lake. Off to the left of the highway is a geologic phenomenon known as **Elephant Feet.** These massive eroded sandstone buttes make a good photo. Northwest of here at the end of a graded dirt road in Navajo backcountry is **White Mesa Natural Bridge,** a massive arch of white sandstone that extends from the edge of White Mesa. The long **Black Mesa** plateau runs for about 15 mi along U.S. 160. Above the prominent escarpments of this land formation, mining operations—a major source of revenue for the Navajo Nation—delve into the more than 20 billion tons of coal deposited there.

NAVAJO NATION NORTH

The magnificent Monument Valley stretches to the northeast of Kayenta into Utah. At a base altitude of about 5,500 ft, this sprawling, arid expanse was once populated by Anasazi, and in the last few centuries has been home to generations of Navajo farmers. The soaring red buttes, eroded mesas, deep canyons, and naturally sculpted rock formations of Monument Valley are easy to enjoy on a leisurely drive. Scenes from many movies—among them *National Lampoon's Vacation, How the West Was Won, Forrest Gump, Stagecoach,* and *2001: A Space Odyssey*—have been filmed here, and Monument Valley is the world's most popular backdrop for TV and magazine advertisements.

Kayenta

🔟 *80 mi northeast of Tuba City, on U.S. 160.*

Kayenta, a small town with a few grocery stores, three motels, and a hospital, is a good base for exploring nearby Monument Valley Navajo Tribal Park and the Navajo National Monument (☞ *below*).

Dining and Lodging

$ ✕ **Golden Sands Restaurant.** The decor and the service at this local café next to the Best Western Wetherill Inn (☞ *below*) are equally unrefined, but you can fuel up on hamburgers, Navajo tacos, and other regional specialties. It's also a good place to learn about the area from residents who stop in for coffee. ⊠ *U.S. 163,* ☎ *520/697–3684. No credit cards.*

$$ ✕▥ **Holiday Inn Kayenta.** This contemporary southwestern-style accommodation about ½ mi from Monument Valley has everything you would expect from a Holiday Inn; it also has one of the few swimming pools in the western section of the region. The on-site Wagonwheel Restaurant offers both standard and Native American fare, and the gift shop offers traditional local arts and crafts. ⊠ *At the junction of U.S. 160 and U.S. 163, mailing address: Box 307, 86033,* ☎ *520/697–3221 or 800/465–4329,* 🅵🅰🆇 *520/697–3349. 164 rooms. Restaurant, pool. AE, D, DC, MC, V.*

$–$$ ✕▥ **Anasazi Inn at Tsegi.** This unpretentious roadside motel, convenient to the Navajo National Monument and Monument Valley, offers striking views of Tsegi Canyon from its rear-facing rooms. Its restaurant sells tasty Navajo fry-bread sandwiches and tacos. In the middle of nowhere, this is really the place to get away from it all. The rooms also have no phones. ⊠ *U.S. 160, 10 mi west of Kayenta, mailing address: Box 1543, 86033,* ☎ 🅵🅰🆇 *520/697–3793. 59 rooms. Restaurant. AE, D, DC, MC, V.*

$–$$ ▥ **Best Western Wetherill Inn.** Named for John Wetherill, a frontiersman who discovered prehistoric Native American ruins in Arizona, this clean two-story motel has southwestern decor and a well-stocked gift shop. ⊠ *U.S. 163, mailing address: Box 175, 86033,* ☎ *520/697–3231 or 800/528–1234. 54 rooms. Indoor pool. AE, D, DC, MC, V.*

$ ▥ **Roland's B&B.** This American Indian–owned and –run B&B near Monument Valley offers rooms for up to six people. Roland also has smaller rooms, and, unique to the area, there are authentic teepees that can accommodate up to 20 people. Teepees require a minimum of two guests and are put up and taken down as guests arrive and depart; teepee guests use the baths in the main house. Continental breakfast is provided for both house guests and teepee guests. ⊠ *U.S. 163, 25 mi south of Monument Valley, mailing address: Box 1542, 86003,* ☎ *520/697–3524. 4 rooms. No credit cards.*

Monument Valley Navajo Tribal Park

⓫ *24 mi northeast of Kayenta, off U.S. 163.*

Within Monument Valley lies the 30,000-acre Monument Valley Navajo Tribal Park. A 17-mi self-guided driving tour on a rough dirt road (there's only one road, so you can't get lost) passes the memorable **Mittens and Totem Pole formations,** among others. Drive slowly, and be sure to walk (15 minutes round-trip) from North Window around the end of Cly Butte for the views. The park has a 100-site campground, which closes from early October through April (☞ Camping, *below*). Be sure to call ahead for road conditions in winter.

The Monument Valley **visitor center** holds a crafts shop and exhibits devoted to ancient and modern Native American history. Most of the independent guided tours here use enclosed vans and charge about $15 for 2½ hours; you can generally find Native American guides in the center. ⊠ *Visitor center: 3½ mi off U.S. 163,* ☎ *435/727–3353.* 🖃 *Park $2.50.* ⊙ *Visitor center May–Sept., daily 7–7; Oct.–Apr., daily 8–5.*

Camping

⚠ **Mitten View Campground.** The sites here have tables, grills, and decks. Water is available, but there are no hookups. All of the 99 sites are open in summer, but only a dozen or so are open year-round. ✉ *Monument Valley Navajo Tribal Park, near visitor center, off U.S. 163, 25 mi north of Kayenta 86003,* ☎ *435/727–3287.* ☞ *$5 (additional charge for showers in winter).*

Outdoor Activities and Sports

HORSEBACK RIDING & TOURS

If you've always wanted to ride off into the sunset at Monument Valley or go on a rafting trip down the San Juan River, get in touch with **Ed Black's Horseback Riding Tours** (✉ Box 155, Mexican Hat, UT 84531, ☎ 800/551–4039). Jeep tours of the Valley from hour-long to overnight can be arranged through Roland Cody Dixon at **Roland's Navajoland Tours** (✉ Box 1542, Kayenta 86033, ☎ 520/697–3524). **Sacred Mountain Horseback Tours** (☎ 435/727–3227), at the Monument Valley visitor center (☞ *above*), offers hourly and overnight tours into Monument Valley.

OFF THE
BEATEN PATH

FOUR CORNERS MONUMENT – An inlaid concrete slab marks the only point in the United States where four states meet: Arizona, New Mexico, Colorado, and Utah. Most visitors—in summer, nearly 2,000 a day—stay only long enough to snap a photo; you'll see many a starfish-posed tourist trying to get an arm or a leg in each state. The monument, a 75-mi drive from Kayenta, is administered by the Navajo Nation Parks and Recreation Department. ✉ *Off U.S. 160, 7 mi northwest of the U.S. 160 and NM 502 junction (near Teec Nos Pos),* ☎ *520/871–6647.*

Goosenecks, Utah

⑫ *33 mi north of Monument Valley Navajo Tribal Park, on Utah S.R. 316.*

Monument Valley's scenic route, U.S. 163, continues from Arizona into Utah, where the land is crossed, east to west, by a stretch of the San Juan River known as the Goosenecks—so named for the myriad twists and curves it takes at the bottom of a wildly carved canyon. This barren, erosion-blasted gorge has a stark beauty that is nearly as awesome as that of the Grand Canyon. The scenic overlook for the Goosenecks is reached by turning west from U.S. 163 onto UT 261, 4 mi north of the small community of **Mexican Hat** (named for the sombrero-like rock formation you'll see on the hills to your right as you drive north), then proceeding on UT 261 for 1 mi to a directional sign at the road's junction with UT 316. Turn left onto UT 316 and proceed 4 mi to the vista-point parking lot.

Dining and Lodging

$ ✕▦ **San Juan Inn & Trading Post.** This spot is a well-known take-out
★ point for white-water runners on the San Juan, a river which vacationing sleuths will recognize as the setting of many of Tony Hillerman's Jim Chee mystery novels. The inn's southwestern-style, rustic rooms overlooking the river at Mexican Hat are clean and well maintained. Diners can watch the river flow by at the on-premises Old Bridge Bar & Grill, which serves great grilled steak for $9.95 and hamburgers for $6. Fresh trout and inexpensive Navajo dishes add variety to the menu. ✉ *U.S. 163 at the San Juan River south of Mexican Hat, mailing address: Box 535, Mexican Hat, UT 84531,* ☎ *435/663–2220 or 800/447–2022,* ⅏ *435/683–2210. 36 rooms. Restaurant. AE, D, DC, MC, V.*

Goulding's Trading Post

⑬ *8 mi northwest of Monument Valley Navajo Tribal Park, off U.S. 163 on Indian Hwy. 42.*

Established in 1924 by Harry Goulding and his wife, this remote, historic spot was used as a headquarters by director John Ford when he filmed the western classic *Stagecoach,* and numerous westerns shot in the area have brought the site a measure of international fame. The Goulding Museum displays Indian artifacts and Goulding family memorabilia as well as Navajo artifacts and an excellent multimedia show about Monument Valley. Goulding's Lodge is ideal for an overnight stay (☞ Dining and Lodging, *below*). Call in advance for reservations. There are other motels in nearby Kayenta (☞ *above*).

Dining and Lodging

$$ ✕⬚ **Goulding's Lodge.** With spectacular views of Monument Valley
★ from each room's private balcony, this comfortable motel often serves as headquarters for film crews. The lodge has handsome pueblo-style stucco buildings that blend in with the surrounding red-rock formations. The cozy rooms are furnished in contemporary style, with southwestern colors and Navajo-design bedspreads. The on-premises Stagecoach restaurant, serving good American fare, is decorated with western movie memorabilia; the view and the service are excellent. Goulding's can also arrange custom guided tours of Monument Valley and provide Navajo guides into the backcountry. ✉ *2 mi west of U.S. 163, just north of Utah border, mailing address: Box 360001, Monument Valley, UT 84536, ☎ 435/727–3231. 62 rooms. Restaurant, pool, travel services. AE, D, DC, MC, V.*

⛺ **Goulding's Good Sam Campground.** This full-service campground with over 50 tent sites and 66 full-hookup RV sites is open year-round with limited service from mid-March to mid-October. There's a heated indoor pool, cable TV, and electrical hookups. Check in at the Goulding's Lodge grocery store. Admission includes access to the 17-mi loop drive around Monument Valley (☞ Monument Valley Navajo Tribal Park, *above*). ✉ *Off U.S. 163, near Goulding's Trading Post, 27 mi north of Kayenta 84536, ☎ 435/727–3231 ext. 425. ▦ $14 (basic) and $22 (with hookup).*

Navajo National Monument

⑭ *53 mi southwest of Goulding's Trading Post, on AZ 564 north of U.S. 160.*

At the Navajo National Monument, two unoccupied 13th-century cliff pueblos, Keet Seel and Betatakin, stand under the overhang of orange and ocher cliffs. The largest ancient dwellings in Arizona, these stone-and-mortar complexes were built by the Anasazi, obviously for permanent occupancy, but abandoned in less than half a century.

The well-preserved, 135-room **Betatakin** (Navajo for "ledge house") seems to hang in midair before a sheer sandstone wall. When discovered in 1907 by a passing American rancher, the apartments were full of baskets, pottery, and preserved grains and ears of corn—as if the occupants had been chased away in the middle of a meal. For an impressive view of Betatakin, walk to the rim overlook about ½ mi from the visitor center. Ranger-led tours (a 5-mi, four-hour, strenuous round-trip hike including a 700-ft descent into the canyon) leave once a day in early May, most of September, and early October, and twice a day from Memorial Day to Labor Day at 9 and noon. No reservations are accepted; groups of no more than 25 form on a first-come, first-served basis.

Keet Seel (Navajo for "broken pottery") is also in good condition in a serene setting, with 160 rooms and five kivas. Explorations of Keet Seel, which lies at an elevation of 7,000 ft and is 17 mi (round-trip) from the visitor center, are restricted: Only 20 people are allowed to visit per day, and only between Memorial Day and Labor Day, when a ranger is present at the site. A permit—which also allows campers to stay overnight near the ruins—is required. Those interested in horseback trips can make arrangements at the visitor center to rent horses and guides from a Navajo family. Trips to Keet Seel are very popular, so reservations are taken up to two months in advance. Anyone who suffers from vertigo might want to avoid this trip: The trail leads down a 1,100-ft near-vertical rock face.

The **visitor center** houses a small museum, exhibits of prehistoric pottery, and a crafts shop. Free campground and picnic areas are nearby, and rangers sometimes present campfire programs in summer. No food, gasoline, or hotel lodging is available at the monument. ⊠ *Navajo National Monument, HC 71, Box 3, Tonalea 86044,* ☎ *520/ 672–2366.* 🎫 *Free.* ☼ *Daily 8–5, tours Memorial Day–Labor Day.*

Camping
🏕 **Navajo National Monument.** The free campground here has 30 RV and tent sites (plus three large group sites), water, and rest rooms, but no hookups. Because of its remote locale, the campground always has available sites. Winter snows can block the road. ⊠ *Reached by turnoff on U.S. 160, 21 mi south of Kayenta 86033,* ☎ *520/672–2366.* ☼ *Year-round.*

Outdoor Activities and Sports
HORSEBACK RIDING

Native American guides conduct daily **horseback tours** to Keet Seel at Navajo National Monument from Memorial Day weekend through Labor Day weekend; rates are about $60 per day. Only 20 people are allowed in per day, and riders must be experienced on horseback. Contact the rangers at the visitor center for reservations. Occasionally no guides are available and tours get canceled, so even if you have made a reservation, always call ahead. The park and gift shop are open year-round. ⊠ *Navajo National Monument, HC 71, Box 3, Tonalea, 86044,* ☎ *520/672–2366 or 520/672–2367. Reservations are taken up to 2 months in advance.*

Shopping
The gift shop at **Navajo National Monument** (☎ 520/672–2366) has an excellent selection of Native American jewelry and is open year-round.

GLEN CANYON DAM AND LAKE POWELL

Lake Powell, with more than 1,900 mi of shoreline, is the heart of the huge 1,255,400-acre **Glen Canyon National Recreation Area.** Created by the barrier of Glen Canyon Dam and fed by the mighty Colorado and five other rivers, the lake extends through terrain so rugged it was the last major area of the United States to be mapped. Lake Powell is ringed by red cliffs that twist off into 96 major canyons and countless inlets, and huge sandstone buttes jut from the emerald waters at random: Seeing the stark geography of Lake Powell is like visiting another planet.

With only 8 inches of annual rainfall, the Lake Powell area enjoys blue skies nearly year-round. Summer temperatures range from the 60s to the 90s (occasionally rising to 100°F). Fall and spring are usually balmy, with daytime temperatures often in the 70s and 80s, but chilly weather can set in. Nights are cool even in the summer, and in winter the risk of a cold spell increases, but all-weather houseboats and tour boats make for year-round cruising.

South of Lake Powell the landscape gives way to the **Echo Cliffs,** orange sandstone formations rising 1,000 ft and more above the highway in places. At **Bitter Springs,** the road ascends the cliffs and provides a spectacular view of the 9,000-square-mi Arizona Strip to the west and the 3,000-ft Vermilion Cliffs to the northwest.

The entry fee at Glen Canyon National Recreation Area and Lake Powell is $5 per vehicle; $3 for hikers, motorcyclists, and bicyclists; and a $10 per week boating fee for boaters. *Boaters and campers should note that regulations require the use of portable toilets on the lake and lakeshore. Park authorities vigorously enforce this rule to prevent water pollution.*

Page

⑮ *96 mi west of the Navajo National Monument, 136 mi north of Flagstaff, on U.S. 89.*

Built in 1957 as a Glen Canyon Dam construction camp, Page is now a tourist spot and a popular base for day trips to Lake Powell; it has become a major point of entry to the Navajo Nation. The town's population of 10,000 makes it the largest community in far-northern Arizona, and most of the motels, restaurants, and shopping centers are concentrated along **Lake Powell Boulevard,** the name given to U.S. 89 as it loops through the business district. Page also has 15 churches of various denominations.

At the corner of North Navajo Drive and Lake Powell Boulevard is the **John Wesley Powell Memorial Museum,** whose namesake led the first known expeditions down the Green River and the rapids-choked Colorado through the Grand Canyon between 1869 and 1872. Powell mapped and kept detailed records of his trips, naming the Grand Canyon and many other geographic points of interest in northern Arizona. Artifacts from his expeditions are displayed in the museum, which has a good selection of regional books and maps, and visitors can get area information and book boating tours, scenic flights, or slot-canyon tours. All accommodations in Page can be booked at the museum. ⊠ *6 N. Lake Powell Blvd.,* ☎ *520/645–9496.* ⌨ *Requested donation $1.* ☉ *Daily, year-round.*

Dining and Lodging

$ ✕ **Dos Amigos.** This small, cheerful Mexican restaurant with simple but authentic Mexican decor offers familiar, satisfying Mexican fare. It's well known around Page for its fajitas and margaritas. ⊠ *608-D Elm St. (in the Safeway Plaza),* ☎ *520/645–3036. AE, MC, V.*

$ ✕ **Zapata's.** A local favorite, Zapata's Sonoran food is a bit spicier than the fare typical of other Mexican regions, but it is very tasty. Specials include chiles rellenos and enchiladas. The basic, clean restaurant is decorated with piñatas, ristras (strings of dried red chili peppers), and pottery. ⊠ *614 N. Navajo Dr.,* ☎ *520/645–9006. D, MC, V.*

$$ ✕▥ **Ramada Inn, Lake Powell.** This modern facility offers rooms with views of the Vermilion Cliffs adjacent to its 18-hole, par-72 golf course. All accommodations are decorated in a territorial motif but have the expected conveniences of a Ramada Inn. The on-site Family Tree Restaurant serves Navajo and American breakfast, lunch, and dinner. Try the grilled pork chops with applesauce and vegetables ($9.60), or

the popular Friday seafood buffet ($15.95), which includes soup, salad, and dessert. The inn also has a cocktail lounge and picnic area. ✉ *287 N. Lake Powell Blvd., off Hwy. 89, mailing address: Box 1867, 86040,* ☎ *520/645–8851 or 800/272–6232. 129 rooms. Bar, pool, meeting rooms. AE, D, DC, MC, V.*

$–$$ ✕⊡ **Courtyard by Marriott.** A sumptuous motel on the grounds of Lake Powell National Golf Course, the Courtyard has very comfortable rooms, extensive health and fitness facilities, and on-premises dining in Peppers, an upscale eatery specializing in American fare. ✉ *Box 4150, 600 Clubhouse Dr., 86040,* ☎ *520/645–5000. 153 rooms. Restaurant, bar, pool, sauna, exercise room. AE, D, DC, MC, V.*

$–$$ ⊡ **Best Western Arizona Inn.** This modern, well-run motel on a high bluff at the northern end of Page has large rooms with queen-size beds and southwestern-print bedspreads. Butterfield Steakhouse has Southwest and standard American fare. ✉ *716 Rim View Dr., mailing address: Box 250, 86040,* ☎ *520/645–2466 or 800/826–2718. 103 rooms. Restaurant, bar, pool, hot tub, meeting rooms. AE, D, DC, MC, V.*

$–$$ ⊡ **Best Western at Lake Powell.** Guests awake to dazzling views of the Vermilion Cliffs in this modern, three-story motel on a high bluff overlooking Glen Canyon Dam. The large rooms are functional and the beds are comfortable. A light breakfast bar (not included in room rate) is offered in the lobby. Facilities are available for disabled travelers. Deluxe rooms have a microwave oven. ✉ *208 N. Lake Powell Blvd., 86040,* ☎ *520/645–5988 or 888/794–2888. 132 rooms. Pool, hot tub, exercise room, meeting rooms. AE, D, DC, MC, V.*

$ ⊡ **Canyon Colors B&B.** The oldest B&B in Page is run by New England transplants to this desert community and offers travelers a personal touch. The Sunflower Room and the Paisley Room, which can accommodate up to five and four respectively, have queen beds and futons. Two more rooms with queen-size beds were added during a recent renovation. The B&B also has an extensive video library including many videos of Lake Powell and the Navajo Nation. Reservations, recommended in summer, can be made up to a year in advance. ✉ *225 S. Navajo Dr., mailing address: Box 3657, 86040,* ☎ ⊞ *520/645–5979, 520/645–9411, or 800/536–2530. 4 rooms. Full breakfast. AE, D, MC, V.*

$ ⊡ **Thatcher's.** Nita Thatcher runs this reasonably priced three-room B&B. There is a common living room and lounge for guests, and Nita makes hearty American breakfasts for all. The room with a king-size bed has its own bath; the other two rooms share a bath. Summer reservations should be made at least six months in advance. ✉ *Box 421, 86040,* ☎ *520/645–3335 or 800/645–6836. 3 rooms, 1 with bath. Full breakfast. No credit cards.*

    ⚠ **Page–Lake Powell Campground.** You can make reservations for the more than 85 full-hookup RV sites and 20 tent sites here. Campers have access to a coin laundry, an indoor swimming pool, rest rooms, and showers. ✉ *849 S. Coppermine Rd., 86040,* ☎ *520/645–3374.* ⊞ *$15–$20.* ☺ *Year-round.*

Nightlife

The Bowl (✉ 24 N. Lake Powell Blvd., ☎ 520/645–2682) is a 10-lane bowling alley and coffee shop. **Ken's Old West Restaurant & Lounge** (✉ 718 Vista Ave., ☎ 520/645–5160) has country-and-western music and dancing; you can also get a pretty good steak, prime rib, seafood, or barbecued-chicken dinner. **Mesa Theater** (✉ 42 S. Lake Powell Blvd., ☎ 520/645–9565) is Page's movie house.

Outdoor Activities and Sports

CRUISES

Wilderness River Adventures (☎ 520/645–3279 or 800/992–8022) offers a variety of tours, including a 4½-hour guided rafting excursion down a white water–less portion of the Colorado River ($49). The scenery—multicolored sandstone cliffs adorned with Indian petroglyphs—is spectacular. The point of departure is in Page, but transportation is furnished both to the launch site and back from Lees Ferry, where the trip ends.

GOLF

Lake Powell National Golf Course (⊠ 400 Clubhouse Dr. off AZ 98, ☎ 520/645–2023) has wide fairways, tiered greens, and a generous lack of hazards. An 18-hole, par-72 and a 9-hole, par-36 municipal course overlook Glen Canyon Dam and Lake Powell.

Shopping

There are numerous gift shops and clothing stores in the downtown area along Lake Powell Boulevard. **Big Lake Trading Post** (⊠ 1501 Hwy. 98, ☎ 520/645–2404) has Indian artifacts, a museum, and a hobby shop. The Post also has a gas station, convenience store, car wash, and laundromat.

Antelope Canyon

⑯ *4 mi east of Page on the Navajo reservation, on AZ 98.*

You've probably already seen a photograph of Antelope Canyon in a magazine or book: A narrow, red sandstone slot canyon with convoluted corkscrew formations, dramatically illuminated by a ray of light streaming down from above. And you're likely to see assorted shutterbugs waiting patiently for just the right shot of these colorful, photogenic rocks, which are actually petrified sand dunes of a prehistoric ocean that once filled this portion of North America. If you don't have a four-wheel-drive vehicle (or the time to wait for the rather erratic—and limited—hours that the gate to the site is open), book a tour (generally available in spring and summer) from Page (☞ Guided Tours *in* The Northeast A to Z, *below*).

Glen Canyon Dam

⑰ *2 mi west of Page on U.S. 89.*

Once you leave the Page business district heading northwest, the Glen Canyon Dam and Lake Powell behind it immediately become visible. This concrete-arch dam—all 5 million cubic ft of it—was completed in September 1963, its power plant an engineering feat that rivaled Hoover Dam. The dam's crest is 1,560 ft across and rises 710 ft from bedrock and 583 ft above the waters of the Colorado River. When Lake Powell is full, it is 560 ft deep at the dam.

Just off the highway at the north end of the bridge is the **Carl Hayden Visitor Center,** where visitors learn about the creation of Glen Canyon Dam and Lake Powell and enjoy panoramic views of both. Between May and October, free tours of the dam are offered daily between 8 and 4, every hour on the half hour. The rest of the year, visitors can take a 40-minute self-guided tour through the complex. ⊠ *2 mi west of Page on U.S. 89,* ☎ *520/608–6404.* ⌨ *Free.* ⊙ *Memorial Day–Labor Day, daily 7–7; Labor Day–Memorial Day, daily 8–5.*

Wahweap

⑱ *5 mi north of Glen Canyon Dam on U.S. 89.*

Most recreational activity in the region takes place around this vacation village, where everything needed for a lakeside holiday is available: fishing, boat rentals, dinner cruises, and much more. Stop at

Wahweap Lodge (☞ Dining and Lodging, *below*) for an excellent view of the lake area.

★ ⑲ The best way to appreciate the beauty of Lake Powell is by boat. If you don't have access to one, the five-hour excursion cruise to **Rainbow Bridge National Monument** is the way to go. Along the 52-mi route (one-way from Wahweap Marina), you're treated to ever-changing, beautiful, and bizarre scenery, including huge monoliths that look like people turned into stone and a butte that resembles a dinosaur. The boat docks near Rainbow Bridge, the 290-ft red sandstone arch that straddles a cove of the lake. The world's largest natural stone bridge, it can be reached only by water or an arduous hike from a remote point on the Navajo reservation (☞ Cruises *and* Hiking *in* Outdoor Activities and Sports, *below*).

The excursion boats, which leave Wahweap daily, are two-tier craft with sundecks upstairs and enclosed seating downstairs. Experienced pilots provide commentary throughout the trip. Pack a lunch or take snacks; no food is sold on the boats, though coffee and water are provided. Other cruises are offered at the Wahweap Marina, including an all-day trip that stops at Rainbow Bridge and then proceeds farther into the Utah portion of the lake (☞ Boating *and* Cruises *in* Outdoor Activities and Sports, *below*).

Dining and Lodging

$$ ✕🏨 **Wahweap Lodge.** The lodge, on a promontory above Lake Powell, serves as the center for recreational activities in the area. This landscaped property offers accommodations with oak furnishings and balconies or patios; many of the rooms have a lake view (rates are a bit higher for these). The brightly colored, southwestern-style suites in the newest building are particularly attractive. The lodge's semicircular Rainbow Room restaurant offers an extensive southwestern, standard American, and Continental menu in a beautiful setting with panoramic views of Lake Powell. Guests can also enjoy two pools, a cocktail lounge, a marina, and, in season, decent pizzas from Itza Pizza. ⊠ *Box 1597 (on U.S. 89, 5 mi north of Page), Page 86040,* ☎ *520/645–2433 or 800/528–6154. 350 rooms. Restaurant, bar, boating, waterskiing, fishing, travel services. AE, D, DC, MC, V.*

🏕 **Wahweap Campground.** The 208 sites, some near the marina, are available on a first-come, first-served basis. Campers can use the coin laundry and showers ($2 extra) at the adjacent RV park (☞ *below*). ⊠ *5 mi north of Page on U.S. 89 near shore of Lake Powell 86040,* ☎ *520/645–1059.* ▣ *$11.* ☾ *Apr.–Oct.*

🏕 **Wahweap RV Park.** This RV park has 120 full-service hookups, showers, and a laundromat. It's open year-round, and reservations are accepted. ⊠ *5 mi north of Page on U.S. 89 near shore of Lake Powell 86040,* ☎ *520/645–1004 or 800/528–6154.* ▣ *$22.50.*

Nightlife

Nightlife in Wahweap revolves around **Wahweap Lodge** (☞ Dining and Lodging, *above*), which has a cocktail lounge and offers a sunset dinner cruise.

Outdoor Activities and Sports

BOATING

Docks and launching ramps are available at **State Line Marina,** 1½ mi north of Wahweap Lodge. **Wahweap Marina** (☎ 520/645–2433) is the largest of the four full-service marinas on Lake Powell (☞ Boating *in* The Northeast A to Z, *below*), with 850 slips and the most facilities, including a decent diner.

CRUISES

Excursions on double-decker scenic cruisers piloted by experienced guides leave from the dock of Lake Powell's Wahweap Lodge (☞ Dining and Lodging, *above*). The most popular is the one to Rainbow Bridge National Monument; a half-day cruise costs $66, full day $91. A 2½-hour sunset dinner cruise costs $52 and also departs from Wahweap Lodge: A prime-rib dinner is served on the fully enclosed decks of the 95-ft *Canyon King* paddle wheeler, a 19th-century riverboat, and the *Desert Shadow,* a newer paddle wheeler. The dinner cruise is approximately 50 mi dock to dock, and visits some of the most beautiful sights on the lake, including otherworldly red sandstone shapes and buttes, rincons, and bluffs.

HIKING

Only seasoned hikers in good physical condition will want to try either of the two trails leading to Rainbow Bridge; both trails are about 26–28 mi round-trip. Take Indian Highway 16 north toward the Utah state border. At the fork in the road, take either direction for about 5 mi and you'll come to a trailhead leading to Rainbow Bridge. Excursion boats pull in at the dock at the arch, but no supplies are sold there. You must get a permit for this hike from the Navajo Nation Parks and Recreation Department (☞ Hiking *in* The Northeast A to Z, *below*) in Window Rock.

THE NORTHEAST A TO Z

Arriving and Departing

By Bus

Greyhound Lines (☎ 800/231–2222) has numerous Arizona destinations, but there is no service into the reservations. If you're coming from out of state and wish to tour northeastern Arizona, take a bus to Phoenix or Flagstaff and then rent a car.

By Car

Travel by car is the absolute best way to tour the Navajo and Hopi nations. Bus travel is more or less dependable, but infrequent, and there is no rail or public air travel available within this area. If you are arriving from southern California or southern Arizona, Flagstaff is the best jumping-off point into northeastern Arizona (☞ Flagstaff *in* Chapter 3). If you are traveling from Utah or Nevada, you might choose to come in from Utah on U.S. 89, starting your tour at Page, Arizona. For those driving south from Colorado, logical entry points are Farmington and Shiprock, New Mexico, via U.S. 64 (what looks like a more direct route to Canyon de Chelly through Red Rock ends up crossing an unimproved road). Gallup, New Mexico, to the east, is also a convenient starting point for exploring the area.

By Plane

No major airlines fly directly to the reservations. To get closer to the northeastern part of the state, fly into **Sky Harbor International Airport** (☎ 520/273–3300) in Phoenix, the primary hub for air travel coming into Arizona from points out of state, and make connections for either the **Flagstaff Pullium Airport** (☎ 520/556–1234) or the **Page Municipal Airport** (☎ 520/645–2494). **Scenic Airlines** (☎ 800/245–8668 or 800/634–6801) has two daily flights from Phoenix to Page; you can rent a car in town.

By Train

Amtrak (☎ 800/872–7245) stops daily in Flagstaff. No passenger trains enter the interior of the Navajo or Hopi reservations.

Getting Around

By Bus

The **Navajo Transit System** (✉ Drawer 1330, Window Rock 86515, ☎ 520/729–4002 or 520/729–5457) has extensive, fixed routes throughout the Navajo reservation as well as charter service; write or phone for schedules. The buses are modern, in good condition, and generally on time, but they do not make frequent runs and when they do run they can be slow. Fares range from 25¢ for local rides to a high of $13.05 (Window Rock to Tuba City). This can be an up-close-and-personal way to travel the Navajo Nation and meet the people who live here as they go about their daily business.

By Car

Because a tour of Navajo–Hopi country involves driving long distances among widely scattered communities, a detailed, up-to-date road map is absolutely essential. A wrong turn could send you many miles out of your way. Gas stations carry adequate state maps, but two other maps are particularly recommended: the AAA (Automobile Association of America) guide to Navajo–Hopi country and the excellent map of the northeastern region prepared by the **Navajo Tourism Department** (☞ Visitor Information *in* Contacts and Resources, *below*).

Most of the 25,000 square mi of the Navajo reservation and other areas of northeastern Arizona are off the beaten track. It isn't easy to find a place to service your car here, so have your car inspected and serviced before your trip. Many visitors to the northeast generally stay on the well-maintained paved thoroughfares, which are patrolled by police officers. If you don't have the equipment for wilderness travel—including a four-wheel-drive vehicle and provisions—and do not have backcountry experience, stay off the dirt roads unless they are signed and graded, and the skies are clear. Seek weather information if you see ominous rain clouds in summer or signs of snow in winter. Never drive into dips or low-lying road areas during a heavy rainstorm; they could be flooded or could flood suddenly. If you heed these simple precautions (☞ Road Service *and* Weather, *below,* for more tips and information), car travel through the region will be as safe as anywhere else. While driving around the Navajo Nation, tune in to the following stations for local news and weather: 660 AM (KTNN), 770 AM, 97.9 FM, or 107.3 FM (KOB).

Contacts and Resources

Banks

Wells Fargo has branch offices with automated-teller machines (ATMs) in Window Rock, Kayenta, and Tuba City on the Navajo reservation. Adjacent to the reservation, Flagstaff, Page, Winslow, and Holbrook have banks and ATMs.

Bicycling

Biking enthusiasts will find miles of paved roads and light traffic. But the mostly two-lane highways do not have paved shoulders, and motorists are unaccustomed to encountering cyclists. The roads at Canyon de Chelly National Monument, Navajo National Monument, Monument Valley Navajo Tribal Park, and Kinlichee Navajo Tribal Park are your best bets. There are no bicycle rental companies in Navajo–Hopi country, so come prepared.

Boating

There are four full-service marinas at Lake Powell where you can rent small or excursion boats, including houseboats, and water-sports equipment, water sleds, and motorized wave cutters: **Wahweap** (☎ 520/

645–2433), **Bullfrog** (☎ 435/684–3000), **Halls Crossing** (☎ 435/684–7000), and **Hite Marina** (☎ 435/684–2278).

Houseboats—which should be reserved well in advance—range widely in size, amenities, and price; one that sleeps six (three double beds) may cost $800 for three nights; an 18-ft powerboat for eight passengers runs about $200 per day. Most of these prices drop after the summer months. Boat tour and lodging packages are also available. For information on all the Lake Powell options and prices, contact **ARA Leisure Services** (✉ Box 56909, Phoenix 85079, ☎ 800/528–6154, FAX 602/331–5258).

Camping and RV Parks

If you plan to stay in national monument and park areas, camping permission can be obtained on-site; for other camping locations, contact the **Navajo Nation Parks and Recreation Department** (☞ Hiking, *below*) to find out whether you need a permit. Be careful not to camp in low-lying areas, which are subject to extremely dangerous flash floods during the summer.

Car Rentals

For car-rental companies serving Phoenix and Flagstaff, *see* Car Rental *in* Smart Travel Tips A to Z.

Emergencies

POLICE

Canyon de Chelly police (☎ 520/674–2111 or 520/674–2112). **Hopi tribal police: Hopi Mesas** (☎ 520/738–2233, 520/738–2234, 520/738–2235, or 520/738–2236). **Navajo tribal police: Chinle** (☎ 520/674–2111 or 520/674–2112), **Tuba City** (☎ 520/283–3111 or 520/283–3112), **Window Rock** (☎ 520/871–6111 or 520/871–6112), **Kayenta** (☎ 520/697–5600).

HOSPITALS/MEDICAL CLINICS

Medical care in Navajo–Hopi country is not easily accessible: People with chronic medical conditions or those in frail health may wish to avoid a trip into Arizona's sparsely populated northeast. Hospital emergency care is generally not more than 60 minutes' driving time from any location on a paved highway.

Kayenta Ambulance (☎ 520/697–4101). **Kayenta Clinic** (☎ 435/727–3241) only offers emergency medical services. **Page Hospital** (✉ 501 N. Navajo Ave., ☎ 520/645–2424) is a complete facility with emergency-room service. **Sage Memorial Hospital** (✉ Ganado, on the Navajo reservation, ☎ 520/755–3411), a public hospital, offers surgery, medical, dental, and emergency services. Emergency care through the **U.S. Public Health Service Indian Hospitals** is available in the reservation communities of Fort Defiance (☎ 520/729–5741), Chinle (☎ 520/674–7001), Tuba City (☎ 520/283–6211), and Keams Canyon (☎ 520/738–2211).

PHARMACIES

There are no pharmacies on the Navajo or Hopi reservation. For emergency medical supplies, *see* the private or public hospitals noted in the Hospitals/Medical Clinics section, *above*.

In Page, **Safeway** (✉ Page Plaza, ☎ 520/645–5714 or 520/645–5068) is open weekdays 9–9, Saturday 9–6, and Sunday 10–4. There is also a **Wal-Mart** pharmacy (✉ Gateway Plaza, ☎ 520/645–2917) open weekdays and Saturday 9–6; it's closed Sunday.

Fishing

Contact the **Navajo Nation Fish and Wildlife Office** (✉ Box 1480, Window Rock 86515, ☎ 520/871–6451 or 520/871–6452) for permits to fish anywhere on the reservation. Fishing permits are available on site or in advance by mail. For the Lake Powell region, fishing licenses are available at the **Wahweap Marina** (✉ U.S. 89, 5 mi north of Page, ☎ 520/645–2243) and at **Stix Market** (✉ 5 S. Lake Powell Blvd., Page, ☎ 520/645–2891). Ask locally for fishing guides. *See also* Sports *in* Smart Travel Tips A to Z.

Guided Tours

Except during winter months, the **Navajo Transit System** (☞ Getting Around by Bus, *above*) operates tours departing from Window Rock. Destinations include Canyon de Chelly and the Painted Desert.

Nava-Hopi Tours, Inc. (☎ 520/774–5003 or 800/892–8687), schedules tours into the Navajo reservation from Flagstaff to the Four Corners area. **Goulding's Monument Valley Tours** (☎ 435/727–3231) departs from Goulding's Lodge (☞ Dining and Lodging *in* Goulding's Trading Post, *above*). Half- and full-day truck and Jeep tours into Canyon de Chelly on the Navajo reservation depart from nearby **Thunderbird Lodge** (☎ 800/679–2473; ☞ Dining and Lodging *in* Canyon de Chelly, *above*). The half-day tours leave twice daily (when there is a minimum of six passengers) throughout the year. Full-day tours are available only from April to October. The newspaper published by the **Navajo Tourism Department** (☞ Visitor Information, *below*) has a listing of operators offering Jeep and horseback tours on the Navajo reservation. Unless you have a four-wheel-drive vehicle or don't mind hiking 8 mi (round-trip) through sand, you'll want to take a guided tour to Antelope Canyon (☞ Antelope Canyon, *above*), one of the most arresting sights in the Page–Lake Powell area. Call the **Page Chamber of Commerce** (☎ 520/645–2741) or the **John Wesley Powell Museum** (☎ 520/645–9496) for information about tour operators.

Hiking

Bring plenty of water and electrolyte-rich beverages such as Gatorade when hiking, and drink often. The **Glen Canyon Natural History Association** (✉ Box 581, Page 86040, ☎ FAX 520/645–3532) sells good topographical maps of the region and useful hiking publications. For a backcountry hiking permit, contact the **Navajo Nation Parks and Recreation Department** (✉ Box 9000, Window Rock 86515, ☎ 520/871–6647). Trails are often poorly marked and not maintained in this wilderness area.

Road Service

Road service, auto repairs, and other automotive services are few and far between, so service your vehicle before venturing into the Navajo and Hopi reservations and carry emergency equipment and supplies. If you need assistance, ask a local for the nearest auto repair service or contact **Car Quest Auto Parts** (auto parts only; ✉ U.S. 163, Kayenta, ☎ 520/697–3200) or **Diamond Towing,** a 24-hr emergency road service (✉ Kayenta, ☎ 520/697–8437).

Shopping

Although you may feel more comfortable shopping at an established store, reservation roadside vendors often have exactly what you want at a good price. If you would like some tips on quality, the **Navajo Tourism Department** (☞ Visitor Information, *below*) has printed material on the subject.

Groceries, over-the-counter medicine, gasoline, and other supplies can be purchased in all of the major communities and trading posts on the

Navajo and Hopi reservations, including Page, Window Rock, Fort Defiance, Ganado, Chinle, Hopi Second Mesa, Keams Canyon, Tuba City, Kayenta, Goulding's Trading Post, and Cameron Trading Post. Plan your gas stops for the locations cited.

Telephone lines—and thus connections with credit-card verification sources—can be unreliable at the Hopi Mesas. It's a good idea to carry cash or traveler's checks to make purchases here or anywhere else outside of the trading posts.

Time

Unlike the rest of Arizona (including the Hopi reservation), the Navajo reservation observes daylight saving time. Thus for half the year—April to October—it's an hour later on the Navajo reservation than everywhere else in the state.

Visitor Information

Hopi Tribe Office of Public Relations (⊠ Box 123, Kykotsmovi 86039, ☎ 520/734–2441; www.nau.edu/áhcop-p/visit/index.html). **National Park Service/Glen Canyon Recreation Area** (⊠ Box 1507, Page 86040–1507, ☎ 520/608–6200 or 520/608–6404). **Native American Tourism Center** (⊠ 4130 N. Goldwater Blvd., Scottsdale 85251, ☎ 602/945–0771). **Navajo Tourism Department** (⊠ Box 663, Window Rock 86515, ☎ 520/871–6436 or 520/871–7371; www.navajo.org). **Page/Lake Powell Chamber of Commerce & Visitor Bureau** (⊠ Box 727, 644 N. Navajo Dr., Page 86040, ☎ 520/645–2741).

Weather

Summer temperatures in northeastern Arizona average about 87°F but can climb beyond 100°F. Winter daytime temperatures range from the 30s to the 60s but can drop to zero or below at night, especially in mountainous areas. Although the region gets less than 10 inches of rainfall in an average year, fierce summer thunderstorms can instantly flood low-lying areas. Heavy snows sometimes stop all traffic on dirt backroads, and it is not uncommon for remote villages to be snowed in for weeks at a time, particularly in the higher elevations.

KTNN radio (660 AM), the "voice of the Navajo Nation," provides periodic weather information. This station serves the Hopi and Navajo reservations from studios in Window Rock. Some programming is in Navajo, but there are news and weather reports in English. Another radio station you might also tune to for news and weather is **KOB** (770 AM, 107.3 FM, or 97.9 FM). You can also call the Navajo or Hopi tribal police (☞ Emergencies, *above*) for weather updates.

3 NORTH-CENTRAL ARIZONA

Antiquity, the Wild West—the real one and Hollywood's version—and the New Age all converge (harmoniously, of course) in north-central Arizona. Flagstaff, the area's largest city, has many historic buildings, an active nightlife, and winter sports in the dramatic San Francisco Peaks. Beyond the city, small towns and desert settings provide glimpses into generations past.

By Edie Jarolim

Updated by
Kim
Westerman

RICH IN NATURAL attractions, north-central Arizona is also rich in artifacts from its earliest inhabitants: Several national and state parks—among them Walnut Canyon, Wupatki, Montezuma Castle, and Tuzigoot national monuments—hold well-preserved evidence of the architectural accomplishments of Native American Sinagua and other ancestral Puebloans who made their homes in the Verde Valley and the region near the San Francisco Peaks. Flagstaff, the largest city in north-central Arizona and home to two important observatories, is a convenient jumping-off point for tours.

Those interested in exploring the West's wild and woolly days will enjoy a visit to the preserved fort at Camp Verde, which gives an excellent feel for frontier life, and the funky former mining town, Jerome. The many Victorian houses in temperate Prescott attest to the attempt to bring "civilization" to Arizona's territorial capital.

The Verde Valley towns of Cornville, Clarkdale, and Cottonwood are as sleepy as their names suggest. Sedona couldn't provide a greater contrast, with its sophisticated restaurants, upscale shops and accommodations, and New Age entrepreneurs. Drive just a few miles, though, and you're among soaring red rocks. U.S. 89A, which heads north out of Sedona through wooded Oak Creek Canyon en route to Flagstaff, is one of the most scenic drives in the state.

Pleasures and Pastimes

Camping
The Prescott and Coconino national forests cover a large part of north-central Arizona. Campgrounds close to Sedona often fill up in summer, especially those along Oak Creek in Oak Creek Canyon; if you want to camp near the red rocks, two good places to try are Manzanita and Banjo Bill. In Coconino National Forest near Flagstaff, the campgrounds near Mormon Lake and Lake Mary—including Pinegrove, Lakeview, Forked Pine, Double Springs, and Dairy Springs—are popular to the point of overcrowding in summer. Sites near Prescott and Jerome in the Prescott National Forest are generally less visited; Potato Patch and Granite Basin are both scenic, and sleeping out on top of Mingus Mountain is unforgettable.

Dining
Sedona remains at the front guard of north-central Arizona's haute-cuisine incursion, but Jerome, Flagstaff, and Prescott have interesting new dining rooms as well. Elsewhere, the fare runs more toward meat and potatoes.

Hiking
You can hike through thickly wooded areas in the Verde Valley and the Prescott National Forest in the state's highest alpine region (and even ascend a volcano), and among the rock formations around Sedona. National Forest Service offices in Camp Verde, Prescott, Sedona, and Flagstaff direct trekkers to the best trails.

Lodging
Flagstaff has many comfortable motels (all the familiar U.S. chains are represented) and pleasant bed-and-breakfasts but no real luxury. You'll find stunning settings and outstanding amenities in Sedona, but few bargains. Many of Prescott's hotels have fabled pasts. Little Jerome has one historic hotel, along with a few reliable B&Bs, but it's smart to call ahead if you think you might want to spend the night here.

Native American Culture

The achievements of the Sinagua people, who lived in north-central Arizona from the 8th through the 15th centuries, reached their height in the 12th and 13th centuries, when various related groups occupied most of the San Francisco Volcanic Field and a large portion of the upper and middle Verde Valley. The Sinagua sites around modern-day Camp Verde, Clarkdale, and Flagstaff provide a window onto this remarkable culture.

Exploring North-Central Arizona

The Verde Valley, in the southern part of the area covered in this chapter, is undervisited, but nearby Prescott, which has always been a Phoenician beat-the-heat getaway, is becoming popular among out-of-towners. It's hard to believe that Sedona, which is adding movie screens, chic restaurants, and B&Bs at an alarming rate, was fairly sedate just 10 years ago. Flagstaff has long been the population hub for north-central Arizona.

Numbers in the text correspond to numbers in the margin and on the North-Central Arizona, Prescott, and Flagstaff maps.

Great Itineraries

A short stay can give you a little taste of this rich part of the state, but at least five days are necessary for the full flavor. Linger longer if you want to savor the region's history and landscape or enjoy some outdoor activities. The following itineraries assume you'll start out in Phoenix, as most visitors do, and head north.

IF YOU HAVE 3 DAYS

Spend the first two nights in 🏨 **Sedona** ⑬. Take a Jeep tour or a hike in **Red Rock State Park,** and then explore the town's shops, especially those in the chic Tlaquepaque complex, adjacent to Los Abrigados Resort, and sights. On the next day, visit the ghost town of **Jerome** ⑥. On your third day, drive through scenic **Oak Creek Canyon** to 🏨 **Flagstaff** ⑭–㉑, where you can visit the **Riordon Historic State Park** or the **Museum of Northern Arizona** in the afternoon and the **Lowell Observatory** at night.

IF YOU HAVE 5 DAYS

Expand your time in 🏨 **Sedona** ⑬ by exploring Oak Creek Canyon and Red Rock State Park on the first day and shopping or exploring the town on the second. Enjoy a good part of the third day in **Jerome** ⑥ then continue on to 🏨 **Prescott** ⑦–⑫, where you can spend the night in one of the many Victorian-era lodgings. Next day, poke around the town's antiques shops and **Sharlot Hall Museum,** and in the late afternoon drive up to 🏨 **Flagstaff** ⑭–㉑. History lovers and hikers will enjoy an excursion to the adjacent **Sunset Crater** ㉔ and **Wupatki** ㉕ national monuments, where Native American artifacts may be explored in an inactive volcanic field.

IF YOU HAVE 7 OR MORE DAYS

Take your time driving up from Phoenix to Sedona, spending the morning of the first day at **Fort Verde State Historic Park** ① and **Montezuma Castle National Monument** ②. In the afternoon, ride the **Verde River Canyon Excursion Train** and spend the night in 🏨 **Jerome** ⑥. Continue on to 🏨 **Prescott** ⑦–⑫ for a day or two before heading over to 🏨 **Flagstaff** ⑭–㉑, where you can ski in the winter or view the entire San Francisco Peaks region from the Agassi ski lift in summer. If you conclude your trip in 🏨 **Sedona** ⑬, you'll have made a very satisfying circle of the area.

North-Central Arizona

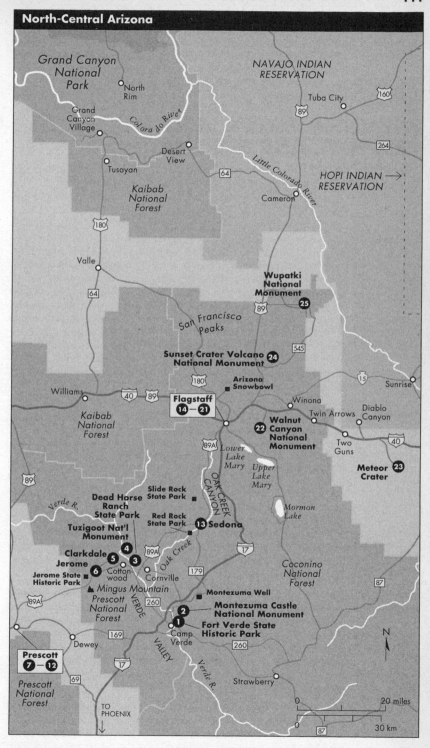

Grand Canyon National Park

North Rim

NAVAJO INDIAN RESERVATION

Tuba City

160

89

Grand Canyon Village

Colorado River

Desert View

64

Little Colorado River

264

HOPI INDIAN RESERVATION →

Tusayan

Cameron

Kaibab National Forest

180

Valle

64

San Francisco Peaks

Wupatki National Monument

89

25

Sunset Crater Volcano National Monument **24**

545

15

Sunrise

Williams

40 89

Kaibab National Forest

180

Flagstaff
14 — **21**

Arizona Snowbowl

Winona

Twin Arrows

Diablo Canyon

22 Walnut Canyon National Monument

89A

Lower Lake Mary

Upper Lake Mary

OAK CREEK CANYON

Two Guns

40

Meteor Crater **23**

89

Verde R.

Dead Horse Ranch State Park

Slide Rock State Park

Red Rock State Park

13 Sedona

Mormon Lake

Tuzigoot Nat'l Monument

89A

Oak Creek

17

Coconino National Forest

87

Clarkdale
Jerome

5

4

3

Cotton-wood

Cornville

179

Jerome State Historic Park

6

▲ Mingus Mountain

Prescott National Forest

VERDE

260

Montezuma Well

Montezuma Castle National Monument

89

Verde R.

2

1

Fort Verde State Historic Park

Camp Verde

260

N ↑

Prescott
7 — **12**

Dewey

169

VALLEY

Verde R.

Strawberry

17

89A

69

Prescott National Forest

TO PHOENIX ↓

0   20 miles

0   30 km

87

When to Tour North-Central Arizona

If you're not committed to warm weather, winter is an excellent time to visit: It's often easier to find a hotel (except in Sedona around Christmas), and, in Flagstaff and Prescott, rooms are less expensive. Prescott and Flagstaff hold most of their festivals and cultural events in summer. Sedona's biggest event, the Jazz on the Rocks Festival, takes place in September.

THE VERDE VALLEY, JEROME, PRESCOTT, AND SEDONA

About 90 mi north of Phoenix, as you round a curve approaching Exit 285 of I–17, the valley of the Verde River suddenly unfolds in a panorama of grayish-white cliffs, tinted red in the distance and dotted with desert scrub, cottonwood, and pine. For hundreds of years many Native American communities, especially those of the southern Sinagua people, lined the Verde River. Rumors of great mineral deposits brought Europeans to the Verde Valley as early as 1583, when Hopi Indians guided Antonio de Espejo here, but it wasn't until the second half of the 19th century that this wealth was commercially exploited. The discovery of silver and gold in the Black Hills, which border the valley on the southwest, gave rise to such boomtowns as Jerome—and to military installations such as Fort Verde, set up to protect the white settlers and wealth seekers from the Native American tribes they displaced. Mineral wealth was also the impetus behind the establishment of Prescott, across the Mingus Mountains from Verde Valley, as a territorial capital by President Lincoln and other Unionists who wanted to keep the riches out of Confederate hands.

Camp Verde

94 mi north of Phoenix on I–17.

❶ The military post for which **Fort Verde State Historic Park** is named was established in 1871–73 as the third of three fortifications in this part of the Arizona Territory. To protect the Verde Valley's farmers and miners from Tonto Apache and Yavapai raids, the fort's administrators oversaw the movement of nearly 1,500 Indians to the San Carlos and Fort Apache reservations. A museum details the history of the area's military installations, and three furnished officers' quarters show the day-to-day living conditions of the top brass. Signs from any of I–17's three Camp Verde exits will direct you to the 10-acre park. ✉ *125 Hollamon St., Camp Verde,* ☎ *520/567–3275.* ☞ *$2.* ⊙ *Daily 8–5.*

❷ The five-story 20-room cliff dwelling at **Montezuma Castle National Monument** was named by explorers who believed it had been erected by the Aztecs. Southern Sinagua Indians actually built the structure, one of the best-preserved prehistoric ruins in North America—and one of the most accessible. An easy paved trail (⅓ mi round-trip) leads to the dwelling and to adjacent Castle A, a badly deteriorated six-story living space with about 45 rooms. Visitors are not permitted to enter the ruins, but the viewing area is very close by.

Somewhat less accessible but equally striking is the **Montezuma Well** unit of the national monument. Although there are some Sinagua and Hohokam ruins here, the limestone sinkhole with a limpid blue-green pool lying in the middle of the desert is the site's main attraction. This cavity—55 ft deep and 365 ft across—is all that's left of an ancient subterranean cavern; the water remains at a constant 76°F year-round. It's a short hike up here, but the peaceful setting and the views of the

Verde Valley reward the effort. To reach Montezuma Well from Montezuma Castle, return to I–17 and go north one exit; you'll see the signs for the well, which is 4 mi east of the freeway. The drive includes a short section of dirt road. ⊠ *From Camp Verde, take Main St. to Montezuma Castle Rd.,* ☎ *520/567–4521 (Montezuma Well); 520/567–3322 ext. 12 (ranger); 520/567–3322 ext. 15 (bookstore).* 🎫 *$2.* ☉ *8–5 (hrs sometimes longer in spring and summer).*

Outdoor Activities and Sports

The Verde Ranger District office of the **Prescott National Forest** (⊠ 300 E. Hwy. 260, Camp Verde, ☎ 520/567–4121; 520/567–1119 TTY) is a good resource for places to hike—as well as to fish and boat—along the Verde River.

Dead Horse Ranch State Park

❸ *20 mi northwest of Montezuma Castle National Monument, 1 mi north of Cottonwood, off Main St.*

In the late 1940s, when Calvin "Cap" Ireys asked his family to help him choose among the ranches he was thinking about buying in the Verde Valley, his son immediately picked "the one with the dead horse on it." Ireys sold the land to the state in 1973 at one-third of its value, with the stipulation that the park into which it was to be converted retain the ranch's colorful name.

The 325-acre spread, which combines high-desert and wetlands habitats, is a pleasant place to while away the day. You can fish in the Verde River or the well-stocked Park Lagoon or hike on some 6 mi of trails that begin in a shaded picnic area and wind along the banks of the river; adjoining forest-service pathways are available for those who enjoy longer treks. Birders can check off more than 100 species from the Arizona Audubon Society lists provided by the rangers. Many visitors are especially eager to see the bald eagles that perch along the Verde River in winter and the common black hawks—a misnomer for these threatened avians—that nest here in summer. ⊠ *675 Dead Horse Ranch Rd., Cottonwood 86236,* ☎ *520/634–5283.* 🎫 *$4 per car for day use; $10 for camping without electricity, $15 with electricity.* ☉ *Daily 8–6.*

Dining

$$–$$$ ✕ **The Kramers at the Manzanita Restaurant & Lounge.** You wouldn't
★ expect to find sophisticated cooking in Cornville, 6 mi west of Cottonwood, but here a European-born chef (who came to the Verde Valley via Los Angeles) prepares Continental fare using organic produce and locally raised meat whenever possible. Roast duckling in orange sauce and rack of lamb are beautifully presented; try the mushroom soup if it's available. The hours here are not as cosmopolitan as the food: Dinner ends at 8 every night. ⊠ *11425 E. Cornville Rd., Cornville,* ☎ *520/634–8851. MC, V. Closed Mon. and Tues.*

$–$$ ✕ **Page Springs Bar & Restaurant.** Come to these two rustic wood-panel rooms on the loop to the town of Page Springs off U.S. 89A for down-home western chow: great chili, burgers, and steaks. You'll get a bosky setting and an Oak Creek view for a lot less than you'd pay closer to Sedona. ⊠ *1975 N. Page Springs Rd., Page Springs,* ☎ *520/ 634–9954. No credit cards.*

$ ✕ **Gabriela's Mexican Food.** You'll find traditional Mexican food in this tiny house off the main Camp Verde drag. Try the carne asada (marinated beef) tacos and the chicken burros (Arizona slang for burritos). ⊠ *154 Holloman St., Camp Verde,* ☎ *520/567–4484. No credit cards. Closed Sun.*

Tuzigoot National Monument

④ *3 mi north of Cottonwood.*

Not as well preserved as Montezuma Castle (☞ *above*) but more impressive in scope, Tuzigoot is another complex of ruins of the Sinagua people, who lived on this land overlooking the Verde Valley from about AD 1000 to AD 1400. Items used for food preparation, as well as jewelry, weapons, and farming tools excavated from the site, are displayed in the visitor center, where there is also a reconstructed room from the pueblo. ✉ *Broadway Rd., between Cottonwood's Old Town and Clarkdale, Clarkdale 86324,* ☎ *520/634–5564.* 🎫 *$2.* ☉ *Daily 8–5; extended summer hrs.*

Clarkdale

⑤ *19 mi northwest of Camp Verde, AZ 260 to U.S. 89A, 23 mi southwest of Sedona on U.S. 89A, 2 mi southwest of Tuzigoot National Monument.*

There's little to see in Clarkdale, but the town was once home to the smelter for the copper mines in nearby Jerome. Said to have arisen from a colony of prostitutes and hard-core gamblers who were tossed out of a rowdy mining camp in one of its periodic purges of sinners, Clarkdale quickly mellowed into a company town.

★ ☾ Train buffs come to catch the 22-mi **Verde River Canyon Excursion Train** (✉ Arizona Central Railroad, 300 N. Broadway, Clarkdale 86324, ☎ 800/293–7245), whose knowledgeable announcers regale riders with the area's colorful history and point out natural attractions along the way—in winter, you're likely to see bald eagles. This trip, which takes about four hours, is especially popular in fall-foliage season and in the spring, when the desert wildflowers bloom; make reservations well in advance. Round-trip rides cost $35.95. For $54.95 you can ride the living-room-like first-class cars, where hot hors d'oeuvres, coffee, and a cocktail are included in the price.

Jerome

★ **⑥** *3½ mi southwest of Clarkdale, 20 mi northwest of Camp Verde, 33 mi northeast of Prescott, 25 mi southwest of Sedona on U.S. 89A.*

Jerome was once known as the Billion Dollar Copper Camp, but after the last mines closed in 1953, the booming population of 15,000 dwindled to 50 determined souls, earning Jerome the "ghost town" designation it still holds, though its population has risen back to almost 500. It's hard to imagine that this town, which doesn't have a single convenience store, once was home to Arizona's largest JCPenney department store and one of the state's first Safeway supermarkets. Jerome saw its first revival during the mid-1960s, when hippies moved in and turned it into an art colony of sorts, and it's now becoming a tourist attraction. In addition to its shops and historic sites, Jerome is worth visiting for its scenery: It's built into the side of Cleopatra Hill, and from here you can see Sedona's red rocks, Flagstaff's San Francisco Peaks, and even eastern Arizona's Mogollon Rim country.

Jerome is about a mile above sea level, but structures within town sit at elevations that vary by as much as 1,500 ft, depending on whether they're on Cleopatra Hill or at its foot. Blasting at the United Verde (later Phelps Dodge) mine regularly shook buildings off their foundations—the town's jail slid across a road and down a hillside, where it sits today. That's not all that was unsteady about Jerome. In 1903 a reporter from a New York newspaper called Jerome "the wickedest town in America" due to its abundance of drinking and gaming establishments; town records from 1880 list 24 saloons. Whether due to divine retribution or to drunken accidents, the town was burned down several times. The mine's financial backers were a bit more respectable: Eugene Jerome, for whom the town was named, was first cousin to Jenny Jerome, Winston Churchill's mother.

Jerome has 50 retail establishments (that's more than one for every 10 residents). You can get a map of the town's shops and its attractions at the visitor-information trailer on U.S. 89A. Except for the state-run historic park, attractions and businesses don't always stay open as long as their stated hours when things are slow.

Of the three mining museums in town, the most inclusive is part of **Jerome State Historic Park.** Just outside town, signs on U.S. 89A will direct you to the turnoff for the park, reached by a short, precipitous road. The museum occupies the 1917 mansion of Jerome's mining king, Dr. James "Rawhide Jimmy" Douglas, Jr., who purchased Little Daisy Mine in 1912. You can see some of the tools and heavy equipment used to grind ore, but accounts of the town's wilder elements—such as the House of Joy brothel—are not so prominently displayed. ⊠ *State Park Rd.,* ☎ *520/634–5381.* ⬭ *$2.* ☉ *Daily 8–5.*

The **Mine Museum** in downtown Jerome is staffed by the Jerome Historical Society. The museum's collection of mining stock certificates alone is worth the (small) price of admission—the amount of money that changed hands in this town 100 years ago boggles the mind. ⊠ *200 Main St.,* ☎ *520/634–5477.* ⬭ *$1.* ☉ *Daily 9–4:30.*

One of the most unusual testaments to Jerome's days of mineral acquisition is the **Gold King Mine and Ghost Town.** This mélange of rusting and refurbished antique trucks and mining artifacts, roamed by sheep, goats, and a donkey, lies 1 mi northeast of town on the site of Haynes, a suburb of Jerome where gold was struck. Remnants of the mining operation include an old shaft, a former miner's hut, a workers' baseball field, and a boardinghouse. It's hard to sort the history from the junk; take a tour with owner Don Robertson for the full experience. ⊠ *Perkinsville Rd.,* ☎ *520/634–0053.* ⬭ *$3.* ☉ *Daily 9–5.*

Dining and Lodging

$$$ ✗ **House of Joy.** The two dimly lit dining rooms at this restaurant in a former bordello are strung with red lights, but it's the stuffed animals and dolls in the windows that put the kitsch factor over the top. Book a table several weeks in advance—this popular restaurant is open only on Saturday and Sunday and only for dinner. Classic Continental dishes such as chicken Kiev and veal cordon bleu are well prepared. Sample the tasty hot muffins, home-baked breads, and desserts. ⊠ *Hull Ave., just off Main St.,* ☎ *520/634–5339. No credit cards; personal checks accepted. Closed weekdays. No lunch.*

$ ✗ **Flatiron Cafe.** Ask where to have lunch or a late afternoon snack and nearly every Main Street shop owner will direct you to a tiny eatery at the fork in the road. The menu includes healthful sandwiches, such as black-bean hummus with feta cheese, and many coffee drinks. Breakfast is also served here. ⊠ *416 Main St.,* ☎ *520/634–2733. Reservations not accepted. No credit cards. Closed Wed. No dinner.*

$ ✗ **Haunted Hamburger/Jerome Palace.** After the climb up the stairs from Main Street to this former boardinghouse, you'll be ready for the hearty burgers, chili, cheese steaks, and ribs that dominate the menu. Lighter fare, including meatless selections like the guacamole quesadilla, is also available. An outdoor deck that overlooks Verde Valley helps to overcome the often indifferent service. ⊠ *410 Clark St.,* ☎ *520/634–0554. MC, V.*

$ ✕ **Jerome Brewery.** The newest restaurant in Jerome remains true to the town's casual nature. Good beer, burgers, and sandwiches are served in the small, attractive dining room on Main St. ⊠ *111 Main St.,* ☎ *520/639–8477. No credit cards.*

$–$$ 🏨 **Jerome Grand Hotel.** A welcome event in room-short Jerome was the 1996 opening of a full-service hotel—the first in more than 40 years—in a former hospital built by the United Verde Mine Company in 1927. Some accommodations are still being converted, but the finished portions include a restaurant and a handsome lounge with an oak bar and an antique nickelodeon. The hotel is on Cleopatra Hill, so many rooms have splendid views. All rooms have TVs with VCRs. ⊠ *200 Hill St., 86331,* ☎ *520/634–8200,* ᶠᴬˣ *520/639–0299. 22 rooms, 1 suite. Restaurant, lounge, shop. AE, D, MC, V.*

$–$$ 🏨 **Surgeon's House.** Abundant plants, knickknacks, bright colors,
★   and plenty of sunlight make this Mediterranean-style home that once belonged to Jerome's sawbones a most welcoming place to stay. The friendly ministrations of innkeeper Andrea Prince enhance the experience. Her multicourse gourmet breakfasts might include potato sour-cream soup, overstuffed burritos, or a marinated fruit compote. There are two suites, a former chauffeur's quarters, and a cottage with a skylight and private patio. You'll enjoy knockout vistas from almost everywhere in the house. ⊠ *101 Hill St., 86331,* ☎ *520/639–1452 or 800/639–1452. 2 suites, 1 cottage. Full breakfast. AE, MC, V.*

$ 🏨 **Ghost City Inn.** The outdoor veranda at this 1898 B&B affords sweeping views of the Verde Valley and Sedona. Most rooms are decorated in Victorian style, but two have contemporary western touches. Afternoon tea and turndown with chocolates are unexpected luxuries in a formerly rough-and-ready town. ⊠ *541 N. Main St., 86331,* ☎ ᶠᴬˣ *520/634–4678 or 888/634–4678. 4 rooms with 2 shared baths, 1 room with private bath. Full breakfast. AE, D, MC, V.*

Nightlife

Paul & Jerry's Saloon (⊠ Main St., ☎ 520/634–2603) attracts a rowdy crowd to its two pool tables and old wooden bar. On weekends there's live music and a lively scene at the **Spirit Room** (⊠ Main St. and U.S. 89, ☎ 520/634–8809); the mural over the bar harks back to the days when it was a dining spot for the "ladies" of the red-light district.

Outdoor Activities and Sports

CAMPING

For information about camping near Jerome at Mingus Mountain, Playground, or Potato Patch—all open May–October—contact the Prescott National Forest's **Verde Ranger District** (⊠ 300 E. Hwy. 260, Camp Verde, ☎ 520/567–4121; 520/567–1119 TTY).

Shopping

Jerome has its share of art galleries (some perched precariously on Cleopatra Hill along with boutiques), but they're funkier than those in Sedona. An exception is the **Anderson-Mandette Art Studios** (⊠ Old Mingus High School, Bldg. C, ☎ 520/634–3438). Robin Anderson and Margo Mandette made the building their workplace in 1978; at 20,000 square ft, it's possibly the largest private art studio and gallery in the United States.

Main Street and Hull Avenue, just around the bend from Main, are Jerome's two main shopping streets. Your eyes may begin to glaze over after browsing through one boutique after another, most offering tasteful southwestern paraphernalia.

Aurum (⊠ 369 Main St., ☎ 520/634–3330) focuses on contemporary art jewelry in silver and gold; about 30 artists are represented. **Designs on You** (⊠ 233 Main St., ☎ 520/634–7879) carries attractively styled women's clothing. **Jerome Artists Cooperative Gallery** (⊠ 502 Main St., ☎ 520/639–4276) specializes in jewelry, sculpture, painting, and pottery by local artists. **The Jewel** (⊠ 420 Hull Ave., ☎ 520/639–0259) specializes in Australian opals. **Nellie Bly** (⊠ 136 Main St., ☎ 520/634–0255) stocks walking sticks, perfume bottles, jewelry, and outstanding kaleidoscopes. **Sky Fire** (⊠ 140 Main St., ☎ 520/634–8081) has two floors of items to adorn your person and your house, from Native American pattern dishes to handcrafted mission-style hutches.

En Route The drive down a mountainous section of U.S. 89A from Jerome to Prescott is gorgeous (if somewhat harrowing in bad weather), filled with twists and turns through Prescott National Forest. If you're coming from Phoenix, the route that crosses the Mogollon Rim, overlooking the Verde Valley, is scenic but less precipitous.

Prescott

33 mi southwest of Jerome on U.S. 89A to U.S. 89, 100 mi northwest of Phoenix I–17 to AZ 69.

In a forested bowl 5,300 ft above sea level, Prescott is a prime summer refuge for Phoenix-area dwellers. It was proclaimed the first capital of the Arizona Territory in 1864 and settled by Yankees to ensure that gold-rich northern Arizona would remain a Union resource. (Tucson and southern Arizona were strongly pro-Confederacy.) It is believed that ancestors of the Yavapai Indians, whose reservation is today on the outskirts of town, were the area's original inhabitants, but early territorial settlers thought that ruins in the area were of Aztec origin. You can see the results of this notion—inspired by *The History and Conquest of Mexico,* a popular book by historian William Hickling Prescott, for whom the town was named—in such street names as Montezuma, Cortez, and Alarcon.

Despite a devastating downtown fire in 1900, Prescott remains the Southwest's richest store of late-19th-century New England–style architecture (some have called it the "West's most Eastern town"). With two institutions of higher education, Yavapai College and Prescott College, Prescott could be called a college town, but it doesn't really feel like one, perhaps because so many retirees also reside here, drawn by the temperate climate and low cost of living.

The city's main drag is Gurley Street, named after John Addison Gurley, who was slated to be the first governor; he died days before he was ❼ to move to the Arizona Territory. **Courthouse Plaza,** bounded by Gurley and Goodwin streets to the north and south and by Cortez and Montezuma streets to the west and east, is the heart of the city: Here the 1916 Yavapai County Courthouse stands, guarded by an equestrian bronze of turn-of-the-century journalist and lawmaker Bucky O'Neill, who died while charging San Juan Hill in Cuba with Teddy Roosevelt during the Spanish-American War. At the south end of the plaza, across from the courthouse's main entrance, the **Chamber of Commerce** is a good place to get your bearings; those interested in architecture should be sure to get a map of the town's Victorian neighborhoods. Most are within walking distance of the chamber office. Many Queen Annes have been beautifully restored, and a number of them are now bed-and-breakfasts. Antiques and collectibles shops line both sides of Cortez Street to the north of the courthouse.

118

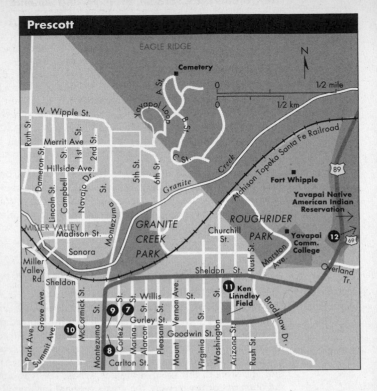

8 Whiskey Row, named for a string of pioneer taverns, runs along Montezuma Street, flanking Courthouse Plaza's west side; it once held 20 saloons and houses of pleasure. Social activity is more subdued these days, and the historic bars provide an escape from the street's many boutiques.

9 The little **Bead Museum,** which sits demurely on Whiskey Row, tells an intriguing story of international trade and intricate bead craft from 3000 BC through today. ☒ *140 S. Montezuma St.,* ☎ *520/445–2431.* ☒ *Free.* ⊗ *Mon.–Sat. 9:30–4:30, Sun. by appointment.*

★ **10** The remarkable **Sharlot Hall Museum** documents local history. Along with the original ponderosa-pine log cabin that housed the territorial governor and the museum named for historian and poet Sharlot Hall, the parklike setting contains three fully restored period homes and a transportation museum. Territorial times are the focus, but natural history and artifacts of the area's prehistoric peoples are on display. ☒ *415 W. Gurley St., 2 blocks west of Courthouse Plaza,* ☎ *520/445–3122.* ☒ *$5 donation requested per family.* ⊗ *Apr.–Oct., Mon.–Sat. 10–5, Sun. 1–5; Nov.–Mar., Mon.–Sat. 10–4, Sun. 1–5.*

11 The 1935 stone-and-log **Smoki Museum** is almost as interesting as the Native American artifacts inside. Priceless baskets and katsinas, as well as pottery, rugs, and beadwork, comprise this fine collection, which represents Indian culture from the Pre-Columbian period to the present. ☒ *147 N. Arizona St.,* ☎ *520/445–1230.* ☒ *$2.* ⊗ *May–Sept., Mon., Tues., Thurs.–Sat. 10–4, Sun. 1–4; Oct., Fri.–Sun. 10–4; Nov.–Apr. phone for appointment.*

12 Included in the permanent collection of the respected **Phippen Museum of Western Art,** about 5 mi north of downtown, is work by many prominent artists of the West, along with the paintings and bronze sculptures of George Phippen. ⊠ *4701 Hwy. 89 N,* ☎ *520/778–1385.* ☷ *$3.* ☉ *Mon. and Wed.–Sat. 10–4, Sun. 1–4.*

Dining and Lodging

$$–$$$ ✕ **Murphy's.** Mesquite-grilled meats and beer brewed exclusively for the restaurant are the specialties here. The baby back ribs, fresh steamed clams, and fresh fried catfish are all good choices. ⊠ *201 N. Cortez St.,* ☎ *520/445–4044. AE, D, MC, V.*

$$ ✕ **The Palace.** Legend has it that the patrons who saved the Palace's ornately carved 1880s Brunswick bar from a Whiskey Row fire in 1900 continued drinking at it while the rest of the row burned across the street. Whatever the case, the bar remains the centerpiece of the beautifully restored turn-of-the-century structure with a high, tin-embossed ceiling. Steaks and chops are the stars here, but the grilled fish and hearty corn chowder are fine, too. ⊠ *120 S. Montezuma St.,* ☎ *520/541–1996. AE, MC, V.*

$–$$ ✕ **Zuma's Woodfire Café.** One of the more sophisticated restaurants in town, Zuma's offers pizzas made in a wood-burning oven, with such toppings as goat cheese, grilled onions, and fresh basil. The large menu also includes salads, pastas, and grilled meats and fish. The current chef moved over from the Hassayampa Inn, Zuma's biggest competition. ⊠ *124 N. Montezuma St.,* ☎ *520/541–1400. AE, D, MC, V.*

$ ✕ **Genovese.** Low-price classic southern Italian fare made this restaurant near Courthouse Plaza an instant local favorite. Try the cannelloni stuffed with shrimp, crab, ricotta cheese, and spinach. The cheese-and-sauce-laden lasagna will satisfy the largest appetite. Toppings on the crispy thin-crust pizza include Gorgonzola, artichokes, and ham along with the standards. ⊠ *217 W. Gurley St.,* ☎ *520/541–9089. AE, MC, V.*

$ ✕ **Kendall's Famous Burgers and Ice Cream.** A great diner in the middle of downtown, Kendall's serves hamburgers cooked to order with your choice of 14 condiments. Be sure to try the homemade french fries. ⊠ *113 S. Cortez St.,* ☎ *520/778–3658. No credit cards.*

$ ✕ **Prescott Brewing Company.** Good beer, good food, good service, and good prices—for a casual meal, it's hard to beat this cheerful, multilevel restaurant. In addition to the chili, fish-and-chips, and British-style bangers (sausage) and mash, you'll also find vegetarian enchiladas made with tofu and a pasta salad with sun-dried tomatoes, avocado, broccoli, and two types of cheese. Fresh-baked beer bread comes with many of the entrées. ⊠ *130 W. Gurley St.,* ☎ *520/771–2795. AE, D, DC, MC, V.*

$$ ✕▥ **Hassayampa Inn.** Built in 1927 for early automobile travelers, the ★ Hassayampa Inn oozes character (be sure to look up at the hand-painted ceiling in the lobby), and some rooms still have the original furnishings. A complimentary cocktail at the lounge and free breakfast at the restaurant gild the lily of reasonable rates. The Peacock Room, the hotel's pretty, if overly formal, dining room, has tapestried booths, dim lighting, and better than average Continental food. ⊠ *122 E. Gurley St., 86301,* ☎ *520/778–9434; 800/322–1927 in AZ;* ℻ *520/445–8590. 58 rooms, 10 suites. Restaurant, bar. Full breakfast. AE, D, DC, MC, V.*

$$–$$$ ▥ **Prescott Resort Conference Center and Casino.** On a hill on the outskirts of town, this upscale property has views of the mountain ranges surrounding Prescott or the valley. Many guests hardly notice, so riveted are they by the poker machines and slots in Arizona's only hotel casino. There are plenty of recreational facilities to occupy those able to resist the one-armed bandits. ⊠ *1500 AZ 69, 86301,* ☎ *520/776–1666 or 800/967–4637,* ℻ *520/776–8544. 161 rooms and suites. Restaurant, coffee shop, piano bar, indoor-outdoor pool, hot tub,*

sauna, 4 tennis courts, exercise room, racquetball, casino. AE, D, DC, MC, V.

$–$$ 🏨 **Mark's House.** Victoria still reigns at this bed-and-breakfast, once owned by the mayor of territorial Prescott. It now belongs to Beth Maitland, star of the daytime soap *The Young and the Restless*, and is ably managed by her parents. Rooms are impeccably furnished with period antiques: The suite in the circular turret, overlooking Thumb Butte, is particularly impressive. Breakfast is served in the formal dining room. ✉ *203 E. Union St., 86303,* ☎ *520/778–4632. 2 rooms with private bath, 2 suites. Full breakfast. D, MC, V.*

$ 🏨 **Hotel St. Michael.** Don't expect serenity on the busiest corner of Courthouse Plaza, but for low rates and historic atmosphere it's hard to beat this hotel. In operation since 1900, the inn has rooms with 1920s wallpaper and furnishings; some face the plaza and others look out on Thumb Butte. The first-floor Caffé St. Michael serves great coffee and croissants. ✉ *205 W. Gurley St., 86303,* ☎ *520/776–1999 or 800/678–3757,* FAX *520/776–7318. 71 rooms. Coffee shop, shops. AE, D, MC, V.*

$ 🏨 **Hotel Vendome.** This World War I–era hostelry has seen miners, health seekers, and celebrities like cowboy star Tom Mix walk through its doors. Old-fashioned touches such as the original claw-foot tubs remain. Like many other historic properties, the Vendome has its obligatory resident ghost (her room costs slightly more). Only a block from Courthouse Plaza, this is a good choice for those who want to combine sightseeing, modern comforts, and good value. ✉ *230 Cortez St., 86303,* ☎ *520/776–0900,* FAX *520/771–0395. 17 rooms, 4 suites. Continental breakfast. AE, D, DC, MC, V.*

Nightlife and the Arts

Montezuma Street's Whiskey Row, just off the central Courthouse Plaza, is nowhere near as wild as it was in its historic heyday, but most bars have live music—and a lively collegiate crowd—on the weekends. For a more refined atmosphere, head over to the art nouveau piano bar at the **Hassayampa Inn** (✉ 122 E. Gurley St., ☎ 520/778–9434); there's always someone tickling the ivories on the weekend. The bar at **Lizzard's Lounge** (✉ 120 N. Cortez St., ☎ 520/778–2244) was shipped from overseas via the Colorado River. **Nolaz** (✉ 216 W. Gurley St., ☎ 520/445–3765) often features good blues and jazz bands. The main source of entertainment at the **Prescott Resort** (✉ 1500 AZ 69, ☎ 520/776–1666) is Bucky's Casino, but the mellow tunes of a piano are an alternative to the clank of the slots on Friday and Saturday nights.

The **Prescott Fine Arts Association** (✉ 208 N. Marina St., ☎ 520/445–3286) sponsors musicals and dramas, a series of plays for children, and a variety of concerts. The association's gallery also presents rotating exhibits by local, regional, and national artists. The **Prescott Jazz Society** (✉ 129½ N. Cortez St., ☎ 520/445–0000) has an intimate storefront lounge. The **Satisfied Mind Bookstore** (✉ 113 W. Goodwin St., ☎ 520/776–9766) next door to the Chamber of Commerce is a good place to find out about poetry readings and other literary goings-on about town. The **Yavapai Symphony Association** (✉ 107 N. Cortez St., Suite 105B, ☎ 520/776–4255) hosts performances by the Phoenix and Flagstaff symphonies; call ahead for schedules and venues.

Prescott's popular **Bluegrass Festival on the Square** takes place in June. The town, which had its first organized cowboy competition in 1888, lays claim to having the world's oldest rodeo: the annual **Frontier Days** (✉ Box 2037, Prescott 86302, ☎ 800/358–1888) roundup, held on the Fourth of July weekend at the Yavapai County Fairgrounds. In August, the **Cowboy Poets Gathering** brings together campfire bards from around the country. The major event in December is the **Christ-**

mas Parade and Courthouse Lighting. Call the **Chamber of Commerce** (☎ 800/266–7534) for contact phone numbers and other details on all these events.

Outdoor Activities and Sports

CAMPING

Campgrounds near Prescott in the Prescott National Forest are generally not crowded. Contact the **Bradshaw Ranger District** (⊠ 2230 E. Hwy. 69, Prescott 86301, ☎ 520/445–7253) for information about the section of the forest south of town and extending down to Horse Thief Basin.

GOLF

The city-owned **Antelope Hills** (⊠ 1 Perkins Dr., ☎ 520/445–0583; 800/ 972–6818 in AZ), just outside Prescott, offers 36 holes on two courses, one of them a Gary Panks creation. The 18-hole **Prescott Country Club Golf Course** (⊠ AZ 69, 14 mi east of Prescott, ☎ 520/772–8984) is set in the foothills of Bradshaw Mountain.

HIKING

More than a million acres of national forest land surround Prescott. Thumb Butte is a popular hiking spot, but there are lots of other trekking and overnighting options. Contact the **Bradshaw Ranger District** (☞ Camping, *above*) of the **Prescott National Forest** for information on campsites and trails.

HORSEBACK RIDING

Granite Mountain Stables (⊠ 2400 W. Shane Dr., 7 mi northeast of Prescott, ☎ 520/771–9551) has daily guided rides as well as group specials, such as hay-wagon outings.

Shopping

Shops selling antiques and collectibles line Cortez Street, just north of Courthouse Plaza. You'll find fun stuff—especially western kitsch— and some good buys on valuable pieces. Many of the stores gather together groups of retailers; at 14,000 square ft, the **Merchandise Mart Antique Mall** (⊠ 205 N. Cortez St., ☎ 520/776–1728) is the largest of these collections of collectors. When your eyes glaze over, stop in at **Déjà Vu Antiques** (⊠ 134 N. Cortez St., ☎ 520/445–6732) for a bit of refreshment at an old-time soda fountain.

Courthouse Plaza, especially along Montezuma Street, is lined with specialty and gift shops. Many match those in Sedona for quality and price. Be sure to check out **Arts Prescott** (⊠ 134 S. Montezuma St., ☎ 520/ 776–7717), a cooperative gallery of talented local craftspeople and artists. **Bashford Courts** (⊠ 130 Gurley St., ☎ 520/445–9798) has three floors of artsy stores. **St. Michael's Alley,** adjoining the Montezuma Street hotel of the same name, is home to interesting retailers, including Robert Shields Design (don't miss his wonderful ceramic snakes) and Desparado General Store where the displays are almost as imaginative as the local arts and crafts sold. **Prescott Newsstand** (⊠ 123 N. Cortez St., ☎ 520/ 778–0072) is a civilized spot that carries magazines, *The New York Times,* and a few international newspapers.

Sedona and Environs

13 *119 mi north of Phoenix, I–17 to AZ 17 to U.S. 89A; 60 mi northeast of Prescott, U.S. 89 to U.S. 89A; 27 mi south of Flagstaff on U.S. 89A.*

It's easy to see what draws so many visitors to Sedona. Red-rock buttes—Cathedral Rock, Bear Mountain, Courthouse Rock, and Bell Rock, among others—reach up into an almost always clear blue sky,

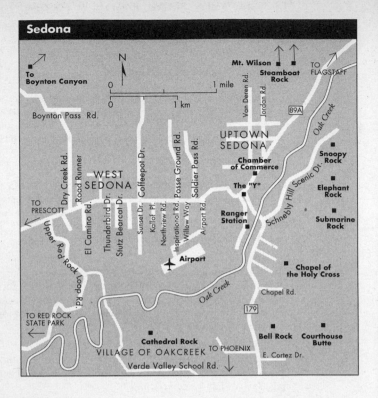

Sedona

both colors intensified by dark-green pine forests. The rugged landscape, at the north rim of the Verde Valley, once attracted surrealist Max Ernst, writer Zane Grey, and many filmmakers (more than 80 westerns were shot in the area in the 1940s and '50s alone).

These days, Sedona lures enterprising restaurateurs and gallery owners from the East and West coasts. New Age followers, who believe that the area contains some of the earth's more important vortices (energy centers), also come in great numbers in the belief that the area's "vibe" confers a sense of balance and well-being and enhances creativity. Several entrepreneurs have set up crystal shops and New Age bookshops that cater to the curious and true devotees.

Expansion since the early 1980s has been rapid, and lack of planning has taken its toll in unattractive developments and increased traffic, especially on weekends and during busy summer months, when Phoenix residents flee north to cooler elevations. Still, the future looks promising. The town has been chosen to take part in the federally sponsored Main Street program, which means, among other things, that a number of Red Rock Territorial–style buildings in the Uptown section will be preserved and that a separate parking district will be built. A proposed bridge over Oak Creek should help alleviate some of the traffic but it will also impinge on the natural glory of Red Rock Crossing, one of the town's most photographed vistas.

Canyons, creeks, Indian ruins, and the red rocks are readily accessible on foot; the area is thrilling and easy to hike (☞ Hiking *in* Outdoor Activities and Sports, *below*). Another option is to take one of the ubiquitous Jeep tours (☞ Guided Tours *in* North-Central Arizona A to Z, *below*).

Those with their own wheels might want to take the drive out to **Boynton Canyon,** sacred to the Yavapai Apache, who believe it was their ancient birthplace. It's home to the Enchantment Resort, where all are welcome to hike the canyon and stop in for lunch or a late-afternoon drink. Weather permitting, the rather bumpy **Schnebly Hill Scenic Drive** is another ooh-and-ah–inspiring option, and the vistas of Sedona from **Airport Mesa** at sunset can't be beat. The **Upper Red Rock Loop** will likely consume a roll or two of film. Many of the most picturesque spots in Sedona are considered energy centers; vortex maps of the area are available at most of Sedona's New Age stores.

You needn't be religious to be inspired by the setting and the architecture of the **Chapel of the Holy Cross.** Built by Marguerite Brunwige Staude in 1956, a disciple of Frank Lloyd Wright, this modern landmark, with a huge cross on the facade, rises between two red-rock peaks. Vistas of the town and the surrounding area are spectacular. There are no regular services, but visitors are welcome for quiet meditation. A small gift shop sells religious articles and books. A trail east of the chapel leads you—after a 20-minute walk over occasional loose-rock surfaces—to a seat surrounded by voluptuous red-limestone walls, worlds away from the bustle and commerce around the chapel. ⊠ *Chapel Rd. (off AZ 179),* ☎ *520/282-4069.* ☞ *Free.* ☉ *Daily 9–5.*

Although it's set in an area that was inhabited by Native Americans for centuries, the town of Sedona itself is very new—it wasn't incorporated until 1988—so there are few historical sights. The town's main activity is shopping, mostly for southwestern-style paintings, clothing, rugs, jewelry, and Native American artifacts (☞ Shopping, *below*). During warmer months visit air-conditioned shops at midday and save hiking and Jeep tours for the early morning or late afternoon, when the light is softer and the heat less oppressive.

Two miles west of Sedona on Highway 89A is the turnoff for the 286-acre **Red Rock State Park,** a less crowded (though nonswimming) alternative to the popular Slide Rock State Park (☞ *below*). The 5 mi of interconnected park trails are well marked and provide beautiful vistas. There are daily nature walks; bird-watching excursions on Wednesday, Thursday, and Saturday; and a guided hike to Eagle's Nest scenic overlook—the highest point in the park—every Saturday. Call ahead for times, which change with the season. ⊠ *4050 Red Rock Loop Rd., Sedona 86336,* ☎ *520/282-6907.* ☞ *$5 per car.* ☉ *Daily 8–5.*

★ Whether you want to swim, hike, picnic, or enjoy beautiful scenery framed through a car window, head north on Highway 89A through the wooded **Oak Creek Canyon,** which begins about 1 mi north of Sedona. It's the most attractive route to Flagstaff and the Grand Canyon and worth a drive-through even if you're not heading north. Although the forest is primarily evergreen, the fall foliage is glorious. The road winds through a steep-walled canyon, and visitors crane their necks for views of the dramatic rock formations above. Oak Creek, which runs along the bottom of the canyon, is lined with tent campgrounds, fishing camps, cabins, motels, and restaurants.

☾ Anglers young and old will enjoy the sure catch at the **Rainbow Trout Farm.** For $1 you'll get a cane pole with a hook and bait. There's no charge if your catch is under 8 inches; above that it's $2.85 to $5.85, depending on the length. The real bargain is that the staff will clean and pack your fish for 50¢ each. ⊠ *3500 N. Hwy. 89A, 3 mi north of Sedona,* ☎ *520/282-3379.* ☞ *$1.* ☉ *Daily 9–5; summer, daily 8–6, weather permitting.*

☾ **Slide Rock State Park,** 7 mi north of Sedona, is a good place for a picnic. On a hot day, you can plunge down a natural rock slide into a swimming hole (bring an extra pair of jeans to wear on the slide). The only downside to this trip is the traffic, particularly on summer weekends; you might have to wait to get in. ⊠ *6871 N. Hwy. 89A,* ☎ *520/ 282–3034.* 🎫 *$5 per car (4 people maximum).* ☉ *Daily 8–5 winter, 8–6 spring, 8–7 summer.*

Dining and Lodging

Some Sedona restaurants close in January and February, so call before you go; make reservations in high season (April to October).

$$$ ✕ **Pietro's.** Good northern Italian cuisine, a friendly and attentive
★ staff, and a lively yet casual atmosphere have made this one of Sedona's most popular dining spots. Try *gamberi giardinieri* (grilled shrimp with shiitake mushrooms in white wine) for a starter, followed by fettuccine with duck, cabbage, and figs, or a veal *piccata* entrée. ⊠ *2445 W. Hwy. 89A,* ☎ *520/282–2525. AE, D, DC, MC, V. No lunch.*

$$$ ✕ **Rene's.** Ease into the plush banquettes of this pretty lace-curtained restaurant for classic Continental dishes. Recommended starters include a delicate French onion soup and the salade Walter—baby spinach leaves and sautéed mushrooms in a hazelnut vinaigrette. Rack of lamb is the house specialty, but the tender antelope in juniper sauce is a worthy competitor. The three-course prix-fixe dinner is under $30. Service is formal, as befits the room and menu, but casual attire is acceptable. ⊠ *Tlaquepaque, B-117, Hwy. 179,* ☎ *520/282–9225. AE, MC, V.*

$$–$$$ ✕ **Heartline Café.** Fresh flowers and innovative southwestern cuisine are this attractive café's hallmarks. The oak-grilled salmon marinated in tequila and lime and the chicken breast with prickly-pear sauce are two options. Appealing vegetarian plates are also on the menu. On nice days grab a seat on the rosebush-lined terrace. ⊠ *1610 W. Hwy. 89A,* ☎ *520/282–0785. AE, D, MC, V. No lunch Sun.*

$$–$$$ ✕ **Sasaki.** Somewhat off the tourist path in the Village of Oak Creek, this understated restaurant serves a limited variety of impeccably fresh sushi and sashimi. There's a full Japanese menu, too; pork katsu (lightly battered and fried cubes of pork) and ten-zura (cold buckwheat noodles with tempura) are good cooked options. The service couldn't be friendlier. ⊠ *65 Bell Rock Rd.,* ☎ *520/284–1757. AE, MC, V.*

$$–$$$ ✕ **Sedona Swiss.** It's hard to go wrong at this European-style restaurant: Breakfast pastry in the adjoining café is light and buttery, and such classic dinner entrées as veal tenderloin Zurichoise, with a sauce containing mushrooms, cream, and cognac, are delicately seasoned. Lighter alternatives like pasta with fresh salmon are also available. A low-price buffet lunch draws in the tour-bus crowd, but in the evening the chalet-style dining room is suitably sedate and romantic. ⊠ *350 Jordan Rd.,* ☎ *520/282–7959. MC, V. Closed Sun.*

$$–$$$ ✕ **Shugrue's Hillside.** One of the better restaurants in Sedona, Shugrue's provides high quality in a wide range of categories, but the salads and meats are particularly good. Rack of lamb and filet mignon are prepared and presented simply. There's a small, thoughtful, and well-priced wine list as well. Don't be confused: Shugrue's Hillside is not owned by the same folks who own Shugrue's West, a less appealing restaurant. It's a good idea to make reservations. ⊠ *671 Hwy. 179,* ☎ *520/ 282–5300. AE, DC, MC, V.*

$$–$$$ ✕ **Takashi.** Those seeking some serenity and a respite from heavy meals will enjoy this Japanese restaurant, which provides aesthetic pleasure in everything from tea (with little bits of floating popcorn and brown rice) to dessert (sweet ginger or red-bean ice cream). Salads include a spicy sushi tuna with Japanese mayonnaise on a bed of cabbage and fresh vegetables. Combination dinners such as sashimi and tempura or teriyaki let you sample a little bit of everything. ⊠ *465 Jordan Rd.,* ☎ *520/282–2334. AE, DC, MC, V. Closed Mon. No lunch Sun.*

$$ ✕ **Top of Sedona.** Don't be put off by the Quality Inn location and non-descript dining room. This restaurant has some of the best red-rock views in town, especially from its outdoor deck, and owners Matt and Corey Erwin have toiled in some of Arizona's finest resort kitchens. Try a grilled polenta appetizer with Gorgonzola and mushrooms, an eggplant Napoleon entrée layered with ratatouille, vegetables, and rice, or well-prepared grilled lamb chops. The chef prides herself on fulfilling special orders (it's best to phone these ahead). ⊠ *771 Hwy. 179,* ☎ *520/282–1662. AE, MC, V.*

$–$$ ✕ **The Hideaway.** There's nothing pretentious about this red-sauce southern Italian restaurant and pizzeria with a wood-beam ceiling and red-and-white-check tablecloths. But what a setting: Every one of the many decks has eye-popping vistas of Oak Creek and the towering buttes. Try one of the large salads at lunch and the hearty lasagna or manicotti at dinner. This is a place that visitors stumble upon and locals tend to keep to themselves. ⊠ *Country Square, AZ 179 (just south of the "Y"),* ☎ *520/282–4204. AE, D, DC, MC, V.*

$ ✕ **Mandarin House.** Its name notwithstanding, the Mandarin House serves everything from Cantonese to Szechuan and Hunan fare, with dishes ranging from the exotic (shark-fin salad) to the old standbys (egg foo yong). The lemon chicken is particularly recommended. Everything is fresh—even the noodles and egg rolls are made on the premises. ⊠ *6486 AZ 179, Suite 114,* ☎ *520/284–9088. AE, D, MC, V.*

$ ✕ **Mesquite Tree Barbecue.** Though it offers outdoor seating only, this uptown Sedona hideaway behind a long row of tourist shops is worth a visit. Follow your nose to the mesquite-burning grill, where you can watch beef, chicken, and pork cook slowly and fall off the bone. The sauce has a slight kick, and the homemade french fries are fabulous. ⊠ *250 Jordan Rd., No. 9,* ☎ *520/282–6533. No credit cards.*

$ ✕ **Tamale Mama's.** The best Mexican food in Sedona is found in this tiny takeout place with two picnic tables out front. Homemade tamales are the specialty, but chile verde and enchiladas are also good. Everything here is lard-free. ⊠ *1595 W. Hwy. 89A,* ☎ *520/204–1744. No credit cards. Closed Sun.*

$$$$ ✕⊞ **Enchantment Resort.** Designed as a tennis resort, Enchantment does
★ indeed have excellent sports facilities, but it's the serene Boynton Canyon setting that makes this place unique. Southwest-style rooms and suites nestle in casitas; haciendas with kitchens have one or two bedrooms. Many accommodations have beehive fireplaces or balconies, and all have superb views. Fresh-squeezed orange juice and a newspaper greet guests each morning, along with a listing of the upcoming day's events and offerings. The Yavapai Room serves excellent Continental and southwestern cuisine. Uqualla, the resort's Havasupai Indian concierge, can direct you to the best places in the canyon to hike or bicycle. ⊠ *525 Boynton Canyon Rd., 86336,* ☎ *520/ 282–2900 or 800/826–4180,* ℻ *520/282–9249. 107 rooms, 115 suites. Restaurant, bar, kitchenettes, 4 outdoor pools, 12 tennis courts, aerobics, croquet, health club, hiking, mountain bikes, pro shop, children's programs. AE, D, MC, V.*

$$$–$$$$ ✕⊞ **L'Auberge de Sedona Resort.** This tri-level resort consists of a central lodge building; a motel-style structure called The Orchards reached by means of a "hillovator"; and—the major attraction—cabins in a wooded setting along Oak Creek. Phoenix couples flock to these country-French hideaways and dine in the hotel's French restaurant, one of the most romantic eateries in Arizona. The six-course prix-fixe dinner runs $60—a bit steep even for Sedona—but it comes with a view of Oak Creek; jacket and reservations are required. ⊠ *L'Auberge La., Box B, 86336,* ☎ *520/282–1661 or 800/272–6777,* ℻ *520/282–*

2885. 69 rooms, 30 cottages. 2 restaurants, pool, hot tub. AE, D, DC, MC, V.

$$$ ✕🏨 **Garland's Oak Creek Lodge.** In the heart of Oak Creek Canyon, this 1930s lodge owned by Gary and Mary Garland has 16 comfortably furnished cabins, some including fireplaces and pullout beds for extra guests. At an elevation of 5,000 ft, this 17-acre spread has its own apple orchard, and accommodations look out over the rugged cliffs of the canyon or the creek. Excellent breakfasts and dinners are included in the room price, along with afternoon tea. Garland's is often booked solid a year in advance—it's open only from April 1 to November 15—but it's worth a call to check for vacancies. ✉ *Hwy. 89A, 8 mi north of Sedona, Box 152, 86339,* ☎ *520/282–3343. 16 cabins with bath. Restaurant, tennis court, croquet, volleyball, fishing. MAP. MC, V.*

$$$–$$$$ 🏨 **Los Abrigados.** This place sparkles at Christmas, when more than a million tiny lights illuminate the grounds, but it's a dazzler year-round. All the suites, attractively decorated in earth tones, have microwaves, refrigerators, coffeemakers, and two TVs; some have private whirlpool tubs and fireplaces. A state-of-the-art health club, including a luxurious spa, will help you burn off any calories picked up at Joey Bistro, the resort's southern Italian restaurant. Another eatery, Steak & Sticks, has a billiards lounge. If you're interested in something more rustic (and less expensive) ask about the affiliated Lomacasi Cottages, arrayed along the banks of Oak Creek. ✉ *160 Portal La., 86336,* ☎ *520/282–1777 or 800/521–3131,* 𝙁𝘼𝙓 *520/282–2614. 175 suites. 3 restaurants, bar, grill, 2 pools, 2 tennis courts, basketball, health club, volleyball, baby-sitting, children's programs. AE, D, DC, MC, V.*

$$$ 🏨 **Alma de Sedona.** One of Sedona's newest and most enchanting accommodations, this family operation run by Lynn McCarroll is bound to attract attention. The large rooms have spectacular views and ultracomfortable beds. Decor is understated, elegant, and inviting. When the inn was designed two years ago by McCarroll and her husband, Ron, they told their architect that their top priorities were views and privacy; they've achieved both unequivocally. ✉ *50 Hozoni Dr., 86336,* ☎ *520/282–2737 or 800/923–2282,* 𝙁𝘼𝙓 *520/203–4141. 12 rooms (1 handicapped accessible). Breakfast room, heated pool, meeting room. AE, MC, V.*

$$–$$$$ 🏨 **Briar Patch Inn.** Set in a verdant canyon with a rushing creek, this ★ bed-and-breakfast has wood cabins (in Native American and Mexican styles), some with decks overlooking Oak Creek. On summer mornings you can sit outside and enjoy home-baked breads and fresh egg dishes while listening to live classical music. New Age and crafts workshops are sometimes held on the premises. Winter is equally beautiful; request a cabin with a fireplace and wake to see icicles hanging from the trees. If you're lucky, the resident shih tzu, Brittany, will greet you. ✉ *3190 N. Hwy. 89A, 86336,* ☎ *520/282–2342,* 𝙁𝘼𝙓 *520/ 282–2399. 13 two-person cabins, 4 four-person cabins. Kitchenettes, massage, fishing, library, meeting room. Full breakfast. MC, V.*

$$–$$$$ 🏨 **Graham Inn and Adobe Village.** The attractive rooms at this inn ✳ ★ south of Sedona in the Village of Oak Creek have TVs with VCRs (there's a good video library), and some have Jacuzzi tubs and balconies that look out onto the red rocks. A few rooms in the main house have been recently remodeled. On the lot next door are four large casitas: one done in vibrant Taos style and another, Lonesome Dove, that evokes the Wild West. All the casitas have fireplaces that open into both the sitting area and the bathroom, and two-person Jacuzzi tubs. What makes this place special, though, is the impeccable yet casual service. Carol and Roger Redenbaugh haven't overlooked a single detail. ✉ *150 Canyon Circle Dr., Oak Creek 86351,* ☎ *520/284–1425 or 800/228–*

1425, FAX 520/284–0767. 4 rooms with bath, 2 suites, 4 casitas. Kitch-enettes, outdoor pool, hot tub, library. Full breakfast. D, MC, V.

$$-$$$ ☒ **Apple Orchard Inn.** Within walking distance of uptown Sedona, nes-tled among pine and juniper trees, Apple Orchard Inn is a newly re-modeled B&B worth considering. Each room has a different theme, and the inn boasts a personal guide to the area, available on request. The massage room is an especially nice feature. ☒ *656 Jordan Rd., 86336,* ☎ *520/282–5328 or 800/663–6968,* FAX *520/204–0044. 7 rooms. Breakfast room, outdoor pool. AE, MC, V.*

$$-$$$ ☒ **Casa Sedona.** Amid all the modern amenities—whirlpool bathtubs for two, air-conditioning and heating units—commune with nature at this appealing spot designed by a protégé of Frank Lloyd Wright. A large redwood deck where breakfast is served has stunning red-rock views. Accommodations have a Southwest decor, but there's one sa-fari-style room and another with a cowboy motif. All have refrigera-tors and gas fireplaces and the newest suite has a full kitchen. ☒ *55 Hozoni Dr., 86336,* ☎ *520/282–2938 or 800/525–3756,* FAX *520/282–2259. 16 rooms. Outdoor hot tub. Full breakfast. MC, V.*

$$-$$$ ☒ **Lodge at Sedona.** A first-class operation—including a professional
★ chef who prepares breakfast and afternoon hors d'oeuvres—the Lodge still manages to feel intimate and friendly. Rooms in this rambling wood-and-stone house run from romantic Renaissance to cowboy kitsch; some have fireplaces, redwood decks, or hot tubs, and one has a gentle res-ident ghost. They've recently added remote temperature control in all the rooms. Of the five public areas where guests can mingle, perhaps the best is the lace-curtained breakfast nook, shaded by trees and look-ing out onto the red rocks in the distance. For solitude, walk the seven-path classical labyrinth (made of local rock) outside. ☒ *125 Kallof Pl., 86336,* ☎ *520/204–1942 or 800/619–4467,* FAX *520/204–2128. 14 rooms with bath, 3 suites. Shop, library, meeting room. Full breakfast. D, MC, V.*

$$ ☒ **Wishing Well.** It's less than a mile from Uptown Sedona, but this
★ bed-and-breakfast on a plateau at the mouth of Oak Creek Canyon will make you forget there's a town nearby. All the rooms have romantic views of Cathedral Rock; one has a private outdoor hot tub. A hiking trail behind the house once served as a cattle route for the area's Na-tive American inhabitants. Hosts Valda and Esper Esau make you feel welcome while respecting your privacy. Breakfast is served on fine china in your room. ☒ *995 N. Hwy. 89A, 86336,* ☎ *520/282–4914 or 800/728–9474,* FAX *520/204–9766. 4 rooms. Continental breakfast. MC, V.*

$-$$ ☒ **Sky Ranch Lodge.** There may be no better vantage point in town from which to view Sedona's red-rock canyons than the private patios and balconies at Sky Ranch Lodge, near the top of Airport Mesa. Some rooms have stone fireplaces and some have kitchenettes; a few are a bit worn, but all are very clean. Paths on the grounds wind around foun-tains and, in summer, through colorful flower gardens. This is an excellent value, primarily because of the views. ☒ *Airport Rd., 86339,* ☎ *520/282–6400,* FAX *520/282–7682. 92 rooms, 2 cottages. Pool. MC, V.*

Nightlife and the Arts

Nightlife in Sedona tends to be fairly sedate. On high-season weekends, there's usually live music at the **Enchantment Resort** and **Shugrue's Hill-side** (☞ Dining and Lodging, *above*). You can find someone playing year-round in nearby Oak Creek at **Irene's** (☒ 6466 AZ 179, ☎ 520/284–2240) and the **Bell Rock Inn** (☒ 6246 AZ 179, ☎ 520/282–4161). The offerings vary from jazz to rock and pop; in all cases, call ahead. The closest you'll come to a rollicking cowboy bar is **Rainbow's End** (☒ 3235 W. Hwy. 89A, ☎ 520/282–1593), a steak house with a large dance floor and country-and-western bands on weekends.

Find out about cultural events in Sedona at the **Book Loft** (✉ 175 AZ 179, just south of the "Y," ☎ 520/282–5173), which often hosts poetry readings, theatrical readings, book signings, and lectures. The Sedona **Jazz on the Rocks Festival** (☎ 520/282–1985), held every September, always attracts a sellout crowd that fills the town to capacity. The **Sedona Arts Center** (✉ N. Hwy. 89A and Art Barn Rd., ☎ 520/282–3809) sponsors events ranging from classical concerts to plays; there's an innovative and growing film festival every March. The **Sedona Heritage Day Festival** (☎ 520/282–7038), a family-oriented event in early October, includes pioneer storytellers, square-dance exhibitions, music, and a barbecue.

Outdoor Activities and Sports

CAMPING

For information on the six **forest-service campgrounds** in the Sedona–Oak Creek Canyon area, call 520/282–4119.

GOLF

The **Beaver Creek Golf Resort** (✉ Montezuma Ave. and Lakeshore Dr., 20 mi from Sedona off I–17, ☎ 520/567–4487) is a championship par-71 course. The **Oak Creek Country Club** (✉ 690 Bell Rock Blvd., ☎ 520/284–1660) is a good semiprivate option. The 18-hole **Sedona Golf Resort** (✉ 7260 AZ 179, Oak Creek, ☎ 520/284–9355) was designed by Gary Panks to take advantage of the many changes in elevation and scenery. The 10th hole, said to be the most photographed hole in all of Arizona, takes in a sweeping view of the Sedona Valley's red rocks.

HIKING

For free detailed maps and hiking advice, contact the rangers at the **Sedona Ranger District Office** (✉ 250 Brewer Rd., 86339, ☎ 520/282–4119), which is open Monday through Friday 7:30–4:30 and Saturday 7:30–4. Ask here or at your hotel for directions to trailheads for Doe's Mountain (an easy ascent, with many switchbacks), Loy Canyon, Devil's Kitchen, and Long Canyon.

Among the forest-service paths you can hike in the Oak Creek Canyon is the popular **West Fork Trail.** A walk through the woods and a dip in the stream make a great summer combination. You'll find the trailhead about 3 mi north of Slide Rock State Park.

HORSEBACK RIDING

El Rojo Grande Ranch & Stables (✉ 7 mi west of Uptown Sedona on Hwy. 89A, ☎ 520/282–1898 or 800/362–2692), a 143-acre equestrian center, offers stagecoach excursions, trail rides, and lessons. Among the equine tour options at **Trail Horse Adventures** (✉ 5 J La., Lower Red Rock Loop Rd., West Sedona, ☎ 520/282–7252) are a midday picnic and an Oak Creek swim and a full-moon ride with a campfire cookout.

Shopping

Many stores in what is known as the Uptown area, running along U.S. 89A to the east of its intersection with AZ 179, cater to the tour-bus trade. Exceptions include **Native & Nature** (✉ 248 N. Hwy. 89A, ☎ 520/282–7870), outstanding for its regional books and Southwest artifacts. **Looking West** (✉ 242 N. Hwy. 89A, ☎ 520/282–4877) sells the spiffiest cowgirl-style getups in town. Check out **Robert Shields Design** (✉ Sacajawea Plaza, 301 N. Hwy. 89A, ☎ 520/204–9253) for colorful clay snakes and unusual silver jewelry (and yes, it's the same Shields who used to perform with Yarnell).

For upscale shopping, **Tlaquepaque** (⊠ AZ 179, just south of the "Y," ☎ 520/282–4838) gathers together more than 100 artisans, many of them painters and sculptors. The complex of red-tile-roof buildings arranged around a series of courtyards shares its name and architectural style with a crafts village just outside Guadalajara. It's a lovely place to browse, but prices tend to be high; locals joke that it's pronounced "to-lock-your-pocket." A good bet for southwestern art is **El Prado Gallery by the Creek** (⊠ No. 101, Bldg. E, ☎ 520/282–7390). **Estebans** (⊠ No. 103, Bldg. B, ☎ 520/282–4686) focuses on ceramics and Native American crafts. **Isadora** (⊠ No. 120, Bldg. A, ☎ 520/282–6232) has beautiful handwoven jackets and shawls. **Kuivato** (⊠ No. 122, Bldg. B, ☎ 520/282–1212) carries gorgeous glassware.

At the junction of AZ 179 and Schnebly Hill Road, a small strip of shops includes **Garland's Navajo Rugs** (⊠ 411 AZ 179, ☎ 520/282–4070), with its dazzling collection of new and antique carpets, as well as Native American katsina dolls, pottery, and baskets. In the same building **Sedona Pottery** (⊠ 411 AZ 179, ☎ 520/282–1192) sells unusual pieces, including flower-arranging bowls, egg separators, and life-size ceramic statues by shop owner Mary Margaret Sather.

The **Hozho Center** (⊠ 431 AZ 179, ☎ 520/204–2257) is a small, upscale complex in a beige Santa Fe–style building. **Lanning Gallery** (☎ 520/282–6865) sells attractive southwestern art and jewelry. **James Ratliff Gallery** (☎ 520/282–1404) has fun and functional pieces by not-yet-established artists. Drive a minute or two south of the Hozho Center on AZ 179 and you'll come to the **Hillside Courtyard & Marketplace** (⊠ 671 AZ 179, ☎ 520/282–4500). Among Hillside's 23 shops and galleries, the **Clay Pigeon** (☎ 520/282–2845) carries boldly designed dishes and sculptures with a Western accent.

West Sedona, the more residential area that stretches west of the "Y" along U.S. 89A, doesn't have such concentrated areas of shops as Uptown and AZ 179, but it's worth a trip over to **Artisans Galleria** (⊠ 1420 W. Hwy. 89A, ☎ 520/284–0077), which showcases the output of more than 100 artists and craftspeople.

Inveterate bargain hunters will want to head south on AZ 179 2 mi past Chapel of the Holy Cross to the village of Oak Creek. At the **Oak Creek Factory Outlets** (⊠ 6601 S. AZ 179, ☎ 520/284–2150) are such stores as Corning/Revere, Mikasa, Anne Klein, Bass, Jones New York, and Van Heusen.

FLAGSTAFF

146 mi northwest of Phoenix, 27 mi north of Sedona via Oak Creek Canyon.

Few visitors slow down long enough to explore Flagstaff, a town of 54,000, known locally as "Flag." Most stop only to spend the night at one of the town's many motels before making the last leg of the trip to the Grand Canyon, 80 mi north. But the city, set against a lovely backdrop of pine forests and the snowcapped San Francisco Peaks, retains a frontier flavor downtown. Flag makes a good base for day trips to Native American ruins and the Navajo and Hopi reservations, as well as to the Petrified Forest National Park and the Painted Desert (☞ Chapter 5).

Flagstaff has more fast-food outlets per permanent resident than most cities, no doubt because of the incredible demand for it: Two major interstate highways crisscross the town; thousands of tourists drive through; thousands of students attending Northern Arizona University reside here; and many Native Americans come in from nearby reservations. During the summer, Phoenix residents head here, seeking relief from the desert heat. At any time of the year, temperatures in Flagstaff are about 20°F cooler than in Phoenix.

Phoenicians also come to Flagstaff in winter to ski at the small Arizona Snowbowl, about 15 mi northeast of town among the San Francisco Peaks. Accommodation rates are low at this time of year, making winter visits an excellent option for downhill and cross-country enthusiasts. Flagstaff has many accommodations (though no major hotels or resorts), but you should make reservations, especially during the summer.

Exploring Flagstaff

A Good Tour

Start your exploration of Flagstaff at the restored **Santa Fe Depot** on Route 66, still a functioning train station and also a visitor center. Drive east (right) from here to reach the raucous **Museum Club** ⑭; head west to reach the **Lowell Observatory** ⑮. To the southwest, Route 66 branches off into Milton Road, which will take you to a turnoff for **Riordon State Historic Park** ⑯ and, a little farther to the south, one for the **Northern Arizona University Observatory** ⑰. Directly across Route 66 to the north is the **Historic Downtown District** ⑱. After walking around here, drive north on Humphreys Street, a major downtown thoroughfare; about a mile after it becomes Fort Valley Road, you'll reach Fort Valley Park, home to the **Pioneer Museum** ⑲. Continue north for just a few minutes on Fort Valley Road to reach the **Museum of Northern Arizona** ⑳. Five miles farther along the same road is the turnoff for **Arizona Snowbowl** ㉑.

TIMING

You can see almost all of Flagstaff's attractions in a single day if you can visit the Lowell Observatory or the Northern Arizona University Observatory in the evening—which is also when the Museum Club is best experienced. Consult the schedule of tour times if you want to visit the Riordon State Historic Park. Plan on devoting at least an hour to the excellent Museum of Northern Arizona. The Historic Railroad District is a good place to have lunch. If you're a skier, you might be spending a good part of a winter's day at Arizona Snowbowl; in summer, allot a couple of hours to the skyride and scenic trails at the top.

Sights to See

㉑ **Arizona Snowbowl.** One of Flagstaff's most popular winter attractions (☞ Skiing *and* Snowboarding *in* Outdoor Activities and Sports, *below*) also lures patrons in the summer, when the Agassi ski lift, which climbs to a height of 11,500 ft in 25 minutes, doubles as a skyride through the Coconino National Forest. From this vantage point, you can see up to 70 mi; views include the North Rim of the Grand Canyon. There's a lodge nearby with a restaurant and bar. ✉ *U.S. 180 to Snowbowl Rd., then 7 mi to skyride entrance,* ☎ *520/779–1951.* ☞ *$9.* ☉ *Skyride operates mid-June–Labor Day, daily 10–4; Labor Day–mid-Oct., Fri.–Sun. only (weather permitting) 10–4.*

⑱ **Historic Downtown District.** Flagstaff downtown recently underwent a major restoration. Some excellent examples of late Victorian, Tudor Revival, and early art deco architecture in this district give a feel for life in this former logging and railroad town. A walking-tour map of the area is available at the visitor center in the Tudor Revival–style **Santa Fe Depot** (✉ 1 E. Rte. 66), an excellent place to begin sightseeing.

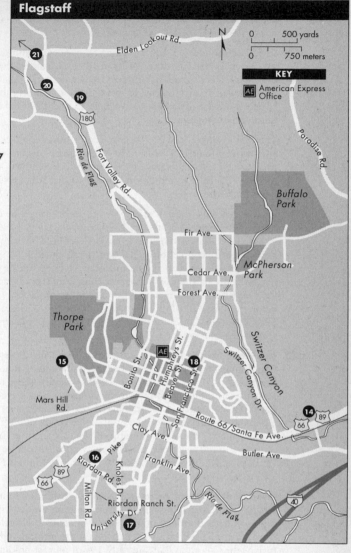

Highlights include the 1927 **Hotel Monte Vista** (⊠ 100 N. San Francisco St.), built after a community drive raised $200,000 in 60 days. The 1888 **Babbitt Brothers Building** (⊠ 12 E. Aspen Ave.) was constructed as a building-supply store and then turned into a department store by David Babbitt, the mastermind of the Babbitt empire (one of Flagstaff's wealthiest founding families; former Arizona governor and current Secretary of the Interior Bruce Babbitt is the latest member of the family to wield power and influence). Most of the area's first businesses were saloons catering to railroad construction workers, which was the case with the 1888 **Vail Building** (⊠ 1 N. San Francisco St.), a brick art deco–influenced structure covered with stucco in 1939. It now houses the Sweet Life ice-cream parlor.

The town's most interesting shops are concentrated here, and there are a couple of brewpubs and some spots where you can grab a quick bite. Students, skiers, new and aging hippies, and just about everyone else who likes good coffee, jams into **Macy's** (⊠ 14 S. Beaver St., ☎ 520/

774–2243) for the best cup in town. The **Black Bean** (✉ 12 E. Rte.
66, ☏ 520/779–9905) is the place for do-it-yourself burritos, as healthy
or as guacamole-smothered as you like.

⑮ Lowell Observatory. Boston businessman, author, and scientist Perci-
val Lowell founded the observatory in 1894 and studied the planet Mars
from here. His predictions of the existence of a ninth planet led to the
discovery of Pluto at Lowell in 1930 by Clyde Tombaugh. V. M.
Slipher's observations here between 1912 and 1920 led to the theory
of the expanding universe.

The 6,500-square-ft Steele Visitor Center hosts exhibits and lectures
and has a gift shop; a "Tools of the Astronomer" display explains what
professional stargazers do. Several interactive exhibits—among them
the Pluto Walk, a scaled-down version of our solar system—will interest children.

On some evenings the public is invited to peer through the 24-inch Clark
telescope, which celebrated its 100th anniversary in 1996, or through
a more up-to-date 16-inch reflecting telescope. Four viewings a week
are offered from June through August; call ahead for a schedule. The
observatory dome is open and unheated, so dress for the outdoors. To
reach the observatory, which is less than 2 mi from downtown, drive
west on Route 66, which resumes its former name, Santa Fe Avenue,
before it merges into Mars Hill Road. ✉ *1400 W. Mars Hill Rd.,* ☏
520/774–2096. ✆ *$3.* ☉ *Visitor center and night viewing hrs change
seasonally; call ahead.*

⑭ Museum Club. For real Route 66 color, don't miss this local institution, fondly known as the Zoo because the building housed an extensive taxidermy collection in the 1930s. Luckily, most of the stuffed
animals—including such bizarre specimens as a one-eyed sheep—are
gone, but some owls still perch above the dance floor of what is now
a popular country-and-western club. Even if you don't like crowds or
country music, it's worth coming to see this gigantic log cabin constructed around five trees; the entryway consists of a huge wishbone-
shape pine. ✉ *3404 E. Rte. 66,* ☏ *520/526–9434.* ✆ *Free.* ☉ *Sun.–
Thurs. noon–1 AM, Fri. and Sat. noon–3 AM.*

★ ⑳ Museum of Northern Arizona. It's worth visiting the museum for its
setting alone, a striking native-stone building shaded with trees. But
the institution, founded in 1928, is also respected worldwide for its
research and its collections centering on the natural and cultural history of the Colorado Plateau; only 1% of its vast holdings on the archaeology, ethnology, geology, biology, and fine arts of the region is
on display at any given time. Among the permanent exhibitions are an
extensive collection of Navajo rugs and an authentic Hopi kiva (men's
ceremonial chamber).

A gallery devoted to area geology is usually a hit with children: It includes a life-size model dilophosaurus, a carnivorous dinosaur that once
roamed northern Arizona. The Harvey W. Branigar Hall hosts a fascinating 27-minute film, *Sacred Lands of the Southwest.* Outdoors, a
life-zone exhibit shows the changing vegetation from the bottom of the
Grand Canyon to the highest peak in Flagstaff. A nature trail, open
only in summer, heads down across a small stream into a canyon and
up into an aspen grove.

In summer the museum hosts exhibits and the works of Native American artists (☞ Nightlife and the Arts, *below*), whose wares are also
sold in the museum gift shop. The museum's education department sponsors excellent tours of the area and as far away as New Mexico and

Utah (☞ Guided Tours *in* North-Central Arizona A to Z, *below*). ✉ *3101 N. Fort Valley Rd.,* ☎ *520/774–5213.* ✇ *$5.* ☉ *Daily 9–5.*

⑰ Northern Arizona University Observatory. This observatory, with its 24-inch telescope, was built in 1952 by Dr. Arthur Adel, a scientist at Lowell Observatory until he joined the college faculty as a professor of mathematics. His work on infrared astronomy pioneered research into molecules that absorb light passing through the earth's atmosphere. Today's studies of our planet's shrinking ozone layer rely on some of Dr. Adel's early work. Visitors to the observatory—which houses one of the largest telescopes that the public is allowed to move and manipulate—are usually hosted by friendly students and faculty members of the university's Department of Physics and Astronomy.

Public viewings take place every clear Friday night from 7:30 to 10. ✉ *Bldg. 47, Northern Arizona Campus Observatory, Dept. of Physics and Astronomy, S. San Francisco St. just north of the Walkup Skydome,* ☎ *520/523–8121 (weekdays); 520/523–7170 (Friday nights).* ✇ *Free; donations appreciated.*

⑲ Pioneer Museum. Operated by the Arizona Historical Society in a volcanic-rock building constructed in 1908—Coconino County's first hospital for the poor—the museum includes among its displays one of the depressingly small nurses' rooms, an old iron lung, and a reconstructed doctor's office. But most of the exhibits touch on more cheerful aspects of Flagstaff history—for example, road signs and children's toys. The museum hosts a folk-crafts festival on the Fourth of July, complete with blacksmiths, weavers, spinners, quilters, and candle makers at work. Their crafts, and those of other local artisans, are sold in the museum's gift shop, a tiny space filled with teddy bears, dolls, hand-dipped candles, and the like. The museum is part of the Fort Valley Park complex, in a wooded residential section at the northwest end of town. ✉ *2340 N. Fort Valley Rd.,* ☎ *520/774–6272.* ✇ *$1 suggested donation per individual, $3 per family.* ☉ *Mon.–Sat. 9–5.*

★ ⑯ Riordan State Historic Park. This must-see artifact of Flagstaff's logging heyday is near Northern Arizona University. Its centerpiece is a mansion built in 1904 for Michael and Timothy Riordan, lumber-baron brothers who married two sisters. The 13,300-square-ft, 40-room log-and-stone structure—designed by Charles Whittlesley, who was also responsible for the El Tovar Hotel at the Grand Canyon—contains furniture by Gustav Stickley, father of the American Arts and Crafts design movement. Fascinating details abound; one room holds "Paul Bunyan's shoes," a 2-ft-long pair of boots made by Timothy in his workshop. Everything on display is original to the house, half of which was occupied by members of the family until 1986. The mansion may be explored on a guided tour only. ✉ *1300 Riordan Ranch St.,* ☎ *520/ 779–4395.* ✇ *$4.* ☉ *May–Sept., daily 8–5, with tours on the hr 9–4; Oct.–Apr., daily 11–5, with tours noon–4.*

Dining and Lodging

By city ordinance, all restaurants in Flagstaff forbid smoking. Some eateries stay open longer in summer, the time of year when lodging prices are also at their highest.

$$$–$$$$ ✕ **Chez Marc Bistro.** More elegant than a traditional bistro, the kitchen turns out classics like rack of lamb with the same adeptness as more innovative dishes like yellowfin sashimi. Desserts, especially the crème brûlée, are wonderful. ✉ *503 Humphreys St.,* ☎ *520/774–1343. AE, MC, V. Closed Sun. No lunch.*

$$–$$$ ✕ **Cottage Place.** An unexpectedly elegant spot in a town known for
★ heavy food and drive-through service, this cozy restaurant in a 50-year-
old cottage has intimate dining rooms with fresh flowers and candles.
The menu strays only slightly from Continental to include some classic American dishes, such as charbroiled lamb chops. Try the artichoke
chicken breast or chateaubriand for two carved tableside. Dinner includes soup and salad, but save room for Chocolate Decadence and
other desserts. In 1996, the restaurant won the Wine Spectator's Award
of Excellence for its wine list. ⊠ *126 W. Cottage Ave.,* ☎ *520/774–
8431. AE, MC, V. Closed Mon. No lunch.*

$$–$$$ ✕ **Down Under New Zealand Restaurant.** At midday, businesspeople
★ flock to the green-and-white dining room or onto an outdoor terrace
for potato-leek soup with sherry and copious Greek salads. In the evening,
when the lights are dim, couples dine on such dishes as grilled rack of
lamb and Cornish game hen with sun-dried cherry stuffing. The emphasis on New Zealand fish and meat and the availability of good Australian wines by the glass attest to the friendly owners' origins. ⊠ *413
N. San Francisco St.,* ☎ *520/774–6677. AE, MC, V. Closed Sun. No
lunch weekends.*

$$ ✕ **Black Bart's Steakhouse Saloon & Old West Theater.** Fans of the Wild
West—or a cornball version thereof—will enjoy the rollicking atmo-
sphere in this brightly lit barn of a restaurant. A throng of diners fills
a sea of tables beneath the beamed ceilings and mounted animal heads,
drinking out of mason jars and devouring steaks grilled over an open
oak fire. The barbecued chicken is tender and flavorful and the bis-
cuits stick to your ribs, but don't expect to see any vegetables on your
plate unless they're deep-fried. Northern Arizona University music
students entertain while they wait on tables, so don't be surprised if
your server suddenly jumps onstage to belt out a couple of show tunes.
⊠ *2760 E. Butler Ave.,* ☎ *520/779–3142. Reservations not accepted
in summer. AE, MC, V. No lunch.*

$$ ✕ **Sakura Restaurant.** The excellent fish at this Japanese restaurant is
flown in every other day from the West Coast, but if sushi doesn't en-
tice you, dine at a large grill table. Even if you haven't set foot in a
Benihana in years, you'll probably enjoy well-seasoned, large portions
of steak or seafood with vegetables being flipped in front of you. ⊠
1175 Rte. 66, ☎ *520/773–9118. AE, D, DC, MC, V. No lunch Sun.*

$–$$ ✕ **Beaver Street Brewery.** Popular among the wood-fired pizzas here
is the Enchanted Forest, with Brie, artichoke pesto, Portobello mushrooms, roasted red pepper, and spinach. Whichever pie you order, expect serious amounts of garlic. Sandwiches, such as the southwestern
chicken with three types of cheese, come with a hefty portion of tasty
fries. You won't regret ordering one of the down-home desserts, like
the supergooey chocolate bread pudding. Among the excellent micro-
brews, the raspberry ale is a local favorite. An outdoor beer garden
opens up in summer. ⊠ *11 S. Beaver St.,* ☎ *520/779–0079. AE, D,
DC, MC, V.*

$–$$ ✕ **Buster's Restaurant.** At lunchtime, families and students from nearby
Northern Arizona University settle into the comfortable booths and
enjoy fresh seafood, homemade soups, salads, giant burgers, and
mesquite-grilled steaks. Try the *lahvosh* appetizer—a giant cracker
heaped with toppings ranging from smoked salmon to mushrooms—
or the Caesar salad with grilled Cajun chicken. At night, upscale single professionals and skiers crowd the bar and work through its
impressive beer selection. ⊠ *1800 S. Milton Rd.,* ☎ *520/774–5155.
AE, D, DC, MC, V.*

$–$$ ✕ **Pasto.** This downtown Italian restaurant, comprising two intimate
dining rooms in adjacent historic buildings, is popular with a young
crowd for good food at reasonable prices. Such southern Italian stan-

dards as lasagna and spaghetti with meatballs appear on the menu along with more innovative fare, like artichoke orzo and salmon Caesar salad. A courtyard in the back, tucked away among higher buildings, has a romantic urban feel. ⊠ *19 E. Aspen St.,* ☎ *520/779–1937. MC, V. No lunch except in high season.*

$ ✕ **Café Espress.** The menu is largely vegetarian at this natural-food restaurant. Stir-fried vegetables, pasta dishes, Mediterranean salads, tempeh burgers, pita pizzas, fish or chicken specials, and wonderful baked goods made on the premises all come at prices that will make you feel good, too. The atmosphere is gallery hip (the work of local artists hangs on the walls) but friendly, and it's open for breakfast every day at 7. ⊠ *16 N. San Francisco St.,* ☎ *520/774–0541. MC, V.*

$ ✕ **Café Olé.** Chili-pepper strings, a neon cactus, and a pastel mural make for an upbeat atmosphere at this little family-run restaurant, popular with local politicos and university professors. Vegetarian green-chili-and-cheese tamales and the best guacamole in town are among the specialties here, and you can sample freshly prepared Mexican dishes in well-priced combination plates. ⊠ *119 San Francisco St.,* ☎ *520/774–8272. Reservations not accepted. No credit cards. Closed weekends in winter, Sun. in summer.*

$ ✕ **Dara Thai.** East meets West at this unusual Route 66 eatery, where one dining area is done up in semiformal Asian style and the other resembles a cowboy diner. But the food in both is consistently Thai and consistently good. Many dishes are prepared with tofu instead of meat or poultry, but strict vegetarians should be aware that fish oil is often used as a base. Don't pass up the homemade coconut ice cream served with chopped peanuts. ⊠ *Western Hills Motel, 1580 Rte. 66,* ☎ *520/774–8390 or 520/774–0047. AE, D, DC, MC, V. No lunch Sun.*

$ ✕ **Hunan West Restaurant.** The hands-down local favorite for Chinese food, this west-side restaurant has far more atmosphere than its strip-mall setting would suggest: An imposing dragon decorates the back wall, and white cloths dress the tables. The friendly staff will guide you through a menu of many Hunan specialties along with familiar Cantonese fare. The hot-and-sour soup is super, as is the "eight-treasure" shrimp and chicken. You can order anything in a "spicy," "not spicy," or reduced-fat version. ⊠ *University Plaza Shopping Center, 1302 S. Plaza Way,* ☎ *520/779–2229. AE, D, DC, MC, V. Closed Mon.*

$ ✕ **Salsa Brava.** This cheerful Mexican restaurant, with light-wood booths and colorful designs, eschews heavy Sonoran-style fare in favor of the grilled dishes found in Guadalajara. The fish tacos are particularly good, and this place has the only salsa bar in town. On weekends, come for a huevos rancheros breakfast. ⊠ *1800 S. Milton Rd.,* ☎ *520/774–1083. AE, MC, V.*

$ ✕ **Tea and Sympathy.** How civilized. Flagstaff now has a shop where you can sink down in an overstuffed chair and enjoy an assortment of tea services—a breakfast tea with granola and fruit, or a Sand and Sea tea, with smoked salmon pâté, fruit, and dessert. There's a huge assortment of tea; if you like what you've tried, you can buy it loose. It's open until 6 every day. ⊠ *409 N. Humphreys St.,* ☎ *520/779–2171. AE, D, MC, V.*

$$–$$$ 🏠 **Comfi Cottages of Flagstaff.** Ideal for people who dislike the coldness of motels but don't enjoy breakfasting with strangers in a traditional B&B environment, these appealing individual cottages come well stocked with breakfast fixings. Most of the conveniences of home are provided, plus picnic tables, bicycles, and barbecue grills. Choose from a variety of styles (English country or southwestern, for example) and sizes in a residential neighborhood less than ½ mi from downtown. If you're traveling with family or with a group of friends, you can't beat the convenience and price. ⊠ *1612 N. Aztec, 86001,* ☎ *520/774–0731*

or 888/774–0731. One 1-bedroom cottage, three 2-bedroom cottages, two 3-bedroom cottages. Bicycles. Full breakfast. D, MC, V.

$$ 🔲 **Inn at Four Ten.** An inviting alternative to the chain motels in
★ Flagstaff, this bed-and-breakfast has a quiet but convenient downtown setting. All the accommodations in the beautifully restored 1907 residence are suites with private baths. Some have private entrances, fireplaces, or hot tubs; all have refrigerators and coffeemakers. Monet's Garden is a recently remodeled room, a lovely Jacuzzi suite with fireplace. The breakfasts are delicious and healthful; in the afternoon fresh-baked cookies are served. The innkeepers, Sally and Howard Krueger, offer concierge service akin to that of small hotels. ✉ *410 N. Leroux St., 86001,* ☎ *520/774–0088 or 800/774–2008,* FAX *520/774– 6354. 9 suites. Refrigerators. Full breakfast. MC, V.*

$$ 🔲 **Little America of Flagstaff.** The biggest hotel in town is a deservedly
★ popular place. It's far from the roar of the trains, the grounds are surrounded by evergreen forests, and it's one of the few places in Flagstaff with room service. Plush rooms have brass chandeliers, comfortable sitting areas with French provincial–style furniture, phones in bathrooms, large stereo TVs, and small refrigerators. Other pluses are courtesy van service to the airport and Amtrak station and a 24-hour gift shop with great southwestern stuff. ✉ *2515 E. Butler Ave., 86004,* ☎ *520/779– 2741 or 800/352–4386,* FAX *520/779–7983. 248 rooms. Restaurant, bar, coffee shop, kitchenettes, refrigerators, room service, outdoor pool, exercise room, hiking, playground, coin laundry, airport shuttle. AE, D, DC, MC, V.*

$$ 🔲 **Radisson Woodlands Plaza Hotel.** This hotel is near downtown and major outbound roads; rooms are large, comfortable, and furnished in southwestern pastels. Sakura (☞ *above*) is one of the two good restaurants on the premises. ✉ *1175 W. Rte. 66, 86001,* ☎ *520/773–8888 or 800/333–3333,* FAX *520/773–0597. 183 rooms. Bar, pool, sauna, spa, steam room, exercise room. AE, D, DC, MC, V.*

$–$$ 🔲 **Birch Tree Inn.** This historic home in a tree-filled neighborhood near downtown is nicely appointed with antiques. The atmosphere is relaxed, in part because the hosts (two friendly couples who trade off innkeeping stints) enjoy chatting with their guests. The billiard table adjoining the living room gets visitors talking to each other, too. You'll start your day well fueled for sightseeing: The morning meal might consist of a cheese, sausage, and potato casserole accompanied by fresh fruit and banana bread made on the premises. ✉ *824 W. Birch Ave., 86001,* ☎ *520/774–1042 or 800/645–5805. 3 rooms with private bath, 2 rooms with shared bath. Outdoor hot tub. Full breakfast. AE, MC, V.*

$–$$ 🔲 **Hotel Monte Vista.** Over the years many Hollywood stars have stayed at this historic downtown hotel built in 1926; some of the guest rooms bear their names. The restored southwestern-deco lobby, with its shoe-shine stand and curved archways, is appealing, and rates are low, but rooms and hallways are somewhat dark, and the men buying racing forms who hang out at the front desk make this an iffy choice for female travelers. Bunk-bed rooms at less than $15 per person are available. ✉ *100 N. San Francisco St., 86001,* ☎ *520/779–6971 or 800/545–3068,* FAX *520/779–2904. 48 rooms. Restaurant, 2 bars. AE, D, DC, MC, V.*

$ 🔲 **Jeanette's.** If you prefer the clean lines of 1920s design to Victorian frou-frou, consider staying at stylish Jeannette's. Rooms in this residence on the city's east side are all beautifully appointed with art deco pieces; one room has a private porch, another a fireplace. Details such as handmade soap and fine china at breakfast enhance the time-travel experience, as does owner Jeanette's devotion to antique clothing, which she often dons. ⊠ *3380 E. Lockett Rd., 86004,* ☎ *520/ 527–1912 or 800/752–1912. 4 rooms. Full breakfast. MC, V.*

Nightlife and the Arts

For current information on what's going on in town, pick up the free *Flagstaff Live.*

Flagstaff's large college contingent has plenty of places to gather after dark, most of them in the historic downtown district and most of them charging little or no cover. It's easy to walk from one rowdy spot to the next.

Club Depot (⊠ 26 S. San Francisco St., ☎ 520/773–9550) inspires dancing fools to move to either live or DJ sounds. For live entertainment nightly—everything from bluegrass to jazz and rock—in a low-key atmosphere, try the **Main Street Bar and Grill** (⊠ 14 S. San Francisco St., ☎ 520/774–1519); the food's good, too, so come early for dinner. **The Monsoons** (⊠ 22 E. Rte. 66, ☎ 520/774–7929) books live music, from alternative to world beat. The **Monte Vista Lounge** (⊠ 100 N. San Francisco St., ☎ 520/774–2403) packs them in with nightly live blues, jazz, classic rock, punk, and an open mike on Wednesday. The ground floor of the **Weatherford Hotel** (⊠ 23 N. Leroux St., ☎ 520/779–1919) is home to both **Charly's,** featuring late-night jazz and blues bands, and the **Exchange Pub,** which tends to attract folksy ensembles.

On the east side, the **Museum Club** (⊠ 3404 E. Rte. 66, ☎ 520/526– 9434) is the town's cowboy honky-tonk, offering free dance lessons on Thursday night and good country-and-western bands like Mogollon on the weekends.

Between the **Flagstaff Symphony Orchestra** (☎ 520/774–5107), **Theatrikos Theater Company** (⊠ 11 W. Cherry Ave., ☎ 520/774–1662), and Northern Arizona University's **College of Creative and Performing Arts** (⊠ Ardrey Auditorium, Knoles and Riordon Rds., ☎ 520/523– 5661), there's bound to be something cultural going on in Flagstaff when you visit. This is especially true in summer: During the month of August, the **Flagstaff Festival of the Arts** (☎ 520/774–7750 or 800/266– 7740) fills the air with the sounds of classical-music and pops performances, many by world-renowned artists.

Flagstaff SummerFest, held the first weekend in August (⊠ Fort Tuthill Coconino County Park, S. Hwy. 89A, ☎ 520/774–5130), includes an arts-and-crafts fair. **A Celebration of Native American Art,** featuring exhibits of work by Zuni, Hopi, and Navajo artists, is held at the Museum of Northern Arizona (⊠ 3101 N. Fort Valley Rd., ☎ 520/774– 5211) from late May through September. Flagstaff's observatories help make September's **Festival of Science** (☎ 800/842–7293 for information) a stellar attraction.

Outdoor Activities and Sports

BIKING

A map of the **Urban Trails System,** available at the Flagstaff Visitors Center (⊠ 1 E. Rte. 66, ☎ 520/774–9541 or 800/842–7293), details biking options in the area. From mid-June through mid-October, the **Flagstaff Nordic Center** (☎ 520/779–1951) opens its cross-country trails to mountain bikers, gratis if you bring your own wheels; rentals are also available.

In town you can rent mountain bikes at **Absolute Bikes** (⊠ 18 N. San Francisco St., ☎ 520/779–5969) or **Mountain Sports** (⊠ 1800 S. Milton Rd., ☎ 520/779–5156 or 800/286–5156). **Arizona Mountain Bike Tours** (⊠ Box 816, Flagstaff 86002, ☎ 520/779–4161; 800/277–7985 in AZ) can guide you along the Colorado Plateau or the volcanic craters near Flagstaff.

CAMPING

Contact the **Coconino National Forest** (✉ 2323 Greenlaw La., ☎ 520/527–3600) for information on camping in the area.

GOLF

In addition to many private clubs in the area, golfers will find semiprivate courses, which accept a limited number of nonmembers, as well as public courses. The best club open to the public in the Flagstaff vicinity is the **Elden Hill Golf Course** (✉ 2380 N. Oakmont Dr., ☎ 520/527–7999 for tee times; 520/527–7997 for the pro shop).

HIKING AND ROCK CLIMBING

You can explore Arizona's alpine tundra in the San Francisco Peaks, where more than 80 species of plants grow on the upper elevations. The habitat is fragile, so hikers are asked to stay on established trails (and there are lots of them). The altitude here will make even the hardiest hikers breathe a little harder, so individuals with cardiac or respiratory problems should be cautious of overexertion. The **Humphreys Peak Trail** is 9 mi round-trip, with a vertical climb of 3,843 ft to the summit of Arizona's highest mountain (12,643 ft). Those who don't want a long hike can do just the first mile of the 5-mi-long **Kachina;** completely flat, this route is surrounded by huge stands of aspen and offers fantastic vistas. It's particularly worthwhile in fall, when changing leaves paint the landscape shades of yellow, russet, and amber. You'll find the Humphreys Peak and Kachina trailheads at the Arizona Snowbowl (☞ Skiing, *below*). Others, such as the short but rewarding **Fatmans Loop** on Mt. Eldin, can be accessed in town.

Contact the **Coconino National Forest** (✉ 2323 Greenlaw La., ☎ 520/527–3600), which maintains these and other trails, for details on hiking in the area; it's open Monday–Friday 7:30–4:30. The **Peaks Ranger Station** (✉ 5075 N. U.S. 89, ☎ 520/527–3630) also has excellent hiking and recreational guides.

Flagstaff Mountain Guides (✉ Box 2383, Flagstaff 86003, ☎ 520/635–0145) facilitates peak rock climbing experiences around town or as far away as Sedona. If you'd prefer to hone your skills first, **Vertical Relief Rock Gym** (✉ 205 S. San Francisco St., ☎ 520/556–9909) provides the tallest indoor climbing walls in the Southwest.

HORSEBACK RIDING

The wranglers at **Hitchin' Post Stables** (✉ 4848 Lake Mary Rd., ☎ 520/774–1719) lead rides into Walnut Canyon and operate horseback or horse-drawn wagon rides with sunset barbecues. In winter, they'll take you through Coconino National Forest on a sleigh—bells and all.

SKIING

CROSS-COUNTRY: The **Flagstaff Nordic Center,** owned and operated by Arizona Snowbowl (☞ Downhill, *below*), is 9 mi north of Snowbowl Rd. on U.S. 180. There are 25 mi of well-groomed trails here. Instruction packages and rental combinations are available. The **Mormon Lake Ski Center** (✉ 28 mi southeast of Flagstaff by way of Lake Mary Rd., Mormon Lake, ☎ 520/354–2240), with trails in the Coconino National Forest, is another option. Instruction, equipment rentals, and moonlight tours on full-moon weekends are available.

DOWNHILL: The ski season usually starts in mid-December and ends in mid-April. **Arizona Snowbowl** (✉ 7 mi north of Flagstaff on U.S. 180, ☎ 520/779–1951) has 30 runs (37% beginner, 42% intermediate, and 21% advanced), four chairlifts, and a vertical drop of 2,300 ft. Those who have skied Colorado's Rockies might find Snowbowl disappointing—there are a couple of good bump runs, but it's better for skiers of beginning or moderate ability. Still, it's a fun place to spend the day. The Hart Prairie Lodge has an equipment-rental shop and a SKIwee center for ages four–eight.

All-day adult lift tickets are $35. Half-day discounts are available, and group-lesson packages (including two hours of instruction, an all-day lift ticket, and equipment rental) are a good buy at $47. A kids' program (which includes lunch, progress card, and full supervision 9–3:30) runs $50. Many Flagstaff motels offer **ski packages,** including transportation to Snowbowl; call 800/828–7285 for details. For the current **snow report,** call 520/779–4577.

SNOWBOARDING

Snowboarders share trails with downhill skiers at the **Arizona Snowbowl** (☞ Skiing, *above*) and can rent equipment there; an all-day Snowboard Package (board, boots, all-day lift ticket, and two-hour lesson) runs $60.

SNOWMOBILING

Adult Toyz Center (☎ 520/522–0018) rents snowmobiles and conducts guided tours (including ones by moonlight).

Shopping

Flagstaff's prime shopping area is downtown. Even if you're not looking for anything in particular, it's fun to stroll along San Francisco Street and Route 66.

For fine arts and crafts—everything from ceramics and stained glass to weaving and painting—visit the **Artists Gallery** (✉ 17 N. San Francisco St., ☎ 520/773–0958), a local artists' cooperative. You can pick up sporting-goods items at **Babbitt's Backcountry Outfitters** (✉ 12 E. Aspen Ave., ☎ 520/774–4775). The 20-odd vendors at **Carriage House Antique and Gift Mall** (✉ 413 N. San Francisco St., ☎ 520/774–1337) sell vintage clothing and jewelry, furniture, fine china, and other collectibles. **Four Winds Traders** (✉ 118 W. Rte. 66, ☎ 520/774–1067) has good buys on pawned and new Native American jewelry. **The Kitchen Source** (✉ 112 E. Rte. 66, ☎ 520/779–2302) sells every cooking implement imaginable. Come to **McGaugh's Newsstand** (✉ 24 N. San Francisco St., ☎ 520/774–2131) for international newspapers and books; even some nonsmokers enjoy the aroma of the pipe tobacco sold in back. **Winter Sun Trading Company** (✉ 107 N. San Francisco St., ☎ 520/774–2884) carries medicinal herbs, jewelry, and crafts in a soothing New Age atmosphere. **Zani** (✉ 111-C S. San Francisco St., ☎ 520/774–9409) stocks hip home furnishings and greeting cards in addition to futons.

The gift shop at the **Museum of Northern Arizona** (☞ Sights to See, *above*) carries high-quality jewelry and crafts.

The **Flagstaff Mall** (✉ 4650 N. U.S. 89, ☎ 520/526–4827) is just east of town off I–40's Exit 201. This mall has the greatest number of department and specialty stores in the area, including Dillards, Sears, and JCPenney. There's also a food court and a two-screen cinema.

SIDE TRIPS NEAR FLAGSTAFF

Visitors who head straight out of town for the Grand Canyon often neglect the area north and east of Flagstaff. But a detour has its rewards. If you don't have enough time to do everything, take a quick drive to Walnut Canyon—only about 15 minutes out of town.

East of Flagstaff

★ ㉒ **Walnut Canyon National Monument** consists of a group of cliff-dwelling homes constructed by the Sinagua people, who lived and farmed in and around the canyon starting around AD 700. The more than 300 dwellings here were built between 1080 and 1250 and abandoned, like those at so many other settlements in Arizona and New Mexico, around 1300. The Sinagua traded far and wide with other Native Americans, including people at Wupatki (☞ Side Trip to the San Francisco Volcanic Field, *below*). Even macaw feathers, which would have come from tribes in what is now Mexico, have been excavated in the canyon. The area wasn't explored by Europeans until 1883, when early Flagstaff settlers shamelessly looted the site for pots and "treasure." Woodrow Wilson declared the site a national monument in 1915, which began a 30-year process of stabilizing the ruins.

Walnut Canyon is fascinating, in part because of the opportunity to enter the dwellings and feel ancient life at close range. Some of the Sinagua homes are in near-perfect condition, in spite of all the looting, because of the dry, hot climate and the protection of overhanging cliffs. You can reach them by descending 185 ft on the 1-mi stepped Island Trail, which starts at the visitor center. As you follow the trail, look across the canyon for other dwellings not accessible on the path.

Island Trail takes about an hour to complete at a normal pace. Those with health concerns should opt for the easier ½-mi Rim Trail, which has overlooks from which dwellings, as well as an excavated, reconstructed pit house, can be viewed. Attractive picnic areas dot the grounds and line the roads leading to the park. Guides conduct tours on Wednesday, Saturday, and Sunday from Memorial Day through Labor Day. Visitors are permitted to enter about two dozen ruins. ⊠ *Walnut Canyon Rd., 3 mi south of I–40 Exit 204,* ☎ *520/526–3367.* ☞ *$3 per person.* ⊙ *Daily 9–5; hrs extended during summer.*

㉓ **Meteor Crater,** a natural phenomenon, set in a privately owned park 43 mi east of Flagstaff, is impressive if for no other reason than its sheer size. A hole in the ground 600 ft deep, nearly 1 mi across, and more than 3 mi in circumference, Meteor Crater is large enough to accommodate the Washington Monument or 20 football fields. It was created when a meteorite came hurtling through space at a speed of 43,000 mi per hour and crashed here 49,000 years ago. The area looks so much like the surface of the moon that NASA made it one of the official training sites for the Project Apollo astronauts.

Visitors can't descend into the crater because of the efforts of its owners to maintain its condition—scientists consider this to be the best-preserved crater on earth—but guided rim tours, given every hour on the hour from 9 to 3, give visitors a bird's-eye view of the hole. There's a small snack bar, and rock hounds will enjoy the Rock Shop's raw specimens from the area and jewelry made from native stones. ⊠ *I–40 east of Flagstaff to Exit 233, then 6 mi south on Meteor Crater Rd.,* ☎ *520/289–2362.* ☞ *$8.* ⊙ *May 16–Sept. 14, daily 6–6; Sept. 15–May 15, daily 8–5.*

San Francisco Volcanic Field

The San Francisco Volcanic Field north of Flagstaff encompasses 2,000 square mi of fascinating geological phenomena—ancient volcanoes, cinder cones, and valleys carved by water and ice, and the San Francisco Peaks themselves, some of which soar to almost 13,000 ft—as well as some of the most extensive Native American ruins in the Southwest: Don't miss Sunset Crater and Wupatki. These national monuments can be explored in relative solitude during much of the year. The area is short on services, so fill up on gas and consider taking along a picnic. A good source for hiking and camping information in this area is the **Peaks Ranger Station** (✉ 5075 N. U.S. 89, ☎ 520/526–0866). If you camp, do not pitch your tent in a low-lying area, where dangerous flash floods can literally wipe you out.

★ ㉔ **Sunset Crater Volcano National Monument** lies 19 mi northeast of Flagstaff off U.S. 89. **Sunset Crater,** a cinder cone that rises 1,000 ft, was an active volcano 900 years ago. The final eruption contained iron and sulfur, which gives the rim of the crater its glow and thus its name, Sunset. You can walk around the base, but you can't descend into the huge, fragile cone. If you take the Lava Flow Trail, a half-hour, mile-long, self-guided walk, you'll have a good view of the evidence of the volcano's fiery power: lava formations and holes in the rock where volcanic gases vented to the surface. Three smaller cones to the southeast were formed at the same time and along the same fissure.

If you're interested in hiking a volcano, head to **Lenox Crater,** about 1 mi east of the visitor center, and climb the 280 ft to the top of the cinder cone. Wear closed, sturdy shoes; the cinder is soft and crumbly. From **O'Leary Peak,** 5 mi from the visitor center on Forest Route 545A, great views can be had of the San Francisco Peaks, the Painted Desert, and beyond; the road is unpaved and rutted, however, so it's advisable to take only high-clearance vehicles, especially in winter. In addition, there's a gate, about halfway along the route, which is usually closed. This will mean a steep 2½-mi hike to the top on foot. ✉ *From Flagstaff, take Santa Fe Ave. east to U.S. 89, head north for 17 mi; turn right onto the road marked Sunset Crater and go another 2 mi to the visitor center,* ☎ *520/556–7042.* 🎫 *$3 per person; admission includes Wupatki National Monument and Doney Mountain (☞ below).* ☉ *Daily 8–5; hrs may be extended in summer.*

★ ㉕ Families from the Sinagua and other ancestral Puebloans are believed to have lived together in harmony on the site that is now **Wupatki National Monument,** farming and trading with one another and with those who passed through their "city." The eruption of Sunset Crater may have caused migration to this area—and may have disrupted the settlement more than once around AD 1064. Although there is evidence of earlier habitation, most of the settlers moved here around 1100 and left the pueblo by about 1250. The 2,700 identified sites contain archaeological evidence of Native American settlement.

The site for which the national monument was named, the **Wupatki** (meaning "tall house" in Hopi), was originally three stories high, built above an unexplored system of underground fissures. The structure had almost 100 rooms and an open ball court—evidence in itself of southwestern trade with Mesoamerican tribes for whom ball games were a central ritual. Next to the ball court is a blowhole, a geologic phenomenon in which air is forced upward by underground pressure; scientists speculate that early inhabitants may have attached some spiritual significance to the region's many blowholes.

Other ruins to visit are **Wukoki, Lomaki,** and the **Citadel,** a pueblo on a knoll above a limestone sink. Although the largest remnants of Native American settlements at Wupatki National Monument are open to the public, other sites are off-limits to casual visitors. Rules regarding entering closed sites are strictly enforced. If you are interested in an in-depth tour, consider taking a ranger-led overnight hike to the **Crack-in-Rock Ruin.** The 14-mi (round-trip) trek covers areas marked by ancient petroglyphs and dotted with well-preserved ruins. The trips are conducted in April and October; call by February or August if you'd like to take part in the lottery for one of the 100 available places on these $25 hikes.

Between the Wupatki and Citadel ruins, the **Doney Mountain** affords 360-degree views of the Painted Desert and the San Francisco Volcanic Field. It's a perfect spot for a sunset picnic. In summer, rangers give lectures. ⊠ *Wupatki National Monument: 20 mi north of the Sunset Crater visitor center along the unmarked Sunset Loop Rd. (☞ above for directions from Flagstaff to Sunset Crater); HC 33, Box 444A,Flagstaff 86004,* ☎ *520/556–7040.* ☉ *Daily 8–5; hrs may be extended in summer.*

NORTH-CENTRAL ARIZONA A TO Z

Arriving and Departing

By Air
America West (☎ 800/235–9292) has daily flights from Phoenix to Flagstaff Pullium Airport (☎ 520/556–1234), 3 mi south of town off I–17 at Exit 337.

A taxi ride from the airport to the downtown area should cost about $9 to $11. Cabs are not regulated; some, but not all, have meters. It's wise to agree on a rate before you leave with a driver for your destination. **A Friendly Cab** (☎ 520/774–4444) and **Sun Taxi** (☎ 520/774–7400) are two reliable options.

If you've rented a car in the Flagstaff airport and want to get downtown, follow signs to I–17 (the airport is just off the highway). Turn right (north) on I–17, and in about 3 mi exit at the downtown turnoff.

America West (☎ 800/235–9292) flies frequently from Phoenix into **Prescott Municipal Airport** (☎ 520/445–7860), 8 mi north of town on U.S. 89.

By Bus
Greyhound (⊠ 399 S. Malpais La., Flagstaff, ☎ 520/774–4573 or 800/231–2222) has daily connections from throughout the west to Flagstaff, but none to Sedona. Buses also run between Prescott (⊠ 820 E. Sheldon Ave., ☎ 520/445–5470) and Phoenix Sky Harbor airport. **Nava-Hopi** buses depart daily to the Grand Canyon. *See* Guided Tours, *below,* for information about Nava-Hopi sightseeing trips to Sedona.

The **Sedona/Phoenix Shuttle Service** (⊠ Box 3342, West Sedona 86340, ☎ 520/282–2066; 800/448–7988 in AZ) makes six trips daily between those cities; the fare is $30 one-way, $55 round-trip. The bus leaves from three terminals of Sky Harbor International Airport in Phoenix. Reservations are required.

By Car
The most direct route to Prescott from Phoenix is to take I–17 north for 60 mi to Cordes Junction, and then drive northwest on AZ 69 for 36 mi into town. A four-lane divided highway, I–17 has several steep inclines and descents (you'll see a number of runaway-truck ramps). However, it's generally an easy and scenic thoroughfare. If you want to take the more leisurely route through Verde Valley to Prescott, continue north on I–17 another 25 mi past Cordes Junction until you see the turnoff for AZ 260, which will take you to Cottonwood in 12 mi. Here you can pick up U.S. 89A, which leads southwest to Prescott (41 mi) or northeast to Sedona (19 mi).

To reach Sedona more directly from Phoenix, take I–17 north for 113 mi until you come to AZ 179; it's another 15 mi on that road into town. The trip should take about 2½ hours. The 27-mi drive from Sedona to Flagstaff on U.S. 89A, which winds its way through Oak Creek Canyon, is breathtaking.

Flagstaff lies at the intersection of I–40 (east–west) and I–17 (running south from Flagstaff), 134 mi north of Phoenix via I–17.

By Train
Amtrak (⊠ 1 E. Rte. 66, ☎ 520/774–8679 or 800/872–7245) comes into the downtown Flagstaff station twice daily. There is no rail service into Prescott or Sedona.

Getting Around

Flagstaff
Flagstaff is a compact town, much of it along the railroad tracks. Just north of the tracks is the busy street that was called Santa Fe Avenue for many years. In 1992 it officially resumed its famous original name, Route 66. I–40 lies south of the tracks and also runs east–west. The main north–south thoroughfare is I–17, which turns into Milton Road, Humphreys Street, and then U.S. 180 as you drive north through town.

Because Flagstaff is the gateway to the Grand Canyon, most people on the road here are from out of town; keep that in mind when you ask for directions.

BY BUS
Pine Country Transit (☎ 520/779–6624) provides clean and reliable service throughout Flagstaff for 75¢. Three bus lines run weekdays from 6:15 AM to 7:10 PM; only one bus line, on a more limited schedule, operates Saturday and holidays, and there is no service on Sunday. Passengers with disabilities should check with the office to find out which buses can accommodate wheelchairs.

BY CAR
It makes sense to rent a car at the airport if you fly into Flagstaff (☞ Car and Jeep Rentals, *below*), and there are some rental agencies near the Amtrak station.

Prescott
In Prescott, U.S. 89 turns into Gurley Street, the main drag, lined with motels and businesses. Gurley leads into Courthouse Square, the heart of town. The most interesting shops, restaurants, and historic hotels are located within a 10-block radius, and you'll be able to do most of your sightseeing on foot. The local bus service is not very regular; call **Ace City Cab** (☎ 520/445–1616) if you don't have a car.

Sedona
Sedona stretches along U.S. 89A (also called Highway 89A), its main thoroughfare, which runs roughly east–west through town. U.S. 89A is bisected by AZ 179. The more commercial section of U.S. 89A east of AZ 179 is known as Uptown; locals tend to frequent the shops on the other side, called West Sedona. To the south of U.S. 89A, AZ 179 is lined with upscale retailers for a couple of miles. There is no public transportation in Sedona; if you don't have your own wheels, you'll need to rent some (☞ Car and Jeep Rentals, *below*) or rely on the services of **Bob's Sedona Taxi** (☎ 520/282–1234) or **Bell Rock Taxi** (☎ 520/282–4222).

Contacts and Resources

Camping and Hiking

For a listing of campgrounds in the Sedona, Prescott, and Jerome areas, consult the *Arizona Camping and Campgrounds Guide,* available from the **Arizona Office of Tourism** (☞ Visitor Information *in* Smart Travel Tips). Reservations for many campgrounds are handled by **The National Recreation Reservations Service** (☎ 800/280–2267).

If you're staying outside in winter, remember that this area gets quite cold, with frequent snowstorms. In summer, night temperatures can dip to 40°F, whereas daytime temperatures can reach 90°F. Be sure to bring plenty of water with you when hiking and drink often to avoid dehydration. Be careful not to camp in low-lying areas, which are subject to extremely dangerous flash flooding during sudden summer rains.

Car and Jeep Rentals

FLAGSTAFF

Agencies represented at the Flagstaff Pullium Airport include **Avis** (☎ 520/774–8421), **Budget** (☎ 520/779–0306), and **Hertz** (☎ 520/774–4452). Budget also has a downtown office, as do **Sears** (✉ 100 N. Humphreys St., ☎ 520/774–1879 or 800/527–0770), **National** (✉ Holiday Inn, 2320 E. Lucky La., ☎ 520/779–1975), and **Enterprise** (✉ 800 W. Rte. 66, ☎ 520/774–9407).

PRESCOTT

Budget (✉ 1031 Commerce Dr., ☎ 520/778–3806), **Enterprise** (✉ 202 S. Montezuma, ☎ 520/778–6506), and **Hertz** (✉ Airport, ☎ 520/776–1399) all have offices in Prescott.

SEDONA

Budget (☎ 520/282–4602) has an office at the Sedona Airport. If you want to explore the back roads of Sedona's red rocks on your own, you can rent a four-wheel-drive vehicle from **Sedona Jeep Rentals** (✉ Sedona Airport, ☎ 520/282–2227 or 800/879–5337) or **Canyon Jeep Rentals** (✉ Oak Creek Terrace Resort, 4548 Hwy. 89A, ☎ 520/282–6061 or 800/224–2229).

Emergencies

Ambulance (☎ 911). **Fire** (☎ 911). **Police** (☎ 911).

FLAGSTAFF

At an altitude of nearly 7,000 ft, Flagstaff has "thin" air; heart and respiratory patients may experience difficulty here, particularly upon exertion.

Flagstaff Medical Center (✉ 1200 N. Beaver St., ☎ 520/779–3366), a full-service hospital, has a 24-hour emergency room downtown, about nine blocks north of Route 66. The facility also provides referrals to local doctors and dentists.

The pharmacy at the **Flagstaff Medical Center** (☞ *above*) is open 24 hours. The pharmacy at **Smith's Food and Drug** (✉ 201 N. Switzer Canyon Dr., at Rte. 66, ☎ 520/774–3389) is open Monday through Saturday 9–9, Sunday 10–4.

Walgreen's (✉ 1500 E. Cedar Ave., ☎ 520/773–1011), a few blocks north of downtown, is open Monday through Saturday 9 AM–10 PM, Sunday 10–6.

PRESCOTT

Yavapai Regional Medical Center (✉ 1003 Willow Creek Rd., ☎ 520/445–2700).

The **Goodwin Street Pharmacy** (✉ 406 W. Goodwin St., ☎ 520/776–9939) has a 24-hour prescription service.

SEDONA

The **Sedona Medical Center** (✉ 3700 W. Hwy. 89A, ☎ 520/204–4900) has a doctor on call 24 hours. Walk-in hours are weekdays 8–5, most Saturdays 9–2.

The pharmacy at **Payless** (✉ 2350 W. Hwy. 89A, ☎ 520/282–9577) closes at 8 PM on weekdays, 6 on Saturday, and 5 on Sunday. **Walgreen's** (✉ 180 Coffee Pot Dr., ☎ 520/282–2528) stays open until 9 PM Monday–Saturday, until 8 on Sunday.

Guided Tours

FLAGSTAFF

Gray Line of Flagstaff, operated by **Nava-Hopi Tours** (✉ Box 339, 114 W. Rte. 66, Flagstaff 86002, ☎ 520/774–5003 or 800/892–8687), runs bus trips from its downtown bus station to the Grand Canyon; $38 for a nine-hour round-trip tour, not including park entry fee. A tour of Sedona costs $36 per person plus a $2 entry fee for Montezuma Castle. The company has other package tours, such as an 11½-hour trip to the Navajo reservation for $74 round-trip. All require reservations, which are taken until two hours before departure.

The Ventures program, run by the education department of the **Museum of Northern Arizona** (✉ 3101 N. Fort Valley Rd., Flagstaff 86001, ☎ 520/774–5213), offers tours of the area led by local scientists, artists, and historians. Trips might include rafting excursions down the San Juan River, treks into the Grand Canyon or Colorado Plateau backcountry, or bus tours into the Navajo reservation to visit with Native American artists. Prices start at about $400 and go up to $1,200, with most tours in the $500–$600 range.

PRESCOTT

On Monday and Friday at 10 AM from Memorial Day through Labor Day, volunteer guides offer free orientation tours of Prescott that leave from the **Chamber of Commerce** (✉ 1 E. Rte. 66). The rest of the year, tours can be booked with **Melissa Roughner** (☎ 520/445–4567), who'll be wearing period clothing from Arizona's territorial days when she guides you around town.

SEDONA

Orientation: Sedona Trolley (☎ 520/282–6826 or 520/282–5400) offers two types of daily orientation tours, both departing from the main bus stop in Uptown and lasting less than an hour. One goes along AZ 179 to the Chapel of the Holy Cross, with stops at Tlaquepaque and some galleries; the other passes through West Sedona to Boynton Canyon (Enchantment Resort). Rates are $7 each or $11 for both.

Special-Interest Tours: Several Jeep tour operators headquartered along Sedona's main Uptown drag conduct various excursions, some focusing on geology, some on astronomy, some on vortices, some on all three. You can even find a combination Jeep tour and horseback ride. The ubiquitous **Pink Jeep Tours** (✉ 204 N. Hwy. 89A, Box 1447, Sedona 86339, ☎ 520/282–5000 or 800/873–3662), as well as **Sedona Adventures** (✉ 276 N. Hwy. 89A, Suite A, Box 1476, Sedona 86339, ☎ 520/282–3500 or 800/888–9494) and **Sedona Red Rock Jeep Tours** (✉ 270 N. Hwy. 89A, Box 10305, Sedona 86339, ☎ 520/282–6826 or 800/848–7728), are all reliable operators. Prices start at about $22 per person for one hour and go up to $65 per person for four hours. Although all the excursions are safe, many are not for those who dislike heights or bumps.

Prices for hot-air-balloon tours generally start at $135 per person for a one- to two-hour tour. The only two companies with permits to fly over Sedona are **Northern Light Balloon Expeditions** (✉ Box 1695, Sedona 86339, ☎ 520/282–2274 or 800/230–6222), open since 1974 and the longest operating in Northern Arizona, and **Red Rock Balloon Adventures** (✉ Box 2759, Sedona 86339, ☎ 520/284–0040 or 800/ 258–3754).

Sedona Art Tours (✉ Box 10578, Sedona 86339, ☎ 520/282–0788) guides visitors through the town's art galleries.

Sedona Photo Tours (✉ 252 N. Hwy. 89A, Box 1650, Sedona 86339, ☎ 520/282–4320 or 800/973–3662) will take you to all the prime spots and help you take your best (photographic) shot. Rates are $35 per person for a basic two-hour tour.

Visitor Information

Camp Verde Chamber of Commerce (✉ 435 S. Main St., 86322, ☎ 520/567–9294). **Clarkdale Chamber of Commerce** (✉ Box 161, 86324, ☎ 520/634–3382). **Cottonwood/Verde Valley Chamber of Commerce** (✉ 1010 S. Main St., Cottonwood 86326, ☎ 520/634–7593). **Flagstaff Visitors Center** (✉ 1 E. Rte. 66, 86001, ☎ 520/774–9541 or 800/842–7293) is open Monday–Saturday 9–6 and Sunday 8–5. **Jerome Chamber of Commerce** (✉ Box K, 86331, ☎ 520/634–2900). **Prescott Chamber of Commerce** (✉ 117 W. Goodwin St., 86303, ☎ 520/445–2000 or 800/266–7534) is open weekdays 9–5, weekends 10–2. The **Sedona-Oak Creek Canyon Chamber of Commerce** (✉ 331 Forest Rd., at the corner of N. Hwy. 89A, Sedona 86339, ☎ 520/282–7722 or 800/288–7336) is open Monday–Saturday 9–5, Sunday 9–3.

4 PHOENIX AND CENTRAL ARIZONA

The ever-widening Phoenix metropolitan area provides a tremendous variety of activities—from golfing on championship courses and hiking on some of the country's most popular trails to dining on the ultimate in Southwest cuisine and luxuriating at world-class resorts. Scottsdale and the college town of Tempe are packed with great boutiques and art galleries. Outside of metropolitan Phoenix, Wickenburg is an authentic Old West town, and the Apache Trail drive is one of the most scenic routes in America.

Updated by
Deidre Elliott

■ N CENTRAL ARIZONA, one of the world's great deserts meets one of its great mountain ranges, providing a stunning variety of natural environments for visitors to enjoy in a relatively small area. Central Arizona also combines some of the oldest human dwellings in the western hemisphere with the homes of contemporary Native American tribes and America's fastest-growing major urban center: metropolitan Phoenix, a melding of 22 communities and, with a population of almost 1,200,000 people, the seventh-largest city in the United States.

At the heart of central Arizona lies the Valley of the Sun—so called for its 330-plus days of sunshine each year—which lends its name to metropolitan Phoenix's common nickname, the Valley. This 1,000-square-mi valley is the northern tip of the Sonoran Desert, a rolling expanse of prehistoric seabed that stretches from central Arizona deep into northwestern Mexico. The landscape of the Valley is surprising, perhaps, for those who don't realize just how lush the desert can be, studded with cacti, paloverde trees, and creosote bushes, crusted with hard-baked clay and rock, and scorched by summer temperatures that can stay above 100°F for weeks at a time. But its dry skin responds magically to the touch of rainwater. Spring is a miracle of gold and orange poppies, stately saguaro cacti crowned with white flowers, scarlet blossoms bursting from the dry spikes of the ocotillo, hills ablaze with bright yellow creosote, reddish lavender dotting the antlers of the staghorn cholla, and tiny blue flowers clustering on the stems of the desert sage.

As the Hohokam discovered 2,300 years ago, this springtime miracle can be augmented by human hands. Having migrated north from northwestern Mexico, they cultivated cotton, corn, and beans in tilled, rowed, and irrigated fields for about 1,700 years, establishing more than 300 mi of canals—an engineering miracle, particularly when you consider the limited technology available. The Hohokam, whose name comes from the Piman word for "people who have gone before," constructed a great town upon whose ruins modern Phoenix is built, and then vanished. Drought, long winters, and other causes are suggested for their disappearance, but no one is really sure what happened.

From the time the Hohokam left until the Civil War, the once fertile Salt River Valley lay forgotten, used only by occasional small bands of Pima and Maricopa indians. Then, in 1865, the U.S. Army established Fort McDowell in the mountains to the east, where the Verde River flows into the Salt River. To feed the men and the horses stationed there, Jack Swilling, a former Confederate army officer, reopened the Hohokam canals in 1867. Within a year, fields bright with barley and pumpkins earned the area the name of Punkinsville. But by 1870, when the town site was plotted, the 300 inhabitants had decided that their new city would rise "like a phoenix" from the ashes of a vanished civilization.

Phoenix would rise indeed. Within 20 years, it had become large enough—its population was about 3,000—to wrest the title of territorial capital from Prescott. By 1912, when Arizona was admitted as a state, the area, irrigated by the brand-new Roosevelt Dam and Salt River Project, had a burgeoning cotton industry. Copper and cattle were mined and raised elsewhere but were banked and traded in Phoenix, and the cattle were slaughtered and packed here in the largest stockyards outside Chicago.

Meanwhile, the climate, so long a crippling liability, became an asset. Desert air was the prescribed therapy for the respiratory ills rampant in the sooty, factory-filled East; Scottsdale began in 1901 as "30-odd tents and a half dozen adobe houses" put up by health seekers. By 1930, visitors looking for warm winter recreation as well as rejuvenating aridity filled the elegant San Marcos Hotel and Arizona Biltmore, first of the many luxury retreats for which the area is now known worldwide.

Phoenix's main growth spurt occurred in the early 1950s when air-conditioning made summers bearable, and the city has experienced the ups and downs of unbridled growth ever since. It's very much a work still in progress; so much is changing, and so quickly, that even longtime residents have a difficult time keeping up. But at the heart of all the bustle is a way of life that keeps its own pace: Phoenix and central Arizona are low-key places where people take things easy and dress informally. If the heat can be a little overwhelming at noon on a summer day, at least it has the salutary effect of slowing things down to an enjoyable speed. As old desert hands say, you don't begin to see the desert until you've looked at it long enough to see its colors; and you aren't ready to get up and move until you've seen the sun go down.

Pleasures and Pastimes

Dining

Generations of Phoenix school children have learned about Arizona's four C's: copper, cattle, cotton, and climate. Today, a good argument could be made for adding a fifth C: cuisine. For years, eating out in Phoenix meant an encounter either with the tacos and burritos of northern Mexico or with the steak and potatoes favored by the city's midwestern transplants. For the truly adventurous, the city had a smattering of Chinese restaurants. Gourmet dining? Funky ethnic eateries? You had a better chance of seeing snow in July.

During the 1980s and 1990s, however, Phoenix's explosive growth fueled a dramatic culinary boom. Creative chefs working with local ingredients took part in the birth of something called southwestern cooking. They started combining familiar, and sometimes not so familiar, flavors in surprising new ways (polenta topped with wild mushrooms in ancho chili cream sauce), re-inventing traditional preparations (quesadillas filled with duck and smoked Gouda), and introducing new ingredients (curried-lamb-stuffed tamales with peanut sauce).

Phoenix's expansion also saw the arrival of immigrants from around the world, who brought their cuisines to the Valley of the Sun. Southeast Asian immigrants introduced spicy Asian dishes that were instantly welcome in a city accustomed to fiery chiles. Immigrants from Central America and the Middle East brought more variations on familiar themes. Phoenicians can now enjoy everything from tandoori to sushi. At the same time, an increasingly sophisticated dining public fills tables at high-end American, Continental, French, and Italian spots around town. Still, Phoenix has not forgotten its culinary roots. Steak and Mexican food have never gone out of style, and here in the Southwest, they never will.

Golf

Phoenix is a golf mecca, thanks to the warm weather, azure skies, and serene vistas of the desert. The explosive growth of the area has brought lots of new courses to the Valley over the past two decades, many world-class. The city provides an impressive array of courses—golfers may choose lush, manicured fairways with tranquil lakes and fountains or get right out in the wild dunes and scrub brush of the desert.

Hot-Air Ballooning

For a bird's-eye view of the spectacular desert landscape, try a hot-air balloon ride. The peaceful silence hundreds of feet up is unforgettable; since the balloon is carried on the wind, you'll experience no wind yourself. And an added bonus is that you'll see many elusive desert creatures that can be viewed in their natural habitats only from a balloon.

Lodging

If there's one thing the Valley of the Sun knows how to do right, it's lodging. Metropolitan Phoenix has accommodations ranging from world-class resorts to roadside motels, from upscale dude ranches to no-frills family-style operations where you can do your own cooking.

Mountains

The Valley of the Sun is ringed by mountains, which provide many opportunities for outdoor activities. Squaw Peak is just north of downtown Phoenix and Camelback Mountain and the Papago Peaks are landmarks between Phoenix and Scottsdale. South of the city, not 5 mi from downtown, rise the much less lofty peaks of South Mountain Park. This 12-mi-wide chain of dry mountains divides the Valley from the rest of the Sonoran Desert.

Past Tempe (pronounced tem-PEE), and Mesa to the east, the barren peaks of the Superstition Mountains—named for their eerie way of seeming just a few miles away and luring unwary prospectors to a dusty death—are the first of a series of mountains that stretch all the way into New Mexico. To the west, past Glendale and Tolleson, the formidable, barren-seeming White Tank Mountains separate the Valley from the empty lands that slope steadily downward toward the Colorado River and the Mojave Desert of California.

But north of Phoenix, behind the dusty Hieroglyphic Mountains (misnamed for Hohokam petroglyphs found there), rises the gigantic Mogollon Rim. This shelf of land, almost as wide as Arizona, was thrust 2,000 to 5,000 ft into the air back in the Mesozoic age; it got its name for posing an overwhelming mogollon (obstruction) to Spanish-speaking explorers probing northward. These slopes are green with pine trees, and the alpine meadows are lush with grasses and aspen. Here, after gold was found in the early 1860s, President Lincoln sent the Arizona Territory's first governor to found the capital at Prescott (☞ The Verde Valley, Jerome, Prescott, and Sedona *in* Chapter 3) and secure mineral riches for the Union.

Today, the northern mountains serve as a cool, green refuge for Valley dwellers. The bumpy wagon roads up the Black Canyon toward Prescott and Flagstaff were key summer escape routes 100 years ago, and their dramatically engineered successor, the four-lane, split-level I–17, leads tens of thousands on exodus every weekend from May to September.

EXPLORING PHOENIX

The Sun Belt boom began when low-cost air-conditioning made summer heat bearable. From 1950 to 1990, the Phoenix urban area more than quadrupled in population, catapulting real estate and home building into two of the state's biggest industries. Cities planted around Phoenix have become its suburbs, and land that for decades produced cotton and citrus now produces microchips and homes. Glendale and Peoria on the west side, and Tempe, Mesa, Chandler, and Gilbert on the east, make up the nation's third-largest silicon valley.

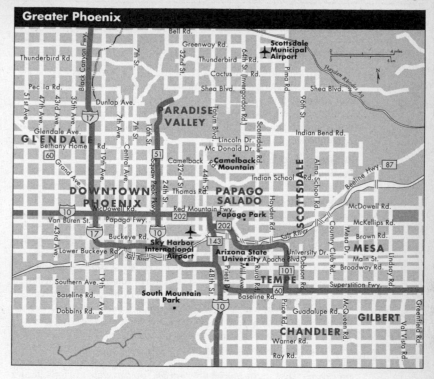

Greater Phoenix

Numbers in the text correspond to numbers in the margin and on the Exploring Downtown and the Cultural Center, Exploring Scottsdale, and Side Trips Near Phoenix maps.

Great Itineraries

IF YOU HAVE 3 DAYS

See the Heard Museum for its internationally acclaimed collection of Native American artifacts, and swing by the Central Library on your way downtown to the Arizona Science Center and Phoenix Museum of History. On day two, rise early and begin your day at Frank Lloyd Wright's Taliesin West; then head south into Scottsdale for a day of gallery browsing and a walk through Old Town. On your final day visit the stunning Desert Botanical Garden, then proceed to Tempe to stroll on Mill Avenue and check out the innovative architecture of the Arizona State University campus.

IF YOU HAVE 5 DAYS

Follow the tour above, and on the fourth day, consider some hiking: Even inexperienced hikers will enjoy the walk up to Papago Park's Hole in the Rock or the 1.2-mi trip to the top of Squaw Peak, whereas the more experienced may choose to ascend Camelback Mountain. South Mountain Park has many trails for hikers of all abilities. Spend the afternoon exploring the stark beauty of the surrounding desert on horseback, in a Jeep, or by hot-air balloon. On your fifth day, drive the loop of the Apache Trail, enjoying breathtaking views of Fish Creek Canyon—or head north to take a tour of Arcosanti or explore the Old West town of Wickenburg.

IF YOU HAVE 7 DAYS

Expand your drive of the Apache Trail to include an overnight stay in Globe. Along the way stop to enjoy the view from Weaver's Needle, stroll through Boyce Thompson Arboretum, or check out the ancient Hohokam ruins at Casa Grande to the south of Phoenix.

Downtown Phoenix

The renovated downtown area gives you a look at Phoenix's past and present, as well as a peek at its future. Restored homes from the original townsite give you an idea of how far the city has come since its inception around the turn of the last century, while several fine museums point to the Valley of the Sun's increasing sophistication in the coming one.

A Good Walk

Park your car in the garage on the southeast corner of 5th and Monroe streets or at any of the many nearby public parking facilities (they're listed on the free map provided by Downtown Phoenix Partnership and available in local restaurants). Begin your tour in the blocks known as the Heritage and Science Park; 5th to 7th streets between Monroe and Adams contain **Heritage Square** ①, the **Arizona Science Center** ②, and the **Phoenix Museum of History** ③. From the corner of 5th and Monroe, walk two blocks west to **St. Mary's Basilica** ④, Phoenix's first Catholic church. Head north one block to Van Buren Street. On the northeast corner of the intersection, you'll see two glass-clad office towers with a lane of royal palms between them. Follow the palm trees: They lead to the **Arizona Center** ⑤. Leaving the Arizona Center, from the corner of 3rd and Van Buren, walk a block west to 2nd Street and two blocks south on 2nd Street, passing the 24-story Hyatt Regency hotel on your right, then another block and a half west on Adams Street to the **Museo Chicano** ⑥. You can walk to Heritage and Science Park from here, catch a DASH shuttle back, or continue on two more blocks west toward the striking facade of the **Orpheum Theatre** ⑦.

If you're really an indefatigable walker, continue south through the plaza on the Orpheum's east side to Washington Street; head east on Washington Street, passing Historic City Hall and the county courthouse on your right. At the intersection of Washington Street and 1st Avenue, you'll see Patriots Square Park on the southeast corner; cross diagonally (southeast) through the park to the corner of Jefferson Street and Central Avenue. Another block east on Jefferson and then a block south on 1st Street will take you to the site of the **America West Arena** ⑧. From the arena, follow Jefferson Street east for two blocks to South 4th Avenue and Phoenix's newest sports venue, **Bank One Ballpark** ⑨, affectionately nicknamed BOB by locals. Afterwards, catch the DASH shuttle back to your car.

TIMING

In moderate weather, this walk is a pleasant daylong tour; from late May to mid-October, it's best to break it up over two days. Be sure to take advantage of the 35¢ DASH (Downtown Area Shuttle; ☞ Getting Around by Bus *in* Phoenix and Central Arizona A to Z, *below*).

Sights to See

❽ **America West Arena.** This 20,000-seat sports palace is the home of the Phoenix Suns, the Arizona Rattlers arena football team, the Phoenix Mercury professional women's basketball team, and the Phoenix Coyotes NHL team. Almost a mall in itself—with cafés and shops, in addition to the team offices—it's interesting to tour even when there's no game on. Check out the video art in the lobby, including the three robot figures fashioned out of small televisions. Tours cost $3, but availability is determined by the arena's schedule of events. Call for current times. ⊠ *201 E. Jefferson St., at 2nd St.,* ☎ *602/379–2000.*

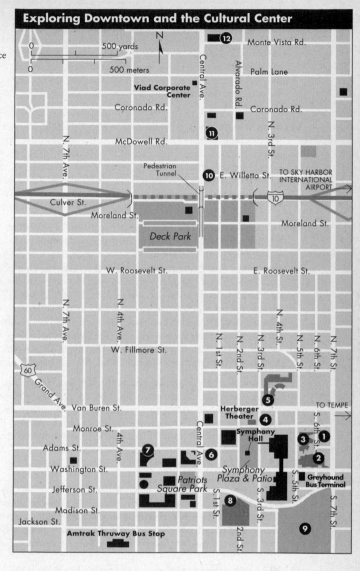

Exploring Downtown and the Cultural Center

❺ Arizona Center. Beyond an oasis of dramatic fountains and sunken gardens stands the curved, two-tiered structure that is downtown's most astonishing shopping venue. The first thing you'll see is the Hooter's at the entrance, which in a way sets the tone for the entire mall. More energetically cheesy than truly elegant, the center boasts a variety of souvenir shops (some with nice merchandise), a dozen restaurants spread over two stories, the state's largest sports bar, and delightful palms, pools, and fountains. There is a variety of chain and specialty stores as well as open-air vendors stationed in the plaza. ✉ *Van Buren St. between 3rd and 5th Sts.,* ☎ *602/271–4000 or 480/949–4386.*

★ ☺ **❷ Arizona Science Center.** This concrete monolith, designed by Antoine Predock, is *the* Phoenix venue for science-related fun and exploration. Lively "please touch" exhibits provide an entertaining educational experience for kids and grown-ups alike—learn about the physics of making gigantic soap bubbles, the technology of satellite weather systems, the launching of hot-air balloons, or how to spin like a figur skater, and listen in to the control tower at Sky Harbor airport. Under the dome of Dorrance Planetarium, dazzling computer graphics simulate orbits and eclipses, as well as three-dimensional space flight. The Irene P. Flinn theater has a 50-ft-high projection screen where such films as "Wolves" and "To Be an Astronaut" are presented in I-WORKS, an IMAX-type technology. ⊠ *600 E. Washington St.,* ☎ *602/716–2000.* ☞ *Museum $8; combination museum, theater, and planetarium $11.* ⊙ *Daily 10–5.*

❾ **Bank One Ballpark.** Also known as Bob, this ballpark—complete with a retractable roof—is the home of the major league team, Arizona Diamondbacks. Tours of the state-of-the-art facility are given on non-game days, Monday through Saturday, at 10:30, noon, 1:30, and 3:00. On game days, tours are scheduled at 10:30 and noon only. At all times, it's a good idea to reserve your tour in advance. ⊠ *401 E. Jefferson St., between S. 4th and S. 7th Sts.,* ☎ *602/462–6000.* ☞ *Tours $6.*

❶ **Heritage Square.** In a parklike setting from 5th to 7th streets between Monroe and Adams, this city-owned block contains the only remaining homes from the original Phoenix townsite. On the south side of the square, along Adams Street, stand several houses built between 1899 and 1901. The midwestern-style **Stevens House** holds the **Arizona Doll and Toy Museum** (⊠ 602 E. Adams St., ☎ 602/253–9337). The **Teeter House,** the third house in the row, is a Victorian-style tearoom. The **Silva House** (☎ 602/236–5451), a bungalow from 1900, has presentations about turn-of-the-century life for settlers in the Phoenix township. On the south side of Adams Street in the **Thomas House** and **Baird Machine Shop** is an Italian bakery/pizzeria combination, **Bianco's** (☞ Dining, *below*).

The queen of Heritage Square is the **Rosson House,** an 1895 Victorian in the Queen Anne style. Built by a physician who served a brief term as mayor, it is the sole survivor of the fewer than two dozen Victorians erected in Phoenix. It was bought and restored by the city in 1974. A 30-minute tour of this classic is worth the modest admission price. ⊠ *6th and Monroe Sts.,* ☎ *602/262–5071.* ☞ *$3.* ⊙ *Wed.–Sat. 10–3:30, Sun. noon–3:30.*

NEED A
BREAK?   The Victorian-style tearoom in the **Teeter House** (⊠ 622 E. Adams St., ☎ 602/252–4682) serves such authentic tea-time fare as Devonshire cream, scones with berries, and cucumber sandwiches. Heartier gourmet sandwiches and salads are also available. The staff will happily box any of your choices, should you prefer to enjoy them on the lawn outside.

❻ **Museo Chicano.** Artistic works of artists from both the United States and Mexico are showcased here. Exhibits display the broad range of classic and modern culture, making this site one of the premier centers for contemporary Latin American art. ⊠ *147 E. Adams St.,* ☎ *602/257–5536.* ☞ *$2.* ⊙ *Tues.–Sat. 10–4.*

❼ **Orpheum Theatre.** The Spanish-colonial–revival architecture and exterior reliefs of this 1929 movie palace have long been admired, and now, after an extensive renovation by artisans and craftspeople, the eclectic ornamental details of the interior have been meticulously restored. Call for details on guided tours and upcoming events. ⊠ *203 W. Adams St.,* ☎ *602/534–5601.*

★ ☺ **❸** **Phoenix Museum of History.** This striking glass-and-steel museum offers a healthy dose of regional history from the 1860s (when Anglo settlement began) through the 1930s. A tour through interactive exhibits allows guests to appreciate the city's multicultural heritage as well as witness its growth. You're invited to play Sniff That Barrel (to guess its contents) at a replica of Hancock Store (an 1860s Circle-K equivalent) or take a turn at packing a toy wagon with color-coded blocks as if for a cross-country trip. ⌧ *105 N. 5th St.,* ☏ *602/253–2734.* ⌨ *$5.* ⊙ *Mon.–Sat. 10–5, Sun. noon–5.*

❹ **St. Mary's Basilica.** Founded in 1881, Phoenix's first Catholic church presents a stunning facade, its pink stucco and twin towers a pleasant anomaly among the modern concrete of downtown. Inside, the basilica, where Pope John Paul II visited in 1987, has magnificent stained-glass windows designed in Munich. Mass is held daily, but call the parish office for visiting hours. ⌧ *N. 3rd and Monroe Sts.,* ☏ *602/252–7651.* ⌨ *Free.* ⊙ *Hrs vary, call for opening times.*

The Cultural Center

The heart of Phoenix's downtown cultural center is the rolling greensward of the Margaret T. Hance Park, also known as Deck Park. Built atop the I–10 tunnel under Central Avenue, it spreads more than 1 mi from 3rd Avenue on the west to 3rd Street on the east, and ¼ mi from Portland Street north to Culver Street. It is the city's second-largest downtown park (the largest is half-century-old Encanto Park, 2 mi northwest). Deck Park is a good place from which to survey revitalized downtown neighborhoods and to appreciate the expansions and renovations of nearly all the area's museums.

A Good Walk

Park free in the lot of the **Phoenix Central Library** ⑩ at the corner of Central Avenue and East Willetta Street. Two blocks north on Central, across McDowell Road, is the modern, green-quartz structure of the **Phoenix Art Museum** ⑪. North of the museum, a slight detour brings a brief respite from the noise and traffic of Central Avenue as well as a glimpse of some lovely residential architecture: Head one block east on Coronado Road to Alvarado Road, then follow Alvarado north for two longish blocks (zigzagging a few feet to the east at Palm Lane) to Monte Vista Road; turn left onto Monte Vista and proceed 50 yards west to the entrance of the **Heard Museum** ⑫. From the Heard, head south on Central Avenue toward the red-granite Viad Tower, with its refreshing fountains and intriguing sculpture garden.

TIMING

Seeing all of the neighborhood's attractions makes a comfortable day tour in moderate weather; in the warm months, it is too much for one day. Bus 0 runs up and down Central Avenue every 10 minutes on weekdays and every 20 minutes on Saturdays.

Sights to See

★ ⓒ ⑫ **Heard Museum.** Pioneer Phoenix settlers Dwight and Maie Heard had a Spanish-colonial–revival building erected on their property to house their impressive collection of southwestern art; today, the site has developed into the nation's premier showcase of Native American art, basketry, pottery, weavings, and bead work. Children will enjoy the interactive art-making exhibits, and events such as the Guild Indian Fair and the Hoop Dancing Competition explore the Native American experience. The museum also has the best gift shop in town; it's not cheap, but you can be sure you're getting authentic, high-quality goods. A major expansion, completed in 1999, doubled the museum's gallery space. ⌧ *2301 N. Central Ave.,* ☏ *602/252–8848 or 602/252–8840.* ⌨ *$6.* ⊙ *Mon.–Sat. 9:30–5, Sun. noon–5.*

The grassy park of the **Viad Corporate Center,** on Central Avenue between McDowell Road and Palm Lane, is a great place to stop for a
rest. A string of tiered fountains snakes through the 2-acre park and
sculpture garden, which contains a collection of lifelike works in
bronze—some so realistic, you might unwittingly pass right by them.
Stop to appreciate their whimsical touches, such as the blue-capped window washer's paperback copy of *Rear Window* tucked in his overalls.

⓫ **Phoenix Art Museum.** The green quartz exterior of this modern museum is another eye-catching piece of architecture on Central Avenue.
More than 13,000 objets d'art are on display inside, including 18th-
and 19th-century European works and the American West collection,
which features painters from Frederic Remington to Georgia O'Keeffe.
A clothing-and-costume collection has pieces from 1750, and the Asian
art gallery is filled with fine Chinese porcelain and pieces of intricate
cloisonné. ⊠ *1625 N. Central Ave.,* ☎ *602/257–1222.* ⊡ *$6; tours
free.* ☉ *Mon.–Wed. and weekends 10–5, Thurs.–Fri. 10–9.*

❿ **Phoenix Central Library.** Architect Will Bruder's magnificent 1995
contribution to Central Avenue is absolutely worth a stop. The curved
building's copper-penny exterior evokes images of the region's sunburnt
mesas; inside, skylights, glass walls, and mirrors keep the structure bathed
in natural light. A five-story glass atrium, known as the Crystal Canyon,
is best appreciated from a speedy ride in one of three glass elevators.
At the top, from the largest reading room in North America, check out
a cable-suspended steel ceiling that appears to float overhead. Free one-
hour tours are offered on Fridays; call to arrange one in advance. ⊠
1221 N. Central Ave., ☎ *602/262–4636; 602/262–6582 tour reservations.* ☉ *Mon.–Thurs. 9–9, Fri.–Sat. 9–6, Sun. 1–5.*

Funky, friendly **Willow House** (⊠ 149 W. McDowell Rd., ☎ 602/252–
0272) is the area's most comfortable coffeehouse. Grab a sandwich,
dessert, or coffee and stretch out in a low-slung couch underneath
brightly painted walls. Check out the various art works on display, as
well as the kaleidoscopic fish swimming along the restroom walls.

South Phoenix

A mostly residential area and home to much of Phoenix's substantial
Hispanic population, South Phoenix is worth a visit for two reasons:
Its family-style restaurants and roadside stands offer some of the best
Mexican food in the city, and it's home to South Mountain Park and
the Mystery Castle, two of Phoenix's most remarkable sights.

A Good Drive

From central Phoenix, take 7th Street south, past Baseline Road, to
the junction of Mineral Road and 7th Street. There you'll find the **Mystery Castle,** a decidedly original home-turned-mini-museum. After a
tour, follow Mineral Road west for about ½ mi to Central Avenue and
the entrance to **South Mountain Park.** Take any of several scenic drives
through this 16,500-acre city-owned wilderness. Labeled as "the most
romantic view" in the park is Dobbins Lookout, from which you can
survey the surrounding peaks and valleys. Maps of all scenic drives as
well as of hiking, mountain biking, and horseback trails are available
at the Gatehouse Entrance just inside the park boundary.

TIMING

Depending on how long you spend in the park, this tour can be ac-
complished in a couple of hours or can last an entire day. Leave about
a half hour each way for driving, an hour to 90 minutes at the castle,

and anywhere from a quick 20-minute drive to an all-day hike in South Mountain.

Sights to See

★ **Mystery Castle.** At the foot of South Mountain lies a curious dwelling fashioned from desert rocks, railroad refuse, and anything else its builder, Boyce Gulley, could get his hands on. Boyce's daughter Mary Lou lives here now and leads tours upon request. Full of fascinating oddities, the castle has 18 rooms with 13 fireplaces, a downstairs grotto tavern, and a roll-away bed with a mining railcar as its frame. The pump organ belonged to Elsie, the Widow of Tombstone, who buried six husbands under suspicious circumstances. ⊠ *800 E. Mineral Rd.,* ☎ *602/268–1581.* ☞ *$4.* ⊙ *Oct.–Jun., Thurs.–Sun. 11–4.*

★ **South Mountain Park.** This desert wonderland, the world's largest city park (almost 17,000 acres), offers an outdoor experience unparalleled in the Valley: a wilderness of mountain/desert trails (☞ Hiking *in* Outdoor Activities and Sports, *below*) for hikers, bikers, and horseback riders. The Environmental Center features a large relief model of the park as well as displays detailing the park's history, from the time of the ancient Hohokam peoples to that of gold-seeking adventurers. Roads climb past buildings constructed by the Civilian Conservation Corps during the New Deal Era, winding through desert flora to the trailheads; scenic overlooks reveal the distant Phoenix skyline, which seems a world away from this wild and luxuriant oasis. Look for ancient petroglyphs; try to spot a desert cottontail rabbit or chuckwalla lizard; or simply stroll among the wondrous vegetation. It's an electrifying experience, all the more startling for being placed right on the edge of a major metropolis. ⊠ *10919 S. Central Ave.,* ☎ *602/495–5078.* ☞ *Free.* ⊙ *Daily 5:30 AM–10:30 PM. Environmental Center Mon.–Sat. 9–5, Sun. 12–5. Group tours and educational programs available by advance reservation only.*

NEED A BREAK?	For a break from Mexican food, check out the Texas-style ribs, brisket, and chicken at **Black's Smokey Hog BBQ** (⊠ 2010 E. Broadway Rd., ☎ 602/305–9693). If you're feeling presidential, stop by **Poncho's** (⊠ 7202 S. Central Ave., ☎ 602/276–2437), where Bill Clinton enjoyed the Fiesta Chiquita, a sampler platter of chimichangas, tacos, tamales, tostadas, and frijoles. Though you're in the middle of the desert, you'll find some of the freshest seafood anywhere at **San Diego Bay Restaurant** (⊠ 9201 S. Avenida Del Yaqui, ☎ 480/839–2991)—try the whole red snapper grilled with tomatoes, onions, garlic, and jalapeños.

Papago Salado

The word "Papago," meaning "bean eater," was a name given by 16th-century Spanish explorers to the Hohokam (as they are more properly called), a vanished native people of the Phoenix area. Farmers of the desert, the Hohokam grew corn, beans, squash, and cotton. They lived in central Arizona from about AD 1 to 1450, at which point their civilization collapsed and disappeared for reasons unknown, abandoning the Salt River (Rio Salado) Valley and leaving behind remains of villages and a complex system of irrigation canals. The Papago Salado region is between Phoenix and Tempe and contains the Pueblo Grande ruins, the Desert Botanical Garden, the Phoenix Zoo, and various recreational opportunities amid the buttes of Papago Park.

A Good Drive

From downtown Phoenix, take Washington Street east to the **Pueblo Grande Museum and Cultural Park,** between 44th Street and the Hohokam Expressway (AZ 143). After a stop at the museum, follow Washington Street east 3½ mi to Priest Drive and turn north. Priest Drive becomes Galvin Parkway north of Van Buren Street; follow signs to entrances for the **Phoenix Zoo** and **Papago Park,** or to the **Desert Botanical Garden.** To visit the **Hall of Flame** afterward, drive south on Galvin Parkway to Van Buren Street; turn east on Van Buren and drive ⅛ mi, turning south onto Project Drive (at the buff-color stone marker that reads SALT RIVER PROJECT).

TIMING

Seeing all the sights requires the better part of a day. You may want to save the Desert Botanical Garden for the end of your tour, as it stays open 8–8 year round and is particularly lovely when lit by the setting sun or by moonlight.

Sights to See

★ ☾ **Desert Botanical Garden.** Opened in 1939 to conserve and showcase the ecology of the desert, these 150 acres contain more than 4,000 different species of cacti, succulents, trees, and flowers. A stroll along the ½-mi-long "Plants and People of the Sonoran Desert" trail is a fascinating lesson in environmental adaptations; children will enjoy playing the self-guiding game "Desert Detective." ✉ *1201 N. Galvin Pkwy.,* ☎ *602/941–1217 or 480/941–1225.* ⊡ *$7.50.* ☾ *Oct.–Apr., daily 8–8; May–Sept., daily 7 AM–8 PM.*

NEED A
BREAK?

If you're headed to the Papago Salado region from downtown Phoenix, stop in **Kohnie's Coffee** (✉ 4225 E. Camelback Rd., ☎ 602/952–9948) for coffee, pastries, bagels, and scones. It's open at 7 AM (8 AM Sunday) and closed by 1 PM (noon on weekends).

☾ **Hall of Flame.** Retired firefighters lead tours through more than 100 restored fire engines and tell harrowing tales of the "world's most dangerous profession." Kids can climb on a 1916 engine, operate alarm systems, and learn lessons of fire safety from the pros. More than 3,000 helmets, badges, and other fire-fighting-related articles are on display, dating from as far back as 1725. ✉ *6101 E. Van Buren St.,* ☎ *602/ 275–3473.* ⊡ *$5.* ☾ *Mon.–Sat. 9–5, Sun. 12–4.*

Papago Park. An amalgam of hilly desert terrain, streams, and lagoons, this park has picnic ramadas (shaded, open air shelters), a playground, hiking and biking trails, and even largemouth bass and trout fishing. (An urban fishing license is required for anglers age 15 and over; you can pick one up at sporting-goods or Circle-K stores.) The hike up to landmark **Hole-in-the-Rock** is popular—but remember that it's much easier to climb up to the hole than to get down. **Governor Hunt's Tomb,** the white pyramid at the top of Ramada 16, commemorates the former Arizona leader and provides a lovely view. ✉ *625 N. Galvin Pkwy.,* ☎ *602/256–3220.* ⊡ *Free.* ☾ *Daily 6 AM–10 PM.*

☾ **Phoenix Zoo.** Four designated trails wind through this 125-acre zoo, which has replicas of such habitats as an African savanna and a tropical rain forest. Meerkats, warthogs, desert bighorn sheep, and the endangered Arabian oryx are among the unusual sights, as is Uco, the endangered spectacled bear from South America. The Discovery Trail at Harmony Farm introduces young visitors to small mammals, and a stop at the big red barn provides a chance to help groom goats and sheep. The 30-minute narrated safari train tour costs $2 and provides a good overview of the park. In December, the popular "Zoo Lights" exhibit transforms the area into an enchanted forest of more than 600,000 twinkling lights, many in the shape of the zoo's residents. ✉

455 N. Galvin Pkwy., ☏ *602/273–1341.* ✉ *$8.50.* ☉ *Sept.–Apr., daily 9–5; May–Aug., daily 7:30–4.*

★ **Pueblo Grande Museum and Cultural Park.** Phoenix's only national landmark, this park was once the site of a 500-acre Hohokam village supporting about 1,000 people and containing homes, storage rooms, cemeteries, and several ball courts. Three exhibition galleries hold displays on the Hohokam culture, archaeological methods, and other Southwest themes; kids will like the hands-on, interactive learning center. View the 10-minute orientation video before heading out on the 1-km Ruin Trail past excavated mounds and ruined structures that give a hint of Hohokam savvy: There's a building whose corner doorway was perfectly placed to watch the summer solstice sunrise. ✉ *4619 E. Washington St.,* ☏ *602/495–0901.* ✉ *$2; free Sun.* ☉ *Mon.–Sat. 9–4:45, Sun. 1–4:45.*

Scottsdale

Historic sites, nationally known art galleries, and souvenir shops fill downtown Scottsdale; a quick walking tour can easily turn into an all-day excursion if you browse. Historic Old Town Scottsdale features the look of the Old West, and 5th Avenue is known for shopping and Native American jewelry and crafts stores. Cross onto Main Street and enter a world frequented by the international art set (Scottsdale has the third-largest artist community in the United States); discover more galleries and interior-design shops along Marshall Way (☞ Shopping, *below*).

A Good Walk

Park in the free public lot on the corner of 2nd Street and Wells Fargo Avenue, east of Scottsdale Road. A portion of the garage has a three-hour limit; go to upper levels that don't carry time restrictions (enforcement on lower levels is strict).

Start your walk by exiting the parking structure from its northeast corner, where a short brick-paved sidewalk leads northward to the plaza of Scottsdale Mall. You'll immediately come upon the **Scottsdale Center for the Arts** ⑬. Be sure to check out the newest addition to this arts complex, the **Scottsdale Museum of Contemporary Art** ⑭, right next door to the main Center building. Stroll counterclockwise around the Mall's lovely grounds, passing Scottsdale's library and municipal buildings, and ending up on the plaza's west side by the **Scottsdale Chamber of Commerce** ⑮ and **Scottsdale Historical Museum** ⑯. Continue west to the intersection of Brown Avenue and Main Street to reach the heart of **Old Town Scottsdale** ⑰, occupying four square blocks from Brown Avenue to Scottsdale Road, between Indian School Road and 2nd Street. From Main Street in Old Town, cross Scottsdale Road to the central drag of the **Main Street Arts District** ⑱. Turn north onto Goldwater Boulevard and gallery-stroll for another two blocks. At Indian School Road, head one block east to the **Marshall Way Arts District** ⑲. Continue two blocks north on Marshall Way to the fountain of prancing Arabian horses that marks **5th Avenue** ⑳. You can catch the trolley back to Scottsdale Mall here, on the south side of the intersection of 5th Avenue and Stetson Drive, or walk the five blocks south on Scottsdale Road and one block east on Main Street.

Not far from from downtown Scottsdale are three other worthy attractions: the **Buffalo Museum, Taliesin West** (Frank Lloyd Wright's winter home), and the lovely **Fleischer Museum.** While in this northern area, see the fascinating metal and ceramic wind chimes at Cosanti Originals studio (☞ Shopping, *below*), made by disciples of Paolo Soleri, the father of the futuristic Arcosanti (☞ Side Trips Near Phoenix, *below*).

TIMING

Plan to spend a full day in Scottsdale, as there's a lot to take in between the countless galleries and shops. Although your tour can easily be completed on foot, a trolley runs through the downtown area and out to several resorts: Ollie the Trolley charges $5 for an all-day pass, though service in downtown Scottsdale is free (☎ 480/970–8130 for information). Also look for horse-drawn **Arizona Carriage Company** (☎ 480/423–1449), whose Cinderella-like carriages provide romantic transportation throughout Old Town Scottsdale ($20 for 15-minute tours, $40 for ½ hour, $70 for an hour for carriages that hold up to six). They're also perfect props for snapshots.

The best option, if you're interested in touring the galleries, is to visit on a Thursday and do the Scottsdale Art Walk (☞ Arts and Crafts *in* Shopping, *below*).

Sights to See

㉑ 5th Avenue. For more than 40 years, this shopping stretch has been home to boutiques and specialty shops. Whether you seek handmade Native American arts and crafts, casual clothing, or cacti, you'll find it here—plus colorful storefronts, friendly merchants, even an old "cigar store" Indian. After a full day of paintings, turquoise jewelry, and knickknacks, children especially may enjoy casting their eyes upon the six-story monster screen of the **IMAX Theater** (⊠ 4343 N. Scottsdale Rd., ☎ 480/945–4629), at the east end of the avenue. ⊠ *Civic Center Rd. and Stetson Dr.*

OFF THE
BEATEN PATH

BUFFALO MUSEUM OF AMERICA – Tucked away in a Scottsdale shopping plaza, this eclectic little museum pays homage to the American bison, or buffalo, and its important role in American history. The museum's contents range from the awesome shaggy beast itself—courtesy of modern taxidermy—to a variety of original works of fine art, to props from the film *Dances with Wolves*. The Buffalo Bill Room showcases the legendary hunter's personal possessions, and the downstairs gift shop is a mélange of all things buffalo—clocks, banks, tins, plates, old stereoscope cards, even a promotional poster from Hunter S. Thompson's novel *Where the Buffalo Roam.* ⊠ *10261 N. Scottsdale Rd.,* ☎ *480/ 951–1022.* ⌑ *$3.* ☉ *Weekdays 9–5.*

FLEISCHER MUSEUM – Housed in the corporate Perimeter Center, this collection is an undiscovered gem. More than 80 artists from the California School of Impressionism, which is noted for its brightly colored plein-air painting, are represented, including William Wendt and Franz A. Bischoff. It's worth a trip to the somewhat out-of-the-way location. ⊠ *17207 N. Perimeter Dr., at the intersection of Pima and Bell Rds.,* ☎ *602/585–3108.* ⌑ *Free.* ☉ *Daily 10–4. Closed holidays.*

TALIESIN WEST – Ten years after visiting Arizona in 1927 to consult on designs for the Biltmore hotel, architect Frank Lloyd Wright chose 600 acres of raw, rugged Sonoran Desert at the foothills of the McDowell Mountains, just outside Scottsdale, as the site for his permanent winter residence. Wright and apprentices constructed a desert camp here, using what he called organic architecture to integrate the buildings with their natural surroundings. An ingenious harmony of indoor and outdoor space is the result. In addition to the living quarters, drafting studio, and small apartments of the Apprentice Court, Taliesin West also has two theaters, a music pavilion, and the "Sun Trap"—a charming structure of sleeping spaces surrounding an open patio and fireplace. Two guided

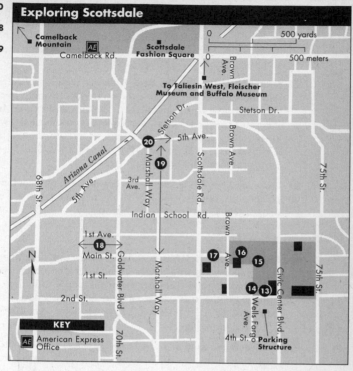

Exploring Scottsdale

tours cover different parts of the interior, and a guided "Desert Walk" winds through the petroglyphs and landscape from which Wright drew his vision, as well as the experimental desert residences designed by his apprentices. Tour times vary, so call ahead; all visitors must be accompanied by a guide. ⊠ *12621 Frank Lloyd Wright Blvd.,* ☎ *480/860–8810 or 480/860–2700.* 🖼 *Guided tour (1 hr) $14 winter, $10 summer; Behind the Scenes tour (3 hrs) $35 winter, $25 summer; Desert Walk tour (90 mins) $20.* ☉ *Oct.–May, daily 8:30–5:30; Jun.–Sept., daily 8:30–5.*

★ **⑱ Main Street Arts District.** Gallery after gallery on Main Street and First Avenue, particularly on the blocks between Scottsdale Road and 69th Street, displays artwork of myriad styles—contemporary, western realism, Native American, and traditional. Several antiques shops are also here; specialties include elegant porcelains and china, jewelry, and Oriental rugs.

NEED A BREAK?

For a light meal during daytime gallery-hopping, try **Arcadia Farms** (⊠ 7014 E. 1st Ave., ☎ 480/941–5665), where such eclectic fare as raspberry–goat cheese salad and rosemary-seasoned focaccia with chicken, roasted eggplant, and feta cheese are prepared lovingly. Enjoy a cool drink or a justly popular lemon roulade pastry on the brick patio shaded by African sumac trees.

⑲ Marshall Way Arts District. Galleries that exhibit predominantly contemporary art line the blocks of Marshall Way north of Indian School Road. Upscale gift and jewelry stores can be found here too. Farther north on Marshall Way across 3rd Avenue, the street is filled with more art galleries and creative stores with a southwestern flair.

⑰ Old Town Scottsdale. Billed as "the West's Most Western Town," this area of Scottsdale has rustic storefronts and wooden sidewalks; it's touristy, but the closest you'll come to experiencing life here as it was 80 years ago. High-quality jewelry, pots, and Mexican imports are sold alongside the expected kitschy souvenirs.

⑬ Scottsdale Center for the Arts. Galleries within this cultural and entertainment complex rotate exhibits frequently, but typically emphasize contemporary art and artists. The airy and bright **Museum Store** (☎ 480/874–4464) has a great collection of unusual jewelry, as well as stationery, posters, and art books. ✉ 7380 E. 2nd St., ☎ 480/994–2787. *Free. ◷ Mon.–Sat. 10–5, Thurs. 10–8, Sun. 12–5; also open during performance intermissions.*

⑮ Scottsdale Chamber of Commerce. Pop inside to pick up some local maps, guidebooks, and brochures. Ask the helpful staff for a walking-tour map of Old Town Scottsdale's historic sites. ✉ 7343 Scottsdale Mall, ☎ 602/945–8481 or 800/877–1117. ◷ Weekdays 8:30–6:30, Sat. 10–5, Sun. 11–5.

⑯ Scottsdale Historical Museum. Scottsdale's first schoolhouse, this red-brick building houses a version of the 1910 schoolroom, as well as photographs, original furniture from the city's founding fathers, and displays of other treasures from Scottsdale's early days. ✉ 7333 Scottsdale Mall, ☎ 602/945–4499. *Free. ◷ Wed.–Sat. 10–5, Sun. noon–5. Closed July–Aug.*

⑭ Scottsdale Museum of Contemporary Art. This museum, next to the Scottsdale Center for the Arts, opened in 1999 in the spectacular Gerard L. Cafesjian Pavilion. When you step through the immense glass entryway designed by New York artist James Fraser Carpenter and stroll through the spaces within the five galleries, you'll realize it's not just the spacious outdoor sculpture garden that makes this a "museum without walls." The opening exhibit featured a variety of contemporary works, including studio glass by Czech artists Stanislav Libensky and Jaroslava Brychtova; mixed-media pieces by Luis Jimenez and William Wegman; and presentations by visual arts performers Jack Massing and Michael Galbreath. New installations are planned every few months, with an emphasis on contemporary art, architecture, and design. ✉ 7380 E. 2nd St., ☎ 480/994–2787. *$5. ◷ Mon.–Sat. 10–5, Thurs. 10–8, Sun. noon–5.*

Tempe

Charles Trumbell Hayden arrived on the east end of the Salt River in the 1860s. There he built a flour mill and began a ferry service to cross the then-flowing Rio Salado (Salt River), founding the town then known as Hayden's Ferry in 1871. Other settlers soon arrived, including an Englishman who felt—upon approaching the town from Phoenix and seeing the butte, river, and fields of green mesquite—that the name should be changed to Tempe after the Vale of Tempe in Greece. Hayden took umbrage at the suggested name change but finally relented in 1879.

Today Tempe is Arizona's sixth-largest city and the home of Arizona State University's main campus and a thriving student population. A 20- to 30-minute drive from Phoenix, the tree- and brick-lined Mill Avenue (on which Hayden's mill still stands) is the main drag, rife with student-oriented hangouts, bookstores, boutiques, eateries, and a repertory movie house.

Tempe's banks of the now-dry Rio Salado are the future site of a sprawling commercial and entertainment district. When completed in several years, the project's centerpiece, the two-mile long Tempe Town Lake (created by placing inflatable dams in a flood control channel), will be ringed by parklands, hotels, and restaurants, and will be the largest urban recreation attraction in Arizona. The lake itself opened in fall 1999, with tour boats, dinner boats, and other pleasure boats plying the man-made waters.

A Good Walk

Parking is available in the public garage at Hayden Square, just north of 5th Street and west of Mill Avenue. Be sure to have your ticket stamped by local merchants to avoid paying parking fees. There's a dearth of free parking in the area and few on-street meters. From **La Casa Vieja,** on the southwest corner of Mill Avenue and 1st Street, cross 1st Street and enjoy your stroll through the **Tempe Arts Center** sculpture garden en route to the center itself. Behind the main building, stroll north to the old Mill Avenue bridge where you can check out the Arts Center's rooftop artwork. (Note: At press time the arts center was embroiled in a battle to keep its lease and may be moving, so call ahead.) Turn around and head to the main part of town; walk south on Mill Avenue, passing the old Hayden flour mill, as well as "A" Mountain to your left. Continue south along shop-lined Mill Avenue until you reach 5th Street; walk a block east on 5th toward the inverted pyramid of **Tempe City Hall.** Follow the pathway west through the grounds of City Hall and Plazita de Descanso, back to Mill Avenue. Head two blocks south on Mill to University Drive and proceed to Gammage Parkway, where you'll find the Grady Gammage Auditorium and ASU art museums and galleries on the southwest corner of the **Arizona State University** campus. You can walk back up Mill Avenue, catch the free FLASH shuttle northward (it stops on the north corner of Gammage Parkway and Mill Avenue (☞ Getting Around by Bus *in* Phoenix and Central Arizona A to Z, *below*), or wind your way northward through the university campus up toward Sun Devil Stadium.

TIMING

If you're planning to shop as well as tour the campus and museums, allow four or five hours for exploring (and periodic breaks) in downtown Tempe.

Sights to See

Arizona State University. What was once the Tempe Normal School for Teachers—in 1886, a four-room redbrick building and 20-acre cow pasture—is now the 750-acre campus of ASU, the largest university in the Southwest. Stop by the **ASU Visitor Information Center** (✉ 826 E. Apache Blvd., at Rural Rd., ☎ 480/965–0100) for a copy of a self-guided walking tour (it's a long walk from Mill Avenue, so you might opt for the short version suggested here). You'll wind past public art and innovative architecture—including a music building that bears a strong resemblance to a wedding cake (designed by Taliesin students to echo Wright's Gammage Auditorium) and a law library shaped like an open book—and end up at the 74,000-seat **ASU Sun Devil Stadium,** home to the school's Sun Devils and headquarters for the NFL's Arizona Cardinals. Admission to all ASU museums is free.

Heralded for its superior acoustics, the circular **Grady Gammage Auditorium** (✉ Mill Ave. at Apache Blvd., ☎ 480/965–4050) was the last public structure completed by architect Frank Lloyd Wright, who detached the rear wall from grand tier and balcony sections in an effort to surround every patron with sound. The stage can accommodate a full symphony orchestra, and there's a 2,909-pipe organ here as well.

Artwork is exhibited in the lobby and in two on-site galleries, and free half-hour tours are offered weekdays 1–3:30 during the school year.

While touring the west end of the campus, stop into the gray-purple stucco **Nelson Fine Arts Center** (☎ 480/965–2787), just north of the Gammage Auditorium. The center's museum houses some fine examples of 19th- and 20th-century painting and sculpture by masters such as Winslow Homer, Edward Hopper, Georgia O'Keeffe, and Rockwell Kent; it's an extensive collection for a small museum. You'll also find works by faculty and student artists and an interesting gift shop. ☉ *Tues. 10–9, Wed.–Sat. 10–5, Sun. 1–5.*

A short walk east, just north of the Hayden Library, ASU's experimental gallery and collection of crockery and ceramics are located in the **Matthews Center** (☎ 480/965–2875). ☉ *Tues.–Sat. 10–5. Closed Jun.–Aug.*

In Matthews Hall, the **Northlight Gallery** (☎ 480/965–6517) exhibits works by both renowned and emerging photographers. ☉ *Mon.–Thurs. 10:30–4:30.*

La Casa Vieja. In 1871, when Tempe was still known as Hayden's Ferry, this old house was built as the home of Charles Hayden. The adobe hacienda is modeled after Spanish mansions and was the town's first building. The late Carl Hayden, former U.S. senator from Arizona, was born here. Now a steak house called Monte's La Casa Vieja, the structure retains its original dimensions; the lobby and dining rooms contain photographs and historical documents pertaining to the frontier history of Tempe. ⊠ *3 W. 1st St.,* ☎ *480/967–7594.* ☉ *Sun.–Thurs. 11–11, Fri.– Sat. 11 AM–midnight.*

Tempe City Hall. Local architects Rolf Osland and Michael Goodwin constructed this inverted pyramid not just to win design awards (which they have) but also to shield city workers from the desert sun. The pyramid is constructed mainly of bronzed glass and stainless steel; the point disappears in a sunken courtyard lushly landscaped with jacaranda, ivy, and flowers, out of which the pyramid widens to the sky: Stand underneath and gaze up for a weird fish-eye perspective. ⊠ *31 E. 5th St., 1 block east of Mill Ave.,* ☎ *480/967–2001.* ⊠ *Free.*

NEED A BREAK?

The outdoor patio of the **Coffee Plantation** (⊠ 680 S. Mill Ave., ☎ 480/829–7878) is a lively scene—students cramming, local residents chatting over a cup of joe, and poets and musicians presenting their latest masterpieces. For a fuller meal, check out **Caffe Boa** (⊠ 709 S. Mill Ave. ☎ 480/968–9112). This friendly spot offers a back courtyard and front patio as well as indoor dining; the upbeat young staff serves creations from panini and crostini to specials like butternut squash soup and seafood ravioli.

DINING

By Howard Seftel

Once a sleepy backwater, the ever-growing Phoenix and its environs draw millions of visitors every year: tourists, conventioneers, and winter snowbirds who roost for months at a time. The population boom has been matched by an astonishing restaurant renaissance. Inventive local chefs have put southwestern cuisine on the world culinary map, and the native dishes of the area's newer ethnic communities—Persian, Ethiopian, Salvadoran, Vietnamese—have added another dimension to the local palette. Authentic Thai, Chinese, and Indian restaurants are thriving, and there's superb south-of-the-border food from every region of Mexico. Travelers with sophisticated tastes will be thrilled with Phoenix's restaurants, some ranked among the country's best.

Restaurants are remarkably casual. Except for a handful of high-end spots, slacks and sports shirt are dressy enough for men; pants or a simple skirt are appropriate for women.

Remember that restaurants change hours, locations, chefs, prices, and menus frequently, so it's best to call ahead to confirm. Show up without notice during tourist season, and you may find the drive-through window the only place in town without a two-hour wait. All listed restaurants serve dinner and are open for lunch unless otherwise specified.

Scottsdale

American

$$$$ ✕ **Terrace Dining Room.** The Phoenician's Terrace Dining Room serves
★ the most lavish (and expensive) Sunday brunch in town. Attention is paid to every detail, from the wheel of costly Parmigiano-Reggiano cheese to the fresh artichoke hearts in the salad. First, wander around the sushi section, the jumbo shrimp table, the homemade pastas, the pâtés, the crepes, and the blintzes and waffles. Then stroll to the main dishes: Salmon and lamb chops are fired up on the grill, while filet mignon and pork tenderloin in port sauce are warmed in trays. Save room for desserts like homemade ice cream, elegant chocolate truffles, or pear-rhubarb tart. Champagne keeps the meal bubbling, so don't plan anything more strenuous than a nap for the afternoon. ⊠ 6000 E. Camelback Rd. (The Phoenician), ☎ 480/423–2530. Reservations essential. AE, D, DC, MC, V.

$$$–$$$$ ✕ **The Grill at the TPC.** Everything is way over par at The Grill: This clubhouse grill is one of the best restaurants in town, but it's not for thrill-seeking foodies after great adventures in modern gastronomy. It is the place for prime steaks, both dry-aged and wet-aged beef, and stunning seafood, flown in fresh daily. For proof, try the house-smoked shark special or phenomenal sesame-crusted ahi tuna. Even nonsmokers will be happy to conclude their meal with a cigar and matchbox made of white chocolate. ⊠ 7575 E. Princess Dr. (Scottsdale Princess Resort), ☎ 480/585–4848. Reservations essential for dinner. AE, D, DC, MC, V.

$$$ ✕ **Golden Swan.** This desert oasis is a great place for a leisurely Sunday champagne brunch. Sit outside under umbrellas or in a covered pavilion that juts into a koi-filled lagoon ringed by palms and hibiscus. The Golden Swan has a unique brunch shtick: Everything except dessert is laid out in the kitchen under the watchful eyes of toque-clad chefs. Try the veal tortellini in lobster sauce, giant prawns, or filet mignon. ⊠ 7500 E. Doubletree Ranch Rd. (Hyatt Regency at Gainey Ranch), ☎ 480/991–3388. Reservations essential. AE, D, DC, MC, V.

American/Casual

$–$$ ✕ **Bandera.** If you're looking for a quick, tasty dinner before a night out on the town, try this casual, high-volume spot. The weekly menu includes wonderfully moist and meaty rotisserie chicken; you'll see the birds spinning in the big window before you even walk through the door. If you're not a poultry fan, salads, fresh fish, prime rib, and meat loaf usually make it on the menu. The mashed potatoes are divine—you'll think mom is in the kitchen peeling spuds. If you get here at prime eating hours, especially on weekends, be prepared to wait for a table. ⊠ 3821 N. Scottsdale Rd., ☎ 480/994–3524. Reservations not accepted. AE, MC, V. No lunch.

$ ✕ **Original Pancake House.** This breakfast landmark does one thing—pancakes—and does it extremely well. These flapjacks inspire worship from local admirers who wait patiently for a table on weekends. Chief among the griddled glories is the signature apple pancake: Homemade batter is poured over sautéed apples and partially baked. Then the con-

166

Phoenix Dining

coction is flipped over, glazed with cinnamon sugar and baked some more. It's creamy, sweet, bubbly . . . and huge. Other varieties, like the German pancake, are also exceptional. ⊠ *6840 E. Camelback Rd.,* ☎ *480/946–4902. Reservations not accepted. No credit cards.*

Contemporary

$$$–$$$$ ✕ **Michael's at the Citadel.** One of this town's best-looking places (check out the brick-lined waterfall at the entrance), Michael's contemporary American fare is as elegant as the setting. The entrées are the real stars here: pan-seared duck paired with foie gras and pearl couscous; sesame-crusted swordfish with green coconut curry; venison with a dried-cherry demiglaze; grilled lamb with a goat-cheese potato tart. If you're celebrating a special occasion, Michael's is the spot. ⊠ *8700 E. Pinnacle Peak Rd.,* ☎ *480/515–2575. AE, D, DC, MC, V.*

$$$–$$$$ ✕ **Rancho Pinot Grill.** The attention to quality paid by the husband-
★   and-wife proprietors here—he manages, she cooks—has made this one of the town's top eating spots. The inventive menu changes daily, depending on what's fresh. If you're lucky, you might come on a day when the kitchen features *posole,* a mouthwatering broth with hominy, salt pork, and cabbage. Entrées include quail with soba noodles, rosemary-infused chicken with Italian sausage, and grilled sea bass atop basmati rice. ⊠ *6208 N. Scottsdale Rd.,* ☎ *602/468–9463. Reservations essential. AE, D, MC, V. Closed Sun.–Mon. and mid-Aug.–mid-Sept. No lunch.*

$$$ ✕ **Cowboy Ciao.** Looking for a culinary kick? This kitchen weds southwestern fare and Italian flair, and it's no shotgun wedding, either. Main dishes, like the Chianti-marinated filet mignon, fennel-seasoned meat loaf, and wild mushrooms in an ancho chili cream sauce heaped over polenta, are creative without going off the deep end. The chocolate lottery—complete with an actual lottery ticket—is a dessert hoot. The imaginative wine list has affordable flights that let you taste several wines with your meal. ⊠ *7133 E. Stetson Dr.,* ☎ *480/946–3111. AE, D, DC, MC, V. No lunch Sun.–Mon.*

$$$ ✕ **Gregory's Grill.** This charming bistro is tiny, with seating for maybe
★   40 patrons. The menu is equally small, but outstanding. Look for appetizers like duck prosciutto, salmon ceviche, and a lovely tower fashioned from veggies and goat cheese. Entrées include beer-marinated beef tenderloin, apple-crusted salmon, and grilled pork chops with quinoa risotto. Note: You can save a bundle by bringing your own beer or wine. ⊠ *7049 E. McDowell Rd. (Papago Plaza shopping center),* ☎ *480/ 946–8700. AE, D, MC, V. Closed Sun. No lunch.*

$$$ ✕ **Razz's Restaurant and Bar.** There's no telling what part of the globe chef-proprietor Erasmo "Razz" Kamnitzer will use for culinary inspiration. However, you can count on his creations to give dormant taste buds a wake-up call: Black bean paella is a twist on a Spanish theme; South American bouillabaisse is a fragrant fish stew, stocked with veggies; and *bah mie goreng* teams noodles with fish, meat, and vegetables, perked up with dried cranberries and almonds. Count on it—Razz'll dazzle. ⊠ *10321 N. Scottsdale Rd.,* ☎ *480/905–1308. AE, DC, MC, V. Closed Sun.–Mon. No lunch.*

$$$ ✕ **Roaring Fork.** The restaurant's name is supposed to reflect what the chef calls "Western American cuisine." It means appetizers like the cornmeal crepe, stuffed with Portobello mushrooms and coated in red pepper sauce, or the smashing cracked-corn stuffing, teamed with turkey confit and dried figs. Two particularly outstanding entrées are skillet-seared pompano, embellished with crawfish and smoked ham hock, and riveting sugar-and-chili-cured duck, served with green chili macaroni. The dessert highlight is the tarte Tatin, here made with pears, not apples, and

goosed up with a vigorous ginger snap. ⊠ *7243 E. Camelback Rd.,* ☎ *480/947–0795. AE, D, DC, MC, V. Closed Sun. No lunch.*

$$ ✕ **L'Ecole.** You'll have no regrets putting yourself in the talented hands of the student-chefs at the Valley's premier cooking academy. You get a three-course dinner for about $20, a real bargain. Look for inventive appetizers like ginger soy gravlax, and main dishes like fillet Rossini. Because the students also pull server duty, you can count on being pampered, too. ⊠ *8100 E. Camelback Rd. (Scottsdale Culinary Institute),* ☎ *480/990–7639. Reservations essential. D, MC, V. Closed weekends.*

French

$$$$ ✕ **Mary Elaine's.** Swanky, formal, and austerely elegant, this is the Phoenician's showcase restaurant, with big picture windows commanding a sweeping view of Phoenix. Two chefs came and went in 1998, leaving the kitchen in chaos, but current chef James Boyce seems to have settled in at the helm. The French/Mediterranean menu leads with starters like calamari and cuttlefish gazpacho and foie gras with caramelized kumquats, then reveals the chef's way with fish. Entrées include monkfish medallions in orange-Burgundy sauce, turbot with fresh hearts of palm, and John Dory accented with fennel. A superb wine list enhances the meal, which might close with nougat glacé with candied grapefruit and Tahitian vanilla sauce. ⊠ *6000 E. Camelback Rd. (The Phoenician),* ☎ *480/941–8200. Reservations essential. Jacket required. AE, D, DC, MC, V. Closed Sun. No lunch.*

Italian

$$$–$$$$ ★ ✕ **Franco's Trattoria.** The Florence-born Franco puts together meals that sing with the flavors of Tuscany. Start with focaccia and hunks of imported Italian cheeses sliced off huge wheels. Next, sample the antipasto or the tasty risotto. Main dishes are hearty and vibrant; naturally, veal is a specialty: The *orecchie d'elefante* (so named because it seems as massive as an elephant's ear) is pounded to millimeter thinness, breaded, fried, and splayed across the plate, coated with tomatoes and shallots, basil, and lemon. ⊠ *8120 N. Hayden Rd.,* ☎ *480/948–6655. AE, MC, V. Closed Sun. and July. No lunch.*

$$$–$$$$ ✕ **Leccabaffi Ristorante.** *Leccabaffi* means "lick the mustache," and that's what you'll want to do after scraping these plates clean. The temptation begins just inside the entrance, where an antipasto table groans with grilled and roasted vegetables. The stars here are the lusty northern Italian meat, fish, and poultry dishes. The *Costoletta alla Valdostana* (a bone-in veal chop with a pocket of fontina cheese) is a triumph. The wine-soaked quail, filet mignon in a Gorgonzola sauce, and Roman-style semolina gnocchi also shine. Finish up with a glass of sweet *vin santo,* Tuscany's classic dessert wine, and a house-made biscottilife is good. ⊠ *9719 N. Hayden Rd.,* ☎ *480/609–0429. AE, D, MC, V. Closed Mon. No lunch.*

$$–$$$ ✕ **Maria's When in Naples.** In a town teeming with Italian restaurants, this is a standout. The antipasto spread laid out just inside the entrance is sure to grab your attention, and it tastes as good as it looks. The homemade pasta is another winner. Check out the *salsiccia Pugliese* (fettuccine topped with homemade sausage, leeks, porcini mushrooms, and white wine sauce), or the *orecchiette Barese* (ear-shape pasta tossed with cauliflower, pancetta, sun-dried tomatoes, olive oil, and cheese). ⊠ *7000 E. Shea Blvd.,* ☎ *480/991–6887. AE, D, DC, MC, V. No lunch weekends.*

$ ✕ **Oregano's.** This happening, jam-packed pizza-pasta-sandwich parlor lures customers with two irresistible come-ons: good food and low prices. Oregano's offers two types of Chicago pizza: stuffed deep-dish and thin-crust, and both are great. So are the untraditional lasagne, particularly the artichoke one, made with whole-wheat pasta (it's worth the

30-minute wait). Sandwich fans will appreciate the baked Italian hoagie, stuffed with pepperoni, capicolla, salami, and provolone, then loaded with tomatoes, onions, peppers, and olives. ⊠ *3622 N. Scottsdale Rd.,* ☎ *480/970–1860. Reservations not accepted. AE, D, MC, V.*

Japanese

$$–$$$ ✕ **Sushi on Shea.** You may be in the middle of the desert, but the Sushi here will make you think you're at the ocean's edge. Yellowtail, toro, shrimp, scallops, freshwater eel, and even monkfish liver pâté are among the long list of delights here. Check out the *nabemono* (hot pot or meals-in-a-bowl) prepared at your table. The best dish? Maybe it's the *una-ju* (broiled freshwater eel with a sublime smoky scent), served over sweet rice. The fact that some people believe eel is an aphrodisiac only adds to its charms. ⊠ *7000 E. Shea Blvd.,* ☎ *480/483–7799. AE, D, DC, MC, V. No lunch.*

Mexican

$$$ ✕ **La Hacienda.** The food here is nothing like the run-from-the-bor-
★   der fare you find at neighborhood taco stands—it's more like the food of Mexico's colonial grandee. The appetizers, such as a mushroom crepe enlivened with *huitlacoche* (a fungus of almost trufflelike intensity), are stunning. The entrées are heavy with seafood: huge, grilled Gulf shrimp; red snapper in a Veracruzana sauce; seared tuna, crusted with wheat flour and served with a roasted poblano and caramelized onion cake. *Cochinillo asado* is La Hacienda's signature dish—roast suck-ling pig, wheeled up to the table and carved to order. Finish with *ca-jeta* ice-cream crepes or the mesmerizing pumpkin-chocolate cheesecake. ⊠ *7575 E. Princess Dr. (Scottsdale Princess Resort),* ☎ *480/585–4848. AE, D, DC, MC, V. No lunch.*

$–$$ ✕ **Carlsbad Tavern.** This is Mexican food served New Mexican style, which means dishes with a hot-chili bite. Get yourself a potent frozen margarita (there's a nice selection of premium tequilas) to wash down starters like red chili potato pancakes and ravioli stuffed with smoked duck and tequila-marinated grilled shrimp. Entrées continue the flavor assault: *Carne adovada* is pork simmered in red chili sauce; the *machaca* tamale duo features two shredded beef tamales, one in green chili sauce, the other coated with spicy red chili; and lamb pierna, a wood-grilled, braised leg of lamb topped with red wine sauce. ⊠ *3315 N. Hayden Rd.,* ☎ *480/970–8156. Reservations not accepted. AE, D, DC, MC, V.*

Middle Eastern

$–$$ ✕ **Al Amir.** Along with traditional appetizer favorites like *baba ghanoush* (mashed eggplant), hummus, falafel, and tabbouleh, this spot serves *ma'anek,* juicy Lebanese sausages zinged with cloves, and *safiha,* canape-size pockets of dough stuffed with ground lamb. Main dishes feature kabobs, but it pays to explore the less familiar options. The *kebbe bil sanyeh* is sensational with layers of heavily seasoned ground beef baked with bulgur wheat and pine nuts. Don't leave without or-dering *knafeh,* a warm cheese pastry smothered in syrup. ⊠ *8989 E. Via Linda,* ☎ *480/661–1137. AE, D, MC, V. Closed Sun.*

Pan-Asian

$$$ ✕ **Restaurant Hapa.** "Hapa" is Hawaiian slang for "half," which de-
★   scribes the half-Japanese, half-American background of the chef. But there's nothing halfway about Hapa's astonishingly flavorful, Asian-inspired cuisine. Appetizers like skillet-roasted mussels coated in a Thai-inspired broth scented with lemongrass, mint, basil, ginger, and coconut let you know you're in for a big-time experience. The signa-ture entrée is beef tenderloin, lined with hot Chinese mustard and caramelized brown sugar. Desserts are just as inspired as the other courses: Look for the skillet of Asian pears with a macadamia-nut crust and Saigon

cinnamon ice cream, or the coconut crème brûlée tart. ⊠ *6204 N. Scottsdale Rd.,* ☎ *480/998–8220. MC, V. Closed Sun. No lunch.*

$$$ ✕ **Roy's.** Roy Yamaguchi, a James Beard award–winning chef and one of the pioneers of Pacific Rim cooking, has restaurants scattered all over the globe. Look for inventive dishes like steamed pork and crab buns with a spicy Maui onion black bean sauce; lemongrass tempura chicken breast; tiger prawns on a lobster Alfredo sauce; and nori-crusted ono with a hot and sour red pepper sauce. It's sophisticated food for sophisticated palates. ⊠ *7001 N. Scottsdale Rd. (Scottsdale Seville),* ☎ *480/905–1155. AE, MC, V. No lunch.*

Seafood

$$$–$$$$ ✕ **Restaurant Oceana.** When you're 400 mi from the nearest ocean, you can expect to pay for your seafood thrills. You'll pay at Restaurant Oceana, but you'll also get plenty of thrills. Everything here was swimming in the sea 24 hours ago. The daily-changing menu may include scallops the size of hockey pucks, Casco Bay cod, Belon oysters from Washington, and mahimahi. Bing cherry shortcake with honey whipped cream, jasmine rice pudding with pineapple soup, and chocolate cake with a molten chocolate center are just three of the can't-miss desserts. ⊠ *8900 E. Pinnacle Peak Rd.,* ☎ *480/515–2277. AE, D, DC, MC, V. Closed Sun.–Mon. No lunch.*

Southwestern

$$$ ✕ **Cafe Terra Cotta.** This Scottsdale branch of the acclaimed Tucson
★ original shows you how the Southwest was won using inventive regional creations and sophisticated flavors. Start off with buffalo carpaccio drizzled with chili-infused oil or a quesadilla filled with duck and smoked Gouda cheese. Next, move to lamb chops in an ancho-chili mole (pronounced mo-lay, this is a spicy chocolate-and-nut-based sauce) or salmon crusted with sunflower seeds and yellow chili sauce. Desserts are just as formidable, especially the orange-curd tart. ⊠ *6166 N. Scottsdale Rd. (Borgata Shopping Center),* ☎ *480/948–8100. AE, D, DC, MC, V.*

Spanish

$$$–$$$$ ✕ **Marquesa.** This gem of a restaurant pays homage to Catalonia, the
★ region around Barcelona. Everything here is right on target, from the setting to the service. Appetizers are extraordinary: *Anec D'Napoleon,* phyllo dough pouches stuffed with a heady blend of duck, foie gras, and mushrooms; and *pebrots del piquillo,* crab and fontina cheese baked into sweet red peppers. Main dishes include monkfish-veal loin duo; pan-roasted rack of lamb; and a first-class paella crammed with lobster, shrimp, mussels, clams, chicken, and *chistora* (a sharp Spanish sausage). For dessert, the Gran Torres cheesecake and flan are equally wonderful. ⊠ *7575 E. Princess Dr. (Scottsdale Princess Resort),* ☎ *480/ 585–4848. Reservations essential. AE, D, DC, MC, V. No lunch.*

Steak

$$$ ✕ **Don & Charlie's.** A favorite with major-leaguers in town for spring training, this venerable chophouse specializes in prime-grade steak and baseball memorabilia—the walls are covered with pictures, autographs, and uniforms. The New York sirloin, prime rib, and double-thick lamb chops are a hit; sides include au gratin potatoes and creamed spinach. Serious carnivores will not strike out here. ⊠ *7501 E. Camelback Rd.,* ☎ *480/990–0900. AE, D, DC, MC, V. No lunch.*

$–$$ ✕ **Pinnacle Peak Patio.** This spot is strictly for tourists, but it's no trap. More than 1,600 diners can sit inside this western restaurant, the largest in the world; another 1,400 can dine under the stars out on the patio. Founded in 1957, the Peak hasn't altered its menu in years—a menu that consists solely of five grilled steaks and hickory-roasted chicken. "Big Marv" Dickson has personally manned the grill since 1961, cooking up more than 2 million pounds of beef himself—he credits delectable porterhouse and T-bones to mesquite smoke's magic, but everyone else knows Marv as a Steak Jedi, with a sixth sense for beef. Country bands play nightly. Wear a tie you don't mind leaving behind. ⊠ *10426 E. Jomax Rd.,* ☏ *480/967–8082. AE, D, DC, MC, V. No lunch Mon.–Sat.*

Thai

$$ ╳ **Malee's on Main.** This fashionable eatery serves up sophisticated, Thai-inspired fare. The recommended *Ahoi Phannee,* a medley of seafood in a bamboo-leaf bowl moistened with red curry sauce redolent of coconut, lime leaf, and Thai basil. The Thai barbecued chicken, grilled to a sizzle and coated with rum, is outstanding. Beware: Take Malee's spices seriously—even the "mild" dishes have a bite. ⊠ *7131 E. Main St.,* ☏ *480/947–6042. AE, DC, MC, V. No lunch Sun.*

North Central Phoenix

American

$$$ ╳ **El Chorro Lodge.** Near the Phoenix Mountains Preserve, El Chorro has been doing business in this picturesque location for 60 years. Sit outside, gaze at the mountains and stars, and try not to make a meal of the famous sticky buns that immediately come to your table. El Chorro's forte is prime-graded meat. Beef Stroganoff, top sirloin, and the chateaubriand for two are tops, and fresh ocean fare like orange roughy and swordfish are also skillfully prepared. The dense chocolate-chip pecan pie makes dessert a must. ⊠ *5550 E. Lincoln Dr.,* ☏ *480/948–5170. AE, D, DC, MC, V.*

Contemporary

$$$–$$$$ ╳ **T. Cook's.** This gorgeous place is among the handful of resort restau-
★ rants that offer top-of-the-line dining for demanding gastronomes. With its brick walls, painted tile, wooden beams, vaulted ceiling, and marble accents, it looks like an Italianate church. The chef's rustic-Mediterranean fare inspires worshipful devotion, featuring exquisite delights like grilled lamb loin teamed with wild mushrooms and Swiss chard; herb-rubbed beef tenderloin with Roquefort potato pie; and sea bass wrapped in Parma ham, brightened with olives and artichokes. Civilized portions mean you can indulge freely in dessert. And that's what you'll want to do when you see the massive *collage de chocolat,* a head-turning sampler for two that will have your brain releasing good-time chemicals for days. ⊠ *5200 E. Camelback Rd. (Royal Palms),* ☏ *602/808–0766. Reservations required. AE, D, DC, MC, V.*

$$$–$$$$ ╳ **Eddie Matney's Epicurean Trio.** One of Phoenix's top chefs has split with his longtime partner, and is charting a new culinary path on his own. The results are often stunning, occasionally offbeat, and once in a while downright weird. In the fine-dining room, guests with three hours (and $70) to spare can get an eight-course prix-fixe meal. Among the highlights are a wild game consomme, melt-in-your-mouth ahi tuna teamed with Peruvian blue potatoes, beef tenderloin in a high-octane wild mushroom ragout, and a unique take on Boston cream pie. At the less formal bistro, try the fanciful East Meets West Seafood Medley, sesame-crusted ahi over braised bok choy, and Parmesan-crusted sea bass on asparagus risotto. A wine-and-cigar room, available for private parties, completes the "Epicurean Trio." ⊠ *2398 E. Camelback Rd.,* ☏ *602/957–3214. Reservations required. AE, D, DC, MC, V. Dining room: Closed Sun.–Mon. Bistro: No lunch weekends.*

$$$–$$$$ ╳ **RoxSand.** With a quirky, risky, and imaginative culinary flair, Chef
★ RoxSand Scocos doesn't follow trends; she sets them at one of the most interesting restaurants in the state. Who else would think to stuff

tamales with curried lamb moistened in a Thai-style peanut sauce? The heavenly *b'stilla* is a Moroccan-inspired appetizer of braised chicken in phyllo dough, covered with almonds and powdered sugar, and specials like mango and wild rice soup tap taste buds you didn't know you had. Air-dried duck is an exotic house specialty, served with buckwheat crepes and a pistachio-onion marmalade. Feta-stuffed chicken breast with polenta-fried shrimp is another offbeat success. Desserts are wicked, especially the B-52 torte, an intoxicating disk of chocolate laced with Kahlua and Bailey's. ✉ *2594 E. Camelback Rd. (Biltmore Fashion Park),* ☎ *602/381–0444. Reservations required. AE, DC, MC, V.*

$$$–$$$$ ✗ **Tarbell's.** Sure it's sleek, smart, and glitzy, but Tarbell's distinguishes itself from the trendoid pack with deftly prepared dishes. The menu changes daily, but you can usually find the vibrant smoked rock shrimp starter. If they're available, order the aromatic mussels, steamed in a heady broth of white wine and shallots. Pricier entrées include a first-rate New York steak with *pommes frites*; on the low end, there's surprisingly good pizza. Your sweet tooth won't be neglected if you opt for the rich Hawaiian chocolate mousse. ✉ *3213 E. Camelback Rd.,* ☎ *602/ 955–8100. Reservations required. AE, D, DC, MC, V. No lunch.*

$$$ ✗ **Lon's at the Hermosa.** A beautifully restored 1930s adobe inn with
★ wood-beamed ceilings and beehive fireplaces, Lon's has a rustic Old Arizona feel, but the menu spans the globe. Appetizers may include grilled polenta pie with wild mushroom ragout, ravioli filled with vegetables and goat cheese, or garlic prawns with pineapple relish. Many of the main dishes are grilled over wood: loin of pork, filet mignon, rack of lamb, ahi tuna, and salmon. Pasta, chicken, duck, and veal are other standouts. For dessert, look for the gingered crème brûlée tart or chocolate truffle pâté. ✉ *5532 N. Palo Cristi Dr. (Hermosa Inn),* ☎ *602/955–7878. Reservations required. AE, D, DC, MC, V. No lunch weekends.*

Delicatessen

$–$$ ✗ **Chompie's Deli.** Run by Brooklyn refugees, this bustling deli brings a bite of the Big Apple to Phoenix with its smoked fish, blintzes, homemade cream cheeses, and herring in cream sauce. The outstanding bagels will remind New York expats of home—about 20 varieties are baked fresh daily. There's also a top-notch bakery on the premises, with rugalach, pies, and coffee cake. Bring a newspaper, or schmooze with your pals. Sometimes you have to stop and smell the bagels. ✉ *3202 E. Greenway Rd.,* ☎ *602/971–8010. Reservations not accepted. AE, MC, V.*

French

$$$–$$$$ ✗ **Christopher & Paola's Fermier Brasserie.** James Beard award–win-
★ ner Christopher Gross is back in business, and locals are grateful. The Fermier Brasserie—it means, roughly, Farmer's Tavern—may sound rustically informal, but the Gallic-themed fare is strictly big-time. Feather-light ravioli, stuffed with escargots and sweetbreads, start the meal off wonderfully. So does the soup of wild mushrooms and foie gras with a touch of port. Entrées include what may be the best steak dish in town, a prime-grade slab of sirloin, marinated, rubbed with truffles, and lightly smoked. Other main dish favorites include a Provençal-style fish stew, a lovely artichoke tart, and cassoulet. Some of the desserts are so stunning that they've been pictured in national foodie magazines: The chocolate tower and the hot and cold chocolate are two of the best. A terrific by-the-glass wine list and six house-brewed beers add to this restaurant's charms. ✉ *2584 E. Camelback Rd. (Biltmore Fashion Park),* ☎ *602/522–2344. AE, D, DC, MC, V.*

$$$ ✗ **Bistro 24.** Smart and stylish, Bistro 24 beckons diners with its parquet floor, colorful murals, and snazzy bar. Mussels steamed in champagne make a lively first course, and the main dishes tilt towards seafood. Grilled salmon, bouillabaisse, and crispy-skin whitefish are deftly done, as is the steak au poivre, served with French-style *frites*. Finish up with a soufflé of tarte Tatin, and rich French-press coffee. Sunday brunch is outstanding. ⊠ *2401 E. Camelback Rd. (Ritz-Carlton Hotel),* ☎ *602/468–0700. AE, D, DC, MC, V.*

Greek

$$-$$$ ✕ **Greekfest.** This pretty place with whitewashed walls feels like an island taverna and brings the flavors of the Aegean to life. Among the appetizers, look for *taramosalata* (mullet roe blended with lemon and olive oil) and *saganaki* (*kefalograviera* cheese flamed with brandy and extinguished with a squirt of lemon). Entrées, many featuring lamb and shrimp, are equally hard-hitting. Try *exohiko* (chunks of lamb mixed with eggplant, peppers, zucchini, and mushrooms). For dessert, the *galaktoboureko* (warm custard pie baked in phyllo dough and scented with cloves and honey) is a triumph of Western civilization. ⊠ *1940 E. Camelback Rd.,* ☎ *602/265–2990. AE, D, DC, MC, V. No lunch Sun.*

Indian

$$ ✕ **Taste of India.** Bread is one of the tests of an Indian kitchen, and the models here—bhatura, naan, paratha, poori—are superb. Just about every spice in the rack is used for dishes like lamb kashmiry and tandoori chicken. Vegetarians will enjoy this spot's wonderful meatless specialties, including *benghan bhartha,* fashioned from eggplant, or *bhindi masala,* a tempting okra dish. Indian desserts include fragrant *ras malai,* a Bengali treat of sweet milk and cheese, with bits of pistachio. ⊠ *1609 E. Bell Rd.,* ☎ *602/788–3190. AE, D, MC, V.*

Italian

$$-$$$$ ✕ **Il Forno.** This is one of the nicest-looking places in town with cherry wood, sleek, shiny mirrors, and eye-catching prints, and the contemporary Italian fare is just as attractive. Chicken breast stuffed with wild mushrooms, figs, and plums, moistened by a sweet white wine sauce, is one of the town's best entrées. Rack of lamb and the seafood stew in a lobster and white wine broth both shine. So does the *pappardelle alla Bolognese,* wide pasta ribbons bathed in a dreamy veal sauce. In a town bursting with Italian restaurants, Il Forno is one of only a handful of standouts. ⊠ *4225 E. Camelback Rd.,* ☎ *602/952–1522. AE, MC, V. No lunch.*

Latin

$$-$$$ ✕ **Havana Patio Cafe.** This Cuban and Latin-American restaurant says "Yanqui, come back" with its flavorful but not too spicy fare. Appetizers are marvelous, particularly the shrimp pancakes, potato croquettes, and Cuban tamale. The best main dishes are the *ropa vieja,* shredded braised beef served with *moros,* a blend of black beans and rice; *pollo Cubano,* chicken breast marinated in lime, orange, and garlic; and *mariscos con salsa verde,* shellfish simmered in a traditional green sauce. Vegetarians will adore the *causa azulada,* a Peruvian platter featuring a blue mashed-potato cake layered with carrot and served on Swiss chard. ⊠ *6245 E. Bell Rd.,* ☎ *480/991–1496. AE, D, DC, MC, V. Closed Mon.*

Mexican

$$ ✕ **Richardson's.** This neighborhood haunt can be noisy and the waitstaff surly, but the fiery fugue of flavors known as New Mexican–style still packs 'em in until midnight. Loose-cushioned, adobe booths surround three sides of a lively bar, and an open kitchen turns out chiles rellenos, enchiladas, and other first-rate standbys. Shrimp, chicken, and chops come off the pecan wood-burning grill with distinctive, savory undertones; Chimayo chicken is flavorfully stuffed with spinach, dried tomatoes, poblano chilies, and asiago cheese, and served with a twice-baked green chili potato. There's a wait on weekends, so don't expect

to linger at the table after dinner. ⊠ *1582 E. Bethany Home Rd.*, ☎ *602/265–5886. AE, MC, V.*

$ ✕ **Blue Burrito Grille.** "Healthy Mexican food" used to be an oxymoron, but not anymore. Here you can find good-for-you, south-of-the-border fare without the lard but with all the taste. Among the heart-healthy menu items are chicken burritos, fish tacos, tamales Mexicanos, enchiladas rancheras, vegetarian burritos, and outstanding blue corn vegetarian tacos. ⊠ *3118 E. Camelback Rd.*, ☎ *602/955–9596. Reservations not accepted. AE, MC, V.*

$ ✕ **El Bravo.** The decor here consists of the collage of bad checks posted
★   by the "Order Here" window. But cognoscenti of Mexican food won't care about the decorating lapses; they come for the town's best Sonoran fare. (Sonora is the Mexican state that borders Arizona.) Burros here are edible works of art, like the *machaca* (shredded beef) *burro.* Enchiladas, chimichangas, and tacos are just as thrilling. If you've got a taste for chili zest, try the red beef popover—it will leave your tongue tingling. Even the sweets are outstanding. Go for the chocolate chimichanga—it's like a creamy Mexican s'more. ⊠ *8338 N. 7th St.*, ☎ *602/943–9753. Reservations not accepted. MC, V.*

Southwestern

$$$–$$$$ ✕ **Vincent Guerithault on Camelback.** It's hard to tell whether Chef
★   Guerithault prepares French food with a southwestern flair, or southwestern fare with a French touch. But whatever this talented chef prepares will be incredibly tempting. Make a meal of the famous appetizers: The duck tamale, smoked salmon quesadilla, and chipotle lobster ravioli are all ravishing. Main dishes are just as strong. The duck confit, rack of lamb, and grilled wild boar loin make choosing difficult, and the sautéed veal sweetbreads with blue cornmeal are out-of-this-world. The signature crème brûlée arrives in three thin pastry cups filled with vanilla, coffee, and coconut custard. ⊠ *3930 E. Camelback Rd.*, ☎ *602/224– 0225. Reservations essential. AE, D, DC, MC, V. No lunch weekends.*

$$ ✕ **Sam's Cafe.** This is the southwestern restaurant that locals bring their skittish Midwestern relatives to with perfect confidence. Nothing's too far out, but most everything is interesting and tasty. The fragrant poblano chicken chowder is fine, as are the Sedona spring rolls, flour tortillas wrapped around chicken and veggies, with a chipotle barbecue sauce. The hands-down main-dish winner is the inventive chicken-fried tuna, a lightly battered slab adorned with a jalapeño cream gravy, served with chili-mashed potatoes. Steaks, chops, tacos, and pastas (try the chicken pasta, flamed with tequila) are outstanding, and the chilled flan, fashioned from yams, drizzled with caramel sauce, and garnished with pecans, is worth a dessert splurge. ⊠ *2566 E. Camelback Rd. (Biltmore Fashion Park)*, ☎ *602/954–7100. AE, D, DC, MC, V.*

Spanish

$$–$$$ ✕ **Altos.** This hot spot attracts sophisticated locals who bask in the scents of Iberia—garlic, sherry, olive oil, saffron. Calamari de Pedro (tender squid dipped in a saffron batter and sizzled in olive oil) is a good appetizer for sharing. *Sombrilla Andaluza* is mesmerizing, a Portobello mushroom marinated in olive oil, garlic, and sherry, then grilled and festooned with red cabbage, parsley, and Serrano ham. Main dishes are also invigorating. The *filete pelon* is a buttery filet mignon topped with cabrales, a creamy Spanish blue cheese. *Lomo en adobo* is pork loin smothered in a lusty sauce with hints of chili, sesame seeds, sugar, and peanuts. The sugar-glazed chocolate espresso crème brûlée may be the single best dessert in Arizona. ⊠ *5029 N. 44th St.*, ☎ *602/808– 0890. AE, D, DC, MC, V. No lunch weekends.*

Steak

$$$–$$$$ ✕ **Morton's.** This national chain doesn't stint on quality and doesn't believe in menus: You have to sit through a 10-minute recital by your server to find out what's served. The New York sirloin is what beef is all about, a ravishing 20-ounce strip that perfectly packages looks, taste and texture, and the juicy 24-ounce porterhouse is heart-stopping. The à la carte side dishes are big enough to split two or three ways, but if you have room for dessert try the chocolate Godiva cake, a moist sponge cake with a molten chocolate interior. ✉ *2425 E. Camelback Rd. (Shops at the Esplanade),* ☎ *602/955–9577. AE, DC, MC, V. No lunch.*

$$ ✕ **Texaz Grill.** The down-home fare here is served in a cowboy setting that oozes with neighborhood charm. The T-bone steak and butter-soft fillet are very satisfying, but it's the he-man-size chicken-fried steak that lures most folks here. The fork-tender beef is encased in crisp batter and ladled with thick, peppery country gravy; the mashed potato side—with the skin mashed in—is a worthy accompaniment. Order yourself a Lone Star Brew, put some coins in the jukebox, and loosen your belt. ✉ *6003 N. 16th St.,* ☎ *602/248–7827. Reservations not accepted. AE, MC, V. No lunch Sun.*

Central Phoenix

American

$$–$$$ ✕ **Montana Grill & Bread Company.** This neighborhood spot is worth a drive from just about anywhere in town. The chef-proprietor is as at home on the range with breads and pastries as he is with the signature entrées, the Montana-style iron-skillet platters. Among the latter are a knockout mixed grill and a gorgeous crispy-on-the-outside, moist-on-the-inside salmon. For dessert, there's an over-the-top chocolate decadent cake, juiced up with caramelized bananas and a shot of Grand Marnier. ✉ *3717 E. Indian School Rd.,* ☎ *602/553–8553. MC, V. Closed Sun.*

Barbecue

$ ✕ **Honey Bear's BBQ.** Honey Bear's motto—"You don't need no teeth to eat our meat"—may fall short on grammar, but this place isn't packed with folks looking to improve their language skills. If you've got barbecue fever, the meaty pork ribs are the cure. This is Tennessee-style barbecue, which means smoky baby backs basted in thick, zippy, slightly sweet sauce with a wonderful orange tang. The sausage-enhanced "cowbro" beans and scallion-studded potato salad are great sides. If a slab of ribs still leaves you hungry, finish up with the homemade sweet potato pie. ✉ *5012 E. Van Buren St.,* ☎ *602/273–9148. Reservations not accepted. AE, D, MC, V.*

Chinese

$–$$ ✕ **Gourmet House of Hong Kong.** This popular Chinese restaurant draws customers who are interested in genuine Chinatown specialties like *chow fun* (thick rice noodles). Try the assorted meat version, topped with chicken, shrimp, pork, and squid. Lobster with black bean sauce may be the world's messiest platter, but it's also one of the tastiest. Don't wear anything that needs to be dry-cleaned. Along with an extensive seafood list, adventurous delights like five-flavor frogs' legs, duck feet with greens, and beef tripe casserole are offered. ✉ *1438 E. McDowell Rd.,* ☎ *602/253–4859. AE, D, DC, MC, V.*

French

$$$ ✕ **Coup Des Tartes.** This cozy, casual, wonderfully homey, BYOB
★   spot—it used to be an antiques store—serves deftly crafted Mediterranean-accented fare. Start off with a charcuterie platter, and move on to delightful main-course fare like fennel-tinged sea bass, ginger-spiked pork tenderloin, and the house specialty, braised lamb shank with

couscous. The chef-proprietor trained as pastry chef, and her signature dessert tarts show she's been well taught. The banana-brulée tart is especially marvelous. ⊠ *4626 N. 16th St.,* ☎ *602/212–1082. AE, D, DC, MC, V. Closed Sun.–Mon. No lunch.*

Italian

$$–$$$ ✕ **La Fontanella.** This outstanding neighborhood Italian restaurant is
★   a winning combination of quality and value. The mom-and-pop proprietors deliver all the hard-hitting flavors of their native land: *suppli,* a Roman specialty, rice croquettes filled with cheese; and escargots, bubbling in garlic and butter, get the meal off to a fast start. All the entrées are first-rate; some are out-of-this-world. Among the latter are lamb *agrassato,* lamb shank braised in wine with raisins, pine nuts, and potatoes; osso buco, gilded with pancetta; seafood *reale,* shrimp and scallops in a sherry cream sauce; and the herb-crusted rack of lamb. For dessert, La Fontanella's homemade gelato puts an exclamation mark on dinner. ⊠ *4231 E. Indian School Rd.,* ☎ *602/955–1213. AE, D, DC, MC, V. No lunch weekends.*

Latin

$ ✕ **Eliana's Restaurant.** This simple, family-run gem features budget-priced El Salvadoran specialties skillfully prepared. You can make a meal of the appetizers: *pupusas* (corn patties stuffed with pork, peppers, and cheese); *pasteles* (meat turnovers); and tamales, filled with chicken and vegetables. Main dishes will wipe out hunger pangs for about the price of a movie ticket. There's *pollo encebollado* (fried chicken with rice and beans), and *mojarra frita,* a whole fried tilapia, an Arizona farm-raised fish popular in Latin America. You can wash your meal down with refreshing homemade fruit drinks. ⊠ *1627 N. 24th St.,* ☎ *602/225–2925. Reservations not accepted. AE, D, MC, V. Closed Mon.*

Mexican

$$–$$$ ✕ **Norman's Arizona.** Chef Norman Fierros has finally gotten his kitchen act together at his latest enterprise. His "Nueva Mexicana" cuisine, aimed at sophisticated locals tired of gringo combination-plate fare, is giving off sparks. Start off with scrumptious *tamalitos,* baby tamales made from vigorous red chilies or sweet green corn. Appetizer salads are also superb, especially the endives tossed with Mexican cheese and roasted pecans. Main dishes are highly energetic, like the chili mash: mashed spuds capped by a poblano chili and surrounded by morsels of chicken in mole. Steak picado, rabbit in a spicy red chili marinade, and grilled sea bass with *culiche* (a squash-and-corn mix) also hit the mark. And no one does south-of-the-border desserts like Norman. His creamy chocolate chimichangas and fabulous banana squash pie are almost legendary. ⊠ *4410 N. 40th St.,* ☎ *602/956–2288. AE, D, MC, V. Closed Mon. No lunch weekends.*

$$–$$$ ✕ **Such Is Life.** No gringo touches here: Authentic, Yucatan-inspired
★   Mexican fare keeps the place packed. For starters, try the *nopal polanco,* a prickly pear cactus pad topped with Chihuahua cheese and chorizo. The lusty, lemon-tinged chicken soup is also thick with poultry, avocado, and hard-boiled egg. Entrées include chicken mole and adobo pork, simmered in a fragrant ancho chili, sesame-orange sauce. If the kitchen has Gulf shrimp, get them grilled in garlic. ⊠ *3602 N. 24th St.,* ☎ *602/955–7822. Reservations essential. AE, D, DC, MC, V. Closed Sun. No lunch Sat.*

$$ ✕ **San Carlos Bay Seafood Restaurant.** From the street, San Carlos Bay
★   doesn't look like much, but the best Mexican seafood in town is served inside. Start off with a seafood cocktail teeming with octopus or shrimp, in a riveting tomato-based liquid spiked with onions, cilantro, lime, and pepper. Among the main dishes, the Veracruz-style filleted snapper is coated with olives, onions, tomatoes, and peppers. The de-

licious, meaty crustaceans come soaked in a devilishly hot sauce. For seafood that doesn't make your nostrils flare, try the well-stocked seven seas stew. ⊠ *1901 E. McDowell Rd.,* ☎ *602/340–0892. Reservations not accepted. No credit cards.*

$–$$ ✕ **Los Dos Molinos.** Is this the place that launched a thousand chips?
★ You bet it is. This restaurant features New-Mexican–style Mexican food. For the uninitiated, that means HOT!—you'll know after one bite. Legions of heat seekers practically worship the Hatch, New Mexico chilies that form the backbone of the dishes here. Adobada ribs, a specialty, feature fall-off-bone meat marinated in red chilies, and the green chili enchilada and beef taco are potentially lethal. But there's flavor in this fire. The *sopaipilla,* a pillow of fried dough doused with cinnamon, honey, or powdered sugar, is the New Mexican antidote to chili flames, but if you can't stand the heat, stay out of this kitchen. ⊠ *8646 S. Central Ave.,* ☎ *602/243–9113. Reservations not accepted. AE, D, MC, V. Closed Mon.*

Pizza

$–$$ ✕ **Pizzeria Bianco.** Bronx-native Chris Bianco makes pizza good enough
★ to inspire memories of Naples, even if you've never been there. The secret? A wood-fired brick oven and a passion for quality. Bianco's pizza crust is a work of art, not too bready, not too light, and just chewy enough to keep your jaws happy. Toppings include imported cheeses, homemade fennel sausage, wood-roasted cremini mushrooms, and the freshest herbs and spices. There's also antipasto and sandwiches on fresh-baked bread. ⊠ *623 E. Adams St.,* ☎ *602/258–8300. MC, V. Closed Mon. No lunch weekends.*

Seafood

$$ ✕ **Steamed Blues.** Crabs in the desert? No, it's not a mirage. This restaurant specializes in blue crabs that are still swimming when you order them. Prepare for the din of pounding mallets as diners attack their dinner—you might think you're in the middle of the "Anvil Chorus" scene in "Il Trovatore." If you prefer not to hammer your meal, there are soft-shell crabs, as well as crab cakes and steamed shrimp. The "Boardwalk" fries—fresh-cut, seasoned, sizzling potatoes—will make you think you're on a Chesapeake Bay pier. ⊠ *4843 N. 8th Pl.,* ☎ *480/966–2722. Reservations not accepted. AE, D, DC, MC, V. No lunch weekends.*

Steak

$$ ✕ **T-Bone Steak House.** You won't see staged gunfights or Indian dances at T-Bone Steak House. You'll just see seriously good steaks in a ranch-house setting. The small menu sticks to the basics: a monstrous 2-pound porterhouse, a 1-pound T-bone, and 12-ounce sirloin, all of them juicy and flavorful. Another bonus: the view. The restaurant sits about halfway up South Mountain. Come at dusk for a great look at the twinkling city lights below. ⊠ *10037 S. 19th Ave.,* ☎ *602/276–0945. AE, DC, MC, V. No lunch.*

East Valley: Tempe, Mesa, Chandler

American

$$$–$$$$ ✕ **Top of the Rock.** The iron law of restaurant physics proclaims that
★ food quality declines the higher off the ground you get (airline food is the ultimate proof). But Top of the Rock seems to be the exception to the rule. This beautiful room, set atop a Tempe butte, has panoramic views of the Valley and food that is simply tops. The lobster napoleon appetizer—lobster layered between crispy wontons lined with Boursin cheese—is good enough to order for entrée and dessert. Main dishes include sugar-spiced barbecue salmon, roasted veal chop, free-range chicken, and mesquite-grilled Black Angus sirloin steak. The house specialty dessert is black bottom pie, with a chocolate praline center and

chocolate mousse topping. This is a great spot for a romantic dinner. ⊠ *2000 Westcourt Way (Buttes Resort), Tempe,* ☎ *602/225–9000. Reservations essential. AE, D, DC, MC, V. No lunch.*

$$–$$$ ✕ **Gordon Biersch.** Though it's in the heart of Mill Avenue, right by Arizona State University, Gordon Biersch is hardly your typical college-town watering hole—it's a high-energy brewpub with a range of sophisticated house brews and a menu made for grown-ups. Big picture windows give a great view of Tempe, and the food is just as visually pleasing. Smoked salmon handrolls, a skillet of roasted mussels, and beer-batter onion rings are good munchies. The cioppino, oyster pan roast, New York steak, and peppered ahi tuna are winning entrées. And drink up: The brewmaster follows the *Reinheitsgebot,* 500-year-old German guidelines for beer making. It's the reason German beer has the reputation it does, and the reason why these suds taste so good. ⊠ *420 S. Mill Ave., Tempe,* ☎ *480/736–0033. AE, D, DC, MC, V.*

Chinese

$$ ✕ **C-Fu Gourmet.** This is serious Chinese food, the kind you'd expect
★ to find on Mott Street in New York City's Chinatown or Grant Street in San Francisco. C-Fu's specialty is fish, and you can see several species in big holding tanks. If you've ever wondered why shrimp is a delicacy, it will be clear once you bite into these crustaceans. After they're fished out of the tank, they're steamed and bathed in a potent garlic sauce. Clams in black bean sauce and tilapia in a ginger-scallion sauce also hit all the right buttons. There's a daily dim sum brunch, too. ⊠ *2051 W. Warner, Chandler,* ☎ *480/899–3888. AE, D, DC, MC, V.*

Contemporary

$$–$$$ ✕ **House of Tricks.** There's nothing up the sleeves of Robert and Robin Trick, the inventive chef-proprietors of this rustic-looking restaurant. The appetizer list is known for its offbeat creations, like cheese and avocado blintzes and stuffed grape leaves in chipotle plum sauce. The main dishes are equally clever. The roast eggplant and goat cheese lasagna is outstanding. Grilled rack of pork with a jalapeño-orange marmalade and scallops in a saffron Pernod sauce also get high marks. The patio bar is a pleasant place to pass a mild Valley evening. ⊠ *114 E. 7th St., Tempe,* ☎ *480/968–1114. AE, D, DC, MC, V. Closed Sun.*

Ethiopian

$ ✕ **Cafe Lalibela.** A trip to the Valley's only Ethiopian restaurant makes for a fun, exotic, and cheap night out. Forget silverware—Ethiopians scoop up their food with *injera,* a soft, spongy, slightly sour bread. Among the dishes you can scoop up here are: *doro wat,* chicken and hard-boiled egg in a robust red chili sauce; *tikil gomen,* lightly spiced cabbage, carrots, and potatoes; *yebeg tibs,* panfried lamb with green pepper and rosemary; and *fosolia,* spicy green beans cooked with carrot. If you're a vegetarian, Cafe Lalibela becomes even more attractive—try *shiro wat,* ground peas in a red chili sauce, touched up with ginger and garlic. ⊠ *849 W. University Dr., Tempe,* ☎ *480/829–1939. AE, D, MC, V. Closed Mon.*

French

$$–$$$ ✕ **Citrus Cafe.** The French proprietors of this café may not boast a fancy Scottsdale address, but they serve some of the best French fare in the Valley. The daily menu is printed on a marker board according to what's fresh in the market. Try the *feuillété aux champignons* (mushrooms in puff pastry) or duck pâté studded with pistachios. The main dishes are pure French comfort food: veal kidneys, sweetbreads, leg of lamb, roast pork, and occasionally even rabbit. For dessert, there's *vacherin,* a marvelous mound of baked meringue that you won't see anyplace else in town. ⊠ *2330 N. Alma School Rd., Chandler,* ☎ *480/899–0502. AE, D, DC, MC, V. Closed Sun.–Mon. and Aug. No lunch.*

German

$–$$ ✗ **Zur Kate.** An unpretentious delight with genuine *gemütlichkeit,* this restaurant has a homey congeniality that no interior designer can manufacture. The place is crammed with beer steins, flags, travel posters and, on weekends, live oom-pah-pah music. The menu covers traditional German territory, which means lots of pork. Some of the favorites are smoked pork chop, ground ham and pork loaf, breaded pork cutlet, and homemade bratwurst. Side dishes are as filling as they are tempting: potato dumplings, home fries, tart potato salad, and pungent sauerkraut. ⊠ *4815 E. Main St., Mesa,* ☎ *480/830–4244. Reservations not accepted. MC, V. Closed Sun. (Sun.–Mon. in summer).*

Italian

$ ✗ **Organ Stop Pizza.** If you're towing around kids, this is the place for dinner. The centerpiece of the operation is the Mighty Wurlitzer Organ, with its 276 keys, 675 stops, and 5,000 pipes. Organists provide continuous entertainment, while the family munches on Italian-American standards—pizza, pasta, sandwiches, and salads. It's all as corny as Kansas in August, and just as wholesome. If you're searching for family values, your search has ended. ⊠ *1149 E. Southern Ave., Mesa,* ☎ *480/813–5700. No credit cards.*

Japanese

$$–$$$ ✗ **Yamakasa.** Yamakasa, one of the Valley's top Japanese restaurants, and its next-door neighbor, C-Fu Gourmet, order their ocean fare in tandem, so you can be sure the high-quality sushi here is fresh. The skilled sushi masters display particular artistry in the hand rolls. Two nabemono (hot pot) dishes are also worth investigating. Another specialty is *shabu-shabu,* thin-sliced beef, swished in a boiling, sake-seasoned, vegetable-filled broth. ("Shabu-shabu" is the hissing sound the meat makes when it hits the liquid.) ⊠ *2051 W. Warner, Chandler,* ☎ *480/899–8868. AE, D, DC, MC, V. Closed Mon. No lunch Sun.*

Mediterranean

$–$$ ✗ **Euro Cafe.** If this place had a motto, it would be "Nothing succeeds like excess" when it comes to portion size and flavor. The southern Mediterranean-theme fare is staggering, in every sense. The Chicken Palm dish, adorned with palm hearts and artichokes heaped over pasta, could feed a small army. The gyros platter, heaped with capers, sun-dried tomatoes, red peppers, and two kinds of Greek cheeses, is equally generous. And beware the penne carbonara, an unconscionable quantity of pasta tubes fattened with ham and bacon, drenched in a creamy cheese sauce. ⊠ *1111 S. Longmore, Mesa,* ☎ *480/962–4224. AE, D, DC, MC, V.*

Mexican

$ ✗ **Rosa's Mexican Grill.** This festive, family-friendly restaurant summons up images of a Baja beach "taqueria" without the flies. The tacos are Rosa's true glory: Beef, pork, and chicken are marinated in fruit juices and herbs for 12 hours, slowly oven-baked for another 10, then shredded and charbroiled. The fish taco, pepped up with cabbage, radishes, and lime, is also in a class by itself. Spoon on one of Rosa's five fresh homemade salsas. But beware the fiery habanero model—it can strip the enamel right off your teeth. ⊠ *328 E. University Dr., Mesa,* ☎ *480/964–5451. No credit cards. Closed Sun.–Mon.*

Middle Eastern

$ ✗ **Tasty Kabob.** Persian food is heavily seasoned, but never spicy hot.
★ Perfumed basmati rice, for example, is often teamed with several grilled kabobs—skewers of ground beef, lamb, chicken, or beef tenderloin. The stews here, called *khoresht* and *polo,* also give you a taste of au-

thentic Persian fare. If *baghali polo* is on the menu, don't hesitate—
it's dill-infused rice tossed with lima beans and lamb shank. ⊠ *1250
E. Apache Blvd., Tempe,* ☎ *480/966–0260. AE, D, MC, V. Closed Mon.*

West Valley: West Phoenix, Glendale, Litchfield Park

Chinese

$–$$
★ ✕ **Silver Dragon.** This is one of the best Chinese restaurants in town—
if you know what you're doing. Non-Asian customers are routinely
seated in a small room on the right, and are handed a snoozy, one-from-
column-A, one-from-column-B menu. Insist on sitting in the big room
to the left, and ask for the Chinese menu (it has brief English descriptions). Your boldness will be rewarded with some of the best Hong Kong–
style Chinese fare between the two coasts. "Crispy Hong Kong–Style
Chicken" is a dream, a plump whole bird steamed, flash-fried, and
hacked into bite-size pieces. The tender, juicy meat and crunchy skin
are what yin and yang are all about. Hot-pot dishes, noodles, fish, and
vegetarian dishes—the "Buddhist Style Rolls" are riveting—make it hard
to eat Chinese food anyplace else in the Valley. ⊠ *8946 N. 19th Ave.,
Phoenix,* ☎ *602/674–0151. AE, MC, V. No lunch Sat.*

German

$$ ✕ **Haus Murphy's.** Neat, tidy, and friendly, this small German restau-
rant has as much charm per square foot as any place in town. (The
soda fountain came from the set of the movie *Murphy's Romance.*) On
weekends, kick back with the old-country accordionist, knock back
some old-country brews, and devour the hearty dishes. Schnitzel is a
specialty, especially the wonderful paprika version, teamed with crispy
chunks of fried potatoes and green beans. Sauerbraten, paired with tart
red cabbage and two huge potato dumplings, is not for the faint of ap-
petite. *Kassler kotellett* (smoked pork chops), *rindergulasch* (a lusty
beef stew), and a variety of sausage platters will also leave you loos-
ening your belt. The sweet, homey desserts—apple strudel, hazelnut
torte—are a nice foil to the smoky, salty fare. ⊠ *5819 W. Glendale
Ave., Glendale,* ☎ *623/939–2480. AE, D, MC, V.*

Mexican

$–$$
★ ✕ **Pepe's Taco Villa.** The neighborhood's not fancy, and neither is this
restaurant. But in a town filled with gringoized, south-of-the-border
fare, this is the real deal. Tacos rancheros—spicy, shredded pork pun-
gently lathered with adobo paste—are a dream. So are the green corn
tamales, *machacado* (air-dried beef), and chiles rellenos. But don't
leave here without trying the sensational mole, a rich, exotic sauce fashioned from chilies and chocolate. ⊠ *2108 W. Camelback Rd., Phoenix,*
☎ *602/242–0379. No credit cards. Closed Tues.*

$ ✕ **Lily's Cafe.** Friendly mom-and-pop proprietors, a jukebox with
south-of-the-border hits, and low-priced fresh Mexican fare have kept
patrons coming here for almost 50 years. Beef is the featured ingredi-
ent. The chimichanga (it's like a deep-fried burrito) is world-class, stuffed
with tender beef and covered with cheese, guacamole, and sour cream.
Fragrant tamales, spunky red chili beef, and chiles rellenos right out of
the fryer also shine. ⊠ *6706 N. 58th Dr., Glendale,* ☎ *623/937–7757.
Reservations not accepted. No credit cards. Closed Mon.–Tues. and Aug.*

Southwestern

$$$–$$$$ ✕ **Arizona Kitchen.** A few years ago, with the help of a researcher who
studies Native American foods, management here put together a bold
southwestern menu. Appetizers like blue corn piki rolls, stuffed with
capon and goat cheese, and the wild boar anasazi bean chili give you
an indication of what's to come. Entrées include grilled sirloin of buf-
falo in cabernet-and-vanilla chili negro sauce, and grilled venison

medallions in blackberry zinfandel cocoa sauce. For dessert, try the chili-spiked ice cream in the striking turquoise "bowl" of hardened sugar. It's worth the 20-minute drive from downtown Phoenix. ⊠ *300 E. Indian School Rd. (Wigwam Resort), Litchfield Park, ☎ 623/935–3811. AE, D, DC, MC, V. Closed Sun.–Mon. and July–Aug. No lunch.*

Vietnamese

$–$$ ✕ **Little Saigon.** Less than a decade ago, you could have counted Phoenix's Vietnamese restaurants on one hand, and had enough fingers left over to put in a bowling ball. These days, though, the Vietnamese community is flourishing, and local Vietnamese in-the-know are eating at Little Saigon. The restaurant has a serenity that's out of step with its shopping mall setting—there's a pretty tiled pool with a graceful arched footbridge. The fare is equally serene. Start off with *banh khot,* doughy oval pancakes tinged with coconut and topped with shrimp. Main dishes show a lot of spunk, especially the charbroiled beef in grape leaves, lemongrass chicken, and sautéed prawns in a sizzling hot pot. Finish up with Vietnamese coffee, filtered tableside into a cup of sweetened condensed milk. The combustible brew of caffeine, sugar, and fat is one of the best legal jolts anywhere. ⊠ *1588 W. Montebello Ave. (Christown Mall), Phoenix, ☎ 602/864–7582. AE, MC, V.*

$–$$ ✕ **Pho Bang.** Tidy and unpretentious, Pho Bang delivers top-notch Vietnamese fare like catfish soup, an outstanding broth zipped up with lemon, pineapple, and fennel. Naturally there's *pho,* meal-size noodle soups stocked with various cuts of beef. Splurge on the shrimp and beef specialty and the server returns with three plates: one with transparently thin slices of marinated beef and raw shrimp; one with piles of mint, lettuce, cilantro, pickled leeks, cucumber, and carrot; and one with rice paper. Fire up the portable grill and cook the beef and shrimp. When they're done, combine with the veggies, roll in rice paper, and dip into the national condiment, fish sauce. It's all as good as it sounds. ⊠ *1702 W. Camelback Rd., Phoenix, ☎ 602/433–9440. Reservations not accepted. MC, V.*

LODGING

If there's one thing the Valley of the Sun knows how to do right, it's lodging, and metropolitan Phoenix has options ranging from world-class resorts to roadside motels, from upscale dude ranches to no-frills family-style operations where you can do your own cooking.

Most resorts lie far from downtown Phoenix, though the renaissance of this area has brought new interest from hoteliers, with historic spots such as the Arizona Biltmore (still Phoenix's nicest) and the charming San Marcos being joined by many others. Most of the other resorts are in the neighboring, tourist-friendly city of Scottsdale, a destination in its own right; a few are scattered 20 to 30 mi to the north in the quickly expanding communities of Carefree and Cave Creek. Dude-ranch territory is 60 mi northwest, in the town of Wickenburg.

Most downtown Phoenix properties are business and family hotels, closer to the heart of the city—and to the average vacationer's budget. Many properties cater to corporate travelers during the week, but lower their rates on weekends to entice leisure travelers; ask about weekend specials when making reservations.

Travelers flee snow and ice to bask in the Valley of the Sun. As a result, winter is the high season, peaking in January through March. Summer season—mid-May through the end of September—is giveaway time, when a night at one of the fanciest resorts often goes for a quarter of the winter price.

Scottsdale

$$$$ 🏨 **Hyatt Regency Scottsdale at Gainey Ranch.** A fun place for families, this resort has a huge water park with waterfalls, 10 pools, a water slide, lagoons plied by gondolas, and waterways that encircle three-quarters of the property. Three golf courses offer a choice of terrains—dunes, arroyo, or lakes—to suit a fancy for sand or water traps. The lobby is filled with stunning Native American sculpture and looks onto a large courtyard where weekend flamenco guitar performances are held. An innovative project, the Hopi Center, provides exhibits and demonstrations, presided over by two Hopi Indians—it's a remarkable venture for a resort, and well worth a visit even for nonguests. Rooms are nicely sized and comfortable. ⊠ *7500 E. Doubletree Ranch Rd., 85258,* ☎ *480/991–3388 or 800/233–1234,* 🆇 *480/483–5550. 493 rooms, 7 casitas. 3 restaurants, 1 bar, 10 pools, three 9-hole golf courses, 8 tennis courts, croquet, health club, concierge floor, business services, free parking. AE, D, DC, MC, V.*

$$$$ 🏨 **Marriott's Camelback Inn.** This historic resort is a swank oasis of
★ comfort and relaxation in the gorgeous valley between Camelback and Mummy mountains, with the best-known spa in the area. Founded in the mid-'30s, the Camelback revels in its Southwest setting, from the stunning cacti adorning the 125-acre grounds to the latilla beam/kiva log lodgings. Rooms are notably spacious and varied in configuration—seven suites even have private swimming pools. A gallery displays Barry Goldwater's historic and landscape photographs, a revelation for those who didn't know of the former senator's talent with a camera. Visit the acclaimed spa, where you can indulge in a massage or in something more exotic like a Para-Joba Body Wrap or an Adobe Mud Purification Treatment. ⊠ *5402 E. Lincoln Dr., 85253,* ☎ *480/948–1700 or 800/242–2635,* 🆇 *480/951–8469. 453 rooms, 27 suites. 5 restaurants, lounge, coffee shop, 3 pools, spa, two 18-hole golf courses, 6 tennis courts, hiking, business services, meeting rooms, free parking. AE, D, DC, MC, V.*

$$$$ 🏨 **The Phoenician.** Guests enter a bright, airy lobby to find towering
★ fountains, gleaming marble, and smiling faces of a service staff who will do handsprings to satisfy. French-provincial decor and authentic Dutch-master paintings are a bit of a surprise in the desert, and create a sumptuous atmosphere. A 2-acre cactus garden showcases hundreds of varieties of cacti and succulents, the Centre for Well Being spa has an inspiring meditation atrium, and the resort's centerpiece pool is lined with mother-of-pearl tiles. Rooms are spacious, with cream walls, tasteful rattan furnishings in muted tones, Italian marble bathrooms, and private patios. Ask for a room facing south, with views of the resort's pools and the city. In a city known for great dining, the Phoenician can lay claim to two of the area's finest restaurants, **Mary Elaine's** and the **Terrace Dining Room** (☞ *Dining, above*). ⊠ *6000 E. Camelback Rd., 85251,* ☎ *480/941–8200 or 800/888–8234. 581 rooms, 73 suites. 4 restaurants, 9 pools, barbershop, beauty salon, sauna, steam room, golf privileges, 12 tennis courts, archery, badminton, basketball, croquet, health club, jogging, volleyball, pro shop, billiards, children's programs, business services, free parking. AE, D, DC, MC, V.*

$$$$ 🏨 **Scottsdale Plaza Resort.** Arched doorways, soft-beige stucco, and tiered stone fountains lend Old World charm to this hotel's Spanish-Mediterranean ambience. Although it lacks the requisite lush golf fairways, this 40-acre independent hotel is out to compete with the five-star big boys. Special-touch amenities—such as the box of chocolate truffles left on the pillow—accompany more pragmatic luxuries like 2-ft-thick walls between rooms. Suites are arranged around a courtyard pool, and the resort boasts Arizona's largest hot tub. The lounge at **Remington's,** the hotel's main restaurant, features jazz combos. ⊠ *7200 N. Scotts-*

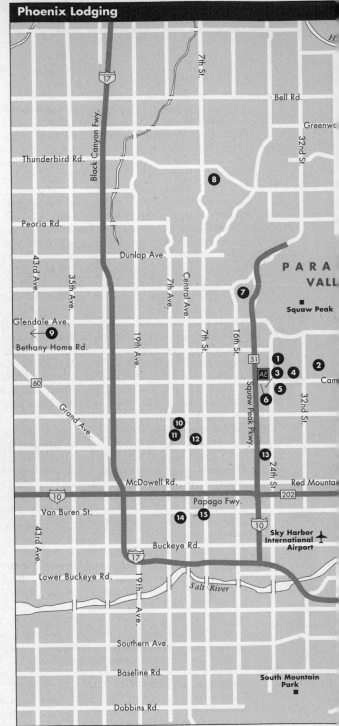

Phoenix Lodging

KEY

A/E American Express Office

0 | 4 miles
0 | 6 km

n Rhodes Aqueduct

TO CAREFREE AND CAVE CREEK

Scottsdale Municipal Airport

SCOTTSDALE

Scottsdale Rd.

Pima Rd.

Thunderbird Rd.

Cactus Rd.

Shea Blvd.

Shea Blvd.

64th St. (Invergordon Rd.)

Scottsdale Rd.

Via De Ventura

96th St.

S E

Tatum Blvd.

Indian Bend Rd.

Lincoln Dr.

Mc Donald Dr.

Camelback Mountain

ck Rd.

Indian School Rd.

Alma School Rd.

Beeline Hwy.

87

44th St.

Thomas Rd.

Scottsdale Rd.

Hayden Rd.

Papago Park

McDowell Rd.

McKellips Rd.

Brown Rd.

Country Club Rd.

Mesa Dr.

202

Salt River

143

Priest Dr.

Arizona State University

Rural Rd.

University Dr.

MESA

Lindsay Rd.

Apache Blvd.

Main St.

Broadway Rd.

Dobson Rd.

Mill Ave.

101

TEMPE

60

Superstition Fwy.

48th St.

10

Baseline Rd.

Price Rd.

Guadalupe Rd.

McQueen Rd.

GILBERT

20 21 22 24 23 17 18 19 25 26 29 28 27 30 31 32 33 34 35 36

dale Rd., 85253, ☎ 480/948–5000 or 800/832–2025, ℻ 480/998–
5971. *224 rooms, 170 suites, 10 lodges. 2 restaurants, 3 lounges, 5 pools,
beauty salon, 3 outdoor spas, putting green, 5 tennis courts, exercise room,
3 racquetball courts, pro shop, free parking. AE, D, DC, MC, V.*

$$$$ ⬚ **Scottsdale Princess.** On the 450 beautifully landscaped acres of this
resort, Mexican-colonial architecture is set against the splendor of the
McDowell Mountains. Built around a series of outdoor areas, the resort has a wonderfully open feel. Rooms in the red-tile-roof main
building and the casitas are furnished in desert-sand tones with pink
accents; the resort's emphasis on spaciousness is echoed in details like
"walk-around" tile showers and immense closets. The **Marquesa**
restaurant has been consistently rated one of the best in the state. Another top-notch restaurant is **The Grill at the TPC,** an upscale steak
and seafood establishment (☞ Dining, *above,* for both). The landscape
director leads tours of the 450-acre grounds, which are lush with
palms, bougainvillea, and rosemary shrubs (each restaurant has its own
herb garden). For perfect sunset-gazing, choose the quiet east pool, where
the distant mountains are perfectly framed by a circle of palms. ⊠ *7575
E. Princess Dr., 85255,* ☎ *480/585–4848 or 800/344–4758,* ℻ *480/
585–0091. 650 rooms, 21 suites, 125 casitas, 75 villas. 5 restaurants,
bar, 3 pools, spa, steam room, two 18-hole golf courses, 7 tennis
courts, health club, racquetball, squash, pro shops, business services,
free parking. AE, D, DC, MC, V.*

$$$–$$$$ ⬚ **Sunburst Resort.** This low-rise hotel may be Scottsdale's best-kept
secret. Five two-story structures line grounds dotted with orange trees
and Adirondack chairs clustered beneath oversized canvas umbrellas.
Roomy accommodations are decorated with patterned bedspreads in
vivid, primary colors, benches upholstered in whimsical cow-print
material, and intricately carved pine furnishings; French doors open
onto private balconies. Motorists will appreciate parking close to the
room. ⊠ *4925 N. Scottsdale Rd., 85251,* ☎ *480/945–7666,* ℻ *480/
945–4056. 205 rooms, 5 suites. Restaurant, bar, pool, refrigerators,
exercise room, meeting rooms, free parking. AE, D, DC, MC, V.*

$$$ ⬚ **Marriott's Mountain Shadows.** Across the street from the more up-
scale Camelback Inn, this Marriott property is a ranch-style resort, per-
fect for families and enviably located, as its name implies, right at the
base of Camelback Mountain. Although the furnishings aren't as distinctive as at its high-class sister property, rooms are large and comfortable, with walk-in closets and spacious sitting areas. Creeks and a
waterfall make the highly regarded golf course a duffer's oasis; you can
even play night golf with glow-in-the-dark balls. If the golf doesn't relax
you, head for the 2 hydrotherapy pools. ⊠ *5641 E. Lincoln Dr.,
85253,* ☎ *480/948–7111 or 800/228–9290,* ℻ *480/951–5430. 318
rooms, 19 suites. 3 restaurants, lounge, 3 pools, massage, sauna, 18-
hole executive golf course, putting green, 8 lighted tennis courts, exercise room, Ping-Pong, pro shops, meeting rooms, airport shuttle, free
parking. AE, D, DC, MC, V.*

$$$ ⬚ **Renaissance Cottonwoods Resort.** Shopaholics will like this 25-acre
resort—it's across the street from the shops and restaurants of the Bor-
gata Shopping Center (☞ Shopping, *below*). Check in among pottery
and large cacti in the low-key lobby; you'll be chauffeured in a golf cart
to your room in one of the adobe buildings. White stucco rooms are pleas-
ant, with light wood furniture, beamed ceilings, and small but well-kept
bathrooms. The suites are much grander, boasting private hot tubs,
large living rooms, and minibars. ⊠ *6160 N. Scottsdale Rd., 85253,* ☎
480/991–1414, ℻ *480/951–3350. 64 rooms, 107 villas. Restaurant, 2
pools, 4 tennis courts, meeting rooms. AE, D, DC, MC, V.*

$$–$$$$ 🏨 **Radisson Resort and Spa.** With myriad sports options, this hotel is the perfect match for active types who desire the facilities of a swank resort in a low-key setting. Two-story buildings house guest rooms, accessible via pathways winding through the well-kept grounds. The large, airy lobby has massive fountains. The spacious rooms are done in teal and peach tones, with patios or balconies, big closets, and sitting areas. Tapps, the resort's pub, features 12 specialty beers on draft. ⊠ *7171 N. Scottsdale Rd., 85253,* ☎ *480/991–3800 or 800/333–3333,* ℻ *602/948–1381. 318 rooms, 32 bi-level suites, 2 luxury suites. Restaurant, 2 bars, patisserie, 4 pools, beauty salon, spa, two 18-hole golf courses, 21 tennis courts, volleyball. D, DC, MC, V.*

$ 🏨 **Motel 6 Scottsdale.** The best bargain in Scottsdale lodging is easy to miss, but it's worth hunting for as it's close to the specialty shops of 5th Avenue and Scottsdale's Civic Plaza. Amenities aren't a priority here, but the price is remarkable considering the stylish and much more expensive resorts found close by. Rooms are small and spare with blue carpets, print bedspreads, and a small desk and wardrobe. And how many Motel 6 properties have a pool surrounded by palms and rooms with a view of Camelback Mountain? ⊠ *6848 E. Camelback Rd., 85251,* ☎ *480/946–2280,* ℻ *480/949–7583. 122 rooms. Pool, hot tub, free parking. AE, D, DC, MC, V.*

$ 🏨 **Scottsdale's 5th Avenue Inn.** The most attractive feature of this three-story, exterior corridor motel is its location within walking distance of Scottsdale's Old Town and boutique/gallery enclave. Modest rooms have standard but serviceable furnishings that include a sofa, coffee table, and petite writing desk, as well as a large open-closet dressing area. Don't come expecting luxury; what you will find is a friendly welcome and a blessedly short stroll to some of the area's finest shopping—which in this city based on the almighty auto is a rarity. ⊠ *6935 5th Ave., 85251,* ☎ *480/994–9461 or 800/528–7396,* ℻ *480/947–1695. 92 rooms. Breakfast room, pool, hot tub, free parking. AE, D, DC, MC, V.*

North of Scottsdale: Carefree and Cave Creek

$$$$ 🏨 **The Boulders.** The Valley's most serene and secluded luxury resort
★ hides among hill-size, 12-million-year-old granite boulders in the foothills town of Carefree, just over the border from Scottsdale. Casitas snuggled into the rocks have exposed log-beam ceilings, ceiling fans, and curved, pueblo-style half-walls and shelves. Each has a patio with a view, a miniature kiva fireplace, and spacious bathrooms with deep tubs. Luxury touches abound, from champagne upon arrival to "couples massages" available in the privacy of your casita. Boutiques and a satellite branch of the Heard Museum are on the property, and golfers stay here to play on two premier courses. ⊠ *34631 N. Tom Darlington Dr., Carefree 85377,* ☎ *480/488–9009 or 800/553–1717,* ℻ *480/488–4118. 160 casitas, 46 patio homes. 5 restaurants, 2 pools, spa, two 18-hole golf courses, 6 tennis courts, exercise room, hiking, horseback riding, jogging, business services, meeting rooms, free parking. AE, D, DC, MC, V.*

North Central Phoenix: Biltmore District

$$$$ 🏨 **Arizona Biltmore.** Designed by Frank Lloyd Wright's colleague Al-
★ bert Chase McArthur, the Biltmore has remained the premier resort in central Phoenix since it opened in 1929. The dramatic lobby, with its stained-glass skylights, wrought-iron pilasters, and cozy sitting alcoves, fills with piano music in the evenings, inviting guests to linger. Impeccably manicured grounds have open walkways, fountains, and flower beds in colorful bloom. Story has it that the Catalina Pool's blue and gold tiles so enchanted former owner William Wrigley, Jr., that he

bought the factory that produced them. Rooms have marble bathrooms and the same low-key elegance as the rest of the hotel, decorated in earth tones and accented with southwestern-patterned accessories. You'll be in good company: Every American president since Herbert Hoover, and various celebrities, have stayed here. ⊠ *24th St. and Missouri Ave., Phoenix 85016,* ☎ *602/955–6600 or 800/950–0086,* FAX *602/381–7600. 720 rooms, 50 villas. 4 restaurants, lobby lounge, 7 pools, two 18-hole golf courses, putting green, 8 tennis courts, health club, jogging, concierge, car rental, free parking. AE, D, DC, MC, V.*

$$$$ ⊡ **Ritz-Carlton.** This sand-color neo-Federal facade facing Biltmore Fashion Park hides a graceful, well-appointed luxury hotel. Large public rooms are decorated with 18th- and 19th-century European paintings and house a handsome china collection. Rooms, done in shades of ice blue and peach, have stocked refrigerators, irons with ironing boards, feather and foam pillows, safes, and white-marble bath basins. Choose between mountain or city vistas. ⊠ *2401 E. Camelback Rd., Phoenix 85016,* ☎ *602/468–0700 or 800/241–3333,* FAX *602/468–0793. 281 rooms, 14 suites. Restaurant, 2 bars, pool, 2 saunas, exercise room, bicycles, concierge floor, business services, parking (fee). AE, D, DC, MC, V.*

$$$ ⊡ **Embassy Suites Biltmore.** Adjacent to Biltmore Fashion Park, this large all-suites hotel has a cheery, informal feel. Huge palms, boulders, and waterfalls punctuate an airy lobby, and mazelike paths lead to lodgings around the atrium. The pleasant suites have small living rooms, larger bedrooms, wet bars, and nicely appointed baths. Complimentary breakfast and afternoon cocktails are thoughtful perks. ⊠ *2630 E. Camelback Rd., Phoenix 85016,* ☎ *602/955–3992 or 800/362–2779,* FAX *602/955–3992. 232 suites. Restaurant, lounge, pool, hot tub, exercise room. AE, D, DC, MC, V.*

$$–$$$ ⊡ **Phoenix Inn.** A block off a popular stretch of Camelback Road, this three-story property is a remarkable bargain, considering it has amenities not generally seen in properties of the same price category—leather love seats, refrigerators, coffeemakers, hair dryers, and microwaves. Several rooms have corner Jacuzzis. Continental breakfast is served daily from 6 to 10, in a pleasant breakfast room with a large television. ⊠ *2310 E. Highland Ave., Phoenix 85016,* ☎ *602/956–5221 or 800/956–5221,* FAX *602/468–7220. 120 suites. Breakfast room, pool, hot tub, exercise room, shop, coin laundry. AE, D, DC, MC, V.*

$$ ⊡ **Camelback Courtyard by Marriott.** Built in 1990, this four-story hostelry delivers compact elegance in its public areas (lots of plants, white tile, and wood) and reliable, no-frills comfort in its rooms and suites. A lap pool and Jacuzzi await in the landscaped courtyard. More than 50 restaurants are within walking distance. ⊠ *2101 E. Camelback Rd., Phoenix 85016,* ☎ *602/955–5200,* FAX *602/955–1101. 154 rooms, 11 suites. Breakfast room, bar, room service, pool, hot tub, exercise room, meeting rooms, free parking. AE, D, DC, MC, V.*

Northeast Phoenix and Paradise Valley

$$$$ ⊡ **Hermosa Inn.** The ranch-style lodge at the heart of this small resort
★   was the home and studio of cowboy artist Lon Megargee in the 1930s; today the adobe structure houses Lon's (☞ Dining, *above*), justly popular for its New American cuisine and amiable staff. The inn, on 6 acres of lush lawn mixed with desert landscaping, is a hidden jewel of hospitality and low-key luxury. Villas as big as private homes and individually decorated casitas hold an enviable collection of art. The secluded Garden Court's hot tub is set in a beautifully designed courtyard. A blessedly peaceful alternative to some of the larger resorts, the Hermosa offers serenity, attention to detail, and alluring accommodations. ⊠ *5532 N. Palo Cristi Rd., Paradise Valley 85253,* ☎ *602/*

955–8614 or 800/241–1210, FAX *602/955–8299. 4 villas, 3 haciendas, 22 casitas, 17 ranchos. Restaurant, bar, kitchenettes, pool, 2 hot tubs, 3 tennis courts, free parking. Full breakfast. AE, D, DC, MC, V.*

$$$$ ⊡ **Royal Palms.** Once the home of Cunard Steamship executive Delos T. Cooke, this Mediterranean-style resort has beautifully maintained courtyards with antique fountains, a stately row of the namesake palms at its entrance, and individually designed, stylish rooms. The deluxe casitas are each done in a different theme—Trompe l'Oeil, Romantic Retreat, Spanish Colonial—by members of the American Society of Interior Designers. The restaurant, **T. Cook's** (☞ *Dining, above*), is one of the most popular in town. ✉ *5200 E. Camelback Rd., Phoenix 85018,* ☎ *602/840–3610 or 800/672–6011,* FAX *602/840–6927. 116 rooms and casitas, 4 suites. Restaurant, bar, pool, tennis court, exercise room, business services, meeting rooms, free parking. AE, D, DC, MC, V.*

$$$–$$$$ ⊡ **Doubletree La Posada Resort.** Camelback Mountain is a spectacular backdrop for this sprawling resort with extensive athletic and sports facilities. The vast Lagoon Pool is the resort's centerpiece, replete with cascading waterfalls, passageways under red boulder formations, and the Grotto Bar. Large rooms sport iron furniture and Navajo-patterned bedspreads; all have patios, data ports, and bathrooms with double vanities. The property's tile floors, mauve/maroon carpets, and amusing chandeliers might make you think you're in a time warp (the place was built in 1978), and the lounge's round, sunken disco floor may fulfill your burning, unresolved "Saturday Night Fever" fantasies. ✉ *4949 E. Lincoln Dr., Paradise Valley 85253,* ☎ *602/ 952–0420 or 800/222–8733,* FAX *602/840–8576. 252 rooms, 10 suites. Restaurant, lounge, 2 pools, 4 hot tubs, beauty salon, massage, sauna, 2 putting greens, 6 tennis courts, exercise room, horseshoes, racquetball, volleyball, pro shop, nightclub, free parking. AE, D, DC, MC, V.*

Central Phoenix

$$–$$$ ⊡ **Embassy Suites Phoenix Airport West.** Just minutes from downtown, this four-story courtyard hotel has lush palms and olive trees surrounding bubbling fountains and a sunken pool. Complimentary breakfast, cooked to order, and an evening social hour are offered in the spacious atrium lounge. Rooms have hair dryers, irons and ironing boards, and wet bars with microwaves, sinks, and mini-refrigerator. ✉ *2333 E. Thomas Rd., 85016,* ☎ *602/957–1910,* FAX *602/955–2861. 183 suites. Restaurant, kitchenettes, refrigerators, pool, hot tub, exercise room, laundry service, airport shuttle, free parking. Full breakfast. AE, D, DC, MC, V.*

$$–$$$ ⊡ **Hyatt Regency Phoenix.** A quintessential Hyatt, this convention-oriented hotel features a spare, seven-story, all-white atrium (there's a surreal, space-station feel here) with huge sculptures and whooshing glass elevators. It also has a revolving restaurant with panoramic views of the Phoenix area. The hotel itself is run efficiently if not warmly, handling the arrival and departure of hundreds of business travelers each day. While not distinctive in any way, rooms are spacious and comfortable. Note: The atrium roof blocks east views on floors 8 to 10. ✉ *122 N. 2nd St., 85004,* ☎ *602/252–1234,* FAX *602/254–9472. 667 rooms. 45 suites. 3 restaurants, bar, pool, exercise rooms, concierge, business services, meeting rooms, car rental, parking (fee). AE, D, DC, MC, V.*

$$ ⊡ **Hilton Suites.** This practical and popular 11-story atrium is a model of excellent design within tight limits. It sits off Central Avenue, 2 mi north of downtown amid the Central Corridor cluster of office towers. The marble-floor, pillared lobby opens into an atrium containing palm trees, natural boulder fountains, glass elevators, and a lantern-lighted café, where guests enjoy a bite. Each room has an exercise bike and VCR, and a large walk-through bathroom between the living room and bedroom. ⊠ *10 E. Thomas Rd., 85012,* ☏ *602/222–1111 or 800/445–8667,* 𝖥𝖠𝖷 *602/265–4841. 226 suites. Restaurant, bar, kitchenettes, refrigerators, in-room VCRs, indoor lap pool, sauna, hot tub, exercise room, free parking. AE, D, DC, MC, V.*

$$ ⊞ **Lexington Hotel.** Phoenix's best bet for fitness enthusiasts and sports-lovers, the Lexington houses a 45,000-square-ft health facility, which includes among other things, a full-size indoor basketball court, a 40-station machine workout center, and a large outdoor waterfall pool. The ambience is bright, modern, and informal. Rooms range in size from moderate (in the cabana wing, first-floor rooms have poolside patios) to very small (tower wing). This is where visiting teams—and fans—like to stay. ⊠ *100 W. Clarendon Ave., 85013,* ☏ *602/279–9811,* 𝖥𝖠𝖷 *602/285–2932. 180 rooms. Sports bar, pool, beauty salon, hot tub, massage, sauna, steam room, health club, basketball, racquetball, free parking. AE, D, DC, MC, V.*

$–$$$ ⊞ **Hotel San Carlos.** Built in 1928, this seven-story hotel is a step back in time: Big-band music, wall tapestries, Austrian crystal chandeliers, shiny copper elevators—Phoenix's first—and an accommodating staff transport you to a more genteel era. Among other distinctions, the San Carlos was the Southwest's first air-conditioned hotel, and suites bear the names of movie star guests like Marilyn Monroe and Spencer Tracy. Rooms, rather snug by modern standards, have attractive period furnishings, plus coffee makers and complimentary movies (and if you think the rooms are small, wait until you see the pool). Room amenities were upgraded in 1999, and restoration of the lobby's original marble floors will be completed by 2000. ⊠ *202 N. Central Ave., 85004,* ☏ *602/253–4121,* 𝖥𝖠𝖷 *602/253–6668. 132 rooms. 3 restaurants, café, pool, exercise room, meeting rooms, parking (fee). AE, D, DC, MC, V.*

$–$$ ⊞ **Quality Hotel & Resort.** With a 1.5-acre Getaway Lagoon ringed by exotic palms and bamboo, the Quality is central Phoenix's best bargain oasis. Rooms and public areas are simply furnished, while the VIP floor offers cabana suites and a private rooftop pool with views of downtown Phoenix's ever-changing skyline. Be prepared for occasional lapses in service. ⊠ *3600 N. 2nd Ave., 85013,* ☏ *602/248–0222 or 800/256–1237,* 𝖥𝖠𝖷 *602/265–6331. 257 rooms, 23 suites. Restaurant, bar, 4 pools, hot tub, putting green, basketball, exercise room, shuffleboard, volleyball, playground, laundry, business services, free parking. AE, D, DC, MC, V.*

North and West Phoenix

$$$$ ⊞ **Wigwam Resort.** Built in 1918 as a retreat for executives of the Goodyear Company, the Wigwam has the pleasing feel of an upscale lodge. You'll still find a wealth of perks, primary among them two top-notch designer golf courses. Casita-style rooms, situated along paths overflowing with cacti, palms, and huge bougainvillea, are decorated in a tasteful southwestern style: distressed-wood furniture, iron lamps, pastel walls, and brightly patterned spreads. Local artwork adorns the walls and all rooms have patios. The business center is in a separate wing so as to not mix business with pleasure, and the immense suites have parlors that can hold up to 300 of your closest friends. It's easy to see how this isolated world of graciousness inspires a fierce loyalty in its guests, some of whom have been returning for more than 50 years. ⊠ *300 Wigwam Blvd., Litchfield Park 85340,* ☏ *623/935–3811 or 800/327–0396,* 𝖥𝖠𝖷 *623/935–3737. 261 rooms, 70 suites. 3 restaurants, 3 bars, 2 pools, 2 hot tubs, beauty salon, 3 golf courses, 9 tennis courts, basketball, croquet, exercise room, Ping-Pong, shuffleboard,* *volleyball, pro shop, children's programs, business services, meeting room, free parking. AE, D, DC, MC, V.*

$$$–$$$$ ⊞ **Pointe Hilton at Squaw Peak.** The most family-oriented of the Pointe group, Squaw Peak features a 9-acre recreation area known as the Hole-in-the-Wall River Ranch with swimming pools fed by man-made waterfalls, a 130-ft water slide, and a 1,000-ft "river" that winds past a mini–golf course, tennis courts, outdoor decks, and artificial buttes with stunning mountain vistas. The Coyote Camp keeps kids busy with activities from gold panning to arts and crafts. Accommodations in the pink stucco buildings vary in size from standard two-room suites to the grand three-bedroom Palacio; all have two or more televisions, wet bars, and balconies. Families prefer the bi-level suites. ⊠ *7677 N. 16th St., Phoenix 85020,* ☎ *602/997–2626 or 800/876–4683,* ⠀ *602/997–2391. 431 suites, 130 casitas, one 3-bedroom house. 3 restaurants, 2 lounges, 7 pools, spa, 18-hole golf course, miniature golf, tennis courts, exercise room, hiking, Ping-Pong, mountain bikes, shops, children's programs, meeting rooms. AE, D, DC, MC, V.*

$$–$$$$ ⊞ **Pointe Hilton at Tapatio Cliffs.** This oasis, snuggled into 400 acres at the base of Phoenix North Mountain Desert Park, has some of the Valley's most spectacular views. The lobby has an open, airy feel, with beamed chalet-type ceilings, so the bright purple carpeting and bold bedspreads in the rooms come as something of a surprise. But the white-washed wood furniture, tin mirrors, marble counters, and well-chosen art are all nice touches. The resort's centerpiece is "The Falls," an award-winning 3-acre creation: A 40-ft cascade fed by mountain waterfalls ends in 12 travertine pools, surrounded by tiled terraces and flower gardens. ⊠ *11111 N. 7th St., 85020,* ☎ *602/866–7500 or 800/876–4683,* ⠀ *602/993–0276. 584 suites. 3 restaurants, 3 lounges, 7 swimming pools, spa, 18-hole golf course, 11 tennis courts, exercise room, hiking, horseback riding, jogging, business services, meeting rooms, airport shuttle, parking (fee). AE, D, DC, MC, V.*

Near Sky Harbor Airport

$$$–$$$$ ⊞ **Pointe Hilton on South Mountain.** The Southwest's largest resort, 15 minutes from downtown, sits next to South Mountain Park, a 16,000-acre desert preserve. Rooms and public areas are serviceable, but the facilities are the real draw: The Pointe offers a premier four-story sports center, four restaurants, and various outdoor activities, from golf and tennis to horseback riding and mountain biking. Landscaped walkways and roads link everything on the 750-acre property; carts and drivers are always on call. ⊠ *7777 S. Pointe Pkwy., Phoenix 85044,* ☎ *602/438–9000 or 800/876–4683,* ⠀ *602/431–6535. 638 suites. 4 restaurants, 6 pools, saunas, 18-hole golf course, 10 tennis courts, health club, hiking, horseback riding, jogging, racquetball, volleyball, mountain bikes, pro shop, coin laundry, meeting rooms, free parking. AE, D, DC, MC, V.*

$$ ⊞ **Doubletree Guest Suites.** In the Gateway Center, just 1½ mi north of the airport, this honeycomb of six-story towers is the best of a dozen choices for the traveler who wants to get off the plane and into a comfortable, centrally located property. Rooms have wet bars with microwaves and refrigerators. Vacationers beware: Bedroom furnishings cater to corporate guests traveling light—two-drawer credenzas serve as bureaus and dinky wardrobes function as closets. ⊠ *320 N. 44th St., Phoenix 85008,* ☎ *602/225–0500 or 800/800–3098,* ⠀ *602/225–0957. 242 suites. Restaurant, bar, pool, sauna, exercise room, meeting rooms, free parking. AE, D, DC, MC, V.*

$$ ⊞ **Hampton Inn Airport.** This four-story, interior-corridor hotel 9 mi from downtown is affordable and accommodating. Rooms are moderate size, appointed with handsome armoires and bright-colored leaf or fish prints for drapes and bedspreads. Free Continental breakfast is available in the lobby, where a good-size television is tuned to the local wake-up news show. Take advantage of the hotel shuttle running from 5 AM to midnight. ⊠ *4234 S. 48th St., Phoenix 85040,* ☎ *602/ 438–8688,* FAX *602/431–8339. 130 rooms, 4 suites. Pool, hot tub, jogging, in-room VCRs, meeting rooms, airport shuttle, free parking. Continental breakfast. AE, D, DC, MC, V.*

East Valley: Tempe and Mesa

$$$–$$$$ ⊞ **The Buttes.** Two miles east of Sky Harbor, nestled in desert buttes at I–10 and AZ 60, this hotel joins dramatic architecture (the lobby's back wall is the volcanic rock itself) and classic Southwest design (pine and saguaro-rib furniture, works by major regional artists) with stunning Valley views. "Radial" rooms are largest, with the widest views; inside rooms face the huge free-form pools, with waterfall, hot tubs, and poolside cantina. The elegant **Top of the Rock** restaurant (☞ Dining, *above*) is a definite plus. ⊠ *2000 Westcourt Way, Tempe 85282,* ☎ *602/225–9000 or 800/843–1986,* FAX *602/438–8622. 353 rooms. 2 restaurants, 3 bars, 2 pools, 4 hot tubs, sauna, 4 tennis courts, exercise room, hiking, jogging, bicycles, shop, concierge floor, business services, meeting rooms, free parking. AE, D, DC, MC, V.*

$$$ ⊞ **Tempe Mission Palms Hotel.** Set between the Arizona State University campus and Old Town Tempe, this three-story courtyard hotel is handy to the East Valley and downtown Phoenix. The tone is set by a handsome, casual lobby—Matisse-inspired upholstery on overstuffed chairs—and an energetic young staff. It's a particularly convenient place to stay if you're attending ASU sports and pro-football Cardinals events (the stadium is virtually next door). Rooms are bright, simple southwestern, and comfortable. The hotel's "Harry's Bar" becomes a lively sports lounge at game time. ⊠ *60 E. 5th St., Tempe 85281,* ☎ *480/894–1400 or 800/547–8705,* FAX *480/968–7677. 303 rooms. Restaurant, bar, pool, sauna, 3 tennis courts, exercise room, business services, meeting rooms, airport shuttle, free parking. AE, D, DC, MC, V.*

$$–$$$ ⊞ **Hilton Pavilion.** This sand-and-rose-color eight-story property has a southwestern look. Rooms are medium size, with plum and teal carpeting, average-size baths, small closets, and a large lighted table; corner suites and the top two floors have the best views. The hotel is in the heart of the East Valley, just off AZ 60, and the immense Fiesta Mall is across the street; downtown Phoenix is 18 mi away. ⊠ *1011 W. Holmes Ave., Mesa 85210,* ☎ *480/833–5555 or 800/544–5866,* FAX *480/649–1380. 201 rooms, 62 suites. Restaurant, 2 bars, refrigerators, pool, hot tub, exercise room, business services, free parking. AE, D, DC, MC, V.*

$$ ⊞ **Twin Palms Hotel.** Across the street from ASU's Gammage Auditorium and minutes from Old Town Tempe, this seven-story high-rise hotel has a domed-window facade. Faux finishes creatively mask dated, textured walls in the rooms, and corner basins strike strategic blows to cramped bathrooms. Guests receive free admission to facilities at the nearby ASU Recreation Complex with three Olympic-size pools, badminton and squash courts, and aerobics classes. ⊠ *225 E. Apache Blvd., Tempe 85281,* ☎ *480/967–9431 or 800/367–0835,* FAX *480/303– 6602. 140 rooms, 1 suite. Bar, pool, concierge floor, airport shuttle, free parking. AE, DC, MC, V.*

In case you want to see the world.

At American Express, we're here to make your journey a smooth one. So we have over 1,700 travel service locations in over 130 countries ready to help. What else would you expect from the world's largest travel agency?

do more

Travel

Call 1 800 AXP-3429 or visit
www.americanexpress.com/travel

In case you want to be welcomed there.

We're here to see that you're always welcomed at establishments everywhere. That's why millions of people carry the American Express® Card – for peace of mind, confidence, and security, around the world or just around the corner.

do more

Cards

In case you're running low.

We're here to help with more than 190,000 Express Cash locations around the world. In order to enroll, just call American Express at 1 800 CASH-NOW before you start your vacation.

do more AMERICAN EXPRESS

Express Cash

And in case you'd rather be safe than sorry.

We're here with American Express® Travelers Cheques. They're the safe way to carry money on your vacation, because if they're ever lost or stolen you can get a refund, practically anywhere or anytime. To find the nearest place to buy Travelers Cheques, call 1 800 495-1153. Another way we help you do more.

do more

Travelers Cheques

NIGHTLIFE AND THE ARTS

The Arts

Phoenix's performing-arts groups have grown rapidly in number and sophistication, especially over the past two decades. The permanent home of the Arizona Theatre Company, Actors Theatre of Phoenix, and Ballet Arizona, the **Herberger Theater Center** (⊠ 222 E. Monroe St., ☎ 602/252–8497) also presents a variety of visiting dance troupes and orchestras.

The **Orpheum Theatre** (⊠ 203 W. Adams St., ☎ 602/252–9678; ☞ Downtown Phoenix *in* Exploring Phoenix, *above*) showcases various performing arts, including children's theater, and film festivals. Facing the Herberger Theater, **Symphony Hall** (⊠ 225 E. Adams St., ☎ 602/262–7272) is home to the Phoenix Symphony and Arizona Opera as well as a venue for pop concerts by top-name performers. Arizona State University offers a variety of events ranging from touring Broadway shows to jazz, pop, and classical concerts at three fine venues: the **Gammage Auditorium** (⊠ Mill Ave. at Apache Blvd., Tempe, ☎ 480/965–3434), **Kerr Cultural Center** (⊠ 6110 N. Scottsdale Rd., Scottsdale, ☎ 480/965–5377), and the **Sundome Center** (⊠ 19403 R. H. Johnson Blvd., Sun City West, ☎ 623/975–1900).

The most comprehensive ticket agencies for ASU events are the **Arizona State University Public Events Box Office** (⊠ Gammage Center, Tempe, ☎ 480/965–3434) and **Dillard's ticket line** (☎ 480/503–5555 or 800/638–4253).

For weekly listings of theater, arts, and music events, check out *The Rep Entertainment Guide,* in Thursday's *Arizona Republic,* or pick up an issue of the independent weekly, *New Times,* from street corner boxes.

Classical Music
Arizona Opera (⊠ 4600 N. 12th St., Phoenix, ☎ 602/266–7464), one of the nation's most respected regional companies, stages an opera season, primarily classical, in Tucson and Phoenix. The Phoenix season runs October to March at Symphony Hall (☞ *above*).

Phoenix Symphony Orchestra (⊠ 455 N. 3rd St., Suite 390, Phoenix, ☎ 602/495–1999), the resident company at Symphony Hall (☞ *above*), has reached the top rank of American regional symphonies. Its season includes orchestral works from classical and contemporary literature, a chamber series, composer festivals, and outdoor pops concerts.

Dance
A. Ludwig Co. (☎ 480/966–3391), the Valley's foremost modern dance troupe, includes choreography by founder-director Ann Ludwig, an ASU faculty member, in its repertoire of contemporary works.

Ballet Arizona (⊠ 3645 E. Indian School Rd., ☎ 602/381–1096), the state's professional ballet company, presents a full season of classical and contemporary works (including pieces commissioned for the company) in Tucson and in Phoenix, where it performs at the Herberger Theater Center, Symphony Hall, and Gammage Auditorium (☞ *above*).

Film
If you're looking for something besides the latest blockbuster, the **Valley Art Theatre** (⊠ 509 S. Mill Ave., Tempe, ☎ 480/829–6668) shows major foreign releases and domestic art films.

Galleries

The gallery scene in Phoenix and Scottsdale is so extensive that your best bet is to consult the "art exhibits" listings in the weekly *New Times* or Thursday's *The Rep Entertainment Guide* put out by the *Arizona Republic*. Or simply stroll down to Main Street and Marshall Way in downtown Scottsdale to view the best art the Valley has to offer.

Theater and Shows

Actors Theatre of Phoenix (☎ 602/253–6701 or 602/252–8497) is the resident theater troupe at the Herberger (☞ *above*). The theater presents a full season of drama, comedy, and musical productions.

Arizona Theatre Company (✉ 502 W. Roosevelt, ☎ 602/256–6995 or 602/252–8497) is the only resident company in the country with a two-city (Tucson and Phoenix) operation. Productions range from classical dramas to musicals and new works by emerging playwrights, with all performances held at the Herberger Theater (☞ *above*).

Black Theater Troupe (✉ 333 E. Portland St., ☎ 602/258–8128) performs at its own house, the Helen K. Mason Center, a half block from the city's Performing Arts Building on Deck Park. It presents original and contemporary dramas and musical revues, as well as adventurous adaptations.

Childsplay (☎ 480/350–8112) is the state's professional theater company for young audiences and families. Rotating through many a venue—Herberger Theater Center, Scottsdale Center for the Arts, and Tempe Performing Arts Center—these players deliver colorful, high-energy performances of works ranging from adaptations of *Charlotte's Web* and *The Velveteen Rabbit* to a theatrical salute to surrealist painter René Magritte and the power of imagination.

Great Arizona Puppet Theatre (✉ 302 W. Latham St., ☎ 602/262–2050), happily relocated to a historic building featuring lots of theater and exhibit space, mounts a yearlong cycle of inventive puppet productions that change frequently; it also offers puppetry classes.

DINNER THEATER

Copper State Dinner Theatre (✉ 6727 N. 47th Ave., Glendale, ☎ 623/937–1671), the Valley's oldest troupe, stages light comedy at Max's, a West Valley sports bar, Friday and Saturday nights.

WILD WEST SHOWS

At **Rawhide Western Town & Steakhouse** (✉ 23023 N. Scottsdale Rd., Scottsdale, ☎ 480/502–1880), the false fronts on the dusty Main Street contain a train depot, saloons, gift shops, and craftspeople. Reenacted Old West shootouts and cheesy souvenirs make this a venue for down-home tacky fun. City slickers can take a ride on a stagecoach or gentle burro and kids will enjoy the Petting Ranch's barnyard animals. Hayrides travel a short distance into the desert for weekend "Sundown Cookouts" under the stars.

Rockin' R Ranch (✉ 6136 E. Baseline Rd., Mesa, ☎ 480/832–1539) includes a petting zoo, a reenactment of a wild shoot-out, and—the main attraction—a nightly cookout with a western stage show. Pan for gold or take a wagon ride until the "vittles" are served, followed by music and entertainment. Similar to its competitor, Rawhide, Rockin' R is a better deal as it's all-inclusive.

Nightlife

From brew pubs, sports bars, and coffeehouses, to dance clubs, mega-concerts, and country venues, the Valley of the Sun offers nightlife of all types. Nightclubs, comedy clubs, and upscale lounges—whatever your choice for fun, nightlife abounds in downtown Phoenix, along Camelback Road in north-central Phoenix, and in Scottsdale, Tempe, and other suburbs.

Among music and dancing styles, country-and-western has the longest tradition here; jazz, surprisingly, runs a close second. Rock clubs and hotel lounges are also numerous and varied. The Valley attracts a steady stream of pop and rock acts. Phoenix is getting hipper and more cosmopolitan as it gets older: Cigar-lovers and martini-sippers will find a wealth of opportunities to indulge their tastes. There are also more than 30 gay and lesbian bars, centered primarily on 7th Avenue, 7th Street, and the stretch of Camelback Road between the two.

You can find listings and reviews in the *New Times* free weekly news-paper, distributed Wednesday, and the *Rep Entertainment Guide* of the *Arizona Republic*. *PHX Downtown,* a free monthly available in down-town establishments, has an extensive calendar for the neighborhood's events from art exhibits and poetry readings to professional sporting events. For concert tickets, try **Dillard's** (☎ 480/503–5555 or 800/638–4253).

Bars and Lounges

America's Original Sports Bar (✉ 455 N. 3rd St., Arizona Center, ☎ 602/252–2112) offers more than 40,000 square ft of boisterous fun, with 62 TVs (seven giant screens among them).

AZ88 (✉ 7353 Scottsdale Mall, Scottsdale, ☎ 480/994–5576) has the vibe of a big-city bar and an artful interior. Casual dining and com-fortable surroundings make this a perennial favorite of all ages.

Beeloe's Cafe and Underground Bar (✉ 501 S. Mill Ave., Tempe, ☎ 480/894–1230) is everything you'd expect in this hip college town, with eclectic presentations of visual and musical artists. As the name im-plies, the bar is located in the basement.

Cajun House (✉ 7117 E. 3rd Ave., Scottsdale, ☎ 480/945–5150), cur-rently one of the hottest spots in the area, is the Valley's only Louisiana-themed venue. Join locals who sip Hurricanes while listening to rock, jazz, and Cajun music; on weekends there's a line to get in.

The Famous Door (✉ 7419 Indian Plaza, Scottsdale, ☎ 480/970–5150) specializes in martinis and cigars. Relax to the sounds of local jazz artists on weekends.

Liquori's (✉ 2309 E. Indian School Rd., Phoenix, ☎ 602/957–2444) features one of the longest happy hours in Phoenix (10 AM–8 PM). As you shoot pool or play pinball, the jukebox turns out hard rock, al-ternative rock, and blues.

Majerle's Sports Grill (✉ 24 N. 2nd St., ☎ 602/253–9004), operated by former Suns basketball player Dan Majerle, is within striking dis-tance of the major sports facilities and offers a comprehensive menu as well as a bar for post-game celebrations (or sorrow-drowning).

Top of the Rock Bar (✉ 2000 W. Westcourt Way, Tempe, ☎ 602/431–2370), the lounge in Top of the Rock restaurant (☞ Dining, *above*) at the Buttes, attracts an older, professional crowd to drink in cocktails and the city's most spectacular view.

Casinos

Just northeast of Scottsdale, **Fort McDowell Casino** (2 mi east of Shea Blvd. on AZ 87, ☎ 602/843–3678 or 800/843–3678) is popular with the Scottsdale-resort crowd. In addition to the cards, slots, and keno games, offtrack greyhound wagering takes place in a classy, mahogany room with 18 giant video screens. Take advantage of the casino's Valley-wide shuttle.

Clubs

Axis and Radius (⊠ 7340 E. Indian Plaza Rd., Scottsdale, ☎ 480/970–1112) is the dress-to-kill locale where you can party and hobnob with celebrities. Michael Jordan, George Clooney, and Cher are just some of the beautiful people who've rocked at these side-by-side clubs. Axis features high-energy dance music and top-40 hits, while Radius pumps up the high-energy funk.

Bobby McGee's (⊠ 7000 E. Shea Blvd., Scottsdale, ☎ 480/998–5591) is the one of the Valley's most popular spots for DJ-spun music.

Downside Risk (⊠ 7419 E. Indian Plaza Rd., Scottsdale, ☎ 480/945–3304) is a sure bet for a happening young crowd in the mood to libate and gyrate.

Martini Ranch & MR Sports Bar (⊠ 7295 E. Stetson Dr., Scottsdale, ☎ 480/970–0500) attracts singles to its patio where alternative and classic rock bands play Tuesday through Saturday.

Tapas Papa Frita (⊠ 6826 E. 5th Ave., Scottsdale, ☎ 480/424–7777) really turns up the heat. Fiery salsa rhythms will have you up and dancing the merengue, the cha-cha, and the mambo.

Coffeehouses

Willow House (⊠ 149 W. McDowell Rd., Phoenix, ☎ 602/252–0272) is a self-described artist's cove that draws scores of artsy, bohemiantypes—a uniquely fun and funky spot in a city not overflowing with great coffeehouses. Thursday-night poetry readings are a big draw. The espresso flows until midnight on weeknights, 1 AM on weekends.

Comedy

The Improv (⊠ 930 E. University Dr., Tempe, ☎ 480/921–9877), part of a national chain, showcases better-known headliners Thursday–Sunday; shows cost between $10 and $20.

Star Theater (⊠ 7117 E. McDowell Rd., Scottsdale, ☎ 480/423–0120) features comedy for people of all ages, including kids, performed by Oxymoron'Z Improvisational Troupe on Friday and Saturday nights and stand-up comics the last two Thursdays of each month; reservations are required.

Country and Western

Handlebar-J (⊠ 7116 E. Becker La., Scottsdale, ☎ 480/948–0110) has a lively, 10-gallon-hat–wearing crowd.

At **Mr. Lucky's** (⊠ 3660 W. Grand Ave., ☎ 602/246–0686), the grand-daddy of Phoenix western clubs, you can dance the two-step all night (or learn how, if you haven't before).

The **Red River Music Hall** (⊠ 730 N. Mill Ave., Tempe, ☎ 480/829–6779) is a lively venue that hosts all kinds of concerts, including a jazz series, country music concerts, and special Christmas shows.

The Rockin' Horse Saloon (⊠ 7316 E. Stetson Dr., Scottsdale, ☎ 480/949–0992) features baby back ribs, live Western music, and dancing in a setting guaranteed to bring out the cowboy or cowgirl in you.

Gay and Lesbian Bars

Ain't Nobody's Business (⊠ 3001 E. Indian School Rd., Phoenix, ☎ 602/224–9977) is the most popular lesbian bar in town; you'll also find a few gay men at this male-friendly establishment, well-known as one of the most fun in town.

B.S. West (✉ 7125 5th Ave., Scottsdale, ☎ 480/945–9028) draws a stylish, well-heeled crowd to this location tucked in a shopping center on Scottsdale's main shopping drag.

Charlie's (✉ 727 W. Camelback Rd., Phoenix, ☎ 602/265–0224), a longtime favorite of local gay men, has a country-western look (cowboy hats are the accessory of choice) and friendly staff.

Young men go to the **Crow Bar** (✉ 710 N. Central Ave., Phoenix, ☎ 602/258–8343) to see and be seen; it's where Phoenix's beautiful people hang out.

Jazz

For a current schedule of jazz happenings, call the **Jazz in AZ Hotline** (☎ 602/254–4545).

J. Chew & Co. (✉ 7320 Scottsdale Mall, Scottsdale, ☎ 480/946–2733) is a cozy, popular spot with indoor and outdoor seating. It's the place to find up-and-coming jazz performers while enjoying a tasty hot or cold sandwich.

Orbit Cafe (✉ 40 E. Camelback Rd., Phoenix, ☎ 602/265–2354) has live jazz and blues every evening in a contemporary art deco–style setting with a casual ambience.

Timothy's (✉ 6335 N. 16th St.,Phoenix, ☎ 602/277–7634) brings together fine French-influenced southwestern cuisine with top jazz performances from 8:30 to 12:30 nightly, and there's no cover charge.

Microbreweries

Bandersnatch Brew Pub (✉ 125 E. 5th St., Tempe, ☎ 480/966–4438) is a popular, unhurried student hangout that brews several *cervezas* daily.

Coyote Springs Brewing Co. (✉ 4883 N. 20th St., at Camelback Rd., Phoenix, ☎ 602/468–0403; ✉ 122 E. Washington St., Phoenix, ☎ 602/256–6645), the oldest brewpub in Phoenix, has delicious handcrafted ales and lagers, and a thriving patio scene at the 20th Street location. Try a raspberry brew.

Hops! Bistro & Brewery (✉ 7000 E. Camelback Rd., Scottsdale Fashion Square, ☎ 480/946–1272; ✉ 8668 E. Shea Blvd., Scottsdale, ☎ 480/998–7777) serves up bistro cuisine and fills chilled mugs with amber and wheat drafts from the display brewery.

Rock and Blues

The **Blue Note** (✉ 8040 E. McDowell Rd., Scottsdale, ☎ 480/946–6227) is a blues club with live shows every night. Friday and Saturday there's a $5 cover.

Char's Has the Blues (✉ 4631 N. 7th Ave., ☎ 602/230–0205) is the top Valley blues club with nightly bands.

Long Wong's on Mill (✉ 701 S. Mill Ave., Tempe, ☎ 480/966–3147) may not be the most elegant joint you'll ever see, but huge crowds of students and other grungy types pack the crowded, graffiti-covered room to catch the sounds of local musicians playing acoustic, rockabilly, rock, and blues.

Mason Jar (✉ 2303 E. Indian School Rd., Phoenix, ☎ 602/956–6271) has nightly shows, mostly hard rock.

Rhythm Room (✉ 1019 E. Indian School Rd., Phoenix, ☎ 602/265–4842) hosts a variety of local and touring blues artists.

OUTDOOR ACTIVITIES AND SPORTS

Participant Sports

Central Arizona has ample opportunity for outdoor recreation, but the area's dry desert heat imposes particular restraints—even in winter, hikers and cyclists should wear lightweight opaque clothing, a hat or visor, and high UV-rated sunglasses and should carry a quart of water for each hour of activity. The intensity of the sun makes strong sunscreen (SPF 15 or higher) a must, and don't forget to apply it to your hands and feet. From May 1 to October 1, you shouldn't jog or hike from one hour after sunrise until a half hour before sunset. During those times, the air is so hot and dry that your body will lose moisture at a dangerous, potentially lethal rate. Don't head out to desert areas at night, however, to jog or hike in the summer; that's when rattlesnakes and scorpions are on the prowl.

Bicycling

Although the terrain is relatively level, the desert climate can be tough on cyclists; note the advice on hours and clothing, *above.* Be sure to have a helmet and a mirror when riding in the streets: There are few adequate bike lanes in the Valley.

Scottsdale's Indian Bend Wash (along Hayden Road, from Shea Boulevard south to Indian School Road) has bikeable paths winding among its golf courses and ponds. **Pinnacle Peak,** about 25 mi northeast of downtown Phoenix, is a popular place to take bikes for the ride north to Carefree and Cave Creek, or east and south over the mountain pass and down to the Verde River, toward Fountain Hills. Mountain bikers will want to check out the **Trail 100,** which runs throughout the Phoenix Mountain preserve (enter at Dreamy Draw park, just east of the intersection of Northern Avenue and 16th Street). **Cave Creek** and **Carefree,** in the foothills about 30 mi northeast of Phoenix, offer pleasant riding with a wide range of stopover options. **South Mountain Park** (☞ Hiking, *below*) is the prime site for mountain bikers, with its 40-plus mi of trails—some of them with challenging ascents and all of them quiet and scenic.

For rentals, contact **Wheels N' Gear** (✉ 7607 E. McDowell Rd., Scottsdale, ☎ 480/945–2881). For detailed maps of bike paths, contact **Phoenix Parks and Recreation** (☎ 602/262–6861). To get in touch with fellow bike enthusiasts and find out about regular and special-event rides, contact the **Arizona Bicycle Club** (Gene or Sylvia Berlatsky, ☎ 602/264–5478), the state's largest group. Popular Sunday-morning rides start in Phoenix's **Granada Park** (✉ 20th St. and Maryland Ave.) and end up at a local breakfast spot. **Desert Biking Adventures** (☎ 602/ 320–4602 or 888/249–2453) offers two-, three-, and four-hour mountain-biking excursions through the Sonoran desert.

Four-Wheeling

Taking a Jeep or a wide-track Humvee through the backcountry has become a popular way to experience the desert terrain's saguaro-covered mountains and curious rock formations. A number of companies offer four-wheeling packages for $50–$75 for short excursions.

Arizona Awareness Desert Jeep Tours (☎ 480/860–1777) ventures down to the Verde River on its own trail and offers wilderness cookouts.

Arrowhead Desert Jeep Tours (☎ 602/942–3361 or 800/514–9063), run by a self-described "hard-core prospector that fell in love with tourism," offers adventures that include gold panning on a private claim, cookouts, cattle drives, river crossings, and Native American dance demonstrations.

Rawhide Land and Cattle Company (☎ 480/488–0023 or 800/294–5337) travels into the Tonto National Forest on rugged old stage and mining roads, stopping for botany lessons, explorations of Hohokam ruins and a gold mine, and a six-gun target shoot along the way.

Scottsdale Jeep Rentals (☎ 480/951–2191) rents Jeeps and provides free trail maps to those who prefer to drive themselves and forgo the company of a talkative guide.

Golf

Arizona boasts more golf courses per capita than any other state west of the Mississippi River, an embarrassment of riches that, coupled with its surfeit of sunny days, makes the Grand Canyon State a golfer's paradise. The world-class courses are among Arizona's major industries, with new spots popping up seemingly on a daily basis: More than 100 courses are available (some lighted at night), and the PGA's Southwest section has its headquarters here. For a detailed listing, contact the **Arizona Golf Association** (✉ 7226 N. 16th St., Phoenix 85020, ☎ 602/944–3035 or 800/458–8484).

Ahwatukee Country Club (✉ 12432 S. 48th St., ☎ 480/893–9772), an upscale course just south of South Mountain Park, is semiprivate but also has a public driving range.

Arizona Biltmore (✉ 24th St. and Missouri Ave., ☎ 602/955–9655), the granddaddy of Phoenix golf courses, offers two 18-hole PGA championship courses, lessons, and clinics.

One of the latest entries into the Valley's golf scene, **Chiricauhua at Desert Mountain** (✉ 10333 Rockaway Hills, Scottsdale, ☎ 480/488–1362) is a player-friendly course designed by Jack Nicklaus.

Encanto Park (✉ 2775 N. 15th Ave., Phoenix, ☎ 602/253–3963) is an attractive, affordable public course.

Gold Canyon Golf Club (✉ 6100 S. Kings Ranch Rd., Gold Canyon, ☎ 480/982–9090) is a desert course backed by the stunning Superstition Mountains.

The championship **Grayhawk Golf Club** (✉ 8620 E. Thompson Peak Pkwy., Scottsdale, ☎ 480/502–1800) is pricey, but it's rated one of the top public courses in Arizona. Designed by Tom Fazio, the course is immaculately groomed.

Hillcrest Golf Club (✉ 20002 N. Star Ridge, Sun City West, ☎ 623/584–1500) is the best course in the Sun Cities, with 179 acres of well-designed turf.

Papago Golf Course (✉ 5595 E. Moreland St., ☎ 602/275–8428) is a low-price public course in a scenic city setting and Phoenix's best municipal course.

Raven Golf Club at South Mountain (✉ 3636 E. Baseline Rd., Phoenix, ☎ 602/243–3636) has thousands of drought-resistant Aleppo pines and Lombardy poplars, making it a cool, shady haven for summertime golfers.

Sun Ridge Canyon (✉ 13100 N. Sun Ridge Dr., Fountain Hills, ☎ 480/837–5100) is an 18-hole championship course with an inspiring view of the canyon scenery.

Thunderbird Country Club (⊠ 701 E. Thunderbird Trail, Phoenix, ☎ 602/243–1262) has 18 holes of championship-rated play on the north slopes of South Mountain. Sweeping views of the city are a bonus.

Tournament Players Club of Scottsdale (⊠ 17020 N. Hayden Rd., Scottsdale, ☎ 480/585–3600), a 36-hole course by Tom Weiskopf and Jay Morrish, is the site of the PGA Phoenix Open.

Troon North (⊠ 10320 E. Dynamite Blvd., Scottsdale, ☎ 480/585–5300) offers a challenging 36-hole course, designed by Weiskopf and Morrish, that makes excellent use of the desert landscape.

Health Clubs

The **Arizona Athletic Club** (⊠ 1425 W. 14th St., Tempe, ☎ 480/894–2281), near the airport at the border between Tempe and Scottsdale, is the Valley's largest facility. Nonmembers pay a day rate of $12, but the club has arrangements with some area hotels.

Jazzercise (☎ 800/348–4748) has 13 franchised sites in the Valley.

Naturally Women (⊠ 2827 W. Peoria Ave., Phoenix, ☎ 602/678–4000; ⊠ 3320 S. Price Rd., Tempe, ☎ 602/838–8800), closed Sunday, focuses on women's needs, from health profiles to diet and exercise programs; it offers one free visit, and a daily rate of $10 thereafter.

The **YMCA** (☎ 602/528–5540) offers full facilities—including weight rooms, aerobics classes, pool, and racquetball privileges—to nonmembers at several Valley locations. Pool rates are $8 per day.

Hiking

The Valley has some of the best desert mountain hiking in the world—the **Phoenix Mountain Preserve System** (☎ 602/262–6861), in the mountains that surround the city, has its own park rangers who can help plan your hikes. Phoenix's hiking trails are some of the most heavily used in the world—and for good reason.

Camelback Mountain (⊠ North of Camelback Rd. on 48th St., ☎ 602/256–3220), another landmark hike, has no park, and the trails are more difficult. This is for intermediate to experienced hikers.

The **Papago Peaks** (⊠ Van Buren St. and Galvin Pkwy., ☎ 602/256–3220) were sacred sites for the Tohono O'odham tribe and probably the Hohokam before them. The soft sandstone peaks contain accessible caves, some petroglyphs, and splendid views of much of the Valley. This is another good spot for family hikes.

South Mountain Park (⊠ 10919 S. Central Ave., ☎ 602/261–8457) is the jewel of the city's Mountain Park Preserves. Its mountains and arroyos contain more than 40 mi of marked and maintained trails—all open to hikers, horseback riders, and mountain bikers. It also has three auto-accessible lookout points, with 65-mi sight lines. Rangers can help you plan hikes to view some of the 200 petroglyph sites.

Squaw Peak Summit Trail (⊠ 2701 E. Squaw Peak Dr., just north of Lincoln Dr., ☎ 602/262–7901) ascends the landmark mountain at a steep 19% grade, but children can handle the 1.2-mi hike if adults take it slowly—allow about 1½ hours for each direction. Call ahead to schedule an easy hike with a ranger who will introduce desert geology, flora, and fauna.

Horseback Riding

More than two dozen stables and equestrian tour outfitters in the Valley attest to the saddle's enduring importance in Arizona—even in this auto-dominated metropolis.

All Western Stables (✉ 10220 S. Central Ave., Phoenix, ☎ 602/276–5862), one of several stables at the entrance to South Mountain Park, offers rentals, guided rides, hayrides, and cookouts.

MacDonald's Ranch (✉ 26540 N. Scottsdale Rd., Scottsdale, ☎ 480/585–0239) offers one- and two-hour trail rides and guided breakfast, lunch, and dinner rides through desert foothills above Scottsdale.

Superstition Stables (✉ Windsong and Meridian Rds., Apache Junction, ☎ 480/982–6353) is licensed to lead tours throughout the entire Superstition Mountains area for more experienced riders; easier rides are also available.

Hot-Air Ballooning

A sunrise or sunset hot-air-balloon ascent is a remarkable desert sightseeing experience. The average fee—there are more than three dozen companies to chose from—is $135 per person and hotel pickup is usually included. Since flight paths and landing sites vary with wind speeds and directions, a roving land crew follows each balloon in flight. Time in the air is generally between 1 and 1½ hours, but allow three hours for the total excursion. Be prepared for changing temperatures as the sun rises or sets, but it's not actually any colder up in the balloon.

Adventures Out West (☎ 602/996–6100 or 800/755–0935) will send you home with a free video of your flight taped from the balloon.

Hot Air Expeditions (☎ 480/502–6999 or 800/831–7610) offers the best ballooning in Phoenix. Flights are long, the staff is charming, and the gourmet treats are out of this world.

Unicorn Balloon Company (☎ 480/991–3666 or 800/468–2478), operating since 1978, is run by the state's ballooning examiner for the FAA. Located at Scottsdale Airport, it offers free pickup at many area hotels.

Jogging

Phoenix's unique 200-mi network of canals provides a naturally cooled (and often landscaped) scenic track throughout the metro area. Two other popular jogging areas are Phoenix's **Encanto Park,** 3 mi northwest of Civic Plaza, and Scottsdale's **Indian Bend Wash,** which runs for more than 5 mi along Hayden Road. Both have lagoons and treeshaded greens.

Sailplaning

At the Estrella Sailport, **Arizona Soaring Inc.** (☎ 480/821–2903 or 800/861–2318) gives sailplane rides in a basic trainer or high-performance plane for prices ranging from $69 to $89. The adventuresome can opt for a wild 15-minute acrobatic flight for $99.

Tennis

Hole-in-the-Wall Racquet Club (✉ 7677 N. 16th St., ☎ 602/997–2626), at the Pointe Hilton at Squaw Peak (☞ Lodging, *above*), has eight paved courts available for same-day reservation at $18 per half hour.

Kiwanis Park Recreation Center (✉ 6111 S. All America Way, Tempe, ☎ 480/350–5201 ext. 4) has 15 lighted premier-surface courts (all for same-day or one-day-advance reserve). Before 5 PM, courts rent for $4.50, after 5 PM, the rate is $6; $2 drop-in programs are offered for single players weekdays, 10:30–noon.

Mountain View Tennis Center (✉ 1104 E. Grovers Ave., ☎ 602/788–6088), just north of Bell Road, is a Phoenix city facility with 20 lighted courts that can be reserved for $3 for 90 minutes of singles play during the day; after dark, the light fee is $2.20.

Phoenix Civic Plaza Sports Complex (✉ 121 E. Adams St., ☎ 602/256–4120) has three lighted rooftop courts available for $4–$6.

Phoenix Tennis Center (✉ 6330 N. 21st Ave., ☎ 602/249–3712), a city facility with 22 lighted hard courts, charges $1.50 per person for 1½ hours on the courts; if it's after dark, add a $2.20 light fee.

Watering Hole Racquet Club (✉ 901-C E. Saguaro Dr., ☎ 602/997–7237) has nine hard, lighted courts that rent for $15 per hour.

Tubing

In a region not known for water, one indigenous aquatic sport has developed: Tubing—riding an inner tube down calm water and mild rapids—has become a very popular tradition on the Salt and Verde rivers. Outfitters that rent tubes include **Salt River Recreation** (✉ Usery Pass and Power Rds., Mesa, ☎ 480/984–3305), conveniently located and offering shuttle-bus service to and from your starting point. Tubes are $9 per day, all day 9–4; tubing season runs May–September.

Spectator Sports

Auto Racing
Phoenix International Raceway (✉ 7602 S. 115th Ave., Avondale, ☎ 602/252–3833), the Valley's NASCAR track, hosts the Skoal Bandit Copper World Classic, Phoenix 200 Indy Car race, and Phoenix 500 NASCAR race.

Balloon Racing
The **Thunderbird Hot-Air-Balloon Classic** (☎ 602/978–7208) has grown into two days of festivities surrounding the national invitational balloon race, held the first weekend in November. You haven't lived till you've seen the Valley skies filled with brightly colored balloons.

Baseball
Many professional baseball teams conduct spring training in Arizona (*see* Close-up box, "Spring Training: Baseball in Arizona"). Games start at the end of February; **Dillard's** (☎ 480/503–5555) sells tickets. To obtain more information about spring training in Arizona, contact the following Cactus League teams:

Anaheim Angels, Tempe Diablo Stadium, Tempe, AZ 602/784–4444

Arizona Diamondbacks, Tucson Electric Park, Tucson, AZ 888/777–4664

Chicago Cubs, HoHoKam Park, Mesa, AZ 602/503–5555

Chicago White Sox, Tucson Electric Park, Tucson, AZ 800/638–4253

Colorado Rockies, Hi Corbett Field, Tucson, AZ 520/327–9467

Milwaukee Brewers, Maryvale Baseball Park, Phoenix, AZ 602/895–1200

Oakland A's, Phoenix Municipal Stadium, Peoria, AZ 602/392–0217

San Francisco Giants, Scottsdale stadium, Scottsdale, AZ 602/990–7972

Seattle Mariners, Peoria Stadium, Peoria, AZ 602/412–9000

The **Arizona Diamondbacks** (☎ 602/514–8400), Phoenix's Major League team, plays at the Bank One Ballpark (☞ Downtown Phoenix *in* Exploring Phoenix, *above*). The 48,500-seat stadium has a re-

SPRING TRAINING: BASEBALL IN ARIZONA

ONE SURE WAY FOR BASEBALL fans to cure the wintertime blues is to visit one of Arizona's many ballparks and see the Boys of Summer at work during spring training—months before they play in other parts of the country.

For most teams, preliminary workouts start in the middle of February while actual games don't begin until the following month. Spring training continues to occupy the entire month of March with teams playing around 15 games during March and into the first week of April.

Spring training is a great time to meet and collect autographs from favorite players. While teams are definitely serious about spring training regimens, the atmosphere around parks is more relaxed than during the regular season. Players often come up to the side of the fields to greet fans as they leave games. Special events such as fireworks nights, bat and T-shirt giveaways, and visits from sports mascots such as "The Famous Chicken" add to the festive atmosphere of spring training.

Tickets for some teams go on sale as early as December. Brochures list game schedules and ticket information and are available by calling each Arizona team's venue. Plus, tickets to spring training games are a real entertainment bargain! Because prices range from around $5 for bleacher seats to around $15 for reserved seats, the whole family can enjoy an evening at the ballpark.

Ballpark Alert! Arizona continues to create state-of-the art ballparks. Bank One Ballpark in downtown Phoenix, known locally as simply "Bob," is home to the major league Arizona Diamondbacks. Tours of this unique sports stadium run Monday through Saturday throughout the year, excluding game days and holidays. Walk-up tickets are available ($6 for adults, $4 children 7–12 and seniors) or, in advance, call 602/462–6543.

For a truly relaxed venue, try Tucson Electric Park, home of spring training for two major league teams (Arizona Diamondbacks and Chicago White Sox) and a minor league team (Tucson Sidewinders). TEP features a sunken field where fans enter at the top of the stadium and walk down to their seats. All concourses are on the inside of the stadium, which means that baseball aficionados won't miss any action while ordering beverages or food. Family-style picnic areas on grass berms (just beyond the outfield wall) offer plenty of space to stretch out a blanket and watch the game. Concessions at TEP include typical ballpark fare such as hamburgers and hot dogs as well as barbecue chicken and beef, southwestern-style pizza, oysters, Caesar salad, beer, soda, wine coolers, and margaritas.

—Deidre Elliott

tractable roof, a natural grass playing surface, and a slew of restaurants, luxury boxes, and party suites.

Basketball

The **Phoenix Suns** (☎ 602/379–7867) continue to fill all 19,000 spectator seats in the America West Arena (☞ Downtown Phoenix *in* Exploring Phoenix, *above*); Valley basketball fans are fiercely loyal to the team. Tip-off is usually at 7 PM.

Football

The **Arizona Cardinals** (☎ 602/379–0102), the area's professional football team, plays at ASU's Sun Devil Stadium in Tempe.

On New Year's Eve at Sun Devil Stadium is the **Fiesta Bowl** (☎ 480/350–0911), one of college football's most important bowl games.

Golf

The **Phoenix Open** (☎ 602/870–0163), in January at the Tournament Players Club of Scottsdale, is a major PGA Tour event and draws an estimated 400,000 spectators each year. In March, women compete in the **Standard Register PING Tournament** (☎ 602/942–0000), at the Moon Valley Country Club.

Hockey

The **Phoenix Coyotes** (☎ 602/379–7825) face off in the America West Arena (☞ Downtown Phoenix *in* Exploring Phoenix, *above*); whether you come for the checking, hooking, or to watch the Zamboni, take a moment to enjoy the small irony of artificial ice in the desert.

Rodeos

The **Parada del Sol** (☞ Festivals and Seasonal Events *in* Smart Travel Tips A to Z *in* Chapter 8), held each January by the Scottsdale Jaycees (☎ 480/990–3179), includes a rodeo, a lavish parade famed for its silver-studded saddles, and a 200-mi daredevil ride from Holbrook down the Mogollon Rim to Scottsdale by the Hashknife Pony Express. The **Rodeo of Rodeos,** sponsored in March by the Phoenix Jaycees (✉ 4133 N. 7th St., ☎ 602/263–8671), opens with one of the Southwest's oldest and best parades.

SHOPPING

Since its resorts began multiplying in the 1930s and 1940s, Phoenix has acquired a healthy share of high-style clothiers and leisure-wear boutiques. But long before that, western clothes dominated fashion here—jeans and boots, cotton shirts and dresses, 10-gallon hats and bola ties (the state's official neckwear). In many places around town, they still do.

On the scene as well, of course, were the arts of the Southwest's true natives—Navajo weavers, sand painters, and silversmiths; Hopi weavers and katsina-doll carvers; Pima and Tohono O'odham (Papago) basket makers and potters, and many more. Inspired by the region's rich cultural traditions, contemporary artists have flourished here, making Phoenix—and in particular Scottsdale, a city with more art galleries than gas stations—one of the Southwest's largest art centers (alongside Santa Fe, New Mexico).

Today's shoppers will find the best of the old and the new—all presented with southwestern style. Cowboy collectibles, handwoven rugs, traditional Mexican folk art, contemporary turquoise jewelry . . . you'll find them all in the Valley of the Sun. One-of-a-kind shops, upscale stores, and outlet malls offer shoppers everything from cutting-edge, contemporary fashion to more relaxed, down-home styles.

Most of the Valley's power shopping is concentrated in central Phoenix and downtown Scottsdale. But auctions and antiques shops cluster in odd places—and as treasure hunters know, you've always got to keep your eyes open.

Antiques and Collectibles

Downtown **Glendale** along Glendale Avenue and the side streets between 57th and 59th avenues has dozens of antiques stores and a "Gaslight Antique Walk" on the third Thursday evening of each month (every Thursday in December). **Glendale Square Antiques** (⊠ 7009 N. 58th Ave., ☎ 623/435–9952) has a nice collection of glassware, china, and vintage watches. **House of Gera** (⊠ 7025 N. 58th Ave., ☎ 623/842–4631) specializes in Victoriana, particularly jewelry, and houses the offbeat Rosato Nursing Museum. **The Mad Hatter** (⊠ 5734 W. Glendale Ave., ☎ 623/931–1991) is a cavernous space with everything from crystal and Fiestaware to old metal wheels and dusty saddles.

Scottsdale Antique Destination is a group of four stores: **Antique Centre** (⊠ 2012 N. Scottsdale Rd., ☎ 480/675–9500), **Antique Trove** (⊠ 2020 N. Scottsdale Rd., ☎ 480/947–6074), and **Antiques Super-Mall** (⊠ 1900 N. Scottsdale Rd., ☎ 480/874–2900) all have fine antiques and offbeat collectibles, and **Razmataz** (⊠ 2012 N. Scottsdale Rd., ☎ 480/946–9748) offers imported antique and new furniture and decorative items, primarily from Mexico.

Arts and Crafts

The best option, if you're interested in touring Scottsdale's galleries, is the **Art Walk** (☎ 480/990–3939), held from 7 PM to 9 PM each Thursday year-round (except Thanksgiving). Main Street and Marshall Way, the two major gallery strips, take on a party atmosphere during the evening hours when tourists and locals are browsing.

Art One (⊠ 4120 N. Marshall Way, Scottsdale, ☎ 480/946–5076) features works by local art students; much of what is found here is quite interesting.

Suzanne Brown Galleries (⊠ 7160 Main St., Scottsdale, ☎ 480/945–8475) has a fabulous collection of innovative glasswork, painting, and other fine arts.

Cosanti Originals (⊠ 6433 Doubletree Ranch Rd., Scottsdale, ☎ 480/948–6145) is the studio where architect Paolo Soleri's famous bronze and ceramic wind chimes are made and sold. You can watch the craftspeople hard at work, then pick out your own—prices are surprisingly reasonable.

The **Heard Museum Shop** (⊠ 22 E. Monte Vista Rd., Phoenix, ☎ 602/252–8344) is hands-down the best place in town for southwestern Native American arts and crafts, both traditional and modern. Prices tend to be high but quality is assured, with many one-of-a-kind items among their collection of rugs, katsina dolls, pottery, and other crafts; there's also a wide selection of lower-priced gifts. The back room gallery has the latest in native painting and lithographs.

LeKAE Galleries (⊠ 7175 E. Main St., Scottsdale, ☎ 480/874–2624) is a low-pressure, pleasant place to admire some of today's most exciting work. The friendly and discerning staff has scoured the Southwest and beyond for the best in contemporary painting and sculpture.

Mind's Eye (⊠ 4200 N. Marshall Way, Scottsdale, ☎ 480/941–2494) offers an eclectic selection of whimsical art furniture, quilted baskets, bright pottery, and beautifully offbeat kaleidoscopes fashioned from Italian glass, German jewels, and other bits and pieces.

Two Gray Hills (⌧ 7142 E. 5th Ave., Scottsdale, ☎ 480/947–1997 or 888/947–7504) deals in native jewelry, crafts, and katsina dolls. The knowledgeable staff will walk you through the styles and lore of traditional jewelry. They pledge to beat the price of any neighborhood competitor.

Markets

Two of metropolitan Phoenix's best markets can be found in the tiny town of Guadalupe, which is tucked between Interstate 10, Baseline Rd., and Warner Rd., almost entirely surrounded by the affluent suburb of Tempe. Take I–10 south to Baseline Rd., go east ½ mile and turn south on Avenida del Yaqui to find open-air vegetable stalls, roadside fruit stands, and tidy houses covered in flowering vines. **Guadalupe Farmer's Market** (⌧ 9210 S. Av. del Yaqui, Guadalupe, ☎ 480/730–1945) has all the fresh ingredients you'd find in a rural Mexican market—tomatillos, varieties of chili peppers (fresh and dried), freshground *masa* (cornmeal) for tortillas, cumin and cilantro, and on and on. **Mercado Mexico** (⌧ 8212 S. Av. del Yaqui, Guadalupe, ☎ 480/831–5925) carries ceramic, paper, tin, and lacquerware, all at unbeatable prices.

In Phoenix, **Patriot's Square Marketplace** (⌧ Patriot's Square Park, Washington St. and Central Ave., ☎ 623/848–1234) sells arts and crafts, locally grown produce, baked goods, and homemade jams and salsas, livening up downtown every Wednesday from 10 AM to 2 PM, October through April.

Shopping Centers

Arizona Mills (⌧ 5000 Arizona Mills Circle, Tempe, ☎ 480/491–9700), the latest entry in the discount shopping sweepstakes, is a mammoth center featuring almost 200 outlet stores, a food court, cinemas, and faux rain forest.

Biltmore Fashion Park (⌧ 24th St. and Camelback Rd., Phoenix, ☎ 602/955–8400) has posh shops lining its open-air walkways, as well as some of the city's most popular restaurants and cafés. **Macy's** and **Saks Fifth Avenue** are its anchors, and high-end designer boutiques are its stock-in-trade—**Via Veneto, Gucci,** and **Polo by Ralph Lauren** are among them. **Cornelia Park** offers an awe-inspiring collection of MacKenzie-Childs, Ltd., glassware as well as furnishings, tiles, and linens. Home to RoxSand, Sam's Cafe, and Christopher & Paola's Fermier Brasserie, this center has more fine eating in a small radius than anywhere else in Arizona (☞ Dining, *above*).

The Borgata (⌧ 6166 N. Scottsdale Rd., ☎ 480/998–1822), a re-creation of the Italian village of San Gimignano, is one of the Valley's most fashionable places to shop and home to some of Scottsdale's most popular restaurants, including Cafe Terra Cotta (☞ Dining, *above*). Shops include **Capriccio** for women's wear, **Stefan Mann** for leather goods, **DaVinci** for menswear, and scores of others. Check out the affordable and intriguing **Mineral & Fossil Gallery** near the Coffee Plantation.

Two-tiered **El Pedregal Festival Marketplace** (⌧ Scottsdale Rd. and Carefree Hwy., ☎ 480/488–1072), 30 minutes north of downtown Scottsdale, is an attractive shopping plaza. At the foot of a 250-ft boulder formation, it contains posh boutiques and the **Heard Museum North** (☎ 480/488–9817), a satellite of the downtown Heard with its own gift shop. Visit **Casualis** for men's sportswear, **Carefree Casuals** for wearable art for women, **Conrad** for custom leather goods, and **Canyon Lifestyles** for southwestern furniture and decor items. In the spring and summer there are open-air Thursday-night concerts in the courtyard amphitheater.

Metrocenter (✉ I–17 and Peoria Ave., ☎ 602/997–2641), on the west side of Phoenix, is the kind of enclosed double-deck, Muzak-choked sterile environment that made mall a four-letter word. Anchor department stores are **Dillard's, JCPenney, Macy's, Robinsons-May,** and **Sears.** Adjacent to the mall, a roller coaster zips through Taj-Mahal-esque minarets at **Castles 'N' Coasters** (✉ 9445 N. Metro Pkwy. E, ☎ 602/997–7575), where a miniature-golf park and video-game palace round out the fun.

Mill Avenue in Tempe is the main drag for ASU's student population; small, interesting shops and eateries make for great browsing or just hanging out. **Urban Outfitters** (✉ 545 S. Mill Ave., ☎ 480/966–7250) sells rough-edged, trendy gear and affordable housewares. The very cool **Changing Hands Bookstore** (✉ 414 Mill Ave., ☎ 480/966–0203) has three stories of new and used books and an inviting atmosphere that will tempt you to linger—as many students do.

Paradise Valley Mall (✉ Cactus Rd. and Tatum Blvd., ☎ 480/996–8840), in northeastern Phoenix, is an older mall with a Macy's department store.

At boisterous **Scottsdale Fashion Square** (✉ Scottsdale and Camelback Rds., Scottsdale, ☎ 480/941–2140), retractable skylights open to reveal sunny skies above. Besides Robinsons-May and Dillard's, there is **Neiman Marcus** (check out the hanging Paolo Soleri sculpture above the Neiman's elevator). The collection of stores runs toward the pricey chains including **J. Crew** and **Artafax. FAO Schwarz,** the **Disney Store,** and **Warner Bros. Studio Store** are attractions for kids.

Superstition Springs Center (✉ AZ 60 and Superstition Springs Rd., Mesa, ☎ 480/832–0212), 30 mi east of Phoenix, has the usual complement of shops and eateries, plus a pleasant outdoor cactus garden to stroll in. The handsome indoor carousel and 15-ft Gila-monster slide keep the kids occupied.

SIDE TRIPS NEAR PHOENIX

All the following sites are within a 1½-hour drive of Phoenix. To the north, Arcosanti and Wickenburg make satisfying half-day or day trips from Phoenix. Stop along the way to visit the petroglyphs of Deer Valley Rock Art Center and the reenactments of Arizona territorial life at the Pioneer Arizona Living History Museum. You also might consider Arcosanti and Wickenburg as stopovers on the way to or from Flagstaff, Prescott, or Sedona (☞ Chapter 3).

South of Phoenix, an hour's drive takes you back to prehistoric times and the site of Arizona's first known civilization, as well as one of its major pioneer western towns. Florence, one of central Arizona's first cities, is rich in examples of territorial architecture. The Casa Grande Ruins National Monument captures vivid reminders of the Hohokam, who began farming this area more than 1,500 years ago.

Deer Valley Rock Art Center

15 mi north of downtown Phoenix on I–17. Exit at W. Deer Valley Rd. and drive 2 mi west.

On the lower slopes of the Hedgepeth Hills, Deer Valley Rock Art Center has the largest concentration of ancient petroglyphs in the metropolitan Phoenix area. Some 1,500 of the cryptic symbols are found here, left behind by various Native American cultures that have lived in the Valley (or passed through) over the past thousand years. After watching one of the videos about the petroglyphs, pick up a pair of binoculars for $1 and an informative trail map and set out on the ¼-mi path. Telescopic tubes point to some of the most well-formed petroglyphs, but you'll soon be picking them out everywhere: Mysterious, enduring, and beautiful, they range from human and animal forms to more abstract figures. Even the cars whizzing by in the distance can't spoil this trip through ancient art and culture. ⊠ *3711 W. Deer Valley Rd., Phoenix,* ☎ *623/582–8007.* ☞ *$3.* ☉ *Tues.–Sat. 9–5, Sun. noon–5.*

Pioneer Arizona Living History Museum

✤ ㉑ *25 mi north of downtown Phoenix on I–17, just north of the Carefree Highway (AZ 74).*

The Pioneer Arizona Living History Museum contains 28 original and reconstructed buildings from throughout territorial Arizona. Costumed guides filter through the bank, schoolhouse, and print shop, as well as the Pioneer Opera House, where classic melodramas are performed daily. This museum is popular with the grade-school-field-trip set and it's your lucky day if you can tag along for their tour of the site—particularly when John-the-Blacksmith forges, smelts, and answers sixth-graders' questions that adults are too know-it-all to ask. For an extra $5 per adult, tour the grounds via a reproduction Conestoga wagon. ⊠ *Pioneer Rd. exit (Exit 225) off I–17,* ☎ *623/465–1052.* ☞ *$5.75.* ☉ *Wed.–Sun. 9–5.*

Wickenburg

㉒ *65 mi from Phoenix. Follow I–17 north for about 25 minutes to the Carefree Highway (AZ 74) junction. About 30 mi west on AZ 74, take the AZ 89/93 north and go another 10 mi to Wickenburg.*

This city, land of dude ranches and tall tales, is named for Henry Wickenburg, whose nearby Vulture Mine was the richest gold strike in the Arizona Territory. By the late 1800s, these banks of the (now-dry) Hassayampa River hosted a booming mining town with the seemingly endless supply of gold, copper, and silver. Resident miners developed a reputation for waxing overenthusiastic about the area's potential wealth, helping to coin the phrase "Hassayamper" for tellers-of-tales throughout the Old West. Legend has it that a drink from the Hassayampa River will cause one to fib forevermore—a tough claim to test, since for most of the river's 100-mi course it flows underground. Nowadays, Wickenburg's Old West atmosphere attracts visitors with its dude ranches, old-timey downtown, and western museum. Antiques buffs will enjoy a choice collection of shops, most of which are found on Tegner and Frontier streets. Maps for self-guided walking tours of the town's historic buildings are available at the **Wickenburg Chamber of Commerce** (⊠ 216 N. Frontier St., ☎ 520/684–5479), in the city's old Santa Fe Depot.

Those interested in the lore of the American West will find the 20,000-square-ft **Desert Caballeros Western Museum** (⊠ 21 N. Frontier St., ☎ 520/684–7075 or 520/684–2272) a worthwhile stop; kids enjoy recreations of a turn-of-the-century general store and local street scene. On the northeast corner of Wickenburg Way and Tegner streets, check out the **Jail Tree,** to which prisoners were chained, the desert heat sometimes finishing them off before their sentences were served.

The self-guided trails of **Hassayampa River Preserve** wind through lush cottonwood-willow forests, dense mesquite bosquets, and around a 4-acre, spring-fed pond and marsh habitat. You'll spot wildlife a-plenty, but it's rare birds that abound here, including waterfowl, herons, and

Side Trips Near Phoenix

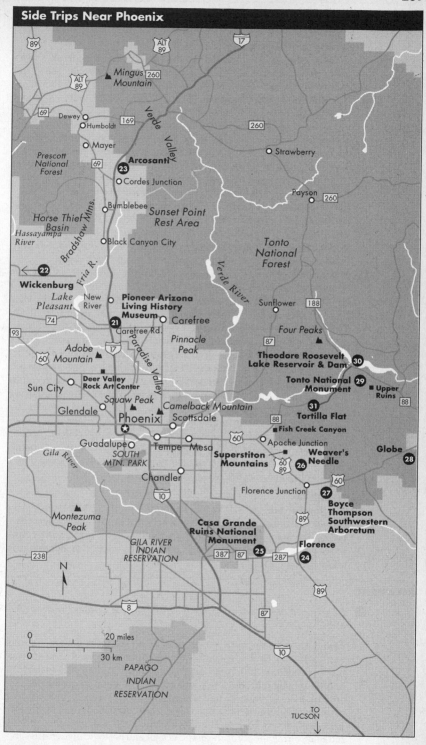

89

ALT 89

17

Mingus Mountain ▲ 260

260

ALT 89

169

Verde Valley

69 Dewey ○

○ Humboldt

○ Mayer

69

Arcosanti ●**23**

Strawberry ○

Payson ○ 260

Prescott National Forest

○ Cordes Junction

Bumblebee ○

Sunset Point Rest Area

Tonto National Forest

Horse Thief Basin

Bradshaw Mtns.

Hassayampa River

○ Black Canyon City

Agua Fria R.

Verde River

●←**22**

Wickenburg

Lake Pleasant

New River

74

Pioneer Arizona Living History Museum

Carefree Rd.

●**21** 17

Carefree

Pinnacle Peak

Sunflower ○

188

Four Peaks ▲

87

Theodore Roosevelt Lake Reservoir & Dam ●**30**

Tonto National Monument ●**29**

■ Upper Ruins

88

93

60 **Adobe Mountain** ▲

Paradise Valley

Deer Valley Rock Art Center

Sun City

Squaw Peak ▲

Glendale

Phoenix ☆

Scottsdale

Camelback Mountain

●**31** **Tortilla Flat**

88

■ Fish Creek Canyon

60

Guadalupe ○

Gila River

SOUTH MTN. PARK

Tempe **Mesa**

Apache Junction

Superstiton Mountains

60 89

●**26**

Weaver's Needle

Globe

●**28**

Chandler

10

Montezuma Peak ▲

Florence Junction

●**27**

60

89

Boyce Thompson Southwestern Arboretum

238

GILA RIVER INDIAN RESERVATION

N ↑

Casa Grande Ruins National Monument

387 87 ●**25** 287

Florence

●**24**

89

8

0 ___ 20 miles
0 ___ 30 km

87

10

PAPAGO INDIAN RESERVATION

TO TUCSON ↓

Arizona's rarest raptors. ⊠ *3 mi southeast of Wickenburg on U.S. 60,* ☎ *520/684–2772.* ☉ *Wed.–Sun.; hrs vary seasonally, call ahead.*

Dining and Lodging

$ ✕ **Anita's Cocina.** Reliable TexMex fare is featured here—fresh, steaming tamales are especially tasty, for either lunch or dinner. Try a fruit burrito for dessert. ⊠ *57 N. Valentine St.,* ☎ *520/684–5777. MC, V.*

$$$$ ✕🏨 **Rancho de los Caballeros.** This 20,000-acre property combines the dude-ranch experience with first-class amenities. Meals are served in the lodge's bright, festive dining room; guests are asked to dress for each night's sit-down dinner—jackets or western vests for men. Rooms are spacious, done in low-key southwestern decor. Some contain two queen-size beds and can be creatively configured—through a system of adjoining doors—to annex separate living rooms or sleeping quarters for children. *Daily,* the Pasa Tiempo newsletter, lists scheduled activities, or guests can simply lounge by the fireplace in the lodge's original 1948 *sala* (living room). ⊠ *1551 S. Vulture Mine Rd., 85390,* ☎ *520/ 684–5484,* 🖷 *520/684–2267. 79 rooms. Dining room, lounge, pool, driving range, 18-hole golf course, 4 tennis courts, horseback riding, children's programs. Closed mid-May–Oct. No credit cards.*

$$$ ✕🏨 **Kay El Bar Ranch.** Tucked into a hollow by the Hassayampa River 3½ mi north of town (go north on U.S. 89/93 for 2 mi, turn onto Rincon Road and follow the signs for 1½ mi to the ranch), this is what dude ranches used to be—personable, low-key, and away from it all. This National Historic Site is run by congenial John and Nancy Loftis, and accepts only 24 guests at a time. Some of the biggest mesquite trees in Arizona shade the eight-room lodge; a two-bedroom, two-bath cottage with private patio (built in 1914); and charming adobe cookhouse, where family-style meals are served three times a day. Each room in the lodge has a small, modern bathroom, but these compact quarters are designed for sleeping rather than hanging out. In the evenings the action is in the living room, where guests enjoy cocktails and homemade hors d'oeuvres by the stone fireplace. ⊠ *37500 S. Rincon Rd., Box 2480, Wickenburg 85358,* ☎ *520/684–7593. 9 rooms, 1 homestead house, 1 cottage. Bar, pool, golf privileges, horseback riding, Ping-Pong, volleyball, library. MC, V. Closed May–mid-Oct.*

Nightlife

The **Rancher Bar** (⊠ 910 W. Wickenburg Way, ☎ 520/684–5957) has a modern-day saloon atmosphere, where real live wranglers and cowboys meet up to shoot some pool after a hard day's work; a live country-music combo plays weekend nights, when the two-stepping locals really file in.

Arcosanti

㉓ *65 mi north of Phoenix on I–17, near the exit for Cordes Junction (AZ 69).*

Two miles down a partly paved road northeast from the gas stations and cafés, the evolving complex and community of Arcosanti was masterminded by Italian architect Paolo Soleri to be a self-sustaining habitat in which architecture and ecology function in symbiosis. Arcosanti is being built by its residents as a totally energy-independent town. It looks almost like a huge playground or contemporary-art theme park, with desert-rock retaining walls and huge solar greenhouses; it's full of inspiring ideas for dramatic design and ecologically sensitive living. It's worth taking the time out for a tour, a bite at the café, and a little shopping for one of the hand-cast bronze wind-bells made at the site. ⊠ *I–17 at Cordes Junction, near the town of Mayer,* ☎ *520/632–7135.* 🎟 *$5 donation.* ☉ *Daily 9–5; tours hourly 10–4.*

En Route If you're continuing from Arcosanti to Prescott, consider stopping in at **Young's Farm** (✉ Junction of AZ 69 and AZ 169, Dewey, ☎ 520/ 632–7272). Family-run since 1947, Young's has hayrides, a nursery, a petting zoo, and a potbellied pig named Clementswine. The store has become a beloved purveyor of fresh vegetables, potpies and pumpkins, sweet corn and cider, honey and fresh bread.

Florence

㉔ *Take U.S. 60 east (Superstition Freeway) to Florence Junction (U.S. 60 and AZ 79) and head south 16 mi on AZ 79 to Florence.*

This old western town southeast of Phoenix is distinguished by an American Victorian courthouse and more than 150 other sites listed on the National Register of Historic Places. You may recognize Florence as the location where *Murphy's Romance* was filmed.

The **Pinal County Historical Society** (✉ 715 S. Main St., ☎ 520/868– 4382) displays furnishings from 1900s houses and Native American crafts and tools. Open Thursday through Monday, **McFarland Historical State Park** (✉ Main and Ruggles Sts., ☎ 520/868–5216) houses memorabilia of former Governor and U.S. Senator Ernest W. McFarland in the circa-1878 Pinal County Courthouse. The **Pinal County Visitor's Center** (✉ 330 W. Butte St., ☎ 520/868–4331) answers questions and provides brochures weekdays 8–3 September through May and 9–2 June through August.

Casa Grande Ruins National Monument

㉕ *9 mi west of Florence on AZ 287 or, from I-10, 16 mi east on AZ 387 and AZ 87. Note: Follow the signs to the ruins, not to the town of Casa Grande. When leaving the ruins, take AZ 87 north 35 mi back to U.S. 60.*

Established in 1918, the Casa Grande Ruins National Monument was unknown to European explorers until Father Kino, a Jesuit missionary, first recorded its existence in 1694. Allow an hour to explore the site, longer if park rangers are giving a talk or leading a tour.

Start at the visitor center, where a small museum features artifacts and information on the Hohokam, who lived here and farmed irrigated fields of corn, beans, squash, cotton, tobacco, and other crops until they vanished mysteriously in about AD 1450. Begin your self-guided tour with an inspection of the 35-ft-tall (that's four stories, folks) Casa Grande (Big House), the tallest Hohokam building known, built in the early 14th century. It sits underneath a modern roof erected on posts to protect it from sun and wind, but the grandeur of the centuries shines through. Neighboring structures are much smaller, and only a bit of the 7-ft wall around the compound is still in evidence. The original purpose of Casa Grande still eludes archaeologists; some think it was an ancient astronomical observatory or a center of government, religion, trade, or education. On your way out, cross the parking lot by the covered picnic grounds and climb the platform for a view of a ball court and two platform mounds, said to date from the 1100s. Although only a few prehistoric sites can be viewed, more than 60 are included in the monument area. ✉ *Just north of Coolidge St. on AZ 87,* ☎ *520/723– 3172.* 🎫 *$2, or $4 per carload.* ☉ *Daily 8–5.*

Dining

$ ✕ **Old Pueblo Restaurant.** Of the down-home Mexican and American fare served here, the steak fajita burros, chimichangas, and *carne asada* (grilled beefsteak) are favorites. The Friday-night all-you-can-eat shrimp and catfish dinner really packs in the locals. ⊠ *505 S. Main St., Florence,* ☏ *520/868–4784. AE, D, DC, MC, V. Closed Sat.*

SIDE TRIPS AROUND THE APACHE TRAIL

Making a large loop east of Phoenix, this 150-mi drive was called by President Theodore Roosevelt "the most awe-inspiring and most sublimely beautiful panorama nature ever created." A stretch of winding highway, the AZ 88 portion of the Apache Trail follows closely the route forged through wilderness in 1906 to move construction supplies to build Roosevelt Dam, which lies at the northernmost part of the loop. Take a day or two to drive the trail, drink in the marvelous vistas, and stop to explore along the way.

From the town of Apache Junction, you can choose to drive the trail in either direction; there are advantages to both. If you begin the loop in a clockwise direction—heading eastward on AZ 88—your drive may be more relaxing; you'll be on the farthest side of this narrow dirt road some refer to as the "white-knuckle route," with its switchbacks and drop-offs straight down into spectacular Fish Creek Canyon. If you follow the route in the counterclockwise direction—continuing on U.S. 60 past the town of Apache Junction—you'll be passing from attraction to attraction such that they can be most appreciated.

The tour below follows the route counterclockwise. Although the drive itself can be completed in one day, we recommend spending a night in Globe, and continuing the loop back to Phoenix the following day.

Superstition Mountains

From Phoenix, take I–10 and then U.S. 60 (the Superstition Freeway) east through the suburbs of Tempe, Mesa, and Apache Junction.

As the Phoenix metro area gives way to cactus- and creosote-dotted desert, the massive escarpment of the Superstition Mountains heaves into view and slides by to the north. The Superstitions are supposedly home to the legendary **Lost Dutchman Mine,** the location—not to mention the existence—of which has been hotly debated since pioneer days.

Weaver's Needle

26 *About 11½ mi southeast of Apache Junction, off U.S. 60, take the Peralta Trail Rd. (just past King's Ranch Rd.). An 8-mi, rough gravel road leads to the start of the Peralta Trail.*

The 4-mi round-trip Peralta Trail winds 1,400 ft up a small valley for a spectacular view of Weaver's Needle, a monolithic rock formation that is one of Arizona's more famous sights. Allow a few hours for this rugged and challenging hike, bring plenty of water and a snack or lunch, and don't hike it in the middle of the day in summer.

Boyce Thompson Southwestern Arboretum

★ **27** *12 mi east of Florence Junction (U.S. 60 and AZ 79).*

At the foot of Picketpost Mountain, the **Boyce Thompson Southwestern Arboretum** is one of the treasures of the Sonoran Desert. From the visitor center, well-marked, self-guided trails traverse 35 acres, winding through all of the desert's varied habitats—from gravelly open desert to lush creekside glades. Native flora coexists alongside imported exotic specimens such as Canary Islands date palms and Australian eucalyptus. The **Smith Interpretive Center,** a National Historic Site, has two greenhouses and displays on geology, plant propagation, and native basketry. Benches with built-in misters are a relief on hot days, and natural exhibits illustrate such subjects as herbs used in traditional Sonoran healing. Bring a picnic lunch and enjoy the arboretum's lovely picnic grounds. ⊠ *37615 Hwy. 60, Superior,* ☎ *520/ 689–2811.* ☞ *$5.* ☉ *Daily 8–5.*

En Route A few miles farther past the arboretum, **Superior** is the first of several modest mining towns and the launching point for a dramatic winding ascent through the Mescals to a 4,195-ft pass that affords panoramic views of this copper-rich range and its huge, dormant, open-pit mines. Collectors will want to watch for antiques shops through these hills, but be forewarned that quality varies considerably. A gradual descent will take you into **Miami** and **Claypool,** once-thriving boomtowns that have carried on quietly since major-corporation mining ground to a halt in the 1970s. Working-class buildings are dwarfed by the mountainous piles of copper tailings to the north. At a stoplight in Claypool, AZ 88 splits off northward to the Apache Trail, but continue on U.S. 60 another 3 mi to make the stop in the city of Globe.

Globe

28 *U.S. 60, 51 mi east of Apache Junction, 25 mi east of Superior, and 3 mi east of Claypool's AZ 88 turnoff.*

On the southern reaches of Tonto National Forest, the city of Globe is the most cosmopolitan of the area's mining towns. Initially, it was gold and silver that brought miners here—the city allegedly got its name from a large circular silver boulder of silver, with lines like continents, found by prospectors—though the region is now renowned as one of North America's richest copper deposits. If you're driving the Apache Trail loop, be sure to stop in Globe to fill up the tank, as it is the last chance to gas up until looping all the way back to U.S. 60 at Apache Junction.

Swing by the **Globe Chamber of Commerce** (⊠ 1¼ mi north of downtown on U.S. 60, ☎ 520/425–4495 or 800/804–5623) to pick up brochures detailing the self-guided **Historic Downtown Walking Tour,** and stop in the nearby **Gila County Historical Museum** (⊠ 1330 N. Broad St., ☎ 520/425–7385) to see the collection of memorabilia from the area's mining days. Then head "downtown" to central Globe's historic Broad Street for shopping and a visit to the local artists' co-op.

The restored late-19th-century Gila County Courthouse houses the **Cobre Valley Center for the Arts** (⊠ 101 N. Broad St., ☎ 520/425–0884), showcasing works by local artists; be sure to visit the ladies and their looms in the basement **Weaver's Studio,** open Thursday–Saturday 10–3.

For a step 800 years back in time, tour the 2 acres of excavated Salado Indian ruins on the southeastern side of town at the **Besh-Ba-Gowah Ruins and Museum.** After a trip through the small museum and a video introduction, enter the area full of remnants of more than 200 rooms occupied here by the Salado during the 13th and 14th centuries. You'll also see public areas such as the central plaza (also the principal burial ground; archaeologists have uncovered over 150 burials), roasting pits, and open patios. Besh Ba Gowah is a name given by the Apaches, who—arriving in the 17th century—found the pueblo abandoned and moved in; loosely translated, the name means "metal camp," as remains left on the site point to it as part of an extensive commerce and trading network. ⊠ *150 N. Pine St.,* ☎ *520/425–0320.* ☞ *$3.* ☉ *Daily 9–5.*

Dining & Lodging

$$–$$$ ✕ **Blue Ribbon Cafe.** Beyond the curtained windows of the entry parlor, this charismatic coffee shop and dining room is the local favorite, serving up three meals a day. Their specialty is the English pasty (pronounced pass-tee); this seasoned meat-and-potato pie has long been a miner's favorite. ⊠ *4805 E. Hwy. 60,* ☎ *520/425–4423. AE, D, DC, MC, V.*

$ ✕ **Chalo's.** This casual roadside spot offers some of the best Mexican food you'll find north of the border. Try an order of their savory stuffed *sopaipillas* (puffed Indian bread), which they fill with pork and beef, beans, and red or green chilies. ⊠ *902 E. Ash St.,* ☎ *520/425–0515. MC, V.*

$ 🏨 **El Rey Motel.** Hosts Rebecca and Ricardo Bernal lovingly operate this quintessential roadside motel where wagon wheels and potted plants dot the grounds. This vintage motor court offers small, immaculate rooms, covered parking spaces, and a shared central picnic and barbecue area. ⊠ *1201 E. Ash St., 85501,* ☎ *520/425–4427,* 𝔽𝔸𝕏 *520/402–9147. 23 rooms. AE, D, MC, V.*

$ 🏨 **Noftsger Hill Inn.** Built in 1907, this bed-and-breakfast was originally the North Globe Schoolhouse; now, classrooms serve as guest rooms with private baths, filled with mining-era antiques and affording fantastic views of the Pinal mountains and historic Old Dominion mine. Innkeepers Frank and Pam Hulme promise you'll enjoy walking off "miner-size" portions of their Sonoran-style breakfasts with the hike through the scenic Copper Hills behind the old school. ⊠ *425 North St., 85501,* ☎ *520/425–2260. 5 rooms. Full breakfast. MC, V.*

Nightlife

Run by the San Carlos Apache tribe, **Apache Gold** (5 mi east of Globe on U.S. 70, ☎ 520/425–7800 or 800/272–2433) has more than 500 slots, Keno, and video and live poker; call about the free shuttle from most of Globe's hotels and motels.

Shopping

Broad Street, Globe's main drag, is lined with a number of antiques and gift shops. **Blue Mule** (⊠ 656 N. Broad St., ☎ 520/425–4920) sells everything from paintings and pottery to stained glass, carved wood, and offbeat sculpture. On Ash between Hill and South East streets **Copper City Rock Shop** (⊠ 566 Ash St., ☎ 520/425–7885) specializes in mineral products, many from Arizona. **Past Times** (⊠ 1068 Adonis Ave., ☎ 520/473–3791) carries antiques. **Simply Sarah** (⊠ 294 N. Broad St., ☎ 520/425–2248), with its ornately carved stone arch, has upscale ladies clothing in predominantly natural fibers and high-quality accessories. Try **Turquoise Ladies** (⊠ 996 N. Broad St., ☎ 520/425–6288) for owner June Stratton's collection of uniquely Globe souvenirs and stories.

En Route   At the stoplight 3 mi south of Globe on U.S. 60, AZ 88 splits off to the northwest. About 25 mi later on AZ 88, heading toward the Tonto National Monument, you'll see towering quartzite cliffs about 2 mi in the distance—look up and to the left for glimpses of the 40-room **Upper Ruins,** 14th-century condos left behind by the Salado people. They can't be seen from within the national monument, so make sure you've got binoculars.

Tonto National Monument

㉙ *30 mi northwest of U.S. 60 on AZ 88.*

This well-preserved complex of 13th-century Salado Indian cliff dwellings is worth a stop. The self-guided walking tour of the **Lower**

Cliff Dwellings is interesting, but the more adventurous will opt to take a ranger-led tour of the 40-room **Upper Cliff Dwellings,** offered on selected mornings from November to April; tour reservations are required, and should be made as far as a month in advance. To reach Tonto National Monument, go northwest on AZ 88, 30 mi beyond the intersection of U.S. 60 and AZ 88. ✉ *HC 02, Box 4602, Roosevelt 85545,* ☎ *520/467–2241.* ⌷ *$4 per carload.* ☉ *Daily 8–5; Nov.–Apr., tours Thurs., weekends at 9:30 AM; May–Oct., tours Tues., Thurs., weekends at 9:30 AM.*

Theodore Roosevelt Lake Reservoir and Dam

㉚ *5 mi northwest of Tonto National Monument on AZ 88.*

Flanked by the desolate Mazatzal and Sierra Anchas mountain ranges, this aquatic recreational area is a favorite with bass anglers, water-skiers, and boaters. Not only is this the largest masonry dam on the planet, but the massive bridge is the longest two-lane, single span, steel-arch bridge in the nation.

En Route Past the reservoir, AZ 88 turns west and becomes a meandering dirt road, eventually winding its way back to Apache Junction via the magnificent, bronze-hued volcanic cliff walls of **Fish Creek Canyon,** with views of the sparkling lakes, towering saguaros, and a vast array of wildflowers.

Tortilla Flat

㉛ *AZ 88, 38 mi southeast of Roosevelt Dam; 18 mi northeast of Apache Junction.*

Close to the end of the Apache Trail are the old-time restaurant and country store of authentic stagecoach stop **Tortilla Flat** (✉ 1 Main St./AZ 88, ☎ 602/984–1776). This is a fun place to stop for a well-earned rest and refreshment—miner- and cowboy-style grub, of course—before heading back the last 18 mi to civilization. Enjoy a hearty bowl of killer chili and save room for prickly-pear-cactus ice cream.

PHOENIX AND CENTRAL ARIZONA A TO Z

Arriving and Departing

By Bus
Greyhound Lines (✉ 2115 E. Buckeye Rd., ☎ 602/389–4200 or 800/231–2222) has statewide and national routes from its main terminal near Sky Harbor airport.

By Car
If you're coming to Phoenix from the west, you'll probably come in on I–10. This transcontinental superhighway's last link was joined in 1990 in a tunnel under downtown Phoenix. The trip from the Los Angeles basin, via Palm Springs, takes six to eight hours, depending on where you start. From San Diego, I–8 slices across low desert to Yuma and on toward the Valley on what the Spanish called El Camino del Diablo (the Devil's Highway); at Gila Bend, take AZ 85 up to I–10. The trip takes a total of six to seven hours. From the east, I–10 takes you from El Paso, across southern New Mexico, and through Chiricahua Apache country into Tucson, then north to Phoenix (a total of about 9–11 hours).

From the northwest, I–40 crosses over from California and runs along old Route 66 to Flagstaff. East of Kingman, however, U.S. 93 branches off diagonally to the southeast, becoming U.S. 60 at Wickenburg and continuing into Phoenix.

The northeastern route, I–40 from Albuquerque, crosses Hopi and Navajo historic lands to Flagstaff, where I–17 takes you south to Phoenix—an eight-hour journey. For a scenic shortcut, take AZ 377 south at Holbrook to Heber and the pines of the Mogollon Rim; then take AZ 260 down the 2,000-ft drop to Payson and AZ 87 through the forests of saguaro cactus into Phoenix.

By Plane

Most air travelers visiting Arizona fly into **Sky Harbor International Airport** (☎ 602/273–3300). Just 3 mi east of downtown Phoenix, it is surrounded by freeways linking it to almost every part of the metro area.

AIRLINES

For flights from Phoenix to Flagstaff, the Grand Canyon, Lake Havasu, Page, Prescott, Yuma, and other Arizona points, try **America West** (☎ 800/235–9292), **Sun Air** (☎ 800/445–8738), and commuter **Skywest** (☎ 800/453–9417).

BETWEEN THE AIRPORT AND DOWNTOWN

It's easy to get from Sky Harbor to downtown Phoenix (3 mi west) and Tempe (3 mi east). The airport is also only 20 minutes by freeway from Glendale (to the west) and Mesa (to the east). Scottsdale (to the northeast) can be reached via the Squaw Peak Parkway (AZ 51), but is a route of all surface streets (depending on destination, 44th Street from the Airport, then Camelback Road into Scottsdale is usually the easiest); both options take about a half hour by car, depending on traffic.

Sky Harbor has limited bus service, ample taxi service, and very good shuttle service to points throughout the metro area. Very few hotels offer a complimentary limo or shuttle, but most resorts do. You should definitely rent a car, either at the airport or wherever you are staying (most rental firms deliver).

By Bus. In about 20 minutes, **Valley Metro buses** (☎ 602/253–5000) will get you directly from Terminal 2, 3, or 4 to the bus terminal downtown (at 1st and Washington streets) or to Tempe (Mill and University avenues). With free transfers, the bus can take you from the airport to most other Valley cities (Glendale, Sun City, Scottsdale, etc.), but the trip is likely to be slow unless you take an express line. Fare is $1.25.

The **Red Line** runs westbound to Phoenix every half hour from about 6 AM until after 9 PM weekdays. Saturday, you take Bus 13 and transfer at Central Avenue to Bus 0 north; there is no Sunday service. The Red Line runs eastbound to Tempe every half hour from 3:30 AM to 7 PM weekdays (no weekend service); in another 25 minutes, it takes you to downtown Mesa (Center and Main streets).

By Car. Tempe is 10 minutes from the airport by car; Glendale and Mesa are 25 minutes away; and Scottsdale and Sun City, 30–45 minutes. The following companies have airport booths or free pickup from nearby lots: **ABC** (☎ 888/899–9997), **Alamo** (☎ 800/327–9633), **Avis** (☎ 800/831–2847), **Budget** (☎ 800/527–0700), **Dollar** (☎ 800/800–4000), **Enterprise** (☎ 800/829–1853), **Hertz** (☎ 800/654–3131), **National** (☎ 800/227–7368), **Thrifty** (☎ 800/367–2277), and, if you care more about your wallet than about appearances, **Rent-a-Wreck** (☎ 602/252–4897 or 800/828–5975).

By Limousine. A few limousine firms cruise Sky Harbor, and many more provide airport pickups by reservation. **Scottsdale Limousine** (☎ 480/946–8446) requires reservations but offers a toll-free number (☎ 800/747–8234); rates start at $65 (plus tip).

By Shuttle. The blue vans of **Supershuttle** (☎ 602/244–9000 or 800/258–3826) cruise Sky Harbor, each taking up to seven passengers to their individual destinations, with no luggage fee or airport surcharge. Wheelchair vans are also available. Drivers accept credit cards and expect tips.

By Taxi. Only a few firms are licensed to pick up at Sky Harbor's commercial terminals. All add a $1 surcharge for airport pickups, do not charge for luggage, and are available 24 hours a day. A trip to downtown Phoenix can range from $8 to $12. The fare to downtown Scottsdale averages about $18. **Checker/Yellow Cab** (☎ 602/252–5252) and **Courier Cab** (☎ 602/232–2222) charge about $3 for the first mile and $1.50 per mile thereafter (not including tips).

By Train

Amtrak (☎ 800/872–7245) provides train service in Arizona with bus transfers to Phoenix. Eastbound train passengers will stop in Flagstaff, where Amtrak buses depart daily for Phoenix each morning. Westbound train travelers will likely make the transfer in Tucson, where Amtrak-run buses have limited service to Phoenix on Sunday, Tuesday, and Thursday nights. What used to be Phoenix's downtown train terminal is now the **Amtrak Thruway Bus Stop** (✉ 4th Ave. and Harrison St., ☎ 602/253–0121).

Getting Around

To get around Phoenix, *you will need a car.* Only a few downtowns (Phoenix, Scottsdale, Tempe) are pedestrian-friendly. There is no mass transit beyond a bus system that does not even run seven days a week.

By Bus

Valley Metro (☎ 602/253–5000) has 21 express lines and 51 regular routes that reach most of the Valley suburbs. But there are no 24-hour routes; only a skeletal few lines run between sundown and 10:30 PM or on Saturday, and there is no Sunday service. Fares are $1.25 for regular service, $1.75 for express, with free transfers. The City of Phoenix also runs a 35¢ **Downtown Area Shuttle (DASH),** with purple minibuses circling the area between the Arizona Center and the state capitol at 15-minute intervals. The system also serves major thoroughfares in several suburbs—Glendale, Scottsdale, Tempe, Mesa, and Chandler. The City of Tempe operates the **Free Local Area Shuttle (FLASH),** which serves the downtown Tempe and Arizona State University area from 7 AM until 8 PM. In addition, **Dial-a-Ride** services (☎ 602/253–4000), normally reserved for seniors and people with disabilities during the weekdays and on Saturdays, are available throughout the Valley on Sundays. Charges begin at $1.20 for the first "zone," or section, of Phoenix in which you travel; each additional zone is 60¢.

By Car

In the Valley of the Sun, rain and fog are rare, and snow gets major headlines. Most metro-area streets are well marked and well lighted, and the freeway system is making gradual progress in linking Valley areas. Arizona requires seat belts on front-seat passengers and children 16 and under. (For car-rental agencies, *see* Between the Airport and Downtown, *above.*)

Around downtown Phoenix, AZ 202 (Papago Freeway), AZ 143 (Hohokam Freeway), and I–10 (Maricopa Freeway) make an elongated east–west loop, encompassing the state capitol area to the west and Tempe to the east. At mid-loop, AZ 51 (Squaw Peak Freeway) runs north into Paradise Valley. And from the loop's east end, I–10 runs south to Tucson, 100 mi away (though it's still referred to as I–10 east, as it is eventually headed that way); U.S. 60 (Superstition Freeway) branches east to Tempe and Mesa.

Roads in Phoenix and its suburbs are laid out on a single, 800-sq-mi grid. Even the freeways run predominantly north–south and east–west. (Grand Avenue, running about 20 mi from northwest downtown to Sun City, is the *only* diagonal.)

Camera devices are mounted on several street lights to catch speeders and red-light runners, and their location is constantly changing. You may think you've gotten away with a few miles over the limit and return home only to find a ticket waiting for you. Smart commuters know to avoid Paradise Valley, where incomes are sky high and speed limits ridiculously low; and locals swear that Indian School Road is a better street than Camelback for driving between Phoenix and Scottsdale.

Central Avenue is the main north–south grid axis: All roads parallel to and west of Central are numbered *avenues*; all roads parallel to and east of Central are numbered *streets*. The numbering begins at Central and increases in each direction.

Weekdays, 6 AM–9 AM and 4 PM–6 PM, the center or left-turn lanes on the major surface arteries of 7th Street and 7th Avenue become one-way traffic-flow lanes between McDowell Road and Dunlap Avenue. These specially marked lanes are dedicated mornings to north–south traffic (into downtown) and afternoons to south–north traffic (out of downtown).

By Taxi

Taxi fares are unregulated in Phoenix, except at the airport (☞ Between the Airport and Downtown, *above*). The 800-square-mi metro area is so large that one-way fares in excess of $50 are not uncommon; you might want to ask what the damages will be before you get in. Except within a compact area, such as central Phoenix, travel by taxi is not recommended.

Contacts and Resources

Emergencies

Police, fire, ambulance, or **highway** emergencies (☎ 911). The **Poison Control Center** (☎ 602/253–3334).

DOCTORS AND DENTISTS

The **Maricopa County Medical Society** (☎ 602/252–2844) and the **Arizona Osteopathic Medical Association** (☎ 602/840–0460) offer referrals during business hours on weekdays. The **American Dental Association Valley chapter** (☎ 602/957–4864) has a 24-hour referral hot line.

HOSPITALS

Samaritan Health Service (☎ 602/230–2273) has four Valley hospitals—Good Samaritan (downtown), Desert Samaritan (east), Ahwautukee Foothills (south), and Thunderbird Samaritan (northwest); all share a 24-hour hot line. **Scottsdale Memorial Hospital** (☎ 480/481–4000 or 480/860–3000) has two campuses in the northeastern Valley. **Maricopa County Medical Center** (☎ 602/267–5011) has been rated one of the nation's best public hospitals.

Walgreen's has fourteen 24-hour locations throughout the Valley. Call
☎ 800/925–4733 to find the one nearest you. **Osco Drug** (☎ 888/443–
5701) has 24-hour outlets, including central Phoenix (✉ 3320 N. 7th
Ave., ☎ 602/266–5501), west Phoenix (✉ 35th and Glendale Aves.,
☎ 602/841–7861), Scottsdale (✉ Scottsdale and Shea Rds., ☎ 480/
998–3500), and Mesa (✉ 1836 W. Baseline Rd., ☎ 480/831–0212).

Guided Tours

Reservations for tours are a must all year, with seats often filling up
quickly in the busy season, October–April. All tours provide pickup
services at area resorts, but some offer lower prices if you drive to the
tour's point of origin. For various outdoor excursions, *see* Outdoor
Activities and Sports, *above*.

ORIENTATION TOURS
Gray Line Tours (✉ Box 21126, Phoenix 85036, ☎ 602/495–9100 or
800/732–0327) gives seasonal, three-hour narrated tours including
downtown Phoenix, the Arizona Biltmore hotel, Camelback Mountain, mansions in Paradise Valley, Arizona State University, Papago Park,
and Scottsdale's Old Town; the price is about $30.

Open Road Tours (✉ 748 E. Dunlap, No. 2, Phoenix 85020, ☎ 602/
997–6474 or 800/766–7117) offers excursions to Sedona and the
Grand Canyon, Phoenix city tours, and Native American–culture trips
to the Salt River Pima–Maricopa Indian Reservation.

For $38, **Vaughan's Southwest Custom Tours** (✉ Box 31250, Phoenix
85046, ☎ 602/971–1381 or 800/513–1381) gives a 4½-hour city tour
for 11 or fewer passengers in custom vans, stopping at the Heard Museum, the Arizona Biltmore, and the state capitol building. Vaughan's
will also take you east of Phoenix on the Apache Trail. The tour is offered on Tuesday, Friday, and Saturday; the cost is $65.

SPECIAL-INTEREST TOURS
Arizona Carriage Company (✉ 7228 E. 2nd St., Scottsdale 85251, ☎
480/423–1449) leads 15-minute to one-hour horse-drawn-carriage
tours around Old Scottsdale for $20–$80.

Cimarron Adventures and River Co. (✉ 7901 E. Pierce St., Scottsdale
85257, ☎ 480/994–1199) arranges half-day float trips down the Salt
and Verde rivers. Trips cost about $35 per person.

Desert Storm Hummer Tours (✉ 15525 N. 83rd Way, No. 8, Scottsdale 85260, ☎ 480/922–0020) conducts 4-hour nature tours for $90
per person, climbing 4,000 feet up the rugged trails of Tonto National
Forest via Hummer.

WALKING TOUR
A 45-minute self-guided walking tour of **Old Scottsdale** takes you to
14 historic sites in the area. Pick up a map of the route in the **Scottsdale Chamber of Commerce** (☞ Visitor Information, *below*).

Opening and Closing Times

Generally, banks are open Monday–Thursday 9–4, Friday 9–6. Selected
banks have Saturday-morning hours, and a few large grocery stores
have bank windows that stay open until 9 PM. Most enclosed shopping malls are open weekdays 10–9, Saturday 10–6, and Sunday noon–
5; some of the major centers (☞ Shopping, *above*) are open later on
weekends. Many grocery stores are open 7 AM–9 PM, but several stores
within major chains throughout the Valley are open 24 hours.

Radio Stations

AM

KTAR 620: news, talk, sports. **KFYI 910:** news, talk. **KISO 1230:** country oldies. **KSLX 1440:** classic rock. **KPHX 1480:** Spanish-language.

FM

KBAQ 89.5: classical. **KJZZ 91.5:** acoustic jazz, National Public Radio. **KKFR 92.3:** contemporary hits. **KOOL 94.5:** oldies. **KMXP 96.9:** adult contemporary. **KSLX 100.7:** classic rock. **KZON 101.5:** alternative rock. **KNIX 102.5:** country. **KEDJ 106.3:** alternative rock. **KVVA 107.1:** Spanish-language.

Visitor Information

Arizona Office of Tourism (✉ 2702 N. 3rd St., Suite 4015, Phoenix 85004, ☎ 602/230–7733 or 888/520–3444), open weekdays 8 AM–5 PM; closed holidays. **Native American Tourism Center** (✉ 4130 N. Goldwater Blvd., Suite 114, ☎ 480/945–0771, FAX 480/945–0264) aids in arranging tourist visits to reservation lands; they can't afford to send information packets, but visitors are welcome to call, fax, or stop in weekdays 8–5. **Phoenix and Valley of the Sun Convention and Visitors Bureau** (✉ Arizona Center, 400 E. Van Buren St., Suite 600, Phoenix 85004; ✉ Hyatt Regency Phoenix, 2nd and Adams Sts.; ☎ 602/254–6500 for both). **Phoenix Chamber of Commerce** (✉ Bank One Plaza, 201 N. Central Ave., Suite 2700, Phoenix 85073, ☎ 602/254–5521). **Scottsdale Chamber of Commerce** (✉ 7343 Scottsdale Mall, ☎ 480/945–8481 or 800/877–1117) is open weekdays 8:30–6:30, Saturday 10–5, and Sunday 11–5.

Weather

The *Arizona Republic*'s **Pressline** (☎ 602/271–5656 then press 1010) gives tomorrow's forecast and up-to-date Valley conditions. **Weatherline** (☎ 602/265–5550) provides three-day forecasts. The **National Weather Service** (☎ 602/379–4000 then press 4) has a local extended forecast recording.

5 EASTERN ARIZONA

Northeast of Phoenix, the trout-filled streams and placid lakes of the White Mountains are a cool escape, even when the saguaro-dotted plains are baking in the merciless desert heat. In the winter, the White Mountains have some of the Southwest's best skiing. Farther north, explore Indian Ruins at Casa Malpais and Homolovi Ruins State Park and marvel at the forces of nature at Petrified Forest National Park and in the Painted Desert.

IN A STATE OF DRAMATIC NATURAL WONDERS, eastern Arizona is often overlooked—truly a tragedy, as it is one of Arizona's great outdoor playgrounds. In the White Mountains, northeast of Phoenix, you can hike amid the largest stand of ponderosa pine in the world while inhaling fresh air; fish for trout in babbling brooks; swim in clear reservoirs fed by unsullied mountain streams; and, at night, camp under the millions of twinkling stars. The region's winter sports are just as varied: You can ski, snowboard, snowshoe, and snowmobile on hundreds of miles of designated trails.

By Jenner Bishop

Updated by Deidre Elliott

An unparalleled natural beauty, however, is what really makes the region remarkable—the White Mountains are unspoiled high country at its best. Certain areas have been designated as primitive wilderness, removed from the touch of man. In these vast tracts, the air is rent with piercing cries of hawks and eagles and majestic herds of elk graze in verdant, wildflower-dotted meadows. Besides the alpine pleasures of fields and forests, the mountains have a number of unique geological characteristics. Past volcanic activity has left the land strewn with cinder cones and the whole region is bounded by the Mogollon Rim—a 200-mi geologic upthrust that splits the state. Much of the plant life is similarly unique; this is one of the only places in the country where such desert plants as juniper and manzanita grow intermixed with mountain pines and aspen.

The human aspects of the landscape are equally appealing. Historic western towns are friendly outposts of down-home hospitality, and the region's many prehistoric ruins are reminders of the rich native cultures that once flourished here. Native Americans are still a vital presence in the region: Nearly half of the White Mountains is Apache reservation. Visitors are welcome to explore most reservation lands. All that's required is a permit—easily obtained from tribal offices.

There's more to eastern Arizona than the White Mountains, however. To the north, along historic Route 66, you'll find the Painted Desert and Petrified Forest National Park and Homolovi Ruins State Park—extraordinary attractions in their own right. The austere mesas of the Painted Desert are world famous for their multihued sedimentary layers. Nature has also worked its wonders on the great fallen logs of the Petrified Forest National Park. In Triassic times, the park was a great steamy swampland; some 225 million years ago, seismic activity forced the swamp's decaying plant matter (and a number of deceased dinosaurs) deep underground, where it eventually turned to stone. Fifty miles west of these unusual geologic remains are remnants of a more recent time: Homolovi Ruins State Park marks the site of four major ancestral Hopi pueblos, one of which contains more than 1,000 rooms. Between these artifacts of times past and the recreational bounty of the White Mountains wilderness, eastern Arizona offers a cultural and outdoor experience that defines the pleasures of Arizona.

Pleasures and Pastimes

Dining

Dining in eastern Arizona offers visitors a range of exciting opportunities. In the White Mountains, you might settle in for a relaxing evening of fine dining at a candlelit restaurant in the pines. Or if cowboy-size steaks and Old West atmosphere are what you seek, choose a more rustic setting at one of the area's many western-style cafés. In and around the Navajo and Hopi reservations, be sure to sample Indian tacos, an authentic treat made with scrumptious fry bread, beans, and chiles.

Indian Ruins

North of Springerville-Eagar, Casa Malpais Archeological Park and the Raven Site Ruins are prehistoric pueblo sites with construction characteristics of both the Anasazi peoples to the north and the Mogollon peoples to the south. Today, both the Hopi and Zuni peoples hotly claim individual affiliations with these sacred ruins—particularly Casa Malpais, thought to have been a prominent religious center with an impressive astronomical calendar and the largest kiva (sunken ceremonial chamber) ever discovered in the United States. Nearby Lyman Lake State Park has petroglyph trails boasting some of the region's more accessible rock art. West of Holbrook, the Homolovi Ruins State Park is home to a large complex of Hopi ancestral pueblos.

Lodging

The communities of Pinetop-Lakeside, Show Low, and Springerville offer a variety of lodging choices, including modern resorts, rustic cabins, and small bed-and-breakfasts. Farther west, near Canyon de Chelly and the Navajo and Hopi reservations, you'll find many establishments run by Native Americans, tribal enterprises intent on offering first-class service and hospitality.

Outdoor Activities and Sports

Although facilities and specific trails are listed under the towns below, some region-wide recreational information is worth noting here.

BIKING

Many White Mountains towns actively promote mountain biking, and there are plenty of rental and service facilities in Pinetop-Lakeside and Show Low. Pedal through the pines on the White Mountains Trailsystem, with its 200 mi of interconnecting multiuse trails.

Many bike routes follow Forest Service roads, which carry heavy traffic during the logging season from April to November; be alert for speeding logging trucks along these bumpy, narrow paths.

CAMPING

The Apache Sitgreaves National Forest has more than 35 campgrounds for both tent camping and RV hookups. The White Mountain Apache Reservation maintains 32 camping areas throughout its 1.6-million-acre reservation. During busy summer months, secure campground reservations 10 days in advance (☞ Outdoor Activities and Sports *in* Eastern Arizona A to Z, *below*).

FISHING

Anglers flock to the more than 65 lakes and reservoirs in the White Mountains where they hook German browns, rainbow and brook trout, as well as the occasional arctic grayling or native Apache trout, the official state fish. Early spring is prime trout-fishing season, but even in the winter, devoted anglers can be found ice fishing out on Nelson Reservoir or on Hawley Lake—which commonly posts the state's coldest wintertime temperatures. High-country warm-water fishing consists mostly of largemouth bass, walleye, bluegill, and catfish. Lyman Lake and Show Low Lake are good bets for catching walleye, hailed as the tastiest catch in the region. An Arizona fishing license is required at these sites; on tribal land, an additional White Mountain Apache fishing license is required.

GOLF

The High Country's links draw many golf enthusiasts from the Valley of the Sun and Tucson. These mountain fairways, with their cool temperatures and thin, pine-scented air, angle through lush forests of Aspen, blue spruce, and ponderosa pine and wind past lakes, streams, and springs.

HIKING

Hikers of all abilities will enjoy the White Mountains' high-desert terrain and wildlife. Pinetop-Lakeside's loop trails can accommodate most any level of proficiency, but advanced hikers should stop by ranger stations for Geological Survey and Forest Service maps and tips on trails and overnight camping hikes. When planning your hike through high-desert country, allow one hour for each 2 mi of trail covered, plus an additional hour for every 1,000 ft gained in altitude. Be aware that poison ivy grows in these wilderness areas; learn to recognize the stuff and steer clear!

Farther north, day hikes through the Painted Desert Wilderness's loose clay and sand are one of the best ways to explore the park's backcountry.

SKIING AND SNOWMOBILING

Famous regionally as a winter skiing destination, the White Mountains offer hilly, wooded landscapes that invite cross-country exploration. Greer is an ideal hub for cross-country skiers: The nearby Pole Knoll Trail System and surrounding Forest Service roads make for 33 mi of cross-country trails. No matter where you stay in the White Mountains, the drive to Sunrise Park Resort—the state's largest ski resort—is never more than an hour away and equipment-rental facilities are located throughout the region. Snowmobilers enjoy the area's dense forest and expansive meadows; the more adventurous enjoy the long-distance routes that connect Sunrise Ski Area to Williams Valley (near the town of Alpine) or Hannagan Meadow.

Volcanoes

A 1,158-square-mi volcanic field extends from Show Low to Springerville and from Greer to just south of St. Johns. Containing more than 405 vents and covers, the Springerville Volcanic Field is a "young" volcanic field—the most recent eruption was 300,000 years ago—and it is the third largest of its kind in the continental United States. These extinct cinder-cone volcanoes and eroded lava flows create an especially unusual landscape.

Exploring Eastern Arizona

A tour of eastern Arizona can best be completed by making a loop. The mountain towns of Pinetop-Lakeside, Greer, and Springerville-Eagar are connected by AZ 260. In winter months you'll have to stick to major thoroughfares, as many Forest Service roads are closed. Call the **White Mountains Road Condition Line** (☎ 520/537–7623) before departing.

Numbers in the text correspond to numbers in the margin and on the Eastern Arizona map.

Great Itineraries

Your White Mountains experience will vary greatly, depending on the season of your visit and your personal interests. The itineraries below assume that you're traveling between March and October, when both primary and secondary roads are passable. If you're visiting during the winter, you may have to rearrange your trip to accommodate seasonal road closures and chain requirements.

IF YOU HAVE 3 DAYS

Your options are limited if you only have three days to explore the mountains, given the distance from Phoenix, and the condition of the roads much of the year. Drive up to **Pinetop-Lakeside** ③, **Greer** ⑤, or

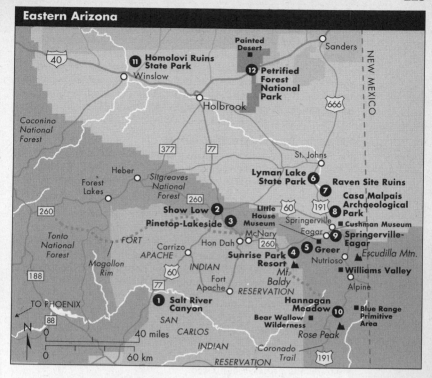

Eastern Arizona

Springerville-Eagar ⑨ and take advantage of a day or two of hiking, fishing, or biking. Snow enthusiasts commonly make the pilgrimage to **Sunrise Park Resort** ④ for just a day or two.

If your main priority is visiting the **Petrified Forest National Park** ⑫, spend the first night in 🏨 **Show Low** ② at any of the motels lining the freeway. On day two tour the park; spend the night in nearby 🏨 Holbrook, or make the scenic 75-mi drive southeast into **Springerville-Eagar** ⑨, where you'll find several lodging options. Another option is to retrace your route back on AZ 77 and head east for accommodations in 🏨 **Pinetop-Lakeside** ③. Spend your third day driving back to Phoenix. You can return via U.S. 60 or opt for the daylong trip down the Coronado Trail, one of the state's most scenic byways.

IF YOU HAVE 5 DAYS

After exploring the **Painted Desert** and **Petrified Forest National Park** ⑫, head south to the White Mountains and spend the night in either 🏨 **Springerville-Eagar** ⑨ or **Pinetop-Lakeside** ③, depending on whether you take AZ 77 or U.S. 180. Indulge in a day of local sightseeing in either of these twin towns, then spend the following day working your way across east–west AZ 260 through the Apache Sitgreaves National Forest and parts of the White Mountain Apache Reservation, making a stop in tiny 🏨 **Greer** ⑤. On the last day, retrace your route back to Phoenix via U.S. 60 or, if departing from Springerville-Eagar, via the Coronado Trail. If you're looking for solitude and remote beauty, skip poking along AZ 260's towns and head straight from the Petrified Forest down U.S. 180 to **Hannagan Meadow** ⑩, returning on the remainder of the Coronado Trail for day five.

IF YOU HAVE 7 OR MORE DAYS

Spend two nights in Holbrook, devoting a full day to the **Painted Desert** and **Petrified Forest National Park** ⑫, and the next half day to touring the **Homolovi Ruins State Park** ⑪ and enjoying the drive south to **Pinetop-Lakeside** ③ or **Springerville-Eagar** ⑨. From either of these points, take advantage of the multitude of recreational opportunities that line east–west AZ 260. Return to Phoenix via the Coronado Trail, stopping for at least one night in Alpine or ☷ **Hannagan Meadow** ⑩; if you don't want to repeat portions of the drive on AZ 260 and you enjoy scenic back roads, pick up a map of Forest Service routes from any ranger station and meander toward Hannagan Meadow and U.S. 191 on Forest Service roads that sprout south and east from AZ 373 and AZ 261.

When to Tour Eastern Arizona

If you're a snow enthusiast, winter is definitely the time to tour the White Mountains; those visiting in the beginning of January who want to witness some real-life mushing should check out the Alpine Annual Sled Dog Races.

During warmer months, take advantage of the wide variety of outdoor activities possible in the area. In the middle of May, the tiny hamlet of Greer comes alive to celebrate Greer Days with a parade, crafts, dances, and a fishing derby. Crowds begin converging on the White Mountains starting in late June, when school is out and Valley of the Sun temperatures start to become uncomfortably warm.

Autumn is a splendid time for a drive down the Coronado Trail, with hairpin turns winding through the yellows and golds of Aspen and Oak. The Pinetop-Lakeside Fall Festival is held the last weekend of September, with a parade and impressive assortment of craft booths. White Mountain Apache Tribal Fair is celebrated Labor Day weekend with a parade and professional rodeo.

THE WHITE MOUNTAINS

With elevations climbing to more than 11,000 ft, the White Mountains of east-central Arizona are a winter wonderland and a summer haven. In the 1870s John Gregory Bourke labeled the region "a strange upheaval, a freak of nature, a mountain canted up on one side; one rides along the edge and looks down two or three thousand feet into . . . a weird scene of grandeur and rugged beauty." It is still grand and rugged, carved by deep river canyons and tall cliffs covered with ponderosa pine. It is also much less remote than it was in Bourke's time, with a full-scale real-estate boom now underway.

Winter travelers through the White Mountains should be aware that weather conditions can change without notice in these higher elevations. Call for weather information before heading out to White Mountains highways (☞ Getting Around by Car *in* Eastern Arizona A to Z, *below*.)

Salt River Canyon

➊ *40 mi past Globe on U.S. 60 north.*

Exposing a time lapse of 500 million years, these multicolored spires, buttes, mesas, and canyon walls have inspired this canyon's nickname as the "mini–Grand Canyon." Approaching the Salt River Canyon from Phoenix, U.S. 60 climbs through rolling hills and the terrain changes to forests of ponderosa pine. After entering the San Carlos Indian Reservation, the highway drops 2,000 ft—from the Natanes Plateau into the canyon's vast gorge—and makes a series of hairpin turns down to cross the Salt River. Stop before crossing the bridge to stretch your legs and wander along the banks of the Salt, enjoying its rock-strewn rapids (on hot Arizona days you can slip your shoes off and dip your feet into the chilly water for a cool respite).

En Route   The road out of the Salt River Canyon climbs along the canyon's northern cliffs, providing views of this truly spectacular chasm, unfairly overlooked in a state full of world-famous gorges. The highway continues some 50 mi northward to the **Mogollon Rim**—a huge geologic ledge that bisects much of Arizona—and its cool upland pine woods.

Show Low

❷ *60 mi north of the Salt River Canyon on U.S. 60.*

Why yes, Show Low *is* an odd name for a town. Local legend has it that two partners, Clark and Cooley, homesteaded the surrounding 100,000 acres in 1870, but found themselves wanting to dissolve the partnership some years later after an argument. The two decided to play cards, after which the winner would buy out the loser. On the last hand of the night, Cooley was a point behind when Clark allegedly offered "show low and you win." Cooley cut the deck and came up with the Deuce of Clubs, thereby winning the game and the land. Part of the partners' then-ranch is now the town of Show Low, and the main drag through town is called Deuce of Clubs.

Show Low has none of the charm of its neighboring White Mountains communities, but it is the main commercial center for the high country. Additionally, the city is a crossing point for east–west traffic along the Mogollon Rim and traffic headed for Holbrook and points north. If you're heading up to the Painted Desert and Petrified Forest from Phoenix, you might want to spend the night here.

Dining and Lodging

$$–$$$ ✕ **Paint Pony Rustic Gourmet.** Rich tapestry booths set the scene for fine dining, which includes filets, pastas, swordfish, and a tableside salad bar. Try "the best hot fudge sundae ever" for dessert. ⊠ *571 W. Deuce of Clubs,* ☎ *520/537–5773. AE, D, MC, V. No dinner Sun.*

$ ✕ **High in the Pines Deli.** A block east of Deuce of Clubs, this quaint deli and coffeehouse has tasty specialty sandwiches—the Garlic Pepper Loin sandwich is out of this world. European-style charcuterie boards include fine selections of pâtés, meats, and cheeses served with a fresh baguette. ⊠ *1201 E. Hall,* ☎ *520/537–1453. No credit cards. Closed Sun. No dinner.*

$ 🏨 **KC Motel.** Victorian decor, including four-poster beds, makes this a not-so-typical establishment. All rooms feature cable TV and refrigerators. ⊠ *60 W. Deuce of Clubs, 85901,* ☎ *520/537–4433. 35 rooms. AE, D, DC, MC, V.*

$ 🏨 **Paint Pony Lodge Best Western.** Guest rooms here feature traditional stucco, wood accents, and large picture windows overlooking Arizona's pine-studded high country. Suites and some rooms include fireplaces. ⊠ *581 W. Deuce of Clubs, 85901,* ☎ *520/537–5773. 48 rooms, 2 suites. AE, D, DC, MC, V.*

Outdoor Activities and Sports

FISHING

Show Low Lake (⊠ 5 mi south of Show Low, 1 mi off AZ 260 on Show Low Lake Rd., ☎ 520/537–4126) has a small bait shop, boat rentals, and a launch on site. **Bill's Lake** (⊠ 7756 White Mountain Lake Rd., ☎ 520/537–8301) is stocked with trout, bass, and catfish, and requires no fishing license; it's a favorite spot for youngsters and nonanglers, who pay by the pound for whatever fish they catch.

GOLF

Show Low Country Club (⊠ Old Linden Rd. and AZ 260, ☎ 520/537–4564) is a par-70 course with a back nine in the pines and a front nine in a more open meadow setting. **Silver Creek Golf Club** (⊠ 2051 Silver Lake Blvd., ☎ 520/537–2744) is an 18-hole championship golf course. **Concho Valley Country Club** (✉ 7 County Rd., off AZ 61; 28 mi northeast of Show Low, ☎ 520/337–4644 or 800/658–8071) is open year-round and has a sparkling spring-fed stream meandering through its par-72 course.

SKIING

In Show Low's Safeway Plaza, **Play It Again Sports** (✉ 161 E. Deuce of Clubs, ☎ 520/537–0451) rents skis, snowboards, bibs, and jackets, and stays open until 7 PM during ski season.

Pinetop-Lakeside

❸ *15 mi southeast of Show Low on AZ 260.*

At 7,200 ft, the community of **Pinetop-Lakeside** is known for its proximity to the world's largest stand of ponderosa pine. Two towns, Pinetop and Lakeside, incorporated in 1984 to form this municipality—although they still retain separate post offices. The modest year-round population is 4,500, but in summer months it can jump as high as 40,000, so the secret about this mountain resort town is now officially out. Once popular only with the retirement- and summer-home-set, the city now lures thousands of "flat-landers" and "desert-rats" up from the Valley of the Sun with its gorgeous scenery, excellent multiuse trails, premier golf courses, and temperatures rarely exceeding 85°F. The main drag is known as both AZ 260 and White Mountain Boulevard.

Dining and Lodging

$$–$$$$ ✕ **Christmas Tree.** Chicken and dumplings "like Grandma's" are the house specialty, but honey duck served with fried apples, lean charbroiled chicken, and broiled lamb chops are also highly recommended. A variety of steaks, chops, lamb, and seafood is also available, as well as a children's menu. Save room for a slice of the Christmas Tree's famous fresh-baked fruit cobbler. ✉ *Woodland Rd. and White Mountain Blvd., Lakeside,* ☎ *520/367–3107. D, MC, V. Closed Mon. and Tues. No lunch.*

$$ ✕ **Pasta House.** Festooned with straw-covered Chianti bottles and lined with casual banquette-seating, this glassed-in sunporch of a converted house offers relaxed, candlelit dining and lovingly prepared Italian cuisine. The bill of fare includes manicotti, lasagna, chicken Sorrentino, and a variety of pastas. Portions here are generous—each entrée includes either salad or minestrone soup and garlic bread—but save room for the tiramisu or cannoli, both made entirely from scratch. ✉ *2188 E. White Mountain Blvd., Pinetop,* ☎ *520/367–2782. AE, D, MC, V. Closed Sun. and Mon. Labor Day–Memorial Day. No lunch.*

$ ✕ **Annie's Gift Shop and Tea Room.** Across the highway from the
★   Lakeside Fire Department, this genteel bistro has specialty sandwiches, quiches, and other delectables that make it the local in-spot for lunch. Don't count on a late one—Annie's closes at 2:30 PM. ✉ *2849 White Mountain Blvd., Lakeside,* ☎ *520/368–5737. AE, D, MC, V. Closed Mon. Labor Day–Memorial Day and Sun. No dinner.*

$ ✕ **Khadija's Bakery.** This breakfast spot—pronounced *Ha-dee-sha's*— offers scrumptious, expertly prepared eggs, bacon, hash browns, and buttermilk pancakes. If you're en route to the slopes or hiking trails, order "Breakfast on the Run"—a gourmet answer to the Egg McMuffin. After 11 AM, enjoy made-daily soups and gourmet sandwiches on fresh-baked breads. Save room for one of Khadija's pastries. ✉ *4945 White Mountain Blvd., Lakeside,* ☎ *520/537–7776. No credit cards. Closed Tues. No dinner.*

$–$$$$ ⚄ **Northwoods Resort.** Each of the cottage-cabins at this mountain re-treat has its own covered porch and barbecue; inside, natural wood paneling, brick fireplaces, and wall-to-wall carpeting add to the homey feel. Full electric kitchens have full-size refrigerators, microwaves, and adjacent dinette sets. Although some of the decor is a far cry from el-egant, proprietors here keep their promise to provide "meticulously maintained" accommodations. The honeymoon cabin features an in-door spa, and the two-story cabins can accommodate 16–18 people. ✉ *Box 397R, AZ 260 at milepost marker 352, Pinetop 85935,* ☎ *520/367–2966 or 800/813–2966,* FAX *520/367–2969. 14 cabins. Refriger-ators, outdoor hot tub, coin laundry. D, MC, V.*

$–$$ ⚄ **Whispering Pines Resort.** These well-maintained cabin-style ac-commodations boast cable TVs, fireplaces, grills, and double hide-a-beds. One- and two-bedroom units—some with efficiency kitchens or second bathrooms—have either handsome knotty-pine or more mod-ern wood-paneling interiors. The four log-construction cabins, three of them studio units, have that rustic hideaway vibe. Couples may want to request one of the Alpine suites with whirlpool tubs. ✉ *Box 307, AZ 260, just beyond milepost marker 352, Pinetop 85935,* ☎ *520/367–4386 or 800/840–3867,* FAX *520/367–3702. 31 cabins. Refriger-ators, indoor hot tub, coin laundry. AE, D, MC, V.*

$ ⚄ **Lakeview Lodge.** Set among the pines, the oldest log guest lodge in Arizona boasts stone fireplaces, rustic antiques, cobblestone walk-ways, and a private fishing lake. The main gathering room features high-backed leather chairs, cushy old-fashioned sofas, and a two-story cathedral ceiling. A lovely chandelier, Indian blankets . . . there's even a stuffed mountain lion above the fireplace. ✉ *Route 3, Box 2251, on AZ 260 8 mi east of Show Low, Pinetop 85901,* ☎ *520/368–5253. 9 rooms. Fishing. MC, V.*

Nightlife and the Arts

FILM

Lakeside Cinema (✉ AZ 260 and Billy Creek Rd., in Safeway Plaza, Pinetop, ☎ 520/367–7469) and **Winchester Theatre** (✉ 1850 S. White Mountain Rd., Lakeside, ☎ 520/367–7469) show first-run movies.

LOUNGES

Charlie Clark's (✉ 1701 E. White Mountain Blvd., Pinetop, ☎ 520/367–4973) lounge has pool tables.

Outdoor Activities and Sports

BIKING

The trailhead for **Country Club Trail** is at the junction of Forest Service Roads 182 and 185; these 3½ mi of moderate-difficulty mountain bik-ing can be spiced up by following the spur-trail to the top of Pat Mullen Mountain and back. The 8-mi **Panorama Trail** affords aston-ishing views from the top of extinct double volcanoes known as the Twin Knolls and passes though a portion of designated wildlife habi-tat area.

Pick up individual trail brochures or a $2 booklet on the **White Moun-tains Trailsystem** from the Lakeside Ranger Station.

FISHING

East of Pinetop-Lakeside and 9 mi south of AZ 260 on AZ 473, 260-acre **Hawley Lake** sits on 8,200-ft Apache territory and yields mostly rainbow trout; rental boats are available in the marina. **Bob's Bang Room & Pawn Shop** (✉ Rte. 3, Box 2581, Lakeside, ☎ 520/368–5040) stocks supplies and deals in pawned fishing equipment.

GOLF

White Mountain Country Club (⊠ AZ 260 and Country Club Dr., ☎ 520/367–4357), the most challenging of Pinetop-Lakeside's courses, is a par-72 private course with steep fairways through ponderosa forests and several doglegs. **Pinetop Country Club** (⊠ 2 mi east of AZ 260 on Buck Springs Rd., ☎ 520/369–4375) boasts several uphill holes, including a wicked number nine played through a dense grove of ponderosa pine. **Pinetop Lakes Golf & Country Club** (⊠ ¼ mi east of AZ 260 on Buck Springs Rd., ☎ 520/369–4184) has fewer trees, but it offers several water hazards by way of compensation. If you want to spend some time on the driving range, visit the **Triple Tee Golf Center** (⊠ 504 N. Woodland Rd., ☎ 520/368–6625).

HIKING

Named one of the country's "Top Ten Trail Towns" by the American Hiking Society, Pinetop-Lakeside is the primary trailhead for the **White Mountains Trailsystem,** roughly 200 mi of interconnecting multiuse loop trails spanning the White Mountains. Pick up a trail booklet at the Lakeside Ranger Station for $2.

☾ Half a mile off AZ 260 on Woodland Rd., **Big Springs Environmental Study Area** is a ½-mi loop trail that wanders by riparian meadows, two streams, and a spring-fed pond; a series of educational signs are devoted to the surrounding flora and fauna.

☾ The well-traveled and very easy **Mogollon Rim Interpretive Trail** follows a small part of the 19th-century **Crook Trail** along the Mogollon Rim; the ¼-mi path, with a trailhead just west of the Pinetop-Lakeside city limits, is well marked with placards describing local wildlife and geography.

HORSEBACK RIDING

Thunderhorse Ranch (⊠ Box 2065, Lakeside 85929, ☎ 520/368–5593) offers horse boarding facilities and a variety of equestrian events.

SKIING AND SNOWBOARDING

All American Rentime (⊠ 4161 White Mountain Blvd., Lakeside, ☎ 520/368–6834) rents downhill ski packages, snowboard packages, and inner-tubes. **Boarderline** (⊠ 1479 White Mountain Blvd., Lakeside, ☎ 520/368–4567) rents snowboards, boots, and apparel daily. The **Skier's Edge** (⊠ 560 W. White Mountain Blvd., Pinetop, ☎ 520/367–6200 or 800/231–3831) has cross-country and downhill ski packages, and rents snowboards with boots for $27 a day.

Shopping

Orchard Antiques (⊠ 1664 W. White Mountain Blvd., Lakeside, ☎ 520/368–6563) is a reliable purveyor of high-quality furniture, glass, and sterling, and deals in some quilts and vintage clothing. **Pinecrest Lane Antiques** (⊠ 50 E. Pinecrest La., Pinetop, ☎ 520/367–0943) has "a house and barn full" of furniture, including iron and brass beds. The log cabin **Harvest Moon Antiques** (⊠ 392 W. White Mountain Blvd., Pinetop, ☎ 520/367–6973) specializes in Old West relics, ranging from buckskins and Apache wares to old guns and U.S. Cavalry items; look for the teepees set up outside.

Hon-Dah

8 mi south of Pinetop-Lakeside on AZ 73.

The name of this small town comes from the Apache phrase "welcome to my house." In this case, the house is White Mountain Apache–owned and –operated **Hon-Dah Casino** (⊠ AZ 73 at AZ 260, ☎ 520/369–0299 or 800/929–8744) with a small poker room, video poker, and blackjack, and hundreds of slot machines, even for nickel and penny wielders. The **Timbers Lounge & Showroom** has live entertainment five nights a week, ranging from musicians—mostly country bands—to magicians and stand-up comics. Besides gambling and entertainment options, the **Indian Pine Restaurant** serves merely passable fare; however, the daily chicken-fried steak breakfast for $5.75 does have some passionate devotees.

Lodging

$ ▦ **Hon-Dah Resort.** This hotel's lobby welcomes guests with a surreal staircase tableau of taxidermed high-country creatures high atop a mountain of boulders. Relax by the oversize fireplace in one of the various sofas and cushioned armchairs. A roofed, open space contains the hotel's all-season heated swimming pool and outdoor hot tub. Rooms all have 25-inch color TVs, refrigerators, and wet bars. The two "Murphy parlour" rooms boast an extra small sitting area with a fold-down wall bed. Because the hotel is connected to the casino, you might pop out to fill the ice bucket but wind up at the blackjack table instead. ⊠ *Box 3250 or AZ 73 at AZ 260, Pinetop 85935,* ☎ *520/369–0299 or 800/929–8744,* ℻ *520/369–7405. 128 rooms, 2 suites. 2 restaurants, 2 lounges, refrigerators, in-room data ports, swimming pool, outdoor hot tub, casino, nightclub. AE, D, MC, V.*

En Route   Named after the McNary Lumber Company, **McNary** was once a thriving company town, supporting more than 2,000 residents. The sawmill was destroyed by fire in 1979, mill owners moved their operation eastward to Eagar, and now McNary is little more than a ramshackle community among the pines of the White Mountain Apache Reservation. During summer months, however, slow down if you see a tent and a sign advertising Indian fry bread. It's worth a stop to try this doughy fried dish with honey or other fillings for a taste of Native American cuisine.

Sunrise Park Resort

❹   *17 mi southeast of McNary; 7 mi south of AZ 260 on AZ 273.*

In winter and early spring, ski-lovers and snow-lovers alike will want to visit this ski area. There's plenty more than downhill and cross-country skiing here, including snowboarding, snowmobiling, and snowshoeing. The resort has 10 lifts and 65 trails on three mountains rising to 11,000 ft. Eighty percent of the downhill runs are for beginning or intermediate skiers and many less intense trails begin at the top so skiers of varying skill levels can enjoy riding the chairlifts together. One-day lift tickets are about $34.

Sunrise's **Snowboard Park** features jumps of all difficulty levels, and its own sound system. Restricted to snowboarders only, the area—between the Pump House and Fairway runs—can support enthusiasts' quests to "get a great ollie, hit the kicker and go big," while simultaneously lessening tension on the hill between boarders and skiers.

Cross-country skiers enjoy 13½ mi of interconnecting trails and snowmobilers have their own 25 mi of separate, designated trails. ⊠ *Box 217, McNary 85930,* ☎ *520/735–7669; 800/554–6835 for snow reports at Sunrise Park. AE, D, MC, V.*

Sunrise Equipment Rentals (⊠ 7 mi south of AZ 260 on AZ 273, ☎ 520/735–7669) has a variety of equipment, from skis, snowboards, and snowshoes in the winter to mountain bikes in the summer. **Action Ski Rental** (⊠ Base of Apache and Cyclone Peaks, ☎ 520/735–7669) offers high-quality downhill and snowboard equipment and offers free hot waxes any time of the day.

Lodging

$–$$ **⊡ Sunrise Resort Hotel.** Catering to visitors who want to be as close as possible to the slopes, this hotel runs a shuttle to the ski resort every half hour, has ski racks in every room, and offers lodging and lift ticket packages. The V.I.P. Suite, with its wet bar, refrigerator, microwave, and hot tub, comes with two lift tickets that grant the holders line-cutting privileges on the slopes. Rooms are comfortable and standard size, but the decor could use a face-lift: The suites of bedroom furniture are passé disco-era relics—the black-lacquer headboard is accented in brass and mirrored panels. ⊠ *Box 217, McNary 85930,* ☎ *520/735–7669 or 800/554–6835,* 𝔽𝔸𝕏 *520/735–7315. 94 rooms, 1 suite. Restaurant, lounge, indoor pool, outdoor hot tub, volleyball, ski shop. AE, D, DC, MC, V.*

Greer

★ ❺   *35 mi southeast of Pinetop-Lakeside and 15 mi southwest of Eagar on AZ 260; 8 mi east of the AZ 273 turnoff, take AZ 373 south.*

The charming community of Greer sits just south of AZ 260 among pine, spruce, and aspens on the banks of the Little Colorado River. This portion of gently sloping National Forest land is covered with meadows and reservoirs and dominated by 11,590-ft Baldy Peak. Much of the surrounding area remains under the control of the Apache tribe, so visitors must take care to respect the land and Apache law. AZ 374 is also Greer's "Main Street"; it winds through the village and crosses the Little Colorado River; eventually coming to a dead end, it's affectionately called "The Road to Nowhere."

Dining and Lodging

$–$$$ **✕ Molly Butler Lodge.** Tasty fare is reliably turned out from the picture-window–lined dining room of Arizona's oldest guest lodge. The menu divides itself between entrées "upstream" (sautéed scallops, halibut, trout almondine) and "downstream" (prime rib au jus, ribs, "hot dang" chili), but it's the hand-cut, aged steaks that draw locals. Sweeping views of Greer's pristine wilderness are enjoyed amidst the lodge's cozy, rustic decor, with kerosene lamps on the tables and mounted hunting trophies on the walls. ⊠ *109 Main St.,* ☎ *520/735–7226. Reservations required weekends and summer. MC, V.*

$ **✕ Greer Mountain Resort Restaurant.** Formerly known as Jaynes restaurant, this plant-hung diner-café is open daily from 7 AM to 3 PM year-round. Grab a seat by the fireplace and sample the homemade ranch beans, a signature grilled-cheese sandwich with green chilies and tomato, and a slice of fresh-baked cobbler. ⊠ *AZ 373, 1½ mi south of AZ 260,* ☎ *520/735–7560. MC, V. No dinner.*

$$ **⊡ The Peaks at Greer.** For those who prefer greater privacy or amenities than Greer's cabin or B&B options, this is the only hotel-style accommodation in town. In addition to a bar and restaurant off the lobby, there's a basement game room. Winter package-rates include lift tickets at nearby Sunrise Ski Resort. During summer months, the deck and patio are lovely spots to enjoy a bite from the restaurant or to relax with a good book. Cabin accommodations have valley views and full-size kitchens. ⊠ *Box 132, Greer 85927,* ☎ *520/735–7777,* 𝔽𝔸𝕏 *520/735–7204. 15 rooms, 3 suites. Restaurant, bar, no-smoking rooms. Continental breakfast. AE, D, MC, V.*

$$ **⊡ Red Setter Inn.** From the vaulted ceilings in the breakfast area, to
★   the antique toy collection, to the player piano in the Gathering Room, this 7,000-square-ft, hand-hewn log inn designed by owners Jim Sankey

and Ken Conant is rich in detail. Many of the rooms have fireplaces, French doors opening onto private decks or balconies, whirlpool bath-tubs, and hand-painted ceramic tiles. From the "Angler's Room," one can fish the river literally steps from a private deck. Guests who set out to hike or fish during the day are sent off with gourmet sack lunches. If it's less-strenuous repose you're seeking, grab an Adiron-dack chair on the redwood deck that overlooks the Little Colorado River, or venture into the game room: There's a video library with more than 300 titles, including every *I Love Lucy* ever made. ⊠ *8 Main St., Box 133, 85927,* ☎ *520/735–7441,* ℻ *520/735–7425. 9 rooms. No-smok-ing rooms, fishing, cross-country skiing, recreation room. Full break-fast. AE, MC, V.*

$–$$$ 🛏 **White Mountain Lodge.** Built in 1892, the Lodge is the oldest build-ing in Greer. Authenticity's unmistakable charm radiates from this B&B, where innkeepers Charlie and Mary Bast are both gracious hosts and well-versed local historians (ask about the fabled night drunken rogues and rocket scientists decided to raise the roof). Rooms in the lodge are appointed in different themes, most of which settle into the cozy, coun-try-decor arena. Separate full-housekeeping cabin units have either wood-burning or gas-log fireplaces, and the Meadow View cabin boasts jetted bathtubs. An always-accessible sideboard is stocked with Mary's homemade cookies and spiced-cider mix, as well as teas and cocoa. ⊠ *Box 143 or 140 Main St., 85927,* ☎ *520/735–7568 or 888/493–7568,* ℻ *520/735–7498. 11 rooms. No-smoking rooms, fishing, cross-coun-try skiing. Full breakfast. D, DC, MC, V.*

$ 🛏 **Greer Mountain Resort.** Budget travelers and families will appreci-ate these cabin accommodations. Each unit is different, but most can sleep up to six people and contain either a fireplace or wood-burning stove. You'll probably want to enjoy breakfast or lunch at the resort's roadside restaurant, but the fully equipped kitchens will appeal to those wanting to whip up their own feast. Cozy, one-bedroom, knotty-pine studio-units have no fireplaces, but they're reasonably priced and a good choice for couples. ⊠ *AZ 373, 1½ mi south of AZ 260 or Box 145, Greer 85927,* ☎ ℻ *520/735–7560. 8 cabins. MC, V.*

⚠ **Rolfe C. Hoyer Campgrounds.** These choice 100 campground units have showers, flush toilets, and the other nearby amenities offered by the town of Greer. Currently the campsite fee is $12, but a surcharge of $8.65 per booking (not per night) is added by the company that han-dles the reservations. Firewood is available for $6 per bag at the en-trance station. The abundant local wildlife is one of this site's draws, but remember to secure campsites from foraging four-legged friends. ⊠ *AZ 373, directly south of AZ 260,* ☎ *520/333–4372; 877/2444–6777 for reservations. Closed Oct.–Apr.*

Nightlife

Tiny Greer's nightlife can be found in the bar and lounge of the **Mol-lie Butler Lodge** (⊠ 109 Main St., ☎ 520/735–7226), where tourists and locals congregate to play a game of pool or sink into cozy seats surrounding a sunken fireplace.

Outdoor Activities and Sports

The **Circle B Market** (⊠ 38940 AZ 373, ☎ 520/735–7540) rents cross-country skis, toboggans, and sleds in winter, and fishing boats and inner tubes the rest of the year; fishing licenses and reservation permits are also for sale.

FISHING

The three **Greer Lakes** are actually the **Bunch, River,** and **Tunnel** reser-voirs. Bait and fly-fishing options are scenic and plentiful; boat launches are available for those partial to trolling. Winding through Greer, the **Little Colorado River's West Fork** is also well stocked with trout.

HIKING

The difficult but still accessible **Mt. Baldy Trail** begins at **Sheeps Crossing**, southwest of Greer on AZ 273. In just under 8 mi (one-way), the trail climbs the northern flank of 11,590-ft Mt. Baldy, the second-highest peak in Arizona where spectacular views of the Salt River Canyon and Mogollon Rim can be seen. Note that the very summit of Baldy is on the White Mountain Apache Reservation; considered sacred land, this final ¼ mi to the summit is off-limits to non-Apaches. The boundary is clearly marked; please respect it, regardless of how much you might wish to continue on to the peak.

HORSEBACK RIDING

Lee Valley Outfitters (☏ 520/735–7454) offers a variety of horseback opportunities: from one- or two-hour horseback rides, to half- or full-day trips. Cookouts and overnight pack trips can also be arranged.

SKIING

Cross-country skiers find Greer an ideally situated hub for some of the mountain's best trails. About 2½ mi west of AZ 373 on AZ 260, a trailhead marks the starting point for the **Pole Knoll Trail System,** more than 30 mi of well-marked, groomed cross-country trails interlacing through the Apache Sitgreaves National Forest and color-coded by experience level. Trail maps are available from both the **Springerville Ranger District office** (✉ 165 S. Mountain Ave. or Box 760, Springerville 85938, ☏ 520/333–4372) and the Alpine Ranger District office (☞ Visitor Information *in* Eastern Arizona A to Z, *below*).

Shopping

At the airy, attractive **Greer Wood Products & Art Gallery** (✉ Main St., ☏ 520/735–7717) you'll likely find the owner crafting a handsome objet d'art—perhaps some juniper-wood furniture—in the back workshop nook. Featuring high-quality crafts and artwork by White Mountains locals, this shop has everything from antler-leg coffee tables and handcrafted wooden jewelry boxes to ceramics and watercolor paintings and definitely merits a stop.

OFF THE
BEATEN PATH

LITTLE HOUSE MUSEUM – This museum's collection of local pioneer and ranching memorabilia is interesting, but it's the mesmerizing tones from a rare collection of automatic musical instruments that you'll come away remembering—that, and the museum's colorful curator, Wink Crigler, with her lore of this region's lively past. The museum is open for 90-minute tours from Memorial Day to Labor Day; arrange winter tours by advance reservation. ✉ 5 mi east of Greer Junction (AZ 260 and AZ 373), turn south on South Fork Rd. and go 3 mi, ☏ 520/333–2286. ☞ $4. ☉ Tours Thurs.–Sat. at 11 and 1:30, Sun. and Mon. at 1:30.

Lyman Lake State Park

❻   *18 mi north of Springerville on U.S. 180/191; 55 mi southeast of Petrified Forest National Park on U.S. 180.*

Created in 1915 by damming the Little Colorado River for irrigation purposes, the 3-mi-long **Lyman Lake** reservoir is popular for boating, waterskiing, wind surfing, and sailing. Designated swimming beaches accommodate those who prefer to stick closer to shore.

Anglers will appreciate a buoyed-off "no-wake" area at the lake's west end, where fishing efforts won't be disturbed by passing speedboats and water-skiers. Contributions to the creel here will include large-mouth bass and crappie, as well as the "good size" (6–8 lbs.) channel catfish that can be pulled up from May to August. Locals recommend early spring as prime season for walleye—the tastiest catch of all; Lyman Lake also has lots of crawdads, a.k.a. "poor man's shrimp."

Between Memorial Day and Labor Day, try to catch one of the ranger-led pontoon-boat rides across the lake to the **Petroglyph Trail**—where some of the state's most wondrous and accessible Native American rock art lies chiseled in basalt.

Other attractions in the 1,200-acre park include a volleyball court, horse-shoe pits, rockhounding opportunities, and the rare chance to observe the park's resident small herd of buffalo. Camping facilities are also available. ⊠ *Box 1428, St. Johns 85936,* ☎ *520/337–4441.*

Raven Site Ruins

❼ *12 mi north of Springerville on U.S. 180/191; 60 mi southeast of Petrified Forest State Park on U.S. 180.*

Overlooking the banks of the Little Colorado River, these prehistoric pueblos contain several kivas, more than 800 rooms, and exhibit cultural features of both the Mogollon peoples to the south and the Anasazi people to the north. Although not as steeped in mysticism as neighboring Casa Malpais, these ruins provide opportunities for hands-on excavation, laboratory analysis, and plenty of "in the grid" field time. At Raven Site Ruins' **White Mountain Archaeological Center,** James and Carol Cunkle lead amateurs, students, and professionals in unearthing the evidence of the pottery-making Native American cultures that flourished here from about AD 1000 to 1450. Self-guided site tours are available all day; make reservations for the guided petroglyph hikes held at various times throughout the day. The tiny combination visitor center, museum, and gift shop is a marvel. ⊠ *HC 30, St. Johns 85936,* ☎ *520/333–5857 or 888/333–5859.* ☒ *$4, including tour, $18 for petroglyph hike.,*⊙ *May–mid-Oct., daily 10–5.*

Casa Malpais Archaeological Park

❽ *2 mi north of downtown Springerville on U.S. 60.*

This 14.5-acre pueblo complex is piquing the interest of a growing number of world-class anthropologists and astronomers. "House of the Badlands" (a sobriquet for the rough-textured ground's effect on bare feet) has a series of narrow terraces lining eroded edges of basalt (hardened lava flow) cliff, as well as an extensive system of subterranean rooms nestled within the earth's fissures underneath. Strategically designed gateways in the walls of the complex allow for streams of sunlight to precisely illuminate significant petroglyphs prior to the setting equinox or solstice sun. Perhaps most importantly, Casa Malpais is home to the 55-ft-diameter Great Kiva—the largest Native American ceremonial chamber known to exist in North America. Strong evidence suggests that these sacred ruins were once inhabited solely by a class of scholars and holy men among the ancient Mogollon peoples. Ask about the ruins' conspicuous lack of excavated cooking apparatus—these lucky guys probably fasted or ordered their room service from up the block (☞ Raven Site Ruins, *above*). ⊠ *Box 807, Springerville 85938,* ☎ *520/333–5375.* ☒ *$4 guided tour.* ⊙ *Guided tours depart daily from the Casa Malpais Museum (⊠ 318 Main St., Springerville, ☎ 520/333–5375) at 9 AM, 11 AM, and 2:30 PM.*

En Route   The junction of U.S. 180/191 and U.S. 60, just north of Springerville, is the perfect jumping-off spot for a driving tour of the **Springerville Volcanic Field.** If you travel 6 mi north on U.S. 180/191, it leads to westward views of the **Twin Knolls**—double volcanoes that erupted twice here about 700,000 years ago. Traveling west on U.S. 60, Green's Peak Rd. and various south-winding Forest Service roads make for a leisurely, hour-long drive past **St. Peter's Dome** and a stop for impressive views from **Green's Peak**, the topographic high point of the Springerville Field. A detailed driving tour brochure is available gratis from the **Round Valley Chamber of Commerce** (⊠ 318 Main St., Springerville 85938, ☏ 520/333–2123).

Springerville-Eagar

🟘   *45 mi east of Pinetop-Lakeside on AZ 260; 67 mi southeast of Petrified Forest National Park on U.S. 180.*

Christened "Valle Redondo," or *Round Valley*, by early Basque settlers of the late 1800s, sister cities Springerville and Eagar are tucked into a circular, high mountain basin. Nestled on the back side of massive 11,000-ft Escudilla Mountain, this self-proclaimed "Gateway to the White Mountains" sits in a different climate belt from nearby Greer and Sunrise Resort; insulated by its unique geography, temperatures and snowfall in Springerville-Eagar are markedly less severe than in neighboring mountain towns. Geographically, the Round Valley also served as a unique Old West haven for the lawless—a great place to conceal stolen cattle and hide out for a while; Butch Cassidy, the Clantons, and the Smith gang all spent time here. So did the late John Wayne, whose former 26-Bar Ranch lies just west of Eagar off AZ 260.

The Round Valley is the favorite of skiers in the know, who appreciate the location as they commute to the lifts at Sunrise with the sun always at their back—important when you consider the glare off those blanketed snowscapes between the resort and Pinetop-Lakeside—and the dramatically lighter traffic on this less-icy stretch of AZ 260.

The **Renée Cushman Art Collection Museum** is only open to the public by special appointment, but a visit here is worth the extra effort. Renée Cushman's extensive collection of objets d'art—some acquired on her travels, some collected with the accumulated resources of three wealthy husbands, some willed to her by her artistic father—is administered by the Church of Latter-Day Saints. Her treasure of goods includes a Rembrandt engraving, Tiepolo pen-and-inks, and an impressive collection of European antiques, some dating back to the 15th century. Call the **Round Valley Chamber of Commerce** (☏ 520/333–2123) to arrange your visit.

Another Round Valley claim-to-fame is the 120,000-sq.-ft **Ensphere,** the only domed high school football stadium in the country. The dome is a gift of Tucson Power & Electric, which moved into these parts and vowed to contribute something to the community. The then-absurd proposal was placed on the ballot, alongside a host of other less-extravagant options, and passed. The shocked TPE, after demanding a recount, made good on their promise.

Dining and Lodging

$ ✕ **Booga Reds.** The delicious home-style cooking here is worth a stop. Fish-and-chips and roast-beef dinners with homemade mashed potatoes and gravy top the menu; should your palette demand something spicier, however, try one of the many Mexican dishes. Save room for an unforgettable piece of the daily fruit or cream pie. Booga Reds opens at 5:30 for an early breakfast, but closes at 9 PM—so make your dinner an early one, too. ⊠ *521 E. Main St., Springerville,* ☎ *520/333–2640. MC, V.*

$ 🗔 **Best Western Sunrise Inn.** This two-story inn is surrounded by grassy areas and red barn fencing. Indoors, there are coffeemakers in each of the rooms. King- or queen-size beds are available, and minisuites feature microwaves and refrigerators. ⊠ *128 N. Main St., Eagar 85925,* ☎ *520/333–2540. 40 rooms. AE, D, DC, MC, V.*

$ 🗔 **Paisley Corner Bed & Breakfast.** Cheryl and Cletus Tisdell have im-
★ peccably restored every inch of this 1910 Colonial-revival–style home and lavished their collection of period antiques throughout. From embossed tin ceilings and stained-glass windows in the parlor to an authentic "soda shop" replete with 1946 Wurlitzer jukebox, not a single detail has been overlooked. Up the handsome oak staircase, four bedrooms (all with private baths) have transom windows, antique beds and armoires, old-fashioned "rib-cage" showers or claw-foot tubs, and pull-chain commodes. You'll find lush terry-cloth robes in your room, as well as wine, fresh fruit, and homemade munchies. Sumptuous breakfasts are prepared on a 1910 stove—rescued from the Old Bisbee Grand hotel—and served at an elegantly set table. Hikers and skiers who want to get an early start can enjoy breakfast as early as they like. ⊠ *287 N. Main St., Eagar 85925,* ☎ *520/333–4665. 4 rooms. Full breakfast. No credit cards.*

$ 🗔 **Reed's Lodge.** The rooms of this mostly single-story, exterior-hallway motor lodge have Western accents like knotty-pine paneling or Navajo-print bedspreads. Thoughtful touches include a game room with pool table and pinball machine, rental video tapes for a nominal fee, and complimentary bicycles for guests. Proprietress Roxanne Knight's knowledge of the city and surrounding environs is not to be surpassed. ⊠ *514 E. Main St., Springerville 85938,* ☎ *520/333–4323 or 800/814–6451,* 🖷 *520/333–5191. 45 rooms, 5 suites. In-room VCRs, outdoor hot tub, bicycles, recreation room. AE, D, DC, MC, V.*

🔥 **Big Lake.** Four campgrounds scattered along the southeast shore of this lake, 30 mi southwest of Round Valley, are popular White Mountains summer spots. The civilized **Rainbow** site offers paved loops to its 150-plus units, access to deluxe rest rooms, an eight-stall shower building, and a store. The lake's smaller sites, **Grayling, Cutthroat,** and **Brookchar,** are less swank, but are within easy walking distance of Rainbow's amenities and share the picturesque tableau of looming 11,590-ft Mt. Baldy. Sites run $10–$12; the lake has a marina where boats and motors are available for rent. ⊠ *24 mi south of AZ 260 on AZ 273,* ☎ *520/735–7313; 877/444–6777 for reservations. Closed early Sept.–mid-May.*

Nightlife

Out on the edge of town where U.S. Highways 60 and 180 enter Springerville, the bright yellow **Little River Lounge** (⊠ 262 W. Main St., ☎ 520/333–5790) is a cowboy-bar with pool tables, darts, and live music and dancing on the weekends. Behind Booga Red's restaurant, **Tequila Red's** (⊠ 521 E. Main St. Springerville, ☎ 520/333–5036) is a popular watering hole, and the place to catch a sporting event.

Outdoor Activities and Sports

For all your mountain-sport needs, stop in at the **Sweat Shop** (⊠ 74 N. Main St., Eagar, ☎ 520/333–2950), which rents skis, snowboards, and mountain bikes and stays open until 10 PM when Sunrise Resort has night skiing.

FISHING

Northwest of Springerville on U.S. 60, **Becker Lake** is a "specialty lake" for trout fishing; check with Pinetop's **State Department of Game &**

Fish (☎ 520/367–4281) for seasonal bait requirements. **Nelson Reservoir** is well stocked with rainbow, brown, and brook trout; the lake is just off U.S. 191, between Springerville-Eagar and the town of Alpine, just north of the hamlet of Nutrioso. **Troutback** (⊠ Box 344, Springerville, ☎ 520/333–2371) will tailor guided half- or full-day fishing trips to novices and seasoned anglers alike; fly rod and reels can be rented for $10 a day.

Sport Shack (⊠ 329 E. Main St., Springerville, ☎ 520/333–2222) sells fishing tackle, hunting and fishing licenses, and reservation permits. **Western Drug** (⊠ 105 E. Main St., Springerville, ☎ 520/333–4321) stays open 365 days a year and has a well-stocked sporting-goods section.

Shopping

K-5 Western Gallery (⊠ 514 E. Main St., at Reed's Lodge, Springerville, ☎ 520/333–4323) sells wares by White Mountains artists and craftspeople, including those from nearby reservations. The gallery also stocks books on local history.

Coronado Trail

★ *123 mi from Springerville to Clifton.*

Surely one of the world's curviest roads, this steep winding portion of U.S. 191 was referred to as the "Devil's Highway" in its prior incarnation as U.S. Route 666. More significantly, the route parallels the one allegedly followed more than 450 years ago by Spanish explorer Francisco Vásquez de Coronado on his search for the legendary Seven Cities of Cíbola with streets paved of gold and jewels.

This 123-mi stretch of highway is renowned for the transitions of its spectacular scenery over a dramatic 5,000-ft elevation change—from rolling meadows to spruce- and ponderosa pine–covered mountains, down into the Sonoran Desert's piñon pine, grassland savannas, juniper stands, and cacti. A trip down the Coronado Trail crosses through Apache Sitgreaves National Forest, as well as the White Mountain Apache and San Carlos Indian reservations.

Cautious switchback-navigating will result in stretches on which motorists barely exceed 10 mph; allow a good four hours to make the drive, more if you plan to stop and leisurely explore—which you should.

Perched on the edge of the Mogollon Rim, about 30 mi outside Alpine, pause at **Blue Vista** to take in views of the Blue Range Mountains to the east, and the succession of tiered valleys dropping some 4,000 ft back down into the Sonoran Desert. Still above the rim, this is one of your last opportunities to enjoy the blue spruce, ponderosa pine, and high-country mountain meadows.

About 17 mi south of Blue Vista, the Coronado Trail continues twisting and turning, eventually crossing under 8,786-ft **Rose Peak**. Named for the wild roses growing on its mountainside, Rose Peak is also home to a fire lookout tower—staffed during the May-through-July dry-lightning season—from which peaks more than 100 mi away can be seen on a clear day. This is a great picnic-lunch stop.

After Rose Peak, enjoy the remaining scenery some 70 more mi until reaching the less attractive towns of Clifton and Morenci, homes to the massive Phelps-Dodge copper mine. U.S. 191 then swings back west, links up with U.S. 70, and provides a fairly straight shot through Safford and across rather uninteresting desert toward Globe.

Alpine

27 mi south of Springerville-Eagar on U.S. 191.

Known as the "Alps of Arizona," the tiny, scenic village of Alpine promotes its variety of winter recreation opportunities, but warmer-month outdoor enthusiasts will find that Alpine, sitting on the lush plains of the San Francisco River, is centrally located to many excellent hiking, fishing, and mountain-biking excursions.

Dining and Lodging

$ ✕🔟 **Hannagan Meadow Lodge.** No kidding—the owners of this re-
★ mote lodge are living-their-dream lottery jackpot winners. They bought the property in 1996 and transformed it into a paragon of casual mountain elegance. Antique bureaus and floral prints in gilded frames impart a genteel, Victorian vibe upstairs in the main lodge, where every room promises a great night's sleep in ornate brass and enamel beds with down pillows. Log cabins are more rustic, although some have kitchenettes and fireplaces. The lodge's dining room is truly the pièce de résistance, with hewn-log beams and ceilings and a glass wall that overlooks the pristine meadow. A general store sells sundries as well as fishing supplies and rents snowmobiles, cross-country skis, and mountain bikes. ⊠ *HC 61, Box 335, Alpine 85920,* ☎ *520/339–4370 or 800/547–1416. 8 rooms, 8 cabins. Restaurant, bar, hiking, horseback riding, fishing, mountain bikes, cross-country skiing, snowmobiling. AE, D, MC, V.*

$ ✕🔟 **Tal-Wi-Wi Lodge.** Facing a lush meadow and distant collection of cool, artesian-fed pools, this lodge's unparalleled setting draws many repeat visitors. Standard rooms are simple and clean, containing either two doubles or one king-size bed, but three of the lodge's most popular rooms have been upgraded to contain wood-burning fireplace-stoves, indoor hot tubs, or both. A soak in the outdoor hot tub is a superb way to drink in the brilliant night sky and moody ponderosa silhouettes. With satellite TV and a karaoke machine, the lodge saloon draws many locals on weekends and for sporting events. The restaurant is a handsome, casual space with a stone fireplace and a moose head mounted above; its standard May–Sept. season sometimes runs longer, depending on snowfall. When the restaurant is open it serves breakfasts on Sat. and Sun. and dinner Wed.–Sat. ⊠ *4 mi north of Alpine on U.S. 191 or Box 169, 85920,* ☎ *520/339–4319,* FAX *520/339–1962. 20 rooms. Restaurant, bar, outdoor hot tub. AE, MC, V.*

Outdoor Activities and Sports

BIKING

The 8-mi **Luna Lake Trail** (⊠ 5 mi east of U.S. 191 on U.S. 180) is a good two-hour cruise for beginning and intermediate cyclists. The trailhead is on the north side of the lake, just before the campground entrance.

FISHING

From May to October, try **Fite's Fishery** (⊠ Box 156, 85920, ☎ 520/ 339–4421). A divergence of the San Francisco River's headwaters, **Luna Lake** (⊠ 5 mi east of U.S. 191 on U.S. 180) is well stocked with rainbow, cut-throat, and brook trout.

GOLF

Alpine Country Club (⊠ 2½ mi east of the U.S. 180 and U.S. 191 junction, Box 526, 85920, ☎ 520/339–4944), at 8,500 ft above sea level, is the highest golf course in the Southwest.

HIKING

The **Escudilla National Recreation Trail** is more picturesque than arduous; the 3-mi trail wends through the Escudilla Wilderness to the summit of towering 10,912-ft **Escudilla Mountain,** Arizona's third-tallest peak. From Alpine, take U.S. 191 north and follow the signs to Hulsey Lake (about 5 mi).

SKIING

Williams Valley Winter Sports Area (✉ 4½ mi west of Alpine on Forest Service Rd. 249, ☎ 520/339–4384) has 12½ mi of cross-country trails of varying difficulty maintained by the Alpine Ranger district. **Toboggan Hill** is a favorite place for families with sleds, toboggans, and tubes.

SNOWMOBILING

Trails begin just off Forest Service Road 249, on the west side of Williams Valley Winter Sports Area, and the network of snow-covered Forest Service roads extends for miles; snowmobilers are asked to respect marked boundaries to the adjacent Bear Wallow Wilderness area, where all motorized equipment is prohibited. Pick up an Apache Sitgreaves National Forest map and Winter Sports brochure from the **Alpine Ranger District** (☞ Visitor Information *in* Eastern Arizona A to Z, *below*) and call for conditions prior to heading out, as weak links in longer routes sometimes "burn out."

Hannagan Meadow

★ ⑩ *50 mi south of Springerville-Eagar on U.S. 191; 23 mi south of Alpine on U.S. 191.*

Surely one of the state's most remote locations, Hannagan Meadow is a pastorally mesmerizing home to splendid camping areas and the site of a famous face-off between the region's sheep and cattle ranchers. Lush and isolated at a 9,500-ft-plus elevation, the meadow is home to elk, deer, and range cattle, as well as blue grouse, wild turkey, and the occasional eagle. Hannagan Meadow is a designated recovery area for the endangered Mexican gray wolf. Adjacent to the meadow, the Blue Range Primitive Area gives access to miles of untouched wilderness and some beautiful rugged terrain.

OFF THE BEATEN PATH

BLUE RANGE PRIMITIVE AREA – Directly east of Hannagan Meadow, this area remains the last designated primitive area in the United States. "The Blue"—as it's lovingly referred to by locals—is home to 170,000 unspoiled acres of diverse terrain surrounding the Blue River. The Blue is all about the deep quiet and solitude of the area's forests and canyon; no motorized or mechanized equipment is allowed—including mountain bikes—and passage is restricted to foot or horseback. Many trails interlace The Blue: prehistoric paths of the ancient native peoples, cowboy trails to move livestock between pastures and water sources, access routes to lookout towers, and fire trails. Most trails on The Blue run between the rim of the canyon and its floor, with dozens of connectors linking main routes and making a variety of daylong loop hikes possible: Avid backpackers and campers will definitely want to spend a few days. The east side of The Blue butts up against New Mexico's Blue Wilderness and offers the least-populated terrain; contact the Alpine Ranger District (☞ Visitor Information *in* Eastern Arizona A to Z, *below*) for trail maps and information.

Camping

⚠ **Hannagan Meadow.** This intimate collection of eight free Forest Service campsites sits under a canopy of trees surrounded by tall, ma-ture forest. There's fresh water but no bathing facilities, though nearby Hannagan Meadow Lodge provides hot showers for $5. ⊠ *U.S. 191 and FS Rd. 576,* ☎ *520/339–4384.* ☉ *Year-round.*

⚠ **KP Cienega.** These five single-unit campsites in a lush meadow are a prime site for viewing the local wildlife. There are no developed facilities, but the campsites are free. ⊠ *U.S. 191 and FS Rd. 25,* ☎ *520/ 339–4384.* ☉ *May–Oct.*

Outdoor Activities and Sports

FISHING

Bear Wallow Wilderness Area (⊠ West of U.S. 191 and bordered by Forest Service Rds. 25 and 54) has a network of cool, flowing streams that are sure bets for native Apache trout. Down in The Blue (☞ Off the Beaten Path, *above*), anglers will want to cast into **KP Creek** and **Grant Creek,** both of which rush through spectacular scenery.

HIKING

Twenty-one miles of maintained trail wind through the 11,000 acres of the **Bear Wallow Wilderness Area** (☎ 520/339–4384). The **Rose Spring Trail** is a pleasant 5.4-mi hike with a moderate gradient and magnificent views from the Mogollon Rim's edge; the trailhead is at the end of Forest Service Road 54. **Reno Trail** and **Gobbler Trail** both drop into the main canyon from well-marked trailheads off Forest Service Road 25 and are 2 and 2½ mi long, respectively. This designated wilderness (and some of its trails) borders the boundaries of the San Carlos Apache Reservation, where an advance permit is required for entry (☞ Visitor Information *in* Eastern Arizona A to Z, *below*).

HORSEBACK RIDING

Don Donnelly Stables (☎ 602/982–7822) offers horseback rides departing from Hannagan Meadow during summer months; hayrides, overnight trail rides, and pack trips can also be arranged.

SKIING

The 8½ mi of groomed cross-country trails of the **Hannagan Meadow Winter Recreation Area** (☎ 520/339–4384) are narrower than the trails of neighboring Williams Valley. The 4½-mi **Clell Lee Loop** is an easy route, partially following U.S. 191; the advanced-level, ungroomed **KP Rim Loop** traverses upper elevations of the Blue Primitive Range and provides some of the most varied (and tranquil) remote skiing in the state.

SNOWMOBILING

The area just northeast of U.S. 191 is a snowmobile playground. Trailheads are located at U.S. 191 and Forest Service Road 576.

PETRIFIED FOREST NATIONAL PARK AND THE PAINTED DESERT

Homolovi Ruins State Park

⓫ *53 mi east of Flagstaff; 33 mi west of Holbrook on I–40.*

Four miles northeast of Winslow off AZ 87 are four major ancestral Hopi pueblos. There are 40 ceremonial kivas thought to date from AD 900, and one pueblo contains more than 1,000 rooms. The Hopi believe their immediate ancestors inhabited this place—it's thought to be one of the last stops of the Anasazi migration—and still hold the site to be sacred. The **Homolovi Visitor's Center** (⊠ HCR 63, Box 5, Winslow 86047, ☎ 520/289–4106) is in the park, about 1½ mi from AZ 87.

VISITING ARIZONA'S NATURAL AND SCENIC WONDERS

HE DESERTS ARE SURPRISINGLY rich in flora and fauna, lakes sparkle behind soaring pine trees, sandstone mesas thrust into sparkling blue skies, and, of course, canyon after awesome canyon cuts deep into the earth's crust. In Arizona, you can explore all these natural marvels and then some.

Flagstaff to Prescott (2 days). Rugged buttes, towering canyon walls, and wind-honed sandstone comprise Oak Creek Canyon's spectacular landscape. Sedona, now favored by travelers and retirees, is surrounded by awe-inspiring crimson buttes. Trails crisscross cool, breezy Prescott National Forest nearby. (☞ The Verde Valley, Jerome, Prescott, and Sedona *in* Chapter 3.)

Central Arizona (1 day). The desert in bloom is a gorgeous explosion of wildflowers and cactus blossoms. To learn more about desert plants, visit Desert Botanical Gardens in Phoenix and Boyce Thompson Arboretum near Superior. (☞ Exploring Phoenix *and* Side Trips Around the Apache Trail *in* Chapter 4.)

Tucson and Environs (1 day). Tremendous mountaintop vistas, trails through cactus forests, and lowland arroyos distinguish Saguaro National Park. For a different kind of view, take the winding road up Kitt Peak to the national observatory, where clear, dry air assures a great view of the heavens. (☞ Exploring Tucson *in* Chapter 6.)

East of Tucson (1 day). High, arid chaparral gives way to a mysterious collection of weathered rocks at Texas Canyon. Chiricahua National Monument contains other bizarre rock formations. (☞ Southeast Arizona *in* Chapter 7.)

The White Mountains (1 day). Head for the White Mountains for fishing, hiking, camping, and wildlife-watching. Then travel the steep, winding Coronado Trail to explore more of the magnificent mountains and valleys. (☞ The White Mountains *below*.)

Painted Desert and Petrified Forest (1 day). You'll marvel at the multicolored palette in the rocks and hills of the Painted Desert, home of prehistoric humans and far more ancient dinosaurs. Similar rainbow hues shimmer from the polished remains of hundreds of fossilized trees in the Petrified Forest. (☞ Petrified Forest National Park and the Painted Desert *below*.)

Monument Valley (1 day). The grandeur of Monument Valley lies in its red sand dunes, giant weathered rock formations, and amazing vistas. Long a favorite location for Hollywood westerns, Monument Valley deserves a firsthand look. (☞ Navajo Nation North *in* Chapter 2.)

Lake Powell (1 day). There's no better way to enjoy the desert than being near—or on—the water. Rimmed by red cliffs and inlets formed by canyons, Lake Powell is otherworldly from both the water and the shore. (☞ Glen Canyon Dam and Lake Powell *in* Chapter 2.)

The Grand Canyon (2 days). The Grand Canyon rivals any scenic or natural wonder in the world for its beauty and geology. Take a sunrise breakfast on the rim, a midday hike among the pines, and an evening stroll to watch the moon rise. Or venture into the canyon for an up close and personal encounter with this truly grand phenomenon. (☞ The South Rim and Environs *and* The North Rim and Environs *in* Chapter 1.)

San Francisco Peaks and Sunset Crater (1 day). On your way back to Flagstaff, stop at Sunset Crater for a look at a dormant volcano cone and the lava flows. All around are the snow-capped San Francisco Peaks, especially beautiful in winter. (☞ Flagstaff *in* Chapter 3.)

Camping

🏕 **Homolovi State Park Campgrounds.** Water and showers are available mid-April to mid-October at these 53 sites. All sites have running water and cost $10 without electrical hookup, $15 with. ☒ *1½ mi from I–40 off AZ 87,* ☏ *520/289–4106.* ☉ *Year-round.*

Petrified Forest National Park

★ ⑫ *54 mi east of Homolovi Ruins State Park and 27 mi east of Holbrook on I–40; 19 mi east of Holbrook on U.S. 180.*

A visit to the Petrified Forest is a trip back in geological time. In 1984 the fossil remains of one of the oldest dinosaurs ever unearthed—dating from the Triassic period of the Mesozoic era 225 million years ago—were discovered here; other plant and animal fossils in the park date from the same period. Remnants of ancient human beings and their artifacts, dating back 8,000 years, have been recovered at more than 500 sites in this national park.

The park derives its name from the fact that the grounds are also covered with petrified tree trunks whose wood cells were fossilized over centuries by brightly hued mineral deposits—silica, iron oxide, manganese, aluminum, copper, lithium, and carbon. In many places, petrified logs scattered about the landscape resemble a fairy-tale forest turned to stone. Most of the park's 93,000 acres include portions of the vast, pink-hued lunarlike landscape known as the Painted Desert. In the northern area of the park, this colorful but essentially barren and waterless series of windswept plains, hills, and mesas is considered by geologists to be part of the Chinle formation, deposited at an early stage of the Triassic period. Colors are most dramatic at dawn and sunset, when oblique light enhances the rainbow of sedimentary layers, making smaller chasms glow deep red.

You can easily spend most of a day on the park's 28 mi of paved roads and walking trails. Lookouts on the north end of the park provide beautiful Painted Desert vistas. Fascinating Native American petroglyphs survive on boulders at **Newspaper Rock** and **Puerco Ruins.** The area around **Jasper Forest** contains stunning hunks of petrified trees scattered on the desert floor. Near the southern end of the park, **Agate House** is a structure assembled from pieces of petrified wood. The self-guided **Giant Logs Trail** starts at the Rainbow Forest Museum and Visitor Center and loops through ½ mi of huge fallen trees. One of the ancient, fallen trunks measures more than 6 ft in diameter.

Because so many looters hauled away large quantities of petrified wood in the early years of this century, President Theodore Roosevelt made the area a national monument in 1906. Since then, it has been illegal (not to mention bad karma) to remove even a small sliver of petrified wood from the park. Plenty of souvenir pieces are available from the park's visitor-center gift shop and surrounding trading posts. Pieces are so cheap that there's really no way to justify this federal offense, with its hefty fines and potential imprisonment. Additionally, don't miss the "Guilt Book" in the south end's Rainbow Forest Museum. This three-ring binder is crammed with letters from guilt-riddled former visitors anxiously returning their purloined souvenirs and detailing directly attributable hexes—from runs of bad luck to husbands turning into "hard-drinking strangers."

At the north entrance of the park, the **Painted Desert Visitor Center** shows a movie entitled *Timeless Impressions,* tracing the natural history of the area. The **Rainbow Forest Museum and Visitor Center** (☒ Near the south entrance, off U.S. 180) displays three skeletons from the Triassic period, including that of "Gertie"—the ferocious phytosaur, a crocodile-like carnivore. The museum has numerous exhibits relating to the world of cycads (tropical plants), ferns, fish, and other early life, as well as artifacts and tools of ancient humans. Within the park's boundaries, visitors also have access to a restaurant and a service station at the north end of the park. Those interested in purchasing books or slides should know that many of the same titles are offered at the Fred Harvey Co. gift shops (there's one at each end of the park) and at the Painted Desert Visitor Center (located at the north end of the park), but only book profits from the Visitor Center fund the continued research and interpretive activities for the park.

Picnicking is allowed inside the park. You may hike into the nearby wilderness areas to camp, but you must obtain a park permit for an overnight stay. Free permits are issued at both visitor centers (☞ *above*) and at the Painted Desert Inn.

Visitors can begin the 27-mi drive through the park either from the northern I–40 entrance or the southern entrance off U.S. 180. Those continuing on to New Mexico will want to enter from the park's south entrance, ending up with I–40's straight shot over the border toward Albuquerque. Visitors with accommodations in Holbrook will probably want to tour the park from south end to north end, saving dramatic sunset vistas of the Painted Desert for last. ✉ *North entrance: off I–40, 30 mi east of Holbrook. South entrance: off U.S. 180, 19 mi southeast of Holbrook. Box 2217, Petrified Forest 86028,* ☎ *520/524–6228.* ✍ *$10 per vehicle; receipt is valid for reentry within the next 7 days.* ☉ *Daily 8–5.*

Dining and Lodging

$$ ✕ **Mesa Italiana Restaurant.** Mesa's chef uses the finest herbs, spices, and other ingredients to create an authentic taste of old Italy. Fresh pastas, calzones, spaghetti with Italian mushrooms, and homemade salads are featured fare. Don't forget the spumoni for dessert. The adjacent sports-themed bar serves pub fare and has off-track betting. ✉ *2318 E. Navajo Blvd., Holbrook 86025,* ☎ *520/524–6696. MC, V. Closed Mon.*

$ 🏨 **Best Western Arizonian Inn.** Each of the large, handsome rooms here is furnished with a suite of formal, ersatz–cherry wood furniture. Some rooms contain microwaves, refrigerators, and data ports. A 24-hour diner is just steps across the parking lot. ✉ *2508 E. Navajo Blvd., Holbrook 86025,* ☎ FAX *520/524–2611. 70 rooms. Pool. AE, D, DC, MC, V.*

$ 🏨 **Days Inn.** This modern southwestern-style structure of stucco walls and Spanish-tile roofs stands amid lava rock landscaping. Inside, southwestern teal hues and whitewashed furniture highlight the decor. Free breakfast, local phone calls, and HBO plus a variety of nearby restaurants make this a pleasant, convenient choice. ✉ *2601 Navajo Blvd., Holbrook 86025,* ☎ *520/524–6949. 51 rooms, 3 suites. Indoor pool, hot tub. AE, D, DC, MC, V.*

$ 🏨 **Wigwam Motel.** Classic Route 66 kitsch, the Wigwam consists of
★ 15 bright white, roadside, cement wigwams where you can sleep inexpensively in a surreal environment. As you might expect, wigwams are phoneless, but—ode to Mother Progress—these wigwams have cable TV. ✉ *811 W. Hopi Dr., Holbrook 86025,* ☎ *520/524–3048. 15 wigwams. MC, V.*

Shopping

McGees Beyond Native Tradition (✉ 2114 E. Navajo Blvd., Holbrook 86025, ☎ 520/524–1977) is the area's premier source of high-quality, Native American jewelry, rugs, Hopi baskets, and katsina dolls; owner

Bruce McGee has long-standing, personal relationships with reservation artisans and a knowledgeable staff that adroitly assists first-time buyers and seasoned collectors alike.

EASTERN ARIZONA A TO Z

Arriving and Departing

By Bus
White Mountain Passenger Lines (☎ 520/537–4539 or 602/275–4245) has service between Phoenix and Show Low; one-way fares are around $40. **Greyhound Lines** (☎ 800/231–2222) travels from Phoenix to Winslow, 50 mi west of Petrified Forest National Park.

By Car
If arriving from points west via Flagstaff, I–40 leads directly to Holbrook, where drivers can take AZ 77 south into Show Low or U.S. 180 southeast to Springerville-Eagar. Those departing from the metropolitan Phoenix area will want to take scenic drive northeast on U.S. 60, or the only-slightly faster AZ 87 North to AZ 260 East, both of which lead to Show Low. From Tucson, AZ 77 North connects with U.S. 60 at Globe and continues through Show Low up to Holbrook. From New Mexico, drivers can enter the state on I–40 and take U.S. 191 south into Springerville-Eagar, or continue on to Holbrook and reach the White Mountains via AZ 77. For those who want to drive the Coronado Trail south-to-north, U.S. 70 and AZ 78 link up with the U.S. 191 from Globe to the west and New Mexico cities to the east, respectively.

By Plane
Show Low Municipal Airport (⌧ U.S. 60 at AZ 77, ☎ 520/537–5629) has two runways; **Express Air** (☎ 602/244–1851) has service to and from Phoenix.

By Train
Amtrak (☎ 800/872–7245) trains depart daily at 6:42 AM from Flagstaff to Winslow. Those traveling from Phoenix will need to take the Amtrak bus—which departs Phoenix-area stations three times daily bound for Flagstaff—and stay overnight in Flagstaff to catch the early morning train to Winslow. From Albuquerque, Winslow is only a three-hour ride, leaving daily at 4:33 PM.

Getting Around

By Car
You'll absolutely need a car to tour Eastern Arizona, especially since most of the region's top scenic attractions are between towns. Rental facilities are few and far between in these parts, so you'll do well to rent a car from your departure point, whether it's Phoenix, Flagstaff, or Albuquerque.

Motorists should travel prepared, with jumper cables, a shovel, tire chains, and—for tire traction on icy roads—a bag of kitty litter. Chain requirements apply to all vehicles, including those with four-wheel drive. Bridges and overpasses freeze first and are often slicker than normal road surfaces; never assume sufficient traction simply because a road appears to be sanded. If you must travel in poor visibility conditions, drivers should turn on the headlights and always keep the highway's white reflectors to their right. For road conditions through the region, contact the **White Mountains Road and Weather Information Line** (☎ 520/537–7623).

CAR RENTALS

Holbrook Auto Sales (✉ 705 Navajo Blvd., ☎ 520/524–3874) offers rental cars in Holbrook. In Show Low try **Enterprise Rent-A-Car** (✉ 980 E. Deuce of Clubs, Show Low 85901, ☎ 520/537–5144). **Fuller's White Mountain Motors** has cars for rent in Show Low (✉ 1920 E. Deuce of Clubs, Show Low 85901, ☎ 520/537–5767) and Round Valley (✉ 225 E. Main St., Springerville 85938, ☎ 520/333–4030).

Contacts and Resources

Emergencies

Halfway between Show Low and Pinetop-Lakeside, **Navapache Regional Medical Center** (✉ 2200 Show Low Lake Rd., Show Low 85901, ☎ 520/537–4375 or 800/300–0361) has a trauma center and 24-hour acute care. **White Mountain Communities Hospital** (✉ 118 S. Mountain Ave., Springerville 85938, ☎ 520/333–4368) has 24-hour emergency room facilities and services the Round Valley area.

Outdoor Activities and Sports

The office of **Arizona State Parks** (✉ 1300 W. Washington St., Phoenix 85007, ☎ 602/542–4174 or 800/285–3703) can provide detailed information about state-run parks and their recreational facilities.

Stop by any White Mountains ranger station and pick up a copy of the 20-page Forest Service brochure entitled "Recreational Opportunities in the Apache Sitgreaves National Forest" for further descriptions of the hiking, horseback riding, camping, bicycling, fishing, and boating options in the area. A similar booklet is available from the White Mountain Apaches detailing opportunities on reservation land.

CAMPING

Call or write the **U.S. Forest Service** (✉ 2022 White Mountain Blvd., Pinetop-Lakeside 85935, ☎ 520/368–5111) for a brochure listing all public camping facilities in the Apache Sitgreaves National Forest, most of which operate from April to November. To assure a site at a fee campground, call **National Forest Service Campground Reservations** (☎ 877/444–6777).

Book your campground site well in advance with the **White Mountain Apache Tribe** (✉ Box 220, Whiteriver 85941, ☎ 520/338–4385).

Visitor Information

CHAMBERS OF COMMERCE

Alpine Chamber of Commerce (✉ Box 410, Alpine 85920, ☎ 520/339–4330). **Holbrook Chamber of Commerce** (✉ 100 E. Arizona Ave., Holbrook 86025, ☎ 520/524–6558 or 800/524–2459). **Pinetop-Lakeside Chamber of Commerce** (✉ 674 E. White Mountain Blvd., Pinetop 85935, ☎ 520/367–4290).

For the Springerville-Eagar area, contact the **Round Valley Chamber of Commerce** (✉ 318 Main St., Box 31, Springerville 85938, ☎ 520/333–2123). **Show Low Chamber of Commerce** (✉ 951 W. Deuce of Clubs or Box 1083, Show Low 85902, ☎ 520/537–2326 or 0888/746–9569).

LAND-MANAGEMENT AGENCIES

Alpine Ranger District (✉ U.S. 191 at U.S. 180/Box 469, Alpine 85920, ☎ 520/339–4384). **Apache Sitgreaves National Forest** (✉ Box 640, Springerville 85938, ☎ 520/333–4301). **Arizona Game & Fish Department** (✉ 2878 E. White Mountain Dr., Pinetop 85935, ☎ 520/367–4281). **Lakeside Ranger District** (✉ 2022 White Mountain Blvd., Lakeside 85935, ☎ 520/368–5111). **Petrified Forest Ranger Office** (✉ Box 2217, Petrified Forest 86028, ☎ 520/524–6228). **San Carlos**

Apache Nation (✉ Box 97, San Carlos 85550, ☎ 520/475–2343 or 888/275–2653). **Springerville Ranger District** (✉ Box 760, 165 S. Mountain Ave., Springerville 85938, ☎ 520/333–4372). **White Mountain Apache Wildlife & Recreation** (✉ Box 220, Whiteriver 85941, ☎ 520/338–4385) is the contact for all reservation fishing, camping, and hiking.

Weather

Call the **White Mountains Road and Weather Information Line** (☎ 520/537–7623) to get the area's latest forecast by phone.

6 TUCSON

Known to residents as the Old Pueblo, Tucson may have buried many of its Spanish roots, but you'll find remnants of this heritage in the 200-year-old Mission San Xavier del Bac, an architectural masterpiece set in the midst of the Tohono O'odham Reservation; in El Presidio, a historic district of adobe-style houses; and in Tucson's myriad Mexican restaurants. Nature-lovers will like the many outdoor options, including Saguaro National Park, which sandwiches the city on its east and west sides, and the Arizona–Sonora Desert Museum, a beautifully landscaped zoo.

Updated by
Andrea Ibáñez

ALTHOUGH IT IS ARIZONA'S second-largest city, Tucson feels like a small town—one enriched by its deep Native American, Spanish, Mexican, and Old West roots. It is at once a bustling center of business and a kicked-back university and resort town. Metropolitan Tucson has more than 700,000 year-round residents, a population increased by the annual migration of "snowbirds," visitors who come in winter to enjoy the warm sun that shines on the city more than 320 days a year. Winter temperatures hover around 65°F during the day and 38°F at night. Summers are unquestionably hot—July averages 104°F during the day and 75°F at night—but, as Tucsonans are fond of saying, "it's a dry heat" (Tucson averages only 11 inches of rain a year).

In a part of the world where everything seems new and buildings more than 50 years old are viewed as historic places, Tucson is an exception. Native Americans have lived along the waterways in this valley for thousands of years. During the 1500s, Spanish explorers arrived to find Pima Indians enjoying the mild weather and growing crops. Father Eusebio Francisco Kino, a Jesuit missionary whose influence is still strongly felt throughout the region, first visited the area in 1687 and returned a few years later to build missions.

The name Tucson came from the Indian word *stjukshon* (pronounced "*stook*-shahn"), meaning "spring at the foot of a black mountain." (The springs at the foot of Sentinel Peak, made of black volcanic rock, are now dry.) The name became Tucson (originally pronounced "*tuk*-son") in the mouths of the Spanish explorers who built the *presidio* (walled city) of San Augustin del Tuguison in 1776 to keep Native Americans from reclaiming the city. At the time it was the northernmost Spanish settlement in the *Pimeria Alta,* and current-day Main Street is a quiet reminder of the former Camino Real, the royal road, that stretched from this tiny walled fort to Mexico City.

Four flags have flown over Tucson—Spanish, Mexican, Confederate, and, finally the Stars and Stripes. Tucson's allegiance changed in 1820 when Mexico declared independence from Spain, and again in 1853 when the Gadsden purchase made it part of the United States (Arizona didn't officially become a state until 1912). In the 1850s the Butterfield stage line was extended to Tucson, bringing adventurers, a few settlers, and more than a handful of outlaws. The arrival of the railroad in 1880 marked another spurt of growth, as did the opening of the University of Arizona in 1891.

Tucson's 20th-century growth occurred after World War I, when veterans with damaged lungs sought the dry air and healing power of the sun, and again during World War II with the opening of Davis-Monthan Air Force Base and the rise of local aeronautical industries. It was also around this time that air-conditioning made the desert climate hospitable year-round. Today, however, many transplants come from the Midwest and nearby California because of the lower housing costs, cleaner environment, and spectacular scenery. High-tech industries have moved into the area, but the economy still relies heavily on tourism and the university, although, come summer, you'd never guess. When the snowbirds and students depart, Tucson has a sleepy feel that reminds you just how much the desert still determines the city's pace.

Pleasures and Pastimes

Dining

Residents have long boasted about Tucson's Mexican food, boldly proclaiming their town "Mexican Food Capital of the U.S." Most of the Mexican food in town is Sonoran style—native to the adjoining Mexican state of Sonora—a cuisine now familiar to most Americans since it uses cheese, mild peppers, corn tortillas, pinto beans, and beef or chicken. Tucson is the birthplace of the "chimichanga" (Spanish for "whachamacallit"), a flour tortilla filled with meat or cheese, rolled and deep-fried. Because traditional Sonoran dishes are notoriously high in calories and saturated fats, many restaurants in Tucson now offer them prepared without lard. All traditional Mexican restaurants serve chips and salsa before the meal, usually with mild and hot salsa, but test carefully since southwesterners have liberal ideas regarding spices. The mark of a fine Mexican restaurant is that its tortilla chips are made fresh and served hot, but not greasy, and that the hand-stretched flour tortillas are parchment-thin. Southwestern cuisine ranges from barbecue and cowboy steaks to light nouvelle recipes that use regional ingredients like cactus and blue corn.

Lodging

In Tucson you can choose from luxurious desert resorts, basic accommodations offered by small motels, or a variety of area bed-and-breakfasts ranging from bedrooms in modest homes to private cottages nestled on wildlife preserves. Southwestern-style guest ranches—some of them former cattle ranches from the 1800s—can be found on the outskirts of town.

Mexican and Native American Culture

Tucsonans of Mexican-American heritage make up almost a fourth of the population and play a major role in all aspects of daily life. The city's south-of-the-border soul is visible in everything from the city's tile-roof architecture to its mariachi festivals and abundance of Mexican restaurants. Native Americans have a strong presence in the area as well: The Tohono O'odham—the name means "desert people who have come from the earth"—reservation borders Tucson, and the Pascua Yaqui have their villages within the city limits. Local events, especially religious festivals around Christmas and Easter, celebrate the culture of these tribes and other Native Americans in Arizona. Native American crafts range from exquisite jewelry and basketry to the more pedestrian (but still authentic) tourist trinkets.

Outdoor Activities

A warm, dry climate and a varied terrain make the Tucson area a year-round sportsman's paradise. Well suited for biking—although it might not seem so with the proliferation of cars—the city has miles of bike paths (shared by joggers and walkers) and plenty of wide open spaces with wonderful desert views. Those same expanses are home to some of the best golf courses in the country, with options ranging from well-manicured links at posh resorts to reasonably priced but excellent municipal courses. Hikers enjoy the myriad desert trails in the winter or cooler treks in nearby mountain ranges during the summer: Saguaro (pronounced "suh-*war*-oh") National Park (both east and west), Mt. Lemmon, Sabino Canyon, "A" Mountain, and Catalina State Park are all within 20 minutes of central Tucson by car. Both equestrians and ersatz cowboys and cowgirls will find horseback riding options to suit them at one of the many area stables and scenic riding trails.

Stargazers can peer through the telescope at the Flandrau Space and Science Center or take part in one of the University of Arizona's astronomy camps. City ordinances against "light pollution"—laws designed to minimize the amount of man-made light emitted into the atmosphere—allow viewing of the usually clear desert skies, even in the city center.

EXPLORING TUCSON

The metropolitan Tucson area covers more than 500 square mi in a valley ringed by mountains—the Santa Catalinas to the north, the Santa Ritas to the south, the Rincons to the east, and the Tucson Mountains to the west. For the most part, touring the area requires a car. The central portion of town, where you'll find most of the shops, restaurants, and businesses, is roughly bounded by Wilmot Road on the east, Oracle Road on the west, River Road to the north, and 22nd Street to the south. The older downtown section, east of I–10 off the Broadway-Congress exit, is much smaller and easy to navigate on foot. Streets downtown don't run true to any sort of grid, however, and many are one-way, so it's best to get a good, detailed map. Remember, too, that the old cliché is reversed here: It's not the humidity—it's the heat. If you are accustomed to humid conditions then chances are you'll be unprepared for Tucson's dry climate, so take frequent fluid breaks if you plan to be outdoors, especially in hot weather.

Numbers in the text correspond to numbers in the margin and on the Downtown Tucson, University of Arizona, Tucson, and Side Trips Near Tucson maps.

Great Itineraries

IF YOU HAVE 1 DAY

You'll get a good feel for the city if you drive out to Saguaro National Park West and the Arizona–Sonora Desert Museum, with a stop at Old Tucson Studios if you're traveling with kids.

IF YOU HAVE 3 DAYS

Follow the first day's itinerary. The next morning, drive out to the Mission San Xavier del Bac and enjoy Indian fry bread for lunch in the plaza. Military buffs should continue south to the Titan Missile Museum; shoppers will enjoy trips in the same direction to Tubac and Nogales, Mexico. On the third day, head downtown to the El Presidio district to explore Tucson's early history and, in the afternoon, visit one of the several museums at the University of Arizona.

IF YOU HAVE 5 DAYS

What you do on the fourth day depends on the weather: If it's hot, visit Sabino Canyon or Mt. Lemmon to cool off; if it's not, you might enjoy breakfast at Tohono Chul Park, followed by a visit to Biosphere 2. On the fifth day, head east, where a hike in Saguaro National Park East can be followed by an underground tour of Colossal Cave.

Downtown

The area bordered by Franklin Street on the north, Cushing Street on the south, Church Avenue on the east, and Main Avenue on the west encompasses more than two centuries of the city's architectural history, dating from the original walled El Presidio de Tucson, a Spanish fortress built when Arizona was still part of New Spain in 1776. A good deal of Tucson's history was destroyed in the 1960s, when large sections of the downtown's barrio were bulldozed to make way for the Tucson Convention Center, high-rises, and parking lots, but it's still possible to explore parts of the original Spanish settlement and to see a number of the posh residences that accompanied the arrival of the railroad.

Much in the way fossils speak silent volumes about the former inhabitants of any geographic region, dwellings that once housed a specific segment of the population tell the history of a neighborhood's past.

El Presidio Historic District, north of the Convention Center and the government buildings that dominate downtown, is a representative mixture of Tucson's historic architecture, a thumbnail of the city's former self. The north–south streets of Court, Meyer, and Main are sprinkled with traditional adobe abodes, typical old-style Mexican construction sitting cheek by jowl with Territorial houses with their wide attics and porches. Drive south on Main and west onto Paseo Redondo for a glimpse of what was once called "Snob Hollow," where the wealthy merchants had their homes.

The area most closely resembling 19th-century Tucson is the **Barrio Historico Neighborhood,** just south of the Convention Center. Come out of Paseo Redondo onto Granada, drive south with the Convention Center to your left and the high-rise Federal Court Building on your right, go left on Cushing and south again on Main Avenue, where El Tiradito shrine is located, and explore the narrow streets of this neighborhood. Proceed east on Kennedy and north on Convent Avenue to see a sampling of the thick-walled adobe houses that huddle close to the street, masking the yards and gardens behind.

To the east, across Stone Avenue, lies **Armory Park Neighborhood,** mostly constructed by and for the railroad workers who settled here after the 1880s. Drive south down Stone Avenue (it's one-way), east on 15th Street, then north on 4th Avenue to view the brick or wood Territorial-style homes, the Victorian era's adaptation to the desert climate.

A Good Tour

Drive up to **"A" Mountain (Sentinel Peak)** ① for a great perspective of downtown Tucson. Come down from on high and head east along Congress Street. Cross the **Santa Cruz River.** Continue east along Congress, then head south on Granada to the **Sosa-Carillo-Fremont House** ② (park at the adjacent Convention Center lot if no events are in progress). Continue south on Granada to the flashing signal and turn east on Cushing Street to the shrine of **El Tiradito (The Castaway)** ③, next to El Minuto's parking lot. One-way streets require you to drive east on Cushing, north on Church, east on Broadway, and then south on Stone Avenue to **St. Augustine Cathedral** ④. To reach the **Tucson Children's Museum** ⑤, head east on McCormick to 6th Avenue. To get to the **Tucson Museum of Art and Historic Block** ⑥, take Church Avenue north to Alameda, then east to Main, where you'll find parking. The complex includes **La Casa Cordova** ⑦, the **J. Knox Corbett House** ⑧, and the **Stevens Home** ⑨. Walk east on Alameda and then south on Church to reach the **Pima County Courthouse** ⑩, downtown's architectural jewel.

TIMING

You can see most of the highlights of downtown, including the Tucson Museum of Art, in about four hours. Although it is all accessible by car, the one-way streets can be frustrating and unnecessarily time consuming, so you might consider parking your car and walking between destinations if they are not far apart. It's a good way to take in downtown, stopping for lunch or a snack along the way.

Sights to See

❶ **"A" Mountain (Sentinel Peak).** The original name of this mountain west of downtown was derived from its function as a lookout point for the

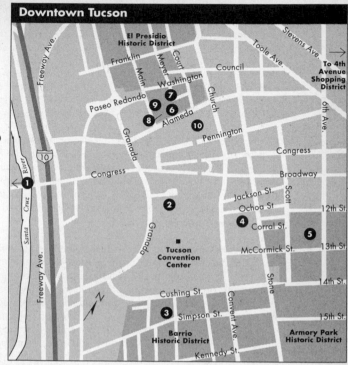

Spanish. In 1915, fans of the University of Arizona football team whitewashed a large "A" on its side to celebrate a victory, and the tradition has been kept up ever since. The Pima Indian village and cultivated fields that once lay at the base of the peak are long gone, although John Warner's renovated 19th-century house at the base still stands. During the day, it's a great place for visitors to get an overview of the town's layout; it is closed at night. ⊠ *Congress St. on Sentinel Peak Rd.*

③ El Tiradito (The Castaway). No one seems to know the details of the story behind this little shrine, but everyone agrees a tragic love triangle was involved. A bronze plaque indicates only that it is dedicated to a sinner who is buried here on unconsecrated ground. The many candles that line the cactus-shrouded spot attest to its continuing importance in local Catholic lore. A modern-day miracle: The shrine's inclusion on the National Register of Historic Places helped prevent a freeway from plowing through this section of the Barrio Historico District. ⊠ *Main Ave., just south of Cushing St.*

⑧ J. Knox Corbett House. Built in 1906–07, this house was occupied by members of the Corbett family until 1963. Tucson's Hi Corbett field (the major league Colorado Rockies use this field for spring training) is named for the grand nephew of the original occupants, J. Knox Corbett, a businessman, and Elizabeth Hughes Corbett, daughter of Tucson pioneer Sam Hughes. The two-story, Mission Revival–style residence has been furnished with American Arts and Crafts pieces; the Stickley brothers, Roycroft, Tiffany, and Morris are among the more famous names represented. ⊠ *180 N. Main Ave.,* ☎ *520/624–2333.* ☞ *Free with admission to TMA (☞ Tucson Museum of Art and Historic Block, below).* ☉ *Mon.–Sat. 10–4, Sun. noon–4.*

⑦ La Casa Cordova. One of the best examples of the simple but elegant Sonoran row house, a Spanish style adapted to adobe construction, La

Casa Cordova is also one of the oldest buildings in Tucson: The original part was constructed in about 1848. It's now home to the Mexican Heritage Museum where you'll find an exhibit of the history of the presidio and furnishings of the Indian and pioneer settlers of the period. After visiting the museum, you'll understand why adobe—brick made of mud and straw, cured in the hot sun—was so widely used in early Tucson. It provides a natural insulation from the heat and cold, and it is durable in Tucson's dry climate. ⊠ *175 N. Meyer Ave.,* ☎ *520/624–2333.* ☜ *Free.* ☉ *Mon.–Sat. 10–4, Sun. noon–4.*

<table>
<tr><td>NEED A
BREAK?</td><td>On the patio of Old Town Artisans, a multiroom marketplace set in a 19th-century adobe building, the pretty **Cocina** (⊠ 186 N. Meyer Ave., ☎ 520/622–0351) restaurant is a pleasant spot for a salad or sandwich. For a meal on the run, **El Rapido** (⊠ 77 W. Washington, ☎ 520/624–4725) is a tiny take-out facility with some of the best flour tortillas in Tucson. You can take your burrito to El Presidio Park and enjoy the beautiful weather nearly year-round.</td></tr>
</table>

★ ❿ **Pima County Courthouse.** This Spanish colonial–style building with its landmark mosaic-tile dome is among Tucson's most beautiful historic structures. It was built in 1927 on the site of the original single-story adobe court of 1869; a portion of the old presidio wall can be seen in the south wing of the courthouse's second floor. To the side of the building, the County Assessor's office has a diorama depicting the area's early days (if the location seems odd, remember that the Spanish were big on taxation, too). The courthouse, still in use, is on the eastern side of **El Presidio Park,** a modern square once occupied by the Plaza de las Armas, the largest of El Presidio's plazas. ⊠ *115 N. Church St., between Alameda and Pennington Sts.*

Santa Cruz River. This is a dry wash or *arroyo* most of the year, but sudden summer thunderstorms and rainwater from upper elevations can turn it into a raging river in a matter of hours. The river has been the location of settlement for thousands of years, and most of the archaeological finds in the valley are located along its banks. When Europeans arrived, the Santa Cruz was a permanent river with wide banks suitable for irrigation. Over time its banks have been narrowed and contained and are now lined by the River Park. Passing over any of the bridges in Tucson, look down into the washes for signs of water, although all you may see are people on horseback.

❷ **Sosa-Carillo-Fremont House.** One of Tucson's oldest adobe residences, this was the only building spared when the surrounding barrio was torn down to build the Tucson Convention Center. Originally purchased by José Maria Sosa in 1860, it was owned by the Carillo family for 80 years and leased at one time to Territorial Governor John C. Fremont. The restored house, now a branch of the Arizona Historical Society, is furnished in 1880s fashion and has changing displays of territorial life. ⊠ *Convention Center Complex, between the Music Hall and the Arena (parking at 151 S. Granada Ave.),* ☎ *520/622–0956.* ☜ *Free; walking tours of the Presidio and Tucson Historic District $4.50.* ☉ *Wed.–Sat. 10–4; walking tours Nov.–Mar., Sat. at 10.*

❹ **St. Augustine Cathedral.** Construction began in 1896 on one of downtown's most striking structures, set in what had earlier been the Plaza de Mesilla. Although the imposing pink building was modeled after the Cathedral of Queretaro in Mexico, a number of its details reflect the desert setting: Above the entryway, next to a bronze statue of St. Augustine, are carvings of a saguaro cactus, yucca, and horned toad. Compared with the magnificent facade, the modernized interior is a bit disappointing. For a unique southwestern experience, attend a mariachi mass celebrated Sundays at 8 AM. ✉ *192 S. Stone Ave.*

❾ Stevens Home. It was here that wealthy politician and cattle rancher Hiram Stevens and his Mexican wife, Petra Santa Cruz, entertained many of Tucson's leaders—including Edward and Maria Fish—during the 1800s. A drought brought the Stevenses' cattle ranching to a halt in 1893, and Stevens killed himself in despair, after unsuccessfully attempting to kill his wife (the bullet was deflected by the comb she wore in her hair). The 1865 house, just north of the Edward Nye Fish House (☞ Tucson Museum of Art and Historic Block, *below*) and architecturally similar, was restored in 1980. ✉ *150 N. Main Ave.* ✆ *Free with admission to TMA.* ☉ *Mon.–Sat. 10–4, Sun. 12–4.*

☚ ❺ Tucson Children's Museum. Kids are encouraged to touch and explore the exhibits here, which are oriented toward science, language, and history: They can crawl inside a giant model of the heart and lungs or turn on the electricity in the streets of a model town. Art supplies and musical instruments add to the fun (and din). The "Take a Hike" program lets girls and boys pretend to take part in a variety of professions, encouraging them to consider careers that have traditionally been restricted by gender. ✉ *200 S. 6th Ave.,* ☎ *520/792–9985.* ✆ *$5.* ☉ *Sat. 10–5, Sun. noon–5; call for weekday hrs.*

★ ❻ Tucson Museum of Art and Historic Block. Tucson's past is interpreted for visitors in downtown's main cultural center. The five historic buildings on this block are listed in the National Register of Historic Places; you can enter **La Casa Cordova** (☞ *above*), the **Stevens Home** (☞ *above*), the **J. Knox Corbett House** (☞ *above*), and the **Edward Nye Fish House** (☞ *below*). The **Romero House,** believed to incorporate a section of the presidio wall, is not open to the public. In the center of the museum complex is the **Plaza of the Pioneers,** honoring Tucson's early citizens.

The **Tucson Museum of Art** building, the only modern structure of the complex, houses a permanent collection of pre-Columbian art and hosts some interesting traveling shows, most of them contemporary. In 1998, the TMA underwent extensive remodeling and expansion, adding 7,000 square ft of exhibit space and incorporating several separate historic buildings into a larger design. The museum's permanent and changing exhibitions of western art fill an 1868 adobe, the **Edward Nye Fish House,** which belonged to an early merchant, entrepreneur, and politician, and his wife, Maria Wakefield Fish, a prominent educator. The building is notable for its 15-ft beamed ceilings and saguaro-cactus-rib supports. Nearby, the **J. Knox Corbett House** is furnished in the Arts and Crafts style. Additions to the central building and expansion into the Stevens house are in the works; take one of the free docent tours for a more complete understanding of the museum's rich history. Those interested in exploring the El Presidio District further can also get a self-guided tour map from the museum. Visitors can park in a large lot at North Main and Paseo Redondo and enter the museum on North Main. ✉ *140 N. Main Ave.,* ☎ *520/624–2333.* ✆ *$2; Tues. free. Free guided tours Wed. and Thurs. at 11 AM.* ☉ *Mon.–Sat. 10–4, Sun. noon–4. Closed Mon. Memorial Day through Labor Day (no guided tours during that period).*

The University of Arizona

A university might not seem to be the most likely spot for a vacation visit, but this one is unusual. Not only is the institution itself of historical importance, but it also supports several museums with exhibitions ranging from astronomy to photography. Call ahead to verify hours for the university's museums, as yearly budget revisions often cause schedule changes. If you drive, leave your car in a university garage or lot; those on 2nd Street between Highland and Mountain avenues, at the junction of Speedway Boulevard and Park Avenue, and on 2nd Street at Euclid Avenue, are the most centrally located. The current rate is $1.25 per hour; on weekends and university holidays parking is free.

The U of A, as the University of Arizona is known locally (versus ASU, its rival state university in Tempe), covers 325 acres and is a major economic influence with a student population of 33,500. The land for the university was "donated" by a couple of gamblers and a saloon owner in 1891 (their benevolence was reputed to have been inspired by a bad hand of cards), and $25,000 of territorial money was used to build Old Main (the original building) and hire six faculty members. Money ran out before Old Main's roof was placed, but a few enlightened local citizens pitched in funds to finish it. Most of the city's populace was less enthusiastic about the institution: They were disgruntled when the 13th Territorial Legislature granted the University of Arizona to Tucson and awarded rival Phoenix with what they considered to be the real prize—an insane asylum and a prison.

A Good Tour

Start your tour on the northwestern corner of campus, at the junction of Speedway Boulevard and Park Avenue, where you'll find a large parking garage. Take the pedestrian underpass to the **Center for Creative Photography** ⑪, located in a gray concrete building on the left. Cater-corner from the center on the right-hand side is the small **University of Arizona Museum of Art** ⑫. Head directly south two blocks on Park Avenue and then go east on 2nd Street to reach the **Arizona Historical Society's Museum** ⑬. One block to the south on University Boulevard, just inside the main gate of the university, is the **Arizona State Museum** ⑭. As you head east, University Boulevard turns into the grassy University Mall; continue on to Cherry Avenue to reach the **Grace H. Flandrau Science Center and Planetarium** ⑮.

TIMING
To see this huge university campus in a single day takes careful planning. During the school semesters, you're better off visiting on the weekend when university parking is free and plentiful; there's no problem in summer when most of the students leave campus.

Sights to See

👆 ⑬ **Arizona Historical Society's Museum.** Flanking the entrance to the museum are statues of two men: Father Kino, the Jesuit who established San Xavier del Bac and a string of other missions, and John Greenaway, indelibly linked to Phelps Dodge, the copper-mining company that helped Arizona earn statehood in 1912. The museum, originally a Pioneer's Society, houses the headquarters of the state Historical Society and has exhibits designed to transport visitors through the history of Southern Arizona, the Southwest United States, and Northern Mexico, starting with the Hohokam Indians and Spanish explorers. Children will enjoy the large exhibit on copper mining (complete with an atmospheric replica of a mine shaft and camp), the stagecoaches in the transportation area, and the pioneer clothing in the costume exhibit. The library houses an extensive collection of historical Arizona photographs and sells inexpensive reprints of most of them. (If you're driving and this is your first stop, park your car in the garage at the corner of 2nd and Euclid streets and then inquire at the museum about the token system.) ✉ *949 E. 2nd St.,* ☎ *520/628–5774.* 🎟 *$3 sug-*

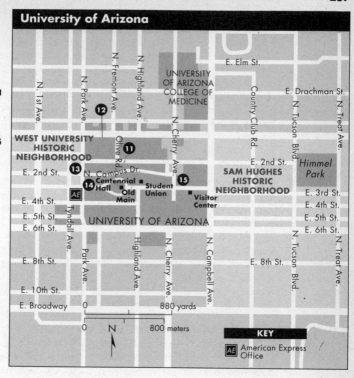

University of Arizona

gested donation. ⊙ *Mon.–Sat. 10–4, Sun. noon–4; library, weekdays
10–4, Sat. 10–1. Library closed Sun.*

⑭ Arizona State Museum. Inside the main gate of the university is the oldest museum in the state, dating from territorial days (1893). Exhibits
in the original (south) building focus on the state's ancient history, including fossils and a fascinating sample of tree-ring dating. *Paths of
Life: American Indians of the Southwest* is a permanent exhibit that
explores the cultural traditions, origins, and contemporary lives of
10 native tribes of Arizona and Sonora, Mexico. ⊠ *Park Ave. at University Ave.,* ☏ *520/621–6302.* ⊡ *Free.* ⊙ *Mon.–Sat. 10–5, Sun.
noon–5.*

NEED A
BREAK?

Just outside the campus gate, University Boulevard is lined with student-
oriented eateries. **Coffee Plantation** (⊠ 845 E. University Blvd., ☏ 520/
628–4300) sells salads and sandwiches and has a view of the passing
University scene. Beer aficionados should head over to **Gentle Ben's** (⊠
865 E. University Blvd., ☏ 520/624–4177), one of Tucson's brewpubs. The patio upstairs affords a good view of the sunset while you
drink the Sampler, the assemblage of all their brews.

★ ⑪ Center for Creative Photography. Ansel Adams conceived the idea of
a photographer's archive and donated the majority of his negatives to
this museum. In addition to its superb collection of his work, the center has works by other major 20th-century photographers including
Paul Strand, W. Eugene Smith, Edward Weston, and Louise Dahl-
Wolfe. Changing exhibits in the main gallery highlight various holdings of the collection, but if you'd like to see the work of a particular
photographer in the center's archives, call to arrange an appointment.
⊠ *1030 N. Olive Rd. (north of 2nd St.),* ☏ *520/621–7968.* ⊡ *$2 sug-
gested donation.* ⊙ *Weekdays 11–5, Sun. noon–5.*

👋 ⑮ **Grace H. Flandrau Science Center and Planetarium.** Attractions here include a 16-inch public telescope; the impressive Star Theatre, where a multimedia show brings astronomy to life; an interactive meteor exhibit; and, in the basement, a Mineral Museum, which exhibits more than 2,000 rocks and gems, some rather rare. Laser light shows are held at night. Bring a camera—special adapters allow you to take pictures through the telescopes. ⊠ *Cherry Ave. and University Blvd.,* ☎ *520/621–4515; 520/621–7827 recorded message.* ☞ *Exhibits $3, laser light show $6, exhibits plus theater $6.* ☉ *Mon.–Tues. 9–5, Wed.–Thurs. 9–5 and 7–9, Fri. 9–5 and 7–midnight, Sat. 1–5 and 7–midnight, Sun. 1–5. Show times vary. Telescope hrs: in summer, Tues.–Sat. 8 PM–10 PM; in winter, Wed.–Sat. 7:30 PM–10 PM.*

⑫ **University of Arizona Museum of Art.** This small museum houses a collection of European paintings from the Renaissance through the 17th century. One of the museum's highlights is the Kress Collection's Retablo from Ciudad Rodrigo, consisting of 26 panels of Fernando Gallego's 1488 altarpiece. The museum also houses the world's second-largest collection of bronze, plaster, and ceramic sculpture by Jacques Lipschitz. ⊠ *Fine Arts Complex, Bldg. 2 (southeast corner of Speedway Blvd. and Park Ave.),* ☎ *520/621–7567.* ☞ *Free.* ☉ *Sept.–mid-May, weekdays 9–5, Sun. noon–4; mid-May–Aug., weekdays 10–3:30, Sun. noon–4. Closed Sat. and university holidays.*

OFF THE
BEATEN PATH

UNIVERSITY NEIGHBORHOODS – When the University of Arizona was built, it stood in the desert on the east side of town and students either lived at home or boarded with residents. Drive slowly along University Boulevard west from the Main Gate of campus through **West University Neighborhood**, a wonderful mixture of stately homes built by former prominent Tucsonans and bungalows constructed for rental to students. On the other side of campus, off Campbell Avenue between Speedway and Broadway, lies **Sam Hughes Neighborhood**, which saw its first homes in the 1920s. Meander along 3rd Street—it is one of Tucson's many bike paths—to see an eclectic mix of Spanish mission revival, bungalow, adobe, and brick homes.

East of I–10 and Central Tucson

The U of A, built in 1891, determined the direction by which the city would grow: Many of the city's major attractions are east of its only major freeway, I–10. Sights worth seeing in central Tucson, as the area near the university is called, include a city park, a zoo, and botanical gardens. Farther to the north lie the imposing Santa Catalina Mountains, and to the far east cacti and caverns rule. Those interested in World War II should take a detour south to see a huge repository of old military aircraft.

A Good Tour

Start your drive at the **Tucson Botanical Gardens** ⑯. One kiddie option is close by: the **Reid Park Zoo** ⑰, less than 10 minutes to the southeast. From here, distances get a bit greater, so some decisions need to be made. You can head north, stopping off at your choice of **Fort Lowell Park and Museum** ⑱, **Sabino Canyon** ⑲, or **De Grazia's Gallery in the Sun** ⑳ en route to **Tohono Chul Park** ㉑ or **Mt. Lemmon** ㉒ (Sabino Canyon and Mt. Lemmon are the most time-consuming of these). Or you can go east to **Saguaro National Park East** ㉓ and **Colossal Cave** ㉔, and south to **Pima Air and Space Museum** ㉕.

TIMING

If it's warm, visit outdoor attractions such as the Tucson Botanical Gardens and Saguaro National Park East in the morning. Sabino Canyon and Mt. Lemmon, on the other hand, are cooler than the rest of the city, the former because of shade provided by Coconino National Forest, the latter due to its elevation. Colossal Cave stays at a constant, comfortable temperature, making it a nice year-round adjunct to a Saguaro National Park East tour.

Sights to See

🐾 ㉔ **Colossal Cave.** The limestone grotto that lies 20 mi east of Tucson (take Broadway Blvd. or E. 22nd St. to Colossal Cave Rd.) is the largest dry cavern in the world. Indeed, parts of it have yet to be explored. Informed guides discuss the fascinating crystal formations and relate the many romantic tales surrounding the cave, including the legend that an enormous sum of money stolen in a stagecoach robbery is still hidden here. Tours last 45 minutes and the wait between them is 30 minutes. A snack bar is on site and picnic benches give a panoramic view to the south and east. ⌧ *Intersection of Colossal Cave Rd. and Old Spanish Trail Rd.,* ☎ *520/647–7275.* ⌧ *$7.50.* ☽ *Oct.–mid-Mar., Mon.–Sat. 9–5, Sun. and holidays 9–6; mid-Mar.–Sept., Mon.–Sat. 8–6, Sun. and holidays 8–7.*

⑳ **De Grazia's Gallery in the Sun.** Arizonan artist Ted De Grazia, who depicted Southwest Indian and Mexican life, built this sprawling, spacious single-story museum with the assistance of Native American friends using only natural material from the surrounding desert. You can visit De Grazia's workshop, former home, and grave. Although the original works are not for sale, the museum's gift shop has a wide selection of prints, ceramics, and books by and about the colorful artist. ⌧ *6300 N. Swan Rd.,* ☎ *520/299–9191.* ⌧ *Free.* ☽ *Daily 10–4.*

⑱ **Fort Lowell Park and Museum.** This restful city park was once the site of a Hohokam Indian village and, centuries later, a fort was built here to protect the fledgling city against the Apaches (1873–91). The former commanding officer's quarters displays artifacts from military life in territorial days. Some of the descendants of the inhabitants of El Fuerte, a Mexican village that arose among the abandoned fort buildings in the 1890s, live in a narrow alley near the museum called El Callejón. ⌧ *2900 N. Craycroft Rd.,* ☎ *520/885–3832.* ⌧ *Free.* ☽ *Wed.–Sat. 10–4.*

㉒ **Mt. Lemmon.** One of the Santa Catalina Mountains, Mt. Lemmon is the southernmost ski slope in the continental United States, but you don't have to be a skier to enjoy a visit. In spring and fall you can picnic and hike among the 150 mi of clearly marked and well-maintained trails; in summer the mountain's 9,157-ft elevation brings welcome relief from the heat. If necessary, check **winter road conditions** by calling 520/741–4991, and gas up before you leave town any time of year as there are no gas stations on Mt. Lemmon Highway, the road that winds and twists its way for 28 mi up the mountainside.

The journey up the mountain is interesting in itself: Every 1,000-ft climb in elevation is equivalent to traveling 300 mi north, so you'll move from typical Sonoran Desert plants in the foothills to vegetation similar to that found in southern Canada at the top. Along the way, you'll see rock formations that look as though they were carefully balanced against each other by architects from another planet.

At milepost 18, on the left-hand side of the road when you're ascending, the **Palisades Ranger Station** can give you current information on the mountain's campgrounds, hiking trails, and picnic spots; it's also a good place to buy maps and books. It's open Friday through Sunday 9 to 5 in winter, daily 9 to 6 in summer. The station does not have a published telephone number, but you can call the Coronado National Forest (☎ 520/749–8700). Admission to the area is $5 per day per vehicle or $20 for an annual pass.

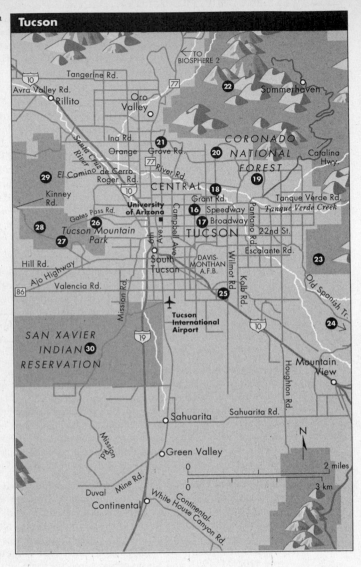

Just before you reach the ski resort, you'll pass through the tiny alpine-style village of **Summerhaven**, which has a couple of casual restaurants, lots of gift shops, and a few pleasant lodges.

Mt. Lemmon Highway ends at **Mt. Lemmon Ski Valley** (☎ 520/576–1321; 520/576–1400 for a recorded snow report). Skiing here depends on natural conditions—there's no artificial snow—so call ahead. There are 16 runs, open daily, ranging from beginner to advanced. Lift tickets cost $27 for an all-day pass and $22 for a half day (starting at 1 PM). Ski equipment can be rented, and instruction is available. In off-season you can take a ride ($6) on the double chairlift that whisks you to the top of the slope—some 9,100 ft. Many ride the lift and then head out on one of several trails that crisscross the summit. ⊠ *Take Tanque Verde Rd. to the Catalina Hwy., which becomes Mt. Lemmon Hwy. as you head north.*

NEED A
BREAK? The **Iron Door** (☎ 520/576–1321) in Mt. Lemmon Ski Valley is open weekends 10–5:30, weekdays 10:30–5:30. In winter, the focus is on burgers, chili, corn bread, and soups; in warmer weather, salads turn up on the menu. This place is popular on the weekends—parking can be tough.

㉕ Pima Air and Space Museum. This huge facility ranks among the largest private collections of aircraft in the world with more than 200 flight machines on display. You'll see a full-scale replica of the Wright brothers' 1903 Wright Flyer and a mock-up of the X-15, the world's fastest aircraft. You can tour a plane used on official business by both John F. Kennedy and Lyndon B. Johnson. World War II veterans find the museum particularly moving, but all ages should enjoy this walk through U.S. aviation history. Hour-long van tours of the nearby Aerospace Maintenance and Regeneration Center (AMARC) at Davis-Monthan Air Force Base provide an eerie glimpse of hundreds of mothballed aircraft lined up in long rows on a vast tract of desert. ⊠ *6000 E. Valencia Rd. (I–10 exit 267),* ☎ *520/574–9658.* ☜ *$7.50, tram ticket $2, AMARC tour (reservations required) $5.* ☉ *Daily 9–5 (last admission at 4).*

☙ **⑰ Reid Park Zoo.** This small but well-designed zoo won't tax the children's—or your—patience. There are plenty of shady places to sit, and a snack bar to rev you up when your energy is flagging. The kids will love the zoo's adorable newborns and the South American enclosure with its rain forest and exotic birds. If you're visiting in the summertime, go early in the day when the animals are active. ⊠ *Reid Park, Lake Shore La., off 22nd St. between Alvernon Way and Country Club Rd.,* ☎ *520/791–4022 recorded info; 520/791–3204 administration.* ☜ *$3.50.* ☉ *Daily 9–4.*

★ **⑲ Sabino Canyon.** Year-round, but especially during summer, locals flock to this oasis in the northeast corner of town. Part of the Coronado National Forest, this is a good spot for hiking, picnicking, or enjoying the waterfalls, streams, swimming holes, and shade trees that provide a respite from the heat. No cars are allowed, but a narrated tram ride (about 45 minutes round-trip) takes you to the top of the canyon; you can hop off and on at any of the nine stops. There's also a tram ride to adjacent Bear Canyon, where you can hike to the popular Seven Falls (it'll take about 1½ hours each way from the drop-off point). ⊠ *Sabino Canyon Rd. in the Santa Catalina foothills,* ☎ *520/749–2861 recorded tram information; 520/749–8700 visitor center.* ☜ *Tram $6, Bear Canyon tram $3. Call for daily tram schedules.* ☉ *Visitor center weekdays 8–4:30, weekends 8:30–4:30.*

㉓ Saguaro National Park East. About 16 mi from the town center, the eastern portion of the national park that sandwiches Tucson covers more than 67,000 acres and climbs through five climate zones, which makes for some dramatic hikes through the foothills of the Rincon Mountains. An 8-mi paved Cactus Forest Drive leads to a variety of trailheads and picnic areas. Ask for a detailed map at the visitor center (☞ Saguaro National Park West, *below,*) for more information about the unique cacti that are concentrated here. ⊠ *Old Spanish Trail (take Speedway Blvd. or 22nd St. E),* ☎ *520/733–5153.* ☜ *$4 per vehicle, $2 individuals entering by bicycle or on foot.* ☉ *Visitor center daily 8:30–5; park roads 7 AM–sunset.*

★ **㉑ Tohono Chul Park.** A 48-acre retreat designed to promote the conservation of arid regions, Tohono Chul—the name means "desert corner" in the language of the Tohono O'odham tribe—uses a demonstration garden, greenhouse, and geology wall to educate visitors about this unique desert area. Enjoy the shady nooks, nature trails, small art gallery, and tearoom (☞ Dining, *below*) at this peaceful spot. ⊠ *7366 N. Paseo del Norte,* ☎ *520/742–6455.* ☜ *$2 suggested donation.* ☺ *Park daily 7 AM–sunset; building Mon.–Sat. 9:30–5, Sun. 11–5.*

⑯ **Tucson Botanical Gardens.** This 5-acre oasis in the center of town includes a tropical greenhouse; a sensory garden, where visitors are encouraged to touch and smell the plants and listen to the abundant birdlife; historical gardens, which display the Mediterranean landscaping that the property's original owners planted in the 1930s; a garden designed to attract birds; and a cactus garden. The grounds are also home to Native Seeds/SEARCH, an organization that helps farmers throughout the Southwest and northern Mexico by collecting, growing, and selling seeds of crops that thrive in arid areas. ⊠ *2150 N. Alvernon Way,* ☎ *520/326–9686.* ☜ *$5.* ☺ *Daily 8:30–4:30.*

OFF THE
BEATEN PATH

BIOSPHERE 2 – In the little town of Oracle, some 45 minutes north of central Tucson, eight people walked into a self-contained, sealed ecosystem in 1992, planning not to come out for two years. The experiment was plagued with problems almost from the start and some of the participants abandoned the project before its end date, but the structure itself remains an interesting phenomenon. Financed by Texas oil billionaire Edward P. Bass, Biosphere 2 is managed by Columbia University's Lamont–Doherty Earth Observatory, which directs all of Biosphere's current scientific, educational, and visitor-center operations.

The miniature world within Biosphere includes tropical rain forest, savanna, desert, thorn scrub, marsh, ocean, and agricultural areas, including almost 4,000 plant and animal species. A film and cutaway model explain the project. Guided walking tours, which last about two hours, don't enter most of the sealed sphere, but the living quarters of the Biospherians are open to the public, and indoor and outdoor observation areas let you peer in at the rest. The Canyon del Oro restaurant, overlooking the Santa Catalina Mountains, has a full menu of sandwiches and hearty entrées; there are also several snack bars. Reasonably priced hotel suites with excellent views are available on Biosphere's premises. ⊠ *AZ 77, mile marker 96.5,* ☎ *520/896–6200 or 800/828–2462.* ☜ *$12.95.* ☺ *Daily 8:30–5; guided tours every ½ hr, 9–4.*

Westside

If you're interested in the flora and fauna of the Sonoran Desert—as well as some of its appearances in the cinema—heed the same advice given the pioneers: Go west.

A Good Tour

From central Tucson, take Speedway Boulevard west; when the houses begin to thin and stands of cacti begin to thicken, you'll see the **International Wildlife Museum** ㉖. Continue west on Speedway to where it joins Anklam Road and becomes Gates Pass Road; at the juncture of Gates Pass and Kinney roads, you'll see signs directing you south to **Old Tucson Studios** ㉗. Return to this juncture and continue north on Kinney Road for about 10 mi until you come to the **Arizona–Sonora Desert Museum** ㉘. It's a short drive farther north along the same road to the Red Hills Information Center, which will introduce you to **Saguaro National Park West** ㉙. Note: The Gates Pass Road can be daunting to a nervous driver and the pass itself is not navigable for large campers, RVs, or cars towing campers. For an alternate route through town, take I–10 to I–19 south to Ajo Road, go west to Kinney Road, and follow the signs. Regardless of which route you choose, take Kinney Road back to I–19 and continue south again. You'll soon come to the turnoff for **Mission San Xavier del Bac** ㉚.

TIMING

Although the attractions in this area are not close together, it's easy to tour all the sights in one day as they're on a fairly direct route to one another. The best plan is to set out in the cooler early morning to Saguaro National Park, which has no shaded areas (it's also the best time to see the wildlife at its liveliest). Spend the rest of the morning at the Desert Museum, where you can have lunch at the Ironwood Terrace (in any case, allow at least two hours for your visit). The hottest time of the afternoon can be spent ducking in and out of attractions at Old Tucson, visiting the air-conditioned International Wildlife Museum, or enjoying the indoor sanctuary of San Xavier Mission.

Sights to See

★ ㉘ **Arizona–Sonora Desert Museum.** The name "museum" is misleading; this delightful site is a beautifully planned zoo and botanical garden featuring the animals and plants of the Sonoran Desert. Hummingbirds, cactus wrens, rattlesnakes, scorpions, bighorn sheep, and prairie dogs all busy themselves in ingeniously designed habitats. An Earth Sciences Center has an artificial limestone cave complete with real bats and a hands-on meteor and mineral display. The coyote exhibit has "invisible" fencing that separates humans from animals. The gift shop carries an impressive selection of books about Arizona and the desert, plus jewelry and crafts. ⊠ *2021 N. Kinney Rd.,* ☎ *520/883–2702.* ⊡ *$8.95.* ☉ *Mar.–Sept., daily 7:30–6; Oct.–Feb., daily 8:30–5. Last ticket sales 1 hr before closing. MC, V.*

☝ ㉖ **International Wildlife Museum.** An imposing turreted structure, this "wildlife" museum has no real life in it at all: 300 species of animals are taxidermed and mounted in re-creations of their natural habitats. A "petting" menagerie allows kids to touch a variety of animal skins; they can also learn about birds and mammals from all over the world via interactive computers. ⊠ *4800 W. Gates Pass Rd.,* ☎ *520/617–1439.* ⊡ *$5.* ☉ *Daily 9–5.*

★ ㉚ **Mission San Xavier del Bac.** The oldest Catholic church in the United States still serving the community for which it was built, San Xavier was founded in 1692 by Father Eusebio Francisco Kino, who established 22 missions in northern Mexico and southern Arizona. The current structure was constructed out of native materials by Franciscan missionaries between 1777 and 1797 and is owned by the Tohono O'odham tribe.

The beauty of the mission, with elements of Spanish, Baroque, and *mudejar* (Spanish Islamic) architectural styles, is highlighted by the stark landscape against which it is set, inspiring an early 20th-century poet to dub it "White Dove of the Desert." Inside, there's a wealth of painted statues, carvings, and frescoes. Paul Schwartzbaum, who helped restore Michelangelo's masterwork in Rome, helped supervise Tohono O'odham artisans in the recent restoration of the mission's artwork; he has called the mission the Sistine Chapel of the United States. Mass is celebrated daily at San Xavier, four times on Sunday morning. Call ahead for information about special celebrations.

Across the parking lot from the mission, **San Xavier Plaza** has a number of Native American crafts shops where you'll find the handiwork of the Tohono O'odham tribe, including jewelry, pottery, friendship bowls, and baskets featuring man-in-the-maze designs. ⊠ *San Xavier Rd., 9 mi southwest of Tucson on I–19,* ☎ *520/294–2624.* ☉ *Church daily 7:30–5:30; gift shop daily 8–5.*

NEED A
BREAK?
For wonderful Indian fry bread—large, round pieces of dough taken fresh from the hot oil and topped with all sorts of delicious possibilities— stop in the **Wa:k Snack Shop** (☎ no phone) at the back of San Xavier Plaza. You can also have breakfast or a Mexican lunch here.

🖐 ㉗ **Old Tucson Studios.** This film set–cum–theme park, seriously damaged by fire in 1995, reopened after a $13 million renovation in early 1997, and many of the adobe structures that were used as movie backdrops (the studio was built for the 1940 motion picture *Arizona*) still stand. Actors in western garb perform and roam the streets talking to visitors, especially children. Kids will enjoy the simulated gunfights, rides, stunt shows, petting farm, and more, while adults might appreciate the screenings of old Westerns and the little-bit-bawdy Grand Palace Hotel's Dance Hall Revue. There are plenty of places to chow down and to buy souvenirs. ⊠ *201 S. Kinney Rd. (inside Tucson Mountain Park),* ☎ *520/883–0100.* ☞ *$14.95.* ☉ *Late Dec.–mid-Apr., daily 9– 7; mid-Apr.–late Dec., daily 10–6.*

★ ㉙ **Saguaro National Park West.** This is the smaller (24,000 acres), more visited section of the national park that flanks Tucson (☞ Saguaro National Park East, *above*). Together the sections are home to the world's largest concentration of the huge saguaro cactus, which is native to the Sonoran Desert and known for its towering height (often 50 ft) and arms that reach out in weird configurations. The cactus is ribbed vertically with accordion-like pleats that expand to store water gathered through its shallow roots during the infrequent desert rain showers. In the springtime (usually April or May), the giant succulent sports a tiny party hat of white blooms. At any time of year, the sight of these kings of the desert ruling over their quiet domain is awe-inspiring.

The slow-growing cacti (they can take up to 15 years to grow 1 ft) are protected by state and federal laws, so enjoy but don't disturb them. In recent years, they have suffered a decline because a decrease in the coyote population has allowed rabbits to proliferate. Rabbits and other small animals nibble at the base of the young saguaro, gathering nutrients and water for survival and thereby hindering or halting the cactus's slow growth.

Before you venture into the desert, it's worth stopping in at the impressive visitor center. A slide show (given every half hour from 8:30 to 4:30) offers a Native American perspective of the saguaro cactus, and a lifelike display simulates the flora and fauna of the region. A loop drive through the park takes ½–2 hours depending on how many stops you make. Ask how to get to Signal Hill, where you can inspect petroglyphs (rock drawings) left by the Hohokam Indians centuries ago. Keep in mind that desert denizens such as snakes and scorpions aren't necessarily hostile unless you crowd them, so just watch your step and respect their habitat. The sun is a more formidable foe; for best protection wear a strong sunscreen on your face and exposed skin at any time of the year, a hat with a minimum four-inch brim, and sunglasses—and don't forget the drinking water. ⊠ *Kinney Rd., 2 mi north of Arizona–Sonora Desert Museum entrance,* ☎ *520/733–5158.* ☞ *Free.* ☉ *Visitor center daily 8:30–5; park roads 6 AM–sunset.*

DINING

Although Tucson's variety of restaurants is impressive, the city doesn't offer much in the way of late-night dining. Most restaurants in town are shuttered by 10 PM. Some spots that keep later hours are noted below.

In addition, two locations of **Coffee, Etc.** (✉ 2830 N. Campbell Ave., ☎ 520/881–8070; ✉ 6091 N. Oracle Rd., ☎ 520/544–8588), with good coffee, a varied menu, and a small gift shop, are open 24 hours.

Northwest Tucson

Continental

$$$$ ✕ **Anthony's.** This is *the* special-occasion restaurant for many Tucsonans. Pink linen, stemmed crystal, pink-rim china, and—on the glassed-in terrace—lighting that precludes seeing your dining companion very well, add to the romantic atmosphere. The view of the city lights and desert are spectacular, and service is uncharacteristically formal for Tucson. Dishes like seafood relleno (an Anaheim chili stuffed with Jack cheese, shrimp, and scallops) and veal Sonoita (sliced veal tenderloin with roasted garlic, sun-dried tomatoes, and goat cheese) put a contemporary spin on the otherwise Continental menu. A nightly pianist draws locals to the cocktail lounge. ✉ *6440 N. Campbell Ave., ☎ 520/ 299–1771. AE, DC, MC, V. Closed for lunch Sat.–Sun.*

French

$$–$$$ ✕ **Café Beaujolais.** Tapestry chairs with wrought-iron ivy designs, pink walls, and the sounds of Mozart or Bach complement the short, classic bistro menu. Mushrooms baked in a puff-pastry shell with a touch of Stilton are a delicious but rich starter; the house salad is crunchy with walnuts and fresh greens. Lamb chops with garlic mashed potatoes are the ultimate in comfort food; the lighter mussels in a white wine and shallot sauce won't disappoint, either. Crème brûlée aficionados will be very happy with the almond-redolent version, which is among the desserts, all made in house. ✉ *5931 N. Oracle Rd., ☎ 520/887–7359. AE, D, MC, V. No lunch weekends.*

Southwestern

$$$–$$$$ ✕ **Café Terra Cotta.** Everything about this restaurant says Southwest— from the decor, with its bright pastels and bleached woods, to the contemporary art, to the food—including modern Southwest specialties such as chicken breast in goat cheese, chiles relleno, pork tenderloin with black beans, and pizza with artichokes and herbed mozzarella. This is the ultimate casual yet classy place to dine, for natives and their out-of-town guests. ✉ *St. Philip's Plaza, 4310 N. Campbell Ave., ☎ 520/577–8100. AE, D, DC, MC, V.*

$$–$$$$ ✕ **Wildflower Grill.** A fresh, bright, and contemporary looking restaurant, this has quickly become known for its creative American fare. Seasonal wild mushrooms topping angel hair pasta create a smoky and substantial meal, while the grilled New York strip steak cries for an accompaniment from the Martini Menu. One of the most popular items on the menu is meat loaf and mashed potatoes. Saturday brunch on the brick patio is a fine treat, fresh in the cool of a spring morning or warmed by spot heaters in winter. ✉ *7037 N. Oracle Rd., ☎ 520/219– 4230. AE, D, DC, MC, V.*

$ ✕ **Tohono Chul Tea Room.** The food is fine, but what's unique here is the setting: The tearoom is nestled in a wildlife sanctuary and surrounded by a cactus garden. Although the interior is typically southwestern, with Mexican tile and light wood and a cobblestone patio, the menu covers southwestern, Mexican, and American dishes. House favorites include seafood corn chowder served with bread and scones baked on the premises, and chicken enchiladas with Monterey Jack cheese, corn, and green chilies. Open daily 8 to 5, the Tea Room has an excellent Sunday brunch—which can mean long waits in high season. ✉ *7366 N. Paseo del Norte, ☎ 520/797–1222. AE, MC, V. No dinner.*

Tucson Dining and Lodging

Dining

Anthony's, **11**

Arizona Inn
Restaurant, **25**

Athens, **32**

Beyond Bread, **18**

Café Beaujolais, **5**

Café Poca Cosa, **35**

Café Terra Cotta, **12**

Cottonwood Cafe, **42**

El Charro Café, **33**

El Minuto Café, **34**

Elle, **38**

Firecracker, **45**

Govinda, **16**

The Grill at Hacienda
del Sol, **14**

Janos at La
Paloma, **15**

Kingfisher Bar and
Grill, **22**

La Fuente, **28**

Le Bistro, **20**

Le Mediterranean, **60**

Le Rendez-vous, **44**

Mariscos
Chihuahua, **29**

New Delhi Palace, **52**

Nonie, **21**

Olive Tree, **57**

Pastiche, **19**

Pinnacle Peak
Steakhouse, **56**

Presidio Grill, **40**

Rancher's Club, **49**

Sakura, **55**

Seri Melaka, **51**

South 4th Avenue, **37**

Tack Room, **59**

Tohono Chul Tea
Room, **1**

Ventana Room, **48**

Vivace, **46**

Wildflower Grill, **4**

Zemam, **39**

Lodging

Adobe Rose Inn, **27**

Arizona Inn, **25**

Best Western Ghost Ranch Lodge, **17**

Canyon Ranch, **61**

Casa Alegre, **65**

Casa Tierra, **23**

Catalina Park Inn, **31**

Clarion Santa Rita, **35**

Cliff Manor Inn, **10**

Doubletree Hotel, **43**

Embassy Suites Tucson-Broadway, **50**

Hacienda del Sol, **14**

Hotel Congress, **36**

Inn Suites Hotel & Resort, **30**

La Tierra Linda Guest Ranch Resort, **24**

Lazy K Bar Guest Ranch, **47**

Loews Ventana Canyon Resort, **48**

Marriott University Park, **64**

Miraval, **9**

Omni Tucson National Golf & Spa resort, **3**

Peppertrees B&B Inn, **63**

Plaza Hotel and Conference Center, **26**

Ramada Inn Foothills, **58**

Sheraton Tucson El Conquistador, **7**

Smugglers Inn, **54**

Tanque Verde Ranch, **62**

Triangle L Ranch Bed & Breakfast, **8**

Tucson Hilton East, **53**

Varsity Clubs of America, **41**

Westin La Paloma, **15**

Westward Look Resort, **5**

White Stallion Ranch, **2**

Windmill Inn at St. Phillip's Plaza, **13**

Downtown Tucson and 4th Avenue

Greek

$$–$$$ ✕ **Athens.** A Greek oasis of tranquillity off bustling 4th Avenue, Athens creates a serene Mediterranean atmosphere with lace curtains, wooden wainscoting, white stucco walls, and potted plants. Order a dish of creamy *taramasalata* (Greek caviar) followed by *kotopoulo stin pita* (grilled chicken breast with a yogurt-cucumber sauce on fresh-baked pita). If it's Greek comfort food you're after, order the moussaka or the *pastitsio* (a pasta-, meat-, and béchamel-filled lasagna). The house favorite is braised lamb shoulder in red wine sauce over pasta—call to reserve your order ahead of time. ⊠ *500 N. 4th Ave., No. 6,* ☏ *520/624–6886. AE, D, DC, MC, V. Closed Sun. No lunch.*

Mexican

$$–$$$ ✕ **La Fuente.** Frank Davis owns and hosts at this family-run restaurant, long a staple of Tucson nightlife. The fairly plain exterior belies the extravagant gardenlike interior that bursts with color, plants, light, and the sound of mariachis nightly. Diners can enjoy tradtional Sonoran cuisine, including sea bass yucatan style and enchiladas *á la bandera*, with one green (guacamole), one white (sour cream), and one red (chili) representing the Mexican flag. For the adventurous, chicken molé poblano—with a spicy, dark sauce based on nuts and chocolate—is an authentic New World dish. ⊠ *1749 N. Oracle Rd.,* ☏ *520/623–3659. AE, DC, MC, V.*

$$ ✕ **Mariscos Chihuahua.** A brightly lit, cheerful, and scrupulously clean setting greets the Tucsonans who come here looking for a change of pace in Mexican restaurants. This one specializes in fresh, by which they mean uncooked, seafood cocktails. *Tostadas ceviche* style loads diced seafood atop a corn tortilla, with plenty of salsa to spice it up. There is a sizable menu of well-prepared cooked seafood as well, highlighted by the Seven Seas Soup with all manner of fish and shellfish, and by the *camarones al mojo de ajo* (shrimp sautéed in garlic). The place has no liquor license, but there is a significant crowd noon and night. ⊠ *1009 N. Grande Ave.,* ☏ *520/623–3563. No credit cards.*

$–$$$ ✕ **El Charro Café.** Started by Monica Flin in 1922 and run by her grandniece and her grandniece's husband today, El Charro still serves excellent versions of the American-Mexican staples Flin claims to have originated—chimichangas (flour tortillas filled with seasoned beef or chicken and deep-fried) and cheese crisps, most notably. Daily "fitness-fare" specials such as seafood enchiladas are delicious as well as healthful. Those in the mood for meat must try a *carne asada* (dried beef) chimichanga, not only because the meat is jerked on premises—on the roof, actually—but because it tastes so good. The adjacent *Toma!* bar serves appetizers and drinks inside or out, and the little shop squeezed between is a great place for regional gifts. ⊠ *311 N. Court Ave.,* ☏ *520/622–1922. AE, D, DC, MC, V.*

$–$$ ✕ **Café Poca Cosa.** Forgoing the cheese-heavy Sonoran standbys fa-
★ miliar to Americans, chef-owner Susana Davila creates exciting recipes inspired by different regions of her native Mexico, at what is arguably Tucson's most innovative Mexican restaurant. The menu, which changes daily, might include *pollo à mole* (chicken in a spicy chocolate-based sauce) or pork *pibil* (made with a tangy Yucatan barbecue seasoning). Servings are plentiful, and each table gets a stack of warm corn tortillas and a bowl of beans to share. Order the daily Plato Poca Cosa, and the chef will select one beef, one chicken, and one vegetarian entrée for you to sample. The tiny original restaurant across the street (⊠ 20 S. Scott Ave.), also a lively treat, is open for breakfast and lunch during the week. ⊠ *88 E. Broadway, beside the Clarion Santa Rita,* ☏ *520/622–6400. Reservations essential. MC, V. Closed Sun.*

$–$$ ✗ **El Minuto Café.** This brightly decorated, bustling restaurant in Tucson's historic barrio is where local families come to eat; it's a good bet for those seeking a late meal downtown. Open until midnight Friday and Saturday and 10 PM the rest of the week, it is equally popular with the business crowd at lunch. In business for more than 50 years, El Minuto serves up *topopo* salads (a variety of goodies, including guacamole, heaped into a crispy tortilla shell); huge burritos; and green corn tamales (in season) made just right. The spicy *menudo* is a great hangover remedy (just don't ask what's in it). ⊠ *354 S. Main Ave.,* ☎ *520/882–4145. AE, D, DC, MC, V.*

South Tucson

Mexican

$–$$ **South 4th Avenue.** Every Tucsonan you meet will argue the merits of a favorite "real" Mexican restaurant, but invariably it's on or near 4th Avenue in South Tucson. South Tucson is a separate, incorporated city surrounded by City of Tucson. It has a predominantly Mexican-American population and thus many authentic and inexpensive places to find good south-of-the-border cuisine. Among the most popular are **Crossroads** (⊠ 2602 S. 4th Ave., ☎ 520/624–0395), **Gran Guadalajara** (⊠ 2527 S. 4th Ave., ☎ 520/620–1321), **Guillermo's Double L** (⊠ 1830 S. 4th Ave., ☎ 520/792–1585), **Micha's** (⊠ 2908 S. 4th Ave., ☎ 520/623–5307), and **Mi Nidito** (⊠ 1813 S. 4th Ave., ☎ 520/622–5081), all open for both lunch and dinner. You'd be hard-pressed to have a bad meal—or a bad time—at any of these friendly, informal places. Many have mariachi bands on the weekends. MasterCard and Visa are accepted at most.

Central Tucson

American

$$–$$$ ✗ **Kingfisher Bar and Grill.** Kingfisher has drawn well deserved critical kudos and a loyal local following. The restaurant's regional American cuisine dazzles much of the time, in a chic setting—low lighting, bright turquoise colors, and neon contrasting with warm brick walls and black banquettes. The innovative menu, which changes seasonally, relies heavily on its good variety of seafood, including soft-shell crab, that is flown in fresh. You might also find mesquite-grilled pork loin chops or crawfish étouffée on the menu. From 10 to midnight, choose from a menu of soups, salads, burgers, and selections from the oyster bar. ⊠ *2564 E. Grant Rd.,* ☎ *520/323–7739. AE, D, DC, MC, V. No lunch weekends.*

American Casual

$ ✗ **Beyond Bread.** This bakery and sandwich place hasn't seen a quiet moment since it opened. Fran's Fromage—brie, lettuce, and tomato on a baguette—or Brad's Beef—roast beef, provolone, onion, green chilies, and Russian dressing on white bread—are wonderfully satisfying meals. Eat inside or on the patio, or order take-out and munch on free bread and butter while you wait. ⊠ *3055 N. Campbell Ave.,* ☎ *520/322–9965,* FAX *520/322–9938. AE, D, MC, V. Closed Sun. after 3 PM; evenings after 6:30 PM.*

Cajun/Creole

$–$$ ✗ **Nonie.** Owned by Elmore Leonard's son, Chris, who named it for his grandmother, this has the the flamboyant style of a New Orleans restaurant with the good food to match. Add friendly, fast service and a hopping dose of Cajun music, and you get the idea. The delicate trout amandine is about as staid as this place ever gets; the crawfish étoufée packs a punch and is more raucously characteristic. It may be hard to

leave room for dessert, but the pecan pie and bread pudding are outstanding. ⊠ *2526 E. Grant Rd.,* ☎ *520/319–1965. AE, MC, V. Closed
Mon. No lunch Sat. or Sun.*

Chinese

$–$$$ ✕ **Firecracker.** Straddling the narrow gulf between Chinese and Pacific
rim fare, this spot enjoys great popularity with lively, youngish patrons
who appreciate fine food. The moo-shu duck with plum-balsamic
glaze and potstickers makes for a flavorful opening. Fireworks chicken
with red chilies and red peppers is zesty but not overpoweringly hot,
and the Mongolian beef is stir-fried to perfection. Bananas Firecracker
(Foster to the rest of us) or madacamia nut tart is a fitting end to a
meal. ⊠ *2990 N. Swan Rd.,* ☎ *520/318–1118. AE, D, MC, V. No
lunch Sat. or Sun.*

Contemporary

$$$–$$$$ ✕ **Elle.** A self-described "wine country restaurant" with French, Ital-
ian, and California influences, this place opened in October '98 in a
shopping center (the first in Tucson) called Historic Broadway Village.
In a wide-open room with contemporary furniture and slate floors, enjoy
the earthy risotto with wild duck and porcini mushrooms or the pork
chop with roasted shallots. Sitting at the edge of several tony residen-
tial areas, this has become the neighborhood restaurant for many lo-
cals. ⊠ *3048 E. Broadway,* ☎ *520/327–0500. AE, DC, MC, V. Closed
Sun. No lunch Sat.*

$$–$$$ ✕ **Pastiche.** Chic and contemporary but still formal enough for linen
tablecloths, this is a nice addition to a street of mostly fast-food venues.
Blackened ahi with mango relish is one of their best dishes, as is the
seafood Newburg served over light, mile-high biscuits. The chef's fa-
vorite is grilled duck breast with chili plum sauce. ⊠ *3025 N. Camp-
bell Ave.,* ☎ *520/325–3333. AE, D, DC, MC, V. No lunch weekends.*

Continental

$$$–$$$$ ✕ **Arizona Inn Restaurant.** Sit out on the patio overlooking the grounds
of this historic inn (☞ Lodging, *below*), or enjoy the view through huge
windows in the dining room, a light, airy place with 1930s southwestern
details. The fire that warms the room on chilly evenings sets the per-
fect stage for veal Oscar. Or you might try steamed fish of the day, served
with ginger and leeks, or the mesquite-smoked quail. Locals come in
for Sunday brunch or a civilized afternoon high tea in the library
(Thanksgiving through Easter only). There is no dress code, but men
will likely feel most comfortable in a jacket. ⊠ *2200 E. Elm St.,* ☎
520/325–1541. AE, MC, V.

Ethiopian

$ ✕ **Zemam.** It can be hard to get a table in this tiny eatery, a favorite
★ with locals. The sampler plate of any three items allows you to try such
dishes as *yesimir wat* (a spicy lentil-based dish), and *zigni* (a milder
beef dish with a tomato sauce). Most of the food has a stewlike con-
sistency; don't come if you feel the need to crunch. Everything is served
on a communal platter topped with *injera,* a spongy bread, and eaten
with the hands. Prices are ridiculously low, considering the food qual-
ity and quantity, and alcohol is bring your own. ⊠ *2731 E. Broad-
way,* ☎ *520/323–9928. Reservations not accepted. MC, V. Closed Mon.*

French

$$$–$$$$ ✕ **Le Rendez-vous.** There is nothing nouvelle about this very traditional
and expensive French restaurant. The chef prepares duck à l'orange
as crispy as it should be, and there are tender veal sweetbreads. A spa
menu and bistro menu are available for those watching their weight
or their wallets. The lunch menu is wide ranging and moderately

priced. ✉ *3844 E. Ft. Lowell Rd.,* ☎ *520/323–7373. AE, D, DC, MC, V. Closed Mon. No lunch weekends.*

$$–$$$ ✕ **Le Bistro.** An Impressionist-style mural beckons you into one of the
★   prettiest restaurants in town. Potted palms tower over tables covered with chic burgundy-and-black cloths splashed with pink flowers, and art nouveau–etched mirrors grace the walls. The elegant setting is matched by the creations of chef-owner Laurent Reux, a young Breton whose fish and shellfish dishes are inspired by his native region. House specialties include salmon in a ginger crust with lime butter, a delicate sea bass, and Long Island duck in a raspberry vinaigrette. Lunch is reasonably priced. ✉ *2574 N. Campbell Ave.,* ☎ *502/327–3086. AE, D, MC, V. No lunch weekends.*

Indian

$–$$ ✕ **New Delhi Palace: Cuisine of India.** Vegetarians, carnivores, and seafood lovers will all find something to enjoy at this elegant Indian restaurant. The congenial staff is helpful in explaining the menu, which features a wide variety of tandoori dishes, curries, rice, and breads. The "heat" of each dish can be adjusted to individual preference by the chef. ✉ *6751 E. Broadway,* ☎ *520/296–8585. AE, DC, MC, V.*

Italian

$$–$$$ ✕ **Vivace.** Daniel Scordato has had his hand in some of the best Ital-
★   ian restaurants in town, and his latest venture fills up with a tony crowd most every night in high season. The interior is industrial chic—gray columns, black iron chairs, open kitchen—but this is still Arizona, which means the black-and-white–clad servers are not SoHo frosty to match. Appetizers are pricey compared with the rest of the menu, though the grilled shrimp in a phyllo cup with tomato, basil, and garlic sauce is hard to resist. For a lighter alternative to such dishes as rich osso buco, try the linguine with grilled salmon. One caveat: The room can get noisy. ✉ *4811 E. Grant Rd., Suite 155,* ☎ *520/795–7221. AE, D, MC, V. No lunch Sun.*

Malaysian

$–$$ ✕ **Seri Melaka.** Malaysian food, like Thai, uses curry, coconut, and other tasty condiments in its sauces. This east side spot has good *satay* (grilled meat on a skewer with peanut sauce) and *lemak* (shrimp or chicken with vegetables in a sweet curry sauce), as well as a variety of well-prepared Chinese dishes. There's a daily lunch buffet and early bird dinner specials weekdays from 4:30 to 6. ✉ *6133 E. Broadway,* ☎ *520/747–7811. AE, D, DC, MC, V.*

Southwestern

$$$–$$$$ ✕ **Presidio Grill.** But for the organ pipe cacti flanking the window, you might think you were in a chic New York eatery with stylish black booths, Art Deco room dividers, and brightly painted girders. The menu, how-ever, has definite southwestern flair. Dinner entrées include chicken Santa Fe, served with black beans, flour tortillas, grilled scallions, and two types of salsa; and prickly pear marinated pork tenderloin with sesame noodles. Across the street from an art cinema in the university area, this popular singles destination is open late (for Tucson) on weekends. ✉ *3352 E. Speedway Blvd.,* ☎ *520/327–4667. AE, MC, V.*

$$–$$$ ✕ **Cottonwood Cafe.** Almost every evening this 1920s hacienda-style complex bustles with folks checking out its hip Southwest scene (which, atypically for Tucson, continues until the witching hour). Rooms are decorated to the tee, with subtle earth tones, distressed-metal sconces, and smooth leather-backed chairs. The grilled calamari appetizer, served with a tangy tapenade, might be followed by lime ancho chicken with grilled peppers and flour tortillas; the chef is into smoked chilies, so their flavor pervades most dishes. The margaritas are as good as

the servers claim. ⊠ *60 N. Alvernon Way,* ☎ *520/326–6000. AE, D, DC, MC, V.*

Steak House

$$$–$$$$ ✕ **Rancher's Club.** Four wood-burning grills are the key to the success
★ of this upscale western-style restaurant, with its mounted animal heads, sidesaddles, and dark wood. The attentive staff will help you choose the right timber—different woods impart different flavors—for your taste buds: Mesquite is offered every day, and hickory, sassafras, and wild cherry alternate during the week. Sauces, butters, and condiments offer more traditional flavorings for the excellent and equally large steaks (sharing is encouraged) and lobster. Local movers and shakers like to gather here for lunch. ⊠ *5151 E. Grant Rd. in the Sheraton,* ☎ *520/321–7621. AE, D, DC, MC, V. Closed Sun. No lunch Sat.*

Vegetarian

$ ✕ **Govinda.** One of the few places in town with a strictly nonmeat menu, this Hare Krishna–run restaurant has reasonably priced all-you-can-eat lunch and dinner buffets that include vegan options. Hot and cold dishes vary daily, but ingredients are consistently fresh and the food is tasty, if not spicy. Choose from three seating areas including an outdoor patio with a snack bar where you can hear the squawks of the resident peacocks. No alcohol is served or permitted. ⊠ *711 E. Blacklidge Dr.,* ☎ *520/792–0630. Reservations not accepted. MC, V. Closed Sun. and Mon. No lunch Tues.*

Northeast Tucson

Continental

$$$–$$$$ ✕ **Ventana Room.** This dining room in the Loews Ventana Canyon Resort (☞ Lodging, *below*) is a triumph of understated elegance: muted colors, low ceilings, and spectacular views—either of the lights of Tucson or the towering waterfall on the property. The contemporary Continental menu, which changes seasonally, has a California-inspired emphasis on lower-fat, lower-cholesterol preparation. Popular à la carte entrées include a buffalo tenderloin and seared ahi tuna, and there's a five-course chef's tasting menu ($55). Jackets are not required, but men may feel more comfortable wearing one. ⊠ *7000 N. Resort Dr.,* ☎ *520/299–2020. AE, D, DC, MC, V. No lunch.*

Mediterranean

$$–$$$$ ✕ **Le Mediterranean.** Pleasant enough in a pastel contemporary mode, the subdued decor gives little hint of the exotic fare on the menu. In addition to Greek dishes like moussaka and lamb kebab, Middle Eastern specialties, such as *shawarma* (beef marinated with tahini sauce) and falafel are available, and the portions are hefty. The smoky-flavored *baba ghanoush* (mashed eggplant) appetizer, for example, comes with a mound of olives, carrots, and radishes. On weekends, a belly dancer livens up the otherwise nondescript dining room. ⊠ *4955 N. Sabino Canyon Rd.,* ☎ *520/529–1330. AE, D, DC, MC, V. Closed Mon. No lunch.*

Southwestern

$$$$ ✕ **Janos at La Paloma.** Chef Janos Wilder was one of the first to rein-
★ vent southwestern cuisine, at his former location downtown. His move to the Westin La Paloma (☞ Lodging, *below*) in the foothills, in the fall of 1998, has only served to expand his culinary horizons. The hillside setting enhances the hacienda's views of the desert, and city lights provide a sparkling backdrop. Among starters, the brie and exotic mushroom relleno (stuffed chile pepper) and the rabbit loin with black bean and roasted corn relish are standouts. Main courses include salmon

with crayfish tails in anise-scented lobster broth, and a venison chop with chorizo-tortilla casserole. The menu, wine list, and service place Janos among the west's finest restaurants. ⊠ *3800 E. Sunrise Dr.,* ☎ *520/615–6100. AE, DC, MC, V. Closed Sun. No lunch.*

$$$$ ✕ **Tack Room.** If the award-winning food and the romantic setting in an elegant old adobe can take your mind off the overly fussy service and the stagnant menu, then it's still worth coming here for a dress-up splurge. Dark-wood beams and furnishings and a blue-and-maroon color scheme are complemented by the dusty-rose linen, and southwestern landscapes by local artists hang on the walls. Arizona four-pepper steak flavored with chilies is a favorite, as are the herb-crusted veal chop and the rack of lamb for two, prepared with mesquite honey, cilantro, and southwestern limes. ⊠ *7300 E. Vactor Ranch Trail,* ☎ *520/722–2800. AE, D, DC, MC, V. Closed Mon., mid-May–mid-Dec., and 1st 2 wks of July. No lunch.*

$$$–$$$$ ✕ **The Grill at Hacienda del Sol.** Opened in 1997, this hotel restaurant (☞ Lodging, *below*) provides a welcome alternative to the chili-laden dishes of southwestern nouvelle cuisine. The roasted garlic, hazelnut, and chèvre tart in puff pastry with Anjou vinaigrette blends disparate flavors admirably. Likewise, the roast pork, cioppino, and other continental entrées take you as far from the Southwest as food alone allows. ⊠ *5601 N. Hacienda del Sol Rd.,* ☎ *520/529–3500. AE, DC, MC, V.*

Eastside

Greek

$$–$$$$ ✕ **Olive Tree.** In an appealing Santa Fe–style building, the Olive Tree serves up fine versions of such Greek standards as moussaka, shish kebab, and stuffed grape leaves, but it has more unusual dishes on its menu as well. The Lamb Bandit is baked in foil with two types of cheese, potatoes, and vegetables. Daily fresh-fish specials are broiled or sautéed in garlic, oregano, and olive oil and served with a well-prepared orzo. This is not light cuisine. If you don't have room for supersweet baklava, a cup of strong Greek coffee makes for a satisfying finish. ⊠ *7000 E. Tanque Verde Rd.,* ☎ *520/298–1845. AE, DC, MC, V. No lunch Sun.*

Japanese

$$ ✕ **Sakura.** Located in the lively "restaurant row" of Tanque Verde Road, this spot really holds its own. Many diners opt for the showmanlike atmosphere provided by the expert teppan chefs who slice, dice, and keep up the pace of humor. This is the best sushi in town and if you're really hungry, you can step up to the sushi bar and tackle the "boat" of raw fish. For the more tame, there are the ever-appealing California rolls or chicken teriyaki. ⊠ *7000 E. Tanque Verde Rd.,* ☎ *520/ 298–7777. AE, DC, MC, V. No lunch Sun.*

Steak House

$–$$ ✕ **Pinnacle Peak Steakhouse.** Anybody caught eating fish tacos or cactus jelly in this pre-nouvelle atmosphere would probably be hanged from the rafters—along with all the ties snipped from loco city slickers. This is a cowboy steak house where excellent mesquite-broiled steak comes with salad and pinto beans. For dessert, try the hot apple cobbler with vanilla ice cream. The restaurant is part of Trail Dust Town, a re-creation of a turn-of-the-century town, complete with cancan girls, a barbershop quartet, souvenir shops, and an old-time photographer's studio. Gunfights are staged in the street outside Tuesday through Saturday at 7 and 8 PM; any night of the week, arrive early in the evening to avoid a long wait for a table. ⊠ *6541 E. Tanque Verde Rd.,* ☎ *520/ 296–0911. Reservations not accepted. AE, D, DC, MC, V. No lunch.*

LODGING

You'll find a dazzling array of lodging options in Tucson, from glitzy resorts and modern hotels to low-key dude ranches, historic inns, and cozy Victorian bed-and-breakfasts.

The **Arizona Association of Bed and Breakfast Inns** (✉ Box 7186, Phoenix 85012, ☎ 800/284–2589) provides referrals to member inns in the area. Seven of the larger, more professionally run inns in town have formed **Premier Bed & Breakfast Inns of Tucson** (✉ 316 E. Speedway Blvd., 85705, ☎ 520/628–1800 or 800/628–5654, 𝖥𝖠𝖷 520/792–1880). Write or call for a brochure. **Old Pueblo HomeStays RSO** (✉ Box 13603, Tucson 85732, ☎ 𝖥𝖠𝖷 520/790–2399 or 800/333–9776) specializes in smaller, more casual bed-and-breakfasts in Arizona and northern Mexico.

Summer rates—April 15 through October 1—are up to 60% lower than those in the winter, and savvy visitors can get bargains if they don't mind visiting during the warmer weather. Note: Unless you book months in advance, you'll be hard-pressed to find a hotel room at any price in Tucson the week before and during the huge gem and mineral show (usually in February).

Unless otherwise indicated, price categories for guest ranches include all meals and most activities.

Northwest Tucson

$$$$ 🏨 **Miraval.** This newcomer 20 mi north of Tucson is giving Canyon
★ Ranch (☞ Northeast Tucson, *below*) a run for its money with a secluded desert setting, beautiful southwestern rooms, and myriad wellness programs, many of them based on Eastern philosophies. Some of the "mindfulness" exercises may strike you as a bit odd—especially the "Equine Experience" or horse therapy (for you, not the horse)—but you'll come away with useful relaxation and meditation techniques. Meals, including tasty buffets (calories and fat content noted, of course), and tips are included. ✉ *5000 E. Via Estancia Miraval, Catalina 85739,* ☎ *520/825–4000 or 800/825–4000,* 𝖥𝖠𝖷 *520/792–5870. 106 rooms. 2 restaurants, bar, 3 pools, spa, 2 tennis courts, croquet, exercise room, horseback riding, bicycles. FAP. AE, D, DC, MC, V.*

$$$$ 🏨 **Omni Tucson National Golf & Spa Resort.** Perfect for couples with separate sybaritic interests, Tucson National is both one of the premier golf resorts in the Southwest (it hosts the Tucson Chrysler Classic) *and* a full-service European-style spa, where you can be coiffed, waxed, wrapped, worked over, and scrubbed to your heart's content. It's smaller than most of Tucson's major resorts but closer to sightseeing and shopping destinations in town. Oddly, of the six levels of accommodations available, the most expensive (hacienda) are the least attractive. ✉ *2727 W. Club Dr., 85741,* ☎ *520/297–2271 or 800/528–4856,* 𝖥𝖠𝖷 *520/297–7544. 167 rooms. 3 restaurants, 2 bars, 2 pools, beauty salon, spa, 27-hole golf course, 4 lighted tennis courts, basketball, exercise room, volleyball. AE, D, DC, MC, V.*

$$$$ 🏨 **Westward Look Resort.** Built as a residence by William and Mary Watson in 1912, this property was converted to a guest ranch in the 1920s, then to a resort in 1943. The lobby is the Watsons' traditionally Southwest-style living room, but the couple probably never envisioned amenities like the New Age wellness center. Guest rooms are done in earthy olive, terra-cotta, and rust tones, with comfy leather chairs, wrought-iron beds, and mission-style furniture; all rooms have coffeemakers. The hotel's fine dining room serves innovative American fare, including ostrich. ✉ *245 E. Ina Rd., 85704,* ☎ *520/297–1151*

or 800/722–2500, FAX 520/297–9023. 236 rooms, 8 suites. 2 restaurants, 3 pools, 3 spas, 8 tennis courts, exercise room, horseback riding, mountain bikes, shops. AE, D, DC, MC, V.

$$$–$$$$ ⊡ **Sheraton Tucson El Conquistador.** You'll know you're in the South-
★ west when you enter the lobby of this golf and tennis resort with its huge copper mural filled with cowboys and cacti, and a wide-window view of the rugged Santa Catalina Mountains. This friendly Sheraton draws families and conventioneers as well as locals, who take advantage of lower summer rates for the excellent sports facilities. Rooms, either in private casitas or the main hotel building, have stylish light-wood furniture with tinwork, pastel-tone spreads and curtains, and balconies or patios (some suites have kiva-shape fireplaces). ⊠ 10000 N. Oracle Rd., 85737, ☎ 520/544–5000 or 800/325–3525, FAX 520/544–1224. 428 rooms. 4 restaurants, piano bar, 4 pools, sauna, one 9-hole and two 18-hole golf courses, 31 tennis courts, basketball, 2 exercise rooms, horseback riding, racquetball, volleyball, bicycles. AE, D, DC, MC, V.

$$$ ⊡ **Westin La Paloma.** Vying with the Sheraton and Loews Ventana for
★ convention business, this sprawling pink resort offers views of the Catalina Mountains above and the city below. It specializes in relaxation: Its golf, fitness, and beauty centers are top-notch and its huge pool has Arizona's longest resort water slide and a swim-up bar and grill for those who can't bear to leave the water. On-site child care and adults- and kids-only pools make for a vacation the whole family will enjoy. Service is excellent all around. ⊠ 3800 E. Sunrise Dr., 85718, ☎ 520/742–6000, FAX 520/577–5878. 487 rooms. 4 restaurants, 2 bars, 3 pools, beauty salon, 3 hot tubs, 27-hole golf course, 12 tennis courts, aerobics, croquet, exercise room, jogging, racquetball, volleyball, business services. AE, D, DC, MC, V.

$$–$$$$ ⊡ **Hacienda del Sol.** This 32-acre facility in the Santa Catalina foothills
★ is part guest ranch, part resort, and entirely gracious. Designed by Josias Joesler, a locally renowned architect, this former finishing school for girls attracted stars—among them Katharine Hepburn and Spencer Tracy—when it was converted to a guest ranch during World War II. Some of the one- and two-bedroom casitas have fireplaces and private porches looking out on the Tucson Mountains. Relaxing activities include yoga, massage, and naturalist-led walks. A lower-priced alternative to larger resorts, this property opened The Grill at Hacienda del Sol (☞ Dining, above) in 1997. ⊠ 5601 N. Hacienda del Sol Rd., 85718, ☎ 520/299–1501, FAX 520/299–5554. 22 rooms, 8 suites. Restaurant, pool, hot tub, tennis court, horseback riding, library. AE, D, MC, V.

$$–$$$$ ⊡ **La Tierra Linda Guest Ranch Resort.** Off a quiet dirt road in the desert, this family-run ranch stands on 30 acres adjacent to Saguaro National Park West. Its adobe casitas, built in the 1930s, have been completely renovated and furnished in typical Southwest style. Accomodations range from double rooms to two-bedroom suites; guests enjoy complimentary breakfast (lunch and dinner are available but not included with the room rate). Riding and hiking trails lead right into the park, and a stable with wranglers offers horseback riding and roping instruction, hayrides, and even cattle drives. ⊠ 7501 N. Wade Rd., 85743, ☎ 520/744–7700, FAX 520/579–9742. 6 rooms, 9 suites. Restaurant, bar, refrigerators, pool, outdoor hot tub, tennis court, hiking, horseback riding, meeting room. AE, D, MC, V.

$$–$$$$ ⊡ **Lazy K Bar Guest Ranch.** In the Tucson Mountains, 16 mi northwest of town at an altitude of 2,300 ft, this family-oriented guest ranch accommodates both greenhorns and more experienced riders. Guest rooms are in eight casitas, or cottages. Those in the older structures, made of Mexican stucco, have fireplaces and wood-beam ceilings; rooms in the newer, adobe-brick buildings are larger and more

modern. ✉ *8401 N. Scenic Dr., 85743,* ☎ *520/744–3050 or 800/321–7018,* ℻ *520/744–7628. 23 rooms. Pool, library. FAP. AE, D, MC, V. 3-night minimum stay.*

$$ 🏨 **Triangle L Ranch Bed & Breakfast.** Buffalo Bill was among the regular visitors to Triangle L, which was built in the 1880s. Cottages are scattered about the property's 80 acres. Co-owner Tom Beeston repairs stringed instruments (there's an amazing collection on the premises) and allows guests a peek inside his studio. The ranch, near Biosphere 2 (☞ Exploring Tucson, *above*) and Catalina State Park, is a birdwatcher's paradise: Songbirds, hawks, ravens, and quail abound. ✉ *2805 N. Triangle L Ranch Rd., Box 900 (about a 45-min drive north of Tucson), Oracle 85623,* ☎ *520/896–2804 or 888/782–9572. 4 private cottages. Continental breakfast. D, MC, V.*

$$ 🏨 **White Stallion Ranch.** Lovers of old Westerns might find this set-
★ ting vaguely familiar: Scenes from the movie *High Chaparral* were shot on this site surrounded by 3,000 acres of mountain desert. The True family—Cynthia, Russell, and Michael—has run the guest ranch for almost 30 years, giving it a homey feel in spite of its 3,000 acres. Large groups are easily accommodated on horseback rides, mountain trail hikes, and cookouts; there's even a weekend rodeo. Peacocks roam the grounds, and children will enjoy the petting zoo's llamas, potbellied pigs, and miniature horses. Renovations in 1998 added an outdoor dining area and two deluxe suites, but most rooms retain their original western furniture. All rooms lack phones and TVs, ensuring a clean getaway for solace-seeking city folk. The room rate is based on a seven-night or longer stay. ✉ *9251 W. Twin Peaks Rd., 85743,* ☎ *520/297–0252 or 888/977–2624,* ℻ *520/744–2786. 32 rooms, 13 suites. Bar, pool, hot tub, 2 tennis courts, basketball, horseback riding, Ping-Pong, shuffleboard, volleyball, billiards. FAP. No credit cards. Closed May–Sept.*

$$ 🏨 **Windmill Inn at St. Philip's Plaza.** This all-suite hotel is in a chic shop-
★ ping plaza filled with glitzy boutiques and good restaurants (☞ Café Terra Cotta *in* Dining, *above*). Each suite has a sitting area, microwave, wet bar, two TVs, three telephones (local calls are free), hair dryer, and iron. A few dollars extra will buy you a view of the pool rather than the parking lot. Complimentary coffee, muffins, and a newspaper are delivered to your door. It's a good deal for the price and centrally located, to boot. ✉ *4250 N. Campbell Ave., 85718,* ☎ *520/577–0007 or 800/547–4747,* ℻ *520/577–0045. 122 suites. Minibars, pool, bicycles, library, laundry. Continental breakfast. AE, D, DC, MC, V.*

$ 🏨 **Cliff Manor Inn.** This unassuming hotel is a nice jumping-off point for hiking, birding, or day trips to the north, and a handy spot when visiting family on the northwest side of Tucson. The hotel offers pleasant, but not overwhelming amenities, and Oracle Road abounds with fine restaurants, two nearby malls, and a movie theater. ✉ *5900 N. Oracle Rd., 85704,* ☎ *520/887–4800,* ℻ *520/292–9861. 61 rooms, 11 casitas. Kitchenettes, pool, nightclub. AE, D, MC, V.*

West of Tucson

$$ 🏨 **Casa Tierra.** For a real desert experience, head out to this bed-and-
★ breakfast on 5 acres near the Arizona–Sonora Desert Museum and Saguaro National Park West. For the last 1½ mi you'll be on a dirt road. All rooms have private baths and private patio entrances and look out onto a lovely central courtyard with a paloverde tree and desert foliage. The southwestern-style furnishings include Mexican *equipales* (chairs with pigskin seats), tiled floors, and viga-beam ceilings. Full vegetarian breakfast is included in the room rate. ✉ *11155 W. Calle Pima, 85743,* ☎ *520/578–3058,* ℻ *520/578–8445. 3 rooms, adjacent*

house sleeps 8. Kitchenettes, hot tub. Full breakfast. No credit cards.
2-night minimum stay. Closed June–mid-Sept.

Downtown Tucson and University of Arizona

$$–$$$ ⊡ **Inn Suites Hotel & Resort.** Located directly off the St. Mary's Road exit of I–10, this is nevertheless a quiet place, just north of downtown and the historic district. The large, peach-and-green southwestern-theme rooms can double as a pleasant office on the road. Most face a lushly green interior courtyard with a sparkling pool and *palapas* (thatched open gazebos) for shade. A complimentary breakfast buffet and free daily newspaper help make this a haven in the center of the bustling city. ⊠ *475 N. Granada Ave., 85701,* ☎ *520/622–3000 or 800/446–6589,* ℻ *520/623–8922. 277 rooms. Bar, restaurant, pool. AE, D, MC, V.*

$$ ⊡ **Adobe Rose Inn.** Located in the historic Sam Hughes Neighborhood just east of the University of Arizona, this B&B is a good bet for those visiting the campus. The historic 1933 adobe features three lodgepole-pine-furnished rooms, two of which have beehive fireplaces and stained-glass windows. Two cottages also grace this property, which is within easy walking distance of the shops, restaurants, and two major bus lines. All rooms have private baths and cable television. Joy Andrews took ownership in June 1999 and maintains the friendly atmosphere. ⊠ *940 N. Olsen Ave., 85719,* ☎ *520/318–4644 or 800/328–4122,* ℻ *520/ 325–0055. 5 rooms. Pool, hot tub. Full breakfast. AE, MC, V.*

$$ ⊡ **Marriott University Park.** This is the place to stay if you are visiting the University of Arizona, less than a block from the front door. The bubbling brook and lush greenery of the atrium lobby make this modern structure, which rose up at the edge of the University of Arizona campus in 1996, a bit incongruous in the desert, but it's a convenient, comfortable, and reasonably priced addition to the local lodging scene. ⊠ *880 E. 2nd St., 85719,* ☎ *520/792–4100,* ℻ *520/882–4100. 250 rooms. Restaurant, lounge, pool, hot tub, sauna, exercise room, video games, concierge floor, business services. AE, D, DC, MC, V.*

$$ ⊡ **Peppertrees B&B Inn.** This restored 1905 Victorian just off the University of Arizona campus allows guests their privacy along with bed-and-breakfast camaraderie. Two appealing contemporary-style guest houses at the rear of the tree-shaded main house have full kitchens, queen beds, private baths, washers and dryers, and individual patios. Rooms are also available in the antiques-filled main house (furnished with pieces from innkeeper Marjorie Martin's family in England) and in a separate studio apartment. Martin, a gourmet cook who has published a book of her recipes, prepares elaborate morning repasts for her visitors. ⊠ *724 E. University Blvd., 85719,* ☎ ℻ *520/622–7167 or 800/348–5763. 4 rooms, 2 two-bedroom guest houses. Full breakfast. D, MC, V.*

$–$$ ⊡ **Catalina Park Inn.** Classical music plays softly in the living room of this beautifully restored 1927 neoclassical house in the West University neighborhood. The original art nouveau tilework and butler's pantry are among many charming architectural details. All rooms have phones, TVs, robes, irons, and hair dryers. Full gourmet breakfast is included. ⊠ *309 E. 1st St., 85705,* ☎ *520/792–4541 or 800/792–4885,* ℻ *520/792–0838. 6 rooms. Full breakfast. MC, V.*

$ ⊡ **Casa Alegre.** You'll enjoy poking around the knickknacks and an-
★ tiques—everything from a hand-hewn Mexican mine shovel to an ornate 19th-century French clock—in Phyllis Florek's "Happy House," which is as comfortable as it is fascinating. The 1915 Arts and Crafts–style bungalow is near the university, 4th Avenue, and downtown, and it's a straight shot west from here to the Desert Museum and other at-

tractions. Resting in the shade of the ramadas (the Southwest's version of a pergola), or taking a plunge into the pool or hot tub is an ideal end to a day of sightseeing. Breakfasts are copious and delicious. ⊠ *316 E. Speedway Blvd., 85705,* ☏ *520/628–1800 or 800/628–5654,* FAX *520/792–1880. 6 rooms. Pool, hot tub, free parking. Full breakfast. D, MC, V.*

$ 🏨 **Clarion Santa Rita.** The lobby of this historic downtown hotel has gleaming marble floors and comfortable couches. The rooms are standard but have coffeemakers, irons, microwaves, and hair dryers. Ask for a room with a view of the outdoor pool, a lovely remnant of the original hotel. It's also home to the excellent Café Poca Cosa (☞ Dining, *above*). Breakfast, newspapers, and local phone calls are all on the house. ⊠ *88 E. Broadway, 85701,* ☏ *520/622–4000 or 800/622–1120,* FAX *520/620–0376. 152 rooms. Restaurant, refrigerators, pool, exercise room, library. Continental breakfast. AE, D, DC, MC, V.*

$ 🏨 **Hotel Congress.** Loved by many for its idiosyncratic charm, this downtown hotel was built in 1919 and restored to its original western version of Art Deco. Each room is different, but all have black-and-white tile baths and the original iron beds, and some have desks and tables. Near the main Sun Tran terminal and close to downtown art galleries and restaurants, this is an excellent choice if you don't have a car, but its convenient location means it can be noisy. ⊠ *311 E. Congress St., 85701,* ☏ *520/622–8848 or 800/722–8848,* FAX *520/792–6366. 40 rooms. Restaurant, bar, beauty salon, nightclub, shop. AE, MC, V.*

$ 🏨 **Plaza Hotel and Conference Center.** Renovated in 1998, the Plaza has a prime location in the very heart of Tucson, across the street from the University of Arizona, two blocks from the University Medical Center, and at the intersection of two major bus routes. A favorite of visiting faculty, prospective students, and parents, it is a no-nonsense hotel with a pool, bar, and pedestrian dining room. Fortunately, there are many restaurants within walking or driving distance along Speedway or Campbell. ⊠ *1900 E. Speedway Blvd., 85719,* ☏ *520/327–7341,* FAX *520/327–0276. 150 rooms. Restaurant, pool. AE, D, MC, V.*

Central Tucson

$$$–$$$$ 🏨 **Arizona Inn.** This sprawling lodging, which has remained in the Greenaway family since it opened in 1930, is an oasis in the center of town: ★ Although close to the university and many sights, the inn's beautifully landscaped 14 acres seem far away from it all. The spacious rooms are spread out in pink stucco houses—all have patios and some have fireplaces—and the luxurious guest houses are reasonably priced when shared by three or more. The Inn also has two fully furnished rental homes: a two-bedroom, two-bath and a five-bedroom, five-bath, both with private gardens. The unobtrusive service sets a standard for hotel hospitality, bringing guests back year after year. In the evening, locals join guests in the hotel's restaurant (☞ Dining, *above*) and cocktail lounge, which often has a pianist. ⊠ *2200 E. Elm St., 85719,* ☏ *520/ 325–1541 or 800/933–1093,* FAX *520/881–5830. 90 rooms. 2 restaurants, bar, tea shop, pool, 2 tennis courts, croquet, Ping-Pong, library. Full breakfast included May–Sept. only. AE, DC, MC, V.*

$$ 🏨 **Doubletree Hotel.** Convenient to the airport and to the center of town, this comfortable, contemporary-style property is across the road from the municipal golf course at Randolph Park, which hosts the LPGA tournament every year. Most of the participants stay here. ⊠ *445 S. Alvernon Way, 85711,* ☏ *520/881–4200,* FAX *520/323–5225. 295 rooms. 2 restaurants, pool, beauty salon, hot tub, 3 tennis courts, exercise room. Full breakfast. AE, D, DC, MC, V.*

$$ ⊞ **Embassy Suites Tucson–Broadway.** This centrally located hotel is 10 mi from Tucson International Airport, 5 mi from downtown, and less than 5 mi from the University of Arizona. Accommodations are two-room suites opening onto a plant-filled atrium. Among the extras are a free cooked-to-order breakfast, a complimentary happy hour every evening, passes to a local gym, and shuttle service to El Con and Park malls. The lounge boasts a large-screen television and billiard tables. ⊠ *5335 E. Broadway, 85711,* ☎ *520/745–2700,* FAX *520/790–9232. 142 suites. Kitchenettes, pool, coin laundry, free parking. Full breakfast. AE, D, DC, MC, V.*

$–$$ ⊞ **Varsity Clubs of America.** Opened in 1998, this time-share facility also doubles as a hotel, so it may have any or all of its suites available for rental at any given time. Its handy location is also a rather busy and noisy one. One- and two-bedroom suites have whirlpool tubs and full kitchens; alternatives to cooking are the Stadium Grill downstairs or any of the several restaurants in walking distance. ⊠ *3855 E. Speedway Blvd., 85716,* ☎ *520/318–3777 or 888/594–2287,* FAX *888/410–9770. 59 suites. Pool, hot tub, exercise room. AE, D, MC, V.*

$ ⊞ **Best Western Ghost Ranch Lodge.** The bleached-out cow skulls pop-
★ ularized by Georgia O'Keeffe are now a Southwest cliché, but they weren't in 1936 when the New Mexico artist gave the then-unusual logo to conservationist Arthur Pack as a wedding gift. The neon sign he made with this design still lights up the entrance to the former hotel Pack, opened in 1941 on the main road into Tucson. The Spanish tile–roof units are spread out over 8 acres that encompass an orange grove and garden with 400 varieties of cacti. Rooms are decorated with modern motel furnishings, but retain original brick walls and sloped wood-beam ceilings. The cottages, with a separate kitchen, sitting area, and carport, are a bargain. ⊠ *801 W. Miracle Mile, 85705,* ☎ *520/791–7565 or 800/456–7565,* FAX *520/791–3898. 83 units. Restaurant, bar, pool, hot tub, shuffleboard. Continental breakfast. AE, D, DC, MC, V.*

Northeast Tucson

$$$$ ⊞ **Canyon Ranch.** Opened in 1979 on the site of the old Double U Guest
★ Ranch, Canyon Ranch draws an international crowd of glitterati to its superb spa facilities. Set on 70 acres in the desert foothills northeast of Tucson, two activity centers include a 62,000-square-ft spa complex and an 8,000-square-ft Health and Healing Center, where dietitians, exercise physiologists, behavioral-health professionals, and medical staff attend to body and soul. Every type of physical activity is possible from Pilates (special stretching and relaxation techniques) to guided hiking, and the food is plentiful and healthy. There is a minimum stay of four nights, and the rate includes all meals, classes, lectures, and sales tax. ⊠ *8600 E. Rockcliff Rd., 85750,* ☎ *520/749–9000 or 800/742–9000,* FAX *520/749–1646. 240 rooms. Indoor pool, 3 outdoor pools, beauty salon, spa, 8 tennis courts, aerobics, health club, basketball, racquetball, squash. FAP. AE, D, MC, V. 4-night minimum stay.*

$$$–$$$$ ⊞ **Loews Ventana Canyon Resort.** One of the newer desert resorts, this one is luxurious, but snootier than most other Tucson properties. Rooms are modern and chic, furnished in soft pastels and light woods; each bath has a miniature TV, an oversize tub, and bubble bath. The center of this spectacular 93-acre property is an 80-ft waterfall that cascades down the Catalina Mountains into a little lake. Guests can enjoy everything from poolside snacks to fine Continental cuisine at the Ventana Room (☞ *Dining, above*). ⊠ *7000 N. Resort Dr., 85750,* ☎ *520/299–2020 or 800/234–5117,* FAX *520/299–6832. 398 rooms. 4 restaurants, bar, lobby lounge, 2 pools, beauty salon, spa, two 18-hole golf courses, 8 tennis courts, exercise room, hiking. AE, D, DC, MC, V.*

$$ ☷ **Ramada Inn Foothills.** Families and business travelers stay in this upscale Ramada on the northeastern side of town, close to many restaurants and Sabino Canyon. An attractive light stucco building with rounded corners, this property has serviceable, if generic rooms, all with hair dryers. A Continental breakfast is complimentary, as are beer and wine in the afternoon. Free passes to a local health club are available, and golf and tennis facilities are nearby. ⊠ *6944 E. Tanque Verde Rd., 85715,* ☎ *520/886–9595 or 800/228–2828,* ℻ *520/721–8466. 113 rooms. Restaurant, lounge, pool, sauna. Continental breakfast. AE, D, DC, MC, V.*

Eastside

$$$$ ☷ **Tanque Verde Ranch.** The most upscale of Tucson's guest ranches
★ and one of the oldest in the country, Tanque Verde sits on more than 600 beautiful acres in the Rincon Mountains between Coronado National Forest and Saguaro National Park East. Rooms in the main ranch house or in private casitas have tasteful southwestern-style furnishings; most have patios, some have fireplaces, and all have picture-window views of the desert. There are breakfast and lunch buffets, and cookouts and barbecues add variety to the daily dinner menu. Horseback picnic excursions are offered for every level of rider, and children can participate in daylong activities, leaving parents to their leisure. Many guests have been coming here year after year to relax and be pampered by the attentive staff. ⊠ *14301 E. Speedway Blvd., 85748,* ☎ *520/ 296–6275 or 800/234–3833,* ℻ *520/721–9426. 82 rooms, 4 houses. Indoor and outdoor pool, spa, 5 tennis courts, basketball, exercise room, horseback riding, horseshoes, volleyball, fishing. FAP. AE, D, MC, V.*

$$–$$$ ☷ **Tucson Hilton East.** This east-side chain property is convenient to Sabino Canyon and Saguaro National Park East as well as to Davis-Monthan Air Force Base. An airy glass-atrium lobby takes full advantage of the view of the Santa Catalina Mountains. The rooms are spacious and well tended, but not particularly distinctive. ⊠ *7600 E. Broadway, 85710,* ☎ *520/721–5600 or 800/648–7177,* ℻ *520/721–5696. 232 rooms. Restaurant, bar, pool, spa, concierge floor. AE, D, DC, MC, V.*

$$ ☷ **Smuggler's Inn.** At the corner of Wilmot/Tanque Verde Road and Speedway Boulevard, this comfortable hotel has easy access to the east-side of Tucson and the "restaurant row" of Tanque Verde Road. A lushly landscaped central courtyard is the focus for the serviceable rooms that have either a balcony or patio. *Mercado de Boutiques,* with its eating establishments and shops, is right next door. ⊠ *6350 E. Speedway Blvd., 85710,* ☎ *520/296–3292 or 800/525–8852,* ℻ *520/722–7391. 150 rooms. Bar, restaurant, pool, hot tub. AE, D, MC, V.*

NIGHTLIFE AND THE ARTS

The Arts

Tucson, known as Arizona's most cultured city, is one of only 14 cities in the United States that is home to a symphony as well as to opera, theater, and ballet companies. Wintertime, when Tucson's population swells with vacationers, is the high season for cultural activities, but the arts are alive and well year-round.

Downtown Saturday Night, an event held the first and third Saturday nights of every month, has downtown art-district galleries, studios, and cafés hopping from 7 to 10. There's often dancing in the street—everything from calypso to square dancing—and musical performances ranging from jazz to gospel. Most of the activity takes place along Congress Street and Broadway (from 4th Ave. to Stone St.) and along 5th and 6th avenues. You can also explore this area via a free, docent-led Thursday Night Artwalk. For more information contact the **Tucson Arts District Partnership, Inc.** (☎ 520/624–9977), which also has material on self-guided gallery and historic district walking tours.

The low cost of Tucson's cultural events comes as a pleasant surprise to those accustomed to paying East or West Coast prices: Symphony tickets are as little as $5 for some performances, and touring Broadway musicals can often be seen for $22. Parking is plentiful and frequently free. Most of the city's cultural activity takes place either downtown in the arts district, near the **Tucson Convention Center** (✉ 260 S. Church St., ☎ 520/791–4101; 520/791–4266 box office) complex and the El Presidio neighborhood, or at the University of Arizona's **Centennial Hall** (✉ 1020 E. University Blvd., ☎ 520/621–3341). Each season brings visiting companies of opera, musicals, and dance; tickets to many events can be purchased through **Dillard's Box Office** (☎ 800/638–4253).

The free *Tucson Weekly,* which hits the stands on Thursday, and the Friday *Starlight* section of the *The Arizona Daily Star* have complete listings of what's going on in town.

Dance

Tucson shares its professional ballet company, **Ballet Arizona** (☎ 888/322–5538), with Phoenix. Performances, which range from classical to contemporary, are held at the Music Hall in the Tucson Convention Center (☞ *above*). The most established of the modern dance companies, **Orts Theatre of Dance** (✉ 930 N. Stone Ave., ☎ 520/624–3799), schedules a variety of outdoor and indoor performances.

Music

From late February through late June, the Tucson Parks and Recreation Department hosts a series of **free concerts** on the weekends. The Tucson Pops Orchestra plays at the De Meester Outdoor Performance Center in Reid Park, and the Arizona Symphonic Winds performs at Morris T. Udall Park (✉ Tanque Verde and Sabino Canyon Rds.). Arrive at least an hour before the music starts (usually at 7:30) to stake your claim on a prime viewing spot. A series of lunchtime concerts takes place downtown at the main library on Wednesdays from late February to early May. Call 520/791–4079 for schedules and directions.

For classical fans, a chamber-music series is hosted by the **Arizona Friends of Chamber Music** (☎ 520/298–5806) at the Leo Rich Theater in the Tucson Convention Center from October through April. The **Arizona Opera Company** (☎ 520/293–4336), based in Tucson, puts on five major productions each year at the Tucson Convention Center's Music Hall. The **Tucson Symphony Orchestra** (✉ 443 S. Stone Ave., ☎ 520/882–8585 box office; 520/792–9155 main office), part of Tucson's cultural scene since 1929, holds concerts in the music hall in the Tucson Convention Center complex and at the Pima Community College Center for the Arts. A variety of concerts and recitals, many of them free, is offered by the **University of Arizona's School of Music and Dance** (☎ 520/621–2998 for a recorded listing of events in the upcoming week).

Tucson's small but vibrant jazz scene encompasses everything from afternoon jam sessions in the park to Sunday jazz brunches at resorts in the foothills. Call the **Tucson Jazz Society Hot Line** (☎ 520/743–3399) for information.

Poetry

The springtime **Tucson Poetry Festival** (☎ 520/620–2045 for details) brings poets, some internationally acclaimed—Amiri Baraka and the late Allen Ginsberg have been participants—to town for three days of readings and related events.

The **University of Arizona Poetry Center** (✉ 1216 N. Cherry Ave., ☎ 520/321–7760) runs a free series open to the public. Phone during fall and spring semesters for information on scheduled readers.

Theater

Theater groups in town include Arizona's state theater, the **Arizona Theatre Company** (☎ 520/884–8210), which performs everything from classical to contemporary drama at the historic **Temple of Music and Art** (✉ 330 S. Scott Ave., ☎ 520/622–2823) from September through May. It's worth coming just to see the beautifully restored Spanish Colonial/Moorish–style theater, and dinner at the adjoining **B&B Cafe** (☎ 520/792–2623) makes a tasty prelude to any performance.

The **a.k.a. theatre** (✉ 125 E. Congress St., ☎ 520/623–7852) specializes in avant-garde productions. **Invisible Theatre** (✉ 1400 N. 1st Ave., ☎ 520/882–9721) presents contemporary plays and musicals. **Pima Community College** mounts productions throughout the academic year (✉ 2202 W. Anklam Rd., ☎ 520/206–6986). The **University of Arizona** drama department presents a fine array of budding talent (✉ Speedway and Olive Sts., ☎ 520/621–1162).

Children of all ages love the old-fashioned melodramas at the **Gaslight Theatre** (✉ 7010 E. Broadway, ☎ 520/886–9428), where hissing the villain and cheering the hero are part of the audience's duty.

Nightlife

Bars and Clubs

Although Tucson doesn't have the huge selection of bars and clubs available in some major cities, there's something here to suit nearly every taste. In addition to the places listed below, most of the major resorts have late-night spots for drinks or dancing.

COUNTRY AND WESTERN

An excellent house band gets the crowd two-stepping every night except Sunday and Monday at the **Maverick** (✉ 4702 E. 22nd St., ☎ 520/748–0456). Follow the crowd over to **The Stampede** (✉ 4385 W. Ina Rd., ☎ 520/744–7744), the Southwest's largest country-and-western nightclub, with two dance floors, pool tables, free dance lessons (call for a schedule), and a western clothing boutique.

JAZZ

There's usually a lively jazz pianist at the **Arizona Inn** (☞ Lodging, *above*). **Cafe Sweetwater** (✉ 340 E. 6th St., ☎ 520/622–6464) consistently attracts high-quality jazz acts—and the food's pretty good, too.

ROCK, BLUES, AND MORE

Berky's (✉ 5769 E. Speedway Blvd., ☎ 520/296–1981) has live R&B and rock and roll every night; there's a newer location on busy 4th Avenue (✉ 424 N. 4th Ave., ☎ 520/622–0376). The **Chicago Bar** (✉ 5954 E. Speedway Blvd., ☎ 520/748–8169) is a good place to catch Tucson blues legend Sam Taylor; other nightly shows include reggae and rock. **Club Congress** (✉ 311 E. Congress St., ☎ 520/622–8848) is the main venue for cutting-edge rock bands on Friday. Downtown's **Empire Cafe and Lounge** (✉ 61 E. Congress St., ☎ 520/885–9779) tends to book bands with an '80s inclination. **The Outback** (✉ 296 N. Stone Ave., ☎ 520/622–4700) hosts performers like Los Lobos, Starship, Cameo, and other bands with a loyal following. Go totally retro at the **Shelter** (✉ 4155 E. Grant Rd., ☎ 520/326–1345), a former bomb shelter where the early '60s still reign.

Casinos

After a long struggle with the state of Arizona, two Native American tribes now operate casinos on their Tucson-area reservations. Both casinos are always open—literally—and because these are located on reservation lands, alcohol is neither sold nor permitted at either location.

Casino of the Sun. Run by the Pascua Yaqui tribe, it has slot and video-gambling machines, keno, high-stakes bingo, and live poker. ⊠ *7406 S. Camino de Oeste,* ☎ *520/883–1700 or 800/344–9435.*

Desert Diamond Bingo and Casino. The Tohono O'odham tribe operates this dazzling venue for 500 one-arm bandits and video poker in addition to live keno, bingo, and poker. ⊠ *7350 S. Old Nogales Hwy.,* ☎ *520/294–7777.*

OUTDOOR ACTIVITIES AND SPORTS

Participant Sports

Ballooning

Balloon America (⊠ Box 31255, Tucson 85751, ☎ 520/299–7744) and **Southern Arizona Balloon Excursions** (⊠ Box 5265, 530 W. Saguaro St., Tucson 85703, ☎ 520/624–3599) offer champagne celebrations and daily flights (in season; usually September or October to May or June) by FAA-certified pilots.

Bicycling

Tucson, ranked among America's top-five bicycling cities by *Bicycling* magazine, has designated bikeways, routes, lanes, and paths all over the city. Most bike stores in Tucson carry the monthly newsletter of the Tucson chapter of **GABA** (Greater Arizona Bicycling Association, ⊠ Box 43273, Tucson 85733), which lists rated group rides; visitors are welcome. You can pick up maps at the office of the **Pima Association of Governments** (⊠ 177 N. Church St., Suite 405, ☎ 520/792–1093). The **Tucson Transportation Department** (☎ 520/791–4372) will mail you city bike maps.

Reliable bike renters include the **Bike Shack** (⊠ 940 E. University Ave., ☎ 520/624–3663) and **Full Cycle** (⊠ 3232 E. Speedway Blvd., ☎ 520/327–3232).

Bird-Watching

Roger Tory Peterson named Tucson one of the country's top birding spots, and avid life listers—birders who keep a list of all the birds they've sighted and identified—soon see why. In the early morning and early evening Sabino Canyon is alive with cactus and canyon wrens, hawks and quail. Spring and summer, when species of migrants come in from Mexico, are great hummingbird seasons. In the nearby Santa Rita Mountains and Madera Canyon (☞ Side Trips Near Tucson, *below*), you can see Elegant Trogans nesting in early spring and species usually found in higher elevations.

You can get the latest word on the bird by phoning the 24-hour line at the **Tucson Audubon Society** (☎ 520/798–1005); sightings of rare or interesting birds in the area are recorded regularly. The society's **Audubon Nature Shop** (⊠ 300 E. University Blvd., Suite 120, ☎ 520/629–0510) carries field guides, bird feeders, binoculars, and natural-history books. The **Wild Bird Store** (⊠ 3522 E. Grant Rd., ☎ 520/322–9466) is an excellent resource for bird-watching books, maps, and trail guides.

Tours are offered by **Borderlands** (⊠ 2550 W. Calle Padilla, Tucson 85745, ☎ 520/882–7650). The Tucson office of the **Nature Conser-**

vancy (⊠ 300 E. University Blvd., Suite 230, ☎ 520/622–3861) arranges seasonal bird-watching tours ranging in length from a few hours to several days; call or write for information. **Wings, Inc.** (⊠ 1643 N. Alvernon Way, Suite 105, Tucson 85712, ☎ 520/320–9868), also leads ornithological expeditions.

Camping

The closest public campground to Tucson is at **Catalina State Park** (⊠ 11570 N. Oracle Rd., ☎ 520/628–5798), about 14 mi north of town on AZ 77 in the desert foothills of the Santa Catalinas. The campground has 49 sites, about half with electrical hookups, accommodating both tents and RVs. Sites cost $15 with electric hookups, $10 without, and the cash-only facility operates on a first-come, first-served basis.

Recreational vehicles can park at several facilities around town. The **Metropolitan Tucson Convention and Visitors Bureau** (☞ Visitor Information *in* Tucson A to Z, *below*) can provide information about specific locations.

Golf

The Tucson & Southern Arizona Golf Guide, published by Madden Publishing, Inc. (⊠ Box 42915, Tucson 85733, ☎ 520/322–0895), describes and rates all the local courses; send $5 for a copy.

The **Golf Stop Inc.** (⊠ 1830 S. Alvernon Way, ☎ 520/790–0941), owned and run by two LPGA pros, can fit you with custom clubs, repair your old irons, or give you lessons. For a local golf package based on your budget, interests, and experience, contact **Tee Time Arrangers** (⊠ 6286 E. Grant Rd., ☎ 520/296–4800 or 800/742–9939). If you're planning to stay a week or more, **Tucson's Resort Golf Card** (⊠ 6286 E. Grant Rd., Tucson 85712, ☎ 520/886–8800), offering year-round discounts at 10 of the area's best courses, is a good deal.

MUNICIPAL COURSES

One of Tucson's best-kept secrets is that the city's five municipal courses are maintained to standards usually found only at the best country clubs. The flagship of these low-priced municipal golf courses (Randolph North, Dell Urich, El Rio, Fred Enke, and Silverbell) is Randolph North, which hosted the PGA and LPGA Tour for many years. To reserve a tee time, contact the **Tucson Parks and Recreation Department** (☎ 520/791–4336) at least a week in advance.

PUBLIC COURSES

Dorado Golf Course (⊠ 6601 E. Speedway Blvd., ☎ 520/885–6751), on the east side of town, has an executive 18-hole course that's good for those who just want to play a few short rounds.

Raven Golf Club at Sabino Springs (⊠ 9777 E. Sabino Greens Dr., ☎ 520/760–1253) is an 18-hole, par-71 course in a gorgeous setting.

Rio Rico Resort & Country Club (⊠ 1069 Camino Carampi, ☎ 520/281–8567), south of Tucson, near Nogales, was designed by Robert Trent Jones, Jr.; it's one of Arizona's lesser-known gems.

San Ignacio Golf Club (⊠ 4201 S. Camino del Sol, ☎ 520/648–3468), in Green Valley, was designed by Arthur Hills and is a challenging 18-hole desert course.

Tubac Golf Resort (⊠ 1 Otera Rd., ☎ 520/398–2211 or 520/398–2021), 45 minutes south of Tucson, will look familiar to you if you've seen the film *Tin Cup.*

RESORTS

Avid golfers check into one of the tony local resorts (☞ Lodging, *above*) and head straight for the links. Golf vacations are a specialty at **Lodge at Ventana Canyon** (✉ 6200 N. Clubhouse La., 85750, ☎ 520/577–1400 or 800/828–5701), with its 36-hole Tom Fazio–designed course; **Sheraton Tucson El Conquistador,** its 45 holes in the Santa Catalina foothills affording 360-degree views of the city; **Starr Pass-Golf Resort** (✉ 3645 W. Starr Pass Blvd., 85745, ☎ 520/670–0500 or 800/503–2898), which now has guest casitas for those who want to devote as much time as possible to playing its 18 magnificent holes in the Tucson Mountains (the Arnold Palmer–managed club was developed as a Tournament Player's Course and has become a favorite of visiting pros; playing its Number 15 signature hole has been likened to threading a moving needle); **Tucson National Golf & Conference Resort,** cohost of an annual PGA winter open, with 27 holes and beautiful, long par 4s, designed by the great Robert Bruce Harris; and **Westin La Paloma,** which has a 27-hole layout designed by Jack Nicklaus (rated among the top 75 resort courses by *Golf Digest*). Those who don't mind getting up early to beat the heat will find some excellent golf packages at these places in the summer.

Health Clubs

5th Street Fitness (✉ 5555 E. 5th St., ☎ 520/571–7000) has an indoor swimming pool, sauna, hot tub, and aerobics classes. Nonmembers receive a free one-day pass; additional days cost $15 for all facilities.

FIT (Fitness & Health Institute of Tucson) (✉ 11 S. Church Ave., Suite 5030, ☎ 520/623–6300) charges visitors $5 for use of their indoor swimming pool, Nautilus equipment and free weights, racquetball and basketball courts, sauna, and steam room.

Tucson Racquet & Fitness Club (✉ 4001 N. Country Club Rd., ☎ 520/795–6960) has extensive facilities, including 11 racquetball courts, two Olympic-size lap pools, and martial arts classes; it's open 24 hours a day. Visitors pay $10.

Hiking

For hiking inside Tucson city limits, you might test your skills climbing trails up Sentinel Peak ("A" Mountain), but there are literally hundreds of trails in the immediate Tucson area. **Catalina State Park** (☞ Camping, *above*) is crisscrossed by hiking trails. One of them, an easy two-hour walk, leads to the Romero Pools, a series of natural *tinajas*, or stone tanks, filled with water much of the year.

The local chapter of the **Sierra Club** (✉ 738 N. 5th Ave., Suite 214, Tucson 85705, ☎ 520/620–6401) welcomes out-of-town visitors on weekend hikes around the area. There's a $2 suggested donation per person for nonmembers. For hiking on your own, a good source of information is **Summit Hut** (✉ 5045 E. Speedway Blvd., ☎ 520/325–1554), which has a collection of hiking reference materials and a friendly staff who will help you plan and outfit your trip. Packs, tents, bags, and climbing shoes can be rented here.

Horseback Riding

Pusch Ridge Stables (✉ 13700 N. Oracle Rd., ☎ 520/825–1664), adjacent to Catalina State Park, serves up a cowboy-style breakfast at the end of your trail ride; gentle children's walks are also available.

Rockhounding

Check with the proper authorities to make sure you're not illegally removing anything from protected areas such as national parks or Indian reservations. Amateur traders and buyers might consider joining the thousands of professionals who come to town in February for the huge **Tucson Gem and Mineral Show** (⊠ Box 42543, Tucson 85733, ☎ 520/322–5773), the largest of its kind in the world. Many precious stones as well as affordable samples are displayed and sold here.

Tennis

Tennis facilities can be found at area resorts, among them Loews Ventana Canyon, Sheraton Tucson El Conquistador, Westin La Paloma, Westward Look, and Canyon Ranch (☞ Lodging, *above*). **Catalina High School** (⊠ 3645 E. Pima), singer Linda Ronstadt's alma mater, is a favorite among local tennis enthusiasts for its well-lighted, no-charge courts, which are open to the public when school's out. **Fort Lowell Park** (⊠ 2900 N. Craycroft Rd., ☎ 520/791–2584) and **Himmel Park** (⊠ 1000 N. Tucson Blvd., ☎ 520/791–3276) have eight lighted courts apiece and low prices. The **Randolph Tennis Center** (⊠ 50 S. Alvernon Way, ☎ 520/791–4896) has 25 courts, 11 of them lighted, at very reasonable rates.

Spectator Sports

Baseball

The 1998 opening of **Tucson Electric Park** (⊠ 2400 E. Ajo Way, ☎ 520/434–1000), a huge multifield facility with plentiful parking, ushered baseball into Tucson on a large scale. Spring training sees three teams come into the Tucson area, from the end of February until the end of March. Not surprisingly, some visitors plan vacations around scheduled training dates; there are plenty of local fans, too.

The National League expansion team based in Phoenix, the **Arizona Diamondbacks,** practices at Tucson Electric Park, as do the **Chicago White Sox,** who attract many snowbirds from the Midwest: So avid are the Chicago fans that a local cable company had a mutiny on its hands when Chicago's WGN TV station was pulled from the local programming schedule (it has since been restored). For **ticket information** for both teams, call 888/683–3900. The **Colorado Rockies** are located at Hi Corbett Field (⊠ 2400 Camino Campestre, ☎ 520/327–9467), which can be most easily reached by driving south at the junction of East Broadway and Randolph Way. Parking is tight at this facility, so arrive early to enjoy a picnic lunch at one of the many ramadas nearby. If you're visiting in summer catch the **Tucson Sidewinders** (☎ 520/325–2621), a minor league team which also plays at Tucson Electric Park. Remember that desert temperatures drop significantly when the sun goes down, so sitting outside in July is not quite as daunting as it sounds.

Rodeo

In the last week of February, Tucson hosts **Fiesta de Los Vaqueros,** the largest annual winter rodeo in the United States, a five-day extravaganza with more than 600 events and a crowd of more than 44,000 spectators a day at the **Tucson Rodeo Grounds** (⊠ 4823 S. 6th Ave., ☎ 520/294–8896). The rodeo kicks off with a 2-mi parade of horseback riders (western and fancy-dress Mexican *charro*), wagons, stagecoaches, and horse-drawn floats; it's touted as the largest nonmotorized parade in the world. Children especially love the celebration—they get a two-day holiday from school. Daily seats at the rodeo range from $8 to $14.

SHOPPING

San Xavier Plaza, across from San Xavier mission, carries the work of a variety of native tribes, including the Tohono O'odham, upon whose reservation the church is located (☞ *Westside in* Exploring Tucson, *above*). Those looking for work by other regional artists might drive down to Tubac, a community 45 mi south of Tucson. Hard-core bargain hunters usually continue south to the Mexican border and Nogales (☞ Side Trips Near Tucson, *below*).

Much of Tucson's retail activity is focused around malls, but you'll find shops with more character and unique wares in more shopper-friendly areas centered around open plazas: St. Philip's Plaza (River Rd. and Campbell Ave.), Plaza Palomino (Swan and Ft. Lowell Rds.), Casas Adobes Plaza (Oracle and Ina Rds.) and around the junction of Swan Road and Sunrise Drive. Here you can find high quality leather goods, charro suits for women (silver-buttoned bolero jackets with full riding skirts), Southwest-style jewelry, and artwork. **Historic Broadway Village** (Country Club Rd. and Broadway) was the first shopping center in Tucson, and although small, it houses interesting shops such as Clues Unlimited mystery bookshop, Zocalo for colonial Mexican furniture, and Table Talk housewares store. The **4th Avenue** neighborhood near the University of Arizona—especially 4th Avenue between 2nd and 9th streets—is also fertile ground for unusual items to be found in artsy boutiques and secondhand stores.

Specialty Shops

ART GALLERIES

Art Life in Southern Arizona (✉ Box 36777, Tucson 85740, ☎ 520/797–1271), published annually, lists local galleries and artists.

Dinnerware Artists Cooperative (✉ 135 E. Congress St., ☎ 520/792–4503) is a cutting-edge downtown venue. **Etherton Gallery** (✉ 135 S. 6th Ave., ☎ 520/624–7370) specializes in photography, but also represents artists in other media. **Obsidian Gallery** (✉ 4340 N. Campbell Ave., ☎ 520/577–3598) has glass art and jewelry by local artists. **Philabaum Contemporary Glass** (✉ 711 S. 6th Ave., ☎ 520/884–7404) sells the handblown vases, artwork, table settings, and jewelry of Tom Philabaum. You can watch the artists at work blowing glass in the back room. **Rosequist Galleries** (✉ 1615 E. Ft. Lowell Rd., ☎ 520/327–5729) has represented regional artists working in all media for 53 years.

BOOKS

Seekers of books by and about women should stop in at **Antigone** (✉ 411 N. 4th Ave., ☎ 520/792–3715), which also sells creative feminist cards and T-shirts. In central Tucson, the **Book Mark** (✉ 5001 E. Speedway Blvd., ☎ 520/881–6350) carries a wide selection of titles; local writers often give readings here. **The Book Stop** (✉ 2504 N. Campbell Ave., ☎ 520/326–6661) is a wonderful browsing place for used and out-of-print books. For mystery buffs there is **Clues Unlimited** (✉ 3000 E. Broadway, ☎ 520/326–8533). Pick up your topographical maps and specialty guides to Arizona at **Tucson's Map and Flag Center** (✉ 3239 N. 1st Ave., ☎ 520/887–4234).

CACTI

You won't need to stick a cactus in your suitcase if you want to take back a spiny souvenir: **B&B Cactus Farm** (✉ 11550 E. Speedway Blvd., ☎ 520/721–4687), on the far eastern side of town (you'll pass it en route to Saguaro National Park East) has a huge selection of desert plants and will ship anywhere in the country.

GIFTS

Del Sol (✉ 435 N. 4th Ave., ☎ 520/628–8765) specializes in folk art, jewelry, and Southwest-style clothing. **Mrs. Tiggy Winkle's Toys** (✉ 4811 E. Grant Rd., ☎ 520/326–0188) will probably remind you of the toy shops of your childhood, only better, with unique items you won't find in the big-box toy stores. **A Taste of Arizona** (✉ Park Mall, 5870 E.

Broadway, ☎ 520/790–3083) is a good stop for regional souvenir gifts and a wide selection of salsas. Reasonably priced ethnic jewelry, apparel, and crafts can be purchased at the **United Nations Center** (✉ 2911 E. Grant Rd., ☎ 520/881–7060).

JEWELRY

Abbott Taylor (✉ 6372 E. Broadway, ☎ 520/745–5080) creates custom designs in diamonds and precious stones. For a splurge, consider buying something by **Beth Friedman** (✉ Old Town Artisans, 186 S. Meyer Ave., ☎ 520/622–5013); her designs in silver and semiprecious stones are unsurpassed. One of the best known jewelers in the Southwest is **Patania's Sterling Silver Originals** (☎ 520/795–0086), formerly the Thunderbird Shop. The Patania family has been creating unique designs in silver here and in Santa Fe for three generations. They also are the single repository of Salvador Corona's folk-style renderings of Mexico. If you prefer a modern take on southwestern jewelry, **Turquoise Door** (✉ 4340 N. Campbell Ave., ☎ 520/299–7787) creates innovative designs.

MEXICAN GOODS

Antigua de Mexico sells well-made furniture and crafts that you are not likely to find easily elsewhere (✉ 7037 N. Oracle Rd., ☎ 520/742–7114). **Tres Encantos** has hand-carved furniture and decorative accents (✉ 6538 E. Tanque Verde, ☎ 520/885–4522).

NATIVE AMERICAN ARTS AND CRAFTS

Tom Bahti literally wrote the books on Native American art, including an early definitive work on katsinas. **Bahti Indian Arts** (✉ St. Philip's Plaza, 4300 N. Campbell Ave., ☎ 520/577–0290), owned and run by his son, Mark, continues to sell high-quality jewelry, pottery, rugs, art, and more. **Huntington Trading Co.** (✉ 111 E. Congress, ☎ 520/628–8578) carries masks and pottery made by the Yaqui and Tarahumara Indians and beadwork by the Huichols.

Other stores which provide an ample selection of Hopi katsinas, Zuni fetishes, Navajo rugs, and Native American jewelry, baskets, and crafts are: **Desert Son** (✉ 4759 E. Sunrise Dr., ☎ 520/299–0818), **Indian Territory** (✉ 5639 N. Swan Rd., ☎ 520/577–7961), **Kaibab Courtyard Shops** (✉ 2837 N. Campbell Ave., ☎ 520/795–6905), and **Silverbell Trading** (✉ 7007 N. Oracle Rd., ☎ 520/797–6852).

WESTERN WEAR

Tucsonans who wear western gear keep it simple for the most part—jeans, a western shirt, maybe boots. This ain't Santa Fe. **Arizona Hatters** (✉ 3600 N. First Ave., ☎ 520/292–1320) can fit you for that Stetson you've always wanted. **Corral Western Wear** (✉ 4525 E. Broadway Blvd., ☎ 520/322–6001), with a large array of shirts, hats, belts, jewelry, and boots, caters to both urban and authentic cowboys and cowgirls. **Stewart Boot Manufacturing** (✉ 30 W. 28th St., South Tucson, ☎ 520/622–2706) has been making handmade leather boots for more than 50 years. But if you want to go where native Tucsonans shop for their everyday western duds, try **Western Warehouse** (✉ 3030 E. Broadway, ☎ 520/327–8005; ✉ 3719 N. Oracle Rd., ☎ 520/293–1808; and ✉ 6701 E. Broadway, ☎ 520/885–4385).

Malls and Shopping Centers

Casas Adobes Plaza (✉ Southwest corner of Oracle and Ina Rds., ☎ no phone) originally served the ranchers and orange grove owners in this once remote northwest region. Now in the center of the fastest growing area in the Tucson Valley, the strip shopping center has a health food store, a full service grocery with outstanding organic meats and

Finally, a travel companion that doesn't snore on the plane or eat all your peanuts.

When traveling, your MCI WorldCom Card is the best way to keep in touch. Our operators speak your language, so they'll be able to connect you back home—no matter where your travels take you. Plus, your MCI WorldCom Card is easy to use, and even earns you frequent flyer miles every time you use it. When you add in our great rates, you get something even more valuable: peace-of-mind. So go ahead. Travel the world. MCI WorldCom just brought it a whole lot closer.

You can even sign up today at www.mci.com/worldphone or ask your operator to make a collect call to 1-410-314-2938.

EASY TO CALL WORLDWIDE

1 **Just dial the WorldPhone access number of the country you're calling from.**
2 **Dial or give the operator your MCI WorldCom Card number.**
3 **Dial or give the number you're calling.**

Australia ◆	
To call using OPTUS	1-800-551-111
To call using TELSTRA	1-800-881-100
Bahamas/Bermuda	1-800-888-8000
British Virgin Islands	1-800-888-8000
Costa Rica ◆	0-800-012-2222
Denmark	8001-0022
Norway ◆	800 -19912
India	000-127
For collect access	000-126
United States/Canada	1-800-888-8000

For your complete WorldPhone calling guide, dial the WorldPhone access number for the country you're in and ask the operator for Customer Service. In the U.S. call 1-800-431-5402.

◆ Public phones may require deposit of coin or phone card for dial tone.

EARN FREQUENT FLYER MILES

AmericanAirlines®
AAdvantage®

Continental Airlines
OnePass

▲Delta Air Lines
SkyMiles®

☛ MILEAGE PLUS.
United Airlines

U·S AIRWAYS
DIVIDEND MILES

MCI WorldCom, its logo and the names of the products referred to herein are proprietary marks of MCI WorldCom, Inc. All airline names and logos are proprietary marks of the respective airlines. All airline program rules and conditions apply.

Fodor's

Distinctive guides packed with up-to-date expert advice and smart choices for every type of traveler.

Fodor's. For the world of ways you travel.

produce, Wildflowers Grill, and Antigua de Mexico, which offers Mexican-Colonial furniture, wrought iron, and folk art.

El Con Mall (⌧ 3601 E. Broadway at Alvernon Way, ☏ 520/795–9958) is Tucson's oldest mall and is undergoing renovation and expansion. Due for completion in January 2000, improvements will include the addition of a 20-theater cinema. Existing stores that plan to stay are: JCPenney, Robinsons-May, Dillard's, and Montgomery Ward.

Foothills Mall (⌧ 7401 N. La Cholla Blvd., at Ina Rd., ☏ 520/742–7191) has made a comeback with the addition of a Barnes & Noble Superstore and a Saks Fifth Avenue outlet store; other retailers are also moving in. Currently, the mall houses a variety of boutiques and a 16-screen cinema.

Old Town Artisans Complex (⌧ 186 N. Meyer Ave., ☏ 520/623–6024), across from the Tucson Museum of Art, has a large selection of southwestern wares, such as Native American jewelry, baskets, Mexican handicrafts, pottery, and textiles.

Park Mall (⌧ 5870 E. Broadway, at Wilmot Rd., ☏ 520/747-7575) has more than 120 stores, including Sears, Dillard's, and Macy's. The second-oldest mall in Tucson underwent a major face-lift in 1998.

Plaza Palomino (⌧ 2980 N. Swan Rd., at Ft. Lowell Rd., ☏ 520/795–1177) has a stunning array of small shops and clothing boutiques such as Dark Star Leather. Maya Palace and The Strand both offer Mexican imports. Shopping here can be an all-day affair punctuated by lunch at Firecracker (☞ Dining, *above*) or La Placita Cafe.

St. Philip's Plaza (⌧ 4280 N. Campbell Ave., at River Rd., ☏ 502/886–7485) arranges its chic shops around a series of Spanish-style outdoor patios. Shop till you drop for women's clothing at boutiques such as Nicole Miller, Sigi's, Easy Pieces, West Fine Leather, The Bag Company, and Changes. When it's time to recuperate, Café Terra Cotta (☞ Dining, *above*), Ovens, or Daniel's provides chic sustenance.

Tucson Mall (⌧ 4500 N. Oracle Rd., at Wetmore Rd., ☏ 520/293–7330) is the busiest mall in town, with Robinsons-May, Dillard's, Macy's, Mervyn's, Sears, JCPenney, and more than 200 specialty shops. For tasteful southwestern T-shirts, belts, jewelry, and posters, try Señor Coyote, on Arizona Avenue, a section of the first floor devoted to regional items.

SIDE TRIPS NEAR TUCSON

There's something for everyone—history buffs, bird-watchers, hikers, Mexican-food lovers, and folks whose idea of heaven is to shop till they drop—en route from Tucson to Nogales along I–19. The road roughly follows the Camino Real (King's Road), which the conquistadors and missionaries traveled from Mexico up to what was once the northernmost portion of New Spain.

The Asarco Mineral Discovery Center

15 mi south of Tucson off I–19.

Opened in February 1997 by the American Smelting and Refining Co. (ASARCO), this facility is designed to elucidate the importance of mining to our everyday lives. Exhibits in two connected buildings include a walk-through model of an ore crusher, videos that explain various refining processes, and a theater that shows a half-hour film on extraction of minerals from the earth. The big draw, however, is the

yawning open pit of the Mission Mine, some 2 mi long and 1¾ mi wide—
impressive, though it doesn't exactly bolster the case the center tries
to make about how environmentally conscious mining has become. ⊠
1421 W. Pima Mine Rd., ☎ *520/625–0879.* 🖃 *$6.* ☉ *Wed.–Sun. 9–
5. Tours of the Mission Mine open pit, which take about 1 hr, leave
the center on the half hr; the last one starts at 4:30.*

Titan Missile Museum

③ *25 mi south of Tucson, off I–19.*

During the Cold War, Tucson was ringed by 18 Titan II missiles. Of
the 54 such missiles that existed in the United States, the only one left
intact when the Salt II treaty with the Soviet Union was signed has been
turned into this rather sobering museum. Guided tours take visitors
down 55 steps into the command post where a ground crew of four
lived. Among the fascinating sights is a 114-ft, 165-ton, two-stage liq-
uid-fuel rocket. Now empty, it originally held a nuclear payload with
214 times the explosive power of the bomb that destroyed Hiroshima.
⊠ *1580 W. Duval Mine Rd. (I–19 exit 69),* ☎ *520/625–7736.* 🖃 *$6.*
☉ *Nov.–Apr., daily 9–5; May–Oct., Wed.–Sun. 9–4 (last tour at 4).*

Madera Canyon

㉜ *61½ mi southeast of Tucson; exit 63 off I–19, then east on White House
Canyon Rd. for 12.5 mi (it turns into Madera Canyon Rd.).*

At Madera Canyon, the Coronado National Forest meets the Santa Rita
Mountains—among them Mt. Wrightson, the highest peak in southern Arizona at 9,453 ft. With approximately 200 mi of scenic trails,
the **Madera Canyon Recreation Area** (☎ 520/670–5464) is a favorite
destination for hikers. Higher elevations and thick pine cover make it
especially popular in summer with Tucsonans looking to escape the heat.
Birders flock here year-round; about 400 avian species have been spotted in the area. The small, volunteer-run visitor center is open only on
weekends. Nearby, the **Bog Springs Campground** has 13 sites with toilets, potable water, and grills, available on a first-come, first-served basis.
The cost is $5 per vehicle per night.

Tubac

★ **㉝** *45 mi south of Tucson at exit 40 off I-19.*

Established in 1726, Tubac is the site of the first European settlement
in Arizona. A year after the Pima Indian uprising in 1851, a military
garrison was established here to protect early Spanish settlers, missionaries, and peaceful Indian converts of the nearby Tumacacori Mission from further attack. It was from here that Juan Bautista de Anza
led the expedition of 240 colonists across the desert that resulted in
the founding of San Francisco in 1776. Arizona's first newspaper, the
Weekly Arizonian, was printed here in 1859, and in 1860 Tubac was
the largest town in Arizona. Today, the quiet little town is a popular
art colony. Crafts sold in the more than 80 shops range from carved
wooden furniture and hand-thrown pottery to delicately painted tiles
and silk-screen fabrics. The annual **Tubac Festival of the Arts** has been
held in February for more than 30 years. For festival dates or other information about the town, contact the **Tubac Chamber of Commerce**
(☎ 520/398–2704).

There's an archaeological display of portions of the original 1752 fort
at the **Tubac Presidio State Historic Park and Museum** in the center of
town. In addition to the visitor center and the adjoining museum,

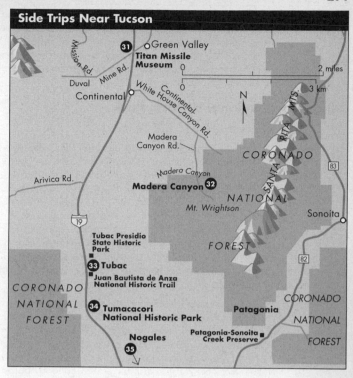

Side Trips Near Tucson

which has detailed the history of the early colony, the park includes Tubac's 1885 schoolhouse and a pleasant picnic area. ✉ *Box 1296 Presidio Dr.,* ☎ *520/398–2252.* ⊞ *$2.* ☉ *Daily 8–5.*

Dining and Lodging

$ ✕ **Tubac Country Market.** Just north of Tubac on the road parallel to I–19, this combination gift shop, deli, and grocery also has a patio restaurant that's open every day for breakfast and lunch. ✉ *2261 E. Frontage Rd.,* ☎ *520/398–9532 or 520/398–9870. MC, V. No dinner.*

$$ ⌂ **Amado Territory Inn.** Although this quiet, friendly bed-and-break-
★   fast is directly off the frontage road of busy I–19 in the town of Amado, it feels worlds away from the highway. Part of a complex that includes a plant nursery and an antiques store and gift shop, the inn, built in 1996, resembles a late-19th-century ranch house, but a soaring ceiling and contemporary southwestern art give it a distinctly modern feel inside. Rooms are furnished with pieces handcrafted in Mexico and have balconies or patios, some with a pretty view of the garden and the Santa Rita Mountains. A full gourmet breakfast (try the huevos rancheros) is included, and there are no phones or televisions in the rooms. ✉ *Box 81, 3001 E. Frontage Rd., Amado 85645,* ☎ *520/398–8684 or 888/398–8684,* ℻ *520/398–8186. 9 rooms. Restaurant, putting green, meeting rooms. Full breakfast. MC, V.*

$$ ⌂ **Burro Inn.** Leave the city behind and wake up to the sounds and sights of burros in the nearly untouched rolling hills just west of Tubac. Al-though the atmosphere is rustic and casual, the two–room suites are modern, with king-size beds, sofa beds, and microwaves. The prop-erty is located 20 ft from National Forest Service land. But it's the *tanque* (reservoir) on the property that's the drawing card for the burros, and you're likely to see other wildlife as well. ✉ *70 W. El Burro La., 85646,* ☎ *520/398–2281. 4 suites. D, MC, V.*

En Route   You can tread the same road as the conquistadors: The first 4½ mi of
              the de Anza National Historic Trail from Tumacacori to Tubac were
              dedicated in 1992. You'll have to cross the Santa Cruz River (which
              is usually pretty low) three times in order to complete the hike, and
              the path is rather sandy, but it's a pleasant journey along the tree-shaded
              banks of the river.

Tumacacori National Historic Park

34   *3 mi south of Tubac; exit 29 off I–19.*

The site where Tumacacori National Historic Park now stands was visited by missionary Father Eusebio Francisco Kino in 1691, but the Jesuits didn't build a church here until 1751. You can still see some ruins
of this simple structure, but the main attraction is the mission of San
José de Tumacacori, built by the Franciscans around 1799–1803. A
combination of circumstances—Apache attacks, a bad winter, and
Mexico's withdrawal of funds and priests—caused the friars to flee in
1848, and persistent rumors of wealth left behind by both the Franciscans and the Jesuits led treasure seekers to pillage the site unsuccessfully. It was finally protected in 1908, when it became a national
monument.

Information about the mission and the de Anza trail is available at the
visitor center, and guided tours are offered daily (more in winter than
in summer). A small museum displays some of the mission's artifacts.
In addition to a Christmas Eve service, costumed historical high masses
are held at Tumacacori in spring and fall. An annual fiesta the first weekend of December features arts and crafts and food booths. ☎ 520/398–
2341. 🔲 $2. ☉ Daily 8–5.

Lodging

$$-$$$ 🔲 **Rio Rico Resort.** Too close to Tucson to be a real getaway, this hotel
languished for many years before finally coming into its own. In a three-
story building without much charm, the rooms are large and comfortable.
Most people come for the golf, the splendid views, and the isolation.
Nogales is a short drive south. ✉ *1069 Camino Caralampi at the I–
19 and Calabasas Interchange, 85648,* ☎ *800/288–4746. 180 rooms.
Restaurant, bar. AE, D, MC, V.*

Nogales

35   *15 mi south of Tumacacori; 63 mi south of Tucson, on I–19 at the Mexican border.*

Nogales, named for the walnuts that grew along the river here, is both
the American town and the huge Mexican city over the border. The
American side was once a focal point for cattle shipping between
Sonora and the United States. Today, Nogales reaps the benefits of
NAFTA, with warehouses and trucking firms dedicated to the distribution of Mexican produce. The American side depends upon the
health of the *peso* and the number of day visitors who cross the border from Mexico to buy American goods. The Mexican side has grown
with the economic success of *maquiladoras*, factories that manufac-
ture goods destined for the United States. There is a great deal of commerce between the two sides of Nogales.

Unfortunately, some of this trade is in narcotics and undocumented workers. Security on the American side is very tight; don't even think about
taking a firearm near the border. You'll also do better not to drive your
car into Mexico: Not only is there a very real possibility it may be stolen,
but you'll face significant delays because of the thorough search you
and your vehicle will receive upon returning. This hassle is unneces-

sary, though, because you can cover Nogales in a day trip and the area of interest to tourists is within easy walking distance of the border crossing. Park on the Arizona side, either on the street or in one of many guarded lots that cost about $4 or $5 for the day, and walk across. If you want to take more time to explore the area, you can spend the night in one of the American-side motels listed here.

Dining and Lodging

$$ ✕ **El Balcon de la Roca.** East of the railroad tracks and off the beaten tourist path on the Mexican side, La Roca is a favorite of Tucsonans. The setting—a series of tiled rooms and courtyards in a stately old stone house, with a balcony overlooking a charming patio—is lovely and the food is very good. Among the variety of meat or seafood dishes is *carne tampiqueña,* an assortment of grilled meats that comes with a chiles relleno and an enchilada. ⊠ *Calle Elias 91,* ☎ *631/2–07–60 or 631/2–08–91. AE, DC, MC, V.*

$ ✕ **Elvira.** The free shot of tequila that comes with each meal will whet your appetite for Elvira's reliable fish dishes, chicken mole, or chiles rellenos. This large, friendly restaurant (divided into intimate dining areas) is at the foot of Avenida Obregón just south of the border and popular with frequent visitors to Nogales. ⊠ *Av. Obregón 1,* ☎ *631/2–47–73. Reservations not accepted. DC, MC, V.*

$ ✕ **Zula's.** Standard, old-fashioned border restaurant fare is served with Greek flair here, Sonoran food (tortillas, cheese, refried beans) alongside gyros and American selections. It makes for an interesting combination. The atmosphere is not as glitzy as at the south-of-the-border places, but the food is just as tasty. ⊠ *982 N. Grand Ave.,* ☎ *520/287–2892. MC, V. No lunch.*

$ ☷ **Americana Motor Hotel.** A serviceable place that has seen better days, the Americana features large, Aztec-style stone sculptures scattered around the grounds. Spacious, and decorated in a Southwest-motel motif, rooms are comfortable, if worn. The restaurant and lounge are casual places to eat American food. ⊠ *639 N. Grand Ave., 85621,* ☎ *520/287–7211 or 800/874–8079. 96 rooms. Pool. AE, MC, V.*

$ ☷ **Days Inn.** This typical chain hotel offers casual, unpretentious border flavor. The small-town service, while friendly, is not particularly quick. ⊠ *844 N. Grand Ave., 85621,* ☎ *520/287–4611 or 800/697–2554,* 𝖥𝖠𝖷 *520/287–0101. 102 rooms. Restaurant, bar, pool, hot tub. AE, MC, V.*

Shopping

The main shopping area is on the Mexican side, on Avenida Obregón, which begins a few blocks west (to your right) of the border entrance and runs north–south; just follow the crowds. You'll find handicrafts, furnishings, and jewelry here, though if you go off on some of the side streets, you might come across more interesting finds at better prices. Except at shops that indicate otherwise, bargaining is not only acceptable but expected. The following shops, however, tend to have fixed prices:

Casa Bonita (⊠ Av. Obregón 134, ☎ 631/2–30–59) sells jewelry, tinwork mirrors, carved wooden chests, and interesting household items.

El Changarro (⊠ Calle Elias 93, ☎ 613/2–05–45) carries high-quality (and high-priced) furniture, antiques, pottery, and handwoven rugs. It's next door to El Balcon de la Roca (☞ Dining and Lodging, *above*).

El Sarape (⊠ Av. Obregón 161, ☎ 631/2–03–09) specializes in sterling silver jewelry from Taxco and designer clothing for women.

Maya de México (⊠ Av. Obregón 150, ☎ no phone) is the place to come for smaller folk art items, including Day of the Dead displays, blue glass, painted dishes, colorful clothing on two levels.

TUCSON A TO Z

Arriving and Departing

By Bus

Buses to Los Angeles, El Paso, Phoenix, Flagstaff, Douglas, and Nogales (Arizona) depart and arrive regularly from Tucson's **Greyhound Lines terminal** (⊠ 2 S. 4th Ave., at E. Broadway, ☎ 520/792–3475). For travel to Phoenix, **Arizona Shuttle Service, Inc.** (☎ 520/795–6771), runs express service from three locations in Tucson every hour on the hour, 4 AM–10 PM every day; the trip takes about 2½ hours. One-way fare is $19. Call 24 hours in advance for reservations. **Arizona Flying Coach** (☎ 520/887–8788) offers similar service; it has fewer vans scheduled but there are four pickup points and prices are slightly lower ($15).

By Car

From Phoenix, 111 mi northwest, I–10 east is the road that will take you to Tucson. Also a major north–south traffic artery through town, I–10 has well-marked exits all along the route. At Casa Grande, 70 mi north of Tucson, I–8 connects with I–10, bringing travelers into the area from Yuma and San Diego. From Nogales, 63 mi south on the Mexican border, take I–19 into Tucson.

By Plane

Check plane fares carefully when planning your trip. Though you may not want to spend time in Phoenix, sometimes it's cheaper to fly into that city and then take a scenic 2½-hour drive down the Pinal Pioneer Parkway (U.S. 79), or a speedier (½-hour) trip on I–10, to Tucson.

Tucson International Airport (☎ 520/573–8000) is 8½ mi south of downtown, west of I–10 off the Valencia exit. Carriers include **Aerocalifornia** (☎ 800/237–6225); **Aeromexico** and its subsidiary, **Aerolitoral** (☎ 520/573–8315); **American** (☎ 800/433–7300); **America West** (☎ 800/235–9292); **Continental** (☎ 520/623–3700); **Delta** (☎ 800/221–1212); **Great Lakes Aviation** (☎ 800/274–0662); **Northwest** (☎ 800/225–2525); **Reno Air** (☎ 800/736–6247); **Southwest** (☎ 800/435–9792); and **United** (☎ 800/241–6522).

BETWEEN THE AIRPORT AND DOWNTOWN

In addition to the transportation options listed below, many hotels provide courtesy airport shuttle service; inquire when making reservations.

By Car. It makes sense to rent at the airport; all the major rental-car agencies—Avis, Budget, Hertz, and National Interrent—are represented, along with Alamo, Dollar, and Value. The driving time from the airport to the center of town varies, but it's usually less than half an hour; add 15 minutes during rush hours (7:30 AM–9 AM and 4:30 PM–6 PM). Parking is not a problem in most parts of town.

By Taxi. Taxi rates vary widely; they are unregulated in Arizona. It's always wise to inquire about the cost of a trip before getting into a cab. You shouldn't pay much more than $18 from the airport to central Tucson. A few of the more reliable cab companies are **ABC** (☎ 520/623–7979), **Airline Taxi** (☎ 520/887–6933), and **Fiesta Taxi** (☎ 520/622–7777), whose drivers speak both English and Spanish.

By Van or Bus. For $8.50–$26, depending on the location, **Arizona Stagecoach** (⊠ Office at airport, ☎ 520/889–1000) takes groups and individuals to all parts of Tucson. If you're traveling light and aren't in a hurry, you can take a city **Sun Tran** (☎ 520/792–9222) bus to central Tucson. Bus 11, which leaves every half hour from a stop at the left of the lower level as you come out of the terminal, goes north on Alvernon Way, and you can transfer to most of the east–west bus lines from this main north–south road; ask the bus driver which one would take you closest to the location you need. You can also transfer to a variety of lines from Bus 25, which leaves less frequently from the same airport location and heads to the Roy Laos center at the south of town (☞ Getting Around, *below*).

By Train
Amtrak (⊠ Station: 400 E. Toole St., ☎ 520/623–4442) serves the city with westbound and eastbound trains three times a week.

Getting Around

A car is a requirement if you're going to thoroughly explore Tucson and southern Arizona. You can get around the small downtown area on foot and by bus or taxi, but Tucson is very spread out and public transportation is somewhat limited when it comes to sightseeing.

By Bus and Trolley
Within the city limits, public transportation is available through **Sun Tran** (☎ 520/792–9222), Tucson's bus system. On weekdays, bus service starts around 5 AM; some lines operate until 10 PM, but most only go until 7 or 8 PM, and weekend service is limited. A one-way ride costs 85¢; transfers are free, but be sure to request them when you pay your fare, for which exact change is required. Those with valid Medicare cards can ride for 35¢. Call for information on Sun Tran bus routes.

The city-run **Van Tran** (☎ 520/620–1234) has specially outfitted vans for riders with disabilities. Call for information and reservations.

By Car
Much of the year, traffic in Tucson isn't especially heavy, but during the busiest winter months (December through March), streets in the central area of town can get congested. There's a seatbelt law in the state, as well as one that requires children under the age of four to ride in a secure child-restraint seat. Don't even think of drinking and driving; if you do, you'll spend your vacation in jail. Arizona's strict laws against driving under the influence are strongly enforced.

Contacts and Resources

Car Rentals
If you haven't rented a car at the airport (☞ Between the Airport and Downtown, *above*), you might try **U-Save Auto Rental** (☎ 520/790–8847), **Enterprise** (☎ 520/881–9400), or **Rent-a-Ride** (☎ 520/750–1900 or 520/622–0162), all in the city center. In addition, **Carefree Rent-a-Car** (☎ 520/790–2655) rents reliable used cars at good rates. If you think you might be interested in driving farther into Mexico than Nogales (where you can park on the U.S. side of the border), check in advance to make sure that the rental company will allow this and that you are covered on your rental insurance policy: Many rental insurance agreements do not cover accidents or theft that occurs outside the United States.

Emergencies
For the **police, ambulance, fire department,** dial 911, a free call from public pay phones.

DOCTORS AND DENTISTS
On weekdays the **Pima County Medical Society** (☎ 520/795–7985) will refer visitors to Tucson physicians. The **Arizona State Dental Association** (☎ 520/881–7237) can recommend a dentist in the area.

HOSPITALS

Columbia El Dorado Hospital (⊠ 1400 N. Wilmot Rd., ☎ 520/886–6361). **Columbia Northwest Medical Center** (⊠ 6200 N. La Cholla Blvd., ☎ 520/742–9000). **St. Joseph's Hospital** (⊠ 350 N. Wilmot Rd., ☎ 520/296–3211). **Tucson General Hospital** (⊠ 3838 N. Campbell Ave., ☎ 520/318–6300). **Tucson Medical Center** (⊠ 5301 E. Grant Rd., ☎ 520/327–5461). **University Medical Center** (⊠ 1501 N. Campbell Ave., ☎ 520/694–0111).

LATE-NIGHT PHARMACIES

Several **Walgreen's** (☎ 800/925–4733) and **Osco** drugstores (☎ 800/654–6726) are open for 24-hour service. Enter the area code and the first three digits of the number from which you are calling for the pharmacy nearest you.

Guided Tours

ADVENTURE AND ECO-TOURS

Sunshine Jeep Tours (☎ 520/742–1943) and **High Desert Convoys** (☎ 520/323–3386) arrange trips to the Sonoran Desert in open-air four-wheel-drive vehicles. **Baja's Frontier Tours** (☎ 520/887–2340 or 800/726–7231) and **Desert Path Tours** (☎ 520/327–7235) explore the natural history of the area. **Arizona Offroad Adventures** (☎ 520/882–6567 or 800/689–2453) offers several mountain-bike excursions, ranging from gentle half-day sessions in Tucson to "extreme" tours through rough terrain and weeklong trips through Arizona. In winter, the Colorado-based **Rocky Mountain Cattle Moo-vers** (☎ 520/682–2088 or 800/826–9666) leads city slickers on a cattle drive from the northwest part of town to the foothills of the Tortolita Mountains.

ORIENTATION TOURS

Great Western Tours (☎ 520/721–0980) and **Tucson Tours & Entertainment** (☎ 520/297–2911) take individuals and groups to such popular sights as Old Tucson, Sabino Canyon, and the Arizona–Sonora Desert Museum. In-depth tours of the city and its neighborhoods are also available. **Old Pueblo Tours** (☎ 520/575–1175), with a slightly different itinerary—including "A" Mountain and San Xavier del Bac Mission—provides a fine historical overview of the area. Many tour operators are on limited schedules (or close altogether) during the summer, but **Off the Beaten Path Tours** (☎ 502/529–6090) has excellent customized excursions year-round.

SPECIAL-INTEREST TOURS

In the spring and fall, those interested in visiting the area's historic missions can contact **Kino Mission Tours** (☎ 520/628–1269), which has professional historians and bilingual guides on staff.

WALKING TOURS

Tucson's historic districts make for great walks. For one easy-to-follow self-guided tour, head for the **Convention and Visitors Bureau** (☞ Visitor Information, *below*). The friendly, knowledgeable docents of the **Arizona Historical Society** (☎ 520/622–0956) conduct walking tours of El Presidio neighborhood (departing from the Sosa-Carillo-Fremont House) every Saturday at 10 from November through March; the cost is $4.50.

Radio Stations

AM

KNST 790: News, talk; **KTKT 990:** Sports Entertainment Network; **KJYK 1490:** Top 40; **KUAT 1550:** National Public Radio, jazz.

FM

KUAT 89.1: National Public Radio; **KUAZ 90.5:** Classical; **KXCI 91.3:** Alternative rock, folk, blues; **KLPX 96.1:** Rock; **KIIM 99.5:** Country.

Visitor Information

The **Metropolitan Tucson Convention and Visitors Bureau** (⊠ 130 S. Scott Ave., 85701, ☎ 520/624–1817 or 800/638–8350) is open weekdays 8–5 and weekends 9–4.

OTHER USEFUL NUMBERS

Chamber of Commerce (☎ 520/792–1212). **Local and state road conditions** (☎ 520/573–7623). **Tucson Parks and Recreation Department** (☎ 520/791–4873). **Weather** (☎ 520/881–3333).

V

7 SOUTHERN ARIZONA

From mountains to grasslands, canyons, and deserts, southern Arizona has some of the most spectacular landscapes in the West, but remains largely undiscovered by travelers. Here you can explore Wild West towns and old mining enclaves at a leisurely pace. Natural lures include the ominous, towering rock formations of Chiricahua National Monument, the rolling grasslands of Patagonia and Sonoita, the many-armed cacti in Organ Pipe National Monument, and a variety of pristine Nature Conservancy preserves.

SOUTHERN ARIZONA CAN DO little to escape its cliché-ridden image as a landscape of cow skulls, tumbleweeds, dried-up riverbeds, and mother lodes—it doesn't need to. The area that evokes such American dime-novel notions as Indian wars, vast land grants, and savage shoot-'em-ups is not simply another part of the Wild West drunk on romanticized images of its former self; local farmers and ranchers here evoke the self-sufficiency and ruggedness of their pioneer ancestors and revel in the area's rowdy past. Abandoned mining towns and sleepy western hamlets dot a lonely landscape of rugged rock formations, deep pine forests, dense mountain ranges, and scrubby grasslands.

Updated by
Andrea Ibáñez

South of Sierra Vista, just above the Mexican border, a stone marker commemorates the spot where the first Europeans set foot in what is now the United States. In 1540, 80 years before the Pilgrims landed at Plymouth Rock, Spanish conquistador Don Francisco Vásquez de Coronado led one of Spain's largest expeditions from Mexico along the fertile San Pedro River valley, where the little towns of Benson and St. David are found today. They had come north to seek the legendary Seven Cities of Cibola where Indian pueblos were rumored to have doors of polished turquoise and streets of solid gold.

The real wealth of the region, however, lay in its rich veins of copper and silver, not tapped until more than 300 years after the Spanish marched on in disappointment. Once word of this cache spread, these parts of the West quickly grew much wilder: Fortune seekers who rushed to the region came face-to-face with the Chiricahua Apaches, led by Cochise and Geronimo, while from rugged mountain hideaways Indian warriors battled encroaching settlers and the U.S. cavalry sent to protect them.

Although the search for mineral booty in southeastern Arizona is much more notorious, the western side of the state wasn't entirely untouched by the rage to plunder the earth. The leaching plant built by the New Cornelia Copper Company in 1917 transformed the sleepy desert community of Ajo into one of the most important mining districts in the state. Interest in going for the gold in California gave rise to the town of Yuma: The Colorado River had to be crossed to get to the west coast, and Fort Yuma was established in part to protect the Anglo ferry business at a good fording point of the river from Indian competitors. The Yuma tribe lost that battle, but another group of Native Americans, the Tohono O'odham, fared better in this part of the state. Known for a long time as the Papago—or "bean eaters," a name given them by the Spanish—they were deeded a large portion of their ancestral homeland by the U.S. Bureau of Indian Affairs. The largest of their three reservations, stretching across an almost completely undeveloped section of southwestern Arizona, encompasses 2,774,370 acres.

Pleasures and Pastimes

Bird-Watching

Southern Arizona has been ranked as one of the five best areas for birdwatching in the United States; nearly 500 species have been spotted in the area. To the east, birders flock to the Patagonia-Sonoita Creek and Ramsey Canyon preserves, the San Pedro Riparian National Conservation Area, the ponds and dry lake beds south of Willcox, and the Portal-Cave Creek area in the Chiricahua Mountains near the New Mexico border. To the west, the Buenos Aires and Imperial national wildlife refuges are among the many places famed for their abundance of avian visitors.

Camping

There are at least 100 camping areas scattered throughout the southern region of Arizona. Though it can get chilly at night in the desert, the weather's usually good enough year-round to make sleeping out under the vast, starry night sky an appealing option. Summertime is the time to camp in the state's cooler higher-altitude campgrounds. Campgrounds in the rural areas of southern Arizona rarely come close to getting full except on holiday weekends, and even then, campers tend to stay close to major cities and towns. Keep in mind that you will find fairly primitive camping conditions (RV hookups are rare); it is advisable to bring your own fresh drinking water and be prepared to carry out what trash you bring in.

Dining

In southern Arizona, cowboy fare is more common than haute cuisine. But there are exceptions to the rule, especially in the wine-growing area and in Bisbee, both popular for weekend outings from Tucson. And of course, a region that shares its border with Mexico is bound to have a fair number of good tacquerias.

Ghost Towns

A number of the smaller mining communities of Cochise County died when their veins of ore ran out, and their adobe buildings gradually melted back into the desert under the summer monsoons. Some of what are termed ghost towns in the area are only heaps of rubble, but others show strong evidence of better days. In addition to Gleeson and Fairbank, a few holdouts remain—enough to keep the post office open— in Dos Cabezas, 15 mi southeast of Willcox, where you'll see the 1885 Wells Fargo station still standing. A tunnel through the mountaintop connects the eastern and western halves of the abandoned town of Hilltop, farther southeast of Willcox. Six miles northwest of Portal in the Chiricahua Mountains, Paradise was active in the 1900s, and a few old-timers still live here. Look for the old town jail among the ruined buildings.

Hiking

You can trek around Nature Conservancy preserves such as Ramsey Canyon, Arivaipa Canyon, the Patagonia-Sonoita Creek Sanctuary, and Muleshoe Ranch; Organ Pipe and Chiricahua national monuments; and dramatic mountain ranges such as the Huachucas, the Patagonias, the Rincons, the Whetstones, and the Dragoons.

Lodging

There are a number of lodgings with character in southern Arizona: Two historic hotels, some guest ranches, a couple of Nature Conservancy properties, and an increasing array of bed-and-breakfasts (including a converted jail and an astronomical observatory) that let you lay down your head surrounded by nature and history. Still, the bulk of the places to stay in the area are of the park-your-car-outside-the-room chain variety.

Stargazing

The telescopes at world-famous Kitt Peak National Observatory are open to the public, and stargazing dinners have recently been initiated there. It's hard to find a more beautiful and remote spot to set an eye to the sky.

Wineries

The term "Arizona Wine Country" may sound odd, but the soil and climate in the Santa Cruz Valley, southeast of Tucson, are ideal for growing grapes. Connoisseurs debate the merits of the various wineries that have sprung up in the region since 1974, but if you want to decide for yourself, tour some of the region's wineries.

Exploring Southern Arizona

Numbers in the text correspond to numbers in the margin and on the Southeast Arizona and Southwest Arizona maps.

Great Itineraries

IF YOU HAVE 2 DAYS

If you are headed east from Tucson, poke around the town of **Patagonia** ② and the Patagonia-Sonoita Creek preserve in the morning, and then continue east to **Tombstone** ④ in the afternoon. After strolling the shoot-'em-up capital, head south to ☒ **Bisbee** ⑤, a good place to spend the night. Take the mine tour the next morning and devote the afternoon to exploring the shops on Main Street.

If you're going west, take a leisurely drive to **Kitt Peak National Observatory** ⑭. Stop at the Tohono O'odham Reservation capital, **Sells** ⑮, en route to ☒ **Ajo** ⑯, where you'll sleep. Plan to spend most of the next day hiking or driving around **Organ Pipe Cactus National Monument** ⑰, but set aside a little time to explore the pleasant mining town.

IF YOU HAVE 4 DAYS

Begin your tour in Arizona Wine Country. First, head to **Patagonia** ② where you can visit the vineyards around **Sonoita** ① and Elgin. Stay overnight in the ☒ **Sierra Vista** ③ area near Ramsey Canyon, where you're likely to be greeted by hummingbirds in the morning. Head out early for **Tombstone** ④ so you can spend the morning exploring the town; in the afternoon head south to see the sights of ☒ **Bisbee** ⑤ and stay overnight. Head north the next day to **Chiricahua National Monument** ⑦ and stay in **Willcox** ⑨. It won't take you long to see that little town's sights; on your way back toward Tucson on I–10, stop at **Texas Canyon** ⑩ and visit the Amerind Foundation's gallery and museum. A few miles farther west is **Benson** ⑪, where you can take a train ride, or go down to **Kartchner Caverns State Park** ⑫ and tour a huge underground world of stalactites and stalagmites.

When to Tour Southern Arizona

As you might expect, the desert areas are popular in winter, and the cooler mountain areas are more heavily visited in summer months. For the most part, prices don't change seasonally, however, so your body's comfort level rather than your purse should be the determining factor in timing a stay.

SOUTHEAST ARIZONA

From the rugged mountain forests to the desert grasslands of Sierra Vista, the southeast corner of Arizona is perhaps the state's most scenic region. Much of this area is part of Cochise County, named in 1881 in honor of the chief of the Chiricahua Apache. Cochise waged war against troops and settlers for 11 years, and he was respected by Indian and non-Indian alike for his integrity and leadership skills. Today Cochise County is dotted by small towns, many of them much smaller— and all much tamer—than they were in their heyday. Cochise County is home to six and part of the seventh of the 12 mountain ranges—including the Huachucas, Mustangs, Whetstones, and Rincons—that compose the 1.7-million-acre Coronado National Forest.

Sonoita

❶ *34 mi southeast of Tucson on I–10 to AZ 83; 57 mi west of Tombstone.*

There's not much to see in Sonoita, once little more than a truck stop at the junction of AZ 83 and AZ 82, but the establishment of a num-

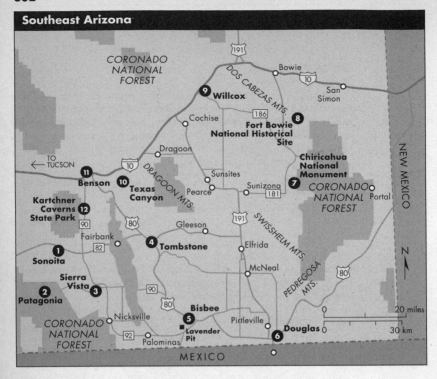

Southeast Arizona

ber of wineries and upscale restaurants here is a sign that the traditional ranching region around the town is changing.

OFF THE
BEATEN PATH

WINE COUNTRY – If you'd like to sample some local product and learn more about wine making, stop at **Dark Mountain Brewery and R. W. Webb Winery** (⊠ 13605 E. Benson Hwy., ☎ 520/762–5777). Take I–10 east about 12 mi, and get off at Vail, Exit 279. This is the only brewery and winery on the same premises in the state. Most of the other growers are in the area where Routes 82 and 83 intersect: Get back on I–10 east for two more exits, and then drive south on Route 83 for 24 mi to Sonoita. Growers in the scenic ranching region nearby include **Callaghan** (⊠ 3 mi south of Elgin, ☎ 520/455–5650), **Sonoita Vineyards** (⊠ 3 mi southeast of Elgin, ☎ 520/455–5893), **Santa Cruz Winery** (right next to the Stage Stop Motel, ☎ 520/394–2888), and **The Village of Elgin Winery** (⊠ Elgin, ☎ 520/455–9309). Others in southeastern Arizona are **Kokopelli Winery** (⊠ Along Route 186 south from Willcox, ☎ 520/384–3800) and **Arizona Vineyards** (⊠ 1830 Patagonia Hwy., 4 mi northeast of Nogales on Rte. 82, ☎ 520/287–7972).

Dining and Lodging

$$$ ✕ **Er Pastaro.** The last thing you'd expect to find in the middle of Marlboro Country is this Italian restaurant, established by a Rome-born former manager of Regine's in New York. The specialty is pasta, with a variety of fresh sauces. There's a good choice of Italian wines. ⊠ 3084 Hwy. 82, ☎ 520/455–5821. *No credit cards. Closed Mon. and Tues. and July–Aug. No lunch.*

$$$ ✕ **Karen's Cafe.** The country French menu, which changes nightly, has salads, a pasta of the day, and two meat or fish entrées—say, a grilled French-cut pork chop in a Calvados cream sauce. Local wines are available by the glass or bottle. One annoyance: The fresh-baked bread, good

though it is, costs extra. ⊠ *471 Upper Elgin Rd., Elgin,* ☏ *520/455–5282. MC, V. Closed Mon.–Tues. No dinner Wed., Sun.*

$ ▥ **Vineyard Bed-and-Breakfast.** A friendly burro, a couple of dogs, and a parrot named Fred all welcome guests to this B&B, which sits on a 20-acre, high-country (5,100-ft) spread just outside Sonoita. Three of the country-style guest rooms occupy a 1916 adobe ranch house. Whether you're lying in a live oak–shaded hammock or swimming in the pool surrounded by plum and peach trees, you'll find this a supremely relaxing setting. Breakfasts, served on a closed-in sunporch, are generous—sourdough pecan waffles, apple fritters, and puff pancakes are all possibilities. Fresh eggs come courtesy of the B&B's hens. ⊠ *92 Los Encinos Rd., Sonoita 85637,* ☏ *520/455–4749. 3 rooms, 1 casita. Pool. No credit cards. Full breakfast.*

Patagonia

❷ *12 mi south of Sonoita via AZ 83.*

Served by a spur of the Atchison, Topeka, and Santa Fe Railroad, Patagonia was a shipping center for cattle and ore. The town declined after the railroad departed in 1962, and the old depot is now the town hall. Today, art galleries and boutiques coexist with real Western saloons in this tiny, tree-lined village in the Patagonia Mountains.

The **Patagonia visitor's center** (⊠ 315 McKoewn Ave., ☏ 520/394–0060) shares quarters with the only kosher winery in Arizona, the **Santa Cruz Winery** (⊠ 154 McKoewn Ave., Patagonia, ☏ 520/394–2888). The **Mesquite Grove Gallery** (⊠ 371 McKoewn Ave., ☏ 520/394–2358) carries an appealing array of local crafts.

At the Nature Conservancy's **Patagonia–Sonoita Creek Preserve,** 1,400 acres of riparian habitat are protected along the Patagonia–Sonoita Creek. More than 275 bird species have been sighted here, along with deer, javelina, coatimundi, desert tortoise, snakes, and more. There is a self-guided nature trail; guided walks are given every Saturday at 9 AM. Three concrete structures near an elevated berm of the Railroad Trail serve as reminders of the land's former use. ⊠ *Make a right on 4th Ave., which comes to a dead end, and then make a left. This paved road soon becomes dirt and leads to the preserve in about ¼ mi;* ☏ *520/394–2400.* ▥ *$5 suggested donation for nonmembers.* ☉ *Wed.–Sun. 7:30–3:30.*

Eleven miles south of town, **Patagonia Lake State Park** is popular for water sports, picnicking, and camping. Formed by the damming of Sonoita Creek, the 265-acre reservoir lures fishers with its largemouth bass, crappie, bluegill, and catfish; it's stocked with trout in the wintertime. You can rent rowboats, paddleboats, canoes, and camping and fishing gear at the marina. Most swimmers head for Boulder Beach. ⊠ *400 Lake Patagonia Rd.,* ☏ *520/287–6965.* ▥ *$5 for day use, $15 camping (partial hookups).* ☉ *Visitor center daily 9–4:30, gates closed 10 PM–4 AM.*

Dining and Lodging

$$ ✕ **Marie's.** Marie's has endeared itself to Patagonia's residents, not only because it's open for dinner most of the week (a rarity here), but also because of the sophisticated Mediterranean fare. Try the freshly made chicken pâté with pistachios, spinach pie, or roast pork loin in white wine and mustard sauce. A good finish is the chocolate hazelnut torte, a house specialty. ⊠ *340 Naugle Ave.,* ☏ *520/394–2812. MC, V. Closed Mon.–Tues. No lunch Wed.–Sat.*

$ ✕ **McGraw's Wagon Wheel Cantina.** The adjoining patio restaurant, serving ribs, chicken, and burgers, is a recent development, but the cowboy bar, with its neon beer signs and mounted moose head, has been around since the early 1900s. This is where every Stetson-wearing ranch hand in the area comes to listen to the country jukebox and down a long neck, maybe accompanied by some poppers (deep-fried hot peppers stuffed with cream cheese). ⊠ *400 W. Naugle St.,* ☎ *520/394–2433. AE, MC, V.*

$ ✕ **Ovens of Patagonia.** Known for its great quiches and salads, this
★ spot also serves dishes with a Cuban-Mexican influence: burritos, pan rellenos, and bread stuffed with fillings such as cinnamon chipotle chicken or chorizo and onions. Don't pass up the key lime pie. ⊠ *Corner 3rd Ave. and AZ 82,* ☎ *520/394–2483. AE, MC, V. No dinner.*

$$$$ ⊞ **Circle Z Ranch.** Built in 1926 as a guest ranch, this facility edged by giant sycamore and cottonwood trees is surrounded by the Patagonia–Sonoita Creek Preserve, home to one of the precious few continually running creeks in the area. Rooms in the adobe-style buildings have hardwood floors with area rugs, king or twin beds, wicker furniture, and antique Monterey wooden chests. Gourmet meals are prepared to suit individual tastes or dietary restrictions, which might explain why more than 60% of business here comes from repeat customers. Guests can bird and hike in the preserve, ride on the adjacent National Forest Land, or just loaf and admire the spectacular setting of movies such as *Red River* as well several episodes of *Gunsmoke.* All meals and amenities are included. ⊠ *Box 194, 85624,* ☎ *520/394–2525. 22 rooms, 2 suites. Pool, tennis courts, shuffleboard. No credit cards. Closed May 15–Oct. 31. FAP.*

$–$$ ⊞ **Stage Stop Inn.** Old Territorial appearance notwithstanding, the building isn't historic and the rooms are standard motel issue, but this is still a good place to lay your hat for the night. The public areas have character, the center-of-town location is prime, and the price is right. ⊠ *303 W. McKeown Ave., 85624,* ☎ *520/394–2211; 800/923–2211 in AZ. 43 rooms. Restaurant, pool. AE, D, DC, MC, V.*

$ ⊞ **Duquesne House.** The rooms of this corrugated tin-roof adobe B&B, built as a miner's boardinghouse at the turn of the century, were decorated with a wonderfully whimsical hand by owner Regina Medley, an artist who also has a gift gallery in town. Western period furniture collected in the Patagonia area fills the house and the four high-ceiling guest units, each with a private entrance. Buffet breakfast may be enjoyed in your room, on the flower-filled screen porch, or in the Santa Fe–style great room. ⊠ *357 Duquesne Ave., Box 772, 85624,* ☎ *520/394–2732. 4 suites. No credit cards. Full breakfast.*

⚠ **Patagonia Lake.** This civilized spot has water, showers, rest rooms, and even a store and marina for those who fish or boat. Arizona has a surprising number of water-recreation lovers, so you can expect the 115 sites (34 with RV hook-up) to fill up quickly. Five miles to the east is the Patagonia–Sonoita Creek Preserve. ⊠ *4 mi southeast of Patagonia on AZ 82 (Patagonia Lake exit),* ☎ *800/285–3703 or 602/542–4174.* ⊠ *$10; $15 with hook-up.* ☉ *Year-round. Reservations not accepted.*

Sierra Vista

❸ *42 mi northeast of Patagonia via AZ 82 to AZ 90.*

A temperate climate year-round has attracted retirees to this town, which is 4,620 ft above sea level. Although Sierra Vista is fairly characterless, with tract housing, RV parks, chain motels, and fast-food restaurants, it's a good base from which to explore some of the area's most interesting sights.

Historic Fort Huachuca, headquarters of the army's Global Information Systems Command, is the last of the great Western forts still in operation. It dates back to 1877, when the Buffalo Soldiers (yes, Bob

Marley fans—*those* Buffalo Soldiers), the first all-black regiment in the U.S. forces, came to aid settlers battling invaders from Mexico, Indian tribes reluctant to give up their homelands, and assorted American desperadoes on the lam from the law back East. Three miles from the fort's main gate is the **Fort Huachuca Museum,** housed in a late-19th-century bachelor officers' quarters. The museum and its annex across the street provide a fascinating record of military life on the frontier. ⊠ *AZ 90, west of Sierra Vista,* ☎ *520/533–5736.* ▦ *Free.* ⊙ *Weekdays 9–4, weekends 1–4.*

Those driving to **Coronado National Memorial,** dedicated to Francisco Vásquez de Coronado, will see many of the same stunning vistas of Arizona and Mexico the conquistador saw when he trod this route in 1540 seeking the mythical Seven Cities of Cibola. It's a little more than 3 mi via a dirt road from the visitor center to Montezuma Pass, and another ½ mi on foot to the top of the nearly 7,000-ft Coronado Peak, where the views are best. Other trails include Joe's Canyon Trail, a steep 3-mi route (one-way) down to the visitor center, and Miller Peak Trail, 12 mi round-trip to the highest point in the Huachuca Mountains (Miller Peak is 9,466 ft). The turnoff for the monument is 16 mi south of Sierra Vista on AZ 92; the visitor center is 5 mi in. ⊠ *4101 E. Montezuma Canyon Rd., Hereford,* ☎ *520/366–5515.* ▦ *Free.* ⊙ *Visitor center daily 8–5.*

Hikers and bird-watchers alike flock to the **Ramsey Canyon Preserve,** managed by the Nature Conservancy. The convergence of two mountain and desert systems—this spot marks the northernmost limit of the Sierra Madre, the southernmost limit of the Rockies, and it's at the edge of the Chihuahuan and Sonoran deserts—as well as the presence of the fresh water of the San Pedro River, makes it a mecca for bird life. Rare species such as the marvelously named Elegant Trogon nest here; between April and October, 14 species of hummingbird come to the area—more than get together anywhere else in the United States. There are only 13 parking spots, which fill up quickly in the busiest months of April, May, and August; advance reservations are required at all times. You'll need to reserve even further in advance for one of the Conservancy's fully equipped cabins in the preserve (consider booking a year ahead of time). Register at the visitor center, where maps and books on the area's natural history, flora, and fauna are available. ⊠ *27 Ramsey Canyon Rd., Hereford (about 6 mi from Sierra Vista; go south on AZ 92 and take a right on Ramsey Canyon Rd.),* ☎ *520/378–2785.* ▦ *$5 suggested donation.* ⊙ *Daily 8–5.*

OFF THE BEATEN PATH

SAN PEDRO RIPARIAN NATIONAL CONSERVATION AREA – Many people view this conservation area from the window of the San Pedro and Southwestern Railroad (☞ Benson, *below*). With the exception of the excursion line, no motorized vehicles are permitted to enter the preserve, but you can walk into the wilderness from parking areas at three bridges on AZ 92, AZ 90, and AZ 82, the last of which is in the town of Fairbank, the site for the preserve's headquarters, run by the Bureau of Land Management.

The San Pedro River, partially rerouted underground by an 1887 earthquake, may not look like much for most of the year but it sustains an impressive array of flora and fauna. In order to maintain this fragile desert ecosystem, 56,000 acres were dedicated a protected riparian area in 1988. (About 70%–80% of the state's wildlife depends on riparian habitats, which now comprise only 0.5% of Arizona's land.) More than 250 species of birds come here, as well as the occasional javelina, bobcat, and mountain lion. Forty thousand years ago, this was the domain of woolly mammoths and mastodons: Many of the huge skeletons in Washington's Smithsonian Institute or New York's Museum of Natural History came from the massive fossil pits in the area. As evidenced by a number of small, unexcavated ruins, the various migratory Indian tribes who passed through centuries later also found this valley hospitable, in part because of its many useful plants. ⊠ *Bureau of Land Management headquarters, Fairbank (8 mi northeast of Sierra Vista),* ☎ *520/458–3559.* ☒ *Free.* ⊙ *Daily 7:45 AM–4:15 PM, conservation area open 24 hrs.*

Lodging

$$ 🏨 **Casa de San Pedro.** Bird-watchers are drawn to this contemporary hacienda-style bed-and-breakfast abutting the San Pedro Riparian National Conservation Area, and the hosts do everything they can to nourish it—they even provide a computer with Robert Tory Peterson software on it, so guests can identify what they spot from the picture windows in the high-ceiling common room. A number of hiking trails pass behind the house, and regular weekend birding courses and tours are offered. Guest quarters are bright and modern, and handcrafted wooden furnishings from northern Mexico lend local character. Breakfasts, which include fresh-baked goods, are as healthy or as indulgent as you like. ⊠ *8933 S. Yell La., Hereford 85615,* ☎ *520/366–1300,* FAX *520/366–9701. 10 rooms. Library. MC, V. Full breakfast.*

$$ 🏨 **Ramsey Canyon Inn Bed & Breakfast.** Bird-watchers find paradise
★ at this country Victorian–style B&B near Ramsey Canyon. Innkeeper Shirlene DeSantis bakes pies and prepares elaborate breakfasts for guests, and her wonderful wood-and-stone inn incorporates local Arizona history with planks from the old post office at Fort Huachuca, the train station at Fairbank, and the Lavender Pit Mine in Bisbee. ⊠ *31 Ramsey Canyon Rd., Hereford 85615,* ☎ *520/378–3010,* FAX *520/378–0487. 6 rooms, two 1-bedroom cottages. No credit cards. Full breakfast.*

$ 🏨 **Windemere Hotel & Conference Center.** Evidence that Sierra Vista is growing in size and sophistication, this large complex incorporates the largest conference space in Cochise County. Just a hop from the airport and the Army Intelligence Center and School, it has large, comfortable, bright rooms, most with sweeping views of the nearby mountains. A breakfast buffet is available to all guests and a restaurant and lounge on site mean you never have to leave the premises, but a drive into town for a meal is worth it to experience a taste of Army town life of days past. Guests have access to a nearby health club. ⊠ *2047 S. Hwy. 92, 85635,* ☎ *520/459–5900 or 800/825–4656,* FAX *520/458–1347. 149 rooms. Pool, hot tub. AE, D, MC, V.*

🏕 **Ramsey Vista.** Though not easy to reach—it's about 7,400 feet up the side of a mountain on an unpaved and winding road—this campground with bathrooms (no showers) but no hook-ups is never crowded and is well worth the trip. The birding is excellent, and you are likely to see coatimundi, javelinas, and deer. ⊠ *7 mi south of Sierra Vista on AZ 92, then 10 mi west on Carr Canyon Rd.,* ☎ *520/670–4552.* ☒ *$10.* ⊙ *May–Oct. Reservations not accepted.*

🏕 **Reef Townsite.** Named for the vanished mining town of Reef, this spot is a mile west of Ramsey Vista, high up on a mountainside in a Ponderosa pine forest. It has rest rooms and drinking water, but no showers or hook-ups. ⊠ *7 mi south of Sierra Vista on AZ 92, then 11 mi west on Carr Canyon Rd.,* ☎ *520/670–4552.* ☒ *$10.* ⊙ *May–Oct. Reservations not accepted.*

Tombstone

❹ *28 mi northeast of Sierra Vista via AZ 90; 24 mi south of Benson via AZ 80.*

It's hard to imagine now, but Tombstone, headquarters for most of the area's gamblers and gunfighters, was once bigger than San Francisco.

These days it derives most of its revenue from tourism. The legendary headquarters of Wild West rowdies, Tombstone was part of an area called Goose Flats in the late 1800s and was prone to attack by nearby Apache tribesmen. Ed Schieffelin, an intrepid prospector, wasn't discouraged by those who cautioned that "all you'll find there is your tombstone." In 1877 he struck one of the West's richest veins of silver in the tough old hills and gave the town its name as an ironic "I told you so." He called the silver mine Lucky Cuss, figuring that he fit the description himself.

The promise of riches attracted all types of folks, including outlaws. Soon gambling halls, saloons, and houses of prostitution sprang up all along Allen Street. In 1881 the Earp family and Doc Holliday battled to the death with the Clanton boys at the famous shoot-out at the OK Corral. Over the past century, scriptwriters and storytellers have done much to rewrite the exact details of the confrontation, but it's a fact that the town was the scene of several gunfights in the 1880s. On Sundays, you can witness replays of some of these on Allen Street.

Tombstone's rough-and-ready heyday was popularized by Hollywood in the 1930s and capitalized on by the local tourist industry in the decades that followed, but there's more to the town than the OK Corral, the souvenir shops on Allen Street, and the staged shoot-outs. "The town too tough to die" (it survived two major fires, an earthquake, the closing of the mines, and the moving of the county seat to Bisbee) was also a cultural center, and many of its original buildings remain intact.

Check with the **Tombstone Chamber of Commerce and Visitor Center** (⊠ 4th and Allen Sts., ☎ 520/457–3929), which is open daily 9 to 5, for a walking tour that includes several of the town's currently unmarked sights. The people behind the counter are happy to fill you in on the best places to go; they can provide a very detailed map and printed description of hotels and restaurants.

Boot Hill Graveyard, where the victims of the OK Corral shoot-out are buried, is on the northwestern corner of town, facing U.S. 80. If you're put off by the commercialism of the place—you enter through a gift shop that sells novelty items in the shape of tombstones—remember that Tombstone itself is the result of crass acquisition, a trait that tends to be decried in the present while its manifestations in the past are romanticized. Chinese names in one section bear testament to the laundry and restaurant workers who came from San Francisco during the height of Tombstone's mining fever. About a third of the more than 350 graves dug here from 1879 to 1974 are unmarked.

For an introduction to the town's—and the area's—past, visit the **Tombstone Courthouse State Historic Park.** Displays include a reconstruction of the original 1882 courtroom, area artifacts, and numerous photographs of prominent—and notorious—town figures. ⊠ *Toughnut and 3rd Sts.,* ☎ *520/457–3311.* ⚄ *$2.50.* ☉ *Daily 8–5.*

Originally a boardinghouse for the Vizina Mining Company and later a popular hotel, the **Rose Tree Inn Museum,** with its 1880s period rooms and huge rosebush (claimed to be the world's largest) on the patio, displays the gentler side of life in Tombstone. ⊠ *Toughnut and 4th Sts.,* ☎ *520/457–3326.* ⚄ *$2.* ☉ *Daily 9–5.*

You'll get a dramatic version of the town's past, narrated by Vincent Price, in the **Historama**—a 26-minute multimedia presentation on Tombstone's history. At the adjoining **OK Corral,** a recorded voice-over details the town's most famous event, while life-size figures of the gunfight's participants stand poised to shoot. Photographer C. S. Fly, whose studio was next door to the corral, didn't record this bit of history, but Geronimo and his pursuers were among the historical figures he did capture with his camera. Many of his fascinating Old West images may be viewed at the **Fly Exhibition Gallery.** ⊠ *Allen St., between 3rd and 4th Sts.,* ☎ *520/457-3456.* 🖾 *Historama $2.50, OK Corral and Fly Exhibition Gallery $2.50, combination ticket $5.* ☉ *Daily 8:30–5; Historama shows every hr on the hr 9–4.*

Allen Street, the town's main drag, is lined with restaurants and curio shops. Many of the street's buildings still bear bullet holes from their livelier days, and some of the remaining artifacts are interesting—including the original printing presses for the town's newspaper, the **Tombstone Epitaph** (⊠ 9 S. 5th St., ☎ 520/457-2211), founded in 1880 and still publishing. If you're looking to wet your whistle, stop by the **Crystal Palace** (⊠ Allen and 5th Sts., ☎ 520/457-3611), where a beautiful mirrored mahogany bar, wrought-iron chandeliers, and tinwork ceilings date back to Tombstone's heyday. Locals come here on weekends to dance to live country-and-western music.

Another Tombstone institution, the **Bird Cage Theater** is a former music hall where Caruso, Sarah Bernhardt, and Lillian Russell—among others—performed. It was also the site of the longest continuous poker game recorded, started when the Bird Cage opened in 1881 and lasting eight years, five months, and three days. Some of the better-known players included Diamond Jim Brady, Adolphus Busch (of brewery fame), and William Randolph Hearst's father. The cards were dealt round the clock; players had to give a 20-minute notice when they were planning to vacate their seats, because there was always a waiting list of at least 10 people ready to shell out $1,000 (the equivalent of about $30,000 today) to get in. In all, some $10 million changed hands.

When the mines closed in 1889, the Bird Cage was abandoned and locked up, but the building has remained in the hands of the same family, who threw nothing out, through five generations. The basement, which served as a bordello, was opened in 1995 to the public for the first time since 1889. All the original furnishings and fixtures are intact, and you can still see the personal belongings left behind by the ladies of the night when the mines closed and they, and their clients, headed for California. ⊠ *6th and Allen Sts.,* ☎ *520/457-3421.* 🖾 *$4.* ☉ *Daily 8–6.*

Dining and Lodging

$$ ✕ **Nellie Cashman's.** You can order anything from a burger to a hearty dinner of juicy pork chops or chicken-fried steak in this homey spot, named for the original owner, a Tombstone pioneer who opened a hotel and restaurant in 1882. Old photographs and postcards decorate the walls. Nellie's is also a great place for a country breakfast complete with biscuits and gravy. ⊠ *5th and Toughnut Sts.,* ☎ *520/457-2212. AE, D, MC, V.*

$ ✕ **The Longhorn Restaurant.** Also home to "Big Nose Kate's Saloon," named for Doc Holliday's girlfriend, this was formerly the "Owl Cafe" and originally the "Bucket of Blood Saloon." Old-time saloon keepers may not have had a way with words, but they sure know what to serve to keep the likes of the Earps, Bat Masterson, and Johnny Ringo coming back for more. Today it's noisier and definitely for the whole family, with American, Mexican, and Italian dishes available: hot dogs, burgers, steaks, ribs, tacos, enchiladas, and spaghetti should keep the kids happy. It may not be cuisine, but it is filling and fun and open for three meals a day. ⊠ *Allen and 5th Sts.,* ☎ *520/457-3405. AE, MC, V.*

$ 🏨 **Best Western Look-Out Lodge.** This motel has spectacular views of the Dragoon Mountains and desert valley below. Touches like western-print bedspreads, Victorian-style lamps, and locally made wood-hewn clocks give the rooms character. A Continental breakfast is included. The front desk and motel switchboard close at 10 PM, so you'll need to check in and receive any phone calls before then. ☒ *U.S. 80 W, Box 787, 85638,* ☎ *520/457–2223 or 800/652–6772,* FAX *520/457– 3870. 40 rooms. Pool. AE, D, DC, MC, V. Continental breakfast.*

$ ⊡ **Priscilla's B&B.** Built in 1904, this is the only remaining two-story, clapboard Victorian house in Tombstone. Considering the tremendous growth of the town, followed by years of neglect and then resurgence, this is indeed a feat. Listed on the National Historic Register, it is painted in authentic Victorian colors and is surrounded by the original picket fence. The decor is Victorian, and in spite of the lace curtains, not overly fussy. Two rooms share a bath while another has private facilities. A full breakfast is served in the exquisitely decorated dining room, just two blocks from all that activity on Allen Street. ☒ *101 N. 3rd St., 85638,* ☎ *520/457–3844. 3 rooms. AE, MC, V.*

$ ⊡ **Tombstone Boarding House Bed & Breakfast.** This friendly bed-and-breakfast is actually two meticulously restored 1880s adobes that sit side by side in a quiet residential neighborhood: Guests sleep in one house and go next door to have a hearty country breakfast (at press time, an on-premise restaurant was in the works). The spotless rooms have hardwood floors and period furnishings collected from around Cochise County. Those seeking a romantic evening should inquire about the inn's candlelight dinners. ☒ *108 N. 4th St., Box 906, 85638,* ☎ *520/457–3716,* FAX *520/ 457–3038. 9 rooms, 1 cabin. MC, V. Full breakfast.*

$ ⊡ **Tombstone Bordello B&B.** This was the last remaining bordello in Tombstone, moved to Allen Street in the 1920s and now enjoying a second career as a B&B. A charming yet small structure, it takes on much more character once you've toured the Birdcage and read a little something about the lives of the "soiled doves" who helped create this town as much as the miners and gunfighters. The porch and balcony give out onto vistas of the Dragoon Mountains while inside the decor is restrained Victorian. Each room comes with queen bed, television, and private bath. Full breakfast is included in the rate. ☒ *101 W. Allen St., 85638,* ☎ *520/457–2394. 2 rooms. Cash or checks only.*

$ ⊡ **Tombstone Motel.** Catercorner from the offices of the *Tombstone Epitaph,* on the town's main through street, this comfortable and well-run motel will remind you of the motor courts of years past. The major attractions of Allen Street are a block away, and rooms have cable television and air-conditioning. ☒ *502 E. Fremont St., 85638,* ☎ *520/ 455–3478 or 888/455–3478. 12 rooms, 1 suite. MC, V.*

Bisbee

⑤ *24 mi south of Tombstone.*

Like Tombstone, Bisbee was a mining boomtown, but its wealth was in copper, not silver, and its success much longer lived. It wasn't until 1975 that the Phelps Dodge Company closed its last mine and the city went into decline. However, it was rediscovered in the early 1980s by burned-out city dwellers and revived as a kind of Woodstock West. The permanent population is a mix of retired miners and their families, aging hippie jewelry makers, and enterprising young restaurateurs and boutique owners. The latter two groups are currently ascendant, and the town is getting a bit touristy, but its complexion is likely to shift again soon: The Phelps Dodge Company has plans to reopen the area's old copper mines.

If you want to head straight into town from U.S. 80, get off at Brewery Gulch interchange. You can park here and cross under the highway, taking Main or Commerce or Brewery Gulch Street, all of which meet here.

Another option is to continue driving on U.S. 80 about ¼ mi to where it intersects with AZ 92. Pull off the highway on the right into a gravel parking lot, where a short, typewritten history of the **Lavender Pit Mine** can be found attached to the hurricane fence surrounding the area (Bisbee isn't big on formal exhibits). The hole left by the copper miners is huge, with piles of lavender-hue "tailings," or waste, creating mountains around it. Arizona's largest pit mine yielded some 94 million tons of copper ore before the town's mining activity came to a halt.

For a lesson in mining history, take the **Copper Queen mine tour.** The mine is less than a half mile to the east of the Lavender Pit, across U.S. 80 from downtown at the Brewery Gulch interchange. Tours are led by one of Bisbee's retired copper miners, who are wont to embellish their official spiel with tales from their mining days. They're also very capable, safety-minded people (any miner who survives to lead tours in his older years would have to be), so don't be concerned about the precautionary dog tags (literally—they're donated by a local veterinarian) issued to each person on the tour.

The tours, which depart daily at 9, 10:30, noon, 2, and 3:30 (you can't enter the mine at any other time), last from 1 to 1½ hours, and visitors go into the shaft via a little open train, like those the miners rode when the mine was active. Before you climb aboard, you're outfitted in miner's garb—a yellow slicker and a hard hat with a light that runs off a battery pack strapped to your waist. You may want to wear a sweater or light coat under your slicker because the temperature in the mine is a brisk 47°F on average. You'll travel by train thousands of feet into the mine, up a grade of 30 ft (not down, as many visitors expect). Those who are a bit claustrophobic might consider taking one of the surface tours that depart from the building at the same times as the mine tours (excluding 9 AM). They cover Old Bisbee and the perimeter of the Lavender Pit mine, as well as the old leaching plant. ⊠ *478 N. Dart Rd.,* ☎ *520/432–2071.* ☜ *Mine tour $8, surface tour $7.*

The **Mining and Historical Museum** is housed in the old redbrick Phelps Dodge general office, across the street from the Copper Queen mine. The museum is filled with old photographs and artifacts from the town's mining days and explores other aspects of the first 40 years of Bisbee's history, from 1887 to 1920. ⊠ *No. 5 Copper Queen Plaza,* ☎ *520/432–7071.* ☜ *$4.* ☉ *Daily 10–4.*

The venerable old **Copper Queen Hotel** (☞ Dining and Lodging, *below*), built a century ago, is behind the Mining and Historical Museum. It has housed the famous as well as the infamous: "Black Jack" Pershing, John Wayne, Teddy Roosevelt, and mining executives from all over the world made this their home away from home.

Brewery Gulch, a short street running north and south, is adjacent to the Copper Queen Hotel (walk out the front door of the Copper Queen, make a left, and you'll be there in about 20 paces). Largely abandoned, it's lined with boarded-up storefronts. In the old days, the brewery housed there allowed the dregs of the beer that was being brewed to flow down the street and into the gutter.

Bisbee's **Main Street** is very much alive and retailing. This hilly commercial thoroughfare is lined with appealing crafts shops, boutiques, and restaurants, many of them in well-preserved turn-of-the-century brick buildings.

Dining and Lodging

$–$$ ✕ Café Roka. Roka is the deserved darling of the hip Bisbee crowd.
★ The constantly changing northern Italian–style evening menu is small,
but you can count on whatever you order—chicken with ricotta and
basil cannelloni, sea scallops with spinach pasta—to be wonderful. Portions are generous, and the entrée price ($11–$18) includes soup,
salad, and a pasta-based main course preceded by a sorbet. The dining room, with exposed brick walls and the original 1906 tinwork ceiling, looks onto a central bar that offers a nice selection of wines and
cognacs. Sunday nights feature jazz, beginning at 6 PM, and a lighter
dinner menu. ⊠ *35 Main St.,* ☎ *520/432–5153. MC, V. Closed Mon.–
Tues. No lunch.*

$–$$ ✕⊡ High Desert Inn. In the heart of downtown Bisbee, the High Desert
★ Inn is housed in the old (1901) Cochise County Jail building, though
you'd never know it. Behind a classical facade highlighted by four mon-
umental Doric columns, this sophisticated but friendly hostelry offers
lovely contemporary-design rooms that include color TV and private
telephones (a rarity in Bisbee accommodations). Decor includes French
wrought-iron beds, wicker and wrought-iron tables, and art moderne
lamps. The inn has a small bar and a dining room, which doubles as
an art gallery. Open for dinner Thursday through Sunday, the restaurant is run by a Cordon Bleu–trained chef. ⊠ *8 Naco Rd., Box 145,
85603,* ☎ *520/432–1442 or 800/281–0510. 5 rooms. Restaurant. D,
MC, V.*

$–$$ ⊡ Copper Queen Hotel. Built by the Copper Queen Mining Company
★ (which later became the Phelps Dodge Corporation) at a time when
Bisbee was the biggest copper-mining town in the world, this hotel in
the heart of downtown has been operating since 1902. Some of the accommodations are small or oddly laid out and the walls between them
are thin, but all have a Victorian charm. Ask for a room that's been
renovated. Guests over the years have included a host of wild and crazy
prospectors as well as more respectable types. Today's visitors are as
likely to include a film producer scouting locations as a retired snow-
bird from Minnesota. ⊠ *11 Howell Ave., Drawer CQ, 85603,* ☎ *520/
432–2216 or 800/247–5829,* ℻ *520/432–4298. 47 rooms. Restaurant,
bar, pool. AE, D, DC, MC, V.*

$ ⊡ School House Inn. You'll flash back to your classroom days at this
bed-and-breakfast, a schoolhouse built in 1918 at the height of Bisbee's mining days. Perched on the side of a hill, the two-story brick
building has a pleasant outdoor patio shaded by an oak tree. In keeping with its educational past, the inn's rooms all have a theme—music,
history, geography, arithmetic—reflected in the decor (though, surprisingly, there is no writing desk in the writing room). Twelve-foot
ceilings contribute to an overall airy effect, but the old floors can be
creaky at night. ⊠ *818 Tombstone Canyon Rd., Box 32, 85603,* ☎
800/537–4333, ☎ ℻ *520/432–2996. 9 rooms. AE, D, DC, MC, V.
Full breakfast.*

Douglas

❻ *23 mi southeast of Bisbee.*

This town on the U.S.–Mexico border has suffered economically in recent years because of weakness in the Mexican peso and the closing
of the Phelps Dodge mine in the 1980s. The town was founded in 1902
by James Douglas to serve as the copper-smelting center for the mines
in Bisbee. Douglas's house, now owned by the Arizona Historical Society, is open to the public (a donation is requested) as the **Dou-
glas/Williams House Museum** (⊠ *1001 D Ave.,* ☎ *520/364–2687*).
There's not much to see here and hours are limited (it's open Tues.–

Thurs. and Sat. 1–4), but there are some interesting old photographs and mementos.

The must-see historic landmark in town and still the center of much of Douglas's activity is the **Gadsden Hotel** (☞ Dining and Lodging, *below*), built in 1907. The lobby contains a solid white Italian-marble staircase, two authentic Tiffany vaulted skylights, and a 42-ft stained-glass mural. One thousand ounces of 14-karat gold leaf were used to decorate the capitals. The bar is lively all day long and still serves as a meeting place for local ranchers. When you leave the hotel and walk out onto G Avenue, Douglas's main thoroughfare, you'll be taking a stroll back through time. A film company shooting here had to do very little to make the restaurants and shop fronts fit its 1940s plot line.

Before Douglas became the smelter for Bisbee, the site was the annual roundup ground for local ranchers, Mexican and American—among them John Slaughter, who was the sheriff of Cochise County after Wyatt Earp. The 140-acre **John Slaughter Ranch/San Bernardino Land Grant,** a National Historic Landmark, gives a glimpse of life near the border in the late 19th and early 20th centuries. You can also visit ruins of a military outpost established here in 1911 during the Mexican civil unrest. Much of the ride out to the ranch is via a graded dirt road that traverses a strikingly western landscape of rolling hills and desert scrub. ⊠ *15 mi east of Douglas (from town, go east on 15th St., which turns into Geronimo Trail and leads to the ranch),* ☎ *520/558–2474.* ⊠ *$3.* ☉ *Wed.–Sun. 10–3.*

Dining and Lodging

$–$$ ✕ **Grand Cafe.** The Marilyn Monroe tribute wall and red velvet–draped dining niche in the back may be a bit kitschy, but the Mexican cooking is taken very seriously. Soups range from a soothing *caldo de queso,* laced with cheese and chunks of fresh potato, to a bracing, nicely spiced *menudo.* The refried beans served on the side of such well-prepared Sonoran specialties as chiles rellenos are wonderfully flavorful. ⊠ *1119 G Ave.,* ☎ *520/364–2344. MC, V.*

$ 🏨 **Gadsden Hotel.** This hotel makes no concessions to the modern idea of what the West should look like: What you see is what you get. The hotel underwent a major renovation in the 1990s, but most of the rugs, drapes, and shower curtains look as though they were installed in the 1970s, and the old plumbing and fixtures aren't always well maintained. Still, the public areas are comfortable and the prices are the best you'll find in Douglas. The bar is still where all the local ranchers hang out when they come into town. Suites and apartments with kitchenettes are available. ⊠ *1046 G Ave., 85607,* ☎ *520/364–4481,* FAX *520/364–4005. 160 rooms. Restaurant, bar, coffee shop, beauty salon. AE, DC, MC, V.*

Chiricahua National Monument

❼   *58 mi northeast of Douglas on AZ 191 to AZ 181.*

Vast fields of desert grass are suddenly transformed into a landscape of forest, mountains, and striking rock formations as you enter the 12,000-acre Chiricahua National Monument. Dubbed the Land of the Standing-Up Rocks by the Chiricahua Apache—who lived in the mountains for centuries and, led by Cochise and Geronimo, tried for 25 years to prevent white pioneers from settling here—this is an unusual site for a variety of reasons. Enormous outcroppings of volcanic rock worn by erosion into strange pinnacles and spires are set in a forest where autumn and spring occur at the same time. Because of the particular balance of sunshine and rain in the area, in April and May visitors will see brown, yellow, and red leaves coexisting with new green foliage. Summer in Chiricahua National Monument is exceptionally wet: From July through September there are thunderstorms nearly every afternoon. In addition, few other areas in the United States have such a variety of plant, bird, and animal life. Deer, coatimundis, peccaries, and lizards live among the aspen, ponderosa pine, Douglas fir, oak, and cypress trees—to name just a few. This is a mecca for birdwatchers, and hikers have more than 17 mi of scenic trails. Some of the most beautiful and untouched camping areas in Arizona are nearby, in the Chiricahua Mountains. ⊠ *Visitor center on AZ 181,* ☎ *520/ 824–3560.* ⊒ *$6 per car.* ⊙ *Daily 8–5.*

| OFF THE BEATEN PATH | **PEARCE –** The gold camp of Pearce, 1 mi off Route 191, 29 mi south of Willcox, has a post office and one viable store; the ruins of the mill, the mine, and many old adobes are very much in evidence. Gold was discovered here in 1894, and the town maintained a thriving population of 1,500 until the mine closed in the 1930s, turning Pearce into a ghost town. |

Lodging

$$$
★
⊞ **Grapevine Canyon Ranch.** This guest ranch in the Dragoon Mountains adjoins a working cattle ranch. Visitors get the chance to watch—and, in some cases, participate in—real day-to-day cowboy activities. Riders of all levels of experience are welcome, and hiking trails crisscross this quintessentially western terrain. Accommodations vary—some are rather plain, others have striking southwestern-style furnishings—but all have spacious decks and porches. Rates include meals and all activities. ⊠ *Box 302, Pearce 85625,* ☎ *520/826–3185 or 800/245– 9202,* ℻ *520/826–3636. 12 rooms. Pool, hot tub, horseback riding, coin laundry. 3-night minimum. AE, D, MC, V. FAP.*

$–$$ ⊞ **Sunglow Guest Ranch.** You can't beat this location in Cottonwood Canyon, about 15 mi south of Chiricahua National Monument. Most of the ranch, except the dining room and kitchen (ask about the history of those rooms once you are settled in), is in a modern structure with courtyard rooms and views of the ponds or the forest beyond. Several meal plans are available, all with healthy ranch-size portions. It is an ideal location for family reunions or retreats because of the quiet setting: Your only disturbance will be the occasional white-tailed deer or coatimundi roaming the open country. ⊠ *HCR1, Box 385, Turkey Creek Rd., Pearce 85625,* ☎ *520/824–3334. 9 suites with kitchenettes. AE, MC, V.*

$ ⊞ **Portal Peak Lodge.** This barracks-style structure, just east of Chiricahua National Monument near the New Mexico border, is notable less for its rooms (clean and pleasant, but nondescript) than for its winged visitors: The Elegant Trogon, 14 types of hummingbird, and 10 species of owl are among the 330 varieties of birds that flock to nearby Cave Creek Canyon. ⊠ *Box 364, Portal 85632,* ☎ *520/558–2223,* ℻ *520/ 558–2473. 16 rooms. Restaurant, grocery. AE, D, MC, V.*

⚲ **Cave Creek Recreational Area.** Here, three campgrounds abut the southeast wall of a canyon that has a creek. In the early spring this spot on the eastern face of the Chiricahuas is one of the known nesting sites of the Elegant Trogan. Later in the spring, hummingbirds migrate up from Mexico to build nests and rear their young. Drinking water and rest rooms (no showers) are available at the campsites. ⊠ *20 mi south of San Simon on unimproved road to Portal, then 5 mi due west on Forest Route 42,* ☎ *520/670–4552.* ⊒ *$10.* ⊙ *May–Oct. Reservations not accepted.*

⚠ **Rucker Canyon.** The site of three campgrounds (Camp Rucker, Cypress Park and Rucker Forest Camp), this canyon is named for the Army outpost that was instrumental in the defeat of Geronimo and his band of Apaches. The sites are on fairly flat ground, with lots of shade and running water nearby. Potable water and rest rooms (no showers) are at each campground. ⊠ *35 mi south of Dragoon on AZ 191 (to milepost 30), then 20 mi east on Rucker Canyon Road,* ☎ *520/670–4552.* ▨ *$10.* ⊗ *May–Oct. Reservations not accepted.*

Fort Bowie National Historical Site

❽ *8 mi northwest of Chiricahua National Monument. To reach the site, take AZ 186 east from Chiricahua National Monument; some 5 mi north of the junction with AZ 181, you'll see signs directing you to the road leading to the fort.*

It's a bit of an outing to this site of Arizona's last battle between Native Americans and U.S. troops in the Dos Cabezas (Two-Headed) Mountains. After driving down a graded but winding gravel road, you'll come to a parking lot where a trail leads 1½ mi to the historic site. The fort itself is virtually in ruins, but there's a small ranger-staffed visitor center with historical displays, rest rooms, and books for sale.

The various points of interest along the way, all indicated by historic markers, include the **Butterfield stage stop**, a crucial link in the journey from east to west in the mid-19th century that happened to be located in the heart of Chiricahua Apache land. Chief Cochise and the stagecoach operators ignored one another until sometime in 1861, when hostilities broke out between U.S. Cavalry troops and the Apache. After an ambush by the chief's warriors at Apache Pass in 1862, U.S. troops decided a fort was desperately needed in the area, and Fort Bowie was built within weeks. There were skirmishes for the next 10 years, followed by a peaceful decade. Renewed fighting broke out in 1881. Geronimo, the new leader of the Indian warriors, finally surrendered in 1886. The fort was abandoned eight years later and fell into disrepair. ⊠ *Visitor Center,* ☎ *520/847–2500.* ▨ *Free.* ⊗ *Daily 8–5.*

Willcox

❾ *26 mi northwest of Fort Bowie National Historical Site on AZ 186.*

Willcox, a major cattle-shipping center, has fewer than 4,000 residents. Its downtown looks like an Old West movie set. An elevation of 4,167 ft renders the climate here moderate in summer and chilly in winter. Apple-pie fans from as far away as Phoenix know this little town as Arizona's apple-growing headquarters and come here to get baked goods. If you visit in winter, you can see some of the more than 10,000 sandhill cranes that roost at the **Willcox Playa,** a 37,000-acre area resembling a dry lake bed 12 mi south of Willcox. They migrate in late fall and head north to nesting sites in February.

Just outside Willcox you'll find the headquarters for the **Muleshoe Ranch Cooperative Management Area** (⊠ Exit 340 off I-10, turn right on Bisbee Ave., take it to Airport Rd., turn right again, after 15 mi take the right fork at a junction just past a group of mailboxes, and continue to end of the road, ☎ 520/586–7072), nearly 49,000 acres of riparian desert land in the foothills of the Galiuro Mountains that are jointly owned and managed by the Nature Conservancy, the U.S. Forest Service, and the U.S. Bureau of Land Management. It's a 30-mi drive on a dirt road to the ranch—it takes about an hour to get there—but the scenery, wildlife, and hiking are well worth the bumps. Backcountry hiking and mountain-biking trips can be arranged by the ranch, and overnight accommodations are available (☞ Lodging, *below*).

The **Rex Allen Arizona Cowboy Museum,** in Willcox's historic district, is a tribute to Willcox's most famous native son, cowboy singer Rex Allen, who now lives in Tucson (he comes back to his hometown the second week of every October for Rex Allen Days, which include an annual rodeo and other Western events). He starred in several rather average cowboy movies during the '40s and '50s for Republic Pictures, but he's probably most famous as the friendly voice that narrated Walt Disney nature films. Check out the glittery suits the star wore on tour—they'd do Liberace proud. ⊠ *155 N. Railroad Ave.,* ☎ *520/384–4583.* ☞ *$2.* ☉ *Daily 10–4.*

The **Willcox Commercial Store** (⊠ 180 N. Railroad Ave., ☎ 520/384–2448), near the Rex Allen Cowboy Museum, was established in 1881 and is the oldest retail establishment in Arizona. Locals like to boast that Geronimo used to shop here. Today it's a clothing store, with a large selection of western wear.

The Chamber of Commerce is home to the one-room **Museum of the Southwest,** which focuses on the Native American and military history of the area. One oddity of the museum is that the memoirs of Civil War general Orlando Willcox, for whom the town was named, don't even mention a visit to Arizona. Across the parking lot, you'll see Stout's Cider Mill (on the frontage road to I–10), where everyone comes to pick up a high-rise apple pie. ⊠ *1500 N. Circle I Rd.,* ☎ *520/384–2272 or 800/200–2272.* ☞ *Free.* ☉ *Mon.–Sat. 9–5, Sun. 1–5.*

Lodging

$ 🏨 **Muleshoe Ranch.** This turn-of-the-century health spa is run by the Arizona chapter of the Nature Conservancy. Five furnished casitas with kitchens or kitchenettes, baths, and linens sit in a pristine setting on a dirt road. There's a visitor center, a nature trail, natural hot springs (for use by casita guests only), and a common room. ⊠ *30 mi northwest of Willcox, R.R. 1, Box 1542, 85643,* ☎ *520/586–7072. 5 units. 2-night minimum Sept.–May and holiday weekends. AE, MC, V.*

Texas Canyon

⑩ *16 mi west of Willcox off I–10.*

A dramatic change of scenery along I–10 will signal that you're entering Texas Canyon. The rock formations here are exceptional—huge boulders appear to be delicately balanced against each other.

Texas Canyon is the home of the **Amerind Foundation** (a contraction of "American" and "Indian"), founded by amateur archaeologist William Fulton in 1937 to foster understanding about Native American cultures. The research facility and museum are housed in a Spanish Colonial Revival–style structure designed by noted Tucson architect H. M. Starkweather. The museum's rotating displays of archaeological materials, crafts, and photographs give an overview of Native American cultures of the Southwest and Mexico. The adjacent Fulton–Hayden Memorial Art Gallery displays an assortment of art collected by William Fulton. ⊠ *Dragoon Rd., 1 mi southeast of I–10 (Exit 318),* ☎ *520/586–3666.* ☞ *$3.* ☉ *Sept.–May, daily 10–4; June–Aug., Wed.–Sun. 10–4.*

Benson

⓫ *On I–10, 12 mi west of Texas Canyon; 50 mi east of Tucson.*

Once the hub of the Southern Pacific Railroad and a stop on the Butterfield Stagecoach route, Benson has for many years been a fairly sleepy
little town. Recently, the town has begun annexing property along Highway 90 and chain hotels have gone up in anticipation of the long-awaited
opening of Kartchner Caverns State Park (☞ *below*). If you walk up
and down central 4th Street, you'll get a flavor for Benson's earlier days
in such buildings as the **Hi Wo Company Grocery** (⊠ 398 E. 4th St.),
still owned by the descendants of the Chinese railroad worker–turned–
entrepreneur who gave the store its name in 1896. One block south
of 4th Street, the little **San Pedro Valley Arts and Historical Society Museum** (⊠ Corner S. San Pedro Ave. and E. 5th St., ☎ 520/586–3070)
has permanent and rotating displays relating to Benson's past.

With the start-up of the **San Pedro and Southwestern Railroad** in early
1995, Benson began to draw a few more visitors. The railroad's *Grey
Hawk* began making regular trips through the San Pedro Riparian National Conservation Area (☞ Sierra Vista, *above*) in 1994. It's the only
motorized vehicle permitted to ride through the preserve, and the outdoor panoramic car is a favorite with bird-watchers. The lively en-route
narration introduces passengers to San Pedro Valley's colorful cast of
boom-time characters, including the inhabitants of the ghost town of
Charleston, where the San Pedro train turns around. The train stops
for lunch and Western-style entertainment in the ghost town of **Fairbank**, which is currently being restored by the Bureau of Land Management. Wander around ramshackle buildings that date back to 1882,
including a post office and a general store established by the Goldwater
brothers, or hike to the ruins of a mill used to crush ore for the Tombstone mines. The four-hour round-trip departs from Benson's new
depot. ⊠ *796 E. Country Club Dr.,* ☎ *520/586–2266 or 800/269–
6314.* ⊡ *$24.* ◷ *Trains run Thurs.–Sun. Call ahead for schedules.*

OFF THE   **SINGING WIND BOOKSHOP** – As you pass through Benson on I–10,
BEATEN PATH   watch for Ocotillo Avenue, Exit 304. Take a left and drive about 2¼ mi,
                  where a mailbox with a backward SW signals that you've come to the
                  turnoff for Singing Wind Bookshop. Make a right at the mailbox and
                  drive ¼ mi until you see a green gate. Let yourself in, close the gate, and
                  go another ¼ mi to the store. If you don't see the proprietor, who also
                  runs the ranch, ring the large gong out front and she's sure to come out
                  and welcome you. This unique bookshop-on-a-ranch has a good selec-
                  tion of books on Arizona wildlife, history, and geology. ⊠ *Ocotillo
                  Ave.,* ☎ *520/586–2425.*

Dining and Lodging

$–$$ ✕ **Horseshoe Cafe.** For a good green-chili burrito or a patty melt, stop
in at this funky café, which has graced Benson's main street for more
than 50 years. You know you're in cowboy country when you see the
neon horseshoe on the ceiling, the macramés of local cattle brands, and
the large Wurlitzer jukebox with its selection of sad C&W sounds. ⊠
154 E. 4th St., ☎ *520/586–3303. MC, V.*

$ ✕ **Reb's Cafe & Coffee Shop.** For another take on real Southwest
food—none of that newfangled nouvelle stuff—this unpretentious spot
is of the cowboy variety. It serves Mexican food and what passes for Italian, but it really prides itself on steaks and hamburgers, and a darned good
breakfast. ⊠ *1020 W. 4th St.,* ☎ *520/586–3856. No credit cards.*

$ ✕ **Ruiz Restaurant.** In this part of the world, the name is pronounced "Reese" and the food is just as regional as the name. Located on the main street, it draws customers who stop here on their way to the big city for tacos, enchiladas, and the famous soup. The decor is functional and the service is fast and pleasant. ⊠ *687 W. 4th St.,* ☎ *520/586–2707. AE, MC, V.*

$ ⊞ **Best Western Quail Hollow.** Benson itself might not have a lot to see, but it is strategically located at the gateway to the Old West in Arizona. The Ocotillo Road exit off I–10 offers easy access to this modern facility, decorated in comfortable style. There is no restaurant on the premises, but several are within walking distance. ⊠ *977 Ocotillo St., 85602,* ☎ *520/586–3646 or 800/322–1850. 89 rooms. AE, MC, V.*

$ ⊞ **Days Inn.** The stretch of road between Tucson and points east is uninhabited except for the occasional cow; under such circumstances, even a chain hotel can be a welcome sight. The rooms are standard issue, large and clean and comfortable, and there is always the nearby train for atmosphere. Complimentary breakfast is offered and restaurants are within walking distance. ⊠ *621 Commerce Dr., 85602,* ☎ *520/586–3000 or 800/329–7466. 61 rooms. AE, MC, V.*

$ ⊞ **Skywatcher's Inn.** You don't have to be an astronomer to enjoy staying at this bed-and-breakfast on the grounds of the private Vega-Bray Observatory. Even with the unaided eye, you'll marvel at the night sky that spreads out from this hilltop property near Benson; six powerful telescopes here, however, bring the universe even closer. The B&B, built in 1995 to accommodate the demands of sleepy stargazers, reflects the owners' delight in science: The comfortable rooms have gadgets like lamps that simulate lightning, and one has the constellations painted on the ceiling, visible in black light. Another room is decorated in a Star Wars motif and yet another looks Eygptian. During the day, you can peruse books, fossils, and minerals in a classroom, or gaze out at ducks swimming in one of three nearby ponds through a telescope in the breakfast room. ⊠ *Astronomers Rd., 2 mi southeast of I–10 (Exit 306). Reservations:* ⊠ *420 S. Essex La., Tucson 85711,* ☎ fax *520/745–2390. 1 room with shared bath (with daytime observatory guests), 2 suites. MC, V. Full breakfast.*

Kartchner Caverns State Park

⑫ *9 mi south of Benson on AZ 90.*

Discovered in 1974 by two Tucson spelunkers who kept it a secret until 1988, this limestone cavern finally opened to the public in late 1999. Great precautions have been taken to protect the wet cave system—which comprises 13,000 feet of passages and two chambers as long as football fields—from damage by light and dryness. In the summer, a colony of bats roosts in a portion of the cave to raise their young; that area remains off-limits to visitors for the time being. The sophisticated Discovery Center introduces visitors to the cave and its formations (such as the world's longest known soda straw stalactite), and hour-long guided tours take small groups into the upper cave, including the large Rotunda and Throne rooms. Advance reservations are required for tours; hiking trails, picnic areas, and campsites are available on the park's 550 acres. ⊠ *AZ 90, 9 mi south of exit 302 off I–10,* ☎ *520/586–4100.* ⊠ *$10 per vehicle up to 4 people, $1 each additional person; tours $14.* ☉ *Daily 8–6.*

SOUTHWEST ARIZONA

Many people speed through southwest Arizona on their way to California, but the area has much to offer those willing to slow down for

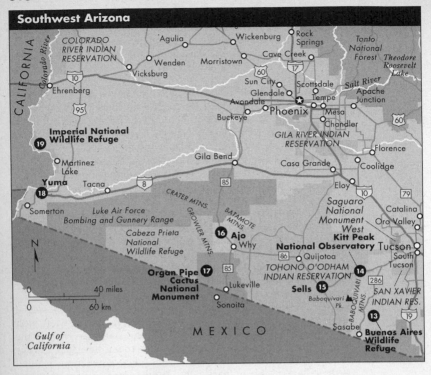

Southwest Arizona

a closer look. The turbulent history of the West is writ large in this now-sleepy part of the state. It's home to the Tohono O'odham Indian Reservation (the largest in the country after the Navajo Nation's) and towns like Ajo, created—and almost undone—by the copper-mining industry. Yuma, abutting the California border, was a major crossing point of the Colorado River as far back as the time of the conquistadors.

Natural attractions are a lure in this starkly scenic region: Organ Pipe Cactus National Monument provides a number of trails for desert hikers, and Buenos Aires and Imperial wildlife refuges—homes to many unusual species—are havens for birders and other nature watchers.

On warm weekends and especially during semester breaks, the 130-mi route from Tucson to Ajo is busy with traffic headed southwest to Puerto Penasco (Rocky Point), Mexico, the closest outlet to the sea for Arizonans. Much of the time, however, the only companions you'll have on this trek are the low-lying scrub and cactus and the mesquite, ironwood, and paloverde trees.

Buenos Aires Wildlife Refuge

⓭ *66 mi southwest of Tucson; from Tucson, take AZ 86 west 22 mi to AZ 286; go south 40 mi to milepost 8, and it's another 3 mi east to the preserve headquarters.*

This remote nature preserve, in the Altar Valley and encircled by seven mountain ranges, is the only place in the United States where the Sonoran/savannah grasslands that once spread over the entire region can still be seen. The fragile ecosystem was almost completely destroyed by overgrazing, and a program to restore native grasses is currently in progress. In 1985 the U.S. Fish and Wildlife Service purchased the Buenos

Aires Ranch—now headquarters for the 115,000-acre preserve—in an attempt to save the masked bobwhite quail, formerly common here but thought to have become extinct. Bird-watchers consider Buenos Aires unique because it's the only place in the United States where they can see a "grand slam" (four species) of quail: Montezuma, Gambel's, scalies, and masked bobwhite. If it rains, the 100-acre Aguirre Lake, 1½ mi north of the headquarters, attracts wading birds, shore birds, and waterfowl—in all, more than 250 avian species have been spotted here. They share the turf with deer, antelope, coatimundi, badgers, bobcats, and mountain lions. Treks to Brown Canyon, accessible only by guided tour, are offered the second and fourth Saturday of every month ($3 per person). ⊠ *Box 109, Sasabe 85633,* ☎ *520/823–4251.* ☞ *Free.* ☉ *Preserve headquarters, weekdays 7–3:30; visitor information office (in Arivaca, on the eastern side of the preserve), daily 8–2.*

Lodging

$$–$$$ 🔲 **Rancho de la Osa.** This guest ranch, set on 250 eucalyptus-shaded acres near the Mexican border and Buenos Aires preserve, is steeped in history. The central hacienda was built in 1889 and two adobe structures were built in the 1920s to accommodate guests, among them Lyndon Johnson, Justice William O. Douglas, and Adlai Stevenson. The recently renovated rooms have modern plumbing and fixtures, woodburning fireplaces, private entrances, and porches with Adirondack chairs. Each room is painted in rich hues—ocher, blue, rust, or green—and furnished in either rustic ranch oak or Mexican antiques. Bread baked on the premises, salads made with ingredients grown in the ranch's garden, and water drawn from the well on the property all contribute to the back-to-basics serenity of a stay here. Rates include all meals. ⊠ *1 La Osa Ranch Rd., Sasabe 85633,* ☎ *520/823–4257 or 800/872–6240,* ᶠᵃˣ *520/823–4238. 16 rooms. Restaurant, lounge, pool, spa, hiking, horseback riding, bicycles, billiards, library. D, MC, V. FAP.*

Kitt Peak National Observatory

⑭ *56 mi southwest of Tucson; to reach Kitt Peak from Tucson, take I–10 to I–19 south, and then AZ 86. After 44 mi on AZ 86, turn left at the AZ 386 junction and follow the winding mountain road 12 mi up to the observatory. (In inclement weather, contact the highway department to confirm that the road is open.)*

Funded by the National Science Foundation and managed by a group of more than 20 universities, Kitt Peak National Observatory is part of the Tohono O'odham Reservation. After much discussion back in the late 1950s, tribal leaders agreed to share a small section of their 4,400 square mi with the observatory's telescopes. Among these is the McMath, the world's largest solar telescope, which uses piped-in liquid coolant. From the visitors' gallery you can see into the telescope's light-path tunnel, which goes down hundreds of feet into the mountain. Kitt Peak scientists use these high-power telescopes to conduct vital solar research and observe distant galaxies. Likely to attract the most attention here is Skywatch—no, not a sci-fi spinoff from *Baywatch*—the world's largest asteroid-hunting telescope, installed in 1997. The scientists and staff are friendly and knowledgeable, and their enthusiasm for astronomy is contagious.

The museum's visitor center has exhibits on astronomy, information about the telescopes, and free hour-long guided tours that depart daily at 10, 11:30, 1, and 2:30. Complimentary brochures enable you to take self-guided tours, and there's a picnic area about 1½ mi below the observatory. The observatory buildings have vending machines, but there are no restaurants or gas stations within 20 mi of Kitt Peak. The observatory now offers stargazing dinner tours ($35 per adult) for up to 20 people; reservations are necessary. ⊠ *Kitt Peak National Observatory,* ☎ *520/318–8726; 520/318–7200 for recorded message.* ✉ *Suggested donation $2 per person.* ☉ *Visitor center daily 9–3:45.*

Sells

⑮ *32 mi southwest of Kitt Peak via AZ 386 to AZ 86.*

The Tohono O'odham Reservation, the second largest in the United States, covers 4,400 square mi between Tucson and Ajo, stretching south to the Mexican border and north almost to the city of Casa Grande. To the south of Kitt Peak, the 7,730-ft Baboquivari Peak is considered sacred by the Tohono O'odham as the home of their deity, I'itoi ("elder brother"). A little less than halfway between Tucson and Ajo, Sells, the tribal capital of the Tohono O'odham, is a good place to stop for gas or a soft drink. If you want something more substantial, head for the Sells Shopping Center where you'll see **Basha's Deli & Bakery** (⊠ Topawa Rd., ☎ 520/383–2546). It's a good-size market and can supply all the makings for a picnic, including a picnic table near the store's entrance. Across the road from Basha's, **Margaret's Arts and Crafts** (⊠ Topawa Rd., ☎ 520/383–2800) sells baskets and other wares made on the reservation. You can also buy crafts at the **Turquoise Turtle** (⊠ AZ 86, near the Chevron Station, ☎ 520/383–2411). Much of the time there's little to see or do in Sells, but in winter an annual rodeo and fair attract thousands of visitors. For details about activities on the reservation, contact the **Tohono O'odham Nation office** (☎ 520/383–2221).

En Route   At Why, about 60 mi from Sells, AZ 86 forks off into the north and south sections of AZ 85. Originally the name of the community at this Y-shape intersection was spelled, simply and descriptively, "Y," but in 1950 the town was told that it had to have a three-letter name in order to be assigned a postal code. Hence the querulous appellation that has kept travelers wondering why Why ever since.

Ajo

⑯ *90 mi northwest of Sells.*

"Ajo" (pronounced "*ah*-ho") is Spanish for garlic, and some say the town got its name from the wild garlic that grows in the area. Others claim the word is a bastardization of the Indian word "au-auho," referring to red paint derived from a local pigment.

For many years Ajo, like Bisbee to the east, was a thriving Phelps Dodge Company town. Copper mining had been attempted in the area in the late 19th century, but it wasn't until the 1911 arrival of John Greenway, general manager of the Calumet & Arizona Mining Company, that the region began to be developed profitably. Calumet and Phelps Dodge merged in 1935, and the huge New Cornelia pit mine produced millions of tons of copper until the mine finally closed in 1985. With the town's main source of revenue gone, Ajo looked for a time as though it might shut down, but many retirees are now being lured here by the warm climate and low-cost housing.

At the center of town is a sparkling white Spanish-style plaza, designed in 1917 by Isabella Greenway, wife of the Calumet mine manager and an important figure in her own right: In the 1930s she opened the Arizona Inn in Tucson, and she was friends with such dignitaries as Eleanor Roosevelt. The shops and restaurants that line the plaza's covered arcade today are rather modest. Unlike Bisbee, Ajo hasn't yet drawn an artistic crowd—or the upscale boutiques and eateries that tend to follow.

You get a panoramic view of the town's huge open pit mine, almost 2 mi wide, from the **New Cornelia Open Pit Mine Lookout Point.** Some of the abandoned equipment remains in the pit, and various stages of mining operations are diagrammed at the visitors' ramada, where there's a 30-minute film about Phelps Dodge's mining operations. ⊠ *Indian Village Rd.,* ☎ *520/387–7746.* ⊡ *$1 suggested donation.* ☉ *Generally 10–4 in high season. Closed Sun. and May–Oct.*

The **Ajo Historical Society Museum** has collected a mélange of articles related to Ajo's past from local townspeople. The displays are rather disorganized, but some of the historical photographs and artifacts are fascinating, and the museum is inside the Territory-style St. Catherine's Indian Mission, built around 1916. ⊠ *160 Mission St.,* ☎ *520/387–7105.* ⊡ *Free.* ☉ *Generally Mon.–Sat. 10–4, Sun. noon–4 in high season; call ahead to confirm. Closed May–Oct.*

The 860,000-acre **Cabeza Prieta National Wildlife Refuge,** about 10 minutes from Ajo, was established in 1939 as a preserve for endangered bighorn sheep and other Sonoran Desert wildlife. A permit is required to enter, and only those with four-wheel-drive vehicles, needed to traverse the rugged terrain, can obtain one. For additional information or for an entry permit, contact the **refuge office** (⊠ 1611 N. 2nd Ave., Ajo 85321, ☎ 520/387–6483).

Dining and Lodging

$ ✕ **Señor Sancho.** Just about everybody in Ajo comes to this unprepossessing roadhouse at the north end of town for generous portions of Mexican food, well prepared and very reasonably priced. This friendly spot has light-wood booths and colorful murals with a Mexican motif. All the standard favorites are on the menu—hearty combination platters, tacos, enchiladas, chili rellenos, flautas, and good chicken mole. ⊠ *663 N. 2nd Ave.,* ☎ *520/387–6226. No credit cards.*

$–$$ ⊞ **Mine Manager's House Inn.** Another remnant of the town's Phelps Dodge heyday, this 5,000-square-ft, 1919 mansion overlooks the entire town from its site atop the highest hill in Ajo. Rest comfortably in queen-size beds and enjoy full breakfasts served on fine china in the former mine superintendent's light-filled formal dining room. ⊠ *601 W. Greenway Dr., 85321,* ☎ *520/387–6505,* 𝔽𝔸𝕏 *520/387–6508. 5 rooms. Hot tub, coin laundry. MC, V.*

$ ⊞ **Guest House Inn.** Built in 1925 to accommodate visiting Phelps Dodge VIPs, this lodging is one of six Southwest "Bird 'n' Breakfast Fly-Inns": Guests can head out early to nearby Organ Pipe National Monument or just sit on the patio and watch the quail, cactus wrens, and other warblers that visit the Sonoran Desert. Rooms are furnished in a range of southwestern styles, from light Santa Fe to rich Spanish Colonial. ⊠ *700 Guest House Rd., 85321,* ☎ *520/387–6133. 4 rooms. DC, MC, V. Full breakfast.*

Organ Pipe Cactus National Monument

⓱ *32 mi southwest of Ajo; from Ajo, backtrack to Why and take AZ 85 south for 22 mi to reach the visitor center.*

Anyone interested in exploring the flora and fauna of the Sonoran Desert should head for Organ Pipe Cactus National Monument, abutting Cabeza Prieta National Wildlife Refuge (☞ Ajo, *above*) but much more accessible to visitors. The monument is the largest gathering spot north of the border for organ pipe cacti. These multiarmed cousins of the saguaro are fairly common in Mexico but rare in the United States. Because they tend to grow on south-facing slopes, you won't be able to see many of them unless you take one of the two scenic loop drives: the 21-mi **Ajo Mountain Drive** or the 53-mi **Puerto Blanco Drive,** both on winding, graded dirt roads. The latter trail, which takes half a day to traverse, brings you to Quitobaquito, a desert oasis with a flowing spring. ⊠ *Rte. 1,* ☎ *520/387–6849.* ☞ *$4 per vehicle.* ☉ *Visitor center daily 8–5.*

Yuma

⑱ *170 mi northwest of Ajo.*

Today, many people think of Yuma as a convenient en route stop—between San Diego and Phoenix or Tucson—and this was equally true in the past. It's difficult to imagine the lower Colorado River, now dammed and bridged, as either a barrier or a means of transportation, but up until the early part of the century, this section of the great waterway was a force to contend with. Records show that since at least 1540 the Spanish were using Yuma (then the site of a Quechan Indian village) as a ford across a relatively shallow juncture of the Colorado.

Three centuries later, the advent of the shallow-draft steamboat made the settlement a point of entry for fortune seekers heading up through the Gulf of California to mining sites in eastern Arizona. Fort Yuma was established in 1850 to guard against Indian attacks, and by 1873 the town was a county seat, a U.S. port of entry, and an army quartermaster depot. The building of the Yuma Territorial Prison in 1876 helped stabilize the economy.

The steamboat shipping business, undermined by the completion of the Southern Pacific Railroad line in 1877, was finished off by the building of Laguna Dam in 1909, which controlled the overflow of the Colorado River and made agricultural development in the area possible. In World War II, Yuma Proving Ground was used to train bomber pilots, and General Patton readied some of his desert war forces for battle at classified areas near the city. Many who served here during the war returned to Yuma to retire, and the city's economy now relies largely on tourism. And one very telling fact may shed some light on why: According to weather bureau statistics, Yuma is the sunniest city in the United States.

Most of the interesting sights in Yuma are at the north end of town. Stop in at the **Convention and Visitors Bureau** (⊠ 377 S. Main St., ☎ 520/783–0071) and pick up a walking-tour guide to the historic downtown area. The adobe-style **Arizona Historical Society Museum,** housed in the Century House, was built around 1870 and exhibits artifacts from Yuma's territorial days and details the military presence in the area. ⊠ *240 S. Madison Ave.,* ☎ *520/782–1841.* ☞ *Free.* ☉ *Tues.–Sat. 10–4.*

If you cross the railroad tracks at the northernmost part of town, you'll come to **Yuma Crossing National Historic Landmark,** which consists of the Quartermaster Depot, the Territorial Prison, and Fort Yuma. The mess hall of Fort Yuma, later used as a school for Indian children, now serves as the small **Fort Yuma Quechan Indian Museum.** Historical photographs, archaeological items, and Quechan arts and crafts are on display. ⊠ *On CA 24, 1 mi north of town,* ☎ *619/572–0661.* ☞ *$1.* ☉ *Weekdays 8–5, Sat. 10–4.*

On the other side of the river from Fort Yuma, the Civil War–period quartermaster depot resupplied Army posts to the north and east and served as a distribution point for steamboat freight headed overland to Arizona forts. The 1853 home of riverboat captain G. A. Johnson is the depot's earliest building and the centerpiece of the **Yuma Crossing State Historic Park.** The residence also served as a weather bureau and home for customs agents, among other functions, and the guided tour through the house provides a complete history. The complex was closed until the fall of 1997, when it reopened as a state park. The new Transportation Museum has stagecoaches, Wells Fargo wagons, and antique surreys, as well as more "modern" modes of transportation like the 1909 Model T and the 1931 Model A pickup. Also new is the re-creation of the Commanding Officer's Quarters, complete with period furnishings and servant's quarters: You'll find the dining room table set with antique china and linens, as if the C.O. himself were expected for dinner. ⊠ *4th Ave. between 1st St. and the Colorado River Bridge,* ☎ *520/329–0471.* 🎫 *$3.* ⊙ *Daily 8–5.*

The most notorious tourist sight in town, **Yuma Territorial Prison** was built for the most part by the convicts who were incarcerated here from 1876 until 1909, when the prison outgrew its location. The hilly site on the Colorado River, chosen for security purposes, precluded further expansion.

Visitors gazing today at the tiny cells that held six inmates each, often in 115°F heat, are likely to be appalled, but the prison—dubbed the Country Club of the Colorado by locals—was considered a model of enlightenment by turn-of-the-century standards: In an era when beatings were common, the only punishments meted out here were solitary confinement and assignment to a dark cell. The complex housed a hospital as well as Yuma's only public library, where the 25¢ that visitors paid for a prison tour financed the acquisition of new books.

The 3,069 prisoners who served time at what was then the territory's only prison included men and women from 21 different countries. They came from all social classes and were sent up for everything from armed robbery and murder to violation of the Mexican Neutrality Act and polygamy. R. L. McDonald, incarcerated for forgery, had been the superintendent of the Phoenix public school system. Chosen as the prison bookkeeper, he absconded with $130 of the inmates' money when he left. Pearl Hart, convicted of stagecoach robbery, gained such notoriety for her crime that she attempted to launch a career in vaudeville after her release.

The mess hall opened as a museum in 1940, and the entire prison complex was designated a State Historic Park in 1961. ⊠ *Near Exit 1 off I–8,* ☎ *520/783–4771.* 🎫 *$3. Free interpretive programs at 11, 2, and 3:30.* ⊙ *Daily 8–5.*

The 40-acre **Saihati Camel Farm** is at the southern end of town. The landscape near Yuma inspired Saudi Arabia native Abdul-Wahed Saihati to raise and breed his favorite animals here along with more exotic desert-loving breeds, such as oryx (antelope) and wildcats. It's fun to help feed the well-groomed, friendly dromedaries—not a biter or spitter among 'em—and to see some rare animal species, many of them purchased from the San Diego Zoo. ⊠ *15672 S. Ave. 1 E (between County 15th and County 16th Sts.),* ☎ *520/627–2553.* 🎫 *Guided tours $3.* ⊙ *Guided tours Mon.–Sat. at 10 and 2, Sun. at 2. Reservations advised.*

Dining and Lodging

$$ ✕ California Bakery. This new restaurant across from Lutes Casino draws raves from locals and visitors both for its menu and ambience. Pasta with shrimp and sun-dried tomatoes is a favorite, as is baked salmon in thyme butter. Simpler preparations, including ribs and chicken are available, too. It's open for breakfast, and there is live music Thursday–Saturday nights until 1 AM. ⊠ *284 S. Main St.* ☎ *520/782–7335. AE, MC, V. Closed Sun.*

$–$$ ✕ Chretin's Mexican Food. A Yuma institution, Chretin's opened as a dance hall in the 1930s before it became one of the first Mexican restaurants in town in 1946. Don't be put off by the nondescript exterior or the entryway, which leads back past the kitchen and cashier's stand into three large dining areas. The food is all made on the premises, right down to the chips and tortillas. Try anything that features *machaca* (shredded spiced beef or chicken). ⊠ *485 S. 15th Ave.,* ☎ *520/782–1291. D, MC, V. Closed Sun.*

$ ✕ Lutes Casino. Almost always packed with locals at lunchtime, this large, funky restaurant and bar claims to be the oldest pool hall and domino parlor in Arizona. It's a great place for a burger and a brew. ⊠ *221 S. Main St.,* ☎ *520/782–2192. Reservations not accepted. No credit cards.*

$$ ☷ Shilo Inn. Remodeled in 1998, this is an excellent family place to stay because of in-room facilities that come as close to a kitchen as you might want on a trip. Rooms are spacious, equipped with microwaves and ironing boards, and most with views of the courtyard and pool. ⊠ *1550 S. Castle Dome Ave., 85365,* ☎ *520/782–9511 or 800/222–2244. 135 rooms, 15 suites. Refrigerator, pool, hot tub, exercise room. AE, D, MC, V. Full breakfast.*

$–$$ ☷ Best Western Coronado Motor Hotel. This Spanish tile–roof lodging, convenient to both the freeway and downtown historical sights, **★** was built in 1938 and is run by the son of the original owner. Bob Hope used to stay here during World War II, when he entertained the gunnery troops training in Yuma. The rooms have such extras as irons and ironing board, microwaves, hair dryers, and modem phone jacks. Yuma Landing Restaurant & Lounge is on site with an impressive collection of historical photos. ⊠ *233 4th Ave., 85364,* ☎ *520/783–4453 or 800/528–1234,* FAX *520/782–7487. 86 rooms. Restaurant, lobby lounge, refrigerators, in-room VCRs, pool, coin laundry. AE, D, DC, MC, V. Full breakfast.*

$–$$ ☷ Radisson Suites Inn. One wing of this sprawling hostelry surrounds a well-manicured courtyard with a fountain and several orange trees; another faces the pool and Cabana Club, where the complimentary Continental breakfast and happy-hour drinks are served. This is an all-suites property, and each accommodation has a coffeemaker, a microwave, and a separate sitting area with a desk. ⊠ *2600 S. 4th Ave., 85364,* ☎ *520/726–4830 or 800/333–3333,* FAX *520/341–1152. 164 suites. Lobby lounge, refrigerators, pool, hot tub, coin laundry, airport shuttle. AE, D, DC, MC, V. Continental breakfast.*

$ ☷ La Fuente Inn. Keep in mind that Yuma's hotels have to compete with huge RV parks, and you begin to see why the rates are reasonable and so many extras are included. La Fuente is particularly popular with military personnel. The decor and setting are unremarkable, but the rooms are good sized and very clean. There is no restaurant on site, but many are within walking or driving distance. ⊠ *1513 E. 16th St., 85365,* ☎ *520/329–1814 or 800/841–1814. 96 rooms. Refrigerators, pool, hot tub, exercise room, coin laundry. AE, D, MC, V. Continental breakfast.*

Imperial National Wildlife Refuge

⑲ *40 mi north of Yuma; from Yuma, take U.S. 95 north past the Proving Ground and follow the signs to the refuge.*

Guided tours (☞ Southern Arizona A to Z, *below*) are the best way to visit the 25,765-acre Imperial National Wildlife Refuge, created by backwaters formed when the Imperial Dam was built. Something of an anomaly, the refuge is home both to species indigenous to marshy rivers and to creatures that inhabit the adjacent Sonoran Desert—desert tortoises, coyotes, bobcats, and bighorn sheep. Most of all, though, this is bird-lovers' heaven. Thousands of waterfowl and shorebirds live here year-round, and migrating flocks of swallows pass through in the spring and fall. During those seasons, expect to see everything from pelicans and cormorants to Canada geese, snowy egrets, and a variety of rarer species. Canoes can be rented at Martinez Lake Marina, 3½ mi southeast of the refuge headquarters. It's best to visit from mid-October through May, when it's cooler and the ever-present mosquitoes are least active. The well-marked Painted Desert Nature Trail, about a mile long, takes you through the different levels of the Sonoran Desert. From an observation tower at the visitor center you can see the river, as well as the fields being planted with rye and millet, on which the migrating birds like to feed. ⊠ *Red Cloud Mine Rd., Box 72217, 85365,* ☎ *520/783–3371.* ⊠ *Free.* ☉ *Visitor center mid-Apr.–mid-Oct., weekdays 8–4:30; rest of yr, weekdays 8–4:30, weekends 9–4.*

SOUTHERN ARIZONA A TO Z

Arriving and Departing

By Air

You'll need to rent a car to tour most of southern Arizona. The best plan is to fly into Tucson, which is the hub of the area, or Phoenix, which has the most flights, and pick up a car at the airport.

SIERRA VISTA

America West (☎ 800/235–9292) has regular flights from Phoenix to the **Libby Army Airfield** at Fort Huachuca (⊠ 2100 Airport Ave., ☎ 520/459–8575).

YUMA

America West Express (☎ 800/235–9292) has direct flights to **Yuma International Airport** (⊠ 2191 32nd St., ☎ 520/726–5882) from Phoenix. **Sky West** (☎ 800/453–9417), a Delta subsidiary, flies nonstop from Los Angeles.

By Bus

SOUTHEASTERN ARIZONA

Greyhound Lines (☎ 800/231–2222) has service from Tucson (⊠ 2 S. 4th Ave., ☎ 520/792–3475) to the stations in Benson (⊠ 242 E. 4th St., ☎ 520/586–3141) and Willcox (⊠ 622 N. Haskell Ave., ☎ 520/384–2183). The line uses **Bridgewater Transport** (⊠ 445 W. 2nd St., ☎ 520/628–8909) in Tucson for its runs to Bisbee (⊠ 7 Okay St., ☎ 520/432–5359), Douglas (⊠ 538 14th St., ☎ 520/364–2233), and Sierra Vista (⊠ 28 Fab Ave., ☎ 520/458–3471). You'll need to book a tour if you want to take the bus to Tombstone.

SOUTHWESTERN ARIZONA

The **Ajo Stage Line** (☎ 800/242–9483) runs buses three times a week from Tucson and four times a week from Phoenix to Ajo. You can get

to the **bus station** in Yuma (✉ 170 E. 17th Pl., ☎ 520/783–4403) from
a variety of directions via **Greyhound Lines** (☎ 800/231–2222).

By Car

SOUTHEASTERN ARIZONA

From Tucson, take I–10 east. When you come to Benson, take U.S. 80
south to reach Tombstone, Bisbee, and Douglas. If you want to go to
Sonoita and Patagonia, or just take a pretty drive, turn off I–10 earlier, at the exit for AZ 83 south; you'll come to Sonoita where this road
intersects AZ 82 and from there you can either continue on south to
Patagonia or head west to Tombstone.

SOUTHWESTERN ARIZONA

Ajo lies on AZ 85 (north–south), Yuma at the junction of I–8 and U.S.
95. For a scenic route to Ajo from Tucson (126 mi), take AZ 86 west
to Why and turn north on AZ 85. Yuma is 170 mi from San Diego on
I–8, and it is 300 mi from Las Vegas on U.S. 95.

By Train

Amtrak (☎ 800/872–7245) trains run three times a week from Tucson east to the Benson depot (✉ 4th St. at San Pedro Ave.) and west
to Yuma (✉ 281 Gila St.). Both are unstaffed stations with no phones.

Getting Around

You can see much of what you'd want to see in Bisbee, Tombstone,
Ajo, and Patagonia by strolling around, but wheels are still an advantage
in almost all of southern Arizona's towns.

By Bus

The **Bisbee Bus** (☎ 520/432–2285) line, operated by Catholic Community Services, has a 1½-hour-long route in and around Bisbee. Buses,
which cost 60¢, run Monday through Friday from 6:50 AM to 6:10
PM; there's wheelchair lift equipment.

Sierra Vista Public Transit (☎ 520/459–0595), also run by Catholic Community services, charges $1 for the general public. Buses operate Mon-
day through Friday 6:30–6:30, Saturday 8:30–4:30.

By Taxi

SOUTHEASTERN ARIZONA

You can phone **Benson Taxi** (☎ 520/586–7688) to get around. For a
cab in Bisbee, call **Sun Arizona Taxi** (☎ 520/432–7899). In Sierra
Vista, **Angel Transport** (☎ 520/458–0027) is reliable.

SOUTHWESTERN ARIZONA

Ajo Stage Lines (☎ 520/387–6467) operates as a taxi service in town.
Friendly Taxi Service (☎ 520/783–1000) and **Yuma City Cab** (☎ 520/
782–0111) have the newest, cleanest taxis in Yuma.

Contacts and Resources

Camping and Hiking

SOUTHEASTERN ARIZONA

Douglas Ranger District (✉ R.R. 1, Box 228-R, Douglas 85607, ☎ 520/
364–3468) and the **Sierra Vista Ranger Station** (✉ 5990 S. Hwy. 92,
Hereford 85615, ☎ 520/378–0311) can give you information about
camping and hiking in the Coronado National Forest, which covers
most of the mountain ranges in southeastern Arizona.

SOUTHWESTERN ARIZONA

Contact the Bureau of Land Management's **Yuma District Office** (✉ 3150
Winsor Ave., Yuma 85365, ☎ 520/726–6300) for details about outdoor recreational activities.

Car Rentals

The following car-rental companies are represented at Yuma International Airport: **Avis** (☎ 520/726–5737); **Budget** (☎ 520/344–1822); and **Hertz** (☎ 520/726–5160).

Emergencies

Call 911 to reach the **fire department, police,** and **emergency medical services.**

SOUTHEASTERN ARIZONA

Bisbee Copper Queen Hospital (✉ 101 Cole St., ☎ 520/432–5383). **Benson Hospital** (✉ 450 S. Octollo St., ☎ 520/586–2261). **Sierra Vista Community Hospital** (✉ 300 El Camino Real, ☎ 520/458–4641). In Willcox, **Northern Cochise Community Hospital** (✉ 901 Rex Allen Dr., ☎ 520/384–2720).

SOUTHWESTERN ARIZONA

For medical problems go to **Ajo Community Health Center** (✉ 410 Malacate St., ☎ 520/387–5651) or **Yuma Regional Medical Center** (✉ 2400 S. Avenue A, ☎ 520/344–2000). The drugstores in most southern Arizona towns shut down at around 5 PM. Yuma, where the following pharmacies stay open until at least 9 on the weekdays, is an exception: **Super Kmart** (✉ 2375 W. 32nd St., ☎ 520/344–0856); **Smith's** (✉ 500 W. 24th St., ☎ 520/782–2529); **Payless** (✉ 600 W. Catalina Dr., ☎ 520/726–7810); **Walgreen's** (✉ 1150 W. 8th St., ☎ 520/783–6834; ✉ 3121 S. 4th Ave., ☎ 520/344–0453).

Guided Tours

BIRD-WATCHING

The **Southeastern Arizona Bird Observatory** (✉ Box 5521, Bisbee 85603, ☎ 520/432–1388) offers a wide array of avian-oriented activities year-round.

RIVER TOURS

You can take a boat ride up the Colorado with **Yuma River Tours** (✉ 1920 Arizona Ave., Yuma 85364, ☎ 520/783–4400). Twelve- to 45-person jet-boat excursions are run by Smokey Knowlton, who has been exploring the area for more than 36 years.

TRAIN EXCURSIONS

The **San Pedro and Southwestern Railroad's** *Grey Hawk* (☎ 520/586–2266 or 800/269–6314) travels through the San Pedro Riparian National Conservation Area (☞ Sierra Vista, *above*).

On Saturdays and Sundays from October through June, you can take a two-hour round-trip jaunt on the **Yuma Valley Railway** (☎ 520/783–3466). The 1922 coach, pulled by one of two historic diesel engines, departs at 1 PM from the 8th Street station in Yuma and runs south alongside the Colorado River for about 11 mi. Tickets cost $10.

Visitor Information

SOUTHEASTERN ARIZONA

Benson–San Pedro Valley Chamber of Commerce (✉ 226 E. 4th St., Box 2255, Benson 85602, ☎ 520/586–2842), open weekdays 9–6, Saturday 9–5. **Bisbee Chamber of Commerce** (✉ 7 Main St., Box BA, Bisbee 85603, ☎ 520/432–5421), open weekdays 9–5, weekends 10–4. **Douglas Chamber of Commerce** (✉ 1125 Pan American, Douglas 85607, ☎ 520/364–2477), open weekdays 9–5, Saturday 10–2. **Patagonia Visitors Center** (✉ Box 241, 315 McKoewn Ave., 85625, ☎ 520/394–0060), open Wednesday–Monday 10–5. **Sierra Vista Chamber of Commerce** (✉ 21 E. Willcox, Sierra Vista 85635, ☎ 520/458–6940 or 800/288–3861), open weekdays 8–5, Saturday 9–1. **Tombstone Chamber of Commerce and Visitor Center** (✉ 4th and Allen Sts., ☎

520/457–3929), open daily 9–5. **Tombstone Office of Tourism** (✉ Box 917, Tombstone 85638, ☎ 520/457–3421 or 800/457–3423), open daily 9–5. **Willcox Chamber of Commerce & Agriculture** (✉ 1500 N. Circle I Rd., Willcox 85643, ☎ 520/384–2272 or 800/200–2272), open Monday–Saturday 9–5, Sunday 1–5.

SOUTHWESTERN ARIZONA

The **Ajo Chamber of Commerce** (✉ AZ 85, just south of the plaza, 321 Taladro, Ajo 85321, ☎ 520/387–7742), open Monday–Saturday 9–4 most of the year but closes down for part of the summer. The **Yuma Convention and Visitors Bureau** (✉ 377 S. Main St., Box 11059, Yuma 85366, ☎ 520/783–0071), open weekdays 9–5.

8 BACKGROUND AND ESSENTIALS

Portraits of Arizona

Books and Videos

Smart Travel Tips A to Z

THE WHAT AND THE WHY OF DESERT COUNTRY

On the brightest and warmest days my desert is most itself because sunshine and warmth are the very essence of its character. The air is lambent. A caressing warmth envelops everything in its ardent embrace. Even when outlanders complain that the sun is too dazzling and too hot, we desert lovers are prone to reply, "At worst that is only too much of a good thing."

Unfortunately, this is the time when the tourist is least likely to see it. Even the winter visitor who comes for a month or more is likely to choose January or February because he is thinking about what he is escaping at home rather than of what he is coming to here. True, the still-warm sun and typically bright skies make a dramatic contrast with what he has left behind. In the gardens of his hotel or guest ranch, flowers still bloom and some of the more obstreperous birds make cheerful sounds, even though they do not exactly sing at this season. The more enthusiastic visitors talk about "perpetual summer" and sometimes ask if we do not find the lack of seasons monotonous. But this is nonsense. Winter is winter, even in the desert.

At Tucson's elevation of 2,300 feet it often gets quite cold at night, even when shade temperatures during the day rise to 75°F or higher. Most vegetation is pausing, though few animals hibernate. This is a sort of neutral time when the desert environment is least characteristic of itself. It is almost like late September or early October, just after the first frost, in southern New England. For those who are thinking of nothing except getting away, rather than learning to know a new world, this is all very well. But you can't become acquainted with the desert itself at that time of year.

By April the desert is just beginning to come into its own. The air and the skies are summery without being hot; roadsides and many of the desert flats are thickly carpeted with a profusion of wildflowers such as only California can rival. The desert is smiling before it begins to laugh, and October and November are much the same. But June is the month for those who want to know the true desert. That is the time to decide once and for all if it is, as for many it turns out to be, "your country."

It so happens that I am writing this not long after the 21st of June, and I took special note of that astronomically significant date. This year, summer began at precisely 10 hours and no minutes, mountain standard time. That means that the sun rose higher and stayed longer in the sky than on any other day of the year. In the north there is often a considerable lag in the seasons as the earth warms up, but here, where it is never very cold, the longest day and the hottest are likely to coincide pretty closely. So it was this year. On June 21 the sun rose almost to the zenith so that at noon it cast almost no shadow. And it was showing what it is capable of.

Even in this dry air, 109°F in the shade is pretty warm. Under the open sky the sun's rays strike with an almost physical force, pouring down from a blue dome unmarked by the faintest suspicion of even a fleck of cloud. The year has been unusually dry (even for the desert). During the four months just past, no rain—not even a light shower—has fallen. The surface of the ground is as dry as powder. And yet, when I look out of the window, the dominant color of the landscape is an incredible green.

On the low foothills surrounding the steep rocky slopes of the mountains, which are in fact 10 to 12 miles away but in the clear air seem much closer, this greenness ends in a curving line following the contour of the mountains' base, inevitably suggesting the waves of a green sea lapping the irregular shoreline of some island rising abruptly from the ocean. Between me and that shoreline the desert is sprinkled with hundreds, probably thousands, of evenly placed shrubs, interrupted now and then by a small tree—usually mesquite or what locals call a cat's-claw acacia.

More than a month ago all the little perennial flowers and weeds, which spring up after winter rains and rush from seed to flower and to seed again in six weeks, gave up the ghost at the end of their short lives. Their hope of posterity lies now invisible, either upon the surface of the bare ground or just below it. Yet even when summer thunderstorms come in late July or August, these seeds will not make the mistake of germinating. They are triggered to explode into life only when they are both moist and cool—which they will be February or March when their season comes again. Neither the shrubs nor the trees seem to know that no rain has fallen during these long months. The leathery, somewhat resinous leaves of the dominant shrub—the attractive plant unattractively dubbed creosote bush—are not at all parched or wilted. Nor are the deciduous leaves of the mesquite.

Earlier in the year the creosote was covered with bright yellow pealike flowers, the mesquite with pale yellow catkins. Now the former is heavy with gray seed and on the mesquite are forming long pods that Indians once ate and that cattle now find an unusually rich food.

It looks almost as though the shrubs and trees could live without water. But of course they cannot. Every desert plant has its secret, though not always the same one. In the case of mesquite and creosote it is that their roots go deep and that, below 6 feet, there is no wet or dry season in the desert. What little moisture is there is pretty constant throughout the year, in dry years as well as wet. Like the temperature in some caves, it never varies. The mesquite and creosote are not compelled to care whether it has rained for four months or not. And unlike many other plants, they flourish whether there has been less or more rain than usual.

Plants with substantial root systems that do not reach very deep are more exuberant some years than others. Thus the Encelia, the brittlebush, which in normal years literally covers many slopes with thousands of yellow, daisylike flowers, demands a normal year. Though I have never seen it fail, I am told that in very dry years it comes into leaf but does not flower, whereas in really catastrophic droughts it does not come up at all, as the roots lie dormant and hope for better times. Even the creosote bush, which never fails, profits from surface water, and when it gets the benefit of a few thunderstorms in late July or August, it will flower and fruit a second time, sprinkling the desert expanse once again with yellow . . .

On such a day as this, even the lizards, so I have noticed, hug the thin shade of the bushes. If I venture out, the zebratails scurry indignantly away, the boldly banded appendages that give them their name curved high over their backs. But I don't venture out very often during the middle of the day. It is more pleasant to sit inside where a cooler keeps the house at a pleasant 80°F. And if you think that an advocate of the simple life should not succumb to a cooler, it is you rather than I who is inconsistent. Even Thoreau had a fire in his cottage at Walden, and it is no more effete to cool oneself in a hot climate than it is to get warm before a stove in a cold one. The gadget involved is newer, but that is all.

In this country "inclemency" means heat. One is "sunbound" instead of snowbound, and I have often noticed that the psychological effect is similar. It is cozy to be shut in, to have a good excuse for looking out of the window or into oneself. A really blazing day slows down the restless activity of a community very much as a blizzard does in regions that have them. Where there is either, a sort of meteorological sabbath is usually observed even by those who keep no other.

Obviously the animals and plants that share this country with me take it for granted. To them it is just "the way things are." By now I am beginning to take it for granted myself. But being a man, I must ask what they cannot: What *is* a desert, and why is it what it is? At 32° latitude one expects the climate to be warm. But the desert is much more than merely warm. It is a consistent world with a special landscape, a special geography, and, to go with them, special flora and fauna adapted to that geography and that climate.

Nearly every striking feature of this world, be it the shape of the mountains or the habits of its plant and animal inhabitants, goes back ultimately to the grand fact of dryness—the dryness of the ground, of the air, of the whole sum total. And the most inclusive cause of dryness is the simple lack of rain.

Some comparisons with wetter regions may bring that into sharper focus. Take, for example, southern New England. By world standards it gets a lot—namely some 40 inches—of rain per year. Certain southern states get even more: about 50 inches for east Tennessee, nearly 60 for New Orleans. Some areas on the West Coast get fantastic amounts, like the 75 inches at Crescent City, California, and the unbelievable 153 inches—nearly four times what New York City gets—recorded one year in Del Norde County, California.

Nevertheless, New England's 40 is a lot of water, either comparatively or absolutely. The region around Paris, for instance, gets little more than half that amount. Forty inches is, in absolute terms, more than most people imagine. One inch of rain falling on an acre of ground means more than 27,000 gallons of water. No wonder irrigation in dry regions is a formidable task even for modern technology.

In terms of vegetation, 40 inches is ample for the kind of agriculture and natural growth that we tend to think of as "normal." It means luxuriant grass, rapid development of second-growth woodland, a veritable jungle of weeds and bushes in midsummer. In inland America, rainfall tends to be less than in coastal regions. Moving west from the Mississippi, it declines sharply and begins to drop below 20 inches a year at about the 100th meridian or, very roughly, at a line drawn from Sioux Falls, South Dakota, through Oklahoma City. This means too little water for most broad-leafed trees and explains why the southern Great Plains were as treeless when the white man first saw them as they are today.

Our true deserts lie farther west still: the Great Basin Desert in Utah and Nevada, the Chihuahuan in New Mexico, the Sonoran in Arizona, and the Mohave in California. The four differ among themselves but they are all arid, and they all fulfill what is probably the most satisfactory definition of "desert": namely, a region where the ground cover is not continuous—where the earth remains bare of vegetation between the plants that manage to grow. Over these American deserts rainfall varies considerably, and with it the character and extent of vegetation. In southern Arizona, for instance, there are about 4 inches of rain at Yuma, nearly 11 around Tucson. Four inches means sand dunes that look like pictures of the Sahara that the word "desert" calls to most people's minds. Eleven means that where soil is suitable, well-separated individuals of such desert plants as cacti and paloverde trees will flourish.

But if scant rainfall makes for deserts, what makes for scant rainfall? To that there are two important answers. One is simply that most nonmountainous regions tend to be dry if they lie in that belt of permanently high atmospheric pressure extending some 30 or 35 degrees on each side of the equator where calms are frequent and winds erratic. Old sailors used to call this region "the horse latitudes," though nobody knows exactly why. (You can take your choice of three equally unconvincing explanations. One is that horses tended to die on ships lying long in the hot calms. Another: The boisterous changeableness of winds when they do come suggests unruly horses. A third is that they were originally named after an English explorer, Ross, whose name Germans mistook for their old word for "horse.") In any event, Tucson falls within the "horse latitudes." Most of the important deserts of the world, including the Sahara and the Gobi, lie within this belt.

Mountains lying across the path of moist winds also make for scant rainfall. In our case, the Coast Ranges of California lie between us and the Pacific. From my front porch, which looks directly across the desert to some of the southernmost Rockies, I can see, on a small scale, what happens. So many times a moisture-laden mass of air reaches as far as these mountains. Dark clouds form, and sometimes the whole range is blotted out. Torrential rain is falling—but not a drop on me. Either the sky is blue overhead or the high clouds that have blown my way dissolve before my eyes as they reach warm air rising from the sun-drenched flats. I live in what geographers call a "rain shadow" cast by the mountains. At their summit rainfall is nearly twice as much as it is down here, and as a result they are clothed with pines from 6,000 or 7,000 feet right up to the 9,000-foot peak. When I do get rain in midwinter and midsummer, it is usually because winds have brought moisture up from the Gulf of Mexico by an unobstructed southern route, or because in summer a purely local thundershower has formed out of hot air rising from the sun-beaten desert floor. Most of the time the sun is hot, even in winter, and the air is usually fantastically dry, the relative humidity being often less than 10.

Naturally the plants and animals living in such a region must be specially adapted to survive under such conditions, but the casual visitor usually notices the strangeness of the landscape before he is aware of flora or fauna. Peculiar features of the landscape are also the result of dryness, even in ways that are not immediately obvious.

The nude mountains reveal their contours, or veil them as lightly as late Greek sculptors veiled their nudes, because only near the mountaintops can anything grow tall enough to obscure the outlines. A little less obvious is the fact that the beautiful "monuments" of northern Arizona and southern Utah owe their unusual forms to the sculpting of windblown sand—or that sheer cliffs often rise from a sloping cone of rocks and boulders because there is not enough draining water to break them down and distribute them over the surrounding plain as they would be distributed in regions with heavier rainfall. But the most striking example of all is the greatest single scenic wonder of the region, the Grand Canyon itself. This narrow gash, cut a mile deep through so many strata that the river now flows over some of the oldest rock exposed anywhere on earth, could have been formed only in a very dry climate.

As recently as 200 years ago the best-informed observer would have taken it for granted that the river was running between those sheer walls at the bottom of the gorge simply because it had found them out. Today few visitors are not aware that the truth is the other way around, that the river cut its own course through the rock. But most laymen do not ask the next questions: Why is the Grand Canyon unique, or why are such canyons, even on a smaller scale, rare? The answer to those questions is that a set of very special conditions was necessary.

First, there must have been a thick series of rock strata slowly rising during a period when a considerable river flowed over it. Second, that considerable river must have carried an unusual amount of hard sand or stone fragments in suspension so that it could cut downward at least as rapidly as the rock over which it flows rose. Third, that considerable river must have coursed through very arid country. Otherwise rain, washing over the edges of the cut, would widen it at the top as the cut went deeper. That is why broad valleys are characteristic of regions with normal rainfall and canyons require arid country.

And the Grand Canyon is the grandest of all canyons because at that particular place all the necessary conditions were fulfilled more exactly than at any other place. The Colorado River carries water from a relatively wet country through a dry one, it bears with it a fantastic amount of abrasive material, the rock over which it flows has been slowly rising during several millions of years, and too little rain falls to rapidly (in geological time) widen the gash that it cuts. Thus in desert country everything from the color of a mouse or the shape of a leaf to the largest features of mountains is more likely than not to have the same explanation: dryness.

So far as living things go, all this adds up to what even an ecologist may call, forgetting himself for a moment, an "unfavorable environment." But like all such pronouncements, this one doesn't mean much unless we ask "unfavorable for what and for whom?" For many plants, for many animals, and for some people it is very favorable indeed. Many of the first two would languish and die if transferred to some region where conditions were "more favorable." It is here, and here only, that they flourish. Likewise, many people feel healthier and happier in the bright dry air than they do anywhere else. And since I happen to be one of them, I not unnaturally have a special interest in the plants and animals that share my liking for just these conditions. For many years now I have been amusing myself by inquiring of them directly what habits and what adjustments they have found most satisfactory. Many of them are delightfully ingenious and eminently sensible . . .

I have lived in this house and been lord of these few acres for nearly five years, and the creatures who share the desert with me have already summed me up as a softy and have grown contemptuously familiar. It is not only that the cactus wrens sit on the backs of my porch chairs. The round-tailed ground squirrels—plain, sand-colored, chipmunk-like animals—are digging rather too many burrows rather too close about the house. The jackrabbits—normally the most timid as well as the fleetest of creatures—take nibbles at the few plants I have set out and refuse to leave off until I arrive shouting and waving my arms a few feet from where they are. Sooner or later something may have to be done to discourage this impudent familiarity, but for the present I am getting some good looks at creatures who usually don't wait to be looked at. Yesterday, for instance, I saw what at first I thought was a bird eating seeds from the upper branches of a creosote bush. It turned out to be a ground squirrel belying his name by climbing several feet above ground among the slender swaying branches of the creosote to eat the small fuzzy seeds. This is doubtless no addition to Knowledge with a capital K. But it is an addition to my knowledge, and that is the next best thing. I like to investigate such matters for myself when I can. "What on earth do they live on?" is a common question from those newcomers not too egotistical to notice that creatures other than those of their own kind do live here somehow. Obviously "creosote seeds" is one answer so far as the ground squirrel is concerned.

People of many races have been known to speak with scorn of those who live where nature makes things easy. In their inclement weather, the stoniness of their soil, or their rigorous winters, they find secret virtues to make even a thing like London fog praiseworthy. Making a virtue out of necessity is not itself a virtue. But there may be something of value in that process. We grow strong against the pressure of a difficulty and test our ingenuity by solving problems. Individuality and character are developed by challenge. We tend to admire trees, as well as people, who bear the stamp of success from struggles with adversity. People who have not had too easy a time of it develop character. And there is no doubt about the fact that desert life has character. Plants and animals are so clearly what they are because of the problems they have solved. They are part of some whole. They belong. Animals and plants, as well as people, become especially interesting when they fit their environment, when to some extent they reveal what their response to it has been. And nowhere more than in the desert do they reveal it.

—Joseph Wood Krutch

Joseph Wood Krutch (1898–1970), one of America's noted natural-history writers, contributed to *The Nation* for many years as a drama and literary critic and lived his last 18 years outside Tucson. *The Voice of the Desert,* from which this essay was excerpted, *Grand Canyon,* and *Henry David Thoreau* are among Krutch's 21 books.

THE NATIVE SOUTHWEST

Considering the aridity of the Southwest, the tremendous cultural productivity of its native civilizations is a fascinating case of people turning the challenges of nature into a meaningful existence. Within the compass of the state of Arizona, Native American pottery and cliff dwellings are the most apparent evidence of this. In fact, they are isolated phenomena on a vast trade route that spanned from the Pacific coast all the way to Mesoamerica, an area in which not only goods, but pottery-making techniques, agricultural technologies, and spiritual beliefs were transmitted.

Some 4,000 years ago—at least 8,000 years after humans crossed the Bering Strait land bridge that once allowed passage on foot between Asia and North America—a major transition in cultures around the world saw people shifting from nomadic hunting-and-gathering lifestyles to more settled agricultural existence. In the southwest, ancient pioneers brought the practice of cultivating corn, squash, and beans north from Mesoamerica. One group in particular, the Hohokam, is believed to have fostered this. In an area straddling the Arizona–New Mexico border, the Hohokam developed a highly productive system. Some archaeologists believe that they migrated from northwestern Mexico with knowledge of planting, growing, and irrigating. Others picture an evolution of Archaic peoples who gradually took on Mesoamerican practices. Either way, they had great success and in turn influenced their northern and eastern neighbors for more than a thousand years. Their artisans produced ritual objects, jewelry, and stone and ceramic wares with great skill. They regularly traded with Mesoamerican tribes, and Pacific-coast exchange brought in raw materials for their own and other regional artisans.

The flowering of Hohokam culture began around 2,300 years ago. The period of their growth, expansion, and eventual decline, when they began to take new ideas in from the north, lasted about 1,500 years—twice as long as the Roman Empire. During that time, they cultivated corn, beans, squash, agave, and cotton, using remarkable irrigation methods. Some of their networks of canals stretched three miles from the Salt and Gila rivers to planted fields. Their contact with Mesoamerican cultures periodically brought new strains of corn to the Southwest along with religious beliefs, ritual practices, and the ball game and ball courts well known from the Maya. The Hohokam culturally fertilized the region, providing a base for the Pueblo culture that has survived into the modern era.

The Mogollon (pronounced mo-go-*yone*) were another group, occupying an area stretching from eastern-central Arizona into New Mexico from 2,000 to 500 years ago. They took on Hohokam and so-called Anasazi cultural patterns, but they never fully embraced an agricultural lifestyle. They became skillful potters, especially those living near the Mimbres River. Their contact with the Anasazi resulted in the production of some of the Southwest's most outstanding pottery. The principle Mimbres Mogollon site is now the Gila Cliff Dwellings National Monument in New Mexico.

Romanticized, mythicized, and perhaps misunderstood, the so-called Anasazi left wondrous architectural remains, most notably at Mesa Verde in Colorado, Chaco Canyon in New Mexico, and Canyon de Chelly, Betatakin, and Keet Seel in Arizona. Composed of various groups living around the Four Corners area, they have generated the most intense interest. For centuries they lived seminomadically, hunting, gathering, and marginally cultivating corn, squash, and beans. They eventually settled into villages and adopted much of the Hohokam culture, more than their Mogollon neighbors did.

These various Ancestral Pueblo peoples were not pueblo dwellers yet, however. They were slow to establish year-round communities. Perhaps they weren't convinced that the Hohokam model would work in their rugged, dry canyonlands. With fewer and smaller rivers, they couldn't irrigate on the Hohokam scale. About 1,500 years ago the Pueblo cultural pattern called Anasazi began to take shape, owing, perhaps, to the introduction of a new, more productive strain of corn.

Ancestral Pueblo peoples made a significant contribution to southwestern culture with their architecture. Their remarkable stone masonry evolved out of a pithouse style used by Archaic peoples. A precursor of the kiva, the pithouse was constructed around a shallow, circular dugout with mud walls packed around vertical pole supports. The new stone-and-mortar houses, on the other hand, were very often rectangular in plan. In small communities they were built on a scale to house groups of a few families. These groups would have individual clan *kivas* (the Hopi word for underground ceremonial chambers) or single great kivas.

The soaring cliff dwellings of Canyon de Chelly, Betatakin, Keet Seel, and Mesa Verde represented another type of settlement, more protected from the elements and, perhaps, from raiders. Villagers cultivated the land around them. All of these communities had kivas, ritual spaces central to the lives of deeply spiritual people.

Ancestral Pueblo culture reached its height about 1,000 years ago. Hitherto Puebloans had continued to refine their use of water, not actually irrigating, but using sporadic rainfall to the greatest advantage. They would line stones across slopes and cut ditches to distribute rainfall and limit erosion. Occasionally they dug canals in order to channel rainwater into planted fields. Unquestionably, they were expert dry farmers, coaxing abundance out of a harsh environment.

At the time of this climax, some people began moving from smaller, widespread communities into larger, denser settlements—perhaps like today's migrations to cities. The volume of trade in nearly all directions was tremendous, and Pueblo artisans were making superb pottery. Decorative techniques varied from region to region: black-on-white, black-on-red, black-on-orange, red-on-orange, and expressive combinations of these. People also etched petroglyphs into, and painted pictograms onto, rock faces. Rock art is found at almost all Anasazi and Sinagua sites. The quantity of artifacts that they left behind—utility and ceremonial items alike—is unparalleled among Native North American groups.

Around 850 years ago, a cultural decline began. Drought and climatic change put pressure on the Pueblos' settled, agricultural lifestyles. Longer winters shortened growing seasons in which less rain fell. Villagers continued to move to more productive areas. By the late 1200s, Canyon de Chelly was unoccupied. Chaco Canyon had been vacant for 100 years. Settlements at Wupatki continued a little longer, into the 1300s. The Hopi Mesas, on the other hand, first built in the 1100s, were growing.

They absorbed some of their migrating neighbors, and their traditions testify to their assimilation of ancient Pueblo culture.

There are also a great number of transitional settlements, many yet to be excavated, that accommodated groups leaving the immediate Four Corners area. Some of them are quite substantial. Considering these transitional settlements, what used to be a question of a culture simply disappearing can now take a more human shape. The Anasazi didn't vanish—they chose to move. Over a couple of centuries they gradually migrated to new locations, slightly altering their lifestyles. (For some of them, that may have been part of a centuries-old practice.) In the process they passed on their knowledge to the people they joined: the Hopi, the New Mexican Zuñi, the Acoma, and other Pueblos. The Zuñi perspective on this migration is telling. As opposed to archaeologists' causes—drought, climatic change, deforestation, disease, warfare—they see it as a process of searching for "the center place," a place of spiritual rightness. And that center place is where present-day Pueblos are living.*

The Sinagua, their name meaning "without water" in Spanish, belonged to a diverse group called the Hakataya, spread out across central Arizona. Wupatki, Walnut Canyon, Tuzigoot, and the inappropriately named Montezuma Castle are all Sinagua sites. These people absorbed Hohokam, Mogollon, and Anasazi cultural patterns: agriculture, village life, and the Mesoamerican ball game; stone masonry and cliff-dwelling architecture; and pottery. Situated in the middle of these three groups, they became a composite but separate culture.

As the so-called Anasazi waned, Hopi and Navajo cultures grew. The Navajo, an Apachean group from the north, gradually migrated southward along the Rocky Mountains about 5,000 years ago and settled in unoccupied places around Pueblo villages. Hunting and gathering were just about all that the land would support

for them. Over time they learned farming techniques from the Pueblos and traded with them and as a result took on a character distinct from other Apachean groups, such as the 19th-century Chiracahua and Mescalero Apache. Living in small, dispersed groups, Navajos also raided Pueblo farms and villages—a practice in retrospect notoriously Apachean.

Soon after the Navajo came the Spanish, invading the Southwest early in the 16th century. Unlike Anglo-European conquerors, they allowed elements of native cultures to survive, provided that they accept a transfusion of Catholicism and alien governance. Of course, their intrusion into southwestern life was far from cordial. Their first contact was with New Mexican Pueblos, whose understandable lack of interest in accepting Spanish rule met with the sword. Pueblo retaliation brought further hostility from the invaders, who murdered hundreds of natives and destroyed villages.

The Spanish didn't have the chance to overrun the Apacheans, whose scattered settlements were more difficult to locate than were pueblos. After the Pueblo Revolt of 1680, which drove the Spanish away, only to have them return 12 years later, the Navajo periodically housed Pueblos seeking refuge from reprisals. In return, the Pueblos taught them rituals, customs, agricultural techniques, and arts—in some of which, like weaving, they eventually surpassed their teachers. In the 1700s, drought led many Hopis to seek refuge among the Navajo in the formerly vacated Canyon de Chelly—a poignant example of the long-standing cooperative relationship of the two groups.

The Navajo also picked up European skills, some of them from the Pueblos. Directly from the Spanish they learned about silversmithing, raising cattle, and riding horses—and they became superior horsemen. Horses extended their gathering range and gave them greater mobility for trading and raiding. The Navajo were not nomadic, however. Many of them had different seasonal residences, log-and-earth hogans, as they continue to do today. These are maintained as permanent dwellings.

After independent Mexico ceded New Mexico to the United States in 1848, the Southwest's new proprietors decided to put an end to Indian raids. Over the next 16 years U.S. troops and the Navajo clashed repeatedly. The United States set up army posts within Navajo territory. They attempted to impose treaties, but U.S. agents often arranged treaties with individual headmen who had no authority that the Navajo as a whole could accept.

This misunderstanding of Navajo organization had tragic results. When raids continued, the U.S. territorial governor believed he had been betrayed. In order to safeguard the so-called frontier, he called in Colonel Kit Carson to destroy Navajo crops and livestock. Over the next few months, the People, as the Navajo call themselves, began to give themselves up. In 1864, as many as 8,000 Navajo made the forced Long Walk to captivity in Fort Sumner, 300 miles to the southeast.

The People were allowed to return to their land after four years of concentration-camp life. Fewer in number and greatly demoralized, they had to reconstruct their lives from scratch, rebuilding customs and lifestyles that had been impossible, if not forbidden, in the camps. Since then, Navajo ingenuity and an impressive ability to seize opportunities have gained them a measure of success in modern America. Their democratically governed community—Navajo Nation—numbers more than 250,000.

The Hopi didn't suffer such brutality. After conflicts with the Spanish—at the end of which they destroyed their own Christianized village of Awatovi in order to maintain the purity of Hopi ritual—their largely noncombative stance with the U.S. government afforded the Hopi more or less hands-off treatment.

In their proper observance of tradition and ritual, the Hopi are unique even among traditional Native Amer-

icans. In fact it was to Hopi spiritual leaders that many Native American traditionalists turned in the 1950s in what eventually became the Indian Unity Movement. Hopi beliefs focus on the relationship between the people, the land, and the Creator. In this strict moral order, prayer and ritual—which include the katsina rain power being dances—are necessary to keep the natural cycle in motion and to ensure the flow of life-sustaining forces. The earth is sacred, and they are its keepers.

The Hopi may well be the best dry farmers on the planet, successfully harvesting crops on a precarious 8 to 15 inches of rain per year—and no irrigation. Doubtless they manage this because they have perfected ancient Ancestral Pueblo techniques. The mesas on which they chose to live contain precious aquifers, particularly essential to life in such an arid territory. These vast water sources no doubt sustained them and their migrant guests when Pueblo peoples left places like Wupatki and Walnut Canyon and Canyon de Chelly 700 years ago. Unfortunately, the Hopi Tribal Council, which represents the progressive Christianized members of the Hopi, has sold sacred land to strip miners who in turn have destroyed parts of Black Mesa and depleted the aquifer. This is one indication of the rift between modernizers and those who continue to practice traditional ways. The traditionalists reside in the villages of Oraibi, Hotevilla, and Shungapovi. They are, understandably, intolerant of whites. They follow the Hopi Way even as contemporary life and the Tribal Council pose ever greater threats to it.

The present-day Tohono O'odham (called Papago by the Spanish) and the Pima, in central-southern Arizona, are descendants of the Hohokam. The Spanish first encountered them in the 17th century cultivating former Hohokam territory, using some of the ancient irrigation canals. Both tribes are Pimans, and both continue some Hohokam practices: living in rancherías along canals and performing costume dances and other rituals that link them to Uto-Aztecan language groups nearby in Mexico. The Pima live on the Salt River Reservation south of Phoenix, and the Tohono O'odham reservation stretches north from the Mexican border.

Like the Southwest's history, perspectives on Native American cultures are complex and fascinating—and have become confused in the clash of Euro-American and Native American ways. Take, for example, the enchanting and mysterious word *Anasazi,* which enters into almost any discussion of native Arizonans. This Navajo word, meaning both "ancient ones" and "enemy ancestors," automatically implies a Navajo perspective. Another of equal value is that of the Hopi, whose name for the ancient culture, *Hisatsinom,* means "people of long ago." Yet another perspective is that of the New Mexican Zuñi, who prefer the word *Enote:que,* "our ancient ones, our ancestors."*

To scientifically trained Euro-American archaeologists, the term *Anasazi* conveniently groups together a variety of ancient Pueblo peoples who had similar lifestyles but often divergent adaptations to southwestern conditions. In past decades researchers encouraged the myth of a lost Anasazi civilization and posed virtually unanswerable questions about who the people were and how and why they "vanished" from the scene. Had they taken the beliefs and statements of the Hopi and of New Mexican Pueblos seriously—acting as both archaeologists and anthropologists—the *Hisatsinom-Enote:que-Anasazi* would have fit seamlessly into the continuity of Native American life.

The perspective we can never know is that of the Ancestral Pueblos themselves—we don't even know what language they spoke. Yet we can try to get a sense of their world view by listening to contemporary Pueblos. If we project their uniquely American customs into the past, aspects of their ancestral culture come to life. And while Western tradition has its own ancient echoes, such as "know yourself" or "love your neighbor," traditional Pueblo ways speak of a life balanced in its relationship with the earth.

Sources

Ancient Ruins of the Southwest: An Archaeological Guide. David Grant Noble. Flagstaff: Northland Publishing Co., 1981.

Indian Country. Peter Mathiessen. New York: The Viking Press, 1984.

The Navaho. Clyde Kluckhon and Dorothea Leighton. Cambridge, Mass.: Harvard University Press, 1974.

Those Who Came Before: Southwestern Archaeology in the National Park System. Robert H. Lister and Florence C. Lister. Flagstaff, Ariz.: Southwestern Parks and Monuments, 1983.

What Happened to the Anasazi? Why Did They Leave? Where Did They Go? A Panel Discussion at the Anasazi Heritage Center. Jerold G. Widdison, ed. Albuquerque: Southwest Natural and Cultural Heritage Association, 1990.

—Stephen Wolf

Stephen Wolf was formerly a staff editor at Fodor's.

WHAT TO READ AND WATCH BEFORE YOU GO

Books

ESSAYS AND FICTION

Going Back to Bisbee, by Richard Shelton, *Frog Mountain Blues,* by Charles Bowden, and *The Mountains Next Day,* by Janice Emily Bowers, are all fine personal accounts of life in southern Arizona. The hipster fiction classic *The Monkey Wrench Gang,* by Edward Abbey, details an ecoanarchist plot to blow up Glen Canyon Dam. *Stolen Gods,* a thriller by Jake Page, is set largely on Arizona's Hopi reservation and in Tucson. Three novels by Tucson-based writers skillfully evoke the interplay between Native American culture and contemporary Southwest life: *Pigs in Heaven,* by Barbara Kingsolver, *Almanac of the Dead,* by Leslie Marmon Silko, and *Yes Is Better Than No,* by Byrd Baylor. Wild West adventure, with all of the mythological glory that Hollywood has tried to capture, abounds in Zane Grey's novels—buy a new copy or look for any of the charming illustrated hardcover editions in used- or out-of-print bookstores. Tony Hillerman's mysteries will put you in an equally southwestern mood.

GENERAL HISTORY

Arizona: A History, by Thomas E. Sheridan, chronicles the Anglo, Mexican, and Native American frontier and details its transformation into the modern-day Sunbelt. *Arizona Cowboys,* by Dane Coolidge, is an illustrated account of the cowboys, Indians, settlers, and explorers of the early 1900s. Buried-treasure hunters will be inspired by *Lost Mines of the Great Southwest,* by John D. Mitchell, which is just enough of a nibble to start you sketching maps and planning strategy. First printed back in 1891, *Some Strange Corners of Our Country,* by Charles F. Lummis, takes readers on a century-old journey to the Grand Canyon, Montezuma Castle,

the Petrified Forest, and other Arizonan "strange corners." For a dip into the backroads of the past, try *Arizona Good Roads Association Illustrated Road Maps and Tour Book,* a 1913 volume, replete with hotel ads, reprinted by *Arizona Highways* magazine. *Roadside History of Arizona,* by Marshall Trimble, will bring you up to date on many of the same thoroughfares. *Ghost Towns of Arizona,* by James E. and Barbara H. Sherman, gives historical details on the abandoned mining towns that dot the state and provides maps to find them. For an anthology that covers the entire state's literature, consult *Named in Stone and Sky: An Arizona Anthology,* edited by Gregory McNamee.

NATIVE AMERICAN HISTORY

Two books provide excellent surveys of the ancient and more recent Native American past and cover in more depth sites mentioned in this guidebook. *Those Who Came Before: Southwestern Archaeology in the National Park System,* by Robert Lister and Florence Lister, provides a well-researched and completely accessible summary of centuries of life in the region informed by both contemporary Indian and archaeological perspectives. David G. Noble's *Ancient Ruins of the Southwest* covers similar territory more briefly and portably and includes directions for driving to sites. *Hohokam Indians of the Tucson Basin,* by Linda Gregonis, offers an in-depth look at this prehistoric tribe. In *Hopi,* by Susanne Page and Jake Page, the daily, ceremonial, and spiritual life of the tribe is explored in detail. Study up on the history of Hopi silversmithing techniques in *Hopi Silver,* by Margaret Wright. The beautifully illustrated *Hopi Indian Kachina Dolls,* by Oscar T. Branson, details the different ceremonial roles of the colorful Native American figurines. Navajo homes, ceremonies, crafts, and tribal traditions are kept alive in *The Enduring Navajo*, by Laura Gilpin. Navajo legends and trends from early days to the present are collected in *The Book of the Navajo*, by Raymond F. Locke.

A superb collection of Native American stories, songs, and poems, *Coming to Light*, edited by Brian Swann, includes material from all over the country, not only the Southwest. *Paths of Life: American Indians of the Southwest and Northern Mexico*, edited by Thomas E. Sheridan and Nancy J. Parezo, offers both contemporary and historical portraits of Native Americans.

NATURAL HISTORY

The Arizona Sonora Desert Museum Book of Answers, by David Lazaroff, covers hundreds of frequently asked natural-history questions. *Gathering the Desert*, by Gary Paul Nabhan, explores the Southwest from an ethnobotanist's viewpoint. *A Guide to Exploring Oak Creek and the Sedona Area*, by Stewart Aitchison, provides natural-history driving tours of this very scenic district. In *100 Desert Wildflowers in Natural Color*, by Natt N. Dodge, you'll find a color photo and brief description of each of the flowers included. Also written by Natt N. Dodge, *Poisonous Dwellers of the Desert* gives precise information on both venomous and nonvenomous creatures of the Southwest. *Venomous Animals of Arizona*, by Robert L. Smith, offers precise information on venomous creatures of the Southwest. *Cacti of the Southwest*, by W. Hubert Earle, depicts some of the best-known species of the region with color photos and descriptive material. For comprehensive information on Grand Canyon geology, history, flora and fauna, plus hiking suggestions, pick up *A Field Guide to the Grand Canyon*, by Steve Whitney. *Grand Canyon Country: Its Majesty and Lore*, by Seymour L. Fishbein, published by National Geographic Books, describes the Grand Canyon through photographs, maps, and firsthand accounts. *Common Edible and Useful Plants of the West*, by Muriel Sweet, gives the layperson descriptions of medicinal and other plants and shrubs, most of which were first discovered by Native Americans. *Roadside Geology of Arizona*, by Halka Chronic, is a good resource for finding the causes of the striking natural formations you'll see throughout the state.

CRAFTS

The Traveler's Guide to American Crafts: West of the Mississippi, by Suzanne Carmichael, gives browsers and buyers alike a useful overview of Arizona's traditional and contemporary handiwork.

GENERAL INTEREST

Arizona Highways, a monthly magazine, features exquisite color photography of this versatile state. Useful general travel information, fine pictures, and well-written historical essays all make the book *Arizona*, by Larry Cheek, a good pretrip resource.

Videos

The Arizona landscape has starred in a slew of films either as itself or as a stand-in for similar terrain—the Sahara Desert, for instance—around the world. *The Postman* (1997) starring Kevin Costner and *Buffalo Soldiers* (1997) starring Danny Glover were filmed around Tucson. The Titan Missile Base near Green Valley was the locale for filming parts of *Star Trek: First Contact* (1996). Sun Devil Stadium in Tempe and Lost Dutchman State Park were featured in the blockbuster hit *Jerry Maguire* (1996). Parts of the Kevin Costner comedy *Tin Cup* (1996) were shot in Tubac. Much of director John Woo's bombastic *Broken Arrow* (1995), starring John Travolta and Christian Slater, was shot around Marble Canyon, which was also used, along with the Page/Lake Powell area, in the Mel Gibson–Jodie Foster vehicle *Maverick* (1994). Tom Hanks trotted through Monument Valley and Flagstaff in *Forrest Gump* (1994). The Tucson area served as the backdrop for much of *Boys on the Side* (1994), starring Whoopi Goldberg, Drew Barrymore, and Mary-Louise Parker. The nouveau westerns *Tombstone* (1993), starring Val Kilmer and Kurt Russell, and Sharon Stone's *The Quick and the Dead* (1995) both made use of various sites in Mescal. Woody Harrelson and Juliette Lewis raged through Holbrook, Winslow, and other towns in *Natural Born Killers* (1994), and the Yuma area was used to otherworldly effect in the science-fiction film *Stargate* (1994). Yuma stands in for a lot of places, including Morocco in Joseph von Sternberg's *Morocco* (1930), starring the sultry Marlene Dietrich, and the Bob Hope comedy *Road to Morocco* (1942).

The famous canyon loomed large in *Grand Canyon* (1991), starring Kevin Kline, Steve Martin, and Danny Glover. The independent cult hit *Red Rock West* (1991), directed by John Dahl and starring Nicolas Cage, was filmed in Willcox and other southeastern Arizona locales. Cage also starred, with Holly Hunter, in *Raising Arizona* (1987). Footage for the Joel Coen–directed film was shot in Scottsdale, Phoenix, and other locations. Chevy Chase frolicked through the Grand Canyon, Monument Valley, and Flagstaff in *National Lampoon's Vacation* (1983). Clint Eastwood stared down all comers in *The Outlaw Josey Wales* (1976), which showcases Patagonia and Mescal. Italian director Michelangelo Antonioni's *Zabriskie Point* (1968) includes scenes of Carefree and Phoenix.

Marilyn Monroe dropped in on Phoenix in *Bus Stop* (1956). Gerd Oswald's noirish *A Kiss Before Dying* (1955), starring Robert Wagner and Joanne Woodward, filmed in Tucson. Parts of *The Bells of St. Mary's* (1954) take place in Old Tucson. Some Arizona locations worked better than the real thing in Fred Zinnemann's *Oklahoma!* (1954). Jean Harlow whooped it up as a harried movie superstar in Victor Fleming's very funny *Bombshell* (1933), which has scenes shot in Tucson proper.

Among the many classic westerns shot in Arizona are *The Searchers* (1956), *She Wore a Yellow Ribbon* (1949), *Fort Apache* (1948), and *Stagecoach* (1939), all directed by John Ford and starring John Wayne, both of whom spent a lot of time filming in the state over the years; *Gunfight at the OK Corral* (1957), starring Burt Lancaster and Kirk Douglas; *Johnny Guitar* (1954), director Nicholas Ray's Freudian take on the Old West that features Joan Crawford in a gender-bending performance as a tough-gal gunslinger; director Howard Hawks's moody *Red River* (1948), which stars John Wayne and Montgomery Clift; and Ford's *My Darling Clementine* (1946), in which Henry Fonda plays a reluctant sheriff.

ESSENTIAL INFORMATION

AIR TRAVEL

BOOKING YOUR FLIGHT

When you book **look for nonstop flights** and **remember that "direct" flights stop at least once.** Try to avoid connecting flights, which require a change of plane.

CARRIERS

➤ MAJOR AIRLINES: **Alaska Airlines** (☎ 800/426–0333) to Phoenix. **American** (☎ 800/433–7300) to Phoenix, Tucson. **America West** (☎ 800/235–9292) to Phoenix, Tucson. **Continental** (☎ 800/525–0280) to Phoenix, Tucson. **Delta** (☎ 800/221–1212) to Phoenix, Tucson. **Northwest** (☎ 800/225–2525) to Phoenix, Tucson. **TWA** (☎ 800/221–2000) to Phoenix. **United** (☎ 800/241–6522) to Phoenix, Tucson. **US Airways** (☎ 800/428–4322) to Phoenix.

➤ SMALLER AIRLINES: **Aero California** (☎ 800/237–6225) to Tucson. **America Trans Air** (☎ 800/225–2995) to Phoenix. **Frontier Airlines** (☎ 800/432–1359) to Phoenix. **Midwest Express** (☎ 800/452–2022) to Phoenix. **Reno Air** (☎ 800/736–6247) to Tucson. **Southwest** (☎ 800/435–9792) to Phoenix, Tucson.

➤ FROM THE U.K.: **American Airlines** (☎ 0345/789–789) from Heathrow via Chicago or from Gatwick via Dallas. **Continental Airlines** (☎ 0800/776–464 or 01293/776–464) from Gatwick via Houston and from Manchester via Newark. **Delta** (☎ 0800/414–767) flies from London's Gatwick Airport to Phoenix via Atlanta or Cincinnati.

➤ WITHIN ARIZONA: Within the state, **America West Express/Mesa** (☎ 800/235–9292) operates regularly scheduled flights from Phoenix to Flagstaff, Prescott, Lake Havasu, Laughlin, Kingman, Sierra Vista, and Yuma. **Eagle Scenic Airlines** (☎ 800/535–4448) flies from Las Vegas to the Grand Canyon.

CHECK-IN & BOARDING

Assuming that not everyone with a ticket will show up, airlines routinely overbook planes. When that happens, airlines ask for volunteers to give up their seats. In return these volunteers usually get a certificate for a free flight and are rebooked on the next flight out. If there are not enough volunteers, the airline must choose who will be denied boarding. The first to get bumped are passengers who checked in late and those flying on discounted tickets, so **get to the gate and check in as early as possible,** especially during peak periods.

Always **bring a government-issued photo ID to the airport.** You may be asked to show it before you are allowed to check in.

CUTTING COSTS

The least-expensive airfares to Arizona must usually be purchased in advance and are nonrefundable. It's smart to **call a number of airlines, and when you are quoted a good price, book it on the spot**—the same fare may not be available the next day. Always **check different routings** and look into using different airports. Travel agents, especially low-fare specialists (☞ Discounts & Deals, *below*), are helpful.

Consolidators are another good source. They buy tickets for scheduled international flights at reduced rates from the airlines, then sell them at prices that beat the best fare available directly from the airlines, usually without restrictions. Sometimes you can even get your money back if you need to return the ticket. Carefully read the fine print detailing penalties for changes and cancellations, and **confirm your consolidator reservation with the airline.**

When you **fly as a courier** you trade your checked-luggage space for a ticket deeply subsidized by a courier service. There are restrictions on when you can book and how long you can stay.

➤ CONSOLIDATORS: **Cheap Tickets** (☎ 800/377–1000). **Up & Away Travel** (☎ 212/889–2345). **Discount Airline Ticket Service** (☎ 800/576–1600). **Unitravel** (☎ 800/325–2222). **World Travel Network** (☎ 800/409–6753).

ENJOYING THE FLIGHT

For more legroom **request an emergency-aisle seat.** Don't sit in the row in front of the emergency aisle or in front of a bulkhead, where seats may not recline. If you have dietary concerns, **ask for special meals when booking.** These can be vegetarian, low-cholesterol, or kosher, for example. On long flights, try to maintain a normal routine, to help fight jetlag. At night **get some sleep.** By day **eat light meals, drink water** (not alcohol), and **move around the cabin** to stretch your legs.

FLYING TIMES

Flying time is 5½ hours from New York, 3½ hours from Chicago, and 1¼ hours from Los Angeles.

HOW TO COMPLAIN

If your baggage goes astray or your flight goes awry, complain right away. Most carriers require that you **file a claim immediately.**

➤ AIRLINE COMPLAINTS: U.S. Department of Transportation **Aviation Consumer Protection Division** (✉ C-75, Room 4107, Washington, DC 20590, ☎ 202/366–2220). **Federal Aviation Administration Consumer Hotline** (☎ 800/322–7873).

AIRPORTS

Major gateways to Arizona include Phoenix Sky Harbor International, about 3 mi east of Phoenix city center, and Tucson International Air Terminal, about 8½ mi south of the central business area.

➤ AIRPORT INFORMATION: **Phoenix Sky Harbor International** (✉ 24th and Buckeye Sts., off I-10, ☎ 602/273–3300). **Tucson International Air Terminal** (✉ Tucson Blvd. and Valen-cia Rd. between 1–10 and I-19, ☎ 520/573–8000).

BIKE TRAVEL

☞ *See* Outdoors & Sports, *below.*

BIKES IN FLIGHT

Most airlines accommodate bikes as luggage, provided they are dismantled and boxed. For bike boxes, often free at bike shops, you'll pay about $5 (at least $100 for bike bags) from airlines. International travelers can sometimes substitute a bike for a piece of checked luggage at no charge; otherwise, the cost is about $100. Domestic and Canadian airlines charge $25–$50.

BUS TRAVEL

Greyhound (☎ 800/231–2222) provides service to many Arizona destinations from most parts of the United States.

CAMERAS & PHOTOGRAPHY

➤ PHOTO HELP: **Kodak Information Center** (☎ 800/242–2424). *Kodak Guide to Shooting Great Travel Pictures,* available in bookstores or from Fodor's Travel Publications (☎ 800/533–6478; $16.50 plus $4 shipping).

EQUIPMENT PRECAUTIONS

Always **keep your film and tape out of the sun.** Carry an extra supply of batteries, and **be prepared to turn on your camera or camcorder** to prove to security personnel that the device is real. Always **ask for hand inspection of film,** which becomes clouded after successive exposures to airport X-ray machines, and **keep videotapes away from metal detectors.**

CAR RENTAL

Rates in Phoenix begin at $34 a day and $140 a week for an economy car with air-conditioning, an automatic transmission, and unlimited mileage. This does not include tax on car rentals, which is 9.5%.

➤ MAJOR AGENCIES: **Alamo** (☎ 800/327–9633; 0181/759–6200 in the U.K.). **Avis** (☎ 800/331–1212; 800/879–2847 in Canada; 02/9353–9000 in Australia; 09/525–1982 in New Zealand). **Budget** (☎ 800/527–0700; 0144/227–6266 in the U.K.). **Dollar**

(☎ 800/800–4000; 0181/897–0811 in the U.K., where it is known as Eurodollar; 02/9223–1444 in Australia). **Hertz** (☎ 800/654–3131; 800/ 263–0600 in Canada; 0181/897– 2072 in the U.K.; 02/9669–2444 in Australia; 03/358–6777 in New Zealand). **National InterRent** (☎ 800/227–7368; 0345/222525 in the U.K., where it is known as Europcar InterRent).

CUTTING COSTS

To get the best deal **book through a travel agent who will shop around.** Also **price local car-rental companies,** although the service and maintenance may not be as good as those of a major player. Remember to ask about required deposits, cancellation penalties, and drop-off charges if you're planning to pick up the car in one city and leave it in another. If you're traveling during a holiday period, also make sure that a confirmed reservation guarantees you a car.

Do **look into wholesalers,** companies that do not own fleets but rent in bulk from those that do and often offer better rates than traditional car-rental operations.

➤ WHOLESALERS: **Auto Europe** (☎ 207/842–2000 or 800/223–5555, FAX 800–235–6321). **Kemwel Holiday Autos** (☎ 914/835–3000 or 800/678– 0678, FAX 914/835–5126).

INSURANCE

When driving a rented car you are generally responsible for any damage to or loss of the vehicle as well as for any property damage or personal injury that you may cause. Before you rent see what coverage your personal auto-insurance policy and credit cards already provide.

For about $15 to $20 per day, rental companies sell protection, known as a collision- or loss-damage waiver (CDW or LDW), that eliminates your liability for damage to the car.

In Arizona, the car-rental company must pay for damage to third parties up to a preset legal limit, beyond which your own liability insurance kicks in. However, **make sure you have enough coverage to pay for the car.** If you do not have auto insurance or an umbrella policy that covers damage to third parties, purchasing liability insurance and a CDW or LDW is highly recommended.

REQUIREMENTS & RESTRICTIONS

In Arizona you must be 21 to rent a car, and rates may be higher if you're under 25. You'll pay extra for child seats (about $3 per day), which are compulsory for children under five, and for additional drivers (about $2 per day). Non-U.S. residents will need a reservation voucher, a passport, a driver's license, and a travel policy that covers each driver, in order to pick up a car.

SURCHARGES

Before you pick up a car in one city and leave it in another **ask about drop-off charges or one-way service fees,** which can be substantial. Note, too, that some rental agencies charge extra if you return the car before the time specified in your contract. To avoid a hefty refueling fee **fill the tank just before you turn in the car,** but be aware that gas stations near the rental outlet may overcharge.

CAR TRAVEL

Major approaches from the east and west are I–40, I–10, I–8, and U.S. 60. Main north–south routes are I–17, I–10 (from Phoenix to Tucson), and U.S. 89. Other artery roads are U.S. 70 and U.S. 64 (U.S. 160 in Arizona) from the east.

Most highways in the state are good to excellent, with easy access, roadside facilities, rest stops, and scenic views. The speed limit on the freeways is now 75 mph, but **don't drive much faster than the limit**—police use sophisticated detection systems to catch violators. Distances between destinations may be longer than you are accustomed to, so allow extra time behind the wheel.

At some point you will probably pass through one or more of the state's 23 Native American reservations. Roads and other areas within reservation boundaries are under the jurisdiction of reservation police and governed by separate rules and regulations. **Observe all signs and respect Native Americans' privacy.** Be careful not to hit any animals, which often wander onto the roads; the penalties can be very high.

AUTO CLUBS

➤ IN AUSTRALIA: **Australian Automobile Association** (☎ 02/6247–7311).

➤ IN CANADA: **Canadian Automobile Association** (CAA, ☎ 613/247–0117).

➤ IN NEW ZEALAND: **New Zealand Automobile Association** (☎ 09/377–4660).

➤ IN THE U.K.: **Automobile Association** (AA, ☎ 0990/500–600). **Royal Automobile Club** (RAC, ☎ 0990/722–722 for membership; 0345/121–345 for insurance).

➤ IN THE U.S.: **American Automobile Association** (☎ 800/564–6222).

EMERGENCIES

Dial 911 to report accidents on the road and to reach police, the Arizona Department of Public Safety, or fire department.

GASOLINE

Prices vary widely depending on location, oil company, and whether you buy full-serve or self-serve gasoline. At press time, regular unleaded gasoline at self-serve stations cost about 99¢ a gallon.

ROAD CONDITIONS

The highways in Arizona are well maintained, but there are some natural conditions you should beware of.

DESERT HEAT. Vehicles and passengers should be well equipped for searing summer heat in the low desert. If you're planning to drive through the desert, **carry plenty of water, a good spare tire, a jack, and emergency supplies.** If you get stranded, stay with your vehicle and wait for help to arrive.

DUST STORMS. These usually occur from mid-July to mid-September (the monsoon months), just before thunderstorms hit, causing extremely low visibility. If you're on the highway, **pull as far off the road as possible, turn on your headlights, and wait for the storm to subside.**

FLASH FLOODS. They may sound apocalyptic or overly cautious, but warnings about flash floods should not be taken lightly. Sudden downpours send torrents of water racing into low-lying areas so dry that they are unable to absorb such a huge quantity of water so quickly. The result is powerful walls of water suddenly descending upon these low-lying areas, devastating anything in their paths. If you see rain clouds or thunderstorms in the area, stay away from dry riverbeds (also called arroyos or washes). If you find yourself in one, get out quickly. If you're with a car in a long gully, leave your car and climb out of the gully. You simply won't be able to outdrive a speeding wave. The idea is to **get to higher ground immediately when it rains.** Major highways are mostly flood-proof, but some smaller roads dip through washes. If showers are nearby, look before you cross. Washes filled with water should not be crossed until you can see the bottom. By all means, don't camp in these areas at any time, interesting as they may seem.

FRAGILE DESERT LIFE. The dry and easily desecrated desert floor takes centuries to overcome human damage. Consequently, it is illegal for four-wheel-drive and all-terrain vehicles and motorcycles to travel off established roadways.

➤ ROAD CONDITIONS: **Arizona Road and Weather Conditions Service** (☎ 602/651–2400 ext. 7623).

ROAD MAPS

The map included at the back of this book and the maps that car-rental agencies provide free cover key areas and major attractions in Arizona. You can buy more detailed maps in bookstores and near the check-out counters in many grocery and drug stores. The Arizona branches of the American Automobile Association (☞ *above*) have state and local maps that are free to members.

RULES OF THE ROAD

During the past few years speed limits have been raised, and many stretches now permit drivers to travel at 75 mph. In the cities, freeway limits are between 55 and 65 mph. Seat belts are required at all times. Tickets can be given for failing to comply. Children under age four must be in child safety seats. Unless otherwise indicated, right turns are allowed on red lights after you've come to a full stop, and left turns onto adjoining one-way streets are allowed on red lights after you've come to a full stop. Driving with a blood-alcohol level higher than .10 will result in arrest and seizure of driver's license. Fines are severe.

CHILDREN IN ARIZONA

Many large resorts and dude ranches have special activities for children, and many offer baby-sitting services. Children of all ages are enthralled by the Wild West flavor around Tucson and the southeastern part of the state, with Tombstone ranking as a particular favorite. If you're driving on long desert stretches, take along plenty of games and snacks. If you are renting a car don't forget to **arrange for a car seat** when you reserve.

➤ LOCAL INFORMATION: The monthly magazine *Raising Arizona Kids* focuses on Phoenix happenings, but also includes a calendar of children-friendly events around the state. You can buy single copies for $1.95 each at Borders, Li'l Things, and Smith stores in Tucson and Phoenix, or send $24.95 for a year's subscription (✉ 2445 E. Shea Blvd., Suite 201, Phoenix 85028, ☎ 602/953–KIDS or in Arizona 888/RAISING, ℻ 602/953–3305).

FLYING

If your children are two or older **ask about children's airfares.** As a general rule, infants under two not occupying a seat fly at greatly reduced fares or even for free.

Experts agree that it's a good idea to use safety seats aloft for children weighing less than 40 pounds. Airlines set their own policies: U.S. carriers usually require that the child be ticketed, even if he or she is young enough to ride free, since the seats must be strapped into regular seats. Do **check your airline's policy about using safety seats during takeoff and landing.** And since safety seats are not allowed just everywhere in the plane, get your seat assignments early.

When reserving, **request children's meals or a freestanding bassinet** if you need them. But note that bulkhead seats, where you must sit to use the bassinet, may lack an overhead bin or storage space on the floor.

LODGING

Most hotels in Arizona allow children under a certain age to stay in their parents' room at no extra charge, but others charge for them as extra adults; be sure to **find out the cutoff age for children's discounts.**

All Holiday Inns allow children under age 19 to stay free when sharing a room with an adult. Westin La Paloma Hotel in Tucson has supervised activities year-round for children ages 6 months–12 years, as well as junior tennis camps for kids 5–14 years old in summer. From Thanksgiving through April, the Tanque Verde Guest Ranch, also in Tucson, offers activities for children 4–11. In the Phoenix area, the Pointe Hilton Resort at Squaw Peak runs its Coyote Camp for children ages 4–12 year-round. The Phoenician Resort in Scottsdale has junior golf and tennis clinics for kids 5–14 throughout the year; Scottsdale's Hyatt Regency also offers a full range of supervised daytime activities geared for kids 3–12. All of the above resorts also have baby-sitting services. ➤ BEST CHOICES: Holiday Inns (☎ 800/465–4329). Westin La Paloma Hotel (☎ 800/228–3000). Tanque Verde Guest Ranch (☎ 800/234–3833). Pointe Hilton Resort at Squaw Peak (☎ 800/934–1000). Phoenician Resort (☎ 800/888–8234). Hyatt Regency (☎ 800/233–1234).

SIGHTS & ATTRACTIONS

Places that are especially good for children are indicated by a rubber duckie icon in the margin.

CONSUMER PROTECTION

Whenever shopping or buying travel services in Arizona, **pay with a major credit card** so you can cancel payment or get reimbursed if there's a problem. If you're doing business with a particular company for the first time, **contact your local Better Business**

Bureau and the attorney general's offices in your state and the company's home state, as well. Have any complaints been filed? Finally, if you're buying a package or tour, always **consider travel insurance** that includes default coverage (☞ Insurance, *below*).

➤ LOCAL BBBs: **Council of Better Business Bureaus** (✉ 4200 Wilson Blvd., Suite 800, Arlington, VA 22203, ☎ 703/276–0100, FAX 703/525–8277).

CUSTOMS & DUTIES

When shopping, **keep receipts** for all purchases. Upon reentering the country, **be ready to show customs officials what you've bought.** If you feel a duty is incorrect or object to the way your clearance was handled, note the inspector's badge number and ask to see a supervisor. If the problem isn't resolved, write to the appropriate authorities, beginning with the port director at your point of entry.

IN AUSTRALIA

Australia residents who are 18 or older may bring home A$400 worth of souvenirs and gifts (including jewelry), 250 cigarettes or 250 grams of tobacco, and 1,125 ml of alcohol (including wine, beer, and spirits). Residents under 18 may bring back A$200 worth of goods. Prohibited items include meat products. Seeds, plants, and fruits need to be declared upon arrival.

➤ INFORMATION: **Australian Customs Service** (Regional Director, ✉ Box 8, Sydney, NSW 2001, ☎ 02/9213–2000, FAX 02/9213–4000).

IN CANADA

Canadian residents who have been out of Canada for at least 7 days may bring home C$500 worth of goods duty-free. If you've been away less than 7 days but more than 48 hours, the duty-free allowance drops to C$200; if your trip lasts 24–48 hours, the allowance is C$50. You may not pool allowances with family members. Goods claimed under the C$500 exemption may follow you by mail; those claimed under the lesser exemptions must accompany you. Alcohol and tobacco products may be included in the 7-day and 48-hour

exemptions but not in the 24-hour exemption. If you meet the age requirements of the province or territory through which you reenter Canada, you may bring in, duty-free, 1.14 liters (40 imperial ounces) of wine or liquor *or* 24 12-ounce cans or bottles of beer or ale. If you are 16 or older you may bring in, duty-free, 200 cigarettes and 50 cigars. Check ahead of time with Revenue Canada or the Department of Agriculture for policies regarding meat products, seeds, plants, and fruits.

You may send an unlimited number of gifts worth up to C$60 each duty-free to Canada. Label the package UNSOLICITED GIFT—VALUE UNDER $60. Alcohol and tobacco are excluded.

➤ INFORMATION: **Revenue Canada** (✉ 2265 St. Laurent Blvd. S, Ottawa, Ontario K1G 4K3, ☎ 613/993–0534; 800/461–9999 in Canada).

IN NEW ZEALAND

Homeward-bound residents 17 or older may bring back $700 worth of souvenirs and gifts. Your duty-free allowance also includes 4.5 liters of wine or beer; one 1,125-ml bottle of spirits; and either 200 cigarettes, 250 grams of tobacco, 50 cigars, or a combination of the three up to 250 grams. Prohibited items include meat products, seeds, plants, and fruits.

➤ INFORMATION: **New Zealand Customs** (Custom House, ✉ 50 Anzac Ave., Box 29, Auckland, New Zealand, ☎ 09/359–6655, FAX 09/359–6732).

IN THE U.K.

From countries outside the EU, including the U.S., you may bring home, duty-free, 200 cigarettes or 50 cigars; 1 liter of spirits or 2 liters of fortified or sparkling wine or liqueurs; 2 liters of still table wine; 60 ml of perfume; 250 ml of toilet water; plus £136 worth of other goods, including gifts and souvenirs. If returning from outside the EU, prohibited items include meat products, seeds, plants, and fruits.

➤ INFORMATION: **HM Customs and Excise** (✉ Dorset House, Stamford St., Bromley Kent BR1 1XX, ☎ 0171/202–4227).

IN THE U.S.

Non-U.S. residents ages 21 and older may import into the United States 200 cigarettes or 50 cigars or 2 kilograms of tobacco, 1 liter of alcohol, and gifts worth $100. Meat products, seeds, plants, and fruits are prohibited.

➤ INFORMATION: **U.S. Customs Service** (inquiries, ✉ 1300 Pennsylvania Ave. NW, Washington, DC 20229, ☎ 202/927–6724; complaints, ✉ Office of Regulations and Rulings, 1300 Pennsylvania Ave. NW, Washington, DC 20229; registration of equipment, ✉ Resource Management, 1300 Pennsylvania Ave. NW, Washington, DC 20229, ☎ 202/927–0540).

DINING

The restaurants we list are the cream of the crop in each price category. Properties indicated by an ✕🏨 are lodging establishments whose restaurant warrants a special trip.

CATEGORY	COST*
$$$$	over $35
$$$	$25–$35
$$	$15–$25
$	under $15

per person for a three-course meal, excluding drinks, service, and sales tax

RESERVATIONS & DRESS

Reservations are always a good idea: we mention them only when they're essential or are not accepted. Book as far ahead as you can, and reconfirm as soon as you arrive. We mention dress only when men are required to wear a jacket or a jacket and tie.

WINE, BEER & SPIRITS

Possession and consumption of alcoholic beverages is illegal on Indian reservations.

DISABILITIES & ACCESSIBILITY

➤ LOCAL RESOURCES: **Southern Arizona Group Office** (☎ 602/640–5250) for information on accessible facilities at specific parks and sites in Arizona.

LODGING

When discussing accessibility with an operator or reservations agent **ask hard questions.** Are there any stairs, inside *or* out? Are there grab bars next to the toilet *and* in the shower/tub? How wide is the doorway to the room? To the bathroom? For the most extensive facilities meeting the latest legal specifications **opt for newer accommodations.**

TRANSPORTATION

➤ BUS: **Greyhound** (☎ 800/752–4841; TTY 800/345–3109), which provides service to many destinations in Arizona, will carry a person with disabilities and a companion for the price of a single fare.

➤ TRAIN: **Amtrak** (✉ National Railroad Passenger Corp., 60 Massachusetts Ave. NE, Washington, DC 20002, ☎ 800/872–7245) advises that you request redcap service, special seats, or wheelchair assistance when you make reservations. Also note that not all stations are equipped to provide these services. All passengers with disabilities are entitled to a 15% discount on the lowest fare, and there are special fares for children with disabilities as well. Contact Amtrak for a free brochure that outlines services for older travelers and people with disabilities.

➤ CAR: **Avis** (☎ 800/331–1212), **Hertz** (☎ 800/654–3131), and **National** (☎ 800/328–4567) can provide hand controls on some rental cars with advance notice.

➤ COMPLAINTS: **Disability Rights Section** (✉ U.S. Department of Justice, Civil Rights Division, Box 66738, Washington, DC 20035-6738, ☎ 202/514–0301; 800/514–0301; 202/514–0301 TTY; 800/514–0301 TTY, ℻ 202/307–1198) for general complaints. **Aviation Consumer Protection Division** (☞ Air Travel, *above*) for airline-related problems. **Civil Rights Office** (✉ U.S. Department of Transportation, Departmental Office of Civil Rights, S-30, 400 7th St. SW, Room 10215, Washington, DC 20590, ☎ 202/366–4648, ℻ 202/366–9371) for problems with surface transportation.

TRAVEL AGENCIES

In the United States, although the Americans with Disabilities Act requires that travel firms serve the needs of all travelers, some agencies specialize in working with people with disabilities.

➤ TRAVELERS WITH MOBILITY PROBLEMS: **Access Adventures** (✉ 206 Chestnut Ridge Rd., Rochester, NY 14624, ☎ 716/889–9096), run by a former physical-rehabilitation counselor. **Accessible Vans of the Rockies, Activity and Travel Agency** (✉ 2040 W. Hamilton Pl., Sheridan, CO 80110, ☎ 303/806–5047 or 888/837–0065, FAX 303/781–2329). **Care-Vacations** (✉ 5-5110 50th Ave., Leduc, Alberta T9E 6V4, ☎ 780/986–6404 or 780/986–8332) has group tours and is especially helpful with cruise vacations. **Flying Wheels Travel** (✉ 143 W. Bridge St., Box 382, Owatonna, MN 55060, ☎ 507/451–5005 or 800/535–6790, FAX 507/451–1685). **Hinsdale Travel Service** (✉ 201 E. Ogden Ave., Suite 100, Hinsdale, IL 60521, ☎ 630/325–1335).

➤ TRAVELERS WITH DEVELOPMENTAL DISABILITIES: **New Directions** (✉ 5276 Hollister Ave., Suite 207, Santa Barbara, CA 93111, ☎ 805/967–2841 or 888/967–2841, FAX 805/964–7344). **Sprout** (✉ 893 Amsterdam Ave., New York, NY 10025, ☎ 212/222–9575 or 888/222–9575, FAX 212/222–9768).

DISCOUNTS & DEALS

Be a smart shopper and **compare all your options** before making decisions. A plane ticket bought with a promotional coupon from travel clubs, coupon books, and direct-mail offers may not be cheaper than the least expensive fare from a discount ticket agency. And always keep in mind that what you get is just as important as what you save.

DISCOUNT RESERVATIONS

To save money **look into discount-reservations services** with toll-free numbers, which use their buying power to get a better price on hotels, airline tickets, even car rentals. When booking a room, always **call the hotel's local toll-free number** (if one is available) rather than the central reservations number—you'll often get a better price. Always ask about special packages or corporate rates.

➤ AIRLINE TICKETS: ☎ 800/FLY–4–LESS. ☎ 800/FLY–ASAP.

➤ HOTEL ROOMS: **Accommodations Express** (☎ 800/444–7666). **Central Reservation Service (CRS)** (☎ 800/548–3311). **Hotel Reservations Network** (☎ 800/964–6835). **Players Express Vacations** (☎ 800/458–6161). **Quickbook** (☎ 800/789–9887). **Room Finders USA** (☎ 800/473–7829). **RMC Travel** (☎ 800/245–5738). **Steigenberger Reservation Service** (☎ 800/223–5652).

PACKAGE DEALS

Don't confuse packages and guided tours. When you buy a package, you travel on your own, just as though you had planned the trip yourself. Fly/drive packages, which combine airfare and car rental, are often a good deal.

ECOTOURISM

Arizona has some of the best-preserved prehistoric sites in the world. Both federal and state law prohibits removal or destruction of artifacts from such sites. In Arizona, it is illegal to uproot or in any way harm a saguaro, and penalties are stiff. Whatever your activity, it is a good idea to tread lightly in natural settings. Remember to extinguish campfires and return the soil to its natural condition by mixing the ashes with dirt and water and covering the site with dirt.

E-MAIL

Checking your e-mail or surfing the Web can sometimes be done in the business centers of major hotels, which usually charge an hourly rate. Web access is also available at many fax and copy centers, many of which are open 24 hours and on weekends. In major cities look for cyber cafés, where tabletop computers allow you to log on while sipping coffee or listening to live jazz. Whether you have e-mail at home or not, you can **arrange to have a free e-mail address** from several services, including one available at www.hotmail.com (the site explains how to apply for an address).

ETIQUETTE

See the individual descriptions of the state's Native American reservations for information about etiquette and behavior.

GAY & LESBIAN TRAVEL

Although there are no state-wide gay and lesbian oriented travel organizations in Arizona, the agencies listed below can help plan gay-friendly vacations. Information on gay establishments in specific cities can be found easily on the Internet.

When planning your trip, check out *Fodor's Gay Guide to the USA* (**Fodor's Travel Publications**, ☎ 800/533–6478 or in bookstores); $20.

➤ GAY- AND LESBIAN-FRIENDLY TRAVEL AGENCIES: **Different Roads Travel** (⌧ 8383 Wilshire Blvd., Suite 902, Beverly Hills, CA 90211, ☎ 323/651–5557 or 800/429–8747, FAX 323/651–3678). **Kennedy Travel** (⌧ 314 Jericho Turnpike, Floral Park, NY 11001, ☎ 516/352–4888 or 800/237–7433, FAX 516/354–8849). **Now Voyager** (⌧ 4406 18th St., San Francisco, CA 94114, ☎ 415/626–1169 or 800/255–6951, FAX 415/626–8626). **Yellowbrick Road** (⌧ 1500 W. Balmoral Ave., Chicago, IL 60640, ☎ 773/561–1800 or 800/642–2488, FAX 773/561–4497). **Skylink Travel and Tour** (⌧ 1006 Mendocino Ave., Santa Rosa, CA 95401, ☎ 707/546–9888 or 800/225–5759, FAX 707/546–9891), serving lesbian travelers.

➤ LOCAL PUBLICATIONS: *Echo* (☎ 602/266–0550) is a gay and lesbian news and entertainment magazine published biweekly and distributed throughout the Southwest and southern California. *Heatstroke* (☎ 602/264–3646) is a Phoenix-based biweekly. The weekly *Observer* (☎ 520/622–7176) covers the Tucson and Phoenix area.

➤ GAY- AND LESBIAN-FRIENDLY TOUR OPERATORS: **Hanns Ebensten Travel** (⌧ 513 Fleming St., Key West, FL 33040, ☎ 305/294–8174, FAX 305/292–9665), one of the oldest operators in the gay market. **Toto Tours** (⌧ 1326 W. Albion Ave., Suite 3W, Chicago, IL 60626, ☎ 773/274–8686 or 800/565–1241, FAX 773/274–8695), for groups.

HIKING

Be sure to take the following precautions when you go for a hike of any length.

ANIMAL BITES

Wherever you're hiking, particularly between April and October, **keep a lookout for rattlesnakes.** You're likely not to have any problems if you maintain distance from snakes that you see—they can strike only half of their length, so a 6-ft clearance should allow you to stay unharmed, especially if you **don't provoke them.** If you are bitten by a rattler, don't panic. Just get to a hospital within two to three hours of the bite. Keep in mind that 30% to 40% of bites are dry bites, where the snake uses no venom (still, get thee to a hospital). **Avoid night hikes without rangers,** when snakes are on the prowl and less visible. You may want to pick up a kit called the Extractor for use if bitten; they're sold in major sporting goods stores in Phoenix and Tucson.

Scorpions and Gila monsters are really less of a concern, since they strike only when provoked. To avoid scorpion encounters, **don't put your hands where you can't see with your eyes,** such as under rocks and in holes. Likewise, if you move a rock to sit down, make sure that scorpions haven't been exposed. Campers should shake out shoes in the morning, since scorpions like warm, moist places. If you are bitten, see a ranger about symptoms that may develop. Chances are good that you won't need to go to a hospital. Children are a different case, however: Scorpion stings can be fatal for them. Always try to keep an eye on what they may be getting their hands into to avoid the scorpion's sting. Gila monsters are relatively rare and bites are even rarer, but bear in mind that the reptiles are most active between April and June, when they do most of their hunting. Should a member of your party be bitten, it is most important to release the gila monster's jaws as soon as possible to minimize the amount of venom released. This can usually be achieved with a stick, an open flame, or by immersing the animal in water.

DEHYDRATION

This underestimated danger can be very serious, especially considering that one of the first major symptoms is the inability to swallow. It may be the easiest hazard to avoid, however;

simply **drink every 10–15 minutes,** up to a gallon of water per day in summer.

HYPOTHERMIA

Temperatures in Arizona can vary widely from day to night—as much as 40°F. Be sure to **bring enough warm clothing for hiking and camping, along with wet weather gear.** Exposure to the degree that body temperature dips below 95°F produces the following symptoms: chills, tiredness, then uncontrollable shivering and irrational behavior, with the victim not always recognizing that he or she is cold. If someone in your party is suffering from any of this, wrap him or her in blankets and/or a warm sleeping bag immediately and try to keep him or her awake. The fastest way to raise body temperature is through skin-to-skin contact in a sleeping bag. Drinking warm liquids also helps.

POTABLE WATER

Never drink from any stream, no matter how clear it may be. Giardia organisms can turn your stomach inside out. The easiest way to purify water is to **dissolve a water purification tablet** in it. Camping-equipment stores also carry purification pumps. **Boil water for 15 minutes,** a reliable method, if time- and fuel-consuming.

SUN PROTECTION

Wear a hat and sunglasses and put on sunblock to protect against the burning Arizona sun. And **watch out for heatstroke.** Symptoms include headache, dizziness, and fatigue, which can turn into convulsions and unconsciousness and can lead to death. If someone in your party develops any of these conditions, have one person seek emergency help while others move the victim into the shade, wrap him or her in wet clothing (is a stream nearby?) to cool him or her down.

HOLIDAYS

Major national holidays include New Year's Day (Jan. 1); Martin Luther King, Jr., Day (3rd Mon. in Jan.); President's Day (3rd Mon. in Feb.); Memorial Day (last Mon. in May); Independence Day (July 4); Labor Day (1st Mon. in Sept.); Thanksgiving Day (4th Thurs. in Nov.); Christmas Eve and Christmas Day (Dec. 24 and 25); and New Year's Eve (Dec. 31).

INSURANCE

The most useful travel insurance plan is a comprehensive policy that includes coverage for trip cancellation and interruption, default, trip delay, and medical expenses (with a waiver for preexisting conditions).

Without insurance you will lose all or most of your money if you cancel your trip, regardless of the reason. Default insurance covers you if your tour operator, airline, or cruise line goes out of business. Trip-delay covers expenses that arise because of bad weather or mechanical delays. Study the fine print when comparing policies.

British and Australian citizens need extra medical coverage when traveling overseas.

Always **buy travel policies directly from the insurance company;** if you buy it from a cruise line, airline, or tour operator that goes out of business you probably will not be covered for the agency or operator's default, a major risk. Before you make any purchase **review your existing health and home-owner's policies** to find what they cover away from home.

➤ TRAVEL INSURERS: In the U.S. Access America (⊠ 6600 W. Broad St., Richmond, VA 23230, ☎ 804/285–3300 or 800/284–8300), **Travel Guard International** (⊠ 1145 Clark St., Stevens Point, WI 54481, ☎ 715/345–0505 or 800/826–1300). In Canada **Voyager Insurance** (⊠ 44 Peel Center Dr., Brampton, Ontario L6T 4M8, ☎ 905/791–8700; 800/668–4342 in Canada).

➤ INSURANCE INFORMATION: In the U.K. the **Association of British Insurers** (⊠ 51–55 Gresham St., London EC2V 7HQ, ☎ 0171/600–3333, FAX 0171/696–8999). In Australia the **Insurance Council of Australia** (☎ 03/9614–1077, FAX 03/9614–7924).

LODGING

Arizona's hotels and motels run the gamut—from world-class resorts to budget chains, and from historic inns, bed-and-breakfasts, and mountain lodges to dude ranches, campgrounds, and RV parks. **Make reservations well in advance for the high season**— winter in the desert south and summer in the high country. Tremendous bargains can be found off-season, when even the most exclusive establishments cut their rates by half.

The lodgings we list are the cream of the crop in each price category. We always list the facilities that are available—but we don't specify whether they cost extra: When pricing accommodations, always ask what's included and what costs extra. Properties indicated by an ✕🔠 are lodging establishments whose restaurant warrants a special trip.

CATEGORY	COST*
$$$$	over $250
$$$	$175–$250
$$	$100–$175
$	under $100

All prices are for a standard double room, excluding service and taxes.

Assume that hotels operate on the European Plan (EP, with no meals) unless we specify that they use the Continental Plan (CP, with a Continental breakfast daily), Modified American Plan (MAP, with breakfast and dinner daily), or the Full American Plan (FAP, with all meals).

APARTMENT & VILLA RENTALS

If you want a home base that's roomy enough for a family and comes with cooking facilities **consider a furnished rental.** These can save you money, especially if you're traveling with a group. Home-exchange directories sometimes list rentals as well as exchanges.

➤ INTERNATIONAL AGENTS: **Europa-Let/Tropical Inn-Let** (✉ 92 N. Main St., Ashland, OR 97520, ☎ 541/482–5806 or 800/462–4486, ⅋ₐ⅋ 541/482–0660). **Hometours International** (✉ Box 11503, Knoxville, TN 37939, ☎ 423/690–8484 or 800/367–4668). **Interhome** (✉ 1990 N.E. 163rd St., Suite 110, Miami Beach, FL 33162, ☎ 305/940–2299 or 800/882–6864, ⅋ₐ⅋ 305/940–2911). **Rent-a-Home International** (✉ 7200 34th Ave. NW, Seattle, WA 98117, ☎ 206/789–9377, ⅋ₐ⅋ 206/789–9379). **Vacation Home Rentals Worldwide** (✉ 235

Kensington Ave., Norwood, NJ 07648, ☎ 201/767–9393 or 800/633–3284, ⅋ₐ⅋ 201/767–5510). **Hideaways International** (✉ 767 Islington St., Portsmouth, NH 03801, ☎ 603/430–4433 or 800/843–4433, ⅋ₐ⅋ 603/430–4444; membership $99).

B&BS

➤ RESERVATION SERVICES: **Arizona Association of Bed and Breakfast Inns** (✉ Box 7186, Phoenix 85012, ☎ 800/284–2589). **Arizona Trails Bed & Breakfast Reservation Service** (✉ Box 18998, Fountain Hills 85269, ☎ 602/837–4284; 888/799–4282). **Bed & Breakfast Southwest** (✉ P.O. Box 51198, Phoenix 85076, ☎ 602/706–8820 or 800/762–9704; 602/874–1316 outside AZ). **Mi Casa Su Casa** (✉ Box 950, Tempe 85280, ☎ 602/990–0682 or 800/456–0682, ⅋ₐ⅋ 602/990–3390; http://www.mi-casa.org). The Arizona Office of Tourism (☞ Visitor Information, *below*) has a statewide list of bed-and-breakfasts.

CAMPING

You can choose from a feast of federal, state, Native American, and private campgrounds in virtually all parts of the state. Facilities range from deluxe parks with swimming pools and recreation rooms to primitive backcountry wilderness sites. Most campgrounds provide toilets, drinking water, showers, and hookups. Camping is also permitted in Arizona's seven national forests, but be forewarned that they have no facilities whatsoever.

Pack according to season, region, and length of trip. Basics include a sleeping bag, a tent (optional, and forbidden in some RV parks), a camp stove, cooking utensils, food and water supplies, a first-aid kit, insect repellent, sunscreen, a lantern, trash bags, a rope, and a tarp. In case you forget something, almost every camping item is available for sale or rent at one of Arizona's many sporting-goods shops.

Individual campgrounds should be contacted before travel for suggestions as to specific equipment to bring, as well as necessary reservations, advance deposits, and permits.

Most state parks have a 15-day maximum-stay limit.

➤ INFORMATION: **National Park Service** (✉ 3121 North 3rd Ave., Suite 142, Phoenix 85013, ☎ 602/640–5250), **Bureau of Land Management** (✉ 222 N. Central Ave., Phoenix 85014, ☎ 602/417–9528), **Arizona State Parks Department** (☞ National Parks, *below*), **Apache Sitgreaves National Forest** (✉ 309 S. Mountain Ave., Springerville 85938, ☎ 520/333–4301), **Coconino National Forest** (✉ 2323 E. Greenlaw La., Flagstaff 86004, ☎ 520/527–3600), **Coronado National Forest** (✉ Federal Bldg., 300 W. Congress St., Tucson 85701, ☎ 520/670–4552), **Prescott National Forest** (✉ 344 S. Cortez St., Prescott 86303, ☎ 520/771–4700, TTY 520/771–4792), or **Tonto National Forest** (✉ 2324 E. McDowell Rd., Phoenix 85006, ☎ 602/225–5200), **Williams-Forest Service Visitor Center** (✉ 200 W. Railroad Ave., Williams 86046, ☎ 520/635–4061).

DUDE RANCHES

Down-home western lifestyle, cooking, and activities are the focus of guest ranches, situated primarily in Tucson and southern Arizona and Wickenburg. Some are resortlike properties where guests are pampered, whereas smaller family-run ranches expect *everyone* to join in the chores. Horseback riding and other outdoor recreational activities are emphasized. Most dude ranches are closed in summer.

➤ INFORMATION: Contact the Arizona Office of Tourism (☞ Visitor Information, *below*) for the names and addresses of dude ranches throughout the state.

HOME EXCHANGES

If you would like to exchange your home for someone else's **join a home-exchange organization,** which will send you its updated listings of available exchanges for a year and will include your own listing in at least one of them. It's up to you to make specific arrangements.

➤ EXCHANGE CLUBS: **HomeLink International** (✉ Box 650, Key West, FL 33041, ☎ 305/294–7766 or 800/

638–3841, FAX 305/294–1448; $88 per year). **Intervac U.S.** (✉ Box 590504, San Francisco, CA 94159, ☎ 800/756–4663, FAX 415/435–7440; $83 per year).

HOSTELS

No matter what your age you can **save on lodging costs by staying at hostels.** In some 5,000 locations in more than 70 countries around the world, Hostelling International (HI), the umbrella group for a number of national youth-hostel associations, offers single-sex, dorm-style beds and, at many hostels, couples rooms and family accommodations. Membership in any HI national hostel association, open to travelers of all ages, allows you to stay in HI-affiliated hostels at member rates (one-year membership is about $25 for adults; hostels run about $10–$25 per night). Members also have priority if the hostel is full; they're eligible for discounts around the world, even on rail and bus travel in some countries.

➤ ORGANIZATIONS: **Australian Youth Hostel Association** (✉ 10 Mallett St., Camperdown, NSW 2050, ☎ 02/9565–1699, FAX 02/9565–1325). **Hostelling International—American Youth Hostels** (✉ 733 15th St. NW, Suite 840, Washington, DC 20005, ☎ 202/783–6161, FAX 202/783–6171). **Hostelling International—Canada** (✉ 400–205 Catherine St., Ottawa, Ontario K2P 1C3, ☎ 613/237–7884, FAX 613/237–7868). **Youth Hostel Association of England and Wales** (✉ Trevelyan House, 8 St. Stephen's Hill, St. Albans, Hertfordshire AL1 2DY, ☎ 01727/855215 or 01727/845047, FAX 01727/844126). **Youth Hostels Association of New Zealand** (✉ Box 436, Christchurch, New Zealand, ☎ 03/379–9970, FAX 03/365–4476). Membership in the U.S. $25, in Canada C$26.75, in the U.K. £9.30, in Australia $44, in New Zealand $24.

HOTELS

Most major hotel chains are represented in Arizona. All hotels listed have private bath unless otherwise noted.

➤ TOLL-FREE NUMBERS: **Baymont Inns** (☎ 800/428–3438). **Best Western** (☎ 800/528–1234). **Choice** (☎

800/221–2222). **Clarion** (☎ 800/252–7466). **Comfort** (☎ 800/228–5150). **Days Inn** (☎ 800/325–2525). **Doubletree and Red Lion Hotels** (☎ 800/222–8733). **Embassy Suites** (☎ 800/362–2779). **Fairfield Inn** (☎ 800/228–2800). **Hilton** (☎ 800/445–8667). **Holiday Inn** (☎ 800/465–4329). **Howard Johnson** (☎ 800/654–4656). **Hyatt Hotels & Resorts** (☎ 800/233–1234). **La Quinta** (☎ 800/531–5900). **Marriott** (☎ 800/228–9290). **Omni** (☎ 800/843–6664). **Quality Inn** (☎ 800/228–5151). **Radisson** (☎ 800/333–3333). **Ramada** (☎ 800/228–2828). **Renaissance Hotels & Resorts** (☎ 800/468–3571). **Ritz-Carlton** (☎ 800/241–3333). **Sheraton** (☎ 800/325–3535). **Sleep Inn** (☎ 800/221–2222). **Westin Hotels & Resorts** (☎ 800/228–3000). **Wyndham Hotels & Resorts** (☎ 800/822-4200).

MOTELS

➤ TOLL-FREE NUMBERS: **Econo Lodge** (☎ 800/553–2666). **Friendship Inns** (☎ 800/453–4511). **Motel 6** (☎ 800/466–8356). **Rodeway** (☎ 800/228–2000). **Super 8** (☎ 800/848–8888).

MEDIA

NEWSPAPERS & MAGAZINES

Major Arizona-interest publications available state-wide are: *Arizona. Business, Arizona Highways,* and *Sunset Magazine.*

MONEY MATTERS

Due to their relative sizes, Phoenix and Tucson tend to have the greatest variety of accommodations and restaurants in the state. There is no real "average" for restaurant or dining prices—rooms can run from $50 a night at a hotel near the airport to $1,500 for a night in one of Phoenix's posh desert spa-resorts. Suffice to say that you'll be able to find a hotel or eatery to fit most any budget. Resorts in Sedona and in some of the smaller, more exclusive desert communities can be pricey due to their growing reputations as destinations in and of themselves, so be prepared to make a day trip of it if you don't want to drop several hundred dollars on a fancy B&B. The Grand Canyon area is equally pricey, but camping options and dorm-style

resorts, such as the Phantom Ranch on the Canyon floor ($65 a night), are more affordable accommodation options. Prices throughout this guide are given for adults. Substantially reduced fees are almost always available for children, students, and senior citizens. For information on taxes, *see* Taxes, *below.*

ATMS

Cirrus (☎ 800/424–7787). **Plus** (☎ 800/843–7587) for locations in the U.S. and Canada, or visit your local bank.

CREDIT CARDS

Throughout this guide, the following abbreviations are used: **AE,** American Express; **D,** Discover; **DC,** Diner's Club; **MC,** Master Card; and **V,** Visa.

➤ REPORTING LOST CARDS: American Express: 800/528–4800; Diner's Club: 800/234–6377; Discover: 800/347–2683; MasterCard: 800/307–7309; Visa: 800/362–7257.

NATIONAL PARKS

Look into discount passes to save money on park entrance fees. The Golden Eagle Pass ($50) gets you and your companions free admission to all parks for one year. (Camping and parking are extra.) Both the Golden Age Passport ($10), for those 62 and older, and the Golden Access Passport (free), for travelers with disabilities, entitle holders to free entry to all national parks, plus 50% off fees for the use of many park facilities and services. You must show proof of age and of U.S. citizenship or permanent residency (such as a U.S. passport, driver's license, or birth certificate) and, if requesting Golden Access, proof of disability. All three passes are available at all national park entrances where entrance fees are charged. Golden Eagle and Golden Access passes are also available by mail.

➤ PASSES BY MAIL: **National Park Service** (✉ National Capitol Area Office, 1100 Ohio Dr. SW, Washington, DC 20242, ☎ 202/208–4747).

➤ STATE PARKS: **Arizona State Parks Department** (✉ 1300 W. Washington St., Phoenix 85007, ☎ 602/542–

4174) for a complete listing of all state parks and their facilities.

BASEBALL

During spring training, the **Chicago Cubs** play at Hohokam Park in Mesa (☎ 602/964–4467), the **Oakland Athletics** at Phoenix Municipal Stadium (☎ 602/392–0217), the **San Francisco Giants** at Scottsdale Stadium (☎ 602/990–7972), the **Anaheim Angels** at Diablo Stadium in Tempe (☎ 602/350–5205), and the **Milwaukee Brewers** at the Compadre Stadium in Chandler (☎ 602/895–1200). Both the **San Diego Padres** and the **Seattle Mariners** train at Peoria Stadium (☎ 602/878–4337) in another Phoenix suburb. The **Colorado Rockies** play at Tucson's Hi Corbett Field (☎ 520/327–9467). For current information on all aspects of Cactus League baseball, contact the **Mesa Convention and Visitor's Bureau** (✉ 120 North Center St., Mesa 85201, ☎ 602/827–4700 or 800/283–6372). The major league **Arizona Diamondbacks** play at the Bank One Ballpark. Call 602/462–6000 for information.

BASKETBALL

The NBA's **Phoenix Suns** strut their stuff at the America West Arena (✉ One Phoenix Suns Plaza, 201 E. Jefferson St., ☎ 602/379–7900).

BICYCLING

Call the county **Parks and Recreation Department** in the area you're visiting for information on nearby bike paths. The **Arizona Bicycle Club, Inc.** (✉ Box 7191, Phoenix, AZ 85011, ☎ 602/264–5478 or 602/279–6674), publishes a schedule of the many bicycle races and tours that take place throughout the state.

FISHING

Fishing licenses are required and can be obtained from the **Arizona Game and Fish Department** (✉ 2222 W. Greenway Rd., Phoenix 85023, ☎ 602/942–3000). For permission to fish San Carlos Lake on the San Carlos Indian reservation call 520/475–2343.

FOOTBALL

The NFL's **Arizona Cardinals** have flown from St. Louis to Phoenix,

where they play at **Sun Devil Stadium** (✉ 5th St. and College Ave., Tempe, ☎ 602/379–0102).

GOLF

For a list of Arizona's golfing facilities, contact the **Arizona Golf Association** (✉ 7226 N. 16th St., Suite 200, Phoenix 85020, ☎ 602/944–3035; 800/458–8484 in AZ).

HIKING

The **Backcountry Office** (☎ 520/638–7888) provides hikers with trail details, weather conditions, and packing suggestions for the Grand Canyon. For hikers who prefer to travel with a group, the **Sierra Club** (☎ 602/253–8633) leads a variety of wilderness treks. Contact the local chapters in Phoenix, Tucson, Kingman, Prescott, Sedona, and Flagstaff for information on guided hikes in these areas.

RIVER RAFTING

Contact the **Arizona Office of Tourism** (☞ Visitor Information, *below*) for an extensive list of rafting outfits, or *see* Tours & Packages, *below*.

ROCKHOUNDING

The Department of Mines and Mineral Resources is an excellent source of information about specimens that can be found in each part of the state.

➤ INFORMATION: **Department of Mines and Mineral Resources** (✉ 1502 W. Washington St., Phoenix 85007, ☎ 602/255–3795).

SKIING

For cross-country skiing, **Arizona Snowbowl & Flagstaff Nordic Center** (☎ 520/779–1951) and **Williams Ski Area** (☎ 520/635–9330), and miles of crisscrossing trails around **Alpine** (✉ Alpine Ranger District, ☎ 520/339–4384) are recommended. Equipment and instruction are readily available. We advise making reservations in the busy season.

For downhill skiing, **Sunrise Ski Resort** (☎ 520/735–7600) in McNary, owned and operated by the White Mountain Apache Indians, encompasses three mountain peaks and is the state's largest ski area. **Arizona Snowbowl** (☞ *above*) and

Mt. Lemmon Ski Valley (☎ 520/576–1321), near Tucson, are also popular. Though they aren't as impressive as those in the Rockies, ski resorts cater to all levels and provide instruction and equipment rental.

TENNIS

Arizona offers a multitude of tennis opportunities, from hard courts at city parks and university campuses to full-scale programs at ultraposh tennis-oriented resorts, such as **Gardiner's Resort on Camelback** (✉ 5700 E. McDonald Dr., Scottsdale 85253, ☎ 602/948–2100 or 800/245–2051), one of the country's best. Most hotels either have their own courts or are affiliated with a private or municipal facility.

PACKING

Wear casual clothing and resort wear in Arizona. When in more elegant restaurants in larger cities, as well as in dining rooms of some resorts, most men wear jackets and appropriate pants (few places require ties). Dressy casual wear is appropriate for women even in the nicest places—take along a silky blouse and chunky silver jewelry and you'll fit in almost anywhere.

Stay cool in cotton fabrics and light colors. T-shirts, polo shirts, sundresses, and lightweight shorts, trousers, skirts, and blouses are useful year-round in the south. **Bring sun hats, swimsuits, sandals, and sunscreen**—mandatory warm-weather items. **Bring a sweater and a warm jacket in winter,** particularly for high-country travel—anywhere around Flagstaff and north of it. And **don't forget jeans and sneakers or sturdy walking shoes**; they're important year-round.

Take along appropriate sports gear, although tennis, golf, ski, and horseback-riding equipment is readily available for rental. In your carry-on luggage **bring an extra pair of eyeglasses or contact lenses** and **enough of any medication you take** to last the entire trip. You may also want your doctor to write a spare prescription using the drug's generic name, since brand names may vary from country to country. In luggage to be checked, **never pack prescription drugs or valuables.** To avoid customs delays, carry medications in their original packaging. And don't forget to copy down and carry addresses of offices that handle refunds of lost traveler's checks.

CHECKING LUGGAGE

How many carry-on bags you can bring with you is up to the airline. Most allow two, but not always, so make sure that everything you carry aboard will fit under your seat, and get to the gate early. Note that if you have a seat at the back of the plane, you'll probably board first, while the overhead bins are still empty.

If you are flying internationally, note that baggage allowances may be determined not by piece but by weight—generally 88 pounds (40 kilograms) in first class, 66 pounds (30 kilograms) in business class, and 44 pounds (20 kilograms) in economy.

Airline liability for baggage is limited to $1,250 per person on flights within the United States. On international flights it amounts to $9.07 per pound or $20 per kilogram for checked baggage (roughly $640 per 70-pound bag) and $400 per passenger for unchecked baggage. You can buy additional coverage at check-in for about $10 per $1,000 of coverage, but it excludes a rather extensive list of items, shown on your airline ticket.

Before departure **itemize your bags' contents** and their worth, and label the bags with your name, address, and phone number. (If you use your home address, cover it so that potential thieves can't see it readily.) Inside each bag **pack a copy of your itinerary.** At check-in **make sure that each bag is correctly tagged** with the destination airport's three-letter code. If your bags arrive damaged or fail to arrive at all, file a written report with the airline before leaving the airport.

PASSPORTS & VISAS

➤ U.K. CITIZENS: **U.S. Embassy Visa Information Line** (☎ 01891/200–290; calls cost 49p per minute, 39p per minute cheap rate) for U.S. visa information. **U.S. Embassy Visa Branch** (✉ 5 Upper Grosvenor Sq., London W1A 1AE) for U.S. visa information; send a self-addressed, stamped envelope. Write the **U.S. Consulate General** (✉ Queen's House, Queen St., Belfast BTI 6EO) if you live in Northern Ireland. Write the **Office of Australia Affairs** (✉ 59th fl., MLC Centre, 19-29 Martin Pl., Sydney NSW 2000) if you live in Australia. Write the **Office of New Zealand Affairs** (✉ 29 Fitzherbert Terr., Thorndon, Wellington) if you live in New Zealand.

PASSPORT OFFICES

The best time to apply for a passport or to renew is during the fall and winter. Before any trip, check your passport's expiration date, and, if necessary, renew it as soon as possible.

➤ Australian Citizens: **Australian Passport Office** (☎ 131–232).

➤ New Zealand Citizens: **New Zealand Passport Office** (☎ 04/494–0700 for information on how to apply; 04/474–8000 or 0800/225–050 in New Zealand for information on applications already submitted).

➤ U.K. Citizens: **London Passport Office** (☎ 0990/210–410) for fees and documentation requirements and to request an emergency passport.

SENIOR-CITIZEN TRAVEL

To qualify for age-related discounts **mention your senior-citizen status up front** when booking hotel reservations (not when checking out) and before you're seated in restaurants (not when paying the bill). When renting a car ask about promotional car-rental discounts, which can be cheaper than senior-citizen rates.

➤ Educational Programs: **Elderhostel** (✉ 75 Federal St., 3rd fl., Boston, MA 02110, ☎ 877/426–8056, ℻ 877/426–2166).

SHOPPING

Keep in mind that the high quality of Native American arts and crafts is reflected in the prices they fetch. Bargaining is the exception, not the rule. In general, the best buys are to be had in the fall, after most of the tourists have gone home. Many uniquely southwestern products—chili pepper strings or locally produced salsas—make inexpensive souvenirs.

STUDENTS IN ARIZONA

➤ Student IDs & Services: **Council on International Educational Exchange** (CIEE, ✉ 205 E. 42nd St., 14th fl., New York, NY 10017, ☎ 212/822–2600 or 888/268–6245, ℻ 212/822–2699) for mail orders only, in the U.S. **Travel Cuts** (✉ 187 College St., Toronto, Ontario M5T 1P7, ☎ 416/979–2406 or 800/667–2887) in Canada.

TAXES

SALES TAX

Arizona state sales tax, which applies to all purchases except food, is 5%. Phoenix and Tucson levy city sales taxes of 2% and Flagstaff taxes purchases at a rate of 1.8%. Sales taxes do not apply on Indian reservations.

TIME

Arizona sets its clocks to mountain standard time—two hours earlier than eastern standard, one hour later than Pacific standard. However, from April to October, when other states switch to daylight saving time, Arizona does *not* change its clocks; during this portion of the year, the mountain standard hour in Arizona is the same as the Pacific daylight hour in California. To complicate matters, the vast Navajo reservation in the northeastern section of the state *does* observe daylight saving time, so that from April to October it's an hour later on the reservation than it is in the rest of the state. Finally, the Hopi reservation, whose borders fall within those of the Navajo reservation, stays on the same non-Navajo, non–daylight saving clock as the remainder of the state.

TIPPING

At restaurants, a 15% tip is standard for waiters; up to 20% may be expected at more expensive establishments. The same goes for taxi drivers, bartenders, and hairdressers. Coat-check operators usually expect $1; bellhops and porters should get 50¢ to $1 per bag; hotel maids in upscale hotels should get about $1 per day of your stay. On package tours, conductors and drivers usually get $10 per day from the group as a whole; check whether this has already been figured into your cost. For local sightseeing tours, you may individually tip the driver-guide $1 if he or she has been helpful or informative. Ushers in theaters do not expect tips.

TOURS & PACKAGES

On a prepackaged tour or independent vacation everything is prearranged so you'll spend less time planning—and often get it all at a good price.

BOOKING WITH AN AGENT

Travel agents are excellent resources. But it's a good idea to collect brochures from several agencies because some agents' suggestions may be influenced by relationships with tour and package firms that reward them for volume sales. If you have a special interest **find an agent with expertise in that area**; ASTA (☞ Travel Agencies, *below*) has a database of specialists worldwide.

Make sure your travel agent knows the accommodations and other services of the place they're recommending. Ask about the hotel's location, room size, beds, and whether it has a pool, room service, or programs for children, if you care about these. Has your agent been there in person or sent others whom you can contact?

Do some homework on your own, too: Local tourism boards can provide information about lesser-known and small-niche operators, some of which may sell only direct.

BUYER BEWARE

Each year consumers are stranded or lose their money when tour operators—even large ones with excellent reputations—go out of business. So **check out the operator.** Ask several travel agents about its reputation, and try to **book with a company that has a consumer-protection program.** (Look for information in the company's brochure.) In the United States, members of the National Tour Association and United States Tour Operators Association are required to set aside funds to cover your payments and travel arrangements in case

the company defaults. It's also a good idea to choose a company that participates in the American Society of Travel Agent's Tour Operator Program (TOP); ASTA will act as mediator in any disputes between you and your tour operator.

Remember that the more your package or tour includes the better you can predict the ultimate cost of your vacation. Make sure you know exactly what is covered, and **beware of hidden costs.** Are taxes, tips, and transfers included? Entertainment and excursions? These can add up.

➤ TOUR-OPERATOR RECOMMENDATIONS: **American Society of Travel Agents** (☞ Travel Agencies, *below*). **National Tour Association** (NTA, ✉ 546 E. Main St., Lexington, KY 40508, ☎ 606/226–4444 or 800/682–8886). **United States Tour Operators Association** (USTOA, ✉ 342 Madison Ave., Suite 1522, New York, NY 10173, ☎ 212/599–6599 or 800/468–7862, FAX 212/599–6744).

GROUP TOURS

Among companies that sell tours to Arizona, the following are nationally known, have a proven reputation, and offer plenty of options. The classifications used below represent different price categories, and you'll probably encounter these terms when talking to a travel agent or tour operator. The key difference is usually in accommodations, which run from budget to better, and better-yet to best.

➤ DELUXE: **Globus & Cosmos** (✉ 5301 S. Federal Circle, Littleton, CO 80123-2980, ☎ 303/797–2800 or 800/221–0090, FAX 303/795–0962). **Tauck Tours** (✉ Box 5027, 276 Post Rd. W, Westport, CT 06881, ☎ 203/226–6911 or 800/468–2825, FAX 203/221–6866).

➤ FIRST-CLASS: **Brendan Tours** (✉ 15137 Califa St., Van Nuys, CA 91411, ☎ 818/785–9696 or 800/421–8446, FAX 818/902–9876). **Caravan Tours** (✉ 401 N. Michigan Ave., Chicago, IL 60611, ☎ 312/321–9800 or 800/227–2826). **Collette Tours** (✉ 162 Middle St., Pawtucket, RI 02860, ☎ 401/728–3805 or 800/340–5158, FAX 401/728–4745). **Mayflower Tours**

(✉ Box 490, 1225 Warren Ave., Downers Grove, IL 60515, ☎ 630/960–3793 or 800/323–7604, FAX 630/960–3575). **Trafalgar Tours** (✉ 11 E. 26th St., New York, NY 10010, ☎ 212/689–8977 or 800/854–0103, FAX 800/457–6644).

➤ BUDGET: **Cosmos** (☞ Globus, *above*).

PACKAGES

Like group tours, independent vacation packages are available from major tour operators and airlines. The companies listed below offer vacation packages in a broad price range.

➤ AIR/HOTEL/CAR: **Certified Vacations** (✉ Box 1525, Fort Lauderdale, FL 33302, ☎ 954/522–1414 or 800/233–7260). **Delta Vacations** (☎ 800/872–7786). **Globetrotters** (✉ 139 Main St., Cambridge, MA 02142, ☎ 617/621–0099 or 800/333–1234). **TWA Getaway Vacations** (☎ 800/438–2929). **United Vacations** (☎ 800/328–6877). **US Airways Vacations** (☎ 800/455–0123).

➤ CUSTOM PACKAGES: **Amtrak Vacations** (☎ 800/321–8684).

➤ FROM THE U.K.: **British Airways Holidays** (✉ Astral Towers, Betts Way, London Rd., Crawley, West Sussex RH10 2XA, ☎ 01293/723–121). **Jetsave Travel Ltd.** (✉ Sussex House, London Rd., East Grinstead, West Sussex RH19 1LD, ☎ 01342/327–711). **Key to America** (✉ 1–3 Station Rd., Ashford, Middlesex TW15 2UW, ☎ 01784/248–777). **Kuoni Travel** (✉ Kuoni House, Dorking, Surrey RH5 4AZ, ☎ 01306/740–500). **Premier Holidays** (✉ Premier Travel Centre, Westbrook, Milton Rd., Cambridge CB4 1YG, ☎ 01223/516–516).

THEME TRIPS

➤ ADVENTURE: **American Wilderness Experience** (✉ Box 1486, Boulder, CO 80306, ☎ 303/444–2622 or 800/444–3833, FAX 303/444–3999).

➤ ARCHAEOLOGY: **Archaeological Conservancy** (✉ 5301 Central Ave. NE, #1218, Albuquerque, NM 87108-1517, ☎ 505/266–1540). **Crow Canyon Archaeological Center** (✉ 23390 Country Rd. K, Cortez,

CO 81321, ☎ 970/565–8975 or 800/422–8975, FAX 970/565–4859). **Earthwatch** (✉ Box 403, 680 Mount Auburn St., Watertown, MA 02272, ☎ 617/926–8200 or 800/776–0188, FAX 617/926–8532). **Nature Expeditions International** (✉ 6400 El Dorado Circle, Suite 210, Tucson, AZ 85715, ☎ 520/721–6712 or 800/869–0639, FAX 520/721–6719). **Southwest Ed-Ventures** (✉ Four Corners School of Outdoor Education, Box 1029, Monticello, UT 84535, ☎ 435/587–2156 or 800/525–4456, FAX 435/587–2193).

➤ BICYCLING: **Backroads** (✉ 801 Cedar St., Berkeley, CA 94710-1800, ☎ 510/527–1555 or 800/462–2848, FAX 510-527–1444). **Cycle America** (✉ Box 485, Cannon Falls, MN 55009, ☎ 507/263–2665 or 800/245–3263). **Timberline** (✉ 7975 E. Harvard, #J, Denver, CO 80231, ☎ 303/759–3804 or 800/417–2453, FAX 303/368–1651).

➤ CULTURAL: **Southwest Ed-Ventures** (☞ Archaeology, *above*).

➤ DUDE RANCHES: **American Wilderness Experience** (☞ Adventure, *above*). **Off the Beaten Path** (☞ Self-Drive, *below*).

➤ GOLF: **Golfpac** (✉ Box 162366, Altamonte Springs, FL 32716-2366, ☎ 407/260–2288 or 800/327–0878, FAX 407/260–8989). **Travel Services Golftrips** (✉ 193 Towne Center Dr., Kissimmee, FL 34759, ☎ 407/933–0032, FAX 407/933–8857).

➤ HIKING: **Backroads** (☞ Bicycling, *above*). **Timberline** (☞ Bicycling, *above*).

➤ HORSEBACK RIDING: **American Wilderness Experience** (☞ Adventure, *above*). **Equitour FITS Equestrian** (✉ Box 807, Dubois, WY 82513, ☎ 307/455–3363 or 800/545–0019, FAX 307/455–2354).

➤ KAYAKING: **Orange Torpedo Trips** (✉ Box 1111, Grants Pass, OR 97526-0294, ☎ 541/479–5061 or 800/635–2925, FAX 541/471–0995).

➤ MOTORCYCLING: **Western States Motorcycle Tours** (✉ 9401 N. 7th Ave., Phoenix, AZ 85021, ☎ 602/943–9030, FAX 602/943–4212).

➤ MUSIC: **Dailey-Thorp Travel** (✉ 330 W. 58th St., #610, New York, NY 10019-1817, ☎ 212/307–1555 or 800/998–4677, FAX 212/974–1420).

➤ NATIVE AMERICAN HISTORY: **Crow Canyon Archaeological Center** (☞ Archaeology, *above*). **Journeys Into American Indian Territory** (✉ Box 929, Westhampton Beach, NY 11978, ☎ 516/878–8655 or 800/458–2632, FAX 516/878–4518). **Southwest Ed-Ventures** (☞ Archaeology, *above*).

➤ NATURAL HISTORY: **Smithsonian Study Tours and Seminars** (✉ 1100 Jefferson Dr. SW, Room 3045, MRC 702, Washington, DC 20560, ☎ 202/357–4700, FAX 202/633–9250). **Victor Emanuel Nature Tours** (✉ Box 33008, Austin, TX 78764, ☎ 512/328–5221 or 800/328–8368, FAX 512/328–2919).

➤ RIVER RAFTING: For trips on the Colorado River: **Action Whitewater Adventures** (✉ Box 1634, Provo, UT 84603, ☎ 801/375–4111 or 800/453–1482, FAX 801/375–4175). **Grand Canyon Dories** (✉ Box 67, Angels Camp, CA 95222, ☎ 209/736–0811 or 800/877–3679, FAX 209/736–2902). **OARS** (✉ Box 67, Angels Camp, CA 95222, ☎ 209/736–4677 or 800/346–6277, FAX 209/736–2902). **World Wide River Expeditions** (✉ 153 E. 7200 S, Midvale, UT 84047, ☎ 801/566–2662 or 800/231–2769, FAX 801/566–2722). Rafting on the Salt River Canyons: **Far Flung Adventures** (✉ Box 377, Terlingua, TX 79852, ☎ 915/371–2489 or 800/359–4138, FAX 915/371–2325).

➤ SELF-DRIVE: **Off the Beaten Path** (✉ 109 E. Main St., Bozeman, MT 59715, ☎ 406/586–1311 or 800/445–2995, FAX 406/587–4147).

➤ SPAS: **Spa-Finders** (✉ 91 5th Ave., #301, New York, NY 10003-3039, ☎ 212/924–6800 or 800/255–7727) represents several spas in Arizona.

➤ WALKING: **Country Walkers** (✉ Box 180, Waterbury, VT 05676-0180, ☎ 802/244–1387 or 800/464–9255, FAX 802/244–5661).

TRAIN TRAVEL

The *Southwest Chief* operates daily between Los Angeles and Chicago, stopping in Kingman, Flagstaff, and Winslow. The *Sunset Limited* travels three times each week between Los Angeles and Miami, with stops at Yuma, Tucson, and Benson. There is a connecting Amtrak bus (a two-hour trip) between Tuscon and Phoenix. For details, contact **Amtrak** (☎ 800/872–7245).

TRAVEL AGENCIES

A good travel agent puts your needs first. Look for an agency that has been in business at least five years, emphasizes customer service, and has someone on staff who specializes in your destination. In addition **make sure the agency belongs to a professional trade organization,** such as ASTA in the United States. If your travel agency is also acting as your tour operator *see* Buyer Beware *in* Tours & Packages, *above*.

➤ LOCAL AGENT REFERRALS: **American Society of Travel Agents** (ASTA, ☎ 800/965–2782 24-hr hot line, FAX 703/684–8319). **Association of British Travel Agents** (✉ 55–57 Newman St., London W1P 4AH, ☎ 0171/637–2444, FAX 0171/637–0713). **Association of Canadian Travel Agents** (✉ 1729 Bank St., Suite 201, Ottawa, Ontario K1V 7Z5, ☎ 613/521–0474, FAX 613/521–0805). **Australian Federation of Travel Agents** (✉ Level 3, 309 Pitt St., Sydney 2000, ☎ 02/9264–3299, FAX 02/9264–1085). **Travel Agents' Association of New Zealand** (✉ Box 1888, Wellington 10033, ☎ 04/499–0104, FAX 04/499–0786).

VISITOR INFORMATION

For general information and brochures contact the Arizona Office of Tourism; for specific information on the state's indigenous culture, contact the Native American attractions.

➤ STATEWIDE INFORMATION: **Arizona Office of Tourism** (✉ 2702 N. Third St., Ste. 4015, Phoenix 85004, ☎ 602/230–7733 or 888/520–3434, FAX 602/240–5475).

➤ NATIVE AMERICAN ATTRACTIONS: **Hopi Tribe Office of the Chairman** (✉ Box 123, Kykotsmovi 86039, ☎ 520/734–2441, FAX 520/734–2435). **Navajo Nation Tourism Office** (✉ Box 663, Window Rock 86515, ☎

520/871–6436 or 871–7371 or 871–6659, FAX 520/871–7381).

WEB SITES

Do **check out the World Wide Web** when you're planning your trip. You'll find everything from up-to-date weather forecasts to virtual tours of famous cities. Fodor's Web site, www.fodors.com, is a great place to start your on-line travels. For more information specifically on Arizona, visit:

➤ GENERAL INFORMATION: The **Arizona Guide** (http://www. arizonaguide.com) is the official Web site of the Arizona Office of Tourism. All of the major cities in the state, as well as Indian reservations, have official sites at this Web address. Here you'll find video clips of popular destinations, information on everything from golfing hot spots to Indian festivals, and links to related websites.

➤ GRAND CANYON: Everything you always wanted to know about this natural wonder can be found at **The Canyon** (http://www.thecanyon.com), the official Web site of the Grand Canyon Chamber of Commerce. Information on parking alternatives, accommodations, and up-to-the-minute updates on park closings and events can be found at this attractive Web site.

➤ THE GREAT OUTDOORS: The **Arizona State Parks Web Site** (http://www.pr.state.az.us) lists basics such as fees and hours for all parks, as well as information about wildlife preservation and listings of special events.

A must-visit for outdoors and adventure travel enthusiasts, the **Great Outdoor Recreation Page** (http://www.gorp.com) is arranged into three easily navigated categories: attractions, activities, and locations.

The **National Park Service site** (http://www.nps.gov), which lists national parks and other lands administered by the park service, has extensive historical, cultural, and environmental information.

➤ NEWSWEEKLIES: The state's newsweeklies are a great source of up-to-the-minute arts and entertainment information, from what shows are on the boards to who's playing the clubs.

Phoenix New Times (http://www.phoenixnewtimes.com) maintains a site with lively features and and insiders' guides to dining, the arts, and nightlife in the Phoenix metro area.

The Web site of *Tucson Weekly* (http://www.tucsonweekly.com) has the lowdown on the Tucson area.

WHEN TO GO

When you travel to Arizona depends on whether you prefer scorching desert or snowy slopes, elbow-to-elbow resorts, or wide-open territory. Our advice: **Visit during spring and autumn,** when the temperatures are milder and the crowds have thinned out.

Winter is prime time in the central and southern parts of the state. The weather is sunny and mild, and the cities bustle with travelers escaping the cold. Conversely, northern Arizona—including the Grand Canyon—can be wintry, with snow, freezing rain, and subzero temperatures; the road to the Grand Canyon's North Rim is closed during this time.

Arizona's desert regions sizzle in summer, and travelers and their vehicles should be adequately prepared. Practically every restaurant and accommodation is air-conditioned, though, and you can get great deals on tony southern Arizona resorts you might not be able to afford in high season. Summer is also a delightful time to visit northern Arizona's high country, when temperatures are 18°F–20°F lower than they are down south—but hotel prices are commensurately high.

CLIMATE

Phoenix averages 300 sunny days and 7 inches of precipitation annually. Tucson gets all of 11 inches of rain each year, and the high mountains see about 25 inches. The Grand Canyon is usually cool on the rim and about 20°F warmer on the floor. During winter months, approximately 6–12 inches of snow falls on the North Rim; the South Rim receives half that amount.

➤ FORECASTS: **Weather Channel Connection** (☎ 900/932–8437), 95¢ per minute from a Touch-Tone phone.

The following average daily maximum and minimum temperatures for two major cities in Arizona offer a representative range of temperatures in the state.

TUCSON

Jan.	64F	18C	May	89F	32C	Sept.	96F	36C
	37	3		57	14		68	20
Feb.	68F	20C	June	98F	37C	Oct.	84F	29C
	39	4		66	19		57	14
Mar.	73F	23C	July	101F	38C	Nov.	73F	23C
	44	7		73	23		44	7
Apr.	82F	28C	Aug.	96F	36C	Dec.	66F	19C
	51	11		71	22		39	4

FLAGSTAFF

Jan.	41F	5C	May	66F	19C	Sept.	71F	22C
	14	−10		33	1		41	5
Feb.	44F	7C	June	77F	25C	Oct.	62F	17C
	17	− 8		41	5		30	− 1
Mar.	48F	9C	July	80F	27C	Nov.	51F	11C
	23	− 5		50	10		21	− 6
Apr.	57F	14C	Aug.	78F	26C	Dec.	42F	6C
	28	− 2		48	9		15	− 9

FESTIVALS AND SEASONAL EVENTS

➤ JAN. 1: Tempe's nationally televised **Fiesta Bowl Footbowl Classic** (☎ 602/350–0911) kicks off the year with a match between the nation's top two college teams.

➤ JAN.: At the **Phoenix Open Golf Tournament** (☎ 602/870–4431) in Scottsdale, top players compete at the Tournament Players Club.

➤ JAN.: The **Dixieland Jazz Festival** (☎ 800/624–7939) at Lake Havasu City uses London Bridge as the backdrop for traditional Dixieland sounds and more, including a parade, riverboat dancing, and Sunday-morning gospel.

➤ JAN.–FEB.: **Parada del Sol Rodeo and Parade** (☎ 602/945–8481), a popular state attraction on Scottsdale Road, features lots of dressed-up cowboys and cowgirls, plus horses and floats.

➤ EARLY FEB.: The **Quartzsite Pow Wow Gem and Mineral Show** (☎ 520/927–6325) is a gigantic flea market, held the first Wednesday through Sunday of the month in Quartzsite, about 19 mi from the California border (take I–10 west of Phoenix and then turn north on AZ 95).

➤ FEB.: At **O'odham Tash** (☎ 520/836–4723) in Casa Grande, Native American tribes from around the country host parades, native dances, a rodeo, costume displays, and food stands.

➤ FEB.: History comes to life during **Wickenburg Gold Rush Days** (☎ 520/684–5479), when the Old West town puts on a rodeo, dances, gold-panning demonstrations, a mineral show, and other activities.

➤ FEB.: **La Fiesta de los Vaqueros** (☎ 520/741–2233) features the world's longest "nonmechanized" parade— horses pull floats and carry dignitaries—launching a four-day rodeo at the Tucson Rodeo Grounds.

➤ FEB.: The huge **Tucson Gem and Mineral Show** (☎ 520/322–5773) attracts rock hounds—amateur and professional—from all over the world who come to buy, sell, and display their geological treasures and to attend lectures and competitive exhibits.

➤ MAR.: In Phoenix, the **Heard Museum Guild Indian Fair and Market** (☎ 602/252–8848) is a prestigious juried show of Native American arts and crafts. Visitors can also enjoy Native American foods, music, and dance.

➤ MAR.: The highlight of the **Ostrich Festival** (☎ 602/963–4571) in Chandler is a race of the big birds; it also features a parade, live entertainment, crafts, and food.

➤ MAR.: For the **Lost Dutchman Gold Mine Superstition Mountain Trek** (☎ 602/258–6016) in Apache Junction, the Dons of Arizona search for the legendary lost mine, pan for gold, and eat lots of barbecue to keep up their strength. There are crafts demonstrations and fireworks, too.

➤ APR.: Tucson hosts the **International Mariachi Conference** (☎ 520/884–9920), four days of mariachi music, along with cultural and educational exhibits.

➤ APR.: During the **Route 66 Fun Run Weekend** (☎ 520/753–5001) from Seligman to Topock, the historic road between Chicago and Los Angeles is feted with classic car rallies, hot-rod and antique-car shows, and various other events—including a 1950s hop.

➤ APR.: **Yaqui Easter** (☎ 520/791–4609) is celebrated in old Pasqua Village (Tucson) on the Saturday nights preceding Palm Sunday and Easter Sunday. Visitors are welcome to watch traditional Yaqui dances and ceremonies.

➤ APR.: Bisbee's **La Vuelta de Bisbee** (☎ 520/432–5421) is Arizona's largest bicycle race and attracts top racers from around the country to the hills of the historic mining town.

➤ MAY: During the **Rendezvous Rendezvous** (☎ 520/635–4061), the townspeople of Williams reenact the annual trek to town by 1800s mountain traders. Events include a steak fry and a Buckskinners black powder shoot.

➤ MAY–JUNE: At Flagstaff's **Trappings of the American West Festival** (☎ 520/779–6921), the featured attraction is cowboy art—everything from painting and sculpture to cowboy poetry readings.

➤ JUNE: Festivities of **Old West Day/Bucket of Blood Races** (☎ 520/524–6558), in Holbrook, include arts

and crafts, western dress, and Native American song and dance, in addition to the 10-km (2-mi) fun run and 20-mi bike ride from Petrified Forest National Park to Holbrook.

➤ JULY: **Prescott Frontier Days and Rodeo** (☎ 520/445–2000), billed as the world's oldest rodeo, finds big crowds and an equally big party on downtown Whiskey Row.

➤ JULY: The **Native American Arts & Crafts Festival** (☎ 520/367–4290) in Pinetop-Lakeside brings storytellers, dancers, musicians, and artists together for two days in a beautiful mountain setting.

➤ AUG.: The **Payson Rodeo** (☎ 520/474–4515), known as the world's oldest continuous rodeo, draws top cowboys from around the country to compete in calf- and steer-roping contests.

➤ AUG.: Flagstaff's **SummerFest** (☎ 520/774–9541) is a gathering of painters, potters, musicians, and other artists from around the United States. They vie with carnival rides and food vendors for the crowd's attention.

➤ AUG.: The **Southwest Wings Birding Festival** (☎ 520/378–0233), held in Sierra Vista, the self-proclaimed Hummingbird Capital of the United States, includes field trips, lectures by recognized Audubon authorities, and other avian-oriented events.

➤ SEPT.: At the **Jazz on the Rocks Festival** (☎ 520/282–1985) in Sedona, six or seven ensembles perform in a spectacular red-rock setting.

➤ SEPT.: The **Navajo Nation Annual Tribal Fair** (☎ 520/871–6436) is the world's largest Native American fair. Held in Window Rock, it includes a rodeo, traditional Navajo music and dances, food booths, and an intertribal powwow.

➤ OCT.: **Rex Allen Days** (☎ 520/384–2272) in Willcox honors the local cowboy film star and narrator for Walt Disney productions with a parade, country fair, rodeo, dances, and more.

➤ OCT.: Spicy food lovers revel at **La Fiesta de Los Chiles** (☎ 520/326–9686), Tucson's two-day salute to the chili, which is cooked, hung, made into art, and otherwise celebrated.

➤ OCT.: At **Tombstone's Helldorado Days** (☎ 520/457–9317) this town relives the spirited Wyatt Earp era and the shoot-out at the OK Corral.

➤ OCT.: A weeklong event, **London Bridge Days** (☎ 520/453–3444) includes a triathlon, a parade, and a variety of British-theme contests in Lake Havasu City.

➤ NOV.: At 110 mi, **El Tour De Tucson** (☎ 520/745–2033) is the largest perimeter bicycling event in the world, attracting international celebrity cyclists.

➤ NOV.: During the **Thunderbird Balloon Classic & Air Show** (☎ 602/978–7208) 150 or more balloons participate in Scottsdale's colorful race.

➤ DEC.: At the **Arizona Temple Gardens & Visitors Center Christmas Lighting** (☎ 602/964–7164), in Mesa, more than 300,000 lights illuminate the walkways, reflection pool, trees, and plants.

➤ DEC.: The waters of Lake Powell alight with the **Festival of Lights Boat Parade** (☎ 520/645–1001) as dozens of illuminated boats glide from Wahweap Lodge to Glen Canyon Dam and back.

➤ DEC.: For the three days of **Old Town Tempe Fall Festival of the Arts** (☎ 602/967–4877) the downtown area closes to traffic for art exhibits, food booths, music, and other entertainment.

INDEX

Arizona

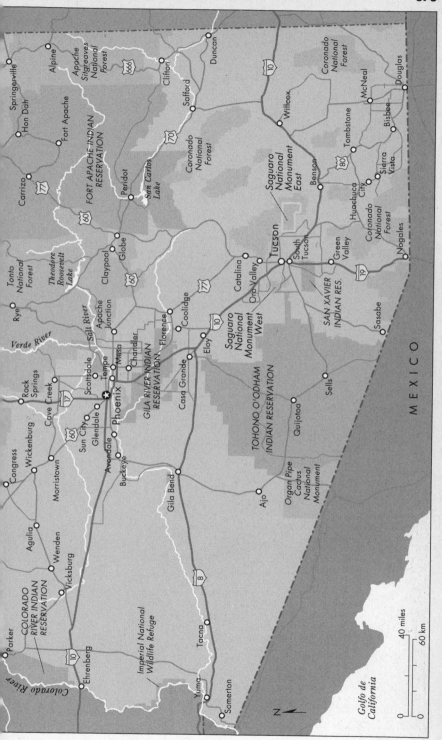

The United States

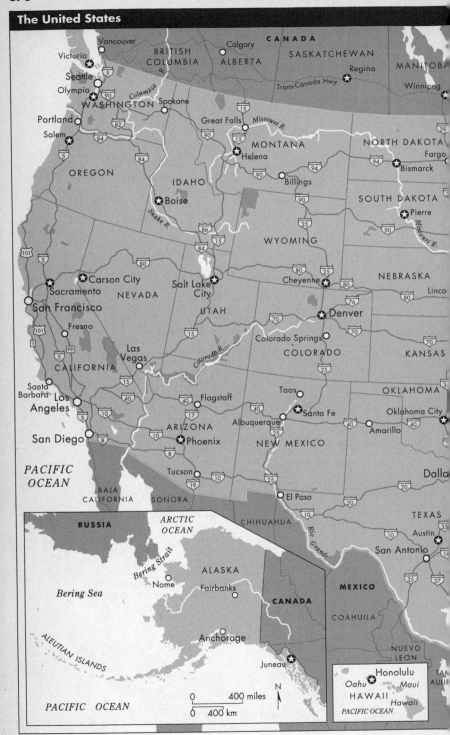

CANADA

BRITISH COLUMBIA

ALBERTA

SASKATCHEWAN

MANITOBA

Vancouver

Victoria ★

Calgary

Regina

Winnipeg

Trans-Canada Hwy.

Seattle ★

Olympia ★

WASHINGTON

Columbia R.

Spokane

5

90

Portland

82

Great Falls

Missouri R.

NORTH DAKOTA

Fargo

Salem

84

84

5

90

Helena ★

MONTANA

94

Bismarck ★

15

OREGON

IDAHO

★ Boise

Billings

SOUTH DAKOTA

Pierre ★

94

Snake R.

86

15

WYOMING

Missouri R.

90

80

84

Carson City ★

Sacramento ★

San Francisco

NEVADA

Salt Lake City

UTAH

Cheyenne

★ Denver

80

25

NEBRASKA

Lincoln

80

76

Fresno

101

99

5

1

Las Vegas

15

Colorado R.

70

Colorado Springs

15

COLORADO

70

KANSAS

70

Santa Barbara

Los Angeles

CALIFORNIA

40

Flagstaff

40

Taos

25

OKLAHOMA

5

10

17

San Diego

Phoenix ★

ARIZONA

10

Albuquerque

★ Santa Fe

Amarillo

Oklahoma City

40

8

8

NEW MEXICO

25

PACIFIC OCEAN

Tucson

19

10

El Paso

25

20

Dallas

BAJA CALIFORNIA

SONORA

CHIHUAHUA

Rio Grande

10

20

TEXAS

Austin

10

San Antonio

35

37

RUSSIA

ARCTIC OCEAN

Bering Strait

Bering Sea

Nome

ALASKA

Fairbanks

CANADA

MEXICO

COAHUILA

NUEVO LEON

Anchorage

ALEUTIAN ISLANDS

Juneau ★

PACIFIC OCEAN

0   400 miles

0   400 km

N

Honolulu ★

Oahu   Maui

HAWAII

Hawaii

PACIFIC OCEAN

TAM AULIP

NOTES

NOTES

NOTES

Looking for a different kind of vacation?

Fodor's makes it easy with a full line of specialty guidebooks to suit a variety of interests—from adventure to romance to language help.

L@@king
@ FOR A
great place to go?

We know just the place. In fact, it attracts more than 125,000 visitors a day, making it one of the world's most popular travel destinations. It's previewtravel.com, the Web's comprehensive resource for travelers. It gives you access to over 500 airlines, 25,000 hotels, rental cars, cruises, vacation packages and support from travel experts 24 hours a day. Plus great information from Fodor's travel guides and travelers just like you. All of which makes previewtravel.com quite a find.

Preview Travel has everything you need to plan & book your next trip.

air, car & hotel reservations

vacation packages & cruises

destination planning & travel tips

24-hour customer service

previewtravel.com

preview travel℠

aol keyword: previewtravel
www.previewtravel.com

FODOR'S ARIZONA 2000

EDITOR: Constance Jones

Editorial Contributors: Stephanie Adler, Deidre Elliott, Andrea Ibáñez, Howard Seftel, Ed Tomchin, Kim Westerman

Editorial Production: Tom Holton

Maps: David Lindroth, *cartographer;* Rebecca Baer and Bob Blake, *map editors*

Design: Fabrizio La Rocca, *creative director;* Guido Caroti, *art director;* Jolie Novak, *photo editor,* Melanie Marin, *photo researcher*

Cover Design: Pentagram

Production/Manufacturing: Robert B. Shields

SPECIAL SALES

Fodor's Travel Publications are available at special discounts for bulk purchases for sales promotions or premiums. Special editions, including personalized covers, excerpts of existing guides, and corporate imprints, can be created in large quantities for special needs. For more information, contact your local bookseller or write to Special Markets, Fodor's Travel Publications, 201 East 50th Street, New York, NY 10022. Inquiries from Canada should be directed to your local Canadian bookseller or sent to Random House of Canada, Ltd., Marketing Department, 2775 Matheson Boulevard East, Mississauga, Ontario L4W 4P7. Inquiries from the United Kingdom should be sent to Fodor's Travel Publications, 20 Vauxhall Bridge Road, London SW1V 2SA, England.

PRINTED IN THE UNITED STATES OF AMERICA

10 9 8 7 6 5 4 3 2 1

IMPORTANT TIP

Although all prices, opening times, and other details in this book are based on information supplied to us at press time, changes occur all the time in the travel world, and Fodor's cannot accept responsibility for facts that become outdated or for inadvertent errors or omissions. So **always confirm information when it matters,** especially if you're making a detour to visit a specific place.

PHOTOGRAPHY

Tony Stone Images: *Rob Boudreau, cover. ("The Mittens," Monument Valley).*

Arizona Inn, *30F.*

Arizona State Parks, *20A.*

The Boulders, *30J.*

Briar Patch Inn, *30A.*

Guido Caroti, *6B, 32.*

John Elkins, *19G.*

Flagstaff Convention & Visitors Bureau: *30I. Gene Balzer, 12B.*

Peter Guttman, *8F, 8G, 8H, 9J, 11D, 13 bottom left, 18F.*

Heard Museum, *3 bottom right, 29B.*

Dave G. Houser, *10A, 11B, 14F, 15H, 15I, 16A, 18E, 21D, 22A, 27D.*

Jan Butchofsky-Houser, *23B, 25I, 26B.*

The Image Bank: *Gill C. Kenny, 24E. Andrea Pistolesi, 13D. Chuck Place, 1, 13E, 14G. Guido A. Rossi, 11C. Thomas Schmitt, 25G. Harald Sund, 12A, 12C, 23C, 30D. A. T. Willett, 23D, 24F, 25H, 26A, 27C, 27E, 30E, 30G.*

Janos, *2 bottom left, 30B.*

Jessen Associates, Inc.: *17B. R. Silberblatt, 2 top right, 17C, 30H.*

Kokopelli's Kitchen, *20C.*

Lake Powell Resorts & Marinas, *3 top right, 3 bottom left.*

E. B. Lane & Associates, *7E.*

Mesa Convention & Visitors Bureau, *2 top left, 3 top left, 19H.*

Metropolitan Tucson Convention & Vistors Bureau: *Thomas Wiewandt, 2 bottom center.*

The Phoenician, *30C.*

The Pointe Hilton Resort, *19I.*

Scottsdale Chamber of Commerce: *Paul Markow, 2 bottom right.*

Sedona–Oak Creek Canyon Chamber of Commerce: *Bob Clemenz, 28A.*

Nik Wheeler, *4–5, 6A, 7C, 7D, 9I, 9K, 15J, 17D, 18 top, 20B.*

ABOUT OUR WRITERS

EVERY Y2K TRIP IS A SIGNIFICANT trip. So if there was ever a time you needed excellent travel information, it's now. Acutely aware of that fact, we've pulled out all stops in preparing *Fodor's Arizona 2000*. To help you zero in on what to see in Arizona, we've gathered some great color photos of the key sights in every region. To show you how to put it all together, we've created great itineraries. And to direct you to the places that are truly worth your time and money in this important year, we've rallied the team of endearingly picky know-it-alls we're pleased to call our writers. Having seen all corners of the areas they cover for us, they're real experts. If you knew them, you'd poll them for tips yourself.

Deidre Elliott, who updated Phoenix and Eastern Arizona, has written for the PBS series *Wild America* and magazines such as *Field and Stream.* Having hiked and rafted throughout the West, she is working on a book of personal essays about the Sonoran Desert.

Tucson and Southern Arizona updater **Andrea Ibáñez** lives in Tucson, where she writes about food, travel, and the Southwest. Phoenix dining critic **Howard Seftel** writes a popular restaurant column in the *New Times,* a weekly alternative newspaper in Phoenix.

Las Vegas-based **Edward Tomchin,** a freelance travel writer, updated the Northeast chapter. His work has appeared in the *Nevada Handbook, Nevada Magazine, Signs of the Times,* and several other publications.

Kim Westerman, who updated the Grand Canyon and North-Central Arizona chapters, moved to the Arizona desert in 1989. She reviews restaurants online for the *Arizona Star* and writes travel pieces for the *New York Times* and other publications.

Don't Forget to Write

We love feedback—positive and negative—and follow up on all suggestions. So contact the Arizona editor at editors@fodors.com or c/o Fodor's, 201 East 50th Street, New York, New York 10022. Have a wonderful trip!

Karen Cure

Karen Cure
Editorial Director